Multinational Finance

PEARSON
Education

We work with leading authors to develop the
strongest educational materials in finance,
bringing cutting edge thinking and best learning
practice to a global market.

Under a range of well-known imprints, including
Financial Times Prentice Hall, we craft high quality
print and electronic publications which help
readers to understand and apply their content,
whether studying or at work.

To find out about the complete range of our
publishing please visit us on the World Wide Web at:
www.pearsoned.co.uk

Multinational Finance

Fifth Edition

ADRIAN BUCKLEY

FT Prentice Hall
FINANCIAL TIMES

An imprint of **Pearson Education**
Harlow, England • London • New York • Boston • San Francisco • Toronto • Sydney • Singapore • Hong Kong
Tokyo • Seoul • Taipei • New Delhi • Cape Town • Madrid • Mexico City • Amsterdam • Munich • Paris • Milan

Pearson Education Limited
Edinburgh Gate
Harlow
Essex CM20 2JE
England

and Associated Companies throughout the world

Visit us on the World Wide Web at:
http://www.pearsoned.co.uk

———————————

First published under the Philip Allan imprint, 1986
Second and third editions published under the Prentice Hall Europe imprint, 1992, 1996
Fourth edition, 2000
Fifth edition, 2004

© Prentice Hall Europe 1992, 1996
© Pearson Education Limited 2000, 2004

ISBN: 978-0-273-68209-7

British Library Cataloging-in-Publication Data
A catalogue record for this book can be obtained from the British Library

10 9 8 7 6 5
09 08

Typeset in 10/12.5pt Sabon by 35
Printed and bound in Malaysia (CTP-VVP)

The publisher's policy is to use paper manufactured from sustainable forests.

Contents

Preface and acknowledgements

This book describes the theory and practice of multinational finance. The increasing internationalization of business, the emergence of the euro and the deregulation of capital markets around the world have made the study of multinational finance far more pertinent than ever before.

Thirty five years ago the majority of financial executives in *The Times* 1,000 companies did not have to appreciate what impelled exchange rates to move, what were the opportunities to raise money outside the United Kingdom, what influenced the evaluation of overseas capital investment projects, and so on. The decisions to move away from the fixed exchange rate system and to abandon exchange controls in the United Kingdom were the most important factors which changed all that. The financial manager in the United Kingdom had to start to learn new tricks in the 1970s. Those who were slow to learn made mistakes. They borrowed in Swiss francs because the interest cost was low; they failed to cover Deutschmark payables as sterling declined precipitously; they failed to realize the opportunities created by the demise of exchange controls; they did not appreciate the benefits that accrue from currency options; and so on.

The majority of financial executives are probably accountants and it is to be regretted that the professional accounting bodies in the United Kingdom responded with too little, too late. In short, they failed to provide an adequate test of knowledge in the field of multinational financial management as part of their professional training and examinations. This lacuna in their training, in conjunction with a paucity of coverage of the total treasury area – corporate finance, currency management, funding management and liquidity management – was one of the reasons for the growth and increasing importance in the United Kingdom of the Association of Corporate Treasurers and similar professional bodies elsewhere. There are few wide-ranging British texts on multinational finance. This book is intended to improve management practice in this most important area of business.

Readership

This text is aimed primarily at students on courses in multinational finance or financial aspects of international business. They may be on MBA courses or pursuing undergraduate or postgraduate studies. But the book is also structured to meet the needs of aspiring accountants, bankers and treasurers. The emphasis on a student market is not to say that the book is inappropriate for the businessperson who needs to know about finance in the international arena. The intention is that it should be relevant to the requirements of financial managers who want to study this special area of finance as well as to non-financial managers who need to know about international money and its implications. My intention is essentially practical. It is that this book should improve performance and awareness in the treasury management area.

Changes to the fifth edition

Nowadays, the field of international financial management is probably the most dynamic segment of all business activity. It is changing at a pace that is no less than staggering. Hence, there have been many things happening in theory and practice since the fourth edition of this book came out in 2000. This fifth edition has been revised and updated. Both the content and number of chapters have been rationalized and reorganized. The reading and learning features are facilitated by the inclusion of end-of-part test banks comprising exercises and multiple-choice questions. Suggested answers to a selection of the exercises and all multiple-choice questions are given at the end of the text allowing for self-assessment. Each chapter ends with an extensive summary, signposted with bullet points to ease the revision of key aspects by students. A new feature is the inclusion of questions at the end of all chapters (except Chapter 1). Answers to all of these appear at the end of the book.

A separately published Teacher's Manual includes teaching notes, case study suggestions, visual aid masters, and suggested answers to the exercises not given in the text.

Acknowledgements

I am most grateful to the Association of Corporate Treasurers for permission to reproduce some of their examination questions in the test banks. And I am especially grateful to Liz Tribe who deciphered my handwriting and cheerfully typed the manuscript. Liz's ability to deal with my quirky sense of humour and to put up with my tendency to lose bits of text is also to be applauded. Errors should be debited to my account though.

I would also like to express my gratitude to the anonymous survey respondents, and to various people who have used the fourth edition of this book and pointed out errors and improvements. That list includes the following: Mark Ashley-Hacker, Ruth Bender, Soumitro Bhattacharyya, Alexei Bogdanov, Abir Clark, Yan Feng, Melisa Hoffman, Ajay Khandelwal, Bryan King, Walter Marques, Jose Olea, Roberto Pace, Jason Parrish, Claudio Santos, Amanda Solomon, Mayan Shah, Louise Streeter and Jianglong Zhou.

Adrian Buckley

Publisher's acknowledgements

We are grateful to the following for permission to reproduce copyright material:

Tables 3.1, 24.2, 24.3 and 24.4 from *Triumph of the Optimists*, copyright © 2002 by Elroy Dimson, Paul March and M. Staunton, reprinted by permission of Princeton University Press; Table 3.11 and Figure 3.1 from *Comparative International Accounting*, 5th edition and 7th edition respectively (Nobes, C. and Parker, R. 1998, 2002) and Appendices 1 and 2 to Chapter 20 from *International Business*, 3rd edition (Rugman, A.M. and Hodgetts, R.M. 2003), reproduced with permission of Pearson Education; Tables 24.5 and 24.6 from *Stocks for the Long Run* (Siegel, J.J. 2002), copyright © 2002, reproduced with permission of The McGraw-Hill Companies; Table 27.6 from 'The credit rating industry', *Quarterly Review*, Vol. 19, No. 2 (Cantor, R. and Packer, F. 1994), reproduced with permission of the Federal Reserve Bank of New York; Table 28.1 from *Issues in Business Taxation* (Tucker, J. 1994), copyright © 1994, reproduced with permission of Ashgate Publishing Limited; Figure 20.4 from *Britain and the Multinationals* (Stopford, J.M. and Turner, L. 1985), copyright 1985 © John Wiley & Sons Limited, reproduced with permission; Figure 20.5 from 'Case studies and failure' by Marquise Cvar, Chapter 15 from *Competition in Global Industries* (Porter, M.E. 1986), Harvard Business School Press, © 1986; Figure 20.6 adapted from *The Competitive Advantage of Nations* (Porter, M.E. 1990), with permission of the Free Press, a Division of Simon & Schuster Adult Publishing Group, copyright © 1990, 1998 by Michael E. Porter, all rights reserved; Figure 32.1 from 'Currency changes and management control: resolving the centralization/decentralization dilemma', *The Accounting Review*, Vol. LII, No. 3, July, pp. 628–37 (Lessard, D.R. and Lorange, P. 1977), copyright © American Accounting Association.

We are grateful to the Association of Corporate Treasurers for permission to include examination questions from a selection of their examination papers, © Association of Corporate Treasurers.

Every effort has been made by the publisher to obtain permission from the appropriate source to reproduce material which appears in this book. In some instances we have been unable to trace the owners of copyright material, and we would appreciate any information that would enable us to do so.

Part A

Essential background

With any topic, there are certain key facts that set the scene and are essential to an understanding of a subject. This is as true of multinational finance as it is of any other subject. In this first section we present some of these key facts about the international monetary system and the internationalization process.

1 Introduction

Financial management traditionally focuses upon three key decisions – the acquisition of funds, their investment and the payment of dividends. The former is termed the financing decision and it is concerned with obtaining funds, either internally or externally, at the lowest cost possible. The second key area of finance is the investment decision, which is concerned with the allocation of funds to opportunities in order to earn the greatest value for the firm. The study of financial management is built upon the hypothesis that judicious financing, investment and dividend decisions positively affect the present value of shareholder wealth. Most writers on financial management arrive at their theories by way of a process of deductive reasoning. They then look at data from empirical tests of these hypotheses and from this base build an armoury of rules and recommendations which help us to analyse opportunities and choose the course of action which maximizes shareholder value.

Domestic financial management is concerned with the costs of financing sources and the payoffs from investment. In the domestic arena, movements in exchange rates are substantially ignored. But when we move outside this purely domestic field, there is no way that we can analyse international financing and investment opportunities without an understanding of the impact of foreign exchange rates upon the basic model of financial management. We are still concerned with raising funds at minimum cost, but there are clearly complications of analysis if a UK-based company is raising funds by way of a Swiss franc borrowing. We are still concerned with investment opportunities chosen to create maximum shareholder value, but what if the income and cash flow of our UK-based company's investments arise from the United States in dollars? Or from Mexico in pesos? And what if exchange controls place barriers on remittances of some proportion of profit?

Obviously multinational finance possesses a dimension that makes it far more complicated than domestic financial management. Indeed we make no bones about it – multinational finance is a complex area of study. It has been sired by the internationalization of business. If money is the language of business, foreign exchange is the language of international business. We are therefore deeply concerned in this book with foreign exchange markets throughout the world and with the pressures that impel exchange rates to move upwards and downwards. In addition to evaluating theories of exchange rate movements, multinational finance is concerned with the risks that flow from holding assets and liabilities denominated in foreign currency. Clearly, the home currency value of such assets and liabilities changes as exchange rates move. Exposure to these changes creates foreign exchange risk. We are concerned not only with defining and classifying foreign exchange risk but also with reporting, managing and controlling this risk. But multinational finance is not only concerned with foreign exchange exposure, it also embraces political risk: that is, the exposure which a firm takes on when it enters into business operations located overseas. Again a practical orientation towards the study of multinational finance suggests that we should focus upon managing and controlling this exposure. A systematic study of finance in the international arena requires that we consider the funding of international trade, the evaluation of cross-frontier investment decisions and the financing of overseas associate and subsidiary companies as well as understanding international financial markets, the impact of tax regimes in different countries and the ways in which exchange controls affect multinational businesses. These topics are the subject matter of this book.

Multinational financial management is so riddled with complications that there is a critical need to put the subject over simply. One of the motivations for writing this book is that most other texts which devote themselves to international money fail to present a clear picture to their readers. When they do, they are invariably excessively wordy. And there are also a good many texts on multinational finance which approach the subject at a high level of abstraction and with an emphasis upon mathematics that could easily be daunting to even the best of MBA students.

Given this background, the intention of the author is that this text should be oriented towards the requirements of students of international finance who need to understand the theory and practice of multinational finance. A certain amount of mathematics is necessary but the intention has been to keep it to a minimum.

The author's assumption is that the readership will be drawn not only from students but also from businesspeople. Among student readers, it is anticipated that some will be aspiring accountants, bankers and treasurers, some will be undergraduates, majoring in multinational business and international finance, and some will be postgraduates on specialist MSc courses as well as on MBA programmes. It is considered that this text should also appeal to businesspeople drawn from the ranks of treasurers, accountants, bankers and corporate planners who require a coherent presentation of the theory and practice of multinational finance. However, inasmuch as there is an increasing need for non-financial managers – line managers and members of a company's top-level decision coalition – to understand finance in the international arena, it is intended that this text should meet their needs too.

It is assumed by the author that readers have a basic knowledge of financial management. This would probably embrace such topics as sources of corporate finance, the investment, financing and dividend decision and the efficient markets hypothesis – but such knowledge is not necessarily expected to be at a high level of competence. The line manager with a general manager's understanding of finance should not be disadvantaged as he or she explores most of the topics in this text. Summarized, it is presumed that readers are familiar with the following foundation stones of corporate finance:

■ The central hypothesis of corporate financial theory is that the value of the firm (V) is a function of the investment decision (I), the financing decision (F), the dividend decision (D) and the management of corporate resources (M). In other words:

$$V = f(I, F, D, M)$$

■ The financing decision is concerned with the obtaining of funds by the corporation; the investment decision is all about the application of resources so obtained and the management of resources (*M*, above) is all about the efficiency of running the corporate entity. The dividend decision concerns flows of monies back to shareholders and, so the hypothesis goes, since equity investors obtain their remuneration via dividend, then enhanced dividend flows increase shareholder value. So much for the theory, what about the empirical evidence?

■ Empirically the evidence suggests that shareholder value is affected by the investment decision, the financing decision and the management of resources. Evidence is inconclusive on dividends.

■ The investment decision affects shareholder value. Relatively high net present value (NPV) projects create relatively high shareholder value.

■ High-returns projects are generally underpinned by market imperfections (for example, barriers to entry, patent protection, product differentiation and so on). After all, for a project in perfect competition circumstances it should earn a normal profit which, when discounted, should give rise to a zero NPV.

■ Over time, the benefits accruing to a project usually erode as the market imperfections themselves are eroded.

■ The successful business gives birth to new products and gains from the market imperfection created. And it regenerates old products by seeking new market imperfections.

■ The successful business also tries to transfer market imperfections from the home market to overseas markets.

■ The financing decision affects shareholder value. The suggestion is that there is an optimum capital structure. Moving towards it creates value for shareholders.

Given the target audience of this book, the mathematics has deliberately been kept at a reasonably unsophisticated level. The author's desire is very much to present a complex subject in the style of a good communicator. And this means that mathematics is our servant, not our god.

It is the intention that this book should be adopted by instructors for class use in teaching multinational finance. Having studied the content of this book, the reader should be able:

■ to appreciate the historic background and existing institutional framework of international money;

■ to understand the history and nature of Economic and Monetary Union in the European Union culminating in the introduction of the single currency, the euro, by various European countries;

■ to understand the roles and significance of equity and bond markets around the world;

■ to understand the workings and methods of quotation in the foreign exchange markets;

- to understand the theoretical relationship between spot and forward exchange rates, interest differentials, expected inflation differentials and expectations of future spot rates, and know how well they stand up in the real world;

- to understand the essence of theories for predicting future exchange rates;

- to understand how to use purchasing power parity data to forecast the future exchange rate;

- to estimate implied future exchange rates via the international Fisher effect;

- to define and distinguish different types of foreign exchange risk and recommend appropriate management action given the existence of these different kinds of exposure;

- to design an information system relevant to a multinational company's need to control, cost-effectively, foreign exchange exposure;

- to appreciate the opportunities which the multinational has to control foreign exchange exposure internally – that is, without the need to enter into contracts with third parties;

- to understand the essence of eliminating foreign exchange risk via forward markets, financial futures and currency options;

- to assess the international capital investment decision in a manner consistent with the parent company's desire to maximize the wealth of its shareholders;

- to obtain a general idea of the mode of working, opportunities and pitfalls created by exchange control regulations in countries in which the multinational corporation operates;

- to understand the sources and nature of country risk and political risk for the international company and, moreover, recommend appropriate management action to mitigate their impact in different circumstances;

- to understand the nature of and participants in the Eurocurrency markets and to assess why there might be opportunities to borrow in the Euromarkets at rates below those in comparable domestic markets;

- to appreciate the problems in financing an overseas subsidiary and make recommendations on the most appropriate financial structure given different sets of circumstances;

- to measure and compare the true cost of borrowing in the international financial arena;

- to appreciate how currency swaps and Euronote markets work and how market imperfections create opportunities in these directions for the astute corporate treasurer;

- to understand how corporate tax rules in many countries create opportunities and pitfalls for international financing and cross-frontier operations;

- to understand the nature of project finance and appreciate how it can create value for shareholders;

- to understand the opportunities available to finance international trade and minimize credit risk;

- to understand the difficulties and possible solutions to the problem of how to measure overseas subsidiary company performance and also appreciate the complexity of treasury performance measurement;

- to understand how and, more importantly, where market imperfections create profitable opportunities for the astute international financial manager.

It is as well for the reader to remember that analysis of international financial and investment opportunities with a view to maximizing shareholder wealth for the multinational investor involves searching out market imperfections and temporary disequilibria. And these are usually far more plentiful in the international arena than in its domestic counterpart. Clearly, avoidance of those that are potentially adverse and exploitation of those from which profitable outturns seem likely is the recommended course of action.

In the remainder of this chapter we describe a few key facts that are pertinent to the study of finance in the multinational arena. They have been set out here because students of the subject repeatedly find themselves asking about these topics. It will therefore be as well for readers to bear them in mind as they peruse the text. The topics briefly considered here are the products that banks market, the creation of Eurocurrency and a range of facts about the size of and participants in the foreign exchange markets.

The reader should be aware that we may denote currencies with their normal abbreviations ($ or €) or their SWIFT codes (USD or EUR). We do this deliberately to get students used to these two approaches. A list of world currencies with their SWIFT codes appears in Appendix 6. (Knowing these stands you in good stead for quizzes!) Where we merely use the term $, it refers to US dollars. For other dollars, like Australian dollars or New Zealand dollars, we tend to use their SWIFT codes, for example AUD and NZD, respectively.

1.1 | What do bankers sell?

Banks play a central role in financial management, whether in the domestic or in the international market place. Too often students of finance accept that banks occupy this vital position without asking themselves what kind of services bankers actually sell.

Most firms have a clearly visible product, for example Ford produces cars and GlaxoSmithKline produces pharmaceuticals. But confusion surrounds what banks actually produce. The answer is that banks basically produce money in the form of demand and time deposits. Demand deposits are those where the investor places money with the bank but the money is repayable to the investor without notice – that is, on demand. This contrasts with time deposits where the investor places money with the bank but the money is only repayable (except with penalty) after the expiration of a fixed time. Most time deposits involve the bank in paying interest to the investor; some demand deposits also attract interest, but some do not. The receipts from these deposits provide the wherewithal to make loans and buy securities and other assets that yield an interest income for the bank. Banks have numerous activities from which they receive fee income. They advise companies, manage trusts and so on. But the bread and butter activity of banking involves trading in demand and time deposits and loans.

Banks deal with two groups of customers – depositors and borrowers. Most borrowers are also depositors; some depositors are also borrowers. Business firms tend to be predominantly borrowers. Households tend to be primarily depositors. Banks are intermediaries between the depositors, who want a safe, secure and convenient place to store some of their wealth, and the borrowers, who want to expand their current production or consumption more rapidly than they can on the basis of their existing wealth and current income. The spread or mark-up between the interest rates bankers charge borrowers as against the cost of borrowing covers their expenses and is the source of their profits.

Profits in banking depend on four factors. The first two of these are their marketing skills in attracting deposits and their investment skills in making loans. Deposits coming in and loans going out appear on the bank's balance sheet respectively as liabilities and assets of the bank. The third source of profit is the banker's marketing, innovative and technical skills in rendering off-balance sheet services such as corporate finance advice and services relating to international trade. The fourth key to a bank's profit is, of course, management skills. Historically, the skills of bankers in terms of attracting deposits have been the key in determining how rapidly their banks grow. More recently, an emphasis upon off-balance sheet factors has become more evident – including the intermediation of money to borrowers from lenders and the practice of innovative services.

Investment skills involve matching the yields on loans and other assets with their risks. Riskier loans should attract higher yields. Banks seek those assets that offer the highest return for the risk. The banks that are best able to determine which assets are underpriced relative to their risks earn the highest returns. Banks that earn the highest returns are better able to increase the interest rates they pay on deposits, and hence they can grow more rapidly than their competitors.

1.2 | The creation of Eurodollars

The traditional definition of a Eurodollar is a dollar deposited in a bank outside the United States.[1] A Euro-yen is a yen deposited in a bank outside Japan. A Eurosterling deposit is created by depositing UK pounds in a bank account outside the United Kingdom. The term 'Eurocurrency' is used to embrace all forms of Eurodeposits. A certain amount of care needs to be exercised when interpreting information in this field because the term 'Eurodollars' is sometimes used as a generic term for all Eurocurrency deposits.

No mystery attaches to the production of Eurodollar deposits. In essence, the process is the same as when an individual with a deposit in one New York bank transfers funds to another bank in New York. The only difference is that the Eurobank in London is across the Atlantic rather than across the Big Apple. If an individual with a dollar deposit in New York decides to move funds to the London branch of the same bank, the bank ends up producing an offshore dollar deposit. The London bank deposits the cheque in its account in a US bank. The investor now holds a dollar deposit in a bank in London as opposed to a dollar deposit in a bank in New York. Total deposits of the banks in the United States are unchanged. Individual investors hold smaller deposits in the United States and they hold larger deposits in London. The London bank now has a larger deposit in the United States. The increase in the London bank's deposits in the New York bank is matched by the increase in dollar deposits for the world as a whole. But it is important to note that the volume of dollar deposits in New York remains unchanged, while the volume in London increases. To illustrate, take an example. Assume that an investor places $5m in a deposit account in a US bank in the United States (transaction A). This same investor subsequently requests his US bank to move his deposit to Londbank, a UK bank in London (transaction B). The T-account entries in the books of the US bank and the UK bank are respectively shown below.

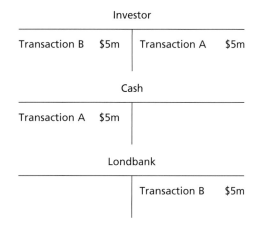

Entries in US bank books

Investor

| Transaction B | $5m | Transaction A | $5m |

Cash

| Transaction A | $5m | | |

Londbank

| | | Transaction B | $5m |

Entries in Londbank books

Investor

| | | Transaction B | $5m |

US bank

| Transaction B | $5m | | |

The T-accounts show that the transaction creating the Eurodollars left unchanged the volume of dollars deposited in the United States and that the Eurodollar deposit in London is backed by dollars in a domestic bank account in the United States.

In the domestic economy, the capacity of banks to expand their deposits is limited by the monetary authorities. They determine both the reserve base of the banking system (the supply of high-powered money) and reserve requirements. But in the external currency market – that is, the Euromarkets – there are no reserve requirements. Eurobanks sell additional deposits whenever the interest rates they are willing to pay are sufficiently high to attract new depositors.

The absence of reserve requirements on offshore deposits does not mean that there is the potential for an infinite expansion of deposits and credit. In the absence of reserve requirements domestically, there would not be an infinite expansion of domestic deposits and credit because bankers themselves would maintain prudential reserves. The growth of offshore deposits is limited by the willingness of investors to acquire such deposits in competition with domestic deposits. For investors, the relevant comparison involves the risk and return on offshore deposits and the risk and return on domestic deposits. The Eurobank system in dollars is an offshore extension of the domestic banking system, just as the Eurobank system in yen is an offshore extension of the domestic yen banking system. Eurobanks are offshore branches of the major international banks.

Dollar deposits in London differ from New York dollar deposits in terms of political risk. They are subject to the actions of a different set of government authorities. Maybe investors who continue to hold dollars in New York believe that London dollars are too risky, and that the additional interest income is not justified in terms of the possible loss if a move of funds back to New York were somehow restricted, perhaps as a package of exchange controls or an attack on the Eurobanking system. The continued growth in external deposits during the 1960s reflected increasing investor confidence that the additional risks attached to external deposits were small. The risks of holding dollars offshore seemed small, particularly when viewed in the light of the differential in dollar interest rates on offshore deposits relative to domestic deposits.

One popular explanation for the genesis of the Eurocurrency markets in the 1950s is that the Soviet government agencies wanted to maintain currency deposits in dollars because the dollar was the most accepted currency for financing their international transactions. They were reluctant to hold their dollars in deposits in New York because of the threat that the US authorities might freeze these deposits. So the Soviet dollars moved to London. The Soviets effectively believed that the political risk of London dollar deposits was lower than in New York.

While the Soviets may have been the cause of the rapid growth of offshore deposits during the 1950s, the big growth in the 1960s reflected other factors. The foremost of these was the increasing differential between Eurodollar and domestic interest rates, which made it increasingly profitable to escape national regulation. On top of this, growth was fuelled by the increasing size of the multinational firm and the great competitive expansion of banks.

Depositors contemplating a move of their funds to the Eurocurrency markets must decide whether to acquire external deposits in London, Zurich, Paris or some other centre. Depositors choose among centres on the basis of their estimates of political risk. This rules out many potential centres where regulation or the threat of regulation is evident. Even though there may be an interest rate that would induce lenders to acquire dollar deposits in Sofia, banks issuing these deposits would not necessarily have the investment opportunities to justify paying such high interest rates.

1.3 | Facts about the foreign exchange markets

For the majority of foreign exchange markets, there are no individual, physical market places. The market is made up of banks and dealers carrying out transactions via telephone and other telecommunication devices. The major players in the market are as follows:

- Commercial banks, investment banks and merchant banks, which may be dealing foreign currency on behalf of their clients engaged in international trade or which may be investing, speculating or hedging on their own account or for customers.

- Central banks, which may be managing their reserves or smoothing fluctuations in their own currency.

- Foreign exchange brokers, which act as intermediaries between other participants.

- Investment funds, moving from one currency to another.

- Corporations, which require foreign currency for trade or which may be hedging or speculating.

- High-net-worth individuals who may be investors or speculators.

The high-street bank customer, requiring foreign exchange for travel or holiday purposes, is an utterly insignificant participant in terms of the overall market.

The total world foreign exchange market is the largest of all markets on Earth. Trading around the world is estimated almost to have doubled between 1989 and 1992 and has increased by around 50 per cent to $1,210bn* per day in 2001, down from $1,450bn in 1998. This is well over 100 times the size of the New York Stock Exchange. The market is a twenty-four hour market which moves from one centre to another – from Tokyo to Hong Kong to Singapore to Bahrain to London to New York to San Francisco to Sydney – as the sun moves round the world.[2] Foreign exchange turnover in 1973 averaged a mere $15bn per day.

The largest centre of foreign exchange dealing is located in London with an estimated 2001 turnover[3] of $504bn per day in 2001, down from $637bn in 1998. This compares with $187bn per day in 1989, $291bn per day in 1982 and $464bn per day in 1995. New York is next in the league table with a daily turnover in 2001

---

* In this book, unless otherwise stated, '$' will always refer to US dollars. One billion means one thousand million.

of \$254bn (1998 – \$351bn, 1995 – \$244bn) and Tokyo's daily turnover is put at \$147bn (1998 – \$149bn, 1995 – \$161bn). Next comes Singapore with a daily figure of \$101bn; Germany, Switzerland, Hong Kong and Australia follow with respective daily turnovers of \$88bn, \$71bn, \$67bn and \$52bn as of 2001. It should be noted that merely aggregating the above figures indicates a total in excess of the estimated world turnover. The apparent anomaly is a result of double counting of individual deals that involve two centres. Between 1998 and 2001, most centres experienced falling turnover as inter-dealer business dropped, being replaced by electronic broking systems. Also, the introduction of the euro resulted in a decline in overall foreign exchange transactions.

Trade accounts for only 2 per cent of all foreign exchange deals. The lion's share of turnover is made up of capital movements from one centre to another and the taking of positions by bankers in different currencies.

Between 90 and 95 per cent of all foreign exchange transactions involve banks. This high preponderance is reflected by banks taking and unravelling positions in currencies and dealing on behalf of corporate customers. Around 90 per cent of all trades involve the US dollar. If a Swiss importer wishes to pay a UK exporter, the bank will calculate the Swiss franc/sterling rate as the combination of the Swiss franc/dollar rate and the dollar/sterling rate.

There is a spot market in which deals are arranged with immediate effect and there is a forward market in which purchase or sale is arranged today at an agreed rate but with delivery some time in the future. Forward markets do not exist for all currencies – for example, there is no forward market for some South American currencies. For a few currencies the forward market goes out to ten years or more; for many it is up to five years; for others it is out to one or two years and for others again it is only in existence for up to six months. The term 'deep market' refers to those currencies that are widely dealt – for example US dollars, euros, sterling. At the opposite end of the spectrum, the term 'shallow' or 'thin market' is applied to currencies such as many developing countries' currencies which are only occasionally traded.

The foreign exchange market is the cheapest market in the world in which to deal. If one were to start with \$1m, switch this into euros and then immediately reverse the transaction so that one returned to US dollars, the proceeds would be less than \$1m by the amount of twice the bid/offer spread (the rate for selling and the rate for buying) for euros against US dollars – after all, two deals have been done. But the total amount by which one would be out of pocket would only be \$250 or so. For major currencies, the large banks act as market-makers. This means that they hold stocks of foreign currencies and are prepared to deal in large amounts at stated prices.

Foreign exchange dealers can make or lose a lot of money for the banks which employ them. While they can make half a million dollars a day for the bank, they can also lose this sum. Their salaries and bonuses are high too. Some make \$1m per annum. But their business life is strenuous – watching currency movements for ten hours per day in the bank (and having a foreign exchange rate screen at home) and dealing on the finest of margins take a toll. Dealers on banks' foreign exchange desks seem to be aged between 20 and just over 30. Perhaps beyond 30, reflexes are slower; perhaps the adrenaline flows more slowly – or maybe dealers have made so much money already that motivation is not quite so great.

1.4 | Summary

- A Eurodollar is a dollar deposited in a bank account outside the United States (with some exceptions – see note 1 at the end of the chapter).

- A Euro-yen is a yen deposited in a bank account outside Japan.

- Eurosterling is represented by pounds deposited in a bank account outside the United Kingdom.

- Eurocurrency embraces all forms of Eurodeposit.

- The term Euro-euro is not used. But euros deposited in a bank account outside the eurozone area become Eurocurrency.

- The term Eurodollars is sometimes used (loosely and strictly incorrectly) to include all Eurocurrency deposits.

- The creation of Eurodollars leaves the volume of dollar deposits in the United States unchanged.

- Eurodollar deposits are backed by dollars in bank accounts in the United States.

- In the domestic banking market, government regulation is exercised through capital adequacy ratios, reserve asset requirements, the 'nod and wink' and other means – usually via the central bank and other monetary authorities.

- In the Euromarkets, there is no regulation, therefore no reserve asset requirements and no other controls.

- Dollars deposited in London or in the United States do not differ in terms of exchange rate risk – but they do in terms of political risk. They do in terms of credit risk, if the deposits are with different bankers.

- Significant participants in the foreign exchange market include commercial banks, investment banks, merchant banks, central banks, foreign exchange brokers, investment funds and institutions, corporations and high-net-worth individuals.

- The foreign exchange market is the largest market on Earth.

- Volume as at 2001 was running at an average of $1,210bn per day – in excess of 100 times that of the New York Stock Exchange. The 1998 figure was around $1,450bn per day.

- The foreign exchange market is a twenty-four hour market.

- The largest trading centre in the foreign exchange (FX) market is London with an estimated 2001 turnover of $504bn per day. Comparable New York figures are of $254bn per day and $147bn per day for Tokyo. Respective figures for 1998 were around $637bn, $351bn and $149bn.

- Trade accounts for only 2 per cent of all FX turnover.

Notes

1. This definition is referred to as 'traditional' because, since December 1981, it has been possible for certain US financial institutions to establish, within the United States, international banking facilities, commonly termed IBFs. The IBFs accepting foreign deposits are exempted from reserve requirements and interest rate restrictions and can make loans to foreign borrowers. In certain circumstances dollars deposited with an IBF effectively become Eurodollars.

2. The author is in no way quietly suggesting a resurgence of the Ptolemaic view of the heavens in preference to the Copernican theory. He merely feels that the above form of words far better conveys the message than saying 'as the world moves around the sun'!

3. Figures include only spot and forward deals and foreign exchange swaps. These transactions are explained in subsequent chapters.

2 The international monetary system

What do we mean by 'the international monetary system'? Essentially it encompasses the institutions, instruments, laws, rules and procedures for handling international payments, in particular those in final settlement of inter-country debts. Money has sometimes been defined as whatever is used in final settlement of debt. Internationally, central banks have come to be the institutions that make final settlements, and hence the assets they use may be termed 'international money'. Central banks hold reserves of international money. These have also been termed 'reserve assets'.

Prior to the Second World War there was no international central bank. Usually central banks of individual countries made final settlements through transfers of gold, sterling or US dollars. A transfer of gold, sterling or US dollars from one country (other than the United Kingdom or the United States) to another (again leaving aside the United Kingdom and the United States) reduced the former's reserve assets and increased the latter's. A transfer of sterling from the United Kingdom to another country could be made by creating sterling deposit liabilities owed to the other country. The same was true for the United States. Thus reserve currency countries (as the United Kingdom and the United States came to be termed) had a different status from that of other countries. They could finance purchases, loans and investments by creating debt. They were effectively bankers to the world. They could create international money. If other countries had deficits in their balance of payments, they had to export gold or sterling or US dollars, thus reducing their holdings of international money. But as long as foreign countries accepted dollars or sterling, the United States and the United Kingdom could settle deficits by creating international money.

In this chapter we trace the international monetary system from before the First World War to the present time.

2.1 The gold standard

The international monetary system that operated immediately prior to the 1914–18 war was termed the 'gold standard'. Then, countries accepted two major assets – gold and sterling – in settlement of international debt. So the term 'gold/sterling standard' might be more appropriate.

Most major countries operated the gold standard system. A unit of a country's currency was defined as a certain weight – a part of an ounce – of gold. It also provided that gold could be obtained from the treasuries of these countries in exchange for money and coin of the country concerned.

The pound sterling could be converted into 113.0015 grains of fine gold, and the US dollar into 23.22 grains. The pound was effectively defined as 113.0015/23.22 times as much gold as the dollar – or 4.8665 times as much gold. Through gold equivalents, the pound was worth $4.8665. This amount of dollars was termed the 'par value' of the pound.

A country is said to be on the gold standard when its central bank is obliged to give gold in exchange for its currency when presented to it. When the United Kingdom was on the gold standard before 1914, anyone could go to the Bank of England and demand gold in exchange for bank notes. The United Kingdom came off the gold standard in 1914, but in 1925 it returned to a modified version termed the 'gold bullion standard'. Individual bank notes were no longer convertible into gold, but gold bars of 400 ounces were sold and bought by the Bank of England. Other countries adopted either this system or the gold exchange standard, under which their central banks would exchange home currency for the currency of some other country on the gold standard rather than for gold itself. The United Kingdom was forced to abandon the gold standard in 1931.

The gold standard was a keystone in the classical economic theory of equilibrium in international trade. The currency of countries on the gold standard was freely convertible into gold at a fixed exchange rate and enabled all international debt settlement to be in gold. A balance of payments surplus caused an inflow of gold into the central bank. This enabled it to expand its domestic money supply without fear of having insufficient gold to meet its liabilities. The increase in the quantity of money tended to raise prices, resulting in a fall in the demand for exports and therefore a reduction in the balance of payments surplus. In the event of a deficit in the balance of payments, the reverse was expected to happen. The outflow of gold would be accompanied by a relative money supply contraction, resulting in exports becoming more competitive and the deficit automatically becoming corrected.

The adoption of the gold standard began in the United Kingdom early in the nineteenth century. An attempt was made in the 1860s by a number of European countries to establish the Latin Monetary Union, involving bimetallism for gold and silver. The intention was that both gold and silver should be used for international debt settlement. But the establishment of the gold standard in Germany in 1871, together with less demand for silver in other areas, led to a diminished use of silver as international money. The United States was forced to abandon redemption of paper money in metal during the Civil War, but the redemption of paper money for gold began in 1879.

Key dates for the adoption of the gold standard in selected countries are summarized in Table 2.1.

The First World War had a serious effect on the international monetary system. The United Kingdom was forced to abandon the gold standard because of the wartime deficit on its balance of payments, and its reluctance at that time to provide gold to settle international differences. This was, perhaps, the beginning of a reduction in confidence in sterling as an international reserve asset.

Table 2.1 Dates for the adoption of the gold standard

United Kingdom	1816
Germany	1871
Sweden, Norway and Denmark	1873
France, Belgium, Switzerland, Italy and Greece	1874
Holland	1875
Uruguay	1876
United States	1879
Austria	1892
Chile	1895
Japan	1897
Russia	1898
Dominican Republic	1901
Panama	1904
Mexico	1905

Source: Chandler (1948).

Many other countries abandoned the gold standard temporarily, but none had the same significance as the action of the United Kingdom because sterling had financed 90 per cent of world payments. The UK government, recognizing the importance of sterling and of UK institutions in international finance, wished to return to the gold standard as soon as possible. Delay occurred because of the recession in the United States in 1920 and 1921, coupled with the post-First World War inflation, which reversed itself as rapidly as it had occurred. Recovery came in the United States, and a degree of recovery also occurred in the United Kingdom. After its disastrous hyperinflation, ending with the value of the mark at 4 trillion to the dollar, Germany also experienced stabilization and returned to the gold standard in 1924.

The gold standard to which major countries returned in the mid-1920s was different from that which had existed before the First World War. The major difference was that instead of two international reserve assets – gold and sterling – there were several. Both the United States and France had become much more important in international finance, and dollar and franc deposits were used for much financing. However, generally speaking, countries other than the United Kingdom had only small amounts of gold. When some countries, including France, accumulated sterling balances, they sometimes attempted to convert these into gold, drawing upon the United Kingdom's gold reserves. When sterling had been the only international currency apart from gold, operating the international monetary system had not been difficult, but when there were a number of countries whose bank deposits constituted international money, and when confidence in different currencies varied, the system became more difficult to operate.

A second important difference was that flexibility in costs and prices no longer existed as it had before the First World War. This was especially important in the United Kingdom which had returned to the gold standard based on pre-war par values. But only with a decline in relative costs and prices could the former par value of the pound have been maintained in the long run. Given that flexibility in costs and prices was lacking, confidence in sterling deteriorated, culminating in the United Kingdom abandoning the gold standard in 1931. Most other countries followed the UK example in quitting the gold standard.

But there were other forces impinging on the United Kingdom in the early 1930s which also had a significant effect on its decision to discard the gold standard. Two of these were the Great Depression of the late 1920s and early 1930s and the international financial crisis of 1931; each of these topics is now summarized with a focus upon their impact on the international monetary system.

2.2 | The Great Depression

A detailed discussion of the causes of the Great Depression is outside the terms of reference of a work of this sort. Nonetheless various questions may spring to the reader's mind. Some of these are pertinent to the international monetary system; some are not. To what extent was the stock market crash in 1929 a cause of the Depression? How did the big contraction in money supply contribute to a decline in business activity? Was the decline in rates of profit, which began in 1929, significant? Some of the explanations propounded do have significance in terms of their effects on the United Kingdom and the gold standard.

One such is the fact that the expansion in money and credit in the late 1920s in the United States was greater than that needed for trade and commerce, and the excess found its way into stock market and real estate speculation. When the credit expansion ceased, stock market levels and real estate prices fell. A relevant question is why the expansion of money and credit did not result in a greater increase in either real output or prices of commodities and services. And one possible answer is that wage rates did not increase much, with the result that consumer spending did not rise sufficiently to cause any marked rise in either real or nominal gross national product (GNP).

Interest rates and the availability of credit in the United States are inextricably linked to the United Kingdom's plight. Following the sharp rise in stock market prices in 1927 to 1929, the Federal Reserve Bank raised the discount rate as part of the classical prescription for slowing the growth of money supply. This resulted in higher interest rates in the United States and this had the tendency to attract foreign funds – particularly from the United Kingdom. Remember that we are talking about an environment with fixed exchange rates. So funds moved out of the United Kingdom to take advantage of higher relative interest rates at the same time as gold was leaving the country because of the United Kingdom's overvalued exchange rate.

Discussing the Depression, Friedman and Schwartz (1963) have argued that what began life as a minor recession was transformed into a major depression because as business declined, the money supply was reduced. With the United States committed to deflation accompanied by a reduction in its money supply, the impact on the rest of the world was devastating. Friedman and Schwartz demonstrate impressive evidence of a correlation between declines in business activity and declines in the money stock, not only during the Great Depression but in the five other instances between 1867 and 1960. They point out that in each case the decline in the money supply preceded the decline in business activity.

Furthermore, the United States had imposed import restrictions in 1922 and again in 1930. Countries heavily dependent upon exports found their incomes falling sharply, their unemployment levels rising and their consumption falling. They could finance their essential imports neither from their exports nor from their reserves.

Add to a world economic system under strain the precariousness of an international monetary system, balanced like an inverse pyramid upon a relatively small base of gold holdings, and our structure is weak indeed. Strains on those countries without substantial gold holdings could cause difficulties for the gold exchange standard countries. Moreover, strains on a gold standard country resulting in a flow of gold reserves to another country could easily precipitate a financial crisis. Many economists are convinced that the supply of gold at that time was inadequate to support the international financial structure of the day.

Exchange rates were out of line with cost structures in different countries. The United Kingdom's return to the old par value for sterling was undoubtedly an error; France's devaluation of the franc in the 1920s was too great; fundamental disequilibria existed. And the system was inadequate to cope with them. Faced with an overvalued currency in deep depression, one of the United Kingdom's responses was to abandon the gold standard.

2.3 | Exchange rates: 1914 to 1944

With the First World War, the stability of exchange rates for major currencies ended. This had been a key feature in the international monetary system before 1914. When the First World War began, the combination of payments via London for imports under bank credits and acceptances of London merchant banks together with utter confidence in sterling – meaning that there were no significant withdrawals of sterling deposits – caused the exchange rate for the pound to rise sharply. Sterling rose as high as $7 to the £. But as wartime expenditures occurred the sterling exchange rate began to fall, and it had dropped as low as $3.18 by early 1920.

As explained earlier in this chapter, the early 1930s saw the international monetary system then in use begin to disintegrate. By the beginning of 1933 the major economies of the world could be categorized as those of the gold bloc (France, Switzerland, the Netherlands and Belgium) which maintained the value of their currencies in terms of gold; those that maintained their currencies' values by strict exchange controls (such as Germany) enforced under a dictatorship; and those that permitted their currencies to depreciate. Many currencies depreciated by as much as 35 to 50 per cent during the first half of the decade. Those countries that did not permit their currencies to depreciate – for example, the United States, France, Belgium, Switzerland and the Netherlands – resorted to strong deflationary pressures. A frequent complaint was that some countries deliberately encouraged currency depreciation, engaging in a beggar-my-neighbour policy. International trade was at a low level, and international capital flows virtually stopped.

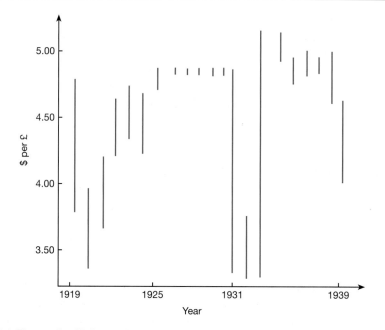

Figure 2.1 The sterling/dollar exchange rate, 1919–39 (range based on monthly averages).

The depreciation of currencies in the 1930s – especially that of the pound (see Figure 2.1) – meant a decline in the foreign exchange component of international reserves relative to the gold component. With limited production of gold and with strong flows thereof to the United States, most countries found their gold holdings reduced. Large fluctuations in exchange rates, accompanied by low levels of international trade and world depression, led to influential calls in the late 1930s and early 1940s in favour of a return to a stable exchange rate environment.

However, the Second World War led to more extensive and tighter controls on international trade and investment. Transactions with enemy countries became illegal, and much of the trade between friendly nations consisted of munitions and warfare supplies. Private markets (as opposed to inter-governmental ones) for most currencies almost ceased to exist. Much of the trade that continued was under various inter-governmental agreements. But even the inter-governmental transactions that took place then were generally either barter transactions or grants made to carry on hostilities against the enemy. There was virtually no role for international finance. Foreign exchange markets, exchange rates and other institutional mechanisms were effectively suspended during the war and were not re-established until the war ended. Trade controls and exchange controls frequently meant that the usual methods of financing could not be used. So the financing of trade was not an urgent problem during the war.

By the end of the Second World War, many commentators, bankers and economists were agreed upon the need for a new monetary system. Sterling's dominance of international trade had gone; the era of the gold standard was passed. Governments might have waited for a new international monetary order to evolve to replace the system that had worked well before 1914 but which had failed in the period from 1914 to 1944. However, this would have meant uncertainty. Action was urgently needed. The action taken stemmed from the Bretton Woods agreement and saw the creation of a new international institution, the International Monetary Fund. The monetary system that emerged from Bretton Woods occupied the international stage for the immediate post-1945 period through to 1971.

2.4 | The Bretton Woods system

The framework for a new international monetary system was created in July 1944 in the United States at Bretton Woods, New Hampshire. The prime movers were John Maynard Keynes and Harry Dexter White, the respective UK and US representatives. The key innovations of the Bretton Woods agreement were as follows:

- A new permanent institution, the International Monetary Fund (IMF), was to be established to promote consultation and collaboration on international monetary problems and to lend to member countries in need due to recurring balance of payments deficits.

- Each fund member would establish, with the approval of the IMF, a par value for its currency and would undertake to maintain exchange rates for its currency within 1 per cent of the declared par value. Countries that freely bought and sold gold in settlement of international transactions were deemed to be adhering to the requirement that they maintain exchange rates within 1 per cent margins. Hence the United States, the only country that met this condition, was not expected to intervene in the foreign exchange markets. Other countries would intervene by buying or selling dollars against their own currencies, to keep their rates within 1 per cent of their parities with the dollar.

- Members would change their par values only after having secured IMF approval. This approval would be granted only if there were evidence that the country was suffering from a fundamental disequilibrium in its balance of payments. It was generally agreed that a long and continuing large loss of reserve assets in support of an exchange rate would be evidence of this fundamental disequilibrium.

- Each IMF member country would pay into the IMF pool a quota, one-quarter being in gold with the remainder in its own currency. The size of the quota was a function of each member's size in the world economy.

- The IMF would be in a position, from the subscription to quotas, to lend to countries in ongoing deficit.

A new monetary framework was thus established which created fixed exchange rates subject to alteration should fundamental disequilibria emerge. Since there was a mechanism for discontinuous adjustment to exchange rates, the system became known as the adjustable peg system.

During its early years, the Bretton Woods system played a positive part in a rapid expansion in world trade. However, its success obscured one of its basic short-comings – there was no provision for expanding the supply of international reserves necessary to support growing trade flows. The unmet demand for international reserves eventually led to increased holdings of national currencies and in particular it strengthened the US dollar's position as an international reserve currency.

The dollar's expanding role in international trade and finance raised new problems in monetary relations. This difficulty has been referred to as the Triffin dilemma after Triffin (1960) who focused attention upon it. Because the US dollar played the part of a reserve currency, US balance of payments deficits were necessary in order to increase international liquidity. But as US liabilities to foreign central banks grew, so confidence in the convertibility of dollars into gold wavered. US gold reserves were becoming a decreasing fraction of foreign liabilities. This method of providing international liquidity could continue only as long as no central bank attempted a run on the US gold reserves. Concern over this dilemma led to the introduction of a new international reserve asset administered by the IMF. This asset, the special drawing right (SDR), was proposed and ratified in 1969.

SDRs were allocated to individual countries by the IMF through the deliberate decision of IMF members to accept them as a new form of international reserve. These credits were allocated to IMF members in proportion to their quotas – rather like a bonus issue of shares in a company. A country holding SDRs may use them to acquire foreign currency by transferring them, via the IMF special drawing account, to another country in exchange for foreign currency. Only member states of the IMF and certain designated official institutions may legally hold SDRs.

2.5 | The role of gold up to 1971

Gold has long existed as a medium of international exchange. But in its role as a reserve asset it has significant shortcomings. First, it is wasteful to use a commodity with a significant positive cost of production to perform a function that could equally well be performed by a financial instrument with a zero cost of production. Secondly, the use of gold gives benefits to the country where the gold is produced and which may not necessarily benefit the world economy. And there have been objections to the political nature of the world's largest gold producer, South Africa. Thirdly, the increase in the supply of gold may not reflect the world's increasing need for extra international liquidity. Indeed increases in gold supplies may be unrelated to the world's needs. They may be influenced, though, by the need for foreign exchange on the part, for example of South Africa.

The price of gold was fixed in 1933 at $35 an ounce and this fixed value held up to the early 1970s. Since the currencies were fixed in relation to the dollar, central banks could exchange their currencies for dollars and with their dollars they could obtain gold. The US Federal Reserve Bank was willing to buy and sell gold at this rate. This willingness of the United States to back the world monetary system is understandable given that the United States, at the end of the Second World War, had a gold stock valued at $20bn or 60 per cent of the total of official gold reserves. As long as the dollar and its gold backing was considered invulnerable, foreign central banks had an incentive to hold currencies, which earned interest, rather than gold, which earned nothing.

In 1954 a gold market was opened in London in which private buyers and sellers could operate. A central bank gold pool of $80m was set up in 1962. The gold pool was an arrangement among eight countries, including the United States, to sell or buy gold in the free market to keep the price close to the official price of $35 an ounce. France left the gold pool in 1967.

By the late 1960s there existed a situation whereby the dollar had become convertible into gold not only by foreign central banks but also by private speculators all over the world. Until 1968, under the gold pool arrangement, major central banks clubbed together to hold the gold price at $35 an ounce. As there was no prospect of the gold price going down, but a good prospect of it going up, this gave speculators a one-way option. In 1968 central banks were forced to set the gold price free for commercial transactions. However, for settlements between themselves, they agreed to stick to the old price and not to sell gold on the free market. The central banks expected that under this two-tier gold system, the free-market gold price would stay within easy reach of the official price. It did not do so for long.

Increasingly, fixed exchange rates were becoming more and more difficult to defend and various governments around the world were very reluctant to devalue and revalue despite what many would have described as fundamental disequilibria. In other words, national governments were abusing the system.

In 1971 the system was clearly under pressure on two fronts – the fixed gold price and fixed exchange rates made little sense. Matters were brought to a head when President Nixon, as a preparation to the 1972 election, sought to expand demand in the United States. Speculation against the dollar mounted and many central banks in continental Europe and Japan were forced to buy dollars to keep their currencies within the narrow bands required by Bretton Woods – rather than rising, which economic and speculative pressures were favouring. The free-market gold price rose sharply. This led several countries to demand conversion of their surplus dollars into gold at the official price of $35 per ounce. The United States, with $10bn in gold reserves versus liabilities of $50bn in other countries' reserves, decided to suspend convertibility in August 1971 and the US dollar was set free to float.

There being considerable anxiety about the international monetary system, a conference of finance ministers was summoned in December 1971 at the Smithsonian Institute in the United States. The so-called Smithsonian Agreement resulted. This increased the fixed exchange rate band spread to 4.5 per cent, allowing central banks more room for manoeuvre before intervention became necessary. At the same time upward revaluations of various currencies against the US dollar were agreed, with the dollar formally devaluing against gold. The price of the metal was increased from $35 per ounce to $38 per ounce – an effective dollar devaluation of 9 per cent.

The dollar-based international monetary system continued to function for just over another year, when the failure of the US balance of payments to respond to the dollar's initial devaluation led to a second realignment. The dollar was devalued again in February 1973; this raised the official gold price to $41.22 per ounce. But this realignment was almost immediately brought under excessive strain when a new exchange crisis emerged in March 1973 and European central banks refused to buy dollars. In mid-March the Bretton Woods era finally crumbled when fourteen major industrial nations abandoned the adjustable peg and allowed their currencies to float against the dollar. But we are not universally in a floating exchange rate world now, as we shall see shortly.

2.6 | The Second Amendment

Following abandonment of pegged exchange rates in March 1973, floating exchange rates were introduced for many countries. In Europe, the opinion was widespread that floating should be only temporary, a view most forcibly expressed by the French. In the United States, opinion favoured a continuing float.

Discussions at summit level moved from Rambouillet in France in November 1975 to Jamaica in January 1976 and culminated in a new IMF article on exchange rate practices. This amendment, the second in the history of the IMF, was ratified by the required majority and became effective on 1 April 1978.

The Second Amendment provided for the reform of three key aspects of international monetary relations. First, it allowed substantially more flexibility in the management of exchange rates and expanded the IMF's responsibility for supervising the international monetary system. Secondly, it altered the nature of the SDR to increase its attractiveness as an international reserve asset. And finally, it simplified and expanded the IMF's ability to assist members in financing short-term imbalances in their international payments accounts.

Under the first innovation, IMF members are expected to 'collaborate with the fund and other members to assure orderly exchange arrangements and to promote a stable system of exchange rates' (IMF, 1978). Their method of collaboration is left to members' discretion.

Members' obligations regarding their exchange practices are specified under Article IV of the fund's Articles of Agreement. Under this amended article (IMF, 1978), each member shall:

- endeavour to direct its economic and financial policies towards the objective of fostering orderly economic growth with reasonable price stability, with due regard to its circumstances;

- seek to promote stability by fostering orderly underlying economic and financial conditions and a monetary system that does not tend to produce erratic disruptions;

- avoid manipulating exchange rates or the international monetary system in order to prevent effective balance of payments adjustment or to gain an unfair competitive advantage over other members.

In April 1977, the IMF adopted principles (IMF, 1977) to provide additional guidance in the choice of an exchange policy. These principles of exchange rate management state that:

■ a member shall avoid manipulating exchange rates or the international monetary system to prevent effective balance of payments adjustment or to gain an unfair competitive advantage over other members;

■ a member should intervene in the exchange market if necessary to counter disorderly conditions, which may be characterized *inter alia* by disruptive short-term movements in the exchange value of its currency;

■ members should take into account in their intervention policies the interests of other members, including those of countries in whose currencies they intervene.

The above principles give members a great deal of latitude in the choice of an exchange rate policy. Members may peg, float or manage their currencies to whatever degree they feel is consistent with their own domestic economic policies. The Second Amendment restricts the role of gold in the international monetary system. Par values may not be set in terms of gold and an official price for gold has been abolished. Members are expected to co-operate in reducing the role of gold with the intention that the SDR should become the primary reserve asset of the international monetary system. The IMF abolished requirements that members make some payments in terms of gold and began to dispose of its gold reserve.

Through its surveillance, the IMF identifies members causing disruptive variations in exchange rates through their domestic economic policies. The IMF may then suggest alternative domestic policies which would have less of an effect on the exchange market.

Providing members with assistance in overcoming payments imbalances continues to be one of the IMF's prime objectives. A member in need of foreign exchange to finance short-term exchange rate intervention may apply to the IMF for borrowing assistance.

2.7 | International reserves

The IMF provides its members with international reserves through the SDR. Changes in the calculation of the value and interest rate earned on excess holdings of SDRs have increased their attractiveness as a reserve asset. The value of the SDR is no longer fixed in terms of the US dollar. Its value is now calculated using a currency basket. The SDR valuation basket consists of the currencies of the five members having the largest exports of goods and services – that is, the US dollar, the euro, the Japanese yen and the pound sterling. Their respective weightings are 42 per cent, 31 per cent, 15 per cent and 12 per cent.

The dollar value of the SDR is computed daily using the average of the buying and selling rates at midday on the London foreign exchange markets. The amounts of currency making up the SDR are fixed; changes in market exchange rates cause changes in the effective weights of the currency amounts over time. The interest rate paid to members holding more than their allocation of SDRs and owed to members holding less than their allocation is determined quarterly as a weighted average of market interest rates. The attractiveness of the SDR has also been increased by expanding the types of transaction in which it can be used. In addition to financing outright purchases of foreign currencies, members can now use SDRs in forward and swap transactions and they can donate SDRs and make SDR-denominated loans to other members and authorized non-member institutions.

2.8 | Exchange rate arrangements

The current exchange rate practices of IMF members span the range of alternatives from pegging to floating. Pegged exchange rates are generally managed on a day-to-day basis through official intervention in the foreign exchange markets and by internal regulations limiting exchange market transactions. Exchange rate parities are set in terms of a foreign currency or group of currencies, and fluctuations in the exchange rate around this parity are managed by official intervention.

Countries that peg their exchange rate may select from a wide range of alternatives. Many nations peg to a single currency, but it has become increasingly common to peg against a group of currencies. Pegging is attractive because it helps reduce the variability of prices in the domestic economy. However, pegging has its costs. These flow from the need to regulate international transactions and intervene in foreign exchange markets.

Generally speaking, floating exchange rates are managed less closely, although practices vary. Some members refrain altogether from intervention, while others intervene strongly. In most cases, nations with developed financial markets prefer floating exchange rates.

The arrangements used by the 186 nations that reported their exchange policies to the IMF on 31 December 2001, are summarized in Table 2.2. Clearly, most currencies operate according to a floating mechanism but there are, in fact, a range of exchange rate regimes around the world.

In truth, countries that allow their currency to float do not commit themselves not to intervene. Indeed they either manage exchange rates informally, or use some set of economic indicators or rely on a co-operative exchange rate agreement such as the European Monetary System. Informal managed floats are the most frequently used. Many of these floaters follow strategies of leaning against the wind. This approach involves official intervention to smooth short-term fluctuations in exchange rates without unduly restricting long-term trends. Other nations with informally managed floats set target exchange rates and intervene to move market rates towards these levels.

Some countries rely on objective indicators to provide signals rather than either using targets or leaning against the wind. These indicators are used to show the economic need for a devaluation or a revaluation. Parities are adjusted frequently, in small amounts, as dictated by the indicators. Exchange market intervention is used to limit exchange rate fluctuations around these central rates.

When a country chooses to peg or float its currency, it is not obliged to co-operate with the IMF or any other nation in the day-to-day management of exchange rates. Although most members value this independence, some nations wish to maintain

Table 2.2 Exchange rate pegging around the world, 31 December 2001

Exchange rate regime	Description	Detail	Number of countries	Examples
Exchange arrangements with no separate currency specific only to the country concerned	The currency of another country circulates as the sole legal tender or the member belongs to a monetary or currency union in which the same legal tender is shared by the members of the union	Eurozone	12	Germany, France, Netherlands etc
		Central Africa Franc (CFA) Zone, West African Economic and Monetary Union (WAEMU)	8	Senegal
		Central African Economic and Monetary Community (CAEMC)	6	Cameroon
		Eastern Caribbean Currency Union (ECCU)	6	Grenada
		Another currency as legal tender	8	Panama
Currency board arrangements	A monetary regime based on an explicit legislative commitment to exchange domestic currency for a specified foreign currency at a fixed exchange rate		8	Lithuania
Other conventional fixed peg arrangements	The country pegs its currency (formally or de facto) at a fixed rate to a major currency or a basket of currencies where the exchange rate fluctuates within a narrow margin of less than ±1 per cent around a central rate	Against a single currency	30	Saudi Arabia
		Against a composite	10	Malta

Table 2.2 (cont'd)

Exchange rate regime	Description	Detail	Number of countries	Examples
Pegged exchange rates within horizontal bands	The value of the currency is maintained within margins of fluctuation around a formal or de facto fixed peg that are wider than at least ±1 per cent around a central rate	Exchange Rate Mechanism of EU	1	Denmark
		Other currency band arrangements	4	Egypt
Crawling pegs	The currency is adjusted periodically in small amounts at a fixed, preannounced rate or in response to changes in certain quantitative indicators		4	Bolivia
Exchange rates within crawling bands	The currency is maintained within certain fluctuation margins around a central rate that is adjusted periodically at a fixed preannounced rate or in response to changes in certain quantitative indicators		6	Uruguay, Venezuela
Managed floating with no preannounced path for exchange rates	The monetary authority influences the movement of the exchange rate through active intervention in the foreign exchange market without specifying, or precommiting to, a preannounced path for the exchange rate		42	Thailand
Independent floating	The exchange rate is market determined, with any foreign exchange intervention aimed at moderating the rate of change and preventing undue fluctuations in the exchange rate, rather than at establishing a level for it		41	USA, UK

closer economic ties with their trading partners. Article IV does not prohibit these nations from co-operating with each other in the management of their bilateral exchange rates. This practice, classified by the IMF as a co-operative exchange arrangement, has become known as group floating, of which the European Monetary System has been the most well known.

2.9 | The European Monetary System

The European Monetary System (EMS) was effectively the embryo that led to the European single currency, the euro. It is worth beginning this section by being clear that the EMS has been neither a pure fixed exchange rate system nor a pure floating rate mechanism.

The EMS was created in 1979 by the European Union (EU) countries with the dual objectives of establishing a zone of exchange rate stability to encourage trade and growth and of accelerating the convergence and integration of economic policies within the EU.

The main characteristic of the EMS was the operation of its exchange rate system. The European Currency Unit (ECU) was the nucleus of the EMS. The ECU comprised a basket of fixed amounts of EU currencies. The ECU was replaced on 1 January 1999, on a one for one basis, by the euro. In other words, one euro equals one ECU.

The ECU was used both as the numeraire of the Exchange Rate Mechanism and as a means of settlement between central banks within the EU. Additionally, it existed as a unit of account for official EU business. The ECU was frequently used as a currency of denomination in the international credit and bond markets. In this respect, the euro has taken over from the ECU.

2.10 | The exchange rate mechanism of the EMS

The central idea underpinning the European Monetary System was to achieve currency stability through co-ordinated exchange rate management. This would facilitate trade within the EU and set the stage for moves towards a single currency towards the end of the twentieth century.

The exchange rate mechanism, a system of flexible exchange rates, was the central plank of the EMS. Countries participating in the ERM would keep the value of their currencies within specified margins (originally $2^{1}/_{4}$ per cent) either side of central rates against the other currencies in the mechanism. Not all EU countries participated in the ERM.

The ERM worked by requiring members to intervene in the foreign exchange markets to prevent currencies breaching their ceilings or floors against the other ERM currencies. Thus, if the peseta fell to its floor within the system, the Bank of Spain would be required to buy pesetas and/or sell other ERM currencies to bolster the peseta against its fellow European exchange rates. Other members would be required to help by intervening on behalf of the weak currency. In our example, this would prop up the peseta before it fell through its floor.

As a second resort, the country whose currency was under pressure could raise its short-term interest rates to make its currency more attractive to investors. If intervention on the foreign exchanges and adjustment of interest rates failed to stop a currency from moving outside its ERM limits, a last resort would be a realignment of the central rates to relieve the tensions in the system. In fact, there were several such realignments.

Economic and Monetary Union

Countries may link their currencies together in various ways. At one end of the spectrum would be a relatively light linkage with little sacrifice of independence of monetary policy; at the other, there might be a convergence of policy such that independence is given up altogether. In 1989, a committee headed by Jacques Delors, the then President of the European Commission, recommended a three-stage transition to a goal of monetary union at the strongly convergent end of the above financial spectrum. The ultimate goal was for Economic and Monetary Union (EMU), a European Union in which national currencies would be replaced by a single EU currency managed by a sole central bank operating on behalf of all EU members.

The Delors vision involved three stages. In the first, all EU members would join the exchange rate mechanism (ERM). In stage 2, exchange rate margins would be narrowed and certain macroeconomic policy decisions placed under more centralized EU control. Stage 3 of the plan would involve the replacement of national currencies by a European currency and the vesting of monetary policy decisions in a European System of Central Banks, similar to the US Federal Reserve System and headed by a European Central Bank.

On 10 December 1991, the leaders of the EU countries met at Maastricht in the province of Limburg at the most southerly tip of the Netherlands. They proposed far-reaching amendments to the Treaty of Rome. These amendments would put the EU squarely on course to EMU. Included in the 250-page Maastricht Treaty were provisions calling for a start to stage 2 of the Delors plan on 1 January 1994 and a start to stage 3 no later than 1 January 1999, which has now been achieved. In addition to its monetary policy provisions, the Maastricht Treaty proposed steps towards harmonizing social policy within the EU (with rules on work-place safety, consumer protection and immigration) and towards centralizing foreign and defence policy decisions of EU members.

In terms of moving to stage 3, convergence criteria were set for individual countries as follows:

- The inflation rate must be within 1.5 percentage points of the average rate of the three EU states with the lowest inflation.

- The long-term interest rates must be within 2 percentage points of the average rate of the three EU states with the lowest interest rates.

- The national budget deficit must be below 3 per cent of GNP.

- The national debt must not exceed 60 per cent of GNP.

- The national currency must not have been devalued for two years and must have remained within the 2.25 per cent fluctuation margin provided for by the EMS.

Despite the optimism of Maastricht, the treaty was viewed with some scepticism, especially in the United Kingdom. Prospects for EMU worsened during 1992 as ERM parities were hit by speculative attacks that led to the UK pound and the Italian lira making their exits from the ERM on 16 September 1992 – coined 'Black Wednesday'. Investors and speculators shifted vast funds out of sterling and the lira into the Deutschmark. Both sank well below their ERM floors as the authorities gave up the struggle to keep them within their old bands. On that day, the UK government tried to maintain the pound exchange rate by intervening heavily in the foreign exchange market and by announcing an increase in interest rates from 10 per cent to 15 per cent. But this was not enough to stem the flow against sterling and, after a steady drain on reserves, the UK government pulled out of the ERM and lowered interest rates back to 10 per cent – and all on the same day.

For the next eleven months or so, relative calm returned to the ERM. But, in August 1993, tensions rose again – this time centred on the French franc. France was in a recession with high unemployment yet was unable to cut its very high interest rates much below Germany's because both were within the same currency zone.

One solution might have been for Germany to lower its lending rates, but the Bundesbank, the German central bank, did not contemplate such a move for fear of encouraging inflation at home. The prime duty of the Bundesbank, an independent Central Bank, as set out in its constitution, was to monitor domestic monetary policy. The Bundesbank was required, by law, to put the need for low German inflation before the troubles of the ERM.

Pressure mounted. Finance ministers of EU countries met to find a solution. Their answer was to widen the currency bands for all, except the Deutschmark and the Dutch guilder, to 15 per cent. The mark/guilder band remained at $2^{1}/_{4}$ per cent.

Despite occasional turbulence within the ERM, by 31 May 1995, the European Commission launched a blueprint for achieving a shift to a single currency by the end of the century. Their green paper adopted a gradual approach but the Commission remained confident that an unspecified number of countries in the then 15-strong European Union would move to a single currency by the beginning of 1999 with the introduction of Euro-banknotes and coins following within a maximum of three years. The green paper proposed three stages in transition towards the adoption of the ECU (now termed the euro) as the new currency of legal tender. These stages were:

- *Phase A*. There would be a gap of one year between commitment by participating countries and locking of exchange rates

- *Phase B*. The European Central Bank would fix parities and begin operating a single monetary policy

■ *Phase C*. The final changeover to the single currency would follow three years later with participating countries' national notes and coins being phased out and the euro becoming their sole legal tender. For participating countries all bank accounts, cheques, transfers and credit cards would be converted into euro.

The 74-page green paper listed the benefits of a single currency as a more efficient single market, stimulation of trade, growth and employment, elimination of transaction costs and an increase in international monetary stability.

The United Kingdom's position outside the first wave towards a common currency was always certain. In the longer term, the United Kingdom's parliamentary system and culture create problems. Most European countries effectively have coalitions in government with the result that the attempt of the ruling party to engineer an economic boom in the run-up to a general election is not so marked as in the United Kingdom. There are many who would argue that the United Kingdom's virtual two-party system is well past its sell-by date. When contrasted with its European counterparts, claims that it achieves superior performance are ludicrous. UK insularity, both in a literal and metaphoric sense, was evidenced when the single currency came into play on 1 January 1999 with the United Kingdom on the sidelines.

2.11 │ The European single currency – the euro

On 1 January 1999, a single European currency (the euro) was introduced in eleven EU countries, with one further entrant two years later. The countries of the euro zone are: Austria, Belgium, Finland, France, Germany, Greece, Ireland, Italy, Luxembourg, Netherlands, Portugal and Spain. We will refer to this group as euroland. The countries of the EU that initially remained outside euroland were the United Kingdom, Denmark, Greece and Sweden. Greece was the late arrival.

The twelve EU countries form an economic and monetary union (EMU) and use the single currency – the euro. These countries locked the exchange rates of their national currencies to the euro and share the new currency.

The twelve countries share a single interest rate, set by the European Central Bank (ECB), and a single foreign exchange rate. The ECB is responsible for the monetary policy of these euro zone countries.

Ever since the European Economic Community (EEC) started in 1957, there were suggestions of more economic co-operation between countries – including a single currency. The creation of the Single Market in 1992 brought the economies of different EU regions closer together, created lower inflation and this increased EU income. Economic convergence between participating countries is the primary condition for a single currency.

EU countries that have decided not to join yet will be able to join when they are ready, provided that they meet the conditions for entry set out in the Maastricht Treaty.

The euro has brought big changes for business both within euroland countries and throughout Europe. For example, there are cheaper transaction costs, exchange rate certainty and transparent price differences. We look at these in turn.

- *Cheaper transaction costs.* The single currency allows firms in countries in the euro zone to trade with each other without changing currencies. This reduces transaction costs. It now costs less for companies to make payments between countries within the euro zone.

- *Stable exchange rates.* The single currency removes exchange rates between countries in the euro zone. This leads to better decision making for its companies.

- *Transparent price differences.* The single currency makes price differences in different countries in the euro zone more obvious. This may affect companies who charge different prices for their products in countries within the euro zone. Also, companies buying from the euro zone will be able to compare prices more easily. Either way, this should sharpen competition.

Even though the United Kingdom has not joined the single currency, the euro zone has had an effect on many UK businesses, especially those that buy and sell products throughout Europe. Some UK companies are using the euro for buying and selling goods and services within the United Kingdom itself. This is the case in supply chains which involve multinational companies. Arrangements for countries which join the single currency after 1 January 1999 will be negotiated at the time they join.

2.12 | Summary

- Immediately prior to 1914 most major countries operated the gold standard system – two major assets, gold and sterling, were accepted in settlement of international debt. A country's central bank was obliged to give gold in exchange for its currency when presented to it.

- In 1914 the United Kingdom, in common with many other countries, left the gold standard.

- In 1925, the United Kingdom adopted the gold bullion standard. Individual bank notes were not convertible into gold but gold bars were sold and bought by the Bank of England. Many other countries adopted this system on the gold exchange standard under which their central banks exchanged home currency for the currency of some other country on the gold standard rather than gold itself.

- The United Kingdom abandoned the gold standard in 1931. Until the Second World War, most countries moved to a system of fluctuating exchange rates while others adopted strict exchange controls.

- The post-war monetary system was created in 1944 at Bretton Woods, New Hampshire.

- The Bretton Woods agreement created the International Monetary Fund (IMF), a world central bank. It established a fixed exchange rate system with countries maintaining their exchange rates within 1 per cent of a declared par value against the US dollar. The United States itself would buy and sell gold in settlement for international transactions. Other countries would intervene in the FX market to keep their currency value within 1 per cent of the declared parity, against the dollar. This parity, the par value, would only be changed with IMF approval. All IMF member countries would pay a quota into the IMF pool and this would be available for loan to countries in need of the wherewithal to intervene in FX markets to keep rates at their par value.

■ The US dollar became the reserve asset of the new monetary order. But with world trade growing, the need for international liquidity grew. To meet this need for international currency, continuing US balance of payments deficits were necessary to put dollars into the system. This shortage of international liquidity reached a head in the late 1960s. The IMF countered in 1969 by creating a new international reserve asset, the SDR (special drawing right).

■ Originally the SDR was equal to a fixed number of dollars, it is now a basket currency consisting of 42 per cent dollars, 31 per cent euros, 15 per cent Japanese yen and 12 per cent sterling.

■ In 1969, SDRs were allocated to IMF members rather like a bonus issue of shares in a company.

■ Strains on the system came to a further head in the early 1970s. The official price of gold had remained fixed at $35 an ounce since 1933. The US Federal Reserve Bank was willing to buy and sell gold at this rate. In 1954 a gold market had been opened in London. As of the early 1970s many countries which should have revalued their currencies had failed to do so – Germany and Japan were two.

■ The fixed exchange rate system and the fixed gold price made little economic sense.

■ With the US president seeking to expand demand prior to the 1972 presidential elections, expectations of dollar devaluation began to materialize.

■ The free-market gold price rose sharply and in August 1971 the United States suspended convertibility and set the dollar free to float. At the Smithsonian Institute in the United States in December 1971, the fixed exchange rate spread was widened from 1 per cent to $4^1/_2$ per cent and the dollar was devalued against gold – from $35 an ounce to $38.

■ This was not enough. In February 1973 the dollar was again devalued to $41.22 per ounce of gold and in March 1973 the Bretton Woods era formally crumbled when fourteen major nations decided to float their currencies.

■ Nowadays, most major currencies around the world have floating exchange rate regimes while many maintain fixed rate systems. Some are fixed against the dollar, some against the euro, some against the SDR. In Europe, twelve countries have adopted the euro as their currency.

■ On 1 January 1999, a single European currency (the euro) was introduced in eleven EU countries. The original eleven countries of the euro zone are Austria,

Belgium, Finland, France, Germany, Ireland, Italy, Luxembourg, Netherlands, Portugal and Spain. Greece has subsequently joined the euro zone.

- The twelve countries share a single interest rate, set by the European Central Bank (ECB), and a single foreign exchange rate. The ECB is responsible for the monetary policy of these euro zone countries.

- Countries whose economies were not ready to join the euro system, and countries that have decided not to join yet, will be able to join when they are ready, provided that they meet the conditions for entry set out in the Maastricht Treaty.

- The euro is the legal currency in the euro zone.

- Euro banknotes and coins were introduced in the euro zone on 1 January 2002 and old national banknotes and coins were withdrawn from circulation.

- Even though the United Kingdom has not joined the single currency, the euro zone has had an effect on many UK businesses, especially those that buy and sell products throughout Europe.

- Arrangements for countries which join the single currency after 1 January 1999 will be negotiated at the time they join.

- For euro-zone businesses and consumers, the euro has brought cheaper transaction costs, exchange rate certainty and transparent prices for transactions within the region.

2.13 | End of chapter questions

Question 1
Compare and contrast the fixed exchange rate, free floating, and managed floating systems.

Question 2
How can central banks use direct intervention to move the value of a currency?

Question 3
List and discuss the advantages and disadvantages of a freely floating exchange rate system versus a fixed exchange rate system?

3 Corporate finance around the world

In introducing the topic of corporate finance around the world, we are immediately confronted with a big problem, namely that corporate finance is not homogeneous – far from it. The stock market plays a bigger part in some countries than in others; shareholder returns as a corporate goal are emphasized to different extents in different countries; corporate governance differs across borders; takeovers are more prevalent in some territories than in others; accounting rules are different and so are tax systems; banks play greater roles in some countries compared with others and they operate in varying ways in various countries. But not everything is different. Many factors are common across borders. So, let us confront the problems head on and examine the world corporate finance environment. In this respect we focus, first of all, upon stock markets in developed economies.

3.1 | World equity markets

In this section, we present a brief overview of equity markets. Table 3.1 summarizes equity market capitalization (the total value of all of companies' ordinary shares in terms of their stock market value) and turnover of the major exchanges in Europe, the United States and Japan. It tells an interesting story. Note that the data in the table relates to the beginning of 2000. Since then, equity markets have fallen dramatically – in many cases in excess of 50 per cent. So the data therein hardly applies nowadays. The point is that by contrasting the magnitude of market capitalization to GDP for different countries, a feeling of equity culture can be gleaned – although in many cases, this may be subsiding. Care must be exercised in doing this. For example, the statistic for Finland is highly affected by the dominance of one key company, Nokia. And there are a number of similar kinds of reservations.

However, in general terms, the large economies of France and Germany display far lower market capitalization to GDP data than the UK. The high ratio for the Dutch market can be attributed, primarily, to a small number of very large multinational firms, such as Royal Dutch Shell and Unilever.

Trends in market capitalization versus GDP for selected countries are summarized in Table 3.2 (overleaf). At the time of writing (early 2003), the percentages shown have, in most cases, been strongly reduced.

Table 3.1 Capitalization of world stock markets at the start of year 2000

Country/region	Market capitalization* $ billion	GDP in 1999 $bn	Market capitalisation* to GDP %
United States	16,635	9,152	182
Japan	4,547	4,347	105
United Kingdom	2,933	1,442	203
France	1,475	1,432	103
Germany	1,432	2,112	68
Canada	801	635	126
Italy	728	1,171	62
The Netherlands	695	394	176
Switzerland	693	259	268
Hong Kong	609	159	383
Australia	478	404	118
Spain	432	596	72
Taiwan	376	288	131
Sweden	373	239	156
Finland	349	130	268
China	331	990	33
South Korea	309	407	76
South Africa	262	131	200
Brazil	228	752	30
Greece	204	125	163
Belgium	185	248	75
Denmark	105	174	60
Ireland	65	93	70
Subtotal	**34,248**	**25,680**	
Other Asia-Pacific	1,065	n/a	
Other Europe	365	n/a	
Other South/Central America	359	n/a	
Other Africa	62	n/a	
World total	**36,099**	n/a	

* Since 2000, equity markets have fallen dramatically so the latest figures would be far lower. The point of the table is to show sharply contrasting equity cultures.
Source: Dimson, Marsh and Staunton (2002).

What about ownership of firms listed on stock markets? Although data are somewhat frail and hardly fully comparable, Table 3.3 (overleaf) summarizes a number of studies of ownership of listed equities in non-financial corporations in six European countries plus the United States and Japan. Of course, given that the studies underpinning data in the table are not fully comparable, very firm conclusions cannot be confidently drawn. Despite this, the high concentration of ownership in continental European and Scandinavian countries, compared with the United Kingdom, Japan and the United States is clear. Generally, the high ownership concentration countries are those where the equity market is less cultivated. Franks, Mayer and Rennebog (1995) report that 79 and 85 per cent respectively of local companies quoted on

Table 3.2 Market capitalizations versus GDP for selected countries (percentages) – 1980, 1994, 1998 and 2000

	1980	*1994*	*1998*	*2000*
France	3.7	34.2	57.9	103.0
Germany	7.9	23.3	47.3	67.8
Italy	1.5	17.7	41.1	62.2
Netherlands	15.2	68.1	160.5	176.4
Switzerland	32.2	125.0	255.5	267.6
UK	20.6	112.7	156.3	203.4
Japan	24.7	74.1	56.5	104.6
USA	23.4	63.9	130.6	181.8

Table 3.3 Ownership concentration in listed firms in various countries (the largest owner's share)

Largest owner's share	*France* (1982)	*Germany* (1985)	*Italy* (1993)	*Spain* (1990)	*Sweden* (1987)	*UK* (1990)	*Japan* (1983)	*US* (1981)
> 50	55	66	89	49	42	5	5	9
30–50					31			
25–30		23	9		12	29		29
20–25	42			49				
15–20					11	27	70	
10–15								10
5–10		12	2		4	30		29
< 5	2			2		9	25	23

Sources: Berglöf (1988), Barca (1995), Galve Gortiz and Salas Fumas (1993), Steil (1996).

stock exchanges in France and Germany in the early 1990s had a single investor with stakes larger than 25 per cent – the corresponding figure for the United Kingdom was only 16 per cent of companies. The overwhelming majority of listed companies in continental Europe are closely held. Although comparisons over time are not always available, the evidence for France, Germany and Sweden shows an increase in ownership concentration over the 1970s and 1980s – see Berglöf (1988). Establishing the identity of controlling holders is often difficult in many countries, especially where bearer securities are the norm and where the beneficiaries of nominee holdings do not have to be disclosed. (Bearer securities contrast with registered securities. The latter involve the name of the owner and his or her address being recorded by the company. This is not so for bearer securities. The ownership of bearer securities passes on mere delivery.) However, the importance of families in the control of corporations is one of the continuing central features distinguishing the continental European business environment from those of the United Kingdom and the United States. This concentration of ownership has also been observed by Steil (1996) who comments upon its relation to liquidity in local equity markets and to the willingness of firms to list on public stock exchanges.

Table 3.4 Ownership of listed equities in various countries by sector
(as of 31 December)

		Private individuals	Non-financial corporations	Government institutions	Financial institutions	Foreign owners
France	1977	41	20	3	24	12
	1992	34	21	2	23	20
Germany	1970	29	41	11	11	8
	1993	17	39	3	29	12
Italy	1993	32	22	28	14	4
UK	1969	50	5	3	36	6
	1993	19	2	1	62	16
Japan	1970	40	23	0	34	3
	1993	20	28	1	43	8
USA	1991	51	15	0	28	6
	1993	48	9	0	37	6

Source: Barca (1995); Berglöf (1988); Lannoo (1994).

In practically all European countries, institutional shareholders have, over the recent past, become more important at the expense of private individuals – see Table 3.4. However, the types of institutions holding shares, and possibly exercising control, are different. In the United Kingdom, the growth of pension funds over the past two decades has been spectacular. The strong portfolio-orientation of institutional investors in the United Kingdom contrasts sharply with the control-orientation of this investor group in, for example Germany.

There are also differences in the nature of the market for corporate control – mergers and acquisitions. In the United Kingdom and the United States, hostile takeovers mounted via purchases in the official stock market play an important role in the world of business. In continental Europe, such transactions are far less the norm. In Germany, the Netherlands and Belgium, this is largely true. Sweden experienced four successful hostile offers during the 1980s, a period of substantial local corporate restructuring. Reversing past passivity, the French authorities have, over the past decade, made a point of activating the market for corporate control and there have been a considerable number of takeovers against the will of incumbent management. But, in general, takeovers in continental Europe have been a mechanism to withdraw firms from the stock exchange rather than as a means of altering control. To some extent, this seems to be changing towards the Anglo-American way. Most control-related trades in continental Europe occur in large blocks of shares outside official markets.

Pension funds also have different levels of importance in the pattern of investment in different European countries. Table 3.5 (overleaf) shows contrasting pension fund asset levels in eleven European countries in the early 1990s. They represented a very high percentage of GDP in the Netherlands, the UK and Ireland. Large variations were apparent on this score. UK pension fund assets amounted to 82 per cent of GDP, a figure only exceeded in Europe by the Netherlands. The contrast of Germany and France, where pension fund assets amounted to only 6 per cent and 3 per cent,

Table 3.5 Assets of pensions funds in various EU countries – end 1993 (US$bn)

	Pension fund assets (end-1993) $bn	% of GDP	% of pension fund assets held in foreign assets
UK	717	82	31
Germany	106	6	8
Netherlands	261	85	21
Sweden (1991)	39	16	1
Denmark	26	19	4
Ireland	18	44	41
France	41	3	2
Italy	12	1	4
Belgium	7	3	37
Spain	10	2	10
Portugal	5	7	10

Includes only independent (private- and public-sector) funded schemes.
Source: European Federation for Retirement Provision/EU Committee.

Table 3.6 Pension funds' portfolio distributions in various EU countries (percentage allocations), 1992

	Equities	Fixed income	Property	Liquidity and deposits
UK	80	11	6	3
Germany	6	80	13	1
Netherlands	24	60	14	2
Sweden	2	90	2	6
Denmark	19	67	12	2
Ireland	66	24	7	3
France	20	67	11	2
Italy	14	72	10	4
Belgium	31	50	8	11
Spain	3	94	2	1
Portugal	18	58	5	19

Source: European Federation for Retirement Provision/EU Committee.

respectively, of GDP, is a marked one. In the EU, foreign assets as a significant percentage of pension fund investments were concentrated in UK, Irish, Belgian and Dutch funds. Equity holdings of pension funds in the early 1990s varied from 80 per cent of the portfolio in the United Kingdom to 6 per cent in Germany and to only 2 per cent in Sweden – see Table 3.6. Apart from the United Kingdom and Ireland, the lion's share of pension fund portfolios was invested in fixed income investments. Since 2001, following the sharp equity market setback, the UK and Ireland have much smaller percentage investments in equities and more in fixed interest securities.

In terms of the history of stock markets, the founding dates for numerous markets are summarized in Table 3.7. Most of the larger markets have longer histories.

Table 3.7 Founding dates of some of the world's stock markets

The Netherlands	1611	Argentina	1872	Indonesia	1912
Germany	1685	New Zealand	1872	Korea	1921
United Kingdom	1698	Brazil	1877	Slovenia	1924
France	1724	India	1877	Uruguay	1926
Austria	1771	Japan	1878	Philippines	1927
United States	1792	Norway	1881	Colombia	1929
Ireland	1799	South Africa	1887	Luxembourg	1929
Belgium	1801	Egypt	1890	Malaysia	1929
Denmark	1808	Hong Kong	1890	Romania	1929
Italy	1808	Chile	1892	Israel	1934
Russia	1810	Greece	1892	Pakistan	1947
Switzerland	1850	Venezuela	1893	Lebanon	1948
Spain	1860	Mexico	1894	Taiwan	1953
Canada	1861	Yugoslavia	1894	Kenya	1954
Hungary	1864	Sri Lanka	1900	Nigeria	1960
Turkey	1866	Sweden	1901	Kuwait	1962
Australia	1871	Portugal	1901	Thailand	1975
Czech Republic	1871	Singapore	1911		
Poland	1871	Finland	1912		

Source: Goetzmann and Jorion (1999), Dimson, Marsh and Staunton (2002).

By 1910, Michie (1992) reports that UK investors owned 24 per cent of the outstanding value of securities worldwide, followed by US citizens with 21 per cent, French with 18 per cent and German with 16 per cent. Russians were reported as holding 5 per cent, Austro-Hungarians 4 per cent and Italians and Japanese 2 per cent each. Most of the balance was held by other western European investors. The data relate to ownership and the figures cover all securities, including bonds. An interesting feature of the markets in 1900 was the prevalence of cross-border investment. Europeans invested heavily in the less developed countries – the Americas, Africa, Russia, South-eastern Europe, Turkey and the Far East. Firms based overseas issued many of the securities traded in London and Paris. Even in such advanced economies as Canada and the USA, Europeans owned a large proportion of all stocks and bonds. Later in the twentieth century, the impact of war, the Wall Street Crash, the Great Depression, currency restrictions, protectionism, and the Cold War made investors become insular and international investment did not return as a major force until the 1970s.

3.2 | World bond markets

Rivalling equities in terms of world market size, bonds are important financial instruments. A bond is a promissory note, under seal, to pay money. The term is generally applied to such instruments, issued by governments and corporations, for debt with an initial maturity of twelve months or more. At the start of 2000, the size of

Table 3.8 Value of world bond markets at the start of year 2000

Country/region	Total outstanding $ billion	% bonds which are government bonds	Bond value as % GDP
United States	14,595	53	159
Japan	5,669	72	130
Germany	3,131	25	148
Italy	1,374	68	117
France	1,227	58	86
United Kingdom	939	50	65
Canada	539	73	85
The Netherlands	458	38	116
Belgium	324	60	131
Spain	304	73	51
Switzerland	269	18	104
Denmark	264	31	152
South Korea	227	52	56
Brazil	209	n/a	28
Australia	198	42	49
Sweden	188	50	79
Austria	149	54	72
India	136	70	30
Greece	88	78	70
China	73	67	7
South Africa	72	65	55
Ireland	32	74	34
Other Asia-Pacific	310	46	29
Other Europe	235	70	28
Other South/Central America	44	n/a	6
World total (40 countries)	**31,054**	**55**	**109**

Source: Merrill Lynch (2000), Dimson, Marsh and Staunton (2002).

the world bond market was $31 trillion, just below the $36 trillion value of world equities. Most developed countries have active markets trading government and corporate bonds. In many countries, their size and trading volume exceed that in equities. The bond markets enable long-term borrowing and lending. In addition, most countries have active money markets for short-term lending and borrowing, trading in securities such as treasury bills, certificates of deposit, and commercial paper. Table 3.8 shows data on the world's major bond markets at the turn of the century.

The table shows that the $14.6 trillion US bond market is the world's largest, representing 47 per cent of the global total. Japan and Germany are in second and third place in terms of market size followed by Italy, France, and the United Kingdom. The United Kingdom has a much smaller bond market versus equities in terms of both absolute size and in terms of capitalization versus GDP. Germany is exactly the opposite, displaying a bond culture rather than an equity culture – perhaps influenced by fifty years of low inflation. Bonds denominated in the world's three main currencies – the USD, EUR and JPY account for 88 per cent of the total world bond markets.

Government issues make up 55 per cent of the world bond market. Of the balance, 26.4 per cent is domestic corporate bonds; 15.1 per cent is made up of Eurobonds; and 3.6 per cent, foreign bonds. Eurobonds are issued internationally, in international markets. Foreign bonds and Eurobonds, like domestic bonds, are issued mainly by governments as well as companies. Foreign bonds are issued in domestic markets but by non-resident entities. Around two-thirds of all outstanding bonds are government issue and one-third are corporate bonds. Japan, Germany and Italy, among others, have larger bond than equity markets. The equity markets of the United Kingdom, Switzerland, Australia, Sweden and South Africa are far larger than their bond markets. The United Kingdom is interesting in this respect. Its bond market is the world's fifth largest and it was less than a third of the size of its equity market at the end of the twentieth century.

Many factors contribute to these differences in equity and bond market sizes. Governments are large bond issuers, so differences in macroeconomic policy, government borrowing, and budget deficits strongly influence national bond market sizes. Countries with larger public sectors and nationalized industries have more government debt. Those that have experienced widespread privatizations have often used the proceeds to retire debt. For the corporate sector, companies operating in countries with bank-based financial systems (that is, with commercial bank board representation – notably Germany, Japan and Italy) have tended to place greater emphasis on debt than equity financing. This has fostered larger corporate bond markets. Another influence is the balance between the usage of short-term debt versus bonds. The Japanese bond market would be even larger but for its government's heavy reliance on short-term borrowing to finance its budget deficit. The US bond market grew significantly from 1990 onwards with a shift away from bank lending towards the capital markets as the key source of funding. At the start of the new millennium, bank loans accounted for 10 per cent of financial assets in the United States, versus 40 per cent in Japan and 50 per cent in the eurozone group of countries.

3.3 | Corporate governance and corporate finance

Corporate governance is concerned with how a company is directed and controlled and, in particular, with the role of the directorate and the need for ensuring that there is an effective framework for accountability of directors to owners. Corporate governance and financial market liquidity are important topics in the finance literature. But they have traditionally been addressed independently of each other. Here we attempt to link the two. The starting point of the corporate governance literature is the agency problem of capitalism. This concerns the credibility problem facing firms when they seek to convince outside investors to contribute funds. In its most extreme form, the agency problem is about how to ensure that management does not steal investors' contributed resources or pay themselves undeserved handsome salaries and so on. The role of corporate governance is to ensure that resources are not dissipated but applied effectively into profitable investment opportunities. There are two generic approaches to the classic agency problem: either key investors are given influence over strategic decisions in the firm (control-oriented finance) or management finds ways of committing to efficient actions and shares in the proceeds from these actions (arm's-length finance).

Under control-oriented finance, investor intervention is typically based on a control block of equity or a position as exclusive or dominant creditor. Intervention may take many forms, from vetoing or blocking inefficient investment decisions to using a voting majority to oust incumbent management.

Under arm's-length finance, investors do not intervene in the company, at least not as long as payment obligations are met. Intervention, if it occurs, typically involves some external mechanism such as renegotiation of corporate control, or a court in the case of bankruptcy. The firm attempts to commit to behave efficiently and to repay investors and, in the meantime, it may provide collateral in the form of contingent property rights to individual well-specified assets or cash flows.

The basic issue of these two approaches to the agency problems is the same – how to convince investors that they will be repaid in the future. The choice of ownership structure has important implications for the way in which the problem is addressed. In the case of control-oriented finance, control is concentrated from the outset, but in the arm's-length case, we rely on the accumulation of controlling stakes – and this, in turn, presupposes the existence of a liquid market through which this is facilitated in the market place.

Systems where control-oriented finance dominates can be expected to be associated with more concentrated ownership structures at the level of the individual firm and with less liquid capital markets. Control-oriented financial systems breed control-oriented investors. The market for corporate control (takeovers) operates outside of the public stock exchanges in the form of occasional trades in large blocks.

Arm's-length systems have dispersed ownership of both debt and equity, and more liquid capital markets. Investors are oriented towards holding portfolios of securities and the market for corporate control operates over public stock markets and this is seen as an important mechanism for the correction of managerial failure. Table 3.9 summarizes hypothesized and observed contrasting characteristics of control-oriented and arm's-length types of financial systems.

Although the link between corporate finance and governance, on the one hand, and corporate law and securities regulation, on the other, is still poorly understood, a recent survey of the corporate governance literature, by Shleifer and Vishny (1995), argues that concentration of ownership is an unavoidable outcome of shortcomings in the legal system. In the absence of well-functioning securities regulation, concentration of ownership is the only way to surmount the agency problem referred to above. Shleifer and Vishny imply that ownership and control patterns are ultimately determined by existing laws. On this front, it is not a coincidence that continental Europe has a legal system founded on codified Roman law whereas the legal systems of England and the United States are rooted in common law. This distinction is worth further comment.

Some countries have a legal system that relies upon a limited amount of statute law and a large amount of case law built up in the courts, supplementing the statutes. Such a common law system is the case in England. It is hence less abstract than codified law. A common law rule seeks to provide an answer to a specific case rather

Table 3.9 Characteristics of control-oriented and arm's-length financial systems

	Type of financial system	
	Control-oriented	*Arm's-length*
Share of control-oriented finance in capital markets	High	Low
Financial markets	Small, less liquid	Large, highly liquid
Number of firms listed on exchanges	Small	Large
Ownership of debt and equity	Concentrated	Dispersed
Investor orientation	Control-oriented	Portfolio-oriented
Turnover of control blocks	Very low	Relatively high
Dominant agency conflict	Controlling *v.* minority shareholders	Shareholders *v.* management
Influence of board of directors	Less important	Important
Role of hostile takeovers	Very limited	Potentially important

Table 3.10 Western legal systems

Common law	*Codified Roman law*
England and Wales	France
Ireland	Italy
United States	Germany
Canada	Spain
Australia	Netherlands
New Zealand	Portugal
	Japan (commercial)

The laws of Scotland, Israel and South Africa, among others, tend to embody elements of both systems.

than to formulate a general rule for the future. Although this common law system emanates from England, it is found in similar forms in many countries influenced by England. For example, the federal law of the United States, the laws of Ireland, India and Australia are, to a greater or lesser extent, modelled on English common law. Other counties have a system of law that is based on the Roman civil law as compiled by Justinian in the sixth century and subsequently developed, at least in Europe, by continental European élites. Here, rules are linked to ideas of justice and morality and they become doctrine and codified in laws. The above distinction has important implications for company law or commercial codes. Table 3.10 illustrates the way in which developed countries' legal systems fall into these two categories.

Nobes and Parker (2002) note the relevance of the above classification in terms of its impact for company accounting – they state that in Germany accounting is 'to a large extent a branch of company law'. The fact that England and continental Europe fall in opposite camps in Table 3.10 may partially explain differences in corporate governance.

3.4 | Corporate reporting around the world

The International Accounting Standards Committee (IASC) was formed in 1973 with the goal of harmonizing international accounting standards. The IASC Board is comprised of representatives from thirteen national standard-setting bodies and up to four other organizations plus a smaller number of non-voting observers. The IASC has recently become a major force in global accounting and financial reporting. Many multinational companies already use the IASC's standards to report their financial performance to international investors. Harmonized standards are important to international investors with a desire to obtain a clear understanding of the risks and performance of the companies in which they invest.

In 1998, the IASC completed a project to develop a comprehensive set of core standards for companies raising capital or listing securities internationally. Several national and international agencies are currently reviewing these standards. The US Securities and Exchange Commission is discussing allowing foreign issuers to use the IASC standards in securities offerings in the United States rather than forcing non-US companies to adopt US generally accepted accounting principles (GAAP). International convergence of accounting standards should ease reporting requirements for multinational corporations and facilitate the free flow of capital.

One of the most interesting developments concerning corporate reporting around the world has been that the European Commission has proposed that by 2005 all EU listed companies must prepare their consolidated financial accounts using International Accounting Standards (IAS). Companies will also have to provide comparative figures for 2004.

Perhaps the most important issue arising from this relates to the adoption of IAS 39 which is concerned with the recognition and treatment of financial instruments, including derivatives. We present more on this topic in Chapter 9.

The historic emergence of different international reporting systems has been widely studied. Following earlier work by Nair and Frank (1980), Nobes and Parker (1998) proposed a hierarchy model of financial reporting. Their classification of fourteen countries is interesting and is summarized in Figure 3.1. By and large, the countries to the right in Figure 3.1 can be characterized by legal systems derived from codified Roman law – see Table 3.10 – and those to the left are mainly rooted in common law. Particularly relevant in Figure 3.1 are the various sources of driving force discernible from country to country – for example the influence of the tax system, and so on. Of course, further territories could be added, for example:

■ Singapore, Hong Kong and Malaysia, under UK influence;

■ Korea, near Japan;

■ Switzerland and Austria, close to Germany;

■ Denmark, close to the Netherlands.

As Nobes (1992) has suggested, EU harmonization of accounting may be in the process of reducing variations in Figure 3.1.

All the European countries in Figure 3.1, except the United Kingdom, Ireland, Denmark and the Netherlands, appear to the right of the tabulation. Were one to

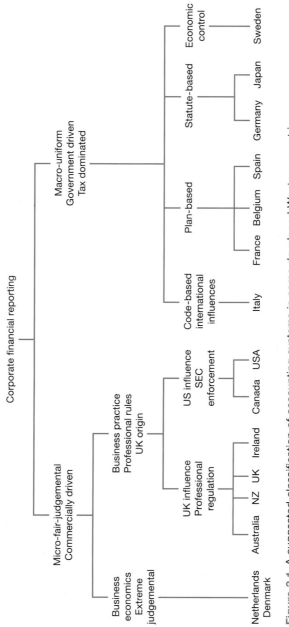

Figure 3.1 A suggested classification of accounting systems in some developed Western countries.
SEC = US Securities and Exchange Commission.

Source: Nobes and Parker, 1998.

wish to put traditional (pre-IAS) accounts from countries on the right-hand side on to a UK-style basis, a number of adjustments would be required. In general terms, according to Alexander and Nobes (1994), these would embrace the following:

- *Conservatism*. Increase net asset values.

- *Historic cost*. Increase net asset values.

- *LIFO* (last in, first out). Increase inventory values for some countries.

- *Consolidation*. Beware lack of consolidation.

- *Associated companies*. Increase net assets and profit where the equity method of accounting is not used.

- *R&D*. Decrease net assets by any capitalized amounts. Adjust profits appropriately.

- *Leases*. Increase fixed assets and liabilities where leases are not capitalized.

- *Pensions*. Examine carefully. Extract any pension provisions from shareholders' funds.

- *Provisions*. Increase shareholders' funds by portion of general provisions.

- *Tax*. Decrease depreciation where reporting is tax-driven.

Some of the most important differences in reporting practices around the world include the following:

- capitalization of research and development is not allowed in Germany and the United States;

- fixed asset revaluations in excess of historic cost are not allowed in the United States, Japan and Germany;

- depreciation charges in accounting reports are tax-based in Germany and in Japan (and to some extent in France too).

3.5 | Different corporate tax systems

Different corporate tax systems across boundaries create another problem in corporate finance. Essentially, the problem arises not from differences in rate, but from differences emanating from the use of the classical system versus the imputation system. How each works precisely is well summarized in Nobes and Parker (2002). So, what is the essential difference between the two systems?

Under a classical system, corporate tax is borne, in the usual way, by the company. But, on payment of a dividend to shareholders, the gross amount of the dividend is subjected to further tax deduction, usually representing shareholder tax at the basic tax rate. The dividend received by the shareholder is net of both corporate tax and shareholder basic rate tax. Higher levels of tax on the dividend may subsequently

Table 3.11 Various corporate tax systems in 2000

Country	System	Corporation tax rate %[a]	Tax credit as % of dividend
Austria	Classical (Split Rate to 1989)	34	–
Belgium	Classical (Imputation 1963–89)	40[b]	–
Denmark	Classical (Imputation 1977–91)	32	–
Finland	Imputation (1990+)	29	40.89
France	Imputation (1965+)	36.66	50
Germany	Imputation (Dividend partially exempt[c])	40[d]	43
Greece	Dividend Exempt (Dividend Deductible to 1992)	40[e]	–
Ireland	Classical (Imputation 1976–99)	20[f]	–
Italy	Imputation (1977+)	50[g]	58.73
Luxembourg	Classical	37[h]	–
Netherlands	Classical	35	–
Portugal	Imputation (1989+)	32	28.23
Spain	Imputation (1986+)	35	40.00
Sweden	Classical	28	–
UK	Imputation (1973+)	30	11
USA	Classical	35	–

[a]Withholding taxes have been ignored throughout.
[b]This Includes a 3% austerity surcharge.
[c]Half of dividends are taxable.
[d]Including a solidarity charge of 5.5% of the tax, and a business tax.
[e]35% for listed companies.
[f]Rate for 2001; it falls to 16% for 2002.
[g]This includes a regional tax.
[h]Including business tax.
Source: Nobes and Parker (2002).

be collected from the shareholder to the extent that he or she falls into high tax brackets. But note particularly the incidence of double taxing.

The imputation tax system is designed to eliminate this double taxing effect. Under it, like the classical tax system, the company pays corporation tax. But when it pays a dividend, it is looked upon as a net dividend and no further shareholder tax is paid, until higher rate calculations are made. The dividend is, though, said to be net of an imputed tax (the tax credit) and it is, of course, the net dividend plus this imputed tax credit which are added together for purposes of income calculation for higher level tax rate calculation, to give the gross dividend.

Nowadays, the Netherlands, Denmark, Austria, Belgium, Sweden, Luxembourg and the United States use the classical tax system. France, Finland, Germany, Ireland, Italy, Portugal, Spain, Australia and New Zealand employ the imputation system. The United Kingdom uses a quasi-imputation system. Rates of corporate tax in the year 2000 and the systems employed are summarized in Table 3.11.

On the topic of corporate taxes, it is worth noting that most tax regimes have statutory rules for depreciation allowances in computing profit for tax purposes. Referring back to Figure 3.1, it is worth noting that most of the countries to the right side in that figure tend to use tax depreciation in their published accounts as the amortization charge for reporting purposes.

Although the EU has plans for harmonization of tax systems and rates, this is an area that is conspicuous for its lack of progress, rather than for any observable move towards co-ordination.

3.6 | Summary

- Corporate finance differs in many ways from one country to another. In the United Kingdom, there is a far greater emphasis upon stock market sourced equity finance than in other countries. France and Germany, for example, rely to a greater extent upon bond markets.

- Corporate governance is concerned with how a company is directed and controlled and how a framework for accountability of directors to owners is established.

- Control-oriented finance and arm's-length finance are important contrasting systems of corporate governance which, probably, have their roots in different legal systems.

- Different corporate governance systems, contrasting legal frameworks and cultures, together with differing orientations towards stock market finance, have created accounting reporting systems which vary sharply around the world. Countries with a greater reliance on stock market equity finance seem to have looser rules on reporting profit to investors.

- Like its contrasting accounting rules, different countries have different tax systems too.

3.7 | End of chapter questions

Question 1
Why do some developed countries have high levels of equity market capitalization to GDP while other developed countries have low levels?

Question 2
How do you suppose the adoption of the European single currency, the euro, has affected the foreign exchange market?

Question 3
How would you expect countries with a more developed bond market versus equities to have experienced past inflation?

Part B

Foreign exchange

Multinational financial management involves manipulation of more than one currency. Its understanding necessarily involves confronting such questions as how foreign exchange markets work and what makes exchange rates move. Making sense of the complexities of international finance has no magic answer – but this section presents in Chapter 4 the single most important theorem of foreign exchange. Without understanding it, the student will always flounder in the dark when confronted with exchange rates and interest rates; but if it is understood, light begins to appear.

4 Exchange rates: the basic equations

Multinational finance and domestic finance have much in common, but there are also many ways in which they differ. International financial management usually involves manipulation with more than one currency. So its understanding necessarily involves questions about how foreign exchange markets work, why exchange rates change, how one can protect oneself against foreign exchange risk and so on.

But before we can begin to approach these topics, there are a number of basic relationships that must be examined. This chapter focuses upon one series of approaches to the determination of foreign exchange rates – but it is by no means the only explanation and we briefly examine some others in Chapter 7.

4.1 | Foreign exchange markets

A US company importing goods from Germany with their price denominated in euros may buy euros to pay for the goods. A US company exporting goods to Germany, again with the price denominated in euros, receives euros which it may then sell in exchange for dollars. The currency aspects of these transactions involve use of the foreign exchange markets.

In most centres, the foreign exchange market has no central, physical market place. Business is conducted by screen trading or by telephone or a number of other telecommunications mechanisms. The main dealers are commercial banks and central banks. Most companies wishing to buy or sell currency usually do so through a commercial bank.

In the United Kingdom, exchange rates are usually quoted in terms of the number of units of foreign currency bought for one unit of home currency, that is £1. This method of quotation is termed the indirect quote. By contrast, exchange rates may be quoted in terms of the number of units of home currency necessary to buy one unit of foreign currency. This is the direct quotation method. In the United States, the convention is to use the direct quote when dealing internally with residents of the United States and the indirect quote when dealing with foreigners. The exception to this latter rule is that the direct US quote is used when dealing with British-based banks or UK businesses. This practice means that New York uses the same figure when talking to foreign dealers as such foreign dealers use for their own transactions and quotations. A quote of $1.6050 per British pound in New York means that each pound costs $1.6050. In other words, to put it in indirect New York terms, there are £0.6231 to the dollar given by 1/1.6050. On the face of it, buying or selling a currency at the spot rate of exchange implies immediate delivery and payment. The practice of the foreign exchange market is for delivery to be at two working days after the deal – but this applies only to spot transactions.

There is also the forward market where deals are for future delivery – usually one, three, six or twelve months' time, although a whole host of other durations, including odd periods (such as twelve days, for example) can be dealt. The forward market enables companies and others to insure themselves against foreign exchange losses (or, of course, to speculate on future movements in exchange rates). If you are going to need CHF100,000 (CHF is the symbol for Swiss francs) in six months' time, you can enter into a six-month forward contract. The forward rate on this contract is the price agreed now to be paid in six months when the CHF100,000 are delivered.

If the six-month forward rate for the pound against the dollar is quoted at $1.6100 per GBP as opposed to the spot rate of $1.6050, the implication is that you pay more dollars if you buy forward than if you buy pounds spot. In this case the dollar is said to trade at a forward discount on the pound. Put another way, the pound trades at a forward premium on the dollar. Expressed as an annual rate, the forward premium is:

$$\frac{1.6100 - 1.6050}{1.6050} \times \frac{12 \text{ months}}{6 \text{ months}} \times 100 = 0.62\% \text{ p.a.}$$

Assuming that forward markets and interest rates are in equilibrium, the currency of the country with the higher interest rate is said to be at a discount on the other currency. At the same time, looking at things from the opposite side of the fence, the currency of the country with lower interest rates will be at a premium on the other currency.

4.2 | Some basic relationships

Why should one currency be quoted at a different rate in the forward market versus the spot market? The hypothesis – the whys and wherefores of which will be examined later in this chapter – is that, in the absence of barriers to international capital movements, there is a relationship between spot exchange rates, forward exchange rates, interest rates and inflation rates. This relationship can be summarized as shown in Figure 4.1. For definitions of all notations used in this chapter, see Table 4.1 (overleaf). The theoretical underpinning to the hypothesized link between variables is now examined.

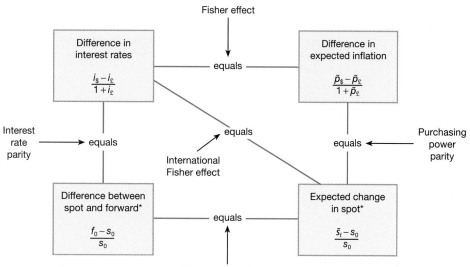

* *Important note*: Using the notation here, f_0, s_0 and $\tilde{s}_t$ must be stated in terms of \$/£: that is, the number of dollars to the pound. If the rate is quoted as £/\$ – that is, the number of pounds to the dollar – the expectations theory boxes should read

$$\frac{s_0 - f_0}{f_0} \text{ and } \frac{s_0 - \tilde{s}_t}{\tilde{s}_t}$$

This should be self-evident.

If it is not, consider the following situation. The £/\$ quotation is equal to $1/(\$/£)$. $(f - s)/s$ can be shown to be equal to $[(1/s) - (1/f)]/(1/f)$. This is demonstrated below.

$$\frac{(1/s) - (1/f)}{(1/f)} = \left(\frac{1}{s} - \frac{1}{f}\right)f$$

$$= \frac{f}{s} - 1$$

$$= \frac{f - s}{s}$$

Great care must be taken on this point on all occasions when using the above formulations. It is recommended that readers use the four-way model as set out above but always use the direct New York quote. When the dollar is not involved in a problem, be careful to get the substitution consistent with the formulations above. To get approximate results, the number of months may be used. In practice, the actual number of days, rather than months, has to be used in calculations. Further modification is necessary inasmuch as bankers and the financial institutions quote all Eurocurrency notes on the basis of a 360-day year. Domestic sterling and most Commonwealth country currencies are based on a 365-day year – all others are quoted by reference to a 360-day year, including domestic US dollars. For purposes of quick approximation, the four-way model relationships may be written as:

$$i_\$ - i_£ = \tilde{p}_\$ - \tilde{p}_£ = \frac{f_0 - s_0}{s_0} = \frac{\tilde{s}_t - s_0}{s_0}$$

But this is very much an approximation.

Figure 4.1 The four-way equivalence in the foreign exchange market.

Table 4.1 Notation used in this chapter

s_0	= spot \$/£ exchange rate now (direct New York quote)
f_0	= forward \$/£ exchange rate now (direct New York quote)
$i_\$$	= Eurodollar interest rate
$i_£$	= Eurosterling interest rate
r	= real return
$\bar{p}_\$$	= expected US inflation
$\bar{p}_£$	= expected UK inflation
$p_\$$	= US price level now
$p_£$	= UK price level now
$\tilde{s}_t$	= expected spot \$/£ exchange rate at time t (direct New York quote)
f_t	= expected forward \$/£ exchange rate at time t (direct New York quote)

4.3 | Interest rates and exchange rates

Assume that an investor has £1m to invest for a period of twelve months. He has a whole spectrum of investment opportunities: he could put the money into sterling or dollar investments, or into yen, or whatever. But for simplicity, suppose we look at only two of these opportunities. The currency markets are quoting the dollar against sterling at \$1.6800 spot and \$1.6066 for twelve months forward. Euromarket fixed interest rates are 13 per cent per annum for twelve months sterling and $8^1/_{16}$ per cent per annum fixed rate for US dollars for a similar period. The investor may:

- either invest £1m in Eurosterling at a 13 per cent per annum fixed interest rate for twelve months;

- or convert £1m into US dollars at \$1.6800; invest the proceeds in the Eurodollar interest market at an $8^1/_{16}$ per cent per annum fixed interest rate for one year and sell the pre-calculated proceeds forward twelve months at a rate of \$1.6066.

What are the expected proceeds? Obviously the sterling investment yields £1,130,000 at the end of twelve months. The dollar investment yields, to all intents and purposes, the same amount. The proceeds from the spot transaction are \$1,680,000. Investing at $8^1/_{16}$ per cent per annum, the proceeds in twelve months' time will total \$1,815,450, and selling this forward at \$1.6066 yields £1,129,995. This is, more or less, the same outcome as from the sterling investment opportunity. If one thinks about it, this is what one would expect. After all, each investment opportunity is of equal risk (the investor carries the credit risk associated with the bank with which he invests, but if he invests with the same Eurobank, the credit risk associated with each opportunity is equal). To the UK company, investment in sterling carries no foreign exchange risk. Neither does the dollar investment when covered via the forward markets. The two investments carry equal risk and should, according to financial theory, promise equal returns.

Were this not the case, arbitrageurs in the foreign exchange and interest rate markets would borrow currency in one centre, convert it to the other, invest there and sell the proceeds forward. Such proceeds would, if equilibrium did not hold, exceed the amount repayable in terms of the borrowing plus accrued interest and thereby yield a virtually riskless profit to the operator. This mechanism is referred to as covered interest arbitrage. The actions of dealers ensure that profitable opportunities of this kind do not last for more than fleeting instants. Exploitation of these brief opportunities creates movements in spot and forward exchange rates and in interest rates – and such movements ensure that the tendency in the currency and interest rate markets is towards equilibrium.

Covered interest arbitrage involves borrowing in centre A for a specified period at a fixed interest rate and shipping the proceeds borrowed to centre B. The sum shipped is deposited there for the same period as the borrowing in centre A, again at a fixed interest rate. The total proceeds of investment in centre B that will accrue at the end of the investment period can be calculated, since the interest rate is fixed. Such proceeds are sold via the forward market for the period of the borrowing and lending, and the sum received in centre A from this forward transaction will more than repay the borrowing in centre A plus accrued interest. This profit is said to be a covered interest arbitrage profit.

By contrast, uncovered interest arbitrage involves a borrowing in centre A for a specified period at a fixed interest rate and shipping the proceeds borrowed to centre B via the spot market. The sum is again placed on deposit for the same period as that for which the borrowing was arranged in centre A and again it is at a fixed rate. This time the investor speculates that the proceeds from lending in centre B, when shipped to centre A at the spot rate prevailing at the end of the investment period, will exceed the borrowing plus accrued interest in centre A. Note that, under uncovered interest arbitrage, the operator speculates on the future spot rate. Any profit earned is a risky profit. Under covered interest arbitrage, the operator is not speculating but making a risk-free profit based on momentary disequilibria in interest differentials and forward and spot rates.

It should be noted in the numerical example above that we have used single (presumably middle) rates for quotations of interest and spot and forward rates. In reality the investor needs to look at buy and sell rates in the spot and forward markets and at borrow and lend rates in interest markets.

It should also be noted that the interest rate differential is termed the 'interest agio'.[1] In the numerical example above it would be given by:

$$\frac{i_\$ - i_£}{1 + i_£} = \frac{8\frac{1}{16}\% - 13\%}{1.13}$$

$$= -0.0437$$

$$= -4.37\%$$

Note that calculating the interest differential in this manner – which is the precisely correct way – differs from taking a straight difference between interest rates: that is, $i_\$ - i_£$. The rationale for using the precise calculation rather than the approximation is demonstrated algebraically at the end of this section.

The annual forward discount is termed the 'exchange agio'.[1] In the numerical example it would be equal to:

$$\frac{f_0 - s_0}{s_0} = \frac{1.6066 - 1.6800}{1.6800}$$

$$= -0.0437$$

$$= -4.37\%$$

If arbitrageurs' actions ensure that opportunities for profitable covered interest arbitrage are eliminated, then the interest agio will equal the exchange agio. This is the essence of interest rate parity theory (see Figure 4.2).

The whole of the above theory is, of course, built upon the assumption that we are looking at markets in which money is internationally mobile. Many governments restrict the mobility of money. But that does not invalidate the hypothesis. Furthermore, governments also frequently place restrictions on lending and borrowing rates charged in domestic interest rate markets. To avoid the effects of this market imperfection we should look at free markets, and these are available in the form of Eurocurrency markets. Clearly, then, in applying the interest rate parity theorem, our attention should focus upon the comparative term structure of interest rates in the Eurocurrency markets.

We now consider the whys and wherefores of using the precise calculation rather than the approximation. Assume that a US exporter is due to receive £A in one year (or at time t where $t = 1$ year), and assume the notation in Table 4.1 (earlier).

The US exporter might avoid foreign exchange risk by using the forward market. His proceeds in US dollars at time t would be $\$f_0 A$. Alternatively, he might avoid the risk by covering in the money markets. He could borrow:

$$\frac{£A}{1 + i_£}$$

in sterling at time $t = 0$. At time $t = 1$, £A will be due to the lender and this will be obtained via payment of the receivable. Meanwhile, the US exporter would convert

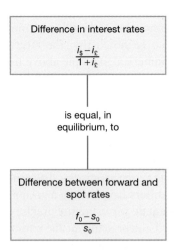

Figure 4.2 The interest rate parity theorem.

$$\frac{£A}{1+i_£}$$

to dollars at time 0 to give:

$$\frac{\$A}{1+i_£} s_0$$

Investing this in the Eurodollar market would yield, at time t:

$$\frac{\$A}{(1+i_£)} s_0(1+i_\$)$$

Assuming equilibrium between money markets and forward markets, each formula of cover will yield the same amount. So we can say that:

$$f_0 A = \frac{A}{(1+i_£)} s_0(1+i_\$)$$

Rearranging this expression, we get:

$$f_0 = s_0 \frac{1+i_\$}{1+i_£}$$

and dividing through by s_0 and then taking 1 from each side gives:

$$\frac{f_0}{s_0} - 1 = \frac{1+i_\$}{1+i_£} - 1$$

This yields the exact interest rate parity[2] formula of:

$$\frac{f_0 - s_0}{s_0} = \frac{i_\$ - i_£}{1+i_£}$$

This precise formulation, rather than the approximate one, is used by traders when dealing or making calculations for foreign exchange purposes. We now turn our attention to the second leg of the theoretical four-way equivalence in the foreign exchange markets.

Exchange rates and inflation rates

Just like the above relationship between interest rates and exchange rates, there exists a similar hypothesis – again underpinned to some extent by the actions of arbitrageurs – relating inflation rates and exchange rates. This relationship is also best approached by a numerical example. If a commodity sells in the United States at $400 per kg, and in the United Kingdom for £250 per kg, and the exchange rate is $1.70 to the pound sterling, then a profitable opportunity exists to buy the commodity in the United States, ship to the United Kingdom and sell there – always assuming, that is, that the gross profit of $25 per kg, given by $(250 \times 1.70) - 400$, exceeds shipping and insurance costs from the United States to the United Kingdom.

Were this profitable opportunity to exist, so the theory goes, arbitrageurs buying in New York and selling in London would increase the price in the United States and depress it in the United Kingdom, and this would go on until the profit potential was eliminated. Arbitrage ensures that, in the absence of market imperfections, the prices of a commodity in two centres should not differ. When talking about prices of a particular good in this way, economists are invoking the law of one price.[3] Applied to the case in point, one could say that:

$$\text{£ price of a commodity} \times \text{price of £} = \text{\$ price of the commodity}$$

That is:

$$\text{Price of £} = \frac{\text{\$ price of the commodity}}{\text{£ price of the commodity}}$$

This kind of relationship should tend to hold for all internationally traded goods. That is:

$$\text{Price of £} = \frac{\text{\$ price of an internationally traded commodity}}{\text{£ price of the internationally traded commodity}}$$

Changes in the ratio of domestic prices of internationally traded goods in two centres should be reflected in changes in the price of currencies – the exchange rate.

In order to take the argument to the next stage, we should, strictly speaking, limit our focus to relative prices of internationally traded goods. But we approximate. Purchasing power parity (PPP) theory uses relative general price changes as a proxy for prices of internationally traded goods. And, applying it to the previous equation, we would obtain:

$$\text{Change in \$ price of £} = \frac{\text{change in \$ price level}}{\text{change in £ price level}}$$

Thus if inflation is 8 per cent p.a. in the United States and 12 per cent p.a. in the United Kingdom, then applying purchasing power parity theory we would expect the pound sterling to fall against the dollar by:

$$\frac{0.08 - 0.12}{1.12}$$

that is, 3.6 per cent p.a. Again this calculation is precise. A quick approximation based merely on straight inflation differentials would suggest a devaluation of 4 per cent p.a. The justification for using the precise formulation, rather than the approximate one, is considered in the algebraic formulation below.

PPP theory, itself an approximation since it uses the general price level as a proxy for the price level of internationally traded goods, suggests that changes in the spot rate of exchange may be estimated by reference to expected inflation differentials. When looking at past exchange rate movements, the hypothesis might be tested by reference to actual price level changes. When making *ex-ante* estimates of spot changes we should look at the expected change in inflation rates. Figure 4.3 summarizes the PPP hypothesis.

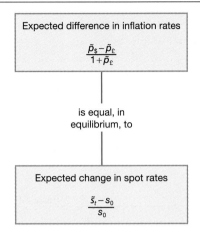

Figure 4.3 The purchasing power parity theorem.

The precise formulation of the PPP theory, illustrated diagrammatically in Figure 4.3, can be easily substantiated by relatively simple algebra. Using the notation in Table 4.1 (earlier) and given that the spot rate of exchange at any date is under-pinned by relative price levels, it follows that the values of the respective spot rates of exchange at time 0 and those expected for time t are given by:

$$s_0 = \frac{p_\$}{p_£}$$

$$\tilde{s}_t = \frac{p_\$(1 + \tilde{p}_\$)}{p_£(1 + \tilde{p}_£)}$$

Substituting, we can obtain:

$$\frac{\tilde{s}_t - s_0}{s_0} = \frac{p_\$}{p_£}\left[\frac{1 + \tilde{p}_\$}{1 + \tilde{p}_£} - 1\right]\frac{p_£}{p_\$}$$

from which it follows that:

$$\frac{\tilde{s}_t - s_0}{s_0} = \frac{\tilde{p}_\$ - \tilde{p}_£}{1 + \tilde{p}_£}$$

At its simplest, then, PPP predicts that the exchange rate changes to compensate for differences in inflation between two countries. Thus, if country A has a higher inflation rate than its trading partners, the exchange rate of the former should weaken to compensate for this relativity. If country A's nominal exchange rate falls and if that fall is an exact compensation for inflation differentials, its real effective exchange rate is said to remain constant. PPP predicts that real effective exchange rates will remain constant through time.

In terms of using purchasing power parity to forecast exchange rates, it should be clear that the predicted equilibrium rate will vary according to which year is chosen as a base date.

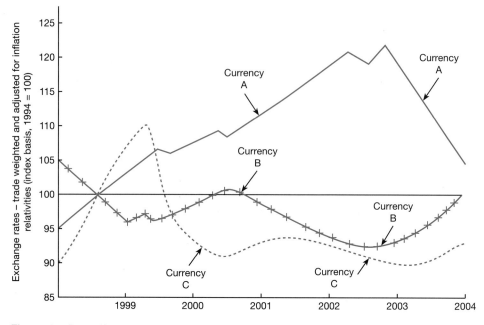

Figure 4.4 Real effective exchange rates.

Thus, referring to Figure 4.4, if 1999 were used as the base year with trade-weighted, inflation-adjusted exchange rates of currencies A, B and C fixed at 100 as of that date, then, as of 2004 currency A would appear overvalued, currency B would appear correctly valued and currency C would appear undervalued. But if 2002 were taken as the base year, currency A would appear undervalued by 2004; at this time currency B would look overvalued and currency C would look correctly valued. So how does one get over this problem?

The answer is that one should start the analysis at a time when the exchange rate of the country being analysed is in equilibrium. And what is meant by the exchange rate being in equilibrium? We believe that the best approach in this area is to commence at a time when the exchange rate is such that the overall balance of trade plus invisibles is equal (or approximately equal) to zero. In one sense, exchange rate equilibrium may be defined as that level at which its impact results in the balance on trade and invisibles coming out at zero overall. This is the approach that we adopt in Section 4.4 headed 'Purchasing power parity applied'. But there are other approaches. For example, Williamson (1994) views the equilibrium exchange rate as that rate which is consistent with overall external balance given underlying capital flows.

One of the biggest problems with PPP is that most applications of it use retail price indices, wholesale price indices or gross domestic product (GDP) deflators. Some international economists have suggested that the use of indices based upon traded goods would better reflect the nature or sentiment of the underpinning theory. They argue that a price index that embraces both traded and non-traded goods can impart a bias into the purchasing power parity calculations, and this is particularly marked when there are significant productivity differences between countries; this is known as the Balassa–Samuelson thesis (see Balassa, 1964, and Samuelson, 1974). As an example, consider two countries producing similar export goods. Country X experiences substantial productivity gains in the export sector, while country Y achieves higher productivity advances in home-consumed goods and services. If productivity increments were of similar proportions as a percentage of their respective economies, both countries would have similar advances in their price indices. But, of course, if exchange rates were to remain constant, country X would, all other things being equal, gain in the export market at the expense of country Y. More probably, the exchange rate of country X would strengthen to reflect its lower export input costs per unit following the productivity gain; clearly, though, PPP calculations based on total data for all output would not pick up this effect. Evidently, care has to be exercised when using purchasing power parity as a model for calculating equilibrium exchange rates. Towards the end of this chapter, PPP is applied to arrive at estimations of where exchange rates should be using macroeconomic data of major world economies. Now let us turn to the theoretical relationship between interest rates and expected inflation rates.

Interest rates and inflation rates

According to the 'Fisher effect', a term coined because it was observed by US economist Irving Fisher, nominal interest rates in a country reflect anticipated real returns adjusted for local inflation expectations. In a world where investors are internationally mobile, expected real rates of return should tend towards equality, reflecting the fact that in search of higher real returns, investors' arbitraging actions will force these returns towards each other. At least this should hold with respect to the free-market Eurocurrency interest rates. Constraints on international capital mobility create imperfections which, among other things, prevent this relationship from holding in domestic interest rate markets. So nominal Eurocurrency interest rates may differ for different currencies, but according to the Fisher effect only by virtue of different inflation expectations. And these inflation differentials should underpin expected changes in the spot rates of exchange. In other words, we would expect US and UK free-market interest investments to yield equal real returns. Differences in nominal returns would reflect expected inflation differentials. This would give us the theoretical relationship summarized in Figure 4.5 (overleaf).

Again, the implications of the Fisher effect (sometimes termed 'Fisher's closed hypothesis') can be followed through algebraically towards the formulation shown in Figure 4.5. Since the Fisher theorem suggests that local interest rates reflect a real expected return adjusted for inflationary expectations, when money is internationally mobile and market imperfections are eliminated, local interest rates will be equal to the international real return adjusted for domestic inflationary expectations. Put algebraically, the following two equivalences are implied:

$$1 + i_\$ = (1 + r)(1 + \tilde{p}_\$)$$

and

$$1 + i_£ = (1 + r)(1 + \tilde{p}_£)$$

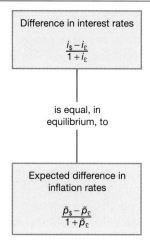

Figure 4.5 The Fisher effect.

Subtracting the latter from the former gives:

$$i_\$ - i_£ = (1 + r)(\tilde{p}_\$ - \tilde{p}_£)$$

And this leads to:

$$\frac{i_\$ - i_£}{1 + r} = \tilde{p}_\$ - \tilde{p}_£$$

Now multiplying through by $1/(1 + \tilde{p}_£)$ we get:

$$\frac{i_\$ - i_£}{1 + i_£} = \frac{\tilde{p}_\$ - \tilde{p}_£}{1 + \tilde{p}_£}$$

We now turn to the relationship between expected changes in the spot rate and the forward discount or premium on a currency.

Changes in the spot rate and the forward discount

This is the fourth side of the quadrilateral and must logically give rise to equality because of the hypothesized equality of the other three sides. This is the expectations theory of exchange rates and its implications are summarized diagrammatically in Figure 4.6.

This hypothesized relationship can be proved by *a priori* reasoning. If users of the foreign exchange market were not interested in risk, then the forward rate of exchange would depend solely on what people expected the future spot rate to be. A twelve-month forward rate on sterling of $1.7635 to the pound would exist only because traders expected the spot rate in twelve months to be $1.7635 to the pound. If they anticipated that it would be higher than this, nobody would sell sterling at the forward rate. By the same token if they expected it to be lower, nobody would buy at the forward rate.

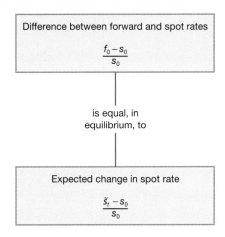

Figure 4.6 The expectations theory of exchange rates.

As traders do care about risk, the forward rate might be higher or lower than the expected spot rate. Suppose that a US exporter is certain to receive £1 million in six months' time. It might wait until six months have elapsed and then convert to dollars, or it might sell the pound forward. The first action involves exchange risk; the latter does not. To avoid foreign exchange risk, the trader may be willing to pay something slightly different from the expected spot price.

On the other side of the equation, there may be traders who wish to buy sterling six months away. To avoid the risk associated with movements in foreign exchange rates, they may be prepared to pay a forward price a little higher than the expected spot price.

Some traders find it safer to sell sterling forward; some traders find it safer to buy sterling forward. If the former group predominates, the forward price of sterling is likely to be less than the expected spot price. If the latter group predominates, the forward price is likely to be greater than the expected spot price. However, the actions of the predominant group are likely to adjust rates until they arrive at the hypothesized position in Figure 4.6.

Interest rate differentials and changes in the spot exchange rate

The hypothesis that differences in interest rate should underpin the expected movement in the spot rate of exchange is termed the 'international Fisher effect'; it is sometimes also called Fisher's open hypothesis. Referring back to Figure 4.1, international Fisher appears as one of the diagonals in the quadrilateral. What international Fisher predicts is summarized in Figure 4.7 (overleaf).

When discussing the interest rate parity theorem, we referred to covered and uncovered interest arbitrage. Effectively, the actions of arbitrageurs eliminate continuing opportunities to make riskless profits by covered interest arbitrage. Their operations bring into equilibrium interest differentials and spot and forward exchange rates.

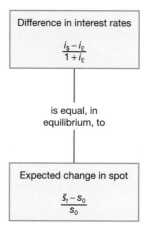

Figure 4.7 The international Fisher effect.

A similar line of reasoning underpins the international Fisher effect, but this time it is uncovered interest arbitrage that is at the heart of the argument. Rational investors may make estimates of future spot rates of exchange. If their views are such as to justify expectations of profit (in excess of that commensurate with the risk involved) from uncovered interest arbitrage, then their actions in purchasing one currency spot and selling another would move exchange rates so as to eliminate excess returns from the uncovered speculation. In a world of efficient markets, investors would use all available information to arrive at fair estimates of spot and future exchange rates, such that the relationship between them would eliminate consistently profitable opportunities of uncovered interest arbitrage. The effect of this would, of course, be to bring interest rate differentials into line with spot exchange rates and expectations of future spot rates.

4.4 | Purchasing power parity applied

In this section we show how current account data may be used to help identify equilibrium exchange rates according to purchasing power parity. It must be remembered that the exercise which follows is approximate only; it claims no precision.

Table 4.2 presents a matrix showing the current account balance as a percentage of GDP for a number of major world economies for the period from 1985 onwards. Data have been presented as a percentage because relative values are far more meaningful than absolute figures. If a current account balance is shown as zero, this may be interpreted as being indicative of exchange rate equilibrium. This was the case for Norway in 1998. For Denmark, no year in the tabulation has a nil balance, but between 1997 and 1998, the current account appears to have flipped from surplus to deficit – it would, for the purposes of this exercise, be acceptable to take 1997 as being as near to equilibrium as is feasible.

Table 4.2 Current account balance as a percentage of GDP for selected countries from 1985

	1985	1986	1987	1988	1989	1990	1991	1992	1993	1994	1995	1996	1997	1998	1999	2000	2001
United States	-3.0	-3.3	-3.4	-2.4	-1.8	-1.4	.1	-.8	-1.2	-1.7	-1.5	-1.5	-1.7	-2.5	-3.5	-4.5	-4.1
Canada	-1.6	-3.1	-3.2	-3.0	-4.0	-3.4	-3.7	-3.6	-3.9	-2.3	-.7	.5	-1.3	-1.3	.2	2.6	2.8
Australia	-5.5	-5.7	-3.9	-4.6	-6.1	-5.2	-3.5	-3.7	-3.3	-5.1	-5.4	-3.9	-3.1	-5.0	-5.9	-4.1	-2.6
Japan	3.7	4.2	3.4	2.7	2.1	1.4	2.0	3.0	3.0	2.7	2.1	1.4	2.2	3.1	2.4	2.5	2.2
New Zealand	-11.9	-9.7	-7.9	-4.2	-3.5	-3.3	-2.8	-2.6	-1.7	-4.6	-4.9	-6.0	-6.6	-4.0	-6.5	-5.4	-3.1
Austria	-.2	.2	-.2	-.2	.2	.7	–	-.4	-.6	-1.5	-2.3	-2.1	-2.5	-2.5			
Belgium-Luxem	.8	2.5	1.9	2.2	2.2	1.7	2.2	2.8	4.9	5.0	4.8	4.8	5.3	4.5			
Finland	-1.5	-1.0	-1.9	-2.5	-5.0	-5.1	-5.5	-4.7	-1.3	1.1	4.0	3.9	5.4	5.7			
France	–	.3	-.5	-.5	-.5	-.8	-.5	.3	.7	.5	.7	1.3	2.7	2.6			
Germany	2.8	4.6	4.2	4.2	4.8	3.2	-1.0	-.9	-.7	-1.0	-.8	-.3	-.1	-.3			
Greece	-9.8	-4.3	-2.6	-1.5	-3.8	-4.3	-1.8	-2.2	-.8	-.1	-2.4	-3.7	-4.0	–	-5.8	-8.7	
Ireland	-3.9	-3.2	-.2	-.1	-1.6	-.8	.6	1.1	3.5	2.9	2.6	2.8	2.3	1.2			
Italy	-1.0	.4	-.3	-.9	-1.5	-1.5	-2.1	-2.4	.8	1.3	2.3	3.2	2.8	1.7			
Luxembourg											13.4	12.1	11.5	8.9			
Netherlands	3.2	2.3	1.8	3.0	4.2	2.7	2.5	2.0	4.1	4.9	6.2	5.2	6.7	3.4			
Portugal	1.8	3.4	1.0	-2.2	.3	-.3	-.9	-.2	.3	-2.5	-.1	-4.8	-6.3	-7.3			
Spain	1.7	1.7	-.1	-1.1	-2.9	-3.7	-3.7	-3.7	-1.2	-1.3	.1	.1	.5	-.6			
Denmark	-4.6	-5.3	-2.8	-1.2	-1.0	1.0	1.5	2.9	3.5	2.1	1.0	1.7	.5	-1.2	1.7	1.6	2.6
Iceland	-3.9	.4	-3.5	-3.9	-1.9	-2.0	-4.0	-2.3	.7	1.7	.8	-1.6	-1.7	-6.9	-6.9	-10.0	
Norway	4.8	-6.0	-4.5	-4.0	.2	3.5	4.3	3.5	3.0	3.1	3.6	7.0	6.5	–	5.5	15.6	15.9
Sweden	-1.0	–	–	-0.3	-1.6	-2.8	-1.9	-3.6	-2.2	.4	2.1	2.2	3.1	1.9	2.5	2.9	3.2
Switzerland	6.3	3.4	3.6	4.7	4.5	3.0	4.5	5.9	7.6	6.7	7.1	7.1	10.4	10.2	10.9	13.6	
United Kingdom	.7	-.2	-1.8	-4.2	-5.1	-3.9	-1.8	-2.2	-1.9	-1.0	-1.3	-1.1	-.2	-.6	-2.2	-2.0	-2.1

Of course, there are a number of problem factors affecting current account data. First of all, they include some items that are not really to do with selling and buying goods and services internationally. Data includes interest and dividends earned and paid overseas; it also includes unilateral transfers. Strictly speaking, these items should be excluded in arriving at our estimate of equilibrium for the exchange rate. If great sophistication is required in the exercise, data may be modified to correct these potential distortions.

Secondly, using current account data as an indicator of equilibrium presents problems for economies that are very substantially affected by earnings from one commodity – for example, sterling was frequently referred to as a petro-currency in the early 1980s, reflecting the large role of oil in the United Kingdom's balance of payments figures. Zambia's balance of payments ebbs and flows in line with copper prices, this mineral being its major export by a very long way. Movements towards equilibrium on Zambia's balance of payments will have more to do with world demand for copper than with exchange rates.

We now move on to Tables 4.3 and 4.4 (overleaf). These show real effective exchange rate indices for a sample of industrialized countries from 1985. Table 4.3 involves a computation of the index on the basis of consumer prices; Table 4.4 is based upon unit labour costs normalized to iron out cyclical effects. For these tables, the 1995 figure is set at 100. Real effective exchange rates have been arrived at in the following manner:

- The nominal exchange rate for country X against its trading partners has been tracked.

- The weighting of trade and services of country X with its trading partners has been extracted from published data.

- Inflation for country X compared with its trading partners has been extracted from published statistics – duly weighted according to aggregate trade and services transactions.

- Nominal exchange rates have been adjusted to a trade-weighted figure by applying weightings in accordance with amounts of trade and services transacted with international partners.

- Such figures have been adjusted to allow for comparative inflation rates of country X and its trading partners.

Notice the dramatic difference obtained by using the different measures in Tables 4.3 and 4.4. This is particularly sharp in the case of the United Kingdom. From 1995 to August 2002, UK figures have moved from 100 to 129.3 according to consumer prices and from 100 to 142.6 if data is based on unit labour costs. In other words, as at 2001, on the basis of the latter figure, the British pound seems more overvalued than on the former criterion.

We now show how the figures can be used to assess whether a currency is overvalued or undervalued. Take the example of the United Kingdom. According to Table 4.2, the current account for the United Kingdom moved, most recently, into approximate balance in 1997 and 1998. With a J-curve effect of twelve months, it is

Table 4.3 Real effective exchange rate indexes based on relative consumer prices

	1987	1988	1989	1990	1991	1992	1993	1994	1995	1996	1997	1998	1999	2000	2001	August 2002
United States	112.4	105.9	109.3	104.7	103.5	101.2	104.7	103.4	100.0	104.3	112.0	120.0	119.3	125.2	134.5	131.1
Canada	114.7	121.0	129.5	128.0	131.9	121.1	113.6	103.3	100.0	101.7	103.2	98.6	97.6	99.5	98.7	96.6
Japan	82.5	88.1	80.7	71.6	76.8	79.2	93.6	98.3	100.0	84.5	80.2	78.9	89.3	95.5	85.5	81.9
Euro area	99.3	95.2	90.9	99.3	96.1	100.8	95.7	95.2	100.0	99.9	90.8	93.0	88.5	79.1	82.3	87.9
Austria	92.6	92.1	90.8	92.4	91.6	93.3	95.7	96.4	100.0	98.0	94.6	94.6	92.8	90.3	91.1	92.5
Belgium	94.8	92.2	90.9	94.8	94.1	95.0	95.0	96.5	100.0	98.2	93.6	93.4	91.8	88.7	89.3	90.6
Finland	110.3	112.8	119.3	122.4	116.9	101.1	86.2	91.7	100.0	96.0	93.0	93.1	90.7	87.1	89.1	90.8
France	99.1	96.9	94.8	98.1	95.1	96.6	97.7	97.4	100.0	99.9	95.6	96.0	93.2	88.4	88.4	90.2
Germany	92.5	90.1	88.1	90.8	87.2	91.5	95.4	95.7	100.0	96.8	92.0	92.5	89.5	84.6	85.6	87.1
Ireland	108.4	104.7	102.4	107.1	104.1	106.9	99.1	99.4	100.0	101.9	101.6	97.1	94.2	91.2	94.5	100.7
Italy	124.0	122.9	125.6	131.5	132.5	130.6	110.5	107.2	100.0	111.6	112.3	113.1	110.9	106.3	107.7	111.0
Netherlands	97.9	95.6	91.8	93.7	92.1	93.7	95.3	96.0	100.0	98.2	93.6	94.4	93.7	89.9	92.7	96.6
Spain	97.5	102.1	108.1	114.8	116.2	115.7	103.1	98.3	100.0	102.2	97.4	97.4	96.7	94.2	95.9	98.4
Denmark	96.2	95.7	93.9	98.1	94.9	96.0	96.4	95.9	100.0	99.3	96.5	98.3	97.5	93.5	94.9	97.4
Norway	105.7	108.3	107.6	106.5	103.2	103.5	99.3	97.2	100.0	99.8	101.1	98.2	97.9	96.1	99.6	109.7
Sweden	108.2	110.9	113.7	118.2	123.9	123.9	101.7	100.2	100.0	108.4	103.0	100.1	97.0	95.1	87.6	89.3
Switzerland	90.0	88.5	83.0	89.2	89.3	87.7	89.7	93.9	100.0	97.3	90.0	91.1	89.4	87.3	89.8	93.3
United Kingdom	104.5	112.8	113.3	117.1	119.8	115.6	103.5	103.7	100.0	102.4	120.5	128.0	127.6	131.9	129.5	129.3

Table 4.4 Real effective exchange rate indexes based on relative normalized unit labour costs

	1987	1988	1989	1990	1991	1992	1993	1994	1995	1996	1997	1998	1999	2000	2001	August 2002
United States	130.9	122.9	124.5	115.8	111.6	109.0	111.1	108.5	100.0	103.6	109.5	116.6	114.8	123.5	135.1	130.6
Canada	94.6	101.4	110.6	113.6	118.8	113.6	107.4	100.8	100.0	100.8	103.5	97.0	95.9	96.0	92.2	91.3
Japan	74.3	79.1	75.7	68.4	73.3	75.6	89.5	95.1	100.0	85.6	81.7	76.3	86.9	93.3	82.6	77.3
Euro area	92.8	89.9	89.9	98.5	95.6	99.6	97.8	95.7	100.0	100.5	90.5	87.5	83.1	74.1	74.0	76.5
Austria	121.5	116.4	111.7	108.8	104.7	105.6	106.2	103.8	100.0	95.2	92.4	89.2	87.4	85.7	85.4	86.1
Belgium	98.7	94.9	94.3	96.4	97.0	96.6	98.0	97.1	100.0	95.8	92.4	91.9	88.4	85.6	86.5	85.9
Finland	126.9	129.7	133.6	134.6	123.7	102.0	86.4	90.6	100.0	92.5	87.2	86.0	82.9	79.0	79.7	79.3
France	108.2	104.5	101.5	102.7	98.4	99.3	100.1	99.0	100.0	96.9	92.9	92.5	91.8	88.2	87.2	88.3
Germany	75.6	76.7	76.8	81.9	81.3	84.9	90.5	93.2	100.0	98.7	92.9	90.5	87.8	82.7	82.0	82.4
Ireland	163.5	155.6	145.3	142.8	129.4	126.0	115.2	107.1	100.0	95.0	89.0	80.5	75.2	68.0	67.4	68.0
Italy	126.8	125.4	131.4	135.8	138.1	134.7	114.9	108.7	100.0	114.6	117.1	114.8	114.3	110.4	109.7	111.9
Netherlands	108.1	102.6	96.5	95.4	92.3	94.6	96.7	97.7	100.0	97.1	92.7	93.9	93.3	91.3	93.1	96.7
Spain	89.7	93.3	100.6	106.5	110.3	115.4	107.5	100.9	100.0	102.6	100.1	102.0	102.3	101.1	103.4	106.7
Denmark	96.3	94.8	93.3	97.7	94.2	95.3	97.9	97.1	100.0	98.2	95.8	97.4	97.2	94.2	95.5	97.6
Norway	96.6	98.4	97.6	97.1	96.5	96.8	94.9	94.7	100.0	102.5	106.9	108.1	113.3	115.5	122.0	139.1
Sweden	115.7	120.0	125.7	124.4	122.4	123.8	100.3	99.4	100.0	112.8	110.0	108.2	104.9	104.2	94.7	96.5
Switzerland	88.1	89.6	85.2	89.7	90.8	86.3	86.8	94.1	100.0	100.2	97.2	102.8	102.5	102.2	107.4	114.1
United Kingdom	104.6	109.7	107.2	107.9	113.0	110.1	101.4	103.6	100.0	103.6	123.5	131.3	133.6	141.0	140.6	142.6

assumed that the 1996 and 1997 exchange rates are around the equilibrium rate. Turning to Table 4.3 – the consumer price tabulation – the real effective index averaged 111.5 for these two years. According to the August 2002 figure (remember that real effective rates in the tables are based upon weighted averages for the year) the British pound index was 129.3. Obviously, the conclusion is that the 2002 value of the pound was overvalued on purchasing power criteria, using consumer prices, against the currencies of its trading partners. By how much is it overvalued? The figure given by 129.3 divided by 111.5 suggests a 16 per cent overvaluation. But if we wish to know whether the GBP is too strong against the US dollar, we need to do another calculation. This involves assessing whether the USD is too strong on PPP criteria. The US current account was near to zero in 1991, and with a twelve-month lag, this suggests that the figure for consumer prices in 1990 might be taken as a starting point. The appropriate index, according to Table 4.3, is 104.7. This suggests an overvaluation of the US dollar by around 25 per cent in August 2002. This is given by the August 2002 figure of 131.1 divided by the 1990 figure of 104.7. The combined effect on the basis of consumer prices is that the USD is overvalued by around 9 per cent against the GBP.

Remember that the estimate is approximate only. We should really question which is the more appropriate index. Certainly if we use unit labour costs, we get a different answer to that based on consumer prices. Would some index based on import and export prices be better? The answer is, in all probability, yes. But there is also a further problem because data are continually being altered and updated. So maybe an approximation is the best we can expect.

As a check, it is useful to run the numbers beginning from two or three current account equilibrium dates. On the same kind of criteria, students are encouraged to do a similar exercise for their own home currency. What do you find? Clearly the tables of real effective exchange rate indices, especially if kept regularly up-to-date, are of great value to companies, investors, speculators and others.

It is worth mentioning that the exchange rate of the euro was set approximately in line with long-run PPP criteria. So the effective start date for evaluations of whether the euro is too strong or too weak might be taken (since it came into effect on 1 January 1999) as the index levels as at 1 January 1999. These are as follows:

- based on relative consumer prices   94.0

- based on relative normalized unit labour costs   88.4

In passing, it should be mentioned that one of the major causes of the Asian financial crisis in 1997 was the fact that so many countries in South East Asia were pegging their currencies to the US dollar at a time of substantial local inflation and when PPP was suggesting significant devaluations. Needless to say, a freely floating currency regime is recommended for most, if not all, currencies.

South American countries have frequently created problems for themselves by failing to adjust their currencies in a devaluation to the figure implied by PPP. They seem to prefer to maintain too strong a rate for their currency, compounding the problems for their economy. Their Ministers of Finance might well be advised to study this book.

4.5 | Big Mac purchasing power parity

We now turn to *The Economist's* Big Mac index. Invented in 1986 as a light-hearted guide to whether currencies are at their right level, the index is based upon the price of a McDonald's Big Mac burger around the world. The Big Mac is produced locally to roughly the same recipe in 118 countries. The Big Mac purchasing power parity methodology aims to calculate the exchange rate that would leave non-USA burgers costing the same as in the United States. *The Economist's* burgernomics compares the Big Mac exchange rate with the actual exchange rate as a test of whether a currency is over- or undervalued. Take an example. It uses prices in April 2003. The price of the Big Mac averaged over New York and Chicago was US$2.71. The price in Britain was £1.99, giving an implied Big Mac PPP rate of £1 = US$1.36. At the time, the actual exchange rate was £1 = US$1.58. If the Big Mac were the only item in your shopping basket, this would imply an overvaluation of the £ against the US$ of 16 per cent.

Light-hearted burgernomics has become a matter of increasing academic interest and has spawned many articles and even a whole book by Ong (2003) of the International Monetary Fund. Little did McDonald's and *The Economist* know what they were starting with the Big Mac the assumed sole constituent of the basket for PPP calculations. Continuing the good humour of this section, may we suggest that your shopping basket should be slightly more diversified.

4.6 | Summary

- The direct quotation method means a rate of exchange quoted in terms of X units of home currency to one unit of foreign currency.

- The indirect quotation method means a rate of exchange quoted in terms of Y units of foreign currency per unit of home currency.

- The United Kingdom generally uses the indirect quotation method; most others usually employ direct quotation.

- The foreign exchange spot market is a currency market for immediate delivery. In practice, payment and delivery are usually two working days after the transaction date.

- The forward market involves rates quoted today for delivery and payment at a future fixed date of a specified amount of one currency against another.

- Forward markets go out to ten years for major currencies, but not for all. Some currencies do not even have a forward market.

- The forward market enables companies and others to insure themselves against foreign exchange loss.

- In the absence of barriers to international capital movements, there is a theoretical relationship between exchange rates, inflation and fixed interest rates.

■ Note how bankers quote interest rates. If the banker wants a 2 per cent return over three months, he or she quotes an annual rate of 8 per cent. In reality, based on compounding every quarter, 2 per cent every three months means an interest rate over a year of 8.24 per cent. But the banker does not quote 8.24 per cent; he or she quotes 8 per cent. Note too that bankers always quote annual rates – even though lending for a week or a month or whatever.

■ Figure 4.1 is most important. Note that dollars and pounds are used in the figure. It can be used for any pair of currencies – simply substitute in the formulae. But remember that the formulae are based on a logic that uses New York direct quotations – that is London indirect. So when you substitute, remember to ensure consistency. Use the direct quote for both currencies as if you were in the centre substituted for dollars in the equations.

■ Interest rate parity concludes that there is a relationship between spot and forward exchange rates which is underpinned by Eurocurrency interest rate differentials. These interest rate differentials are based on fixed – not floating – interest rates for the period concerned. With the notation of Table 4.1 in the text:

$$\frac{f_0 - s_0}{s_0} = \frac{i_\$ - i_\pounds}{1 + i_\pounds}$$

■ Note that in the above formulation, the left-hand side is termed the forward premium or forward discount. The right-hand side is termed the interest differential.

■ Note in the above formula, and indeed all formulae used in this section, that we are using precise relationships based on correct deductive reasoning. In the formulae above, we do not use $(i_\$ - i_\pounds)$ as the interest differential. We actually use this as the numerator in our calculation. There is an essential denominator – and this is given by $(1 + i_\pounds)$.

■ Remember also that if we do calculations connected with a three-month forward rate, we have to use corresponding interest rates – that is for three months. Thus, an 8 per cent rate as quoted by the banker becomes 2 per cent over three months.

■ In reality, in the market place, forward rates are based on numbers of days. In this text, we approximate by using months.

■ The logical proof of interest rate parity is based upon covered interest arbitrage. Note what is entailed in this process – see the text.

■ Some courses on international financial management require you to be able to prove the four-way equivalence model; some do not require this facility. As a matter of information, courses that the author teaches do not demand such proof.

■ Purchasing power parity is concerned with the relationship between movements in spot exchange rates and relative inflation rates. With the notation in the text:

$$\frac{\tilde{s}_t - s_0}{s_0} = \frac{\tilde{p}_\$ - \tilde{p}_\pounds}{1 + \tilde{p}_\pounds}$$

■ This formula is clearly forward-looking since it uses expected movements in exchange rate and inflation rates.

■ A currency whose value moved exactly in line with purchasing power parity would have a real effective exchange rate of 100 throughout the period concerned.

■ If the exchange rate for a currency over time were exactly to reflect inflation differentials as defined above, one would say that its real effective exchange rate (sometimes abbreviated to real exchange rate) was constant.

■ A formulation which is backward-looking (that is, based on historic data) would take the form:

$$\frac{s_t - s_0}{s_0} = \frac{p_\$ - p_£}{1 + p_£}$$

In this form, rather than using expected data, past rates would be used.

■ A currency would be overvalued if it were too strong compared with its purchasing power parity value. It would be undervalued if it were too weak compared with its purchasing power parity values.

■ If purchasing power parity calculations are to reflect a currency's strength against all of its trading partners, it is necessary to weight exchange rate movements and relative inflation rates in accordance with its trade patterns.

■ Note that different purchasing power parity values will be obtained as different base years for calculation are used.

■ The above difficulty may be overcome by using a base date when the exchange rate is in equilibrium. This is perhaps best taken as a time when the country's current account in its balance of payments is zero.

■ A real exchange rate of 100 implies correct valuation. A real effective exchange rate of 100 plus implies overvaluation and a real effective rate of less than 100 implies undervaluation.

■ Note that inflation may be based on consumer prices, wholesale prices, the GDP deflator or export prices. The last of the above four gives the best purchasing power parity valuation. After all, this is the best definition of inflation for international trade purposes.

■ The Fisher effect is concerned with the relationship between interest rates and inflation. With the notation of Table 4.1 it suggests that:

$$\frac{i_\$ - i_£}{1 + i_£} = \frac{\tilde{p}_\$ - \tilde{p}_£}{1 + \tilde{p}_£}$$

■ Expectations theory relates the forward discount and changes in spot rate. It suggests that:

$$\frac{f_0 - s_0}{s_0} = \frac{\tilde{s}_t - s_0}{s_0}$$

■ The international Fisher effect links interest rate differentials with expected changes in spot rates. It suggests that:

$$\frac{i_\$ - i_\pounds}{1 + i_\pounds} = \frac{\tilde{s}_t - s_0}{s_0}$$

■ The four-way equivalence model developed in this chapter is a deductive model. In terms of using it in the real world, we have to ask how will it stand up empirically. Findings are summarized in Chapter 7. In a nutshell, at the level of most corporate users of foreign exchange rate markets it is only interest rate parity that holds in the short term. The other relationships are found to stand up fairly well long term. But more of that later.

4.7 | End of chapter questions

Question 1
All other things being equal, assume that US interest rates fall relative to UK interest rates. Again with all other things being equal, how should this affect the:

(a) US demand for British pounds;

(b) supply of pounds for sale; and

(c) equilibrium value of the pound?

Question 2
What is the expected relationship between the relative real interest rates of two countries and the exchange rate of their currencies?

Question 3
Some Latin American currencies have depreciated against the US dollar on a daily basis. What is the major factor that places such a severe downward pressure on the value of these currencies? What obvious change in Latin American economic policy would prevent the regular depreciation of these currencies?

Notes

1. 'Agio' means the sum payable for the convenience of exchanging one kind of money for another. The term originally derived from Italian moneylending in the Middle Ages.

2. Some textbooks state the interest rate parity formula as:

$$\frac{f_0}{s_0} = \frac{1 + i_\$}{1 + i_\pounds}$$

This is perfectly correct and is merely an adaptation of the formulation used in this book.

3. Like all 'laws' in the social sciences, we should not give this one the status of immutability.

5 Foreign exchange markets

The foreign exchange market is the framework of individuals, firms, banks and brokers who buy and sell foreign currencies. The foreign exchange market for any one currency, for example the US dollar, consists of all the locations such as Paris, London, New York, Zurich, Frankfurt and so on, in which the US dollar is bought and sold for other currencies. Foreign exchange markets tend to be located in national financial centres near the local financial markets. The most important foreign exchange markets are found in London, New York, Tokyo, Frankfurt, Amsterdam, Paris, Zurich, Toronto, Brussels, Milan, Singapore and Hong Kong.

There are four main types of transaction undertaken in these foreign exchange markets: spot transaction, forward deals, futures transactions and currency options.

In the spot market, currencies are bought and sold for immediate delivery. In practice, this means that settlement is made two working days after the spot date. The intervention of these two days allows for necessary paperwork to be completed. In the forward market, currencies are bought and sold at prices agreed now but for future delivery at an agreed date. Not only is delivery made in the future, but payment is also made at the future date.

5.1 | The players

The main participants in the market are companies and individuals, commercial banks, central banks and brokers. Companies and individuals need foreign currency for business or travel reasons. Commercial banks are the source from which companies and individuals obtain their foreign currency. Through their extensive network of dealing rooms, information systems and arbitrage operations (buying in one centre and selling in another), banks ensure that quotations in different centres tend towards the same price. There are also foreign exchange brokers who bring buyers, sellers and banks together and receive commissions on deals arranged. The other main player operating in the market is the central bank, the main part of whose foreign exchange activities involves the buying and selling of the home currency or foreign currencies with a view to ensuring that the exchange rate moves in line with established targets set for it by the government.

Not only are there numerous foreign exchange market centres around the world, but dealers in different locations can communicate with one another via the telephone, telex and computers. The overlapping of time zones means that, apart from weekends, there is always one centre that is open.

5.2 | Methods of quotation

A foreign exchange rate is the price of one currency in terms of another. Foreign exchange dealers quote two prices, one for selling, one for buying. The first area of mystique in foreign exchange quotations arises from the fact that there are two ways of quoting rates: the direct quote and the indirect quote. The former gives the quotation in terms of the number of units of home currency necessary to buy one unit of foreign currency. The latter gives the quotation in terms of the number of units of foreign currency bought with one unit of home currency.

Continental European dealers normally quote via the direct method for their centre. In London dealers generally use the indirect London method. In the United States, both quotation methods are used. When a bank is dealing with a customer within the United States a direct quotation is given, but when dealing with other banks in Europe (except the United Kingdom), the indirect quotation is generally used.

Foreign exchange dealers quote two prices: the rate at which they are prepared to sell a currency and that at which they are prepared to buy. The difference between the bid rate and the offer is the dealer's spread which is one of the potential sources of profit for dealers. Whether using the direct quotation method or the indirect quote, the smaller rate is always termed the bid rate and the higher is called the offer, or ask, rate.

If we assume that the middle quote (that is, halfway between the sell and buy price) for Swiss francs to the US dollar is CHF1.3753 = USD1, then the New York direct quote for this rate would be $0.7271 and the Zurich direct quote is CHF1.3753. Where both centres use the same method of quotation (that is, they both use the direct quote or they both use the indirect method) and when they are both in effect quoting the same price (in other words there are no arbitrage opportunities) the quote in one centre is the reciprocal of the other. Thus the two quotes multiplied together will equal 1.0. To the extent that this condition fails to hold, possibilities for profitable arbitrage (selling in one centre and buying in the other) exist. Of course, operators need to look at the buy rate in one centre and the sell rate in the other in terms of assessing arbitrage opportunities. In carrying out a profitable arbitrage, dealers force the prices in various centres towards equality.

If, in terms of the middle quote, the US dollar/sterling rate is $1.6015 equals £1, then the New York quote (using the local direct method) will be $1.6015 and the London quote (using the indirect method) will also be $1.6015. Where one centre uses the direct quotation method and the other uses the indirect method, the two quotations will, assuming no profitable arbitrage opportunities exist, be exactly the same.

The size of the bid/offer spread varies according to the depth of the market and its stability at any particular time. Depth of a market refers to the volume of transactions in a particular currency. Deep markets have many deals; shallow markets have few. High percentage spreads are associated with high uncertainty (perhaps owing to impending devaluation) and low volumes of transactions in a currency. Lower spreads are associated with stable, high-volume markets. Deep markets usually have narrower spreads than shallow ones.

If US dollars are quoted in terms of sterling as $1.6050 to $1.6060, it means that the dealer is prepared to sell dollars at $1.6050 to the pound, or buy dollars at $1.6060. Conversely, the dealer is prepared to buy pounds at the rate of $1.6050 or sell pounds at $1.6060. In the above example, the spread is equal to $0.0010, or 10 points. A point (or pip, as it is widely referred to) is the last significant figure in the quotation.

Next, it is necessary to consider the meaning of cross-rates. A cross-rate may be defined as an exchange rate that is calculated from two (or more) other rates. Thus the rate for the Swiss franc to the Swedish krona will, most likely, be derived as the cross-rate from the US dollar to the Swiss franc and the US dollar to the krona.

The practice in world foreign exchange markets is that currencies are quoted against the US dollar. If one bank asks another for its Swiss franc rate, that rate will be quoted against the US dollar unless otherwise specified. Most dealings are done against the US dollar, hence it follows that the market rate for a currency at any moment is most accurately reflected in its exchange rate against the US dollar. A bank that was asked to quote sterling against the Swiss franc would normally do so by calculating this rate from the £/$ rate and the $/Sfr rate. It would therefore be using cross-rates to arrive at its quotation.

Let us suppose that we require a quote for the euro against the Swiss franc. The quotation that we would receive would articulate with the quote of both currencies against the US dollar. If these rates against the dollar were $1 = €1.1326/1.1336 and $1 = CHF1.3750/1.3755, it would be possible to derive the cross-rate for the euro against the Swiss franc. Our goal is to derive the selling and buying rates for euros in terms of Swiss francs. If we are selling euros we will be buying Swiss francs. So we begin with the rate for selling euros and buying dollars; we then move to selling dollars and buying Swiss francs. The amalgamation of these two rates gives us the rate for selling euros and buying Swiss francs. The rate for selling euros to the dealer and buying dollars is €1.1336; the rate for selling dollars and buying Swiss francs is CHF1.3750. So selling €1 gives $0.8822. Selling $0.8822 gives CHF1.2130. The rate for selling euros and buying Swiss francs is €1 = CHF1.2130, or CHF1 = €0.8244.

Similarly, in our example, if we are buying euros we will be selling Swiss francs. This time we begin with the rate for buying euros from the dealer and selling dollars, and then we move to buying dollars and selling Swiss francs. Amalgamating these two rates gives us the rate for buying euros and selling Swiss francs. The rate for buying euros and selling dollars is €1.1326; the rate for buying dollars and selling Swiss francs is CHF1.3755. Selling CHF1 gives $0.7270. Selling $0.7270 gives €0.8234. The rate for buying euros and selling Swiss francs is CHF1 = €0.8234, or €1 = CHF1.2145. The cross-rate quotation using direct euro figures would be €0.8234/0.8244 = CHF1, and the direct Zurich quote would be CHF1.2130/1.2145.

It is also worth mentioning the manner of quotation when the market or financial commentators use a slash between two currencies. Take the following example:

EUR/JPY   128.56   ↑ 0.32

This means that you get (or, more precisely it is the middle price of buy and sell prices) JPY128.56 for €1. So the slash means that the currency before the slash should be equated to one and you get the number of units quoted (128.56) of the currency after the slash. Imagine that our quotation is a mid-morning quote in London. The figure of 0.32 with the upward arrow implies that the quote has moved upwards by 0.32 since the opening of the London trading session. So, the opening price was therefore 128.24. The upward arrow means that at mid-morning, in our example, you get more JPY for your € than at the opening. So the upward arrow implies that the currency before the slash (€ in the example) has strengthened in the trading session versus the JPY.

   Take another example. Check it out yourself before going on to the explanatory note below it. Can you understand this quotation? How many Swiss francs are there to one US dollar? How many US dollars are there to one Swiss franc? Which currency has strengthened during the trading session? The quotation is:

US$/CHF   1.3785   ↓ 0.0026

This means that US$1 equals CHF1.3785. And, during the trading session since the opening, the US$ has weakened against the CHF. The opening price was 1.3811 and the dollar has moved down against the Swiss franc to 1.3785. The downward percentage movement is therefore 0.0026 divided by 1.3811 (the opening price) with the result multiplied by 100 – that is 0.19 per cent. Looked at from a reverse position, CHF1 equals US$0.7254. Try working out the quotation with CHF before the slash. Do it without looking at the figures below. The answer should be:

CHF/US$ 0.7254   ↑ 0.0013

Note that the movement upwards is from 1.0 divided by 1.3811, that is 0.7241 at the opening, giving a Swiss franc rise of 0.0013.

5.3 | Forward contracts and quotations

It is necessary to consider next how forward rates are quoted by foreign exchange dealers. A forward foreign exchange contract is an agreement between two parties to exchange one currency for another at some future date. The rate at which the exchange is to be made, the delivery date and the amounts involved are fixed at the time of the agreement.

   One of the major problems that newcomers to foreign exchange markets have is understanding how the forward premium and discount works and how foreign exchange dealers quote for forward delivery. Assume that a quoted currency is more expensive in the future than it is now in terms of the base currency. The quoted currency is then said to stand at a premium in the forward market relative to the base currency. Conversely, the base currency is said to stand at a discount relative to the quoted currency.

Consider an example in which the US dollar is the base currency and the Swiss franc is the quoted currency. Assume that the spot rate is $1 = CHF1.3753. The rate quoted by a bank today for delivery in three months' time (today's three-month forward rate) is $1 = CHF1.3748. In this example, the dollar buys fewer Swiss francs in three months' time than it does today. So the Swiss franc is more expensive in the forward market. Thus the dollar stands at a discount relative to the Swiss franc; conversely, the Swiss franc stands at a premium relative to the dollar. The size of the dollar discount or Swiss franc premium is the difference between 1.3753 and 1.3748, that is, 0.05 centimes. The convention in the foreign exchange market is frequently to quote in terms of points, or hundredths of a unit. Hence 0.05 centimes is frequently quoted as 5 points.

In order to arrive at the forward prices, the Swiss franc premium or dollar discount must be subtracted from the spot rate. Were there a Swiss franc discount or dollar premium, this would be added to the spot rate. But care has to be taken: in our example we used a New York indirect quote. Had we used a New York direct quote, the reverse would apply: in other words, the Swiss franc premium or dollar discount would have to be added to the spot quotation. An easier way to deal with this little problem is always to remember (and this has never, in practice, been found to be otherwise) that the bid/offer spread on the forward quote is always wider than the spread on the spot figure. If this is remembered it is an easy process to compare the two spreads and if the forward spread is narrower than the spot spread, the sums have been done incorrectly and recomputation is necessary.

Just as in the spot market, dealers quote selling and buying rates in the forward market, too. As in the spot market the convention, whether using direct or indirect quotation methods, is that the smaller rate is quoted first. In the above example the spot rate for Swiss francs to US dollar might be quoted as CHF1.3748/1.3758 and the three-month Swiss franc premium (or dollar discount) might be 6/3. Thus, if the foreign exchange dealer is buying dollars forward, there will be a Swiss franc premium of 6 points, or 0.06 centimes. But if he is buying the Swiss franc, the premium will only be 3 points or 0.03 centimes. Using the convention that the forward spread is wider than the spot spread, the full three-month forward quotation comes out at CHF1.3742/1.3755.

	Bid rate	Offer rate	Spread in points
Spot quotation	1.3748	1.3758	10
Forward spread	6	3	3
Subtract to make forward spread 13 points	1.3742	1.3755	13

Sometimes forward quotes are given as −10/+10 or 10P10. In this situation the forward market is said to be 'round par'. Thus, to get the forward rate, 10 points have to be added to either the bid or offer and 10 points have to be subtracted so that the forward spread widens on the spot spread. For example, take the quotations of:

$$1.3748/1.3758 \qquad -10/+10$$

The forward rate could be construed as 1.3738/1.3768, i.e. it may be quoted in full rather than as points distance from spot. This is called the outright forward price. It would be computed as:

	Bid rate	Offer rate	Spread in points
Spot quotation	1.3748	1.3758	10
Forward spread	(10)	10	20
	1.3738	1.3768	30

Sometimes this kind of situation is quoted in terms of the spread from the spot rate as 10 centimes discount, 10 centimes premium.

It is important to bear in mind that the currency quoted at a discount in the forward market relative to another currency will have higher Eurocurrency interest rates than the currency which is at the premium. The rationale for this was discussed in the previous chapter.

As an adjunct to the above methods of quoting forward foreign exchange rates, we sometimes see the percentage per annum cost of forward cover. What does this mean and how is it calculated? The annualized forward premium may be expressed as a percentage by reference to the formula:

$$\frac{\text{Forward rate} - \text{spot rate}}{\text{Spot rate}} \times \frac{12}{n} \times 100$$

where n is the the number of months in the forward contract.[1] It should be noted that small differences in the annual percentage cost of forward cover arise when using the direct quotation method as opposed to using the indirect quote. Slightly different results arise too from using the buying rate as opposed to the selling rate or the middle price. The problem of differing costs of forward cover for buying and selling is easily resolved. While different figures are achieved using mathematics, the relevant figure for a company executive using the forward market is the percentage cost of doing the transaction that he or she wishes to undertake.

Let us look at an example. Suppose again that we have a spot rate of USD1 = CHF1.3748/1.3758 and that the three-month forward quote is 6/3. The forward rate came out (see above) as CHF1.3742/1.3755. If we were a buyer of Swiss francs forward, the forward premium would be obtained by comparing the rates for buying Swiss francs (that is CHF1.3748 spot and CHF1.3742 three months forward). The annualized forward premium for buying Swiss francs would therefore amount to:

$$\frac{1.3742 - 1.3748}{1.3748} \times \frac{12}{3} \times 100 = -0.17\% \text{ p.a.}$$

The Swiss franc is said to be at an annualized premium of 0.17 per cent in the three-month forward market against the US dollar based on rates for buying marks.

5.4 | Spot settlement

A spot foreign exchange deal is made for settlement in two working days' time. So, in normal circumstances, a deal done on Monday is settled on Wednesday. The value date is the date of Wednesday.

A working day is defined as one in which banks for currencies on either side of the deal are open for business in both settlement countries – with one exception. If the deal is done against the US dollar and if the first of the two days is a holiday in the United States but not in the other settlement country, then that day is also counted as a working day.

In the case of a US dollar/Swiss franc deal done on Monday, settlement would normally be on Wednesday. This would not be affected by a US holiday on the Tuesday. But it would be affected by a Swiss holiday on the Tuesday. In the latter case, the spot date would be postponed until Thursday, provided that both centres were open on Thursday. If Tuesday were a normal working day, but Wednesday were a holiday in either the United States or Switzerland, then the spot day would be Thursday, assuming that both centres were open that day.

In the case of a US dollar/Swiss franc deal done, say, in London, the occurrence of UK bank holidays during the spot period is entirely irrelevant. This is because all bank account transfers are made in the settlement country rather than the dealing centre.

In certain countries, such as the United States or Switzerland, bank holidays may affect only part of the country – depending on whether it is a local state holiday, or, if religious, whether the area is mainly Catholic or Protestant. In this case, the date for settlement could vary according to the regional location of the bank accounts involved. This complication is ignored in this book, but it is clearly relevant in the real world.

Settlement of both sides of a foreign exchange deal ought to be made on the same working day. Given time zone differences, settlement on any given working day will take place earlier in the Far East, later in Europe, and later still in the United States. This implies a risk. Using the US dollar/Swiss franc example, a bank selling Swiss francs may deliver them in Zurich before receiving the dollars in New York. Should the recipient in Switzerland go bankrupt before delivering the dollars, losses may arise. Hence the worry about limits and the section devoted to this in Chapter 32. The notion that the two sides of the deal should be completed on the same day is referred to as the principle of *valeur compensée* or compensated value.

The only exception to compensated value arises in deals in Middle Eastern currencies for settlement on Friday. This is a holiday in most Middle East countries. When this happens, the person buying the Middle Eastern currency – for example, Saudi riyals – makes payment, say in US dollars, on Friday. Delivery of the riyals takes place on Saturday, which is a normal business day in the Middle East.

5.5 | Forward value dates

The first step in finding the normal forward value date for periods of one, two, three months, and so on, is to fix the spot value date. The normal forward value date will be the same date in the relevant month. So, if spot is 8 October, one month is 8 November, two months is 8 December and so on.

If the date so calculated is a holiday, then the date is rolled onward to the next day on which banks are open for business in both centres. Assume that we were dealing US dollars/Swiss francs for one month and 8 November is on a weekend or a holiday in New York or Zurich. Then we roll the date onward to the 9th, if that day is a business day in both centres. If it is not, then we keep rolling the date onward until a business day is reached.

Exceptions to this rule arise in the case of month-ends. A month-end date is the last day of a month where banks are open for business in the two settlement countries. In the US dollar/Swiss franc deal, if 30 September is a US holiday, then month-end would be 29 September, provided that day is a business day in both centres.

There are two further exceptions to the standard rule set out in the first paragraph of this section. Both of these concern month-ends. The first is the so-called 'end–end rule'. This says that if the spot value date is a month-end, then all forward value dates are also month-ends. Suppose that the October month-end is 28 October, and the 29th and 30th are on a weekend and 31 October is a public holiday. Then if spot is 28 October (that is, the month-end) the 'end–end rule' makes the one-month date 30 November if that is the November month-end, not 28 November.

The second exception is that forward value dates must not be rolled on beyond the month-end. Suppose the one-month date would normally be 31 March but that is a holiday. We do not roll the one-month date on to 1 April, but roll it back to 30 March.

However, we would also stress that pricing contracts for foreign exchange and interest rates actually depend upon day counts.

5.6 | Main purpose of the forward market

By entering into a forward foreign exchange contract, a UK importer or exporter is able to fix, at the time of the contract, a price for the purchase or sale of a fixed amount of foreign currency for delivery and payment at a specified future time. By so doing, the importer or exporter may eliminate foreign exchange risk due to future exchange rate fluctuations. This enables the exact sterling value of an international commercial contract to be calculated despite the fact that payment is to be made in the future in a foreign currency.

If a foreign currency stands at premium in the forward market, it shows that the currency is 'stronger' than the home currency in that forward market. By contrast, if a foreign currency stands at a discount in the forward market, it shows that the currency is 'weaker' than the home currency in that forward market. The words 'stronger' and 'weaker' are put in inverted commas because, in the context of forward markets, strength and weakness merely take account of interest rate differentials as suggested by the interest rate parity part of the four-way equivalence model encountered in Chapter 4.

5.7 ▎ Summary

- Foreign exchange market transactions may involve spot, forward, futures and options deals and deposit and borrowing market transactions. This chapter does not deal with futures or options.

- In all of these markets, dealers quote bid and offer rates – one for buying, one for selling.

- So, in the spot market, dealers quote bid/offer rates.

- In the forward market, dealers quote the spot bid/offer rate and then quote, as a bid/offer rate, the forward points. The forward points give the distance from spot to forward.

- To obtain the outright forward rate, if the bid and offer on the forward points have the same sign – positive or negative – then, assuming the bid points exceeds the offer points, deduct both from the spot. If both have the same sign but the offer points exceed the bid points, then add both to the spot.

- If the forward points have the opposite sign, a bid that is positive and an offer that is negative or vice versa, one is added and the other deducted from the corresponding bid/offer rate for spot to get the outright forward. In this circumstance, the bid forward points are deducted from the spot bid quote; the offer forward points are added to the spot offer quote. This gives the respective bid/offer quotation for the outright forward rate.

- The forward premium or discount is always calculated as the annualized percentage difference between the spot and forward rates as a proportion of the spot rate, that is:

$$\frac{f_0 - s_0}{s_0} \times \frac{12}{n} \times 100\%$$

- When spot and forward rates are compared, one currency will usually be more expensive forward than spot. The currency that is more expensive in the forward market is said to be at a premium. This currency can be said to be 'strengthening' in the forward market. The term 'strengthening' is in inverted commas because it is not really strengthening as such – its relative strength merely reflects interest differentials.

- If interest rate parity is holding – and at the level that most company treasurers deal, it always holds – then the currency that is 'strengthening' is said to be at a premium and this currency will have lower fixed interest rates. Here is a mnemonic: SPIL means strengthening, premium, interest rates, lower.

- Or how about Spain and Portugal form the Iberian landmass?

- Or here is another: SLIP means strengthening, lower interest rates, premium.

5.8 | End of chapter questions

Question 1
Assume the following information:

	Bank X	Bank Y
Bid price of Swiss francs	$.401	$.398
Ask price of Swiss francs	$.404	$.400

Given this information, is arbitrage possible? If so, explain the steps that would create the arbitrage. Compute the profit from this arbitrage if you had $1,000,000 to use.

Question 2
Based on the information in the previous question, what market forces would occur to eliminate any further possibilities of the locational arbitrage described in your answer to Question 1.

Question 3
Assume the following information for a particular bank:

	Quoted price	
Value of Batavian drac (BTD) in US dollars	USD	.90
Value of Ulerican crown (ULC) in US dollars	USD	.30
Value of Batavian drac in Ulerican crown	ULC	3.02

Given this information, is triangular arbitrage possible? If so, explain the steps that would reflect triangular arbitrage, and calculate the profit from this strategy if you had $1,000,000 to use.

Note

1. Always remember that in the real world the exact number of days must be used rather than months. For simplification purposes, we use months throughout this book.

6 The balance of payments

The balance of payments position of a country is often claimed to be an important piece of information for anyone wishing to predict the future of a currency's strength in exchange rate terms. A recurring current account surplus is often associated with a strengthening of a country's exchange rate; a continual deficit on current account is frequently associated with a fall in a country's exchange rate. A surplus on current account is underpinned by an excess of exports over imports. Suppose that exports from a country are denominated in the home currency. Payment for them involves a foreigner in buying home currency and selling foreign currency. This tends to strengthen the home currency. Hence surpluses and the strengthening of the exchange rate tend to go hand in hand. Conversely, deficits on the current account are associated with an excess of imports over exports. Recurring current account deficits and weakening of the exchange rate are generally related.

There are a good many frailties in a forecasting model based solely on current account outturns. The current account is only part of the balance of payments picture: the capital account has to be considered as well. Before we can truly discuss the problems of using balance of payments data to forecast foreign exchange rates, we need to consider a number of concepts associated with the balance of payments. This chapter attempts to describe these concepts and draws conclusions about foreign exchange rate forecasting using balance of payments information.

6.1 | The essence of international trade

The basis of international trade has been explained in terms of the principle of comparative advantage. This presumes that, for a number of reasons, some individuals and some countries produce some goods and services more efficiently than others. It is conceivable that one particular country might produce every product more efficiently than any other. Even if this were so, it might be to this country's advantage to apply all of its skills and resources towards the production of only those goods or services that gave it the greatest payoff and to buy in other products and services which gave a lower payoff. It is, of course, extremely unlikely that one particular country would produce all goods and services more efficiently than its international competitors. However, as long as one country has an greater advantage, a comparative advantage, in producing certain goods and services, it benefits by specializing in those lines, exporting those goods and services and importing other goods and services from other countries. A country gains then by specializing in products in which it has the greatest comparative advantage because any shift of resources to other products reduces output. Naturally, a country must produce enough of the goods and services in which it possesses a comparative advantage not only to meet its own needs but also to export in exchange for imports of goods and services needed to meet demand.

International trade usually involves the cross-frontier payment of money to pay for goods and services. The word 'usually' is deliberately employed because a significant volume of international trade is by barter. Indeed, in dealing with certain countries that are short of foreign exchange, trade is largely via barter. But for most transactions, barter is as awkward internationally as it is domestically. Unless international trade is by barter alone, it must be financed.

One of the most valuable services rendered by the foreign exchange markets is the provision of a mechanism for transferring the money of one country into the money of another. As long as different currencies exist and as long as international trade embraces payment other than by barter, foreign exchange will be a necessary dimension of international trade.

6.2 | The balance of payments and foreign exchange rates

A foreign exchange rate is the price of one currency in terms of another. The balance of payments summarizes the flow of economic transactions between the residents of a given country and the residents of other countries during a certain period of time.

The balance of payments measures flows rather than stocks. These flows represent payments and receipts. Balance of payments data record only changes in asset holdings and liabilities; they do not present the absolute levels of these items. So the balance of payments of a country is rather like the statement of sources and use of funds of a firm. For a country, sources of funds are acquisitions of external purchasing power, rights a country has to claim goods and services or to invest in another country. For a country, uses of funds, in the context of the balance of payments, means a decrease in its external purchasing power. For balance of payments purposes, a resident is any person, individual, business firm, government agency or other institution legally domiciled in the given country.

The balance of payments measures transactions among countries. Transactions that affect only local residents and involve only the national currency (in contrast to foreign exchange) are not recorded in the balance of payments.

The balance of payments comprises three distinct types of account, namely:

- the current account;

- the capital account;

- the official reserves.

Table 6.1 Simplified balance of payments in Ruritania, 2003 ($m)

CURRENT ACCOUNT			
Trade account			
Exports of goods	2,500		
Imports of goods	−1,500		
Balance of trade		1,000	
Invisibles account			
Receipts from interest and dividends, travel and services such as shipping, property, banking and financial charges	1,000		
Payments for interest and dividends, and services such as shipping, travel, property, banking and financial charges	−500		
Balance of invisibles (services)		500	
Unilateral transfers			
Gifts received from abroad	200		
Grants to foreign countries	−600		
Balance on unilateral transfers		−400	
Current account balance		1,100	
CAPITAL ACCOUNT			
Long-term capital flows			
Direct investment			
Sale of financial assets	1,000		
Purchase of financial assets	−2,000	−1,000	
Portfolio investments			
Sale of financial assets	3,000		
Purchase of financial assets	−1,500	1,500	
Balance on long-term capital		500	
Private short-term capital flows			
Sale of financial assets	5,000		
Purchase of financial assets	−2,000		
Balance on short-term private capital		3,000	
Capital account balance			3,500
OVERALL BALANCE			4,600
OFFICIAL RESERVES ACCOUNT			
Gold decrease (+) or gold increase (−)			−2,400
Decrease (+) or increase (−) in foreign exchange			−2,200
TOTAL OFFICIAL FINANCING			−4,600

Note: Sources of funds are given by +; use of funds is given by −.

Table 6.1 shows a simplified balance of payments format for Ruritania in 2003. It is simplified because it contains merely 23 lines of figures whereas the full balance of payments as published by the IMF in *International Financial Statistics* contains over 50 lines. In terms of putting this rather complex presentation of data into a more manageable design for purposes of forecasting exchange rates, the model used in Table 6.1 is recommended.

Balance of payments information is compiled by government statisticians from questionnaires completed by companies, banks, export agencies and others. The overall balance of payments is, by definition, equal – the sum of the current and capital accounts equals the official financing. If the aggregate of data obtained by government statisticians does not balance, a heading called 'net errors and omissions' is introduced. This item is a permanent feature of balance of payments figures. We now consider, in turn, the content of the current account, the capital account and the official financing parts of the balance of payments. In this description we constantly refer to data in Table 6.1 by way of illustration.

The current account records trade in goods and services and the exchange of gifts among countries. Trade in goods comprises exports and imports. A country increases its exports when it sells goods to foreigners; this is a source of funds. It increases imports when it buys goods from foreigners; this is a use of funds. The difference between exports and imports is called the 'trade balance'. According to Table 6.1, Ruritania has a positive trade balance of $1,000m in 2003. Sources of external purchasing power exceed uses thereof through trade by $1,000m.

The difference on services is called the 'balance of invisibles'. In balance of payments terminology, services include interest, dividends, travel expenses, shipping, property, banking, financial and other consultancy services. The rendering of these services to foreigners is a source of funds and their receipt from foreigners is a use of funds. Respectively, they increase or reduce external purchasing power. From Table 6.1 it is seen that Ruritania has a positive balance on invisibles of $500m. In other words, sources of external purchasing power exceed uses by $500m in respect of transactions in invisibles.

Gifts are recorded in the unilateral transfers account. This account is frequently called 'remittances' or 'unrequited transfers'. It embraces money that migrants send home, and gifts and aid that one country makes to another. A gift represents a use of external purchasing power. Ruritania has a negative balance on unilateral transfers amounting to $400m. Uses of funds exceed sources by this amount.

The overall current account of Ruritania shows a positive balance of $1.1bn, made up of positive balances in trade and invisibles and a negative balance on unilateral transfers.

Turning now to the capital account, this details international movements of financial assets and liabilities. These are classified in the balance of payments according to their maturity and according to the involvement of the owner of the asset or liability. There are a number of sub-divisions such as direct investment, portfolio investment and private short-term capital flows. Direct investment and portfolio investment involve financial assets with an initial maturity of more than a year when issued. Short-term capital movements consist of claims with an original maturity of less than one year. The distinction between direct investment and portfolio investment is made on the basis of the degree of management involvement. In the case of direct investment, considerable management involvement is presumed to exist; this is interpreted as a minimum of 10 per cent ownership in a firm. No management involvement is presumed to exist for portfolio investment.

Ruritania has a deficit on direct investment to the extent of $1,000m. While foreigners invested $1,000m in the country, Ruritania invested $2,000m out of the country in respect of situations when in excess of 10 per cent ownership was acquired.

Under the heading of portfolio investment, Ruritania has an inflow of $3,000m compared with an outflow of $1,500m. Together with the balance on direct investment, this gives a positive balance on long-term capital account of $500m.

In the private short-term capital account, Ruritania increased its liabilities to foreigners – a source of funds for the country – by $5,000m, while Ruritania increased its claims on foreigners (a use of funds for Ruritania) by $2,000m. These two items gave rise to a positive net balance on the short-term capital account of $3,000m.

Summing long-term and short-term capital flows gives the balance on capital account. For Ruritania there is a positive capital account balance of $3,500m.

When the current account and capital account are added up, we get a total that is frequently called the 'overall balance'. For Ruritania, this amounts to $4,600m. In other words, Ruritania has acquired a net source of external purchasing power of this amount.

The official reserves account rounds off the balance of payments. It shows the means of international payment that the monetary authorities of a country have acquired or lost during a particular period. The term 'means of international payment' includes gold and convertible foreign currency. It must be borne in mind that only foreign currency holdings that are freely convertible are included in the official reserves. Really this means that only a handful of currencies find their way into official reserves. Currencies such as the US dollar and sterling qualify as they are freely convertible at the present time. Most governments do not allow their country's currency to be freely converted to others, so holdings of Brazilian reals, Indian rupees, Chinese renminbi yuan and so on would not be classified as official reserves.

If there is a surplus at the overall balance level on a country's balance of payments, the effect will be for there to be an inflow of official reserves. But we must bear in mind the notation used in balance of payments accounting. As we shall see later in this chapter, balance of payments accounting is just a variant of double-entry bookkeeping. For every debit there is a credit; for every plus entry on the balance of payments, there will be a compensating minus entry. So, in the official reserves part of the balance of payments, a negative entry implies an increase in reserves. In Table 6.1, Ruritania has expanded its gold reserves by $2,400m and its foreign exchange reserves by $2,200m. Care must be taken to interpret the sign in front of official reserves data correctly because of the counter-intuitive nature of the way of recording information.

Movements in the official reserves may be interpreted as an indicator of the extent of direct intervention in the foreign exchange markets by the central bank. When the monetary authorities support the home currency (or associated currencies where there is a joint float), they do so by selling reserves and buying the home currency – this would reduce official reserves. Conversely, when they depress the home currency, they do so by buying in convertible currency and selling home currency – this would increase official reserves.

Table 6.2 Balance of payments accounting

Debit (–)	*Credit (+)*
1. Import of goods	
	2. Export of goods
3. Purchase of services from foreigners	
	4. Sale of services to foreigners
5. Interest, dividends, rents and royalties to foreigners	
	6. Interest, dividends, rents and royalties from foreigners
7. Gifts to foreigners	
	8. Gifts from foreigners
9. Direct investment	
• by residents in foreign countries	• by foreigners in home country
10. Portfolio investment	
• by residents in foreign country	• by foreigners in home country
11. Long-term claims on foreigners	
• increase	• decrease
12. Long-term liabilities to foreigners	
• decrease	• increase
13. Short-term claims on foreigners	
• increase	• decrease
14. Short-term liabilities to foreigners	
• decrease	• increase
15. Official reserves of gold	
• increase	• decrease
16. Official reserves of foreign exchange	
• increase	• decrease

6.3 | Balance of payments accounting

The balance of payments always balances. The sum of the debits and credits on the current account, the capital account and the official financing is always equal. This arises because balance of payments tabulations are built on double-entry bookkeeping principles. Table 6.2 summarizes the accounts used in balance of payments accounting. These accounts are numbered so that such numbers can be used as a form of shorthand in subsequent examples. The accounts are classified according to whether they are typically debit or credit – or both.

Through a series of simple examples the essence of balance of payments accounting may be understood.

Example 1

A resident of country X exports goods to a resident of country Y, who signs a bill of exchange, denominated in country Y's currency, which matures in 90 days. In country X's balance of payments, an export has occurred and a short-term claim on a foreigner has been acquired. The debit and credit position is therefore:

Dr   Short-term claims on foreigners (the bill of exchange)
Cr   Export of goods

Example 2

The exporter in Example 1 holds the bill to maturity when he receives payment in country Y's currency. The exporter now has a claim (the payment in Y's currency) on a bank in country Y. Effectively, the debit and credit are therefore in the same account.

Dr   Short-term claims on foreigners (the amount in Y's currency)
Cr   Short-term claims on foreigners (the bill of exchange)

Example 3

The exporter in the two previous examples now decides to convert the payment in country Y's currency to his own. He does this through his own clearing bank. Here the bank buys the foreign currency and sells the home currency in exchange. Now the bank in country X has acquired country Y's currency. The bank now has a short-term claim on foreigners. All that happened is that the short-term claim on foreigners has been shuffled from one resident of country X, the exporter, to another, the clearing bank. From a balance of payments standpoint no entry needs to be made.

Example 4

The clearing bank decides to sell the foreign currency acquired in the previous example to country X's central bank in exchange for home currency. Assume that country Y's currency is freely convertible in the foreign exchange markets. When the central bank acquires gold or freely convertible foreign currency, it increases the official reserves. So in this case the balance of payments entry is:

Dr   Official reserves of foreign currency
Cr   Short-term claims on foreigners (the amount in Y's currency)

Example 5

If the previous example had differed in only one respect, namely that country Y's currency had not been freely convertible, then there would have been no increment to the official reserves. In this case there would be no balance of payments entry – the short-term claim on foreigners would merely have been shuffled from the clearing bank to the central bank, and since the short-term claim was not convertible foreign currency it would not count as part of the official reserves. It would, in fact, remain as a short-term claim on foreigners, but the claim would be held by the central bank rather than the clearing bank.

Example 6

A US resident on holiday in country X changes dollar travellers' cheques for country X's currency at an airport bank. All of this is spent on her vacation. In this case the balance of payments entry would be:

    Dr   Short-term claims on foreigners (the holding of US dollars)
    Cr   Travel services to foreigners (part of account number 4 in Table 6.2)

Example 7

Had the airport bank in the previous example then sold the US dollars to the central bank, this would have increased the official reserves. The balance of payments entry would be:

    Dr   Official reserves of foreign currency
    Cr   Short-term claims on foreigners (the holding of US dollars)

The acquisition of convertible foreign currency within a country does not lead to an entry in the official reserves until that foreign currency finds its way to the central bank. This is a very important feature of balance of payments accounting which needs to be clearly understood.

Example 8

A resident of country X sends a cheque to a relative in Australia. In country X's balance of payments the above transaction is shown as:

    Dr   Gifts to foreigners
    Cr   Short-term liabilities to foreigners (the cheque)

Example 9

A foreign bank uses a deposit in country X's currency to buy country X's treasury bills. This transaction is classified as a reduction in short-term liabilities to foreigners (the deposit in country X's currency) matched by an increase in short-term liabilities to foreigners (the treasury bills). Note that since treasury bills have a maturity of less than twelve months, they do not constitute portfolio investment. So the transaction is:

Dr   Short-term liabilities to foreigners – decrease (the currency deposit)
Cr   Short-term liabilities to foreigners – increase (the treasury bills)

It is worth pointing out that current account and capital account movements are termed *autonomous* in balance of payments parlance. These movements can be considered as a barometer of pressures on the exchange rate of the home currency. Official reserves movements are termed 'compensating' or 'accommodating' items. Sometimes this distinction is expressed in 'above the line' and 'below the line' terms respectively. Accounts 'above the line' embrace autonomous accounts whose balance determines whether the balance of payments is in surplus or deficit. Accounts 'below the line' represent compensating accounts that show how the balance of payments surplus or deficit was financed.

When the balance of payments is in surplus, international purchasing power of the country has increased during the period in question – that is, autonomous receipts exceed autonomous payments. When the balance of payments is in deficit, international purchasing power of the country has decreased during the period in question – thus autonomous payments exceed autonomous receipts. A surplus in the autonomous account is accompanied by an increase in foreign reserves or a decrease in official liabilities in the compensating accounts. This puts an upward pressure on the external value of the home currency. A deficit in the autonomous accounts is associated with a decrease in foreign reserves or an increase in liabilities to foreigners. This tends to put a downward pressure on the external value of the home currency. Countries with continuous deficits in the balance of payments experience international currency depreciation.

In practice, balance of payments statistics are not compiled on an entry-by-entry basis. Only aggregates of transactions are measured for a period. The customs and excise authorities provide the main source for figures on exports and imports; financial institutions, government agencies and industry report the changes in foreign financial assets and in liabilities to foreigners. Hence the almost perennial item in balance of payments accounting – net errors and omissions – arises because sources and uses fail to balance.

6.4 | Forecasting exchange rates and the balance of payments

The use of balance of payments data to forecast foreign exchange rates is predicated upon the assumption that when a country's currency is in equilibrium, that country will display a break-even position in respect of trade and those invisibles that reflect the rendering of services (as opposed to the remuneration of capital: that is, interest and dividends). Although not exactly in accordance with the above formula, this is frequently interpreted as being equivalent to an even current account outturn. The other key assumptions in forecasting foreign exchange rates from the balance of payments are that currencies that are undervalued will have the effect of creating positive current account outturns, while currencies that are overvalued will have the effect of creating negative current account results.

These key underpinnings also assume that no market imperfections exist, such as the absence of any significant valuable raw materials or a trained labour force which typifies so many Third World countries. Often one concludes that, on the basis of balance of payments data, there is no way to identify the exchange rate at which many Third World countries will break even on current account.

There are also frailties of the forecasting model which need to be borne in mind. These concern three key areas.

The first relates to situations when exports are denominated in a third currency and where the exporter continues to hold the proceeds of an export sale in the said currency. Consider an example. Many raw materials are priced in US dollars. This is true of oil. A UK oil exporter will sell petroleum to Europe, for example with the price denominated in US dollars. When the European importer pays the UK oil company it will pay dollars. The export will show as a positive increment to the British balance of payments current account. But if the exporter continues to hold the proceeds of the sale in a US dollar bank account, it will not strengthen the pound sterling. As far as the balance of payments is concerned, the dollar deposit will show as a short-term claim on foreigners. Now if the UK oil company were to sell its dollars for pounds via its clearing bank, then this deal would tend to strengthen sterling. But even if the UK oil company sells its dollars to a clearing bank, the transaction will still show as a short-term claim on foreigners from a balance of payments viewpoint. But the claim is now held by the bank rather than the oil exporter. Clearly, from the standpoint of using balance of payments data to forecast exchange rates with great confidence, we have inadequate information based on the normal package of published figures.

The second frailty involves a country's capital account. While it may experience substantial deficits on current account, a country may have substantial capital inflows from multinationals. These capital flows may exceed the current account deficit, resulting in an overall tendency for a country's currency to strengthen despite its negative current account balance. This situation underpinned the strength of the Mexican peso and the Indonesian rupiah in the early 1970s when inflows from oil companies undertaking exploration activities propped up deficits on current accounts and allowed the governments of both countries to postpone devaluations which were indicated by purchasing power parity.

The third frailty also arises in the area of the capital account. Among other things the capital account includes borrowings from bankers or from the IMF. These would show as long-term liabilities to foreigners. The conversion of such borrowings from, say, US dollars to the home currency would tend to strengthen the home currency in the short term but would not, in the very short term, affect the current account of the country.

Evidently, using current account data as indicators of potential foreign exchange movements is fraught with pitfalls. Forecasters need to tread very warily but, with care, have a useful tool at their disposal.

6.5 | Summary

- The balance of payments summarizes economic transactions between the residents of a given country and the residents of other countries during a given period of time.

- The balance of payments measures flows; these flows represent payments and receipts.

- Balance of payments data do not embrace absolute levels of assets and liabilities – but they do include changes in these items, rather like a source and use of funds statement as opposed to a balance sheet.

- The balance of payments comprises three distinct types of account, namely the current account, the capital account and the official reserves.

- The current account records trade in goods and services and gifts between countries. Trade comprises exports and imports. Services include interest, dividends, travel, shipping, insurance and consulting fees for banking, property and financial matters.

- The difference on trade is called the balance of trade or visibles. The difference on services is called the balance of invisibles.

- The capital account details international movements of financial assets and liabilities.

- Direct investment and portfolio investment relate to situations where investment overseas occurs in respect of assets with a maturity of over one year. Short-term capital movements refer to situations were assets and liabilities have maturities of less than one year.

- The degree of management involvement activity distinguishes direct and portfolio investment. Direct investment implies considerable management involvement, and is interpreted as a minimum of 10 per cent ownership in a venture or firm. No management involvement is presumed for portfolio investment.

- The total of long- and short-term capital movements gives the balance on capital account.

- The capital account would include payables and receivables outstanding on trade or services. It will also include inflows from multinationals and borrowings from bankers or from the IMF.

- There is also the official reserves. It shows changes in the means of international payment held by the monetary authorities of a country during a particular period. The term 'means of international payment' includes gold and convertible foreign currency.

- Movements in official reserves indicate the extent of direct intervention in foreign exchange markets by the central bank. When the home currency is supported, there will be an outflow of official reserves. By a reverse token, pushing down the home currency is reflected by an increase in official reserves.

- The three accounts constituting the balance of payments sum to zero.

- The nearest we have to the idea of a country's currency being in equilibrium is to interpret this as meaning a level at which the country displays a break-even portion on trade and services – which is not exactly the current account balance since interest and dividends should be excluded from invisibles for this purpose.

6.6 | End of chapter questions

Question 1
How would a relatively high home inflation rate affect the home country's current account, all other thing being equal?

Question 2
How would you expect a weakening home currency to affect the home country's current account, all other things being equal?

Question 3
It is sometimes suggested that a floating exchange rate will adjust to reduce or eliminate any current account deficit. Explain why this adjustment would occur. Why does the exchange rate not always adjust to correct a current account deficit?

7 Theories and empiricism on exchange rate movements

Explanations of economic phenomena often conflict. Hypotheses are advanced and tested. For a while it looks as if one particular series of explanatory variables is accounting for changes in the dependent variable, then the relationship breaks down. As social scientists we should not be surprised at the infuriatingly unpredictable way in which our world seems to work.

Multinational finance is no exception. The key question to which we seek a solution is: what makes foreign exchange rates move and can these movements be predicted? We are looking for the typical kind of regression equation in which the future spot rate is the dependent variable and there may be one or more independent variables whose coefficients can be estimated, hopefully with acceptably high levels of significance, and the equation has a high R^2.

Unfortunately, the models that have been developed do not necessarily hold for anything but quite short periods. So we do not have the kind of model upon which we can rely with high degrees of certainty in terms of predicting movements in spot rates.

Summarizing the position about our ability to explain exchange rate movements after the fact, or to forecast them before the event, Meese (1990) highlighted the forecasting superiority of the random walk model versus structural models and argued that:

> Economists do not yet understand the determination of short- to medium-run movements in exchange rates. Neither models of exchange rates based on macroeconomic fundamentals nor the forecasts of market participants as embodied in the forward rate or survey data can explain exchange rate movement better than a naïve alternative such as a random walk model. Worse yet, exchange rate changes are hard to explain after the fact, even with the knowledge of actual fundamental variables. It remains an enigma why the current exchange rate regime has engendered a time series database where macroeconomic variables and exchange rates appear to be independent of one another.

This view was reiterated by Frenkel and Froot (1990) who observed that:

> It is now widely accepted that standard observable macroeconomic variables are not capable of explaining, much less predicting ex ante, the majority of short-term changes in the exchange rate.

But note Frenkel and Froot's reference to the majority of short-term exchange rate changes – they do not say all changes. So what is the evidence? What are the competing hypotheses? And can we do anything at all about predicting movements in foreign exchange rates?

7.1 | Inflation and interest rate differentials

As outlined in Chapter 4, one of the major deductive hypotheses about expected movements in the spot exchange rate is underpinned by the following:

- expected inflation differentials;

- interest rate differentials (and here we should be looking at free-market interest rates such as Eurorates);

- spot and forward rate differentials.

The rationale for the hypothesized relationships was dealt with at length in Chapter 4. The four-way equivalence model developed there is extremely important. It is essential that readers understand the theoretical relationships among inflation differences, interest rate differences, the forward premium/discount and expected spot movements.

However, remember that the existence of non-traded goods logically gives rise to deviations from the purchasing power parity theory of exchange rates. Also systematic deviations from PPP theory are to be expected due to short-term capital flows and current account imbalances.

As we will discuss later in this chapter, the PPP theory of exchange rate movements holds up fairly well in the long term. The fact that short-term deviations abound has stimulated the search for a better model. One such model is the balance of payments approach.

7.2 | The balance of payments approach

There are different balance of payments explanations of exchange rate movements. The emphasis has tended to change through time as the international financial scene has itself undergone change.

In its original form, this explanation tended to ignore capital flows. Prior to the 1960s, this was excusable since most major currencies were not convertible, with the consequence that there were minimal private capital flows. The current account theory can best be explained by approaching it under the two distinct systems of exchange rate regime – namely, fixed and floating.

Assume a fixed exchange rate regime first. The national income model suggests that the current account gets worse as national income rises. The basic tendency is then for the domestic currency to weaken (to pay for the increased imports), and the fixed exchange rate system requires that, should this fall beyond certain narrow limits, this should be countered by support from the domestic government. This might take the form of selling reserves of foreign currency in the foreign exchange markets. Usually this would be accompanied by domestic severity to dampen home demand, evidenced by lower relative money supply growth with consequent lower relative inflation, leading to an improvement in exports and a lowering of imports. According to this formula – which looks fine on paper – the current account deficit is automatically corrected.

So, too, is a surplus. Here, rather than selling foreign exchange reserves, the foreign currency is bought. To pay for this, borrowings are increased – probably by the issue of treasury bills. As treasury bills are a reserve asset, this results in an increase in money supply, which in turn leads, all other things being equal, to higher inflation. Remember we are looking at a fixed parity regime: this means that exports become less competitive and hence the surplus reduces. Again this is an automatic corrective mechanism.

On paper, then, the Bretton Woods system should avoid permanent disequilibria – after all, there are automatically correcting means of achieving current account stability. But empirically, things did not turn out this way as anyone who has examined the evidence of the United Kingdom in the 1950s and 1960s knows.

Of course, devaluation or revaluation was an option designed to counter recurrent disequilibria. Predicting changes in exchange rates in these circumstances became a potentially fruitful area of investigation. An interesting study carried out in the 1970s by Murenbeeld (1975) is worth mentioning. Using discriminant analysis, Murenbeeld studied a series of devaluations and revaluations from the late 1950s to early 1970s and came up with a discriminating equation. His original hypotheses may be summarized in the format shown in Table 7.1.

Having obtained data on a number of currency realignments, the researcher arrives at a Z-score predictor of foreign exchange parity change using respective quarterly and monthly data as follows:

$$Z = -0.487 + 0.732RI + 0.058\Delta R - 0.123\Delta WP - 0.145UNEM - 0.25M + 0.167G$$
$$Z = 0.33 + 0.69RI + 0.17\Delta R - 2.29\Delta WP - 0.45UNEM - 0.66M + 15.35G$$

where the quarterly and monthly independent variables are:

RI = ratio of reserves to imports,
ΔR = % change in reserves,
ΔWP = % change in wholesale price index,
UNEM = change in trend of number becoming unemployed as % of total number unemployed,
M = change in trend of money supply as % of total money supply,
G = change in trend of government budgetary surplus/deficit as % of GNP.

According to Murenbeeld, quarterly Z scores in excess of 2.0 are indicative an upward valuation of the currency concerned and scores below –1.5 are indicative of a devaluation. And for monthly data, discriminating scores are respectively 1.0 and –1.5. Interested readers are referred to the original.[1] In pursuit of an economic and political model which would provide a leading indicator of devaluations, Bilson (1979) examined a monetary model of the exchange rate and an international liquidity variable (measured by the stock of international reserves divided by the

Table 7.1 Murenbeeld's devaluation/revaluation hypotheses

Devaluation		Revaluation
High	Inflation	Low
Up	Trend in unemployment	Down
Low	Ratio of reserves to imports	High
Down	Change in level of reserves	Up

monetary base – that is the money supply, specifically high powered money). He found that his methodology, using these variables, provided a good proxy for the extent of the currency depreciation and a good lead indicator of the timing of the devaluation. When the international liquidity indicator fell substantially relative to its historical norm, the actual exchange rate depreciated thereafter within one to two years. The technique is not guaranteed, but Bilson suggested that these indicators offered exchange rate forecasters useful information and insights. Clearly it is most readily applied to fixed or pegged exchange rate systems.

The economics departments in numerous international banks have similar proprietary models which they use internally and offer to favoured clients.

Having deviated slightly from the mainstream of this chapter, let us now return to it by examining the current account theory of the exchange rate under a floating currency regime.

Again, in terms of illustrating the mechanism, let us begin from an increase in national income and a worsening of the current account balance. If we leave the capital account out of the equation for now, paying for the increased imports results in demand for foreign currency at the expense of the home currency. Buying foreign exchange for domestic currency weakens the local currency, which then makes exports more competitive and (assuming that the Marshall–Lerner[2] conditions on elasticities are met) consequently improves the current account. By a reverse route in the argument, current account surpluses lessen, with a strengthening exchange rate as the corrective mechanism.

So far, of course, our models have been simplistic to the extent that the capital account and the interest rate have been left out of the equation. Extending the argument now to make good this omission, we come up with the essence of the Mundell (1967) and Fleming (1962) models. The overall balance of payments is the current account plus the capital account. Using a simple example to illustrate the workings of the model, let us begin by assuming an increase in national income with an accompanying deterioration in the current account balance. If overall balance of payments equilibrium is to be maintained at zero as national income increases, the domestic rate of interest must also rise – this improves capital flows to compensate for the initial deterioration on the current account. This increase in the interest rate dampens domestic demand, which, in its turn, has the effect of reducing imports and consequently improves the current account. The mechanism of this version of the balance of payments model involves the interest rate increase as a means of avoiding a weakening in the domestic currency. This is in line with conventional wisdom, but does not accord with the monetary approach.

7.3 | The monetary approach

In the world of classical economics, trade deficits were associated directly with money supply changes. In its more modern form, the monetary approach predicts that an excess supply of money domestically will be reflected in an outflow across the foreign exchanges.

Beginning with a growth in national income, under the monetary approach, this will be associated with a growing demand for money for transaction purposes. An excess demand for money can be met in one of two ways: either through domestic credit creation or through a balance of payments surplus. This rationale explains the apparent paradox (remember that the Keynesian model predicts that an increase in national income will be associated with a weakening current account balance) of fast-growing countries such as Germany which have had almost perpetual balance of payments current surpluses. Fast real growth causes a growth in transactions demand for money: the economy induces an inflow of money via the foreign balance to the extent that this money is not created by the central bank.

Assuming that two countries have equal real growth but one increases its money supply more than the other (or there is no money supply growth in either but different real growth rates), rational expectations would suggest that relative interest rates and expected relative inflations would alter. Either through the purchasing power parity theorem or via the mechanism referred to in the previous paragraph, the economy with the high relative money supply growth will have a weakening exchange rate. According to the monetary approach, high nominal interest rates and weakening currencies both flow from high relative money supply growth.

The discussion of the monetary approach so far has been simplistic. It can be made more sophisticated by bringing together purchasing power parity and the quantity theory of money. In this description of exchange rate determination drawing on the above two theories, the usual quantity theory notation is used. That is:

M = money stock,
V = velocity of circulation of money,
P = price of goods,
T = number of transactions per year.

Setting the supply of money equal to its demand, the key quantity theory of money equation suggests that:

$$MV = PT \qquad (7.1)$$

If transactions, T, are a function of real income, Y, then:

$$T = aY$$

and, where k is equal to a/V, it follows that:

$$M = k\,PY \qquad (7.2)$$

Equation (7.2) is, of course, a slight reformulation of the key quantity theory expression set out in equation (7.1). Letting * refer to foreign currency variables, as is the practice in the literature, obviously:

$$M^* = k^* P^* Y^* \tag{7.3}$$

Rearranging terms in the last two equations, clearly:

$$P = \frac{M}{kY} \quad \text{and} \quad P^* = \frac{M^*}{k^* Y^*} \tag{7.4}$$

Purchasing power parity is now brought into the discussion. It will be recalled from Chapter 4 that:

$$\frac{\tilde{p}_\$ - \tilde{p}_\pounds}{1 + \tilde{p}_\pounds} = \frac{\tilde{s}_t - s_0}{s_0} \tag{7.5}$$

As an approximation, we can rewrite equation (7.5) as shown below, where we let a dot over a variable represent a percentage change:

$$\dot{s} = \dot{P} - \dot{P}^* \tag{7.6}$$

Remember that we are always using the New York direct quotation when talking about exchange rates. If, therefore, foreign price levels are inflating at a rate in excess of US prices, the direct New York exchange rate in dollars goes down – in other words, the dollar hardens.

Substituting the expression for P and P^* from equation (7.4) in the last equation, we obtain:

$$\dot{s} = (k^* - k) + (\dot{M} - \dot{M}^*) + (\dot{Y}^* - \dot{Y}) \tag{7.7}$$

Equation (7.7) suggests that the rate of change of the exchange rate is a function of three terms, each of which compares the rate of change of a variable in the home country with the rate of change of the same variable in the foreign country. The first term compares the velocities of money, the second compares the money supplies and the third term compares incomes.

Now we will, for illustrative purposes, change the parameters of the model (while maintaining the relationships in equation (7.4)) and observe how they affect the rate of change of the exchange rate, $\dot{s}$. Thus:

- If $\dot{k}$ rises, this means that the velocity of money is decreasing at home so the rate of inflation is falling. If $\dot{P}^*$ is constant throughout, the home currency should appreciate, or at least not depreciate as fast.

- If $\dot{M}$ rises, the rate of growth of the domestic money supply is increasing, so inflation at home will increase and the currency will depreciate.

- If $\dot{Y}$ rises, the rate of growth of real income has increased, which means, with the rate of growth of the money supply fixed, inflation will decrease and the currency will appreciate.

No one would argue that purchasing power parity holds in the short run – indeed the empirical evidence suggests that purchasing power parity is anything but a short-run phenomenon. It is essentially a long-run tendency. It is not a complete theory of exchange rate determination. The money supply and prices tend to move slowly whereas exchange rates change rapidly – like share price movements. And, again like share prices, movements overshoot the theoretical equilibrium rate. How can we explain this tendency for foreign exchange rates to exaggerate on their path towards equilibrium?

7.4 | Overshooting – the Dornbusch model

A modern version of the Keynesian model – associated with Dornbusch (1976) and endorsed by Driskill (1981), Papell (1985) and Levin (1986) – can be invoked to explain the empirically observed reality of overshooting. Frequently, spot exchange rates seem to move too much given some economic disturbance. And they seem to move contrarily too. For example, country A may have a higher inflation rate than country B, yet the currency of country A may appreciate relative to that of B. Such anomalies may be explained in the context of an overshooting exchange rate model. Our knowledge and experience suggest that financial markets adjust instantaneously to an exogenous shock, whereas goods markets adjust slowly over time. With this background, let us analyse what happens when country A increases its money supply.

For equilibrium to hold in the money market, money demand must equal money supply. If the money supply increases, something must happen to increase money demand. It is assumed that people hold money for transactions purposes and that they also hold bonds that pay an interest rate, i. This assumption allows us to write a money demand equation of the form:

$$M_\mathrm{d} = aY + bi \qquad (7.8)$$

where M_d is the real stock of money demanded – the nominal stock of money divided by the price level – Y is income and i is the interest rate. Money demand is found positively to relate to income: in other words, the coefficient, a, exceeds zero. As Y increases, people tend to demand more of everything, including money. Since the interest rate is the opportunity cost of holding money, there is an inverse relation between money demand and i: in other words, b in equation (7.8) is negative. It is generally found that in the short run, following an increase in the money supply, both income and the price level are relatively constant. As a result, interest rates must drop to equate money demand to money supply. We now consider the effect given a second country.

The interest rate parity relation for countries A and B may be written as:

$$\frac{i_\mathrm{A} - i_\mathrm{B}}{1 + i_\mathrm{B}} = \frac{f - s}{s} \qquad (7.9)$$

Here we use the same notation as in Chapter 4 and quotations for f and s, the forward and spot exchange rates, are in terms of the direct quote in country A. Now, if i_A falls, given the foreign interest rate i_B, then it follows that $(f - s)/s$ – that is, the forward premium/discount – must fall too. When the money supply in country A increases, we would expect that eventually prices in A will rise because we have more

A currency chasing the limited quantity of goods available for purchase. This higher future price level in country A will imply that its currency should weaken to achieve purchasing power parity. This long-run change in the exchange rate, Δs, if it is to be consistent with purchasing power parity, will be given by the approximation:

$$\Delta s = p_A - p_B \tag{7.10}$$

Since p_A is expected to rise over time, given p_B, s will tend to weaken. This weaker expected future spot rate will be reflected in a weaker forward rate now. But if f, the forward rate for country A, weakens while, at the same time, $f - s$ falls to maintain interest rate parity, the current value of s will have to weaken more than f. Subsequently, once prices start rising, real money balances should fall so that the domestic interest rate rises. Over time, as the interest rate increases, s will alter to maintain equilibrium. Therefore, the initial fall in the spot rate of country A will be in excess of the long-run spot rate for country A. In other words, s will overshoot its long-run value.

To summarize the discussion, Figure 7.1 (overleaf) shows the passage of price levels, interest rates and the exchange rate for currency A over time. The initial equilibrium position at time t_0, is given by variables with subscripts 0. When the money supply increases at time t_0, the domestic interest rate falls and the exchange rate weakens, while the price level remains fixed. The eventual long-run equilibrium price p_{LR} and exchange rate s_{LR} will move in proportion to the increase in the money supply. Although the forward rate should move immediately to its new equilibrium f_1, the spot rate will weaken below the eventual equilibrium s_{LR} owing to the need to maintain interest parity – remember that i_A has fallen in the short run. Over time, as prices start to rise, the interest rate increases and the exchange rate converges to the new equilibrium level s_{LR}.

7.5 | The portfolio balance theory

An extension of the monetary model is the portfolio balance theory. In the monetary model, exchange rates are determined by the relative supply and demand for money at home. The portfolio balance model uses this idea but introduces foreign money and foreign bonds as potential substitutes for bonds and money at home. If foreign and domestic bonds are perfect substitutes and assuming that conditions of interest arbitrage hold, the portfolio balance model reduces to the monetary model and exchange rates are determined solely by activities in the money markets. In the portfolio balance theory, they are not perfect substitutes in the short term. Thus, exchange rates are determined in part by the relative demand and supply of money and in part by the relative demand and supply of other assets.

In the monetary approach, the determinants of exchange rates are specified by the long-run steady-state situation. In the portfolio balance model, agents may hold international portfolios of assets denominated in different currencies. This makes the demand for money a more complex function than in the monetary model and an additional determinant of exchange rates is the presence of imperfect substitution

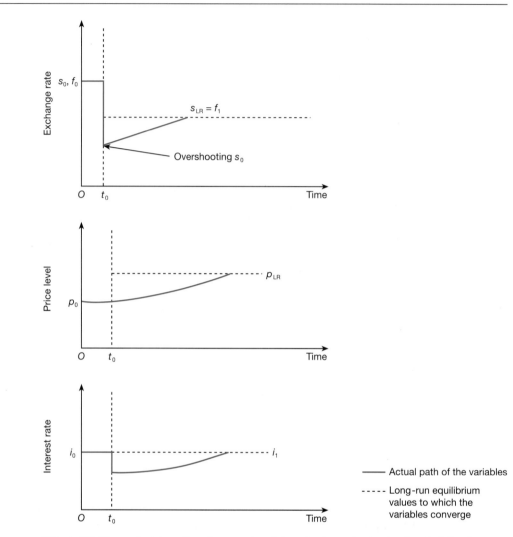

Figure 7.1 Forward and spot exchange rates, interest rate and price level path following increase in domestic money supply.

between assets. Also, in the portfolio balance approach there is a wealth effect – changes in exchange rates impact upon the wealth of holders of assets denominated in foreign currency.

The key assumptions of the portfolio balance model are as follows:

■ Members of the public use their domestic wealth, W, to hold a combination of the following assets – domestic money, M, foreign money, M_F, domestic bonds, B, and foreign bonds, B_F. Residents of the home country can hold assets denominated in foreign currencies, while overseas residents can hold assets denominated in home currency. The exchange rate equation, in these circumstances, can be written as:

$$s = f(M, M_F, B, B_F)$$

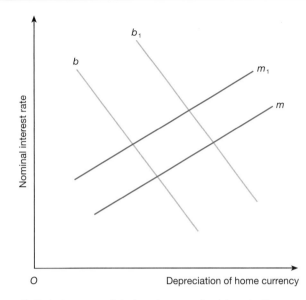

Figure 7.2 The portfolio balance model of exchange rate determination.

- The domestic economy is a price taker in all markets including the international financial markets.

- Foreign interest rates are assumed to be kept constant by the foreign monetary authorities.

- Expectations about forward rates and inflation are assumed to be formed in accordance with rational expectations.

The portfolio balance theory has implications, as shown in Figure 7.2, for interest rates and currency depreciation. In the figure, the vertical axis shows the nominal interest rate, i, and the horizontal axis denotes home exchange rate depreciation.

Curve b in Figure 7.2 shows the combinations of interest rates and exchange rates for which the bond market is in equilibrium. Its negative slope is obtained via the following reasoning. If interest rates at home rise, investors will wish to hold more domestic bonds in their portfolios. If the supply of such bonds is fixed, then an excess demand for domestic bonds emerges and the only way to eliminate this excess demand is by a fall in the domestic currency value of foreign bonds. So the home currency appreciates in value, reducing the real wealth of the portfolio holders, since their foreign bond holdings are now worth less. Through this income effect, so the argument goes, the excess demand for domestic bonds is eliminated. Therefore, with a fixed supply of domestic bonds, equilibrium is maintained by the relation between the exchange rate and the domestic interest rate or via the relationship between the value of the home currency and the interest rate.

Curve m in Figure 7.2 indicates the combination of interest rate and exchange rate for which the domestic money market is in equilibrium. It has a positive slope indicating that as interest rates rise the exchange rate depreciates in order to maintain money market equilibrium assuming, of course, that the money supply is held constant. An increase in interest rates reduces the demand for money, but with a constant money supply, the only way to eliminate the implied excess supply of money is to make people feel wealthier through the income effect which raises the demand for money. This is achieved through depreciation of the home currency which increases the domestic currency value of foreign bonds.

Figure 7.2 shows the effects of an increase in the supply of domestic bonds. The b curve moves to b_1, as domestic residents require higher interest rates if they are to be persuaded to hold more domestic bonds, less money, and fewer foreign bonds. The m curve shifts to the left to m_1. This is because the stock of bonds is increased and, assuming that the government is engaging in open market operations, the money supply falls.

The combined effect of these movements is to raise the interest rate in the home country. The effect on the exchange rate is ambiguous and depends on which curve shifts by more and on the relative gradients of the curves. In Figure 7.2, curve b shifts by more, resulting in a depreciation of the home currency. In this case, domestic bonds and money are closer substitutes than domestic and foreign bonds, and hence the drop in the demand for foreign assets is less than the drop in the demand for money. If the m curve had shifted by more, the domestic currency would have appreciated. In such a case domestic and foreign bonds are closer substitutes than domestic bonds and money. Hence the decline in the demand for foreign bonds is greater than the decline in the demand for money.

Referring to Figure 7.2, an increase in the overall money supply causes the m curve to shift to the right. Individuals find that they are holding an excess of money balances and the resulting readjustment in their portfolios is reflected in an excess demand for foreign and domestic bonds. Thus the domestic rate of interest declines – the price of bonds rises – resulting in a depreciation of the home currency. An increase in the volume of foreign bonds held by home investors is generated by a current account surplus in the home country and this raises wealth at any given exchange rate. With domestic money and bond supplies fixed, wealth must be reduced towards the original level to restore equilibrium. This is achieved by an appreciation of the domestic currency.

7.6 ┃ The role of news

Before we round off this section on theories of exchange rate determination, we must consider the role of news, which has received substantial focus in the literature. Our coverage of exchange rate theories, so far, might lead the reader to conclude that experts should be adept at forecasting future spot exchange rates. In reality, the prediction of future currency paths is very difficult. Research has shown that the theories we have covered are relevant in explaining systematic patterns of exchange rate behaviour. But the value of these theories for predicting exchange rates is limited, first by the fact that some of our theories actually conflict, and secondly by the propensity for the unexpected to occur. The real world is characterized by unpredictable shocks and surprises. When an unexpected event takes place, it is often referred to as news. Interest rates, prices and incomes are often affected by news, and the same is true of exchange rates. Exchange rate changes linked to news will, by definition, be unexpected. Errors in predicting future spot rates are often excused by our inability to forecast sudden shocks. Periods dominated by unexpected announcements of economic policy changes will result in great fluctuations in spot and forward exchange rates as expectations are revised resultant upon these unexpected pieces of news.

An interesting study by Almeida, Goodhart and Payne (1998) examined the response of the DEM/US$ rate to macroeconomic news at five-minute intervals. Another study, by Bosner-Neal, Roley and Sellon (1998), looked at the response of the US$ exchange rate to changes in the interest rate of the US Federal funds target. Both studies found a significant relationship between these news events and unanticipated exchange rate movements.

News also has implications for purchasing power parity. Because exchange rates are financial asset prices that respond quickly to new information, news on prices will have an immediate impact on exchange rates. But exchange rates change much more rapidly than do goods prices, which make up typical price indices. Consequently, during periods dominated by news, we observe exchange rates varying a great deal relative to prices so that large deviations from purchasing power parity are realized. Periods, such as the 1970s, the 1980s and the early 1990s, where many unexpected economic events occurred – oil price rises, international debt problems and so on – are periods of large unexpected exchange rate changes with substantial deviations from purchasing power parity. Volatile exchange rates reflect turbulent times. While world political events remain unpredictable, so exchange rates will remain volatile.

Given the discussion so far in this chapter, it is clear that different economic models may predict different directions of movement in exchange rates consequent, for example, upon a change in interest rates. Invariably, when the student is confronted with a plethora of different explanations for a phenomenon, it is a fair conclusion that we are not sure of what causes what. This is very true of exchange rates in the short run – as we will learn later in this chapter. Indeed it becomes clear then that empirical tests indicate that we would not be well advised to risk large amounts of money on the forecasts produced by econometric models. So what about relying on charts? There seem to be plenty of forecasters of exchange rates who produce charts. And how do charts work anyway?

7.7 | Chartism

Applied to share price movements, commodity price movements and currencies, this technique involves the study of past price movements to seek out potential future trends. Implicit in this possibility is the assumption that past price patterns provide a guide to future movements.

Just in case readers are not familiar with what chartism – sometimes called 'technical analysis' – does, this section attempts to give a very brief description. If readers

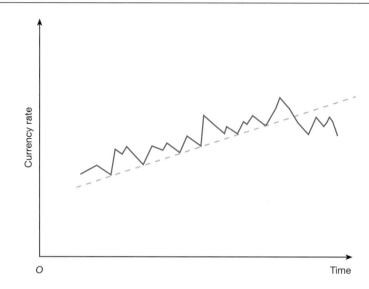

Figure 7.3 Breach of a rising trend.

want a more detailed review, especially of the point and figure approach which is most frequently used, they are referred to other specialist works on chart techniques such as Beckman (1969) and a host of others. Chartists attempt to predict share price movements by assuming that past price patterns will be repeated. There is no real theoretical justification for this. Chartists do not attempt to predict every price change. They are deeply interested in trends and trend reversals – that is, when the price of a share or commodity has been rising for several months but suddenly starts to fall. Features of chartism that are considered important for predicting trend reversals include the following:

- the observance of resistance levels;
- head-and-shoulders patterns;
- double-bottom or double-top patterns.

But there is a great deal more too. All that can be done in a general section of this sort is to give a flavour. So the main features referred to can best be illustrated by examples.

Consider Figure 7.3. In this, the broken line represents the lower resistance level on a rising trend. It will be noted that many of the troughs lie on this line, but only at the end is it breached. The chartist would tend to view this breach as an indication that the trend had been reversed.

In Figure 7.4 the basic trend has been flat with oscillations within a channel. There are upper and lower resistance levels which bound this channel and, according to chartists, the breach of either of these will indicate a new trend. This sort of pattern arises from market indecision, as does the triangular pattern in Figure 7.5. In this figure the breach of the resistance lines is said to indicate a change of trend.

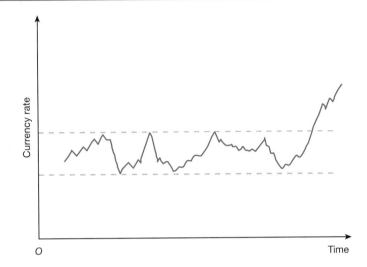

Figure 7.4 Movement out of a channel.

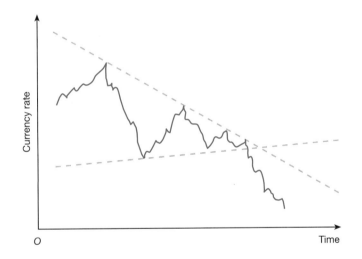

Figure 7.5 Breach of a triangular pattern.

Let us now look at a resistance level on a double top. Suppose that the price of a share has been rising steadily for some time. Recently the price fell as some investors sold to realize profits and it then rose to its maximum level for a second time before starting to fall again. This is known as a double top and, based on experience, the chartist would predict that the trend has reversed. A typical double top might appear as shown in Figure 7.6 (overleaf). Double bottoms are interpreted in a similar – but reverse – way.

Another indication of a trend reversal is the head-and-shoulders formation of the type shown in Figure 7.7 (overleaf). In this kind of situation the chart might be interpreted as follows. The price has been rising for some time. At the peak of the left shoulder, profit taking has caused the price to drop. The price has then risen steeply

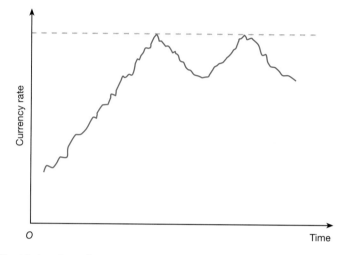

Figure 7.6 Double-top formation.

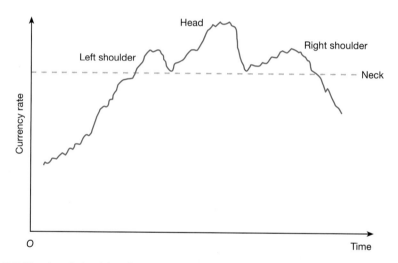

Figure 7.7 Head-and-shoulders formation.

again to the head before more profit taking causes the price to drop to around the same level as before – the neck. Although the price rises again, the gains are not as great as at the head. The level of the right shoulder together with the frequent dips down to the neck suggest to the chartist that the upward trend previously observed is over and that a fall is imminent. The breach of the neckline is the indication to sell. An inverse head and shoulders is interpreted using a reverse, but similar, argument.

In preparing charts of movements, the technical analyst usually employs one of two types of chart. These are the line and bar chart and the point and figure chart. We consider the line and bar chart first.

In this kind of chart, each day's trading is represented by one vertical line with a horizontal bar. The length and position of the vertical line represents the day's trading range in a particular market, and the horizontal bar represents the closing price

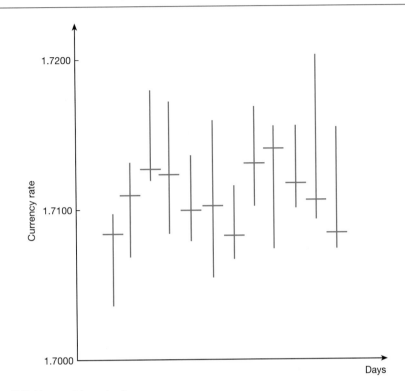

Figure 7.8 Line and bar chart.

in that market. There will thus be a different chart plotted in each time zone of a globally trading foreign exchange market. Consecutive days' lines and bars are plotted consecutively on a time axis as shown in Figure 7.8.

The point and figure chart is different. It is composed of a matrix of boxes in rows and columns. The vertical axis represents the exchange rate, as in the line and bar chart. Each box represents a particular exchange rate movement, say 10 points. Unlike the line and bar chart, a new column is not started each new day, but only when the exchange rate changes direction.

The point and figure chart is therefore composed of a series of columns representing rising and falling sequences of exchange rate movements. Sequences of a rising exchange rate are usually represented by columns of Xs; sequences of falling rates by columns of 0s. As the exchange rate rises, the chartist will add new Xs to the top of the existing column of Xs. Once the rate begins to fall, the chart analyst will abandon the column of Xs and begin a new column of 0s to represent the falling sequence. This new column will be started diagonally down from the last X. A point and figure chart might look like that in Figure 7.9 (overleaf).

The technical analyst has other techniques. Besides charts, oscillators, moving averages and momentum analysis can be used to forecast exchange rates. How do these methods work?

An oscillator is usually taken to mean the difference between the latest closing exchange rate and the closing exchange rate a specified number of days earlier. So,

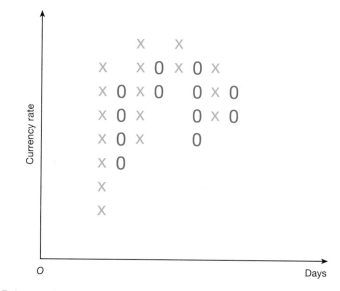

Figure 7.9 Point and figure chart.

a three-day oscillator may be constructed by plotting the difference between the latest closing rate and the closing rate three days earlier. When plotted, oscillators frequently exhibit familiar chart patterns – like those already referred to – and the identification of these patterns can assist the technical analyst in detecting trend reversals.

A moving average is usually taken to mean the average of the closing exchange rates over a specified number of previous days. A ten-day moving average can be constructed by plotting for each day the average of the ten previous closing exchange rates. Moving averages are often plotted against the current spot exchange rate. A moving average tends to lag behind the current spot rate, so the two rates will not cross while a trend remains intact. However, once a trend begins to reverse, the two rates will tend to cross. This indicates a buy or sell signal to the technical analyst, depending upon the direction of cross-over.

Momentum refers to the underlying strength of a particular trend and may be calculated in a number of different ways. One simple way of measuring momentum is to track the difference between two different moving averages. For example, this may involve the difference between the five-day and the ten-day moving averages. While a trend remains intact, both moving averages will lag behind the current spot rate, the ten-day more than the five-day, but the difference between the two will remain relatively constant. When the trend shows signs of tiring, the five-day average will react more quickly than the ten-day. Consequently, the difference between the two moving averages will change, indicating a fall in momentum to the technical analyst. Such falls in momentum provide the technical analyst with the wherewithal to make a buy or sell recommendation.

Modern financial theory based upon efficient markets has little time for chartist techniques in deep markets. But there is some evidence (see later in this chapter) that in foreign exchange markets, at least in the short term, chartism pays greater dividends than does reliance upon econometric models for forecasting exchange rates. Perhaps it is worth reminding readers of the essence of the efficient markets hypothesis.

7.8 | The efficient markets hypothesis

An initial, and very important, premise of an efficient market is that there are a large number of profit-maximizing participants concerned with the analysis and valuation of securities and they are all operating independently of one another. A second assumption is that new information regarding securities comes to the market in a random fashion. The third assumption of an efficient market is especially crucial. Investors adjust security prices rapidly to reflect new information. While the price adjustments made are not always perfect, they are unbiased – sometimes there is an overadjustment; sometimes there is an underadjustment. But one does not know which it will be. Adjustment of security prices takes place rapidly because the market is dominated by profit-maximizing investors. The combined effect of new information being obtained by market participants in a random, independent fashion plus the presence of numerous investors who adjust stock prices rapidly to reflect this new information means, according to efficient market theorists, that price changes are likely to be independent and random. According to chartism, of course, price changes are not independent – they are to some extent a function of past price movements. It is evident why efficient market proponents utterly reject the claims of chartists.

Also, in our brief overview of efficient markets, it should be mentioned that, because security prices adjust to all new information and, therefore, supposedly reflect all public information at any point in time, the security prices that prevail at any point in time should be an unbiased reflection of all currently available information.

Based on this brief description, an efficient market is evidently one in which security prices adjust rapidly to the infusion of new information, and current stock prices fully reflect all available information, including the risk involved. Therefore, the returns implicit in a security's price reflect merely the risk involved, so the expected return on a security is consistent with risk – nothing more. There are three gradations of efficient market: the weak form, the semi-strong form and the strong form.

The weak form of the efficient market hypothesis assumes that current stock prices fully reflect all stock market information, including the historical sequence of prices, price changes and any volume information. Because current prices already reflect all past price changes and any other stock market information, this implies that there should be no relationship between past price changes and future price changes. That is, price changes are independent. In other words, past market data cannot be of any use in predicting future prices.

The semi-strong efficient markets hypothesis asserts that security prices adjust rapidly to the release of all new public information. In short, stock prices fully reflect all publicly available data. Obviously the semi-strong hypothesis encompasses the weak form hypothesis because all public information includes all market information such as past stock prices, trends and so on, plus all non-market information such as earnings, stock splits, economic news and political news. A direct implication of this hypothesis is that investors acting on important new information after it is public cannot derive above-average profits from the transaction, allowing for the cost of trading, because the security price already reflects this new public information.

The strong form of the efficient markets hypothesis contends that stock prices fully reflect all information whether public or otherwise. Hence, it implies that no group of investors has a monopolistic access to information relevant to the formation of prices. Therefore, no group of investors should be able to derive above-average profits consistently. The strong form hypothesis encompasses both the weak and the semi-strong forms. Further, the strong form hypothesis requires not only efficient markets, where prices adjust rapidly to the release of new public information, but also perfect markets in which all information is available to everyone at the same time. This form of the efficient markets hypothesis contends that, because all information is immediately available to everyone and is rapidly discounted by everyone, no group has monopolistic access to important new information and, therefore, no individual trader can consistently derive anything more than the average profit for all traders. Of course, the scandals of insider trading reported at the end of the 1980s and 1990s are evidence that information is not automatically evenly distributed between all players. The extent to which the stock market exhibits market efficiency is considered in various texts, such as Keane (1983). The reality of stock market efficiency is seriously challenged by Shiller (1989), Fama and French (1992), Lakonishok, Shleifer and Vishny (1994), Haugen (1999, 2002), Shefrin (2000), Shleifer (2000) and Montier (2002). However, our concern here is with foreign exchange markets.

It will be recalled that at the beginning of the discussion of the efficient markets hypothesis the basic premise of an efficient market was that there were a large number of profit-maximizing participants. So there are in the foreign exchange markets. But there are also very large non-profit-maximizers – central banks. Their intervention is designed not to make profits but to ease currency price movements in order to achieve a multiplicity of political objectives. The question is: does this intervention stop currency markets from exhibiting market efficiency? This is entirely an empirical question and it is looked at later in this chapter. We now turn to evidence as it relates to purchasing power parity.

7.9 | Empiricism and purchasing power parity

Purchasing power parity (PPP), in its absolute form, maintains that, in competitive markets free of transportation costs and official barriers to trade, such as tariffs, identical goods sold in different countries must sell for the same price where their prices are expressed in terms of the same currency – this is the law of one price. A study by Isard (1977) compared the movements of dollar prices of West German goods relative to their US equivalents for specific tradable goods. His results showed persistent violation of the law of one price. He concluded that 'the law of one price is flagrantly and systematically violated by empirical data'; he went on to say that 'these relative price effects seem to persist for at least several years and cannot be shrugged off as transitory'. Isard's judgement is echoed by McKinnon (1979) who observed that: 'substantial and continually changing deviations from PPP are commonplace. For individual tradable commodities, violations of the law of one price can be striking.' Despite this conclusion, McKinnon is defensive lest he throws out the baby with the bathwater. He observes that 'until a more robust theory replaces it, I shall assume that purchasing power parity among tradable goods tends to hold in the long run in the absence of overt impediments to trade among countries with convertible currencies'.

Purchasing power parity, in its relative forms, maintains that changes in relative prices of a basket of similar goods among countries determine changes in exchange rates. This form of theory reflects that postulated by Cassal (1921), namely that the exchange rate between two currencies in the medium term simply reflects the ratio of prices of a representative basket of goods, both domestic and foreign, in two countries.

The history of empirical work on purchasing power parity has followed a pattern. Prior to the 1980s, there were many and various tests of Cassal's medium-term model. Generally, these found that purchasing power parity held as a long-run phenomenon. Indeed, dynamic exchange rate models, as developed, for example, by Dornbusch (1976) and Mussa (1982), began to rely on purchasing power parity as a long-term condition for equilibrium of foreign exchange rates. In the 1980s, much research challenged this view. The orientation of tests moved towards whether the real effective exchange rate follows a random walk. The findings of these studies are by no means unanimous.

Reverting to Cassal's medium-term model, the consensus of a large number of studies confirms his view – for example, Yeager (1958), Balassa (1964), Treuherz (1969), Aliber (1975a, b) and Aliber and Stickney (1975). Some of these are worth mentioning in more detail.

Treuherz (1969) investigated the relationship between annual inflation rates and devaluation percentages against the US dollar for five South American countries – Argentina, Brazil, Chile, Colombia and Peru – for the fourteen-year period from 1954 to 1967. While Treuherz's results showed that the relationship between the two variables was weak for any individual year on its own, he found an almost perfect relationship between changes in internal purchasing power and the external value of the currency when using averages beyond four years.

Aliber and Stickney (1975) tracked inflation rates, as measured by consumer price indices, and exchange rates for forty-eight countries over the period 1960 to 1971. Like Treuherz, their results are that for individual years there may be substantial deviations from PPP but, as a long-run phenomenon, PPP holds up well. Their investigation shows deviations from PPP to be far greater for developing countries compared to industrialized countries. The authors note that the use of different measures of inflation, such as wholesale price indices, GDP deflators and so on, would have little effect on their findings.

Gailliot (1970) carried out a long-run test of PPP in its relative form using data covering 1900 to 1967 for the United States, Canada, the United Kingdom, France, West Germany, Italy, Japan and Switzerland. His results support PPP as a long-run relationship – even though his study covered a vast number of shocks to the economies of countries examined.

One of those shocks was the German hyperinflation of the early 1920s. This period provided the database for an investigation of the US dollar/mark relationship for 1920 to 1923. Frenkel (1977) found that actual and expected changes in price levels over this period accounted for in excess of 99 per cent of the exchange rate movement. In a not dissimilar empirical exercise based upon the hyperinflation of Germany and Poland during the 1920s, Huang (1984) found that PPP held as expected.

Generally speaking, international finance specialists in the mid-1970s took the view that, empirically, the key determinant of long-run exchange rate movement was relative purchasing power. Indeed, Hodgson and Phelps (1975) concluded that, based upon a statistical model involving exchange rate movements and prior inflation differentials, it takes some eighteen months for PPP corrections to flow through. Folks and Stansell (1975) came to the conclusion that rates moved very rapidly towards PPP equilibrium. Their study, based upon data drawn from the highly inflationary, flexible exchange rate period from 1920 to 1924, concluded that there was only a minimal lag between inflation differentials and exchange rate movements. The authors of this research believe that their finding is consistent with the efficient market view that because relative inflation rates are publicly available data, they should immediately be incorporated into exchange rates. Undoubtedly, however, the experience of the massive inflation in the 1920s was exceptional, and we should be wary about applying these conclusions today. Drawing on more recent evidence for European countries, Thygesen (1977) found that it took five to six years for inflation differentials for the United Kingdom and Italy to come through in terms of restoration of PPP equilibrium. Thygesen observed that three-quarters of this movement was achieved within two years.

From the late 1970s and onwards, an empirically based argument has raged. Does PPP hold, even in the long run? Using various indices to account for inflation differentials, Kravis and Lipsey (1978) found that PPP held more closely for traded goods than for non-traded items, but departures from PPP were substantial, even over long periods and even for traded goods. Similarly, Krugman (1978) found against PPP. In tests of the floating periods of the inter-war years and the 1970s, he concludes that 'there is . . . evidence that there is more to exchange rates than PPP. This evidence is that the deviations from PPP are larger, fairly persistent, and seem to be larger in countries with unstable monetary policies.'

This lack of support for PPP is reinforced by Edison (1985). Using monthly changes in the US dollar/sterling exchange rate over the period from 1973 to 1979, she tested how well three models fared in terms of predicting rates. First, a monetary model was used; then the Dornbusch overshooting model was used; and finally a combined monetary/portfolio balance model was tested. Edison concluded that exchange rate behaviour over the period concerned was inconsistent with PPP. Beginning from 1973, de Grauwe (1988) also found against PPP. Plotting real exchange rates for the US dollar against both the German mark and the Japanese yen for the period 1972 to 1986, real exchange rates were found not to hold and fluctuations were substantial.

Not all recent studies reject PPP. Using average quarterly data for the US dollar/Swiss franc exchange rate from 1973 to 1977, Driskill (1981) found evidence of overshooting in the face of monetary shocks. Such monetary disturbances during a particular quarter caused an overshoot to the extent of a factor of 2. Furthermore, any subsequent tendencies towards correction were found to be irregular. Defining long run as a period of two to three years, Driskill found some evidence to support PPP holding over this time span. However, this study covered a very narrow range of exchange rates. This finding is, to some extent, supported by Everett, George and Blumberg (1980), who have achieved more than a random degree of success in forecasting long-run exchange rate movements based on restoration of PPP. Rush and Husted (1985) have also found long-run support for PPP in Japan, Canada and various European countries. And Manzur (1990), looking at a wide spectrum of exchange rates, investigated currency movements with inflation – due allowance being given in respect of trade weighting. He found that PPP cannot be rejected over the long term but is convincingly found not to hold in the short run. Manzur's evidence suggests that PPP, based on a weighted basket of currencies, tends to reassert itself over a period of about five years.

A new development in testing long-run economic relationships has emerged over the recent past. This is the co-integration technique. Its development and application for the analysis of time series have been associated with Granger (1986) and Engle and Granger (1987). Many economic time series have a long-term change in the mean level – they may show a trend up or down over time in a non-stationary fashion – but groups of variables may be inclined to drift together. If this is the case and there is an inclination for some linear relationship to hold between a group of variables over a long period of time, then co-integration analysis will help to determine this relationship.

Many economic theories are concerned with equilibrium relationships, but the equilibrium relationship may not hold at all times. The distinction is made between the short run and the long run, with deviations from equilibrium in the short run but, in general, the equilibrium relationship holding in the long run. The co-integration techniques applied to time series analysis may provide a formal framework for testing equilibrium relationships of this kind. Co-integration analysis can be used to test the validity of an economic theory, if the theory involves groups of variables that trend up and down over time in a non-stationary fashion.

The PPP relationship is a classic example of an economic theory under which certain variables should not tend to diverge from one another without limit. There have been various recent tests using the co-integration methodology. Taylor (1988) tested nominal exchange rates and relative manufacturing prices for five major countries – the United Kingdom, West Germany, France, Canada and Japan. The PPP hypothesis was tested over the floating exchange rate period since the demise of the Bretton Woods system. The results found little evidence of PPP holding. Taylor was unable to reject the hypothesis that the nominal exchange rates and prices for the different countries tended to drift apart without bound. But Taylor and McMahon (1988), using co-integration techniques, found that, in general, long-run PPP held among the US dollar, the UK pound, the German mark and the French franc during the 1920s. The single exception to this was the dollar/sterling relationship. In an even more rigorous examination, Taylor (1992) looked further at the long-run PPP relationship for the dollar/sterling exchange rate during the 1920s. This time, a stable equilibrium relationship for the exchange rate was found. Taylor argued that the tests used earlier lacked power and the wrong conclusion had been drawn in the earlier analysis.

McNown and Wallace (1990) examined PPP data to determine whether exchange rate adjusted price levels between the United States, Japan, the United Kingdom and Canada formed a co-integrated system. During the fixed rate sub-period, the Japanese and possibly the Canadian wholesale price indices were found to form co-integrated systems with the United States. With the possible exception of Canada, co-integration was rejected for the recent period of flexible exchange rates. In the period from 1957 to 1986, evidence of co-integration was only found for the United States and Japan. No evidence of co-integration was found for any period for Great Britain. Johnson (1990) explored the PPP relationship between Canada and the United States using co-integration techniques. He found strongly in favour of a PPP relationship, particularly over the period 1950–1986; this is in keeping with the findings of McNown and Wallace.

Phylaktis (1992) used co-integration techniques to test the PPP hypothesis between Greece, the United States, France and the United Kingdom for a short period in the 1920s. The evidence supports PPP for the Greek drachma and the US dollar, as well as for the French franc and the UK pound.

Using data for Australia, New Zealand and the United Kingdom, Richards (1993) used co-integration techniques to determine whether a PPP equilibrium was apparent. The tests were carried out over the period from 1948 to 1992. She found some support for long-run PPP having held between New Zealand and the United Kingdom but generally rejected the PPP relationship for the three countries tested.

Another area of interest in recent investigations of PPP has been concerned with testing whether or not the real exchange rate follows a random walk. Important investigations by Roll (1979), by Pigott and Sweeney (1985), by Adler and Lehmann (1983) and by Hakkio (1986) have not been able to reject the hypothesis that real exchange rates do follow a random walk. If this is so, Abuaf and Jorion (1990) conclude that 'the random walk . . . has the disturbing implication that shocks to the real exchange rate are never reversed, which clearly implies that there is no tendency for PPP to hold in the long run'. By contrast, if PPP were to hold, we would experience a mean-reverting process. At least one of the above researchers, Hakkio (1986), is sufficiently doubtful to state that 'though the hypothesis that the exchange rate follows a random walk cannot be rejected, not much weight should be put on this conclusion'. Both Pippinger (1986) and Levi (1996) refer to a number of weaknesses in the statistical tests used in evaluating PPP.

Not all random walk tests have come out against PPP. Work undertaken by Cumby and Obstfeld (1984) and Cumby and Huizinga (1988) on expected exchange rate changes and relative inflation rates found that real exchange rate changes were somewhat predictable. Investigating the behaviour of long-run real exchange rates, Huizinga (1987) found a tendency – albeit statistically insignificant – towards reversion to the mean. Abuaf and Jorion (1990), studying exchange rate data for six European Union countries plus Canada, Japan, Norway and Switzerland for the period from 1973 to 1987, and applying more sophisticated statistical techniques than heretofore, concluded that 'the empirical results . . . cast doubt on the hypothesis that the real exchange rate follows a random walk'. They found clear evidence of a tendency for real exchange rates to revert to their central value. Interestingly, they also conclude that 'a 50 per cent over-appreciation of a currency with respect to PPP would take between 3 and 5 years to be cut in half. Similarly, analyzing annual data over the period 1900–1972 reveals that a period of 3 years is needed for such a reversal.'

If there were a tendency for the real exchange rate to return to its initial value, then it may reasonably be argued that PPP holds in the long run. The tendency for a time series to revert to its mean – mean reversion – is characteristic of a stationary time series. A random walk is an example of a non-stationary time series because it hold no tendency to return to its starting, or any other, value. Meese and Rogoff (1988) and Mark (1990) have been unable to reject the possibility that the real exchange rates evolve as a random walk without any mean reverting properties.

Mark (1995) also provides strong evidence that the long-run path of the exchange rate can be accurately gauged from knowledge of the current level of the rate relative to its equilibrium value in a monetary model. The adjustment path corresponds broadly to the overshooting path described in Figure 7.1. In fact, Mark's results confirm this hypothesis. Mark found that his model explains between 50 and 75 per cent of the variation in the US dollar's exchange rate against the mark, the Swiss franc and the yen over three and four year horizons. But Obstfeld (1995), studying exchange rate changes and inflation over a 20 year period (1973–1993) in the modern floating currency era, has concluded that the long-run variation in exchange rate changes across countries is largely dependent on differences in rates of inflation.

The most complex problem in testing the empirical validity of PPP is that the real exchange rate itself need not be constant. Real variables, such as real income and real interest rates, may change permanently if there is a permanent real disturbance. The real exchange rate might also change on a permanent basis if a real shock affected one country but not its trading partners. That the long-run path of real exchange rates is constant is a convenient assumption. It might plausibly be based on the assumption that while real shocks occur, they affect all countries more or less equally, leaving long-run real exchange rates unchanged. However, for nations that experience country-specific real shocks, such as the discovery of significant new oil resources or the abandonment of distorting market practices, a change in the long-run real exchange rate remains a possibility – see Edison (1987). But evidence of the long run mean reverting behaviour of the real exchange rate is extensive. And this is consistent with PPP working well in the longer term.

So, it seems that PPP offers a reasonably good guide to long run exchange rate movements. Plotting real exchange rates of sixteen leading currencies against the US dollar, over the last one hundred years, Dimson, Marsh and Staunton (2002) show remarkable stability. The substantial deviations that they do note are in respect of the German mark in its colossal inflation period in the early 1920s and also for the same currency following the second World War. The latter period was one in which the inflation calculations were dubious and subject to extensive government manipulation.

In a review of the literature, Rogoff (1996) suggested that, for a broad sample of countries, the half-life of deviations from PPP are around three to five years, implying that deviations from PPP dampen out at a rate of about 15 per cent per year. More recently, Taylor and Peel (2000) have suggested that the speed of return to PPP increases when the deviation is larger. These findings on the tempo of mean reversion are valuable in forecasting exchange rate returns to an equilibrium path.

7.10 | Empiricism and the Fisher effect

It will be recalled that the Fisher effect attributes differences in nominal interest rate in different countries to different inflation expectations for those countries. Fama (1975) found positive evidence of this relationship from 1953 to 1971 in the United States, as did Moazzami (1990), using US evidence from 1953 to 1985. Other notable findings in favour of the Fisher effect come from Gibson (1970, 1972) and Fama and Schwert (1977), all using data derived from the United States.

But the majority of work on the Fisher effect does not point in this direction. Empirical studies of leading industrial economies which reject the Fisher hypothesis have been carried out by Mishkin (1984), Friedman and Schwartz (1982), von Furstenberg (1983), Geske and Roll (1983), Cumby and Obstfeld (1984) and Cumby and Mishkin (1984). Interestingly, the first of this batch of studies, the Mishkin work, found that, based upon quarterly data for the United States, Canada, the United Kingdom, France, Germany, Netherlands and Switzerland from 1967 to 1979, there was a negative correlation between real interest rates and expected inflation over the period concerned. Viren (1989) tested Fisher for eleven countries with data drawn from 1875 to 1984, and the results show a relatively poor relationship between nominal interest rates and inflation. It should be borne in mind, however, that most tests of the Fisher effect have been carried out in conjunction with tests of the associated international Fisher effect which suggests that differences in interest rates between countries are related to expected changes in the spot exchange rate.

7.11 | Empiricism and the international Fisher effect

Aliber and Stickney's (1975) study, referred to above in relation to investigating whether PPP holds, also sought to establish whether the international Fisher effect held. Their results on international Fisher are similar to their findings on PPP. For this part of their investigation they restricted their analysis to the period 1966 to 1971 for seven industrialized countries (Belgium, Canada, France, West Germany, Netherlands, Switzerland and the United Kingdom) and six Latin American countries (Argentina, Brazil, Chile, Colombia, Mexico and Venezuela). They concluded that the average annual deviations seem to suggest a zero net differential as a central tendency, particularly for the developed countries. As with PPP theory, the deviations from the Fisher effect are larger for the developing countries than for the industrialized countries. The magnitude of the maximum annual deviation indicates that there are significant short-term deviations, but these tend to be offset as the period is lengthened.

The conclusion of Aliber and Stickney's study is that the international Fisher effect holds long term. Although this tends to be confirmed by Oxelheim's (1985) study spanning 1974 to 1984 for the Western world's major currencies, this conclusion is by no means substantiated by all of the evidence from other pieces of work, for example Robinson and Warburton's (1980) study which spanned the period from 1972 to 1979 for leading currencies.

If the international Fisher effect were to hold over the medium to long term, investment in interest-bearing monetary assets held for the medium to long term should not be subject to exchange rate risk in the sense that the higher rate of interest would compensate for currency depreciation. Thus, an investor may achieve a higher interest return by placing his money in Eurosterling than by putting it into Euro-Swiss francs. But this should be evened out over the medium to long term by the fact that the Swiss franc should, according to international Fisher, appreciate versus the pound sterling. If we superimpose upon this some of the ideas associated with efficient markets, it should not be possible to formulate a filter rule for investment policy which would consistently outperform the average rate of return achieved from investing in international interest-bearing securities of comparable quality. International Fisher, linked with the efficient markets hypothesis, suggests that the average return over all currencies – taking into account relative interest rates and appreciation/depreciation – should be equal and filter rules should not yield abnormal returns when taking into account associated risk.

Robinson and Warburton (1980) sought empirically to investigate whether this was so. Their study covered the period 1972 to 1979 and they devised four investment rules for placing and switching money in three-month treasury bills or three-month Eurocurrency deposits. The four filter rules were as follows:

- Invest for the highest nominal rate of interest.

- Invest for the highest real rate of interest with inflation expectations based on consumer prices over the preceding six months.

- Invest for the highest real rate of interest with inflation expectations based on wholesale prices over the preceding six months.

- Invest for the highest real rate of interest with a 'correction' factor built in to allow for exchange rates being out of equilibrium.

The investigators' findings are thought-provoking since their filter rules seemed to yield substantial excess returns. These findings seem to cast some doubt about the received wisdom on two fronts. Can they be reconciled with the international Fisher effect? Are foreign exchange markets efficient? Of course, it may just be a quirk that the filter rules produced the kinds of results shown; efficient markets advocates would suggest that finding *ex-post* rules that yield superior returns is not difficult. Also Robinson and Warburton's methodology might be improved. They use a single period of analysis running from 1972 to 1979 and this would have been improved had they used a number of investment periods covering different spans and terminating at varying dates. Given the comment above about ease of finding *ex-post* decision rules which yield superior returns, Bell and Kettell (1983) sought to replicate the Robinson–Warburton experiment for the two further years after their filter rules were published. Surprisingly, their results were not dissimilar; the filter rules continued to yield excess returns. Of course, it is possible that the excess returns simply reflected higher risk.

More replications of this work were carried out by Madura and Nosari (1984). They simulated a speculative strategy in which the currency with the lowest quoted interest rate was borrowed by a US-based speculator and converted and invested in the currency with the highest nominal interest rate. At the end of the speculation period, the funds were repatriated and the loan repaid. Substantial profits were found to result from this policy. This filter rule was repeated for investment with the speculation located in seven other major Western economies and similarly large profits resulted.

Another study by Thomas (1985) in the early 1980s ends up with similar findings. His filter rule involved the purchase and sale of currency futures with underlying high and low interest rates respectively. If the high interest rate currencies depreciate relative to their low interest rate brethren, then no profits should accrue. Thomas reports that 57 per cent of such transactions resulted in profits; therefore there were also a significant number of losses. But the overall profit as an annualized percentage rate of return was 77 per cent per annum over the years of his investigation. As MacDonald (1988) correctly states, the failure of international Fisher 'to hold may be attributable . . . to the existence of a risk premium'. Whether such a risk premium is consistent with the kinds of gain that Thomas reports, and whether such gains would continue to accrue now and into the future are matters for debate. Certainly, the lion's share of Thomas's gains came from the gearing component in the futures contract but what is interesting is that the profit strategy at the core of Thomas's work was written up by Robinson and Warburton before the time of his investigation. Theorists of efficient markets would suggest that reactions by rational players in the market place to the dissemination of the information would close the profit opportunity, again suggesting, perhaps, that the profits simply reflect risk taken on. Clearly we have a problem seeking a solution.

The evidence about the medium- to long-term reliability of the international Fisher effect is therefore conflicting. As financial economists, we should hardly be surprised that our models do not hold immutably for all periods. But there seem to be legitimate questions to be asked about efficient markets in foreign exchange. A discussion on this latter topic follows later in this chapter.

7.12 | Empiricism and interest rate parity

It will be recalled that interest rate parity theory equates the forward premium or discount with interest differentials. Empirical studies have generally confirmed that the covered interest differential is not significantly different from zero except when there are market imperfections such as those created by government controls on capital flows, exchange restrictions, prohibitions on profit remittances and capital repatriations, and so on.

In support of the covered interest differential being zero, Roll and Solnik (1975) found that 'dealers in the Eurocurrency markets actually used the interest rate parity theorem to establish their prices'. This is confirmed by Giddy and Dufey (1975), who found that the foreign exchange markets in Eurodollars, Euro-Canadian dollars, Euro-French francs and Eurosterling operate this process efficiently. These findings are confirmed by various researchers such as Bilson (1975), Aliber (1975b), Marston (1976) and Herring and Marston (1976) while others have identified deviations from interest parity, notably Stein (1965), Branson (1968), Pedersson and Tower (1976) and Frenkel and Levich (1975, 1977). But the majority of references so far in this section have confined themselves to investigating interest rate parity up to twelve months ahead. With the emergence of long-term forwards, what is the evidence?

A study by Hilley, Breidleman and Greenleaf (1981) demonstrated substantial deviations from IRP using forward contracts at three, four and five years to maturity. More recently, Popper (1993) analysed long-term IRP using five-year and seven-year securities and the interest differential implied by currency swaps of matching maturities (currency swap techniques are explained in Chapter 14). For her sample of major countries in the mid-1980s, Popper found that deviations from long-term covered interest parity were only slightly higher (about 0.1 per cent) than deviations from short-term covered interest parity. However, in a similar study, Fletcher and Taylor (1994) examined five-, seven- and ten-year securities for deviations from long-term IRP. They reported that in every market studied there were significant deviations from IRP. They suggested that these represent profit opportunities even after allowing for transaction costs. Deviations of this sort create a window of opportunity for firms and may partly explain the rapid growth in long-term currency swaps – see Chapter 14.

7.13 | Empiricism and expectations theory

Although we would not expect the forward rate today always to equal the future spot rate, expectations theory suggests that, on average, this will tend to be so. This means that the forward rate will exceed the future spot rate as often as it is below it. In other words, the forward rate will be an unbiased predictor of the future spot rate. Once again, empirical evidence casts some doubt upon this.

Work undertaken by Kohlhagen (1978), Giddy and Dufey (1975), Cornell (1977), Levich (1978), Frenkel (1979, 1980) and MacDonald (1983) all indicate that the forward rate is an unbiased predictor of the future spot rate. According to an investigation by Kettell (1979) of US dollar, Deutschmark and Swiss franc forward rates during the decade to 1976, the 30-day forward rate was an unbiased predictor but the 90-day rate was not. Aliber (1975a, b) notes that, while the forward rate is an unbiased predictor, its accuracy diminishes the further forward one looks and it is a less accurate predictor when currencies are floating as opposed to when they are fixed.

Evidence against the unbiased nature of the forward rate as predictor can be found in Roll and Solnik's (1975) study covering forward rates for the period 1950 to 1973. Kaserman (1973) provides similar evidence and adds that the forward rate undervalues the future spot rate when the spot rate is rising, and vice versa. A similar conclusion is reported by Wong (1978) who adds that the forward rate is an unbiased predictor in the very long run but is biased even in the medium term. Studies by Hansen and Hodrick (1980), Bilson (1981), Hakkio (1981), Hsieh (1982), Baillie, Lippens and McMahon (1983), Edwards (1983) and Levy and Nobay (1986) all suggest that the forward rate is a biased predictor. This finding of bias is reinforced by Chang (1986) who, surprisingly, shows that the current spot rate is superior at forecasting future rates than the forward rate. This conclusion has also been reached by Chrystal and Thornton (1988). In an investigation into exchange rates for the dollar, the yen and the Deutschmark, de Grauwe (1988) concluded that movements in spot exchange rates are larger than the forward premium/discount. He noted that systematically lower forward premium/discounts imply systematic underestimation of the size of the exchange rate change. Madura (1989) reaches a somewhat similar conclusion. Tracking movements of the US dollar against sterling from 1974 to 1988, he concludes that during periods of pound strength, forecasts based on the forward rate undervalue sterling, whereas during phases of pound weakness, the forward rate overvalues the UK currency.

As Hodrick (1987) states, in summarizing the 'evidence against the unbiasedness hypothesis [it] appears to be very strong and consistent across currencies, maturities and time periods'. Effectively, the studies reviewed here might be suggesting that the formulation of a forecasting model capable of beating the forward rate can be devised – something of a challenge to the idea of the efficient nature of foreign exchange markets. But we must take great care. Boothe and Longworth (1986) actually produced evidence to the effect that according to the data for the early 1970s to the early 1980s for the Canadian dollar, the French franc, the German mark, the Italian lira, the Japanese yen and the UK pound against the US dollar, these tended to show a reversal in the sign of the future spot rate versus that implied in the forward rate. Put mathematically, their evidence based on the model:

$$(s_{t+1} - s_t) = a_i + a_2(f_t - s_t) + u_{t+1}$$

actually produced an a_2 coefficient close to −1.

7.14 | Empiricism and foreign exchange market efficiency

A market is said to be efficient if current prices quoted therein approximately reflect all currently available information and there are no opportunities for making extraordinary profits by further exploiting such information. In the context of foreign exchange markets, the hypothesis would presumably suggest that profit-seeking market participants act upon information available to them in such a way that the spot exchange rate always reflects all available information that could potentially be useful in earning excess profits. Absolutely definitive empirical evidence about efficiency in the foreign exchange markets is unavailable because of the inadequacy of a comprehensive testing model. However, there has been no lack of empirical work in this complex area – and findings differ.

First of all, evidence favouring efficiency is presented. Giddy and Dufey (1975) examined the behaviour of four major currencies, namely the US dollar, the Canadian dollar, the pound sterling and the French franc over the floating periods 1919 to 1926 and 1971 to 1974. Using various models to establish trading rules based on sequences of past currency movements, they concluded that 'except possibly for very short-term (foreign exchange) forecasts the results provide support for the notion that trading rules are of no use in forecasting exchange rates'. They claim that their evidence is consistent with currency prices following a random walk and they find that the best predictor for an exchange rate in the future is the present exchange rate adjusted for interest rate differentials – that is, the forward rate. Roll (1979) supports Giddy and Dufey's efficiency findings and major studies by Cornell and Dietrich (1978) and Rogalski and Vinso (1977) also indicate that the foreign exchange markets are efficient to some extent. Cornell and Dietrich, whose work drew on evidence from the period 1973 to 1975, produced results that were consistent with the weak form of efficient market. Rogalski and Vinso, analysing the floating period from 1920 to 1924 for six currencies, and the Canadian dollar float of 1953 to 1957, claim that their evidence implies that the semi-strong form of efficient market seems to provide the most appropriate description of exchange rate behaviour in the period studied by them. This finding was confirmed by Caves and Feige (1980) in a study of the float period for 1953 to 1963 for the Canadian dollar against the US dollar. Pippinger's (1973) study of the behaviour of floating exchange rates in Canada, Norway, the United Kingdom, France and Spain indicates that exchange rates are efficient and follow a random walk except in cases of central bank intervention when signs of inefficiency are witnessed.

There is, however, a wealth of studies which conclude that foreign exchange markets do not necessarily behave in a manner altogether consistent with an efficient market. We have already discussed Robinson and Warburton's (1980) work and mentioned those of Hansen and Hodrick (1980), Bilson (1981), Hsieh (1982), Baillie, Lippens and McMahon (1983), Baillie and McMahon (1989) and a significant number of others. To these we should add more. Poole (1967), in a study of the behaviour of nine currencies in the post-First World War period and the Canadian float from 1950 to 1962 used both filter rules and tests of serial dependence and concluded that the substantial evidence of serial correlation implied that the random walk hypothesis should be rejected. Filter rules developed by Poole yielded substantial profits but he did not adjust for interest rates and transaction costs. Grubel (1965), in a study that has rightly been criticized by Kohlhagen (1978) on methodological grounds, found that significant speculative profits would have been yielded by filter rules during the late 1950s. Similarly, in the period from 1973 to 1975, Dooley and Shafer (1976) established significant serial correlation in exchange rate changes and developed filter rules that were 'remarkably profitable' and they deduce this to be inconsistent with an efficient market. Logue and Sweeney (1977) used Poole's filter rule strategy and compare the payoff to a buy-and-hold policy for the French franc/US dollar over the period 1970 to 1974. Taking account of interest and transaction costs, excess profits still remain. MacDonald and Young (1986) also found excess profits from filter rule trading. Upson (1972), in the period from 1960 to 1967, found that the forward pound sterling behaved in a non-random way.

Various writers – for a summary see MacDonald (1988) – have concluded that spot exchange rates appear to move in a lagged way to news events. It must be added that some of the studies are frail on methodology and hence the conclusions are not beyond serious dispute. If exchange rates do fail to react immediately to news events, then there must be some challenge to the efficient nature of currency markets. However, more recent studies by Almeida, Goodhart and Payne (1998) and Bosner-Neal, Roley and Sellon (1998) – already referred to in the middle of section 7.6 – have suggested a strong link between news events and exchange rate movements.

Levich (1978) has identified large profit opportunities in forward speculation and has shown, in a series of surveys in *Euromoney* (1981, 1982 and 1983), that several foreign exchange rate forecasting services, but nothing like all, achieved significant excess profits for users in the period 1977 to 1980. However, their track record deteriorates sharply through 1982 to 1983. But Levich is careful not to reject market efficiency. Following the first of the above studies, he warns:

> Do these results prove that the foreign exchange market is inefficient? No. This is because the forward rate may contain a risk premium. If so, exchange rate forecasters ought to be able to forecast better than the forward rate. The profits earned by speculators who follow these forecasts may represent only a fair return for the extra foreign exchange risk incurred.

Schulmeister (1987, 1988) in an analysis of the $/DM rate over the period from April 1973 to October 1986, developed filter and moving average models and tested a momentum model based on the rate of change in the past exchange rate and a combination model involving both moving averages and momentum models. His results suggest that most of these technical models would have yielded significant profitable trading strategies after adjusting for interest expense and transaction costs. Schulmeister suggests one reason behind the profitability of trading rules: that exchange rate changes and speculative profits appear to be distributed non-normally. So, there are too many small exchange rate changes relative to a normal distribution. But there are also too many large exchange rate swings relative to the normal distribution. The implication of the latter is that once an exchange rate move has started, it seems likely to proceed more or less uninterrupted, allowing technical analysts to identify profitable investment opportunities.

Levich and Thomas (1993) also found evidence on the profitability of filter rules and moving average cross-over rules. They tracked 3,800 daily observations over the period from January 1976 to December 1990 and based their analysis on currency futures prices. Again, filter rules and moving average cross-over rules produce profitable trading signals.

In attempting to show the role of government intervention, Silber (1994) looked at the efficiency of futures markets. He developed filter rules based on past results and took the most profitable rule and applied it in the next period. Silber's evidence suggested that for currencies and short-term interest rates, where governments maintain a significant involvement, there was a tendency for technical trend-following rules to result in profits. Crude oil was another instance where political factors were found strongly to influence market prices. But the markets in gold and silver and in equities showed no tendency for naïve filter rules to yield profits. Silber concluded that the process of government intervention in foreign exchange markets may be a feature that distinguishes currency markets from other financial markets.

Similarly, LeBaron (1999) investigated the profitability of technical trading models from 1979–1992 for the DEM and JPY. LeBaron reported that if the days when the Federal Reserve actively intervened were removed from his observations, there would be a dramatic decline in the level and significance of technical trading profits. But LeBaron warned that it was not clear that the Federal Reserve caused the inefficiencies in the foreign exchange market, or just happened to be around when they occurred. Neely (1998) arrived at similar conclusions.

A study by Kwok and van de Gucht (1991) applied filter rules to the DEM/US$ exchange rate sampled at 30-minute intervals over the period from February 1985 to August 1989. Their results showed strong evidence that their filter rules, applied to high-frequency, intra-day exchange rates, resulted in statistically significant trading profits throughout the period. Hardly surprising that technical models to forecast short-run directional changes in exchange rates are widely used around the world – see two paragraphs hence.

A series of interesting studies has been carried out by Goodman (1978, 1980, 1981, 1982) and Goodman and Jaycobs (1983) who have claimed to show that technically oriented (based on charts) exchange rate forecasting services have both outperformed econometric models and generated recurring exceptional profits. Abuaf (1988) is sufficiently impressed by the evidence on the superiority of chartism to state that 'technical models have prediction power, especially in intra-day trading. However, their prediction power for periods of a month or longer does not seem strong.' The finding of the studies that technical analysis outperforms the forward rate which, in turn, outperforms econometric models in the short term, is supported by Bilik (1982). The superiority of the forward rate over judgemental and econometric models for periods of up to one year is also borne out by Blake, Beenstock and Brasse (1986); unfortunately their study of a very small sample of forecasting services included none based on technical analysis. Goodman (1979) also evaluated the record of six fundamentally oriented forecasting firms on the basis of their forecasting accuracy for six currencies – the Canadian dollar, French franc, German mark, Japanese yen, Swiss franc and UK pound – from January 1976 to June 1979. His study evaluated the performance of these forecasting firms using both accuracy in predicting trend and accuracy in their actual estimates. He used the forward rate as a benchmark to judge the effectiveness of the forecasting firms. No individual firm was found to be significantly more accurate than the forward rate in predicting trend. On average, these firms performed worse than the forward rate. Another study, by Meese and Rogoff (1983), evaluated the forecasting effectiveness of seven models – two based on spot and forward rates, two technical models and three fundamental models – for the time period between November 1976 and June 1981. For the US dollar against the mark, the yen and the pound, forecast rates were obtained for horizons of 1, 6 and 12 months. The market-based forecasts (those based on spot and forward) were more accurate than both the technical and fundamental models. Of the two market-based forecasts, the spot rate performed marginally better than the forward rate. In a different study of 42 Japanese currency forecasters, Elliott and Ito (1995) showed that the currency forecasters were less accurate than a random walk forecast. However, the forecasts of 32 of the 42 forecasters were found to be useful in generating profits at the one-month horizon.

The popularity of chartist techniques in terms of near-term forecasting of exchange rates is evidenced by Takagi (1991). He states that: 'for short run forecasts, the predominant method is chartist or technical analysis; and that, for the longer run forecasts, the common method is fundamental analysis based on such fundamental variables as PPP.' This finding was confirmed in a survey of several hundred London foreign exchange market participants by Taylor and Allen (1992). They reported that 90 per cent of respondents placed greater reliance on technical models for their very short run (intraday to one-week) forecasts. As the future horizon lengthened, more respondents turned to fundamentals to guide their exchange rate forecasts. At a time horizon of one-year or more, roughly 85 per cent of respondents relied primarily on economic fundamentals. But Allen and Taylor (1989), in reviewing the forecasts of London foreign exchange chartists, conclude that, on average, chartists' forecasts performed worse than a random walk.

Although now dated, Kohlhagen (1978) discusses and criticizes the methodology of many of the early studies. MacDonald (1988) and Holland (1993) provide good reviews of the more recent literature.

If there is some evidence suggesting less than complete market efficiency, can we explain it? The answer may lie with the behaviour of central banks. One of the key assumptions about efficient markets is that they comprise profit-maximizing participants all acting independently of one another. Central bank intervention, either directly by dealing in the foreign exchange markets or indirectly by influencing interest rates, is rarely directed towards profit maximization and the banks' behaviour is frequently a function of the effects that other participants are having on the market – for example, if the concerted actions of profit-maximizing market operators were to push the exchange rate towards a sensitive level, sustained central bank intervention might follow. That central banks' operations in foreign exchange markets are not profit oriented is well substantiated by Taylor (1982) who tabulates profits and losses – mainly the latter – accruing to nine major central banks through official intervention in the foreign exchange market during the bulk of the floating period in the 1970s.

Perhaps the conflicting evidence on market efficiency is nothing more than we should expect. Central banks do not intervene all of the time in the market. At times when they are not intervening, we would expect the foreign exchange markets to show all of the features associated with efficiency; at times when central banks are intervening it would be doubtful whether markets would display efficiency. According to this explanation then, foreign exchange markets in some currencies, for some periods, would be seen to be efficient, but for other periods – that is, when the central bank is intervening – they would not.

7.15 | Summary

- We are seeking a model that explains exchange rate movements. The goal is a regression model that works, in which the spot rate is the dependent variable and coefficients can be estimated for a series of independent variables and which has a high statistical significance. The search has been no more successful than the hunt for El Dorado, the fabled South American city rich in gold and treasure sought by Spanish explorers of the 16th century.

- We have, nonetheless, a number of competing theories of exchange rate movements including purchasing power parity theory, balance of payments theories, monetary theories and portfolio balance theory. How do these work?

- Purchasing power parity was summarized in Chapter 4. It is found to be a poor predictor of exchange rates in the short term. But when developed from an equilibrium base year and used as a long-term forecasting device, it seems to work well.

- The balance of payments theory of exchange rate determination has gone through many forms. The original form ignored capital flows and was applied to a fixed exchange rate mechanism. The way it works – simplistically – is as follows. Assume an increase in national income. This results in a pressure for imports to rise. To pay for them, the exchange rate weakens as funds flow out to buy foreign currency. Support for the home currency is necessary – remember we are talking about a fixed rate regime. And worries about the balance of payments current account deficit lead to severity in the home market. This may be manifest in lower money supply growth and lower inflation. The effect should be to dampen demand for imports and force resources into export production, improving the current account – and strengthening the exchange rate.

- The above version of the balance of payments theory has been overtaken by events. Remember that it is based on a fixed exchange rate regime. Balance of payments theory may be approached in a floating exchange rate environment either ignoring capital flows or with them. Let us do the former first. Under such an environment, improvements in national income tend to worsen the current account and weaken the exchange rate. The lower currency rate should, *ceteris paribus*, improve exports and dampen imports with the attendant force to improve the current account and strengthen the currency.

- In the version of balance of payments theory which takes cognizance of floating exchange rates and allows for capital flows, the reasoning is as follows. As national income increases, the current account deteriorates. If official reserve movements are to be avoided, there must be an improvement in capital account. This may be achieved via higher interest rates (assuming underlying inflation remains unchanged this implies higher real interest rates) which has the effect of damping demand – and hence imports. Thus the current account swings back into an improved position. Note that though interest rates increase under this version of balance of payments theory, the exchange rate tends to remain constant.

- This is not so with the monetary theory of exchange rates. Using the route outlined above, improvements to national income result in increased transactions demand for money. To the extent that this is not created by the domestic banking system, it is imported from abroad. The increased money supply tends to push up inflation and interest rates and the exchange rate consequently worsens. The driving force in this model is relative money supplies between the home country and trading partners.

■ The portfolio balance theory suggests that the exchange rate is a function of the relative supply of domestic and foreign bonds. Simplistically, the effect can be seen in an example. Assume that the supply of bonds in a country increases. Its bond prices would then fall but bond yields to redemption should increase. All other things being equal, money flows into the country and forces up the exchange rate. Note that in this model interest rates move up without any effect on inflation – in other words, real interest rates rise. If, of course, expected inflation were to rise too, then the exchange rate should not be enhanced.

■ Empirically, we observe a tendency for exchange rates to overshoot the level implied by economic models.

■ The news explanation of exchange rates is different. It suggests that as unexpected news occurs, these unanticipated pieces of information affect rates appropriately. But remember it is unexpected news that moves markets – expected news should be discounted in present levels.

■ Note how chartist models work. This is explained fairly straightforwardly in the text.

■ The efficient market hypothesis is an important proposition. It is based upon markets for securities being composed of players out to maximize profit. Their pursuit of profit moves security prices rapidly to reflect the effect of new information. Prices achieved are not always perfect – but they are unbiased. Security prices adjust to all new information. The efficient market hypothesis comes in three gradations.

■ The weak form of efficient market is one in which current security prices reflect all market information including the historic sequence of past prices, changes and returns. Thus there should be no relationship between past prices and future prices because past price movements should be impounded in today's security price. This form of efficient market clearly has no time for chartism which predicts on the basis of past prices.

■ The semi-strong efficient market asserts that security prices move in sympathy with all new public information. So stock prices reflect all published available data. The semi-strong form embraces also the weak form.

■ The strong form efficient market implies, by definition, that no group of investors has monopolistic access to information relevant to the formation of security prices and that security prices reflect all information – whether publicly or privately available.

■ By and large, stock markets in advanced Western economies exhibit semi-strong form efficiency for major stocks traded. However, evidence is emerging to challenge this notion.

■ But currency markets are different. They seem to exhibit efficiency some of the time – but not all the time. Chartism seems to work quite well when efficiency is less than perfect. Why might this be so? Why might this biggest market in the world exhibit less than perfect efficiency? Perhaps the answer lies in the fact that the biggest player in the market is not a profit maximizer. And who is the biggest player? Not the big commercial banks. It is, of course, the central banks – they are not profit maximizers. They are more concerned, as a rule, with achieving political, as opposed to economic, goals in their intervention in foreign currency markets.

■ Hardly surprisingly, chartism seems to perform better than econometric models in terms of forecasting exchange rates over the short term. Chartist models should be most superior when foreign exchange market intervention is rife.

■ The four-way equivalence model is an equilibrium model arrived at by deductive reasoning. It should not be surprising if, for lengthy periods, parts of the model do not hold in the real world. Markets move towards equilibrium and the same is true of foreign exchange markets.

■ The test of a good theory is how well it stands up in the real world. Evidence suggests that interest rate parity holds virtually all the time at the level of quotations by banks to companies, but the remaining parts of the model are found to have more of a long-run nature.

■ Purchasing power parity is found to hold up well in the medium to longer term but there are very substantial deviations from it in the short run – so much so that using it as a short-run predictor of exchange rate movements is utterly unjustified by the evidence.

■ Evidence on the international Fisher effect is more conflicting than on purchasing power parity. Some have found international Fisher to work well in the medium to long term while others have found evidence to challenge this conclusion. Tests of international Fisher have found substantial short-term deviations.

■ The same kinds of finding apply in respect of the Fisher effect too.

■ Evidence on interest rate parity suggests that it works really well in the real world in terms of explaining spot versus forward exchange rates by Eurocurrency interest differences. It works outstandingly well for short-term forwards.

■ The forward exchange rate is generally found to be an unbiased predictor of the future spot rate. But, empirically, a bias is found when looking at very short-term movements. Thus the forward rate itself has been found consistently to undervalue the future spot rate when the spot rate is rising strongly, and vice versa.

■ We also have evidence on foreign exchange market efficiency – and this is conflicting too.

■ If foreign exchange markets are efficient, we should not be able to use mechanical dealing rules which consistently yield excess profits. Profits that are achieved should be commensurate with the level of risk undertaken. The empirical evidence is somewhat unclear. Some investigators have found results consistent with market efficiency; others appear to have identified filter rules which consistently yield excess profits over lengthy periods.

■ At first sight, the above evidence may be conflicting. But it is possible that there are periods when the substantial presence of central banks, operating in a non-profit-maximizing way in the foreign exchange markets, may create the environment where operators may beat the market.

7.16 | End of chapter questions

Question 1
Explain the theory of purchasing power parity (PPP). Based on this theory, what is a general forecast of the values of currencies in highly inflated countries?

Question 2
Explain how you could determine whether purchasing power parity exists.

Question 3
For each of the following six scenarios, say whether the value of the dollar will appreciate, depreciate, or remain the same relative to the Japanese yen. Explain each answer. Assume that exchange rates are freely floating and that all other factors are held constant.

(a) The growth rate of national income is higher in the United States than in Japan.

(b) Inflation is higher in the United States than in Japan.

(c) Prices in Japan and the United States are rising at the same rate.

(d) Real interest rates become higher in the United States than in Japan.

(e) The United States imposes new restrictions on the ability of foreigners to buy American companies and real estate.

(f) US wages rise relative to Japanese wages, and American productivity falls behind Japanese productivity.

Notes

1. If one were to use the model, one should study the original Murenbeeld article to obtain the exact definitions of UNEM, M and G.

2. The Marshall–Lerner condition states that, if the sum of the elasticities of demand for a country's exports and that for its imports exceeds unity, then a devaluation will have a positive effect upon its trade balance. Alternatively, if the sum of these elasticities is less than 1 then revaluation should improve the trade balance. The Marshall–Lerner model is built upon a number of grossly simplifying assumptions.

8 Definitions of foreign exchange risk

Foreign exchange risk management begins by identifying what items and amounts a firm has exposed to risk associated with changes in exchange rates. An asset, liability, profit or expected future cash flow stream (whether certain or not) is said to be exposed to exchange risk when a currency movement would change, for better or for worse, its parent or home currency value. The term 'exposure' used in the context of foreign exchange means that a firm has assets, liabilities, profits or expected future cash flow streams such that the home currency value of assets, liabilities, profits or the present value in home currency terms of expected future cash flows changes as exchange rates change. Risk arises because currency movements may alter home currency values.

In this sense, assets, liabilities and expected future cash flow streams denominated in foreign currencies are clearly exposed to foreign exchange risk. But some expected future cash flows denominated in home currency terms may also be exposed. For example, a UK company selling in its home market may be competing with firms based in the Netherlands. In such circumstances changes in the sterling/guilder exchange rate will almost certainly affect the present value of the UK company's expected cash flows by strengthening or weakening its competitive position against its Dutch rivals.

Foreign exchange exposure is usually classified according to whether it falls into one or more of the following categories:

- transaction exposure;
- translation exposure;
- economic exposure.

Transaction exposure arises because a payable or receivable is denominated in a foreign currency. Translation exposure arises on the consolidation of foreign-currency-denominated assets and liabilities in the process of preparing consolidated accounts. This concept is essentially concerned, then, with what might be called accounting exposure. Economic exposure arises because the present value of a stream of expected future operating cash flows denominated in the home currency or in a foreign currency may vary because of changed exchange rates. Transaction and economic exposure are both cash flow exposures. Transaction exposure is a comparatively straightforward concept but translation and economic exposure are more complex. Each of the three categories of exposure is now examined and defined in more detail.

8.1 ▍ Transaction exposure

Transaction exposure arises because the cost or proceeds (in home currency) of settlement of a future payment or receipt denominated in a currency other than the home currency may vary because of changes in exchange rates. Clearly transaction exposure is a cash flow exposure. It may be associated with trading flows (such as foreign-currency-denominated trade debtors and trade creditors), dividend flows or capital flows (such as foreign-currency-denominated dividends or loan repayments).

8.2 ▍ Translation exposure

Consolidation of financial statements that involve foreign-currency-denominated assets and liabilities automatically gives rise to translation exposure, sometimes termed accounting exposure. Consolidation of foreign subsidiaries' accounts into group financial statements denominated in home currency requires the application of a rate or rates of exchange to foreign subsidiaries' accounts, in order that they may be translated into the parent currency. Both balance sheets and income statements must be consolidated and they both give rise to translation exposure. Translating foreign currency profit and loss accounts at either the average exchange rate during the accounting year or at the exchange rate at the end of the accounting year (both methods are currently permissible UK accounting procedures) will mean that expected consolidated profit will vary as the average or the expected closing rate changes. So the whole amount of profit earned in foreign currency is exposed to translation risk in the sense that the home currency consolidated profit may vary as exchange rates vary.

Balance sheet exposure is somewhat more complex. Some items in a foreign subsidiary's balance sheet may be translated at their historical exchange rates (the rate prevailing at the date of acquisition or any subsequent revaluation). Thus their home currency translated value cannot alter as exchange rates alter; such assets and liabilities are not exposed in the accounting sense. Other items may be translated at the closing exchange rate – the rate prevailing at the balance sheet date at the end of the accounting period. While the value of such items is fixed in the foreign subsidiary's currency, the amount translated into the parent currency will alter as the exchange rate alters. Hence all foreign currency items that are consolidated at current rates are exposed in the accounting sense.

Accounting exposure, therefore, reflects the possibility that foreign-currency-denominated items which are consolidated into group published financial statements at current or average rates will show a translation loss or gain as a result. This kind of exposure does not give an indication of the true effects of currency fluctuations on a company's foreign operations.

Economic exposure, to be discussed later, is a far better measure of true value exposure. Translation exposure, as will become clear later, is really a function of the system of accounting for foreign assets and liabilities on consolidation which a group of companies uses. Clearly it has little to do with true value in an economic sense.

There are four basic translation methods. These are the current/non-current method (sometimes called the traditional or working capital method), the all-current (or closing rate) method, the monetary/non-monetary method, and the temporal method. These differing means of translation are considered in detail below. It is worth mentioning that the all-current method is now the most frequently used in the United Kingdom, the United States and many other countries.

The current/non-current method

This approach uses the traditional accounting distinction between current and long-term items and translates the former at the closing rate and the latter at the histor-ical rate. Accounting exposure for a foreign subsidiary at a particular point in time is given by the net figure of assets less liabilities that are exposed to potential change should exchange rates alter. Evidently, according to the current/non-current method, the sum exposed is net current assets.

One of the implications of this method of translation is that inventory is exposed to foreign exchange risk but long-term debt is not. The logic of such an assumption is by no means apparent. Indeed it should be clear that long-term debt is very much exposed to exchange risk. In home currency terms, the cash amount of a foreign-currency-denominated loan (whether a payable or receivable loan) will change as exchange rates change. This lack of logic underpins the move away from the current/non-current method which has been witnessed over recent years.

The all-current (closing rate) method

This method merely translates all foreign-currency-denominated items at the closing rate of exchange. Accounting exposure is given simply by net assets or shareholders' funds (sometimes called equity). This method has become increasingly popular over time and is now the major worldwide method of translating foreign subsidiaries' balance sheets.

The monetary/non-monetary method

Monetary items are assets, liabilities or capital, the amounts of which are fixed by contract in terms of the number of currency units regardless of changes in the value of money. Translation via the monetary/non-monetary method involves monet-ary assets and monetary liabilities being translated at the closing rate while non-monetary items are translated at their historical rate. Accounting exposure under this method is given by net monetary assets.

In terms of development of accounting reporting, this method of translating for-eign subsidiaries' accounts seems to have been a halfway house between the current/non-current method and the all-current method.

The temporal method

The temporal method of translation uses the closing rate method for all items stated at replacement cost, realizable value, market value or expected future value, and uses the historical rate for all items stated at historic cost.

The rationale for the temporal approach is that the translation rate used should preserve the accounting principles used to value assets and liabilities in the original financial statements. According to the temporal method, the translation rate for each asset or liability depends upon the measurement basis used in the foreign subsidiary's original account.

Applied to traditional historic cost accounts, the temporal and monetary/non-monetary methods give almost the same results. The main difference arises in the case of certain items of inventory. Where stock is stated in the original accounts at market value (where it is below historic cost) the temporal method would translate it at the current rate while the monetary/non-monetary approach would use the historic rate of exchange. But it should be emphasized that the temporal method is by no means synonymous with the monetary/non-monetary approach.

Example 1 – a numerical example

It should be clear that identical firms with identical assets, liabilities, capital structures and trading results may show different translation gains and losses and different translated balance sheets depending upon the method used for converting foreign currency items to home currency values. This can be demonstrated by a simple numerical example.

Assume that a UK company sets up a subsidiary in Australia on 1 March and that the opening transactions are booked in the Australian company's accounts according to the prevailing exchange rate of £1 = AUD3. The opening balance sheet is shown in Table 8.1.

Assume, further, that no additional business or transactions go through the Australian company during March and consequently the Australian dollar balance sheet at the end of the month remains as at the beginning. But assume that during March sterling fell against the Australian dollar and the exchange rate at the end of the month was £1 = AUD2.5. This means that the sterling-translated balance sheet of the subsidiary will alter, the extent of the change differing according to whether the current/non-current, all-current, or monetary/non-monetary method of translation is used. Table 8.1 shows the results.

From the table it will be noted that the translation gain or loss is equal to 16.67 per cent of the accounting exposure. This is, of course, consistent with the movement in sterling value versus the Australian dollar from 3 to 2.5. But it will further be noted from the table that translation outturns range from a gain of over £491,000 to a loss of over £349,000. These differences arise merely because of varying accounting methods.

Table 8.1 Example illustrating translation exposure

	Subsidiary's balance sheet as at 1 March AUD000	Subsidiary's balance sheet as at 1 March £000	Subsidiary's balance sheet as at 31 March translated according to:		
			All-current rate £000	Current/ non-current £000	Monetary/ non-monetary £000
Fixed assets	8,400	2,800	3,360*	2,800	2,800
Inventory	4,200	1,400	1,680*	1,680*	1,400
Cash	1,065	355	426*	426*	426*
Total assets	13,665	4,555	5,466	4,906	4,626
Current payables	2,100	700	840*	840*	840*
Long-term debt	4,200	1,400	1,680*	1,400	1,680*
Equity	7,365	2,455	2,946	2,666	2,106
Translation gain/(loss)			491	211	(349)
Accounting exposure as at 31 March exchange rate			2,946	1,266	(2,094)
But accounting exposure is better measured in foreign currency as AUD000			7,365	3,166	(5,234)

* Assets and liabilities exposed, as of 31 March, to translation exposure under different translation conventions.

Example 2 – moving towards a consensus

Internationally, the accounting profession has been concerned about the position on translation of foreign-currency-accounting statements. Indeed, the accounting professions in the United States and the United Kingdom now have almost identical rules for accounting for foreign currencies in published accounts. Generally speaking, translation of foreign balance sheets uses the current rate method. Transaction gains, whether realized or not, are accounted for through the profit and loss account. But there is a major exception. Where a transaction profit or loss arises from taking on a foreign currency borrowing in a situation in which the borrowing can be designated as a hedge for a net investment denominated in the same foreign currency as the borrowing, then the gain or loss on the borrowing, if it is less than the net investment hedged, would be accounted for by movements in reserves rather than through the income statement. If this kind of transaction gain or loss exceeds the amount of the loss or gain respectively on the net investment hedged, the excess gain or loss is to be reported in the profit and loss account. Non-transaction gains and losses are to be dealt with by reserve accounting direct to the balance sheet rather than through the profit and loss account.

According to the US standard FAS 52, translation of foreign currency revenues and costs (the essence of the income statement) is to be made at the average exchange rate during the accounting period. The British standard SSAP 20 allows the use of either the current rate or the average rate for this purpose. However, it is fair to say that opinion in the United States has moved towards the average rate method.

While translation methods affect group balance sheet values, the key point is that they have nothing to do with economic value. The value of the Australian subsidiary in the example should not be affected by adopting a different method of accounting. Its worth will be the same whether the all-current, current/non-current or monetary/non-monetary method is used. In all probability its discounted net present value will have changed as a result of the strengthened guilder. But this changed present value is hardly what we pick up by using different methods of translating balance sheets. Clearly, changes in value resulting from changed exchange rates show in terms of different present values. If we are concerned with how true value has changed because of exchange rate movements, we should be looking at economic value and how it changes in sympathy with moving exchange rates. This is what true exposure to exchange rate movements is all about.

8.3 | Economic exposure

Economic exposure is concerned with the present value of future operating cash flows to be generated by a company's activities and how this present value, expressed in parent currency, changes following exchange rate movement. The concept of economic exposure is most frequently applied to a company's expected future operating cash flows (unhedged) from sales in foreign currency and from foreign operations. But it can equally well be applied to a firm's home territory operations and the extent to which the present value of those operations alters resultant upon changed exchange rates. For the purpose of convenience, the exposition that follows is based on a firm's foreign operations, although an uncovered foreign-currency-denominated receivable or payable will vary as exchange rates vary.

The value of an overseas operation can be expressed as the present value of expected future operating cash flows which are incremental to that overseas activity discounted at the appropriate discount rate. Expressing this present value in terms of the parent currency can be achieved via equation (8.1) – but remember that incremental cash flows to the whole group of companies include management fees, royalties and similar kinds of flow as well as direct cash flows from trading operations. The present value of the foreign subsidiary may be expressed as:

$$PV = \sum_{t=0}^{n} \frac{(CI_t - CO_t)e_t}{(1 + r)^t} \tag{8.1}$$

where PV is the parent currency present value of the foreign business, CI represents estimated future incremental net cash inflows associated with the foreign business expressed in foreign currency, CO is the estimated future incremental net cash outflows associated with the foreign business expressed in foreign currency, e is the expected future exchange rate (expressed in terms of the direct quote in the home territory), r is the appropriate discount rate, namely the rate of return that the parent requires from an investment in the risk class of the overseas business, t is the period for which cash flows are expected and n is the final period for which all flows are expected. Equation (8.1) assumes that all net incremental cash flows accruing to the overseas operation are distributable to the parent company in the home country.

At first sight the reader might conclude that quantifying economic exposure and the impact of changing exchange rates is fairly straightforward. For example, assume that a UK company has a wholly owned Danish subsidiary with a net present value of DKK120m. If the exchange rate is £1 = DKK8 and subsequently moves to £1 = DKK10, presumably the value of the subsidiary has moved from £15m to £12m. Such a conclusion would, in all probability, be incorrect. It is necessary to be far more analytical to reach a worthwhile conclusion on valuation.

Devaluation will affect cash inflows and cash outflows as well as the exchange rate. Consider a company competing in export markets. While devaluation will not affect the total market size, it should have a favourable market share effect. The company in the devaluing country should increase sales or profit margins – in short, it should benefit. Similarly, companies competing with imports in the domestic market should also gain since a devaluation will tend to make imported products more expensive in local currency terms. However, this benefit may be offset to some extent by domestic deflation which frequently accompanies devaluation. So, in the import competing sector of the domestic market there will be beneficial and negative impacts. Next, in the purely domestic market, devaluation may lead to reduced company performance in the short term as a result of deflationary measures at home which so often accompany currency depreciation.

All of the above factors affect cash inflows. Devaluations also affect cash outflows. Imported inputs become more expensive. If devaluation is accompanied by domestic deflation it will probably be the case that suppliers' prices will rise as their financing costs move up. An inverse line of reasoning applies with respect to revaluation of a currency.

Getting to grips with economic exposure involves us in analysing the effects of changing exchange rates on the following items:

■ Export sales, where margins and cash flows should change because devaluation should make exports more competitive.

■ Domestic sales, where margins and cash flows should alter substantially in the import competing sector.

■ Pure domestic sales, where margins and cash flows should change in response to deflationary measures which frequently accompany devaluations.

■ Costs of imported inputs, which should rise in response to a devaluation.

■ Cost of domestic inputs, which may vary with exchange rate changes.

The analysis is clearly complex, but it is necessary in order to assess fully how the home currency present value of overseas operations is likely to alter in response to movements in foreign exchange rates.

So far it has been assumed that the parent's present value of its foreign subsidiary is a function of that subsidiary's estimated future net cash flows. In other words, there is an assumption that all cash flows are distributable to the parent. In fact, host governments frequently restrict distribution to foreign parents by exchange controls. Suffice here to say that where distribution of cash flows to the parent is limited, the present value formula needs to be adjusted a little:

$$PV = \sum_{t=0}^{n} \frac{(\text{Div}_t + \text{OPF}_t)e_t}{(1+r)^t} + \frac{\text{TV}e_n}{(1+r)^n} \qquad (8.2)$$

The notation is as before except that Div represents the expected net dividend inflow in a particular year, OPF represents other parent flows such as royalties and management fees in a particular period, and TV represents the terminal value remittable over the foreign exchanges at the end of the project's life.

The reader should always bear in mind that economic exposure is equally applicable to the home operations of a firm inasmuch as a change in exchange rates is likely to affect the present value of its home operations; this may arise for all of the reasons which would impinge upon foreign businesses.

There is another, related dimension to economic exposure. A UK firm exporting goods to the United States, denominated in dollars, in competition with a German manufacturer will be facing a transaction exposure against the dollar and an economic exposure against the euro. Clearly, as the exchange rate between the pound and the euro changes, so the UK manufacturer is in a stronger or weaker position and this will filter through to sales levels, profit and cash generation. As such, the present value of the UK company's export business will alter as exchange rates change. Just like the previous kind of economic exposure, this subset is difficult to quantify for reasons similar to those mentioned before.

It can be seen that assessing economic exposure necessarily involves us in a substantial amount of work on elasticities of demand and behaviour of costs in response to changes in exchange rates. But the critical question that we would ask is whether economic exposure (or transaction exposure or translation exposure for that matter) is of any relevance to the financial manager of an international company. This question is addressed in Chapter 10.

8.4 | Summary

- Foreign exchange risk concerns risks created by changes in foreign currency levels.

- An asset, liability or profit or cash flow stream, whether certain or not, is said to be exposed to exchange risk when a currency movement would change, for better or worse, its parent, or home, currency value.

- Exposure arises because currency movements may alter home currency values.

- Categorizations of foreign currency exposure vary from text to text. This chapter distinguishes three forms of currency risk. These are transaction exposure, translation exposure and economic exposure. Later, in Chapter 11, a further classification, macroeconomic exposure, is highlighted. But we shall leave this to one side for the moment. In any case it is really more than foreign exchange exposure.

- Transaction exposure arises because a payable or receivable is denominated in a foreign currency.

- Translation exposure (sometimes also called accounting exposure) arises on the consolidation of foreign-currency-denominated assets, liabilities and profits in the process of preparing accounts.

- Economic exposure arises because the present value of a stream of expected future operating cash flows denominated in the home currency or in a foreign currency may vary because of changed exchange rates.

- Note that transaction and economic exposure are both cash flow exposures. Pure translation exposure is not cash flow based.

- A particular item may be classified under more than one heading. For example, a long-term foreign-denominated borrowing is both a transaction exposure (because the home currency equivalent to repay the loan varies as exchange rates change) and a translation exposure.

■ The magnitude of a translation exposure varies according to the accounting convention used for translation of foreign-denominated items. There are four basic translation methods. These are the current/non-current method, the all-current (sometimes called closing rate) method, the monetary/non-monetary method, and the temporal method. The exact mechanisms by which each method works are summarized in the main text.

■ It is worth noting that, nowadays, most advanced economies, including the United States and the United Kingdom, consolidate foreign-denominated balance sheet items according to the all-current method. These countries tend to use either the closing rate or the average rate during an accounting period for the purpose of translating foreign-denominated profit and loss accounts.

■ The relevance of classifying foreign exchange risk according to its transaction, translation or economic nature is that we would advocate that some categories of exposure should be actively managed by the headquarters treasury while our prescription for other categories is that since some of them do not matter, there is little point in applying treasury time in taking action to avoid the risk concerned – more of this later.

8.5 | End of chapter questions

Question 1
Compare and contrast transaction exposure and economic exposure.

Question 2
Why might the cash flows of purely domestic firms be exposed to exchange rate fluctuations?

Question 3
How do most companies deal with economic exposure?

9 Financial accounting and foreign exchange

In Chapter 8, we discussed the nature of translation exposure and showed how it could change with different accounting conventions used to record foreign operations. The accounting profession in much of the capitalist world has addressed itself to this problem and in many countries has come up with a series of rules for reporting to shareholders.

This chapter focuses upon the methods recommended in the United States and in the United Kingdom. These are embodied in Statement of Financial Accounting Standard No. 52 (FAS 52) of the Financial Accounting Standards Board in the United States and Statement of Standard Accounting Practice No. 20 (SSAP 20) in the United Kingdom, which are very similar in terms of their prescriptions. Prior to the introduction of FAS 52 in the United States, there was an extended debate about the implications of the previous accounting standard, FASB 8.

In summary, the recommendations of FAS 52 and of SSAP 20 are as follows. The closing rate method is to be used to convert foreign subsidiaries' balance sheets. Gains and losses on exchange arising from mere translation exposure are to be taken direct to the balance sheet and dealt with as movements on reserves. The only foreign exchange gains or losses to be credited or debited to profit and loss account are transaction (i.e. cash flow) gains or losses.

According to FAS 52, profits earned by foreign subsidiaries and reported in their income statements are to be consolidated in the group accounts in home currency terms at an average exchange rate for the accounting period. The UK standard, SSAP 20, permits the use of either the average method or the closing rate method.

The procedures put forward in the new standards differ substantially from that promulgated by the previous US standard, FASB 8. Under the old standard, both translation and transaction gains and losses were to be recorded in the group income statement – a procedure that resulted in heated debate in the financial community. We shall now look at all three standards in more detail. The section that follows focuses upon FASB 8. This is followed by a good look at FAS 52. This US standard is highlighted more prominently than its UK counterpart, SSAP 20, because it is clearer and more carefully drafted. The UK standard is examined, in the main, through a tabulation of differences between FAS 52 and SSAP 20.

Towards the end of this chapter, we acquaint readers with the contents of the US accounting requirements of FAS 133 which relates to 'accounting for derivative instruments and hedging activities' and with its counterpart IAS 39 (from the International Accounting Standards Board).

9.1 | FASB 8

FASB 8 was issued in 1975 and its objectives were 'to measure and express in dollars and in generally accepted principles the assets, liabilities, revenues, or expenses that are measured or denominated in foreign currency' (FASB, 1975). Under FASB 8, US firms were required to translate financial statements into US dollars according to the temporal method. The stated objective was to produce the same results as if the foreign entity's books had been maintained in the parent currency. Cash, receivables and payables would be translated at the current rate. Assets and liabilities carried at historic prices would be translated at the historical exchange rate. Assets and liabilities carried at current prices or at future exchange prices would be translated at the current exchange rate. Revenues and expenses in the profit and loss account would be translated at average rates for the accounting period, except for those items relating to assets carried at past exchange prices, such as depreciation (relating to fixed assets) and cost of goods sold (relating to inventory). These items would be translated at historical rates. All gains and losses, whether arising on translation of profit and loss accounts or balance sheets, would be taken direct to the income statement.

A substantial section of the US financial community was of the opinion that reporting results according to such a formula produced distortions which would mislead rather than inform. Clearly, the income statement of a US multinational might receive a big increment or decrement as the dollar respectively weakened or strengthened. And this would flow through to earnings per share. The pressure group that built up felt that gains and losses on foreign currency transactions should be taken directly to the consolidated income statement but that gains and losses arising from mere translation should be taken out of income.

Another concern was that certain items were not being translated logically. Inventory, for example, was translated primarily at historical exchange rates. So a rate change in one period might not affect profits until the period in which the inventory was sold. Many accountants were also concerned about the practical problems involved in keeping track of the historic costs and historical exchange rates for inventory, an asset that turns over very quickly. They preferred to translate inventory at current rates.

Another problem area was long-term debt. Although seemingly logically translated at current rates and hence exposed to exchange rate changes, many financial executives considered that it was incorrect to translate a fixed asset at historical rates and to have the asset sheltered from any foreign exchange gain or loss, while the debt used to finance the asset was exposed to exchange rate changes. Commentators were by no means unanimous in their suggestion of alternatives. Some proposed that the asset should be translated at the current rate to match the exposure of the debt. Others suggested that the translation methods for long-term debt and fixed assets were logical but that the gain or loss on the debt translation should be taken out of the income statement.

Mounting influential criticism, coupled with opinions within the Financial Accounting Standards Board and the US accounting profession to the effect that FASB 8 created misleading distortions in the reported profits of multinationals, led to its withdrawal and its replacement by FASB 52, subsequently referred to as FAS 52.

9.2 | FAS 52

In 1982, FAS 52 replaced FASB 8 as the guiding standard for translation of foreign currency accounts by US corporations. The new standard's stated objective was to

> provide information that is generally compatible with the expected economic effects of a rate change on an enterprise's cash flows and equity and, secondly, to reflect in consolidation statements the financial results and relationships of the individual consolidated entities as measured in their functional currencies in conformity with US generally accepted accounting principles. (FASB, 1981)

Unlike FASB 8, which permitted only the temporal method of translating financial statements, FAS 52 permits the use of two different methods, depending upon circumstances.

Before going into the mechanics of FAS 52 it is important to appreciate one of the standard's key concepts – namely that of the functional currency. An entity's functional currency is the currency of the primary economic environment in which the entity operates. In the case of a US exporter, the functional currency is normally the US dollar. In this case, the functional currency is also the reporting currency, as the US exporting company generates its financial statements in US dollars. If a US corporation had an independent subsidiary in France that exported goods to the United Kingdom, the functional currency of the French subsidiary would, most probably, be the euro. However, the reporting currency of the US parent of the French subsidiary would be the US dollar, the currency in which its consolidated financial statements are prepared.

In the case of a US company becoming involved in a foreign currency transaction, each asset, liability, revenue, expense, gain or loss arising from the transaction is to be recorded in the firm's functional currency at the exchange rate in effect at the transaction date. At each subsequent balance sheet date, any balances that are denominated in a currency other than the functional currency of the entity should be recorded at the new balance sheet rate, namely the current rate. So if a US importer expects to pay a UK exporter in pounds sterling for goods bought, the liability is denominated in pounds sterling, and its dollar value must be adjusted on each balance sheet to reflect the current exchange rate. The change in dollar value is treated as a foreign exchange gain or loss and, since it is a transaction gain or loss, it should be included in the determination of net income in the period in which the rate changes.

An example may usefully explain the point here. Assume that a US importer buys goods from a UK exporter on 1 December for £1m with payment to be made on 20 January following. Assume further that the US importer closes its books on 31 December and that the exchange rate moves from $1.6805 = £1 on 1 December to $1.6407 = £1 on 31 December, and to $1.6100 = £1 on 20 January. As can be seen from Table 9.1 (overleaf), the purchase of goods is booked on 1 December at the exchange rate prevailing then. But at the company's year-end, 31 December, the amount payable is revalued at the exchange rate prevailing then and the difference is taken to an exchange gain account which will, in turn, be taken to the credit of the company's profit and loss account. On 20 January settlement of the debt takes place at the exchange rate prevailing on that date, so that a further exchange gain is then booked.

Table 9.1 US company's books: transaction in £ sterling

		Dr	Cr
1 Dec.	Purchases	$1,680,500	
	Accounts payable		$1,680,500
	Purchase of goods of £1m converted @ $1.6805		
31 Dec.	Accounts payable	$39,800	
	Foreign exchange gain		$39,800
	Revaluation of payable of £1m @ $1.6407		
20 Jan.	Accounts payable	$1,640,700	
	Foreign exchange gain		$30,700
	Cash		$1,610,000
	Payment of £1m to creditor @ $1.6100 and		
	foreign exchange gain versus previous balance		

Note that under FAS 52 the gain on foreign exchange goes directly to the income statement in the period when the exchange rate changes, even though the liability has not been settled and the exchange rate could subsequently go the other way before ultimate settlement. In the example, the $39,800 is taken to the credit of the income statement before the debt is settled. This kind of treatment is in breach of the realization principle, one of the canons of accounting. Clearly, it contravenes the prudence concept in accounting under which revenues and profits are not anticipated, but are recognized by inclusion in the profit and loss account only when realized in the form of either cash or other assets, the ultimate cash realization of which can be assumed with reasonable certainty.

In the above example it was assumed that the US importer did not cover the sterling payable. It could have done so by entering into a forward contract. In terms of FAS 52, forward contracts create a number of problems which result in different accounting treatments according to the nature of, and the rationale for, the forward contract.

There are several reasons to enter into a forward contract. The reason may be:

■   to cover a transaction such as the import mentioned above;

■   to speculate on currency movements;

■   to hedge a net investment in a foreign entity;

■   to hedge a foreign currency commitment.

All of these give rise to different accounting treatments under FAS 52.

In the example described above, the US importer must deliver foreign currency to the UK exporter on 20 January and is unsure as to the future spot rate. To avoid this uncertainty, the importer may enter into a forward contract on 1 December with a banker to deliver dollars in return for pounds on 20 January. In these circumstances the cost of goods is effectively $1,680,500 plus or minus the forward discount or premium. Looked at another way, the importer then has a foreign currency receivable from the bank to offset the foreign currency payable to the exporter. Assuming that the size of the forward contract equals the size of the account payable, then every time the exchange rate changes, the value of the receivable changes, giving rise to a gain or loss that is exactly equal and opposite to the gain or loss on the foreign currency account payable. This gain or loss on the forward contract receivable is recognized in the income statement immediately, so it offsets the gain or loss on the account payable. The only accounting cost to the importer would then be the premium or discount on the forward contract, and that is written off over the life of the contract. The accounting treatment of forward contracts to cover a foreign currency transaction creates a neutral income statement effect.

If a firm enters into a forward contract to speculate on expected currency movements rather than to cover an exposure, any gains or losses on that contract are recognized immediately in income. The gain or loss is determined by multiplying the amount of the contract by the difference between the forward rate available on the balance sheet date and the original contracted rate, or the forward rate last used to measure a gain or loss.

If a US parent decides to enter into a forward contract or other foreign currency transaction – like a borrowing in the same currency – to hedge an investment in a foreign entity, the parent may include any gain or loss on the contract as a separate component of stockholders' equity rather than incorporating it in the income statement.

A firm may enter into a foreign currency commitment and hedge it with a forward contract. Here the premium or discount on the contract as well as any gain or loss resulting from exchange rate changes are deferred until the transaction date and are included in the foreign currency transaction. Thus the US importer might have entered into a commitment with the UK exporter in October to receive goods on 1 December. At the same time, the US importer might have entered into a forward contract to hedge its commitment. On 1 December any gains or losses and amortization of premium or discount would be added to the cost of the goods purchased from the exporter.

The idea of a borrowing to hedge an investment in a foreign entity is important. Take the example of a US parent company with a net investment in a Swiss subsidiary, for which the Swiss franc is the functional currency. Assume that the US parent borrows Swiss francs and designates the Swiss franc loan as a hedge of the net investment in the Swiss firm. The loan is in Swiss francs, which are not the functional currency of the US parent. The loan is therefore a foreign currency transaction. The loan is a liability and the net investment in Switzerland is an asset. Should the dollar/Swiss franc exchange rate move subsequently, the adjustment resulting from translation of the Swiss subsidiary's balance sheet would go in the opposite direction to the adjustment resulting from translation of the US parent company's Swiss franc debt. Should the adjustment from translation of the Swiss franc loan (after tax effects, if any) be less than or equal to the adjustment from translation of the Swiss subsidiary's balance sheet, both adjustments would be included in the analysis of changes in the cumulative translation adjustment and would be reflected in equity movements. However, should the adjustment from translation of the US parent's Swiss franc debt (after tax effects, if any) exceed the adjustment from translation of the Swiss subsidiary's balance sheet, the excess is, in FAS 52 terms, a transaction gain or loss which would be included in the consolidated income statement.

Ordinarily, for a borrowing to hedge a net investment, it should be in the same currency as the functional currency of the net investment hedged. But the standard allows for exceptions such as those relating to currencies that move in tandem. Where a foreign currency borrowing is not in the same currency as a net investment in a foreign country, then FAS 52 does not recognize a hedged position and in this case the gain or loss resulting from changes in the exchange rate against the currency of the borrowing would be viewed as an income statement item.

Reverting to forward contracts, it is important to realize that, in order for the separate accounting for forward contracts against foreign currency commitments to hold, two conditions must be met. First, the forward contract must be designated as a hedge on a foreign currency commitment and, secondly, the foreign currency commitment must be firm. The forward contract may be for an amount equal to the commitment on an after-tax basis, but any foreign exchange gains or losses on an amount in excess of that must be taken into the income statement rather than being dealt with via reserve accounting in the balance sheet. The idea of accounting for forward contracts is to match the recognition of contract gains and losses with those of the foreign currency transaction.

Earlier in this chapter, we discussed the relevance of the functional currency for FAS 52 accounting. As defined earlier, the functional currency is that of the primary economic environment where the entity operates. A US-owned French corporation that produces and sells for the French market might consider the euro as its functional currency, and the currency in which it also keeps its books and records. The functional currency would be translated into the parent company's reporting currency using the current rate method. This means that all assets and liabilities – bar equity – would be translated at the current rate. In addition, all revenues and expenses would be translated at a weighted average exchange rate for the accounting period concerned.

If it were decided that the functional currency was something other than the currency of the country where the entity was operating and that in which its books and records were being kept, then those books and records would have to be translated into the functional currency. Generally, in these circumstances management would decide that the reporting currency of the parent would be the functional currency. Translation would take place under the temporal method as with FASB 8. Again the translation process is designed to produce the same results as if the books and records had been maintained in the functional rather than the local currency.

Generally, the functional currency will be the local currency if the local operations are relatively self-contained and integrated with the environment. The parent's reporting currency is normally considered the functional currency if the foreign entity is an extension of and fairly dependent on its dealings with the parent. Management is responsible for deciding which is the functional currency and FAS 52 gives a series of guidelines for its selection. The standard uses a series of indicators which it classifies as follows:

- Cash flow indicators.

- Sales price indicators.

- Sales market indicators.

- Expense indicators.

- Financing indicators.

- Inter-company transactions indicators.

For further detail on these indicators, interested readers are referred to the actual standard, but the gist of the matter is that the choice of functional currency should flow from the question: in what currency are the above indicators designated?

Once the decision has been made as to which currency is the functional currency, translation can take place. The mechanics of translation are not difficult but a few problems need to be resolved. For example, a foreign entity might be conducting multiple business activities through branches or divisions, each with a different functional currency requiring a different translation method. A French subsidiary of a US corporation may have African subsidiaries that are considered an extension of the French firm. The African operations would be translated into euros using the temporal method. If the French firm were considered fairly independent of the US parent, then the French statements would be translated on consolidation into US dollars at the current rate.

Another problem concerns entities operating in highly inflationary countries, defined in FAS 52 as those in which cumulative inflation over a three-year period totals 100 per cent or more. Balance sheets of entities in these countries would be highly distorted if they were translated at the current exchange rate, so the standard requires that the functional currency should be the parent currency, with the use of the temporal method.

Finally, there is the question of how gains and losses are treated. When the functional currency is considered to be the local currency, then any gains or losses that arise merely from translating the financial statements into the parent currency using the current rate method are taken to a separate component of stockholders' equity rather than through the income statement. This is a major departure from FASB 8. If the temporal method is used for cases where the local currency is not considered to be the functional currency, then the foreign exchange gain or loss is taken directly to the income statement, as under FASB 8.

Compared with FASB 8, its successor allows a good deal of flexibility in choosing the method of translating financial statements. This recognizes the fact that there are inherent differences in foreign operations that require different methods of translation. However, lest the standard appear too flexible, it is important to note that, once management decides which is the functional currency of a foreign operation, it is not permitted to change without a significant change in the economic facts and circumstances prevailing relative to those at the time of the original choice.

Much more important, though, is the fact that translation gains and losses, where the functional currency is the local currency, are treated as a separate component of shareholders' equity, thereby taking these gains and losses out of the income statement. Finance directors, accountants and analysts have generally regarded this as a more realistic approach than that proposed by FASB 8.

One of the objectives of FAS 52 is to provide information compatible with the economic effects of a rate change on an enterprise's cash flows and equity. The new standard, for firms whose functional currency is the local rather than the parent currency, will always place such companies in a net exposed asset position because net worth is the only section of the balance sheet that is not translated at the current rate. This means that a parent with a subsidiary operating in a country whose currency is strong relative to the parent currency will recognize foreign exchange gains upon translation, since the home currency value of the net asset position rises as the foreign currency hardens. This is claimed to be consistent with the cash flow picture because the home currency value of dividends also rises as the foreign currency hardens.

The current rate method does not totally eliminate the impact of exchange rate changes on the income statement. This is because the subsidiary's income statement must still be translated into dollars. If the foreign currency is weakening relative to the dollar, then the dollar equivalent of net income will fall. This was experienced by US corporations with operations in Europe during the recession of the early 1980s. Income in local currency was not advancing much because of the recession but the strong dollar magnified this weak income picture. The result was the very weak dollar increments in some cases and declines in others.

Of course, where inflation is exceedingly high, the use of the temporal method is still recommended under FAS 52, so to an extent the objections to the temporal method remain.

Certainly, FAS 52 avoids the distortions in reported profit brought about by taking translation gains and losses to the income statement – as recommended by FASB 8. So it is claimed that published accounts become more relevant to managers and to the financial community. However, most of the serious evidence (see Chapter 10) is that financial analysts were not deceived by the inclusion of translation gains and losses in the income statement and that the reporting requirements of FASB 8 had no significant effect on security values of multinational corporations reporting under the old standard.

9.3 | SSAP 20

The UK accounting profession has made recommendations very similar to its counterpart in the United States. Although much less detailed and rigorous than FAS 52, the application of the UK standard produces such similar results that it would be an exercise in duplication to summarize them in detail here. One minor material difference is that SSAP 20 permits translation of the foreign subsidiary's income statement at either the closing rate or an average exchange rate for the period, provided that the method selected is consistently applied from one period to another. Differences in accounting principles applying to FAS 52 and SSAP 20 are highlighted in Table 9.2.

Table 9.2 Foreign currency translation differences: US and UK standards

United States (FAS 52)	United Kingdom (SSAP 20)
Translation of foreign currency financial statements	*Translation of foreign currency financial statements*
1. The entity's functional currency is defined as the currency of the primary economic environment in which the entity operates. Generally this is the currency of the environment in which the entity generates and expends cash.	1. The entity's local currency is defined as the currency of the primary economic environment in which it operates and generates net cash flows – broadly equivalent to the functional currency as defined in FAS 52.
2. For assets and liabilities, the exchange rate at the balance sheet date is used to convert the financial statements from the functional currency to the reporting currency. Revenues, expenses, gains and losses are to be translated at the exchange rate in effect when these items are recognized. In practice, an appropriately weighted average rate may be used.	2. As in the US standard, assets and liabilities are translated using the exchange rate at the balance sheet date. The profit and loss account may be translated using either the year-end rate or an average for the accounting period. Whichever procedure is adopted, it must be applied consistently.
3. Pure translation adjustments arising from the process of translating an entity's financial statements from the functional currency into the reporting currency should not be included in determining net income but are to be accumulated and reported as a separate component of consolidated shareholders' equity.	3. Pure translation adjustments arising from the process of translating an entity's accounts from its functional currency into the reporting currency as a group should be disclosed as a movement on group reserves – as in the US standard.
4. Highly inflationary economies include those with cumulative inflation of approximately 100% or more over a three-year period. Where the functional currency is that of a highly inflationary economy, the financial statements are to be remeasured as if the functional currency were the reporting currency. Essentially this means translation of non-monetary balance sheet and revenues and expenses related to non-monetary items using historical exchange rates and translation of all other items using the current rate. Gains or losses resulting therefrom are included in the determination of net income.	4. It is recommended that the local currency financial statements denominated in currencies of hyperinflationary economies, which are not defined in the standard, should be adjusted to reflect current price levels and then translated in the normal way.

Table 9.2 (cont'd)

United States (FAS 52)	United Kingdom (SSAP 20)

Foreign currency transactions

Foreign currency transactions

1. Foreign currency transactions are transactions denominated in a currency other than the entity's functional currency. At the date the transaction is recognized, each asset, liability, revenue expense, gain or loss arising from the transaction is to be measured and recorded in the functional currency of the recording entity using the exchange rate in effect at that date. At each balance sheet date, recorded balances that are denominated in a currency other than the functional currency of the recording entity are adjusted to reflect current exchange rate. Resulting remeasurement gains and losses – except for those items noted in (2) and (3) below – are included in the determination of net income for that period.

2. Gains and losses on inter-company foreign currency transactions that are of a long-term nature – that is, settlement is not planned or anticipated in the foreseeable future – are not to be included in determining net income but should be reported separately and accumulated in consolidated stockholders' equity.

3. Gains and losses on foreign currency transactions that are designated as, and are effective as, economic hedges of a net investment in a foreign entity are to be reported separately and accumulated in consolidated stockholders' equity. A foreign currency transaction shall be considered a hedge of an identifiable foreign currency commitment provided both of the following conditions are met:
   - The foreign currency transaction is designated as, and is effective as, a hedge of a foreign currency commitment.
   - The foreign currency commitment is firm. This latter bullet point requirement differs from FAS 80 (Accounting for futures contracts) and FAS 133 (Accounting for derivative instruments and hedging activities).

1. Foreign currency transactions should be translated and recorded at the exchange rate ruling on the transaction date. Monetary assets and liabilities – mainly cash and bank balances, loans (whether short-term or long-term) and receivables and payables – should be translated at the balance sheet date at the exchange rate ruling at that date. Gains or losses on both settled and unsettled transactions – except for those items noted in (2) and (3) below – will normally be taken to the profit and loss account, although in exceptional cases it may be necessary to consider restricting the extent to which gains on long-term monetary items are recognized.

2. Where investments in foreign enterprises have been made by means of long-term loans and inter-company deferred trading balances and such financing is intended to be, for all practical purposes, as permanent as equity, foreign exchange differences arising therefrom should be dealt with as an adjustment to reserves.

3. Where foreign currency borrowings have been used to finance or hedge an investment denominated in foreign currency, then gains and losses shall not be included in determining consolidated net income but rather taken to reserves and offset against the corresponding losses or gains on the underlying investments. The UK standard regarding hedge accounting is not as specific as the US regulation. Hedge accounting treatment is possible even though the foreign currency flow is not a committed one.

Table 9.2 (cont'd)

United States (FAS 52)	United Kingdom (SSAP 20)
4. Generally, a transaction that hedges a net investment should be denominated in the same currency as the functional currency of the net investment hedged. In some cases, it may not be practical or feasible to hedge in the same currency, and therefore a hedging transaction also may be denominated in a currency for which the exchange rate generally moves in tandem with the exchange rate for the functional currency of the investment hedged.	4. Unlike the US standard, the foreign currency borrowings may be in a different currency from that of the investment provided that such borrowings do not exceed the amount of cash which the investments are expected to generate, whether from profits or otherwise.

9.4 | Derivatives

Derivative instruments comprise financial products that have grown up around security, currency and commodity markets. Their price is a function of some underlying security, currency rate or other commodity. The term is usually used to embrace swaps, financial futures, options and a range of financially engineered instruments that are hybrids of other financial products. We have not yet examined these derivatives. In fact, we look at swaps in Chapter 14, financial futures in Chapter 15, options in Chapters 16 and 17, and financial engineering in Chapter 19. But the term derivatives also includes forwards which have already been introduced in this text. The price of a foreign exchange forward is based upon the underlying spot price adjusted for interest rates. In other words, the price of the derivative (the forward) is based upon (a function of) the price of an underlying security (the spot foreign exchange rate) adjusted according to a mathematical relationship. The idea underpinning derivatives is simple. But, as we will see in Part D of this text, their mathematical foundations can be complicated. We have merely introduced this definition here because derivatives become relevant in the remaining parts of this chapter – especially section 9.7.

9.5 | FAS 133

Effective for fiscal years beginning after 15 June 1999, FAS 133 is a US accounting standard concerned with accounting for derivative instruments and hedging activities. It requires that all derivative financial instruments should be reflected on a company's balance sheet at fair value. This concept has gained popularity over the years, but its deceptive simplicity disguises the more difficult question of what to do with movements in fair values between one reporting period and the next. Also, the question

Table 9.3 Examples of fair-value and cash flow hedges

Fair-value hedges
- Foreign currency forward or foreign exchange swap (see Chapter 14) hedging a foreign currency money market deal
- Hedge of an unrecognized firm commitment
- Interest rate swap (see Chapter 14) hedging a fixed rate loan
- Commodity future (see Chapter 15) hedging commodity inventory

Cash flow hedges
- Foreign exchange forward hedging a forecast revenue or expense transaction
- Interest rate swap (see Chapter 14) hedging a floating rate loan
- Option hedging (see Chapters 16 and 17) forecast purchase of a fixed asset
- Commodity future (see Chapter 15) hedging uncommitted purchase or sale of commodity

arises of how fair values are to be determined in situations where there is no readily available market price, for example, for a particular over-the-counter instrument.

In a nutshell, the points in FAS 133 to be noted are as follows. All derivatives are to be recorded at fair value, whether they are assets or liabilities, on the balance sheet. Prior to the introduction of FAS 133, derivatives were recorded on the balance sheet through various methods of measurement other than fair value (such as historic cost, spot or simply nil). Second, the accounting standard requires that unrealized gains and losses resulting from movements in the balance sheet fair values of derivatives between periods should be recorded through the profit and loss account. Essentially, this is merely mark-to-market accounting (an expression that means do the valuation according to market value), but here comes the crunch – two main exceptions to this rule exist: fair-value hedges and cash flow hedges. But what do these mean?

A fair-value hedge is a hedge of an exposure to changes in the fair value of a recognized asset or liability – basically (with exceptions) a hedge of the value of a balance sheet item. Gains and losses resulting from movements in fair values of instruments qualifying as fair-value hedges are to be recorded in the profit and loss account, as are gains and losses resulting from fair-value changes in the hedged item. This should leave no net profit and loss account effect (except that due to any hedge ineffectiveness) since the gains and losses on the hedging and the hedged items should offset each other.

A cash flow hedge is a hedge of an exposure to variability in cash flows of a recognized asset or liability or of a forecast transaction. Essentially, this is a hedge of an uncertain or unquantified flow. Gains and losses from movements in fair values of instruments qualifying as cash flow hedges are to be recorded directly in equity. Subsequently, these gains and losses are to be reclassified into earnings when the hedged item affects earnings. The effect would be to achieve symmetry by cancelling out in the profit and loss account. Thus, the equity section of the balance sheet acts as a holding tank for gains and losses on cash flow hedges until these are recycled to earnings to coincide with the hedged item (for example, a forecast sale, which is being hedged) actually occurring.

Table 9.3 lists some examples of the types of hedge that may qualify for fair-value and cash flow hedging. The effect should be that all derivatives are carried at their fair values on the balance sheet and that earnings logically reflect the effect of hedging (this means no net profit or loss effect other than through any residual hedge ineffectiveness). This is achieved via symmetrical accounting of results on hedging and hedged items. In theory, the objective of marking to market, without putting unnecessary earnings volatility into the profit and loss accounts of companies using derivatives for hedging, is achieved.

However, if companies are to benefit from reduced earnings volatility from the hedge accounting rules of FAS 133, then clear, detailed policies and procedures must be established. This needs to be done to ensure that such hedging activities are compliant with the accounting standard, in terms of documentation, linkage with underlying exposures, measurement of fair values and, most importantly, monitoring of hedging effectiveness, which must remain high throughout the life of the hedge and the hedged item. This requirement for high effectiveness in monitoring may mean that strategies that previously qualified for hedge accounting will no longer meet the rules. The procedural burden is that effectiveness must be measured throughout the life of a hedge, and not just on the basis of a beginning and end valuation.

A similar International Accounting Standard, IAS 39 (Financial Instruments: recognition and measurement), proposes almost identical requirements and is discussed in section 9.7 of this chapter.

9.6 | FRS 13

It should be mentioned that there is a UK accounting standard operative (from April 1999) on disclosures relating to derivatives and other financial instruments. This standard is numbered FRS 13 and requires narrative and numerical disclosures as follows. In respect of narrative disclosure, companies must explain, either in the accounts or in an accompanying document (such as the Operating and Financial Review) cross-referenced to the accounts:

- the role of financial instruments in changing or creating the risks faced by the company;

- the approach of directors of the company to managing these risks, including a description of the objectives, policies and strategies for issuing and holding financial instruments;

- any decision to change these objectives, policies and strategies after the year-end.

Furthermore, companies must give numerical disclosures dealing with the following:

- Interest rate risk (total borrowings by currency sub-analysed into fixed rate, floating rate and interest-free, with the weighted average period until maturity). The analysis is to be done after taking account of swaps, forward contracts and other non-optional derivatives.

- Currency risk (net monetary assets by currency, excluding those on which exchange movements are taken to reserves under SSAP 20). Again, the analysis is to have regard to the effect of non-optional derivatives.

- Liquidity risk (maturity analysis of borrowings and undrawn committed facilities).

- Fair values (for each category of financial instrument, book value compared with either total fair values, or total positive and total negative fair values).

- Financial instruments used for trading (for each category of financial instrument, the net gain or loss in the year and the fair value of assets and liabilities at the year-end).

- Financial instruments used for hedging (unrecognized gains and losses deferred to future periods and those deferred in previous periods recognized in the current period).

The accounting standard refers to derivatives and financial instruments. However, financial instruments are defined in FRS 13 so as to include virtually everything in a company's balance sheet apart from tangible and intangible fixed assets, investments in subsidiaries, associates and joint ventures, inventory, tax and equity shareholders' funds. Even trade debtors and creditors are 'financial instruments' under the FRS 13 usage of the term.

FRS 13 requires all companies covered by the FRS to give narrative disclosures and numerical disclosures. However, these differ between those required for:

- companies not in the financial services sector;

- banks;

- listed financial services companies other than banks.

The summary above deals only with the requirements for companies not in the general financial services sector.

FRS 13 involves a major information-gathering exercise. The detailed requirements are complex. For example, the required analysis of monetary items by currency seems simple, until it is realized that it must, in effect, include only those items on which exchange differences are taken to the group profit and loss account. Thus a US dollar debtor of a UK company would be included in the analysis, but one held by a US subsidiary would not. However, any sterling liability of the US dollar subsidiary (which could include an inter-company balance with the UK parent) would be included.

9.7 │ IAS 39

Listed companies within the European Union must ensure that their annual accounts comply with the International Accounting Standards reporting requirements by no later than 2005.

In essence, the requirements of FAS 133 and IAS 39 follow similar lines. To re-iterate, both sets of guidelines stipulate that companies must report their financial derivatives and any change in their value. In both accounting regimes, an essential distinction is drawn in accordance with the purpose for which derivatives are used. There is a distinction between:

- derivatives that are used as a hedge;

- derivatives that cannot be considered to be a hedge.

A financial derivative is deemed to be a hedge if it seeks to eliminate a foreign exchange and/or interest rate risk pertaining to either a specific asset or liability item in a balance sheet, or any future flow, claim or liability that is not yet reflected in the balance sheet.

Under both standards, derivatives are required to satisfy similar strict criteria to qualify as a hedge. In the first place, a company needs to formulate risk management policies. Then, when it acquires a financial derivative, the company must clearly specify and document its relationship with the relevant asset or liability, future or otherwise. In this respect, the company needs to demonstrate that it is reasonable to assume that the hedge is effective in offsetting value changes. The company will subsequently need to demonstrate that this hedge maintains its effectiveness at all reporting dates. This means that the company must show that the value of the hedge is not less than 80 per cent and not more than 125 per cent of the value of the asset or liability that is being hedged.

In terms of accounting for hedging and non-hedging transactions, any change in the value of a financial derivative that cannot be held to be a hedge, must be accounted for in the profit and loss account of the company in question. This means that the change in value of a financial derivative that can be treated as a hedge is accounted for in the same way as that of the underlying asset or liability that is hedged, whether this is a future item or otherwise. This treatment is precisely consistent with that mentioned in section 9.5 on FAS 133.

Companies that are unable to provide adequate evidence and/or documentation revealing the relationship of the hedge with the relevant underlying asset or liability, together with details of its effectiveness according to these guidelines, run the risk that they will have to account for variations in the value of financial derivatives (which could be considerable) in the profit and loss account.

9.8 | Summary

- The accounting professions in the United States, the United Kingdom and in many other advanced countries now have almost identical rules for accounting for foreign currencies in published accounts.

- Generally speaking, translation of foreign currency items uses the all-current rate method.

- Transaction gains, whether realized or not, are accounted for through the profit and loss account. But there is a major exception – and this relates to a foreign currency denominated borrowing. Where a transaction profit or loss, whether realized or not, arises from taking on a foreign currency borrowing in a situation in which the borrowing can be designated as a hedge for a net investment denominated in foreign currency, then the gain or loss on the borrowing, if it is less than the net investment hedged, would be accounted for by movements in reserves rather than through the income statement. If this kind of transaction gain or loss exceeds the amount of the loss or gain respectively on the net investment hedged, then the excess gain or loss is to be reported in the profit and loss account.

■ Note that under the US standard, to qualify for the above hedge qualification, the foreign borrowing must be in the same currency as the investment hedged or one which moves in tandem with it. The UK standard is not specific on this point.

■ Non-transaction gains and losses are to be dealt with by reserve accounting direct to the balance sheet rather than through the profit and loss account.

■ According to US accounting rules, translations of foreign currency denominated profit and loss accounts are to be made at the average exchange rate during the accounting period. The UK standard allows the use of either the current rate or the average rate for this purpose. It is fair to say that opinion in the United Kingdom is moving towards the average exchange rate method.

■ Note the effects of hedging contractual and forecast flows under FAS 133 and IAS 39. Essentially, should the hedge be totally effective, the item, whether committed or forecast, should not result in earnings volatility since the income statement is to reflect the symmetry of the hedged position.

9.9 | End of chapter questions

Question 1
Consider a period in which the US dollar weakens against most foreign currencies. How does this affect the reported earnings of a US-based MNC with subsidiaries all over the world?

Question 2
Consider a period in which the US dollar strengthens against most foreign currencies. How will this affect the reported earnings of a US-based MNC with subsidiaries all over the world?

Question 3
If US based MNCs are concerned with how shareholders react to changes in consolidated earnings, but prefer not to hedge their translation exposure, how might they attempt to reduce shareholder reaction to a decline in consolidated earnings that results from a strengthening dollar?

Test bank 1

Exercises

Foreign exchange problems

In these problems assume that all interest rates quoted are per annum rates. Calculate 90 day rates by taking one quarter of the annual rate. Also assume that, where only one rate is quoted, rather than a bid/offer rate, deals may be done at this rate whether they are purchase or sale deals, lend or borrow deals. This is, of course, a simplifying assumption. Also disregard any transaction costs; for substantial deals these are generally taken care of in the bid/offer spread. Take one month as one twelfth of a year, two months as one sixth – and so on.

1. The spot rate for the Swiss franc (CHF) in New York is USD0.55.

    (a) What should the spot price for the US dollar to the Swiss franc be in Zurich?
    (b) Should the dollar be quoted at CHF1.85 in Zurich, how would the market react?

2. When the Swiss franc spot rate was quoted at USD0.55 in New York, the US market was quoting sterling at USD1.60.

    (a) What should the price of the pound to the Swiss franc be in Zurich?
    (b) If sterling were quoted at CHF2.80 to the pound sterling in Zurich, what profit opportunities would exist?

3. Your company has to make a USD1m payment in three months' time. The dollars are available now. You decide to invest them for three months and you are given the following information:

    ■ the US dollar deposit rate is 8 per cent p.a.;

    ■ the sterling deposit rate is 10 per cent p.a.;

    ■ the spot exchange rate is GBP1 = USD1.80;

    ■ the three-month forward rate is GBP1 = USD1.78.

    (a) Where should your company invest for the better return?
    (b) Assuming that interest rates and the spot exchange rate remain as above, what forward rate would yield an equilibrium situation?

(c) Assuming that the US dollar interest rate and the spot and forward rates remain as in the original question, where would you invest if the sterling deposit rate were 14 per cent per annum?

(d) With the originally stated spot and forward rates and the same dollar deposit rate, what is the equilibrium sterling deposit rate?

4. The spot rate for the Danish krone is USD0.1500 and the three-month forward rate is USD0.1505. Your company is prepared to speculate that the Danish krone will move to USD0.1650 by the end of three months.

    (a) Are the quotations given direct or indirect Copenhagen quotations?
    (b) How would the speculation be undertaken using the spot market only?
    (c) How would the speculation be arranged using forward markets?
    (d) If your company were prepared to put USD1m at risk on the deal, what would the profit outturns be if expectations were met? Ignore all interest rate implications.
    (e) How would your answer to (d) above differ were you to take into account interest rate implications?

5. A foreign exchange trader gives the following quotes for the Ruritanian doppel spot, one-month, three-month and six-month to a US-based treasurer.

    USD0.02478/80   4/6   9/8   14/11

    (a) Calculate the outright quotes for one, three and six months forward.
    (b) If the treasurer wished to buy Ruritanian doppels three months forward, how much would he or she pay in dollars?
    (c) If he or she wished to purchase US dollars one month forward, how much would the treasurer have to pay in Ruritanian doppels?
    (d) Assuming that Ruritanian doppels are being bought, what is the premium or discount, for the one-, three- and six-month forward rates in annual percentage terms?
    (e) What do the above quotations imply in respect of the term structure of interest rates for US dollars and Ruritanian doppels?

6. You are given the following spot quotations in London:

    USD1 = CHF1.5485/95
    USD1 = AUD1.7935/45
    GBP1 = USD1.6325/35

    Calculate the following bid/offer quotations, also in London:

    (a) CHF against AUD
    (b) GBP against AUD

Foreign exchange rates

Consider the tabulation below which is given by a bank to a customer. For questions 1 to 16, the required rate is against the home currency, which is sterling.

Spot	USD1.6325–35 Premium	AUD2.30–2.30$^3/_4$ Premium	JPY263.15–25
1 month forward	0.75–0.73 cents	$^5/_8$ – $^1/_2$ cents	0.15 yen premium 0.10 yen discount
2 months forward	1.35–1.32 cents	$1^1/_8$ –1 cents	0.17 yen premium 0.08 yen discount
3 months forward	2.03–2.00 cents	$1^5/_8$ –$1^1/_2$ cents	0.19 yen premium 0.06 yen discount

The word 'premium' or 'discount' implies that the foreign currency quoted at the head of each column is at the premium or discount respectively. For questions 1–16, do the calculation against the home currency, that is sterling.

1. At what rate will the bank buy spot USD?

2. At what rate will the customer buy JPY three months forward?

3. At what rate will the customer sell USD one month forward?

4. At what rate will the bank sell spot yen?

5. At what rate will the customer buy AUD spot?

6. At what rate will the bank buy JPY two months forward?

7. At what rate will the customer buy USD two months forward?

8. At what rate will the bank sell USD two months forward?

9. At what rate will the bank buy AUD three months forward?

10. At what rate will the customer sell JPY one month forward?

11. At what rate will the bank buy USD three months forward?

12. At what rate will the customer sell JPY three months forward?

13. At what rate will the customer sell USD three months forward?

14. At what rate will the bank sell JPY one month forward?

15. At what rate will the bank buy AUD one month forward?

16. At what rate will the bank sell AUD three months forward?

For questions 17–22 calculate the annual percentage forward premium/discount, state which currency is at the premium, and indicate where interest rates should be higher if interest rate parity holds.

17. Home currency versus USD, 1 month. Assume you are a buyer of USD.

18. Home currency versus USD, 3 months. Assume you are a buyer of home currency.

19. Home currency versus USD, 3 months. Assume you are a seller of USD.

20. Home currency versus JPY, 3 months. Do the calculation on middle prices.

21. Home currency versus JPY, 3 months. Assume you are a seller of home currency.

22. Home currency versus AUD, 2 months. Assume you are a buyer of home currency.

▍Multiple choice questions

There is one right answer only to each question.

1. If a firm based in the Netherlands wishes to avoid the risk of exchange rate movements, and is due to receive USD100,000 in 90 days, it could:

    (a) enter into a 90-day forward purchase of US dollars for euros;
    (b) enter into a 90-day forward sale of US dollars for euros;
    (c) purchase US dollars 90 days from now at the spot rate;
    (d) sell US dollars 90 days from now at the spot rate.

2. Under a fixed exchange rate system:

    (a) a forward foreign exchange market does not exist as it would be pointless since rates do not move;
    (b) central bank intervention in the foreign exchange market is not necessary since rates do not move;
    (c) central bank intervention in the foreign exchange market is often necessary;
    (d) central bank intervention in the foreign exchange market is not permitted.

3. Given a home country and a foreign country, purchasing power parity suggests that:

    (a) the home currency will depreciate if the current home inflation rate exceeds the current foreign interest rate;
    (b) the home currency will depreciate if the current home interest rate exceeds the current foreign interest rate;
    (c) the home currency will appreciate if the current home inflation rate exceeds the current foreign inflation rate;
    (d) the home currency will depreciate if the current home inflation rate exceeds the current foreign inflation rate.

4. If purchasing power parity were to hold even in the short run, then:

    (a) real exchange rates should tend to increase over time;
    (b) real exchange rates should tend to decrease over time;
    (c) real exchange rates should be stable over time;
    (d) quoted nominal exchange rates should be stable over time.

5. If Euro-sterling interest rates were consistently below Eurodollar interest rates, then for the international Fisher effect to hold:

    (a) the value of the British pound would tend to appreciate against the dollar;
    (b) the value of the British pound would tend to depreciate against the dollar;

(c)   the real value of the British pound would remain constant most of the time;
(d)   the value of the British pound against the dollar would appreciate in some periods and depreciate in others, but on average, there would be a zero rate of appreciation.

6.   The following information is available:

$ deposit rate for 1 year	= 11 per cent
$ borrowing rate for 1 year	= 12 per cent
Ruritanian doppel deposit rate for 1 year	= 8 per cent
Ruritanian doppel borrowing rate for 1 yearm	= 10 per cent
Ruritanian doppel forward rate for 1 year	= $0.40
Ruritanian doppel spot rate	= $0.39

A US exporter denominates its Ruritanian exports in Ruritanian doppels (RUD) and expects to receive RUD600,000 in one year. What will be the approximate value of these exports in 1 year in US dollars if the firm executes a forward hedge?

(a) $234,000
(b) $238,584
(c) $240,000
(d) $236,127

7.   If direct spot quotations in New York and London were $1.5995–1.6000 and £0.6250–0.6254 respectively, arbitrage profits per $1m would be:

(a)   0
(b) $313
(c) $327
(d) $640

8.   Calculate the forward per annum premium or discount given the following quotes. Spot £1 = $1.4000; 3 months forward £1 = $1.4200.

(a)   The $ is at a premium of 1.43 per cent.
(b)   The $ is at a discount of 1.43 per cent.
(c)   The $ is at a premium of 5.71 per cent.
(d)   The $ is at a discount of 5.71 per cent.

9.   The international Fisher effect suggests that should pound interest rates exceed US dollar interest rates:

(a)   the pound's value will remain constant;
(b)   the pound will be at a discount on the dollar;
(c)   the pound will depreciate against the dollar;
(d)   UK inflation rate will decrease.

10.   Inflation in the United States and Sweden is expected to be 4 and 9 per cent, respectively, in the forthcoming year and 6 and 7 per cent, respectively, in the year

following. The current spot rate for the Swedish krona is $0.1050. Based on purchasing power parity, the expected spot value for the Swedish krona in two years would be:

(a) $0.1111
(b) $0.1024
(c) $0.0992
(d) $0.1074

Part C

Hedging

There is a wide range of methods available to minimize foreign exchange risk. This section is devoted to examining whether currency risk should, logically, be managed and then focuses upon internal and the third-party contract (external) means of managing foreign exchange risk.

10 Does foreign exchange exposure matter?

Most of the arguments about whether or not foreign exchange exposure matters draw on material summarized in the earlier chapters on the four-way equivalence model, definitions of foreign exchange exposure and the empirical work on the four-way model. Foreign exchange exposure can be looked at under three separate headings: transaction exposure, economic exposure and translation exposure. Chapter 8 provided a discussion on these different perspectives of foreign exchange exposure. In this chapter we consider the extent to which each should be a relevant factor for the corporate treasurer in the maximization of the present value of the firm.

10.1 ∣ Transaction exposure

Transaction exposure is concerned with how changes in exchange rates affect the value, in home currency terms, of anticipated cash flows denominated in foreign currency relating to transactions already entered into.

According to the bulk of empirical work on the expectations theory part of the four-way equivalence model, the current forward rate is, at least in the longer run, an unbiased predictor of the future spot rate. If in the long term using the forward rate to approximate the future spot rate results in being on the high side as often as on the low side – which is what the term 'unbiased predictor' means – then it follows that covering forward will be of little worth to the firm that has a large number of transactions denominated in foreign currency. It might as well not cover forward but take the spot rate at the time the payable or receivable matures, since the results from adopting the strategy of covering forward will, in the long run, equal the results achieved from running the debt to maturity and taking the spot rate. Indeed, given that foreign exchange dealers charge their customers a wider bid/offer spread on forward contracts compared with spot transactions, it follows that avoiding cover should be more profitable in the long run.

But it can also be an extremely dangerous policy. By failing to cover transaction exposure, a firm may incur a vast loss on a single very large receivable or payable denominated in a foreign currency. This may result in an overall loss for the firm in a particular financial period, which could, in its turn, lead to all sorts of financial distress. It is not much comfort to the finance director of a company which has just failed as a direct result of not covering transaction exposure that it would have been all right in the long run because at some time in the future it could hope to win on another contract the amount that it has just lost on this one. There is little consolation in the company being all right in the long run if it is dead in the short run. Bearing this in mind, the prudent finance director will argue that covering forward reduces potential variability in home currency cash flows as well as in profits. Thus covering forward reduces some of the threat of short-term financial problems. In the longer term, the cost of such insurance against foreign exchange risk is small, since it effectively amounts to the dealer's spread on forward transactions less the spread on spot deals. It may not be the case that this policy maximizes profits in the long run but from the standpoint of a risk-averse satisfier it has clear appeal.

Remember that all of the above argument about expectations theory is based upon the forward rate being an unbiased predictor of the future spot rate in the long run. It needs to be emphasized, and reiterated, that the empirical evidence on this part of the four-way model (see Chapter 7) indicates that, for short periods when a currency can be identified as being in a phase of strength against other currencies, the forward rate tends, on average, to underestimate the strength of the currency being analysed in terms of its future spot rate. And the reverse seems to apply in respect of phases of weakness in the short term.

It is understandable that the firm that enters into very few transactions denominated in foreign currency may cover all of them. It is also understandable that risk-averse managers in companies with a vast number of transactions denominated in foreign currency would make a habit of covering them. However, treasurers in such firms usually adopt policies of selective covering. The rationale of this tactic and its frequent mode of operation are considered further in Chapters 11 and 13.

The same kind of argument, but with some essential differences, applies with respect to lending and borrowing denominated in foreign currencies. Most lending or borrowing involves respective receipt or payment of interest at regular intervals with capital repayment at a specified date. According to the international Fisher effect, the penalty for borrowing in a hard currency will be exactly offset by the benefit of a low interest rate. Perhaps this can best be illustrated by an example. Assume that the expected inflation in the United Kingdom is higher than that in Switzerland. If we begin from a base year in which exchange rates between sterling and the Swiss franc are in equilibrium, then we would anticipate, via purchasing power parity, that the Swiss franc would strengthen against sterling. And, via the Fisher effect, we would expect interest rates in Switzerland to be lower than sterling interest rates. Thus the international Fisher effect would be suggesting a weakening of sterling against the Swiss franc compensated for by lower Swiss franc interest rates. So a company considering raising £5m might do so in sterling and it might expect then to pay a higher interest rate than would be the case were that same company to raise the money in Swiss francs. But raising the money in Swiss francs would have the drawback that when repayment was due the company would probably have to find in excess of £5m sterling because of the strengthening of the Swiss franc during the period that the loan was outstanding. Leaving aside imperfections in the market created by taxation treatment of foreign exchange losses on loans (but note that in the real world these market imperfections created by non-symmetrical tax treatment are far too important to be left aside), the international Fisher effect would predict that the gain resulting from the lower interest rate on the Swiss franc borrowing would be exactly offset by the loss on capital repayment at maturity.

The above kind of situation is illustrative of how the international Fisher effect underpins the argument that foreign exchange exposure on borrowings does not matter. But, of course, we have seen in our overview of empirical investigations of the four-way equivalence relationship that our deductive, theoretical model does not hold too often in the real world. Some studies suggest that international Fisher holds in the medium to long term, but there is other work that suggests that we can wait an awfully long time for international Fisher to assert itself. For the international company these findings are crucial. In the long run our company borrowing in hard currencies might expect to come out even and thus be indifferent about the currency denomination of its borrowings, but in the short run its Swiss borrowing might wipe it out.

This kind of problem has dramatically affected more than a few UK companies. Laker Airways arranged lease finance denominated in US dollars for the bulk of its aircraft. When the dollar strengthened, the company's balance sheet and cash flow ability to service debt came under excessive strain. J. Lyons, another UK company, had a wealth of Swiss franc borrowings on its balance sheet. As sterling weakened against the Swiss franc, its plight became similar to Laker's. Laker went out of business partly, but by no means solely, due to its dollar borrowings; Lyons was rescued when it was taken over by Allied Breweries but its problems stemmed from uncovered hard currency debt.

The problem that treasurers of international companies have is not just that international Fisher is often found empirically to be a long-run phenomenon, but also that when they undertake a borrowing denominated in foreign currency the exchange rates between the home currency and the foreign one may not be in equilibrium. Subsequent correction of the disequilibrium can incur a vast loss (or profit) for the international borrower.

Perhaps it is fair to conclude that, were the four-way equivalence model to hold in the real world immutably and with no time lags, and if tax is ignored, then transaction exposure should not matter. That the real world is not so convenient as the theoretical one, that the four-way equivalence model does involve time lags, and very big ones, and that tax treatment of interest and currency gains and losses are not entirely symmetrical mean that transaction exposure is very important to international financial executives. In short, it needs to be managed.

10.2 | Economic exposure

Economic exposure refers to the possibility that the present value of future operating cash flows of a business, expressed in the parent currency, may change because of a change in foreign exchange rates. According to purchasing power parity theory, exchange rate changes are associated with different relative rates of inflation. The argument that economic exposure does not matter draws on the PPP theorem.

Devaluation of the home currency tends to favour companies competing in export markets. It also has a favourable impact on import-competing areas. And it creates advantages for firms that are domestically sourced (imports become relatively more expensive) and domestically financed. Revaluations have precisely opposite effects.

A relatively high home-country inflation rate, if not accompanied by devaluation, has an adverse effect on companies competing in export markets and those competing domestically with imported goods. It adversely affects firms that are domestically sourced and (because the tendency will be for the home interest rate to rise) domestically financed.

Devaluation creates advantages that correct disadvantages flowing from high relative inflation rates. The benefits created for some firms by devaluation should offset earlier adverse effects created by inflation. If relative inflation rates are being accompanied by appropriate exchange rate adjustments, as predicted by PPP, it may be argued that we have a situation where the overall effect is neutral. The benefits of devaluation exactly offset the earlier penalties of inflation. But should this be universally true? Maybe the above argument would be applicable to the firm all of whose costs were inflating at the same rate as the general level of inflation in the country in which it was based. The devaluation or revaluation would then be exactly offsetting movements in the firm's specific costs. In these circumstances economic exposure would not matter to the firm.

Of course, it is most unusual for the firm's individual costs to move exactly in line with general inflation. And where they do not, economic exposure will matter to the firm. Indeed, multinationals consider relocating or switching manufacture from one country to another, or altering the sourcing of cost inputs, to correct for local costs having inflated in excess of general inflation levels or, more specifically, in excess of competitor nations' costs.

If, then, economic exposure does matter to the international company, should it endeavour to hedge this exposure through forward market purchases or sales of currency? The author believes that the answer to this question veers towards the negative. This is not because economic exposure is based on uncertain cash flows or because it is difficult to quantify since it involves detailed analysis of elasticities of demand, but because there are easier ways to deal with the fact that the present value of expected cash flows accruing from operations may alter in response to changes in exchange rates. This simple way involves financing operations, either partially or wholly, in the foreign currency (or currencies) which is judged as having a significant impact upon the present value of operations. It should be mentioned that this approach does not provide an exact cover for economic exposure. This arises because the hedge via financing is a function of relative inflation rates, with differences corrected via PPP; the changing value of operating cash flows is affected by relative specific price and cost increases and these are only partially corrected by changing exchange rates based on general inflation levels.

It should be mentioned that the author has come across anecdotal evidence of international companies actively managing economic exposure via forward markets and via currency options. This involves the calculation of exposed net present values based on anticipated operating cash flows, deducting from them the hedge effect achieved by financing and then using forward and/or option markets to hedge net exposure should this be deemed the advantageous course of action.

It should be mentioned that there is a strong case for monitoring and managing economic exposure by entering into forward or option markets to protect the present value of expected future cash flows where the tenor of the firm's involvement in a particular overseas environment has a finite time horizon, such as a joint venture which will terminate after, say, three years of operation. Since the firm's involvement does not span sufficient time to ensure a cycle running through to equilibrium, economic exposure can be material. However, this kind of situation has more of a transaction exposure dimension (although the residual cash flow is not yet certain or contracted), since the residual value of the project will, presumably, be remitted to headquarters at the end of the period of overseas involvement.

10.3 | Translation exposure

Translation exposure arises as a result of the process of consolidation of foreign currency items into group financial statements denominated in the currency of the parent company. This was discussed in Chapters 8 and 9. Some items frequently viewed as being solely translation exposure are essentially transaction exposure items. This is the case with respect to borrowings or lendings denominated in foreign currency. Repayment of the loan requires cash to pass from borrower to lender, and this creates a cash flow exposure. With respect to the question of whether foreign exchange exposure matters for these kinds of item, which may be classified as both transaction exposure and translation exposure, the answer should flow from viewing them as transaction, rather than as translation, items.

It will be recalled from earlier chapters that different translation methods may have different impacts upon a firm's reported earnings per share. But do these different accounting methods affect the valuation of the firm? Clearly, from a theoretical standpoint, the accounting methods of reporting for overseas subsidiaries' results should not impact on their own upon valuation of a subsidiary. Its valuation to the parent company should be a function of expected future cash flows which are distributable to the parent. Admittedly, this may alter as exchange rates alter. It can be argued from a theoretical point of view that, should subsidiaries' values change in response to movements in exchange rates, then it is logically a result of their present value, in home currency terms, being perceived by investors to have altered. Note that this theoretical argument has nothing to do with accounting reporting for foreign operations.

But the key question is: how does the investment community interpret changing subsidiary results based on changed translation methods? In other words, whether translation exposure matters is essentially an empirical question. Our answer therefore draws on empirical investigations. Since the relevant studies have not yet been referred to elsewhere in this book, it is necessary to spend some time discussing them.

Under FASB 8, translation gains and losses were included in the group consolidated profit and loss account and caused wide fluctuations in reported corporate profits and earnings per share. The effect of the US standard brought forth such comments as 'nothing is surer to upset a chief executive than an accounting provision that disturbs the smooth year-to-year earnings gains so cherished by securities analysts'. This kind of reasoning on the part of some large multinationals has undoubtedly led to some questionable decisions designed to hedge translation exposure by incurring transaction exposure. Srinivasula (1983) describes a situation where ITT, the US-based multinational, sold forward $600m worth of foreign currencies with a view partially to hedging its balance sheet exposure. The dollar fell relative to most foreign currencies and this resulted in a translation gain and an offsetting loss on forward cover. This gain was unrealized but the forward loss involved a cash loss in the order of $48m. Although ITT achieved its objective of partially hedging balance sheet exposure, it could be argued that such transactions make little or no economic sense. Of course, FAS 52 obviates the need for any company to take this illogical action. It is worth mentioning that ITT was by no means alone in its response to accounting exposure under FASB 8. A number of studies reported similar actions by US-based multinationals designed to counter translation exposure by incurring transaction exposure. A paper by Griffin (1979) summarizes a number of studies by other researchers into the effects FASB 8 had on corporate financial policy. It should be noted, though, that it was a minority of US multinationals which responded to exposure under FASB 8 by taking on transaction exposure in the opposite direction.

But did the reporting requirements of FASB 8 affect the stock market performance of companies reporting translation gains and losses? Clearly, this is entirely an empirical question. There have been at least three major investigations in this area. These have been undertaken by Makin (1977), Dukes (1978) and Garlicki, Fabozzi and Fonfeder (1987); their results are by no means identical. Makin assessed share price performance for three sample groups comprising typical multinational companies, comparable domestic companies and, thirdly, a group of multinationals which were considered to be particularly sensitive to FASB 8 reporting requirements. He found that the accounting standard requirements did not affect share price performance for the typical multinational group, but he did find a downgrading in share price for the sensitive group. While he interprets this as implying that FASB 8 reporting requirements may affect share prices, Giddy (1978a) has challenged this interpretation on the basis that the sensitive group of multinationals would be affected not only in terms of income statement reporting but also in terms of dollar remittances from dividends declared by overseas subsidiaries – an area to which Makin's study failed to address itself.

Dukes (1978) sought to investigate the stock market effect of FASB 8 reporting requirements in a study in which he compared security returns from a sample of 479 multinational companies with a control sample of domestic firms. The empirical results are that the security return behaviour of portfolios of multinational firms, despite the impact of FASB 8 on reported earnings, is not significantly different from the return behaviour of comparable portfolios of domestic firms. Although Dukes' methodology can be challenged, his conclusions are that the US stock market is not fooled by pure translation gains and losses.

Table 10.1 Gearing can make pure translation exposure relevant

	Base case	Subsequent movement to
Exchange rate $ to £	1.80	1.40
Assets (£m)		
In UK	100	100
In USA ($180m)	100	128.6
	200	228.6
Financed by (£m):		
Shareholders' funds	100	100
US$ debt ($180m)	100	128.6
	200	228.6
Debt to equity ratio	1 to 1	1.3 to 1

His findings are reinforced by the more recent Garlicki, Fabozzi and Fonfeder (1987) study. Their work was concerned with estimating shareholder effects pursuant to the announcement of the change in translation guidelines from FASB 8 to FAS 52. The researchers focused their attention in particular upon two announcement dates: the initial exposure draft date, 28 August 1980, and the date of the subsequent statement by the Financial Accounting Standards Board that FAS 52 was to be adopted, 8 December 1981. In respect of neither of these significant dates could the researchers identify any abnormal gain or loss accruing to shares of companies affected by the revised standard. They conclude that this is consistent with shareholders having the sophistication not to be moved by revised accounting translation guidelines. Moreover, the actions of some multinationals in hedging translation exposure with transaction exposure is seen not only to be illogical from a deductive standpoint but also to be unjustified empirically, since stock market analysts seem not to be interested in pure translation gains and losses.

Generally speaking, our interpretation of the available evidence accords with the findings of Dukes and of Garlicki, Fabozzi and Fonfeder, which in turn underlines the theoretical view that pure translation exposure does not matter. But notice the rider at the beginning of the previous sentence – generally speaking. Why such a caveat?

The answer is best given by way of an example. Consider the company in Table 10.1. It is a UK-based corporation with a subsidiary in the United States. Initially, the group appears to have as large an operation, in asset terms, in the United States as in the United Kingdom – £100m in each country – and the US operation's dollar assets are matched by dollar debt. In the base case situation – that is, with an exchange rate of $1.8 to £1 – the group has a consolidated debt to equity ratio of 1 to 1. Imagine further that loan covenants place a figure of 1 to 1 as the maximum gearing allowed, calculated according to the consolidated accounts. It can readily be seen that, should the dollar strengthen against the pound, there is a problem for the company in terms of its loan covenant on gearing. Certainly, as Table 10.1 shows, dollar assets and liabilities are matched, but nonetheless the

Table 10.2 Profit and loss account translation exposure

	Last year (million)			Budget (million)			Actual (million)		
	Local currency	Rate	£	Local currency	Rate	£	Local currency	Rate	£
Home country results									
UK	43		43	48		48	44		44
Overseas results									
USA	32	1.6	20	36	1.5	24	32.4	1.8	18
Switzerland	105	2.1	50	112	2.15	52	114	2.5	45.6
Australia	116	2.9	40	127.6	2.9	44	119	3	39.7
			153			168			147.3
Shares in issue		250m			250m			250m	
Earnings per share		61.2p			67.2p			58.9p	

debt to equity constraint is breached at any time when the dollar is stronger than $1.8 to the pound. A company in this kind of situation will certainly have something to worry about when it is near to its specified debt limitations; it will, quite rightly, be concerned with translation exposure. This prescription is reinforced in Edelshain (1995).

We also have the situation where a firm's overseas subsidiaries' profit and loss account results may change in home currency terms as exchange rates move. Table 10.2 illustrates how an international company's consolidated results may show a drop in reported earnings even though, in all local currencies, trading results have improved. Does this kind of exposure constitute a pure translation exposure? Probably not, because profit after tax, when adjusted for depreciation, fixed and working capital inputs and so on, represents one of the most significant aspects of cash generation. For this reason, profit and loss account exposure must be more than pure translation exposure. If it were not, it would not be suggested that it merited exposure management time and attention. Interpreted as more than just translation exposure, managing foreign subsidiaries' bottom-line profit and loss results is warranted. One instrument to achieve this is the average rate option. But since currency options have not yet been discussed in this book, examination of how to achieve cover for this kind of exposure is deferred until later (see Chapter 16).

Remember that the empirical evidence that has led us to the view that pure translation exposure is of relatively little importance to the corporate treasurer derives from the United States. To conclude that such evidence is applicable, for example, to the United Kingdom or the Netherlands implies that capital markets are of at least a similar magnitude of sophistication in London and Amsterdam as in New York. Whether this is so is a moot point. Before we can be sure one way or the other, further research needs to be done. Clearly there is a need for some caution.

10.4 | Forecasting exchange rates

With the word of warning sounded in the last paragraph, the general conclusion of the foregoing discussion in this chapter is that pure translation exposure can, except in respect of its gearing implications, be ignored for all practical purposes. In the long run, taking on transaction exposure should result in gains equalling losses, but in the short term gains or losses may accrue. From a practical point of view the author recommends selective cover of transaction exposure for the large international company and (perhaps) blanket cover for the very occasional exporter/importer or company which is only casually into cross-frontier financial exposure. Economic exposure is best countered by financing in those currencies that materially create the exposure.

The conclusion in favour of selective covering of transaction exposure begs the question of whether or not buying professional forecasts of exchange rates might be helpful. The rationales of selective cover and of buying forecasts of foreign exchange rates are really interrelated. We now examine the evidence. If forecasts consistently achieve better results than using forward rates, we may wish to buy them to help us to take selective action on transaction exposure. And we may wish to use them to make speculative profits or to undertake leading and lagging operations (which will be discussed in Chapter 12) in advance of devaluations and revaluations of currencies. Aliber's (1983) cynical comments epitomize the negative point of view on buying foreign exchange forecasts. He observes that 'since 1973, about twenty firms have been established to sell forecasts of exchange rate movements. One inference is that they can make more money selling forecasts than using them.' This view may have a lot of substance during those periods when foreign exchange markets are displaying the characteristics associated with market efficiency. The contrary view, namely that forecasting foreign exchange rates can lead to consistently profitable results, is based on evidence to the effect that the foreign exchange market does not always display the typical features associated with efficient markets. Chapter 7 included a review of the available evidence.

That Murenbeeld (1975), Bilson (1979) and various others – for example, Armington (1977) – have developed models for predicting devaluations and revaluations, and that these models have reasonably good track records, presumably argues in favour of forecasting. That Robinson and Warburton (1980), Madura and Nosari (1984), Thomas (1985), Schulmeister (1987, 1988), Kwok and van de Gucht (1991), Levich and Thomas (1993), Silber (1994) and le Baron (1999) (see Chapter 7) have developed filter rules for locating funds for maximum profit, that Goodman (1978, 1980, 1981, 1982) and Goodman and Jaycobs (1983) have shown that some technically based forecasts consistently perform well, and that Levich (1981, 1982, 1983) has identified some (but by no means total) persistence in forecasters' superior performance, all combine to underwrite the potential value that may accrue from selectively using foreign exchange forecasts. Against this it must be emphasized that a study of eight UK forecasting services by Brasse (1983) found them to exhibit less accuracy than the forward rates and only three got the direction of change of rate right. Also Haache and Townsend (1981), in a study of linkages between exchange rates and current account balances, report some forecastability – they also find evidence of J-curve effects with an average lag of two months or so.

Giddy and Dufey's (1975) finding that under clean floats the foreign exchange markets are efficient and do not afford forecasters with opportunities consistently to make profits is reconcilable with the opinion about the virtues of forecasting, since we rarely find ourselves in clean float situations for long.

10.5 | Summary

- Transaction exposure is concerned with how changes in exchange rates affect the home currency value of anticipated foreign-currency-denominated cash flows relating to transactions that have already been entered into.

- Empirically, over long periods, the forward rate is an unbiased predictor of the future spot rate. Hence, failing to take cover but running with the spot rate should yield similar returns – in the long run. However, failing to cover may have disastrous short-term results. Avoiding these potential pitfalls by selective covering is therefore claimed by corporate treasurers to be a logical strategy.

- Economic exposure relates to the possibility that the present value of future cash flows of a firm may change due to foreign currency movements. However, exchange rate changes are related, via purchasing power parity, to differences in relative inflation rates. The firm whose operations experience cost inflation exactly in line with general inflation may be returned to its original position by changes in exchange rate exactly in line with purchasing power parity. In these circumstances, economic exposure may be argued not to matter.

- Most firms, of course, experience specific cost inflations which differ from general inflation. In this situation, which is the most common one, economic exposure does matter.

- One approach to minimizing this kind of exposure is to finance an appropriate part of the firm's operations in the currency to which the firm's value is sensitive.

- Translation exposure arises as a result of the process of consolidation of foreign-currency-denominated items into group financial statements denominated in the currency of the parent company. Whether it matters is entirely an empirical question.

- US-based research has tended to indicate that pure translation exposure does not affect share prices. As such, it seems that pure translation exposure should not matter most of the time. However, when a company is near to its gearing constraints it needs to be actively vigilant about translation exposure lest exchange rate movements precipitate breach of a borrowing covenant.

- There are financial instruments available to enable the company that is concerned with the adverse effects of translation exposure upon its consolidated profit and loss account to insure against the adverse impact on reported earnings per share – one such method involves the average rate option, which is considered in a later chapter.

10.6 | End of chapter questions

Question 1

(a) Present an argument for why translation exposure is relevant to an MNC.

(b) Present an argument for why translation exposure is not relevant to an MNC.

Question 2
Walt Disney Inc built the EuroDisney theme park in France that opened in 1992. How do you suppose this project affected its overall economic exposure to exchange rate movements? Why?

11 Principles of exposure management

In this chapter we focus upon a number of key issues in the management of exposure in general and of foreign exchange exposures in particular. The structure of the chapter involves us, first of all, in looking at the question of why a firm might wish to hedge. This is followed by focusing upon information necessary for foreign exchange management and the chapter ends with a re-examination of economic exposure.

11.1 | Why hedge anyway?

An attempt is first made to summarize the arguments against and in favour of covering corporate exposures to risk. The reader might reasonably raise the point that it is a little bit late in the day to discuss these points – why was such a fundamental issue not raised in Chapter 1?

In defence of the positioning of such a key topic as 'why hedge?' as late as Chapter 11, the author is prepared to advance an argument. But first of all, let it be said that the objection that this chapter could easily have occurred at the very beginning of the book is a valid one. In the end it was felt that because this book is intended as an essentially practical guide to the theory and practice of international financial management, it made more sense to keep the early sections on the practical side. In short, the author did not wish to put the reader off by raising a series of arguments that, to a large extent, derive from the academic literature on financial management. So the defence rests its case on a somewhat pragmatic point, but concedes that an equally strong argument may be advanced to say that the fundamental question – why hedge? – should be addressed immediately and on page 1 of a book on multinational finance. So much for this discussion; let us now turn to answering the poser.

11.2 | What does exposure management aim to achieve?

Hedging exposures, sometimes called risk management or exposure management, is widely resorted to by finance directors, corporate treasurers and portfolio managers. The practice of covering exposure is designed to reduce the volatility of a firm's profits and/or cash generation, and it presumably follows that this will reduce the

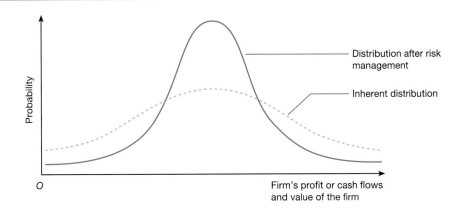

Figure 11.1 The goal of risk management.

volatility of the value of the firm. Figure 11.1 shows graphically what such efforts aim to achieve.

Certainly, among practitioners at least, the overriding view of the virtue of exposure management is as a device to reduce the variability of the firm's profits, cash flow or valuation caused by changes in interest rates and exchange rates. But there is a countervailing argument advanced by a number of financial academics. Its essence is as follows. Reducing the variability of the firm's returns, while leaving their expected level unchanged, should have little or no effect on the value of the firm. This view derives from the capital asset pricing model. The firm's operations are viewed as being risky in the sense that they move or fail to move in tandem with the market as a whole. The proposition continues with the idea that well-diversified international investors should not be willing to pay a premium for corporate hedging activities which they can readily duplicate for themselves simply by adjusting their portfolios. This line of argument leads to the view that hedging to reduce overall variability of profits, cash flow or firm value may be important to managers compensated on the basis of short-term results; however, it is a matter of irrelevance to diversified shareholders. They even out the ups and downs of individual corporate investments by holding well-diversified portfolios. Rather than being interested in how particular corporations hedge their own outturns, what is important is how the portfolio manager diversifies his or her investments.

11.3 | The arguments against corporate hedging

Really, the above argument is but one of a battery of attacks drawing their pedigree from the heavyweights of corporate finance. The range arrayed against hedging represents not only the capital asset pricing model but also purchasing power parity and the disciples of Modigliani and Miller. With such artillery in place, can hedging be remotely justified? As we will show, some arguments are more valid than others. So let us look at the map of the battlefield more closely.

According to purchasing power parity (PPP), movements in exchange rate offset price level changes. If PPP were to hold immutably and with no time lags, there would, so the argument goes, be no such thing as exposure to exchange rate risk and consequently no need to hedge. If the annual rate of inflation in the United Kingdom is 10 per cent higher than that in the United States, the pound will depreciate against the US dollar by an appropriate percentage rate. As a result, it follows that there is no relative price risk. If two units of US wheat exchanged for one unit of UK beef at the beginning of the year, that same exchange ratio would hold at the end of the year. The mere fact that the pound has depreciated is of no concern. The effect on the US exporter of wheat and the UK exporter of beef is of no significance, since the change in nominal prices in their national currencies has been compensated for by the exchange rate change.

There are numerous problems with this highly simplified version of PPP. Empirical tests have confirmed that the adjustment between changes in price levels and exchange rates is anything but immediate – there are long lags in the PPP relationship working in the real world. Even if, over the long-term horizon, PPP seems to have greater empirical validity, there are substantial short-term deviations. If a firm's planning horizon is shorter than that required for PPP to hold, then the firm is exposed to exchange risk – and this is probably the case for most firms.

Furthermore, even if PPP holds in the aggregate with respect to the price level indices of two countries, it need not – and usually does not – hold for every commodity. In short, the law of one price does not hold. If the increase in the price levels of wheat in the United States and beef in the United Kingdom do not correspond to the increases in the inflation levels in their respective countries, there will be a relative price risk. Even if PPP and the law of one price were to hold, prices of a firm's specific inputs and outputs might change relative to each other, and thus expose the firm to risk, which – if caused by unexpected exchange rate changes – must be viewed as exchange rate risk. That there are deviations from PPP and that there are relative price risks for at least some goods imply the presence of exchange risk. The PPP-based argument against hedging is not a substantial one.

Perhaps the capital asset pricing model (CAPM) has more guns arrayed against hedging. According to the CAPM, the essential aspect of risk that matters is systematic risk. If exchange rate risk and interest rate risk are considered to be unsystematic, they can be diversified away by investors in the process of constructing their own portfolios. On the other hand, if currency risk and interest rate risk are systematic and if forward exchange and interest hedge contracts are priced according to the CAPM, all that a firm does by entering into these kinds of contract is to move along the security market line. If this is so, then there is no addition to the value of the firm. As Adler (1982) puts it, 'in the absence of imperfections like transaction costs and default risks, the value of a forward contract would be zero at the instant at which it was initiated'. In reality, there are transaction costs – the bid/offer spread for one. So in the real world, according to this argument, companies could be said to destroy value by entering into forward contracts.

But inevitably there is another point of view. This concerns companies' motivations to avoid financial distress. Greater variability of net cash flow implies a higher probability of bankruptcy. In turn, this affects the firm's cost of funds and its ability to raise finance. To quote Makin (1981), 'costs of capital in the short run can be influenced by the perceived riskiness of claims on multinationals and that perceived riskiness, relative to other multinationals, could be altered in the short run by heavy exposure in foreign currencies'. His view is reinforced by Logue and Oldfield (1977) who observe:

> creditors may be concerned with total variability of cash flows where default is possible . . . gains and losses that a firm experiences due to random currency fluctuations may influence valuation through the effect on debt capacity. Where total variability is important, hedging in the foreign exchange markets may add to the firm's debt capacity.

And Adler (1982) argues that the evidence of default is the most justifiable goal for hedging. He observes:

> on the dimension of default risk, stockholders' and management's interests largely coincide. Stockholders are averse to bankruptcy risk on the grounds that the associated costs can permanently deplete their equity. When the market perceives a rise in default risk, share prices drop. Managers prefer to reduce the probability of default or of cash inadequacy so as to avoid abdicating control in favour of creditors. Jobs may then also be in jeopardy. Large exchange losses can affect the adequacy of reference currency cash flows. Consequently, bankruptcy-risk reduction can partly be achieved by a policy of hedging.

In short, despite countervailing CAPM arguments, there is a strong case that avoidance of default risk justifies minimizing variations in cash flows through hedging.

Turning next to arguments against hedging which derive from the Modigliani–Miller (MM) propositions (1958), it will be recalled that in relation to corporate gearing they advance the argument that what the firm can do, so can the investor. Extending this argument to the foreign exchange or interest rate domain, the same could be said to apply. Modigliani and Miller's argument suggested that a shareholder could obtain 'home-made leverage' by borrowing on his or her own account. In a similar way, why should the shareholder not obtain 'home-made hedging'? And, like MM's argument that home-made leverage would make corporate gearing irrelevant, so would home-made hedging make corporate hedging irrelevant.

Of course, if for any reason hedging by investors is not as effective as corporate hedging, then it will be in the interest of the shareholders to let the firm manage exchange and interest rate risk. As we have seen in this book heretofore, the main hedging instruments are forward markets, options markets, Eurocurrency markets and foreign money markets. Their nature is wholesale and they deal in minimum amounts that tend to be too large for individual investors. Commercial banks tend to limit access to forward and options markets. True, markets for currency futures exist which are readily accessible to individual investors, so some of the arguments about barriers to entry based on size applying to individual investors disappear. But remember that on financial futures exchanges there is a minimum contract size and the individual investor may be seeking cover at below this level.

Furthermore, there are techniques of currency management which are truly only available at the company, rather than the shareholder, level. For example, inter-company invoicing, leading and lagging of inter-company and third-party payments and judicious transfer pricing of both financial and real resources – to name but a few – are techniques for moving funds across borders and thus altering exposure.

And there are opportunities for hedging which are often open only to corporations and not to individual investors – for example, subsidies are sometimes available to hedgers in some countries in the form of special credit facilities, subsidized exchange risk insurance, or special forward rates offered by central banks.

The argument in favour of corporate hedging does not stop here. There is an information-based argument too. For the individual investor to hedge, he or she needs to be aware of the level and timing of currency and interest rate exposure for all the companies in the portfolio. Such information is required not only for today but also for future dates. This information may already have been collected by the firm for planning purposes. For the company, information gathering for hedging purposes may involve no additional opportunity cost. In contrast, an individual may have to incur very large costs to obtain similar information – and it is not just for one company either, but for a whole portfolio of investments.

Even though, in an ideal world, shareholders should be able to manufacture home-made hedging, it is extremely doubtful whether, in the real world, this would be either feasible or economic. And this militates in favour of corporate hedging.

There are other propositions which begin as arguments against corporate hedging and end up pointing in the opposite direction. One of these is the self-insurance and market efficiency argument (see Aliber, 1979, and Feizer and Jacquillat, 1981). It goes as follows. Currency and interest rate markets do not provide bargains – only fair gambles based on fair prices. In other words, by leaving foreign exchange positions uncovered, the firm may gain or it may lose. Such gains and losses will tend to average out, so the argument goes, over the long run. Hence an open position is essentially the same as a hedged position. 'The implication', to quote Dufey and Srinivasulu (1983), 'is that one should aim to maximize the expected value without undue concern for the variance of returns.'

Similarly, it is argued that, since foreign exchange and interest rate markets are efficient in the sense that contracts are priced on the basis of all currently available information, one cannot earn any excess returns in such markets, and hence hedging is of no value. As Shapiro and Rutenberg (1976) observe, 'unless capital market imperfections exist and persist, a treasurer . . . engaged in selective hedging . . . will not be able to earn consistent foreign exchange profits . . . in excess of those due to risk taking'.

But what is the treasurer trying to do by hedging? Surely, even if pursuing a selective hedging policy, the treasurer is not necessarily seeking excess returns, but merely trying to establish a risk/return profile with which the management feels comfortable. Furthermore, several others with interests in the firm are surely interested in reducing the variance of its returns flowing from currency and interest rate risk exposure. These groups include managers, other employees, financial regulators and creditors.

Managers and employees do not have a diversified portfolio of jobs. Their income stream from employment flows from their single job. By definition, investing in their career with one firm implies an undiversified portfolio. Clearly, managers and employees have a strong interest in reducing the variability of profit and cash flows and, in so doing, reducing the risk of financial distress. Another group concerned with reducing the variability of earnings is financial regulators. Governments around the world have increased their regulatory activity related to banks and other financial institutions' foreign exchange exposure policies. And creditors too have an obvious interest in their customers reducing their risk of incurring financial distress.

There is another argument that may be offered against corporate hedging. This concerns the desire of the shareholder for corporate risk. Take a company such as BP (prior to its merger with Amoco). Although a UK company with a substantial sterling base of shareholders, BP's income flows are essentially in dollars since oil is priced in dollars. If the shareholders' consumption patterns were dollar-based or if shareholders wanted to take on dollar risk, it might make sense for BP not to hedge its dollar exposure at all. Of course, companies are unable to know intimately their shareholders' consumption patterns or desires for risk and this line of reasoning leads to the conclusion that the company might hedge its exposures. But the obverse of this argument contends that, should companies leave themselves unhedged and communicate the nature of their exposures to shareholders, it would then be up to investors to make their own decisions about whether they wished to take on the company's risk by investing. In short, the argument is essentially one to the effect that shareholders may actually prefer that a portion of their income stream be exposed to foreign currency risk. In particular, this might be so when exchange controls prevent an investor from diversifying internationally. In any case, if the individual shareholder then wished to do so, he or she would be at liberty to hedge the exposure.

11.4 | The arguments for corporate hedging

If risk management is to be logically justified in financial terms, there has to be a positive answer to the question 'will exposure management increase the value of the firm?' And, furthermore, it is necessary to specify the route by which such value is created.

The fact that a firm is confronted with interest rate, exchange rate and/or commodity price risk is only a necessary condition for the firm to manage that risk. The sufficient condition is that exposure management increases the value of the firm.

The equation that is the cornerstone of finance suggests that the value of the firm (V) is a function of expected future net cash flows – $E(\text{NCF})$ – discounted at the firm's cost of capital, k. It can be written as:

$$V = \sum_{t=0}^{n} \frac{E(\text{NCF}_t)}{(1 + k)^t}$$

From this equation it is immediately apparent that, if the firm's value is to increase, it must do so as a result of either an increase in expected net cash flows or a decrease in the discount rate.

How might hedging affect the firm's discount rate? If we look at the risks that are usually hedged in an exposure management policy – currency risk, interest rate risk and commodity price risk – we can see that all of these may be interpreted, from the standpoint of modern portfolio theory, as diversifiable risks. Shareholders can

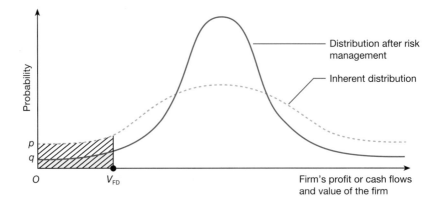

Figure 11.2 Hedging reduces the probability of financial distress.

manage these risks by holding a diversified portfolio. It follows that active management of these risks should have no effect on the firm's cost of capital. Unless the company is held by undiversified owners, risk management should not increase the expected value of the firm through a reduction in the discount rate.

In the case of a company held by well-diversified investors, exposure management can only be expected to increase the value of the firm through an increase in expected net cash flows. A logical question follows: how can hedging affect the value of the firm's expected net cash flows, as opposed to their variability? We would argue that avoidance of financial distress and a reduction in the present value of taxes paid are both potential sources of such value creation via hedging.

In Figure 11.1 it was noted that risk management can reduce the volatility of the cash flows of the firm. Figure 11.2 goes a step further. It indicates that, by reducing cash flow volatility, hedging reduces the probability of the firm getting into financial difficulty and bearing the consequent costs of such distress.

Where V_{FD} is the value of the firm below which financial distress is encountered, it can be seen that hedging reduces the probability of financial distress from point p to point q. Hedging can reduce the costs of financial distress by:

- reducing the probability of financial distress;

- reducing the costs imposed by financial problems.

Clearly, as Figure 11.2 shows, the probability of financial distress may be lowered by hedging.

We can also use the subsequent diagram, Figure 11.3, to point out the virtue of hedging in terms of enabling the firm to achieve its desired corporate strategy, presumably the key to the firm's value. Assume that the cash flow level, CF, on the horizontal axis of Figure 11.3 is that level of cash generation that the firm needs to undertake to pursue its desired investment plans. Clearly, by hedging, the firm reduces the probability that its cash throw-off will be insufficient to enable it to pursue its planned strategy. As can be seen from Figure 11.3, the probability of its being able to pursue the desired policy from self-generated funds increases greatly from level a to level b as a result of exposure management techniques.

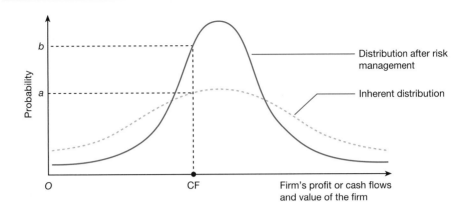

Figure 11.3 Hedging better enables the firm to pursue its desired strategy.

Returning to hedging as a device to lower risk of financial distress, even short of bankruptcy, the possibility of financial distress can impose substantial costs on the firm. These involve higher contracting costs with customers, employees and suppliers. Companies that provide service agreements or warranties make a long-term commitment to their customers. The value customers place on these agreements and warranties depends on their perception of the financial viability of the firm. If the future of the firm is in doubt, customers will place less value on the service back-up and warranties and may turn to a competitor or demand a lower price to compensate. Either way, there is an evident impact upon profit and cash generation of the firm.

The essential argument may be summarized as follows. The marketing of a firm's product may be eased by a stable corporate track record since buyers want some assurance that the firm will stay in business to service the product and to supply parts. By a similar line of argument, potential employees may be scared off by a volatile earnings record which could suggest less job security. To compensate for this, employees may demand higher salaries and perks.

With the probability of financial distress increased by an absence of hedging, suppliers of debt capital might demand higher returns to compensate for higher expected bankruptcy costs and/or they might negotiate tighter debt covenants. Either way, the tendency would be for the cost of debt to increase. In parallel, it could be argued that, *ceteris paribus*, a reduction in the probability of financial distress or default would lower the cost of debt and increase the firm's debt capacity.

The reader might believe that a more realistic model of corporate valuation conforms to that following:

$$V_F = \Sigma V_i - P(\sigma)$$

where V_F is the value of the firm, V_i is the net present value of each of the firm's parts and $P(\sigma)$ is a penalty factor that reflects the impact on after-tax cash flows of the total risk of the firm. Note that this formula, which has some guru support, is not consistent with CAPM ideas – the penalty factor is a function of total risk, not just systematic risk. And, if you think about it, firms are usually bankrupted because of total risk rather than systematic risk. Anyway, the above proposition of corporate value

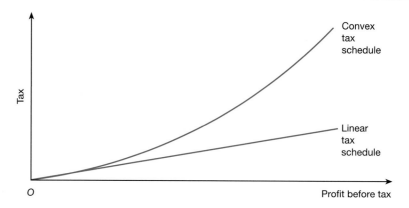

Figure 11.4 A convex tax function.

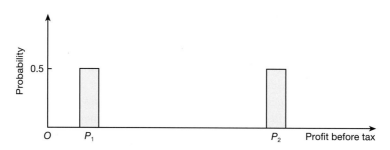

Figure 11.5 Unhedged profit expected outturns.

would obviously suggest that hedging is a good thing for shareholders because, in lowering the penalty factor, corporate value is enhanced.

It was stated earlier that hedging and the tax system interrelate to impact upon the level of net cash flows of the firm. How does this work? If a company is facing an effective tax schedule which is convex, then a reduction in the volatility of profit through hedging can reduce corporate taxes payable. What is meant by a convex tax schedule? Figure 11.4 gives an example – clearly the firm's average effective tax rate rises as pre-tax profit rises.

So how does this give lower total taxes with risk management? Let us assume that, with no hedging at all, the firm faces a distribution of pre-tax income as shown in Figure 11.5. A low profit of P_1 or a high profit of P_2 each has an equal probability of occurrence of 50 per cent. With a profit of P_1 the firm would pay taxes of T_1, and with a profit of P_2 the firm would pay taxes of T_2. Clearly, the expected value of the tax payment $E(T)$ will be equal to:

$$\frac{T_1 + T_2}{2}$$

The position is summarized in Figure 11.6.

If the firm were to hedge, the volatility of its pre-tax income would decline – both P_1 and P_2 would move towards their mean profit level. Suppose that hedging were so successful that the distribution of profit outturns became simply P_{mean}, as shown in

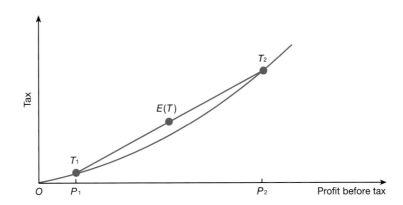

Figure 11.6 Tax payable in unhedged case.

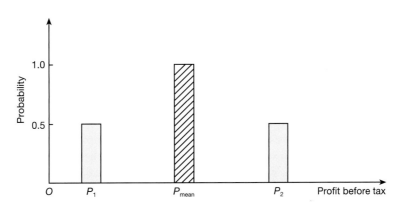

Figure 11.7 Hedged profit versus profit expected outturns.

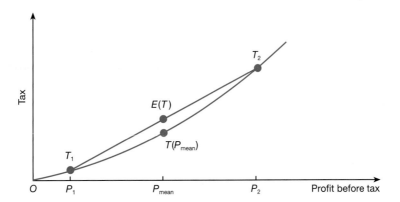

Figure 11.8 Tax payable in hedged case versus tax payable in unhedged case.

Figure 11.7. Then, with profit at this level, taxes payable would become $T(P_{mean})$, as indicated in Figure 11.8. Clearly, with the convex nature of the effective tax schedule, the tax on the hedged income is less than the expected tax if the firm were not to hedge.

The implication of all of the above is that if the tax schedule is convex, hedging can lead to a reduction in the firm's expected taxes. The more convex the tax schedule and the more volatile the firm's pre-tax profits, the greater are the tax benefits that accrue to the company. Corporate tax schedules in the United Kingdom and the United States currently give the firm only minimal, if any, benefits on this front. Nonetheless the principle should be clear.

The line of argument advanced in this section is similar to that of Dufey and Srinivasulu (1983), Abuaf (1988) and Rawls and Smithson (1990).

We now turn to the topic of relevant information for hedging purposes.

11.5 | Information for exposure management

Management of foreign exchange exposure is an integral part of the treasury function in the multinational company. Rational decision taking presupposes that relevant information pertinent to the decision is available. This generalization is no less true of treasury management than it is of any other aspect of business. To make logical decisions on foreign exchange exposure, relevant information is required. This part of the chapter is devoted to the topic of an information system for exposure management.

But what is the problem? Maybe an example would help. Suppose that one wholly owned subsidiary of a US-based group has a receivable of €5m due in three months' time, while another wholly owned subsidiary has a payable of €5m three months away. It would make no sense for the two subsidiaries each to cover their exposure by respectively selling and buying €5m three months forward. Obviously these two exposures cancel out when viewed on a group basis. Perhaps the boards of directors of the two wholly owned subsidiaries would each reach a decision to the effect that they would want to cover their exposure. It is no problem to ensure that for internal management accounting purposes or for performance appraisal a notional hedge is done. Most multinationals achieve this by requiring that divisions wishing to cover foreign exchange exposures do so by buying or selling forward with the group treasury. But reverting to our numerical example, the point is that from a group standpoint there is no need to cover the receivable and payable referred to because setting the long position in one wholly owned subsidiary against the short position in the other wholly owned company provides an exact cancelling out. The difficulty for the multinational in this area is that it needs continuous flows of information from all subsidiaries on their foreign exchange exposure. And this is costly. As in any centralized system, the question needs to be asked when it is initially instituted and regularly reiterated: do the benefits of centralization outweigh its costs?

In this context, savings are likely to accrue in terms of saved bid/offer spreads on deals eliminated – in the numerical example, by not hedging the €5m receivable in one subsidiary and the €5m payable in the other, the effective cash saving is the bid/offer spread because one subsidiary would be dealing at the market rate to buy and the other at the market rate to sell. Benefits will also accrue to a centralized treasury through greater financial control, matching, netting and leading and lagging opportunities (see Chapter 12), better ability to optimize group cash management, tax bills, movement of funds to avoid exchange controls and an ability to raise funds worldwide at lower rates than through a piecemeal approach. To justify a centralized system the value of such benefits has to exceed their costs in terms of expensive manpower such as treasury personnel, dealers, information systems and so on. It should not be taken for granted that the centralized treasury is always superior to the decentralized operation – indeed it rarely is for the small business. Centralization may be difficult to justify when there are many partly owned subsidiaries, since different shareholders may have different attitudes in terms, for example, of risk aversion and so on. Even were centralization justified, as it might have been five years ago, a regular post-audit is really needed to ensure that benefits have accrued and outstripped costs and that it continues to be the rational, cost-effective policy.

However, before getting fully to grips with information for exposure management, we need to ask ourselves with which definition of exposure the firm is concerned. It is to this topic that we now turn.

11.6 What kind of foreign exchange exposure is significant?

We have classified foreign exchange exposure under three headings: transaction exposure, translation exposure and economic exposure. Earlier in this text we argued that the firm should be crucially concerned with transaction exposure and economic exposure, since these two classifications of exposure are essentially underpinned by cash flows. This contrasts with pure translation exposure where differences arise due to accounting conventions in the process of consolidating the financial accounts of companies within a group. Of course, pure translation gains and losses are now dealt with by way of reserve accounting under the consolidation procedures of US and UK companies according to the accounting standards in these two countries. This means that distortions to earnings per share and profit trends which were brought about by the requirements of the US accounting standard FASB 8 have been eliminated. Furthermore the indications of most serious empirical studies – admittedly US-based – are that security analysts are sufficiently sophisticated not to be fooled by the inclusion of these translation gains and losses in income statements, and since they do not seem to affect security prices, the conclusion follows that translation exposure should not matter to the multinational company. And if companies need not worry about translation exposure – except in respect of gearing (see Chapter 10) – it follows that collecting information on it is not a worthwhile process. Furthermore, companies should not enter into transactions to hedge pure translation exposures. As Ross, Clark and Taiyeb (1987) state, 'as a very general . . . first principle, it is uncommercial to hedge a non-cash item with a cash one'. In this connection, it should be reiterated that gains and losses arising from converting borrowings and lendings denominated in foreign currency are classified by this author as transaction gains and losses and are therefore left outside of the definition of pure translation exposure used here. Should information be required on pure translation exposure, the normal rolling budgets which most large companies prepare ought to be sufficient to meet any needs of users.

Having argued against the inclusion of pure translation exposure within the exposure information system, we now turn to economic exposure and transaction exposure. The computation of economic exposure is a complex process, requiring as it does detailed analysis of elasticities of demand, competitor appraisals and other aspects discussed in Chapter 8. Identifying economic exposure presupposes that corporate executives are able to specify how the value of the firm will respond to exchange rate changes. Since we have argued elsewhere in this book that economic exposure matters, presumably treasurers in multinational companies will wish to manage it. The sort of information necessary to manage economic exposure concerns the impact of exchange rate changes upon the value of the firm. With rapidly changing exchange rates and a competitive world, economic exposure may also change regularly. But keeping track of this class of foreign exchange exposure is difficult. It clearly requires the input of very skilled executive time and as such is not easily amenable to being systematized. Given this background we would argue that, if economic exposure is being actively managed, it is regularly necessary to update information about it. But, given that identification of economic exposure should be based upon the sensitivity of the present value of the firm to changes in exchange rates, we believe that this is so complex an issue that we would not recommend that it becomes the subject of a routine, simple information system. However, if a firm is actually managing economic and transaction exposure, it needs to equip itself with current figures on both kinds of exposure. For economic exposure, this would mean that regular net present value details of operating cash flows would be necessary for all of a multinational company's operations, plus details of the extent to which they are hedged by local and other financing. A later part of this chapter is devoted to a more advanced consideration of the difficulties involved in analysing and controlling economic exposure.

The other class of exposure that is also based on cash flows is, of course, transaction exposure. We have argued in Chapter 10 that transaction exposure matters to the firm. Identification of transaction exposure is not difficult, unlike economic exposure. Unmanaged transaction exposure may result in loans denominated in foreign currency being left exposed while the foreign currency strengthens dramatically. This may have very far-reaching effects on the firm, as we pointed out in Chapter 10. And passively managed transaction exposure may result in subsidiary companies in a group pursuing policies which are optimal from their own viewpoint as subsidiaries but which result in sub-optimization from a group standpoint. The example of the €5m exposure is a case (see section 11.5) which would cost the group two bid/offer spreads to cover exposures when an internal cover was already available. Managing transaction exposure presupposes that the group treasury has information on its magnitude and maturity. We shall now attempt to outline an information system for transaction exposure that is relatively easy and inexpensive to operate. It might be implemented even though a fully fledged, centralized treasury is not in existence.

11.7 | The transaction exposure information system

Although no single transaction exposure information system will be universally applicable to every business, there are certain features that should be present in all. First, the information system should be forward looking. Given that we are concerned with taking decisions about future events, it follows that we need information about anticipated outturns. Secondly, the frequency of reporting needs to be adequate. What constitutes sufficient frequency is entirely a practical question but we have found that for most companies, with significant international operations, monthly reports bolstered by computer communication to the centre on additional exposures taken on is adequate. But clearly very large groups or those with vast items denominated in foreign currency may wish to shorten this reporting time-scale. Thirdly, the flow of information should be direct to the treasury rather than being routed via other departments, such as accounting departments, which can create delays. Finally, the need for information must be sold to management in subsidiary companies. It is essential that such managers comprehend the rationale for data on foreign currency commitments and it is essential that subsidiary company performance should not be distorted. Failure in these areas usually results in reduced motivation on the part of subsidiary management and a weak and tardy system of control.

Information systems should be timely, succinct and oriented to decision and control. There is no place for irrelevant information. Thus the routine exposure information system should home in solely upon transaction exposure. McRae and Walker (1980) extend the currency exposure information system to translation exposure. For reasons set out above, the author believes this to be unnecessary and unjustified – except when gearing constraints loom.

Our concern is with transaction exposure, using a minimum monthly reporting frequency. Reports are essentially forecasts specifying receipts and payments to be made in foreign currency. They should focus upon currency of denomination, maturity and cover already taken. It is recommended that reports should distinguish four key data. These embrace inter-company versus third-party flows, capital versus trading items, firm contractual flows versus probable flows and, finally, details of covered and uncovered flows.

Table 11.1 (overleaf) is an example of such an exposure forecast. Although it does not split out capital and trading items or firm and probable flows as such, this can easily be achieved by entering the respective initials C or T and F or P. Thus the treasury at the UK holding company level would require from the US subsidiary a form like the table showing all non-US$ exposures which had been taken on by that subsidiary. Similar schedules would also be required from all other subsidiaries showing transaction exposures in currencies other than the local currency. In addition to these schedules, material changes would be immediately communicated by telex to the group treasury. This enables the group treasury to co-ordinate covering activities in response to the overall transaction exposure position.

Receipt of transaction exposure schedules from all around the world enables the central treasury to prepare a group exposure statement. Like the previous schedule this is usually prepared monthly; an example of such a summary report appears in

Table 11.1 Transaction cash flow exposure schedule (£000)

Company: US Sub Inc. Currency: £
Country: USA Forecast period: 6 mths to 30.6.04
Prepared by: AB
Date prepared: 24.12.03
Rate: $ v. £ as at 24.12.03
Spot: 1.7200 1 mth 1.7300 3 mths 1.7500

	Jan.	Feb.	Mar.	Apr.	May	June	Beyond June
Receipts							
Third party	2,000	3,000	1,000	1,000			Due Sept. 04
Inter-company Swedish sub		2,000					
Total receipts	2,000	5,000	1,000	1,000			1,000
Payments							
Third party	3,000	3,000					2,000 Due Oct. 04
Inter-company German sub			2,000				
Total payments	3,000	3,000	2,000				2,000
Net receipts/(payments)	(1,000)	2,000	(1,000)	1,000			1,000
Cover against receipts		1,000					(2,000) Sept. 04
Cover against payments	1,000		1,000	1,000			2,000 Oct. 04
Net exposure	–	1,000	–	1,000			1,000
Details of forward cover* (specify contract date; settlement date; rate; amount)	1.8.03 Jan. 1.7350 1,000	1.9.03 Feb. 1.7450 1,000	30.9.03 Mar. 1.7550 1,000				16.10.03 Oct. 1.7580 2,000

* Details of forward cover frequently appear on a separate schedule.

Table 11.2 Group cash flow exposure schedule (£000)

Prepared by: .... Date prepared: .... Forecast period: ....

	Jan.	Feb.	Mar.	Apr.	May	June	Beyond June
Currencies with forward market Euros .... Canadian $ .... Japanese yen .... Swedish krone .... Swiss franc .... US$ .... Others (specify)							
Total							
No forward market .... Currency (specify) .... Currency (specify) .... Currency (specify)							
Total							

Table 11.2. In the table, it will be noted that currencies are categorized according to whether a forward market exists or not. This is a useful distinction since ease of action to obtain cover is more readily available when a forward foreign exchange market exists. However, where forward markets do not exist, cover may be synthesized by borrowing or lending in the local currency, assuming that financial markets have sufficient depth for this strategy to be pursued. It is also useful to categorize currencies according to their membership of joint floats. The value of this kind of device lies in the fact that, sometimes, large companies cover against the net cash flow exposure having netted out positions with respect to all currencies in a joint float.

11.8 | Histogramming

Having estimated a company's transaction exposure on a group basis, the question for the group treasurer is what to do about it. Action is clearly a function of the management's view on the directions in which exchange rates are likely to move. Here the histogramming technique is frequently used. This involves obtaining and giving weight to estimates of exchange rate movements from well-informed parties inside and outside the company. Sources inside the company might include the group treasury, the economics department, local management and various others. Sources outside the company would include bankers and forecasting groups. The technique

Table 11.3 Currency forecast (£000)

Forecaster:	Group treasurer		Current spot rate:	$1.7750 = £1
Currency:	£/$		Forward rate:	$1.7800 = £1
Forecast period:	3 months		Date prepared:	....

Expected range	Mid-point	Probability	Forecaster weighting	Weighted probability
1.7400 to 1.7699	1.7550	0.05	0.20	0.0100
1.7700 to 1.7999	1.7850	0.3	0.20	0.0600
1.8000 to 1.8299	1.8150	0.35	0.20	0.0700
1.8300 to 1.8599	1.8450	0.25	0.20	0.0500
1.8600 to 1.8899	1.8750	0.05	0.20	0.0100
		1.00	1.00	0.2000

involves each forecaster assigning probabilities to a range of estimated future exchange rates over various periods. It should be noted that ranges, rather than single point estimates, are usually used. Table 11.3 shows a format that might be used for this process. As can be seen, Table 11.3 contains a weighting factor in addition to the actual forecast. Weightings are built into the process by reference to individual forecasters' previous track records. The sum of the weightings for all forecasters must equal 1.00. With reference to Table 11.3, the probability assigned by the forecaster is multiplied by the forecaster's weighting to give a final weighted probability. These weighted probabilities are brought together in a summary histogram (see Table 11.4) and they may then be compared with the forward rate for the purpose of decision taking.

Reverting to Table 11.3, this shows a format for individual forecasts – in this case it is for the treasury. Forecasts of this kind will be prepared by each of the forecasting participants for one month, two months, three months forward and so on. These forecasts are weighted according to each forecaster's past record – this has been done in Table 11.4 over three months – and histograms as shown at the foot of the table can readily be prepared for one month, two months, three months forward and so on. In the example, the forecasting participants are group treasury, group economics, local treasurer, group financial planning, the company's bankers and a consultant foreign exchange forecasting company. The respective weights given to each party are 20, 15, 15, 20, 15 and 15 per cent.

From Table 11.4 it can be seen that the weighted forecast suggests a very high probability that the exchange rate in three months' time will be within the range 1.77 to 1.83. If the forward rate for three-month dollars is $1.78 to £1 (see Tables 11.3 and 11.4), then if the company expected to be short of dollars against the pound three months away (that is, it has to buy in dollars for pounds in three months' time), it would most probably benefit by waiting and buying dollars through the spot market in three months' time, since, according to the histogram, there is a good chance that the dollar will have weakened in three months' time and the histogram promises a better payoff by using the spot rate in three months' time rather than the forward

Table 11.4 Summary histogram (£/$)

Currency: £/$ Date prepared: ....
Forecast period: 3 months   Forward rate: $1.7800 = £1

	Forecast range				
	1.7400 to 1.7699	1.7700 to 1.7999	1.8000 to 1.8299	1.8300 to 1.8599	1.8600 to 1.8899
Grp treasurer	0.01	0.06	0.07	0.05	0.01
Grp economics	0.01	0.08	0.05	0.01	0
Local treasurer	0	0.08	0.07	0	0
Financial planning	0.01	0.09	0.07	0.02	0.01
Banker	0.01	0.07	0.07	0	0
Forecaster	0.01	0.06	0.07	0.01	0
Total	**0.05**	**0.44**	**0.40**	**0.09**	**0.02**

Summary

Confidence level

50%   44%   40%   25%   9%   5%   2%   0%

1.7400 to 1.7699	1.7700 to 1.7999	1.8000 to 1.8299	1.8300 to 1.8599	1.8600 to 1.8899

rate. Remember that the rationale for the use of selective hedging is that, at least in the short term, the forward rate has been found to be a biased predictor of the future spot rate. Evidence was summarized in Chapter 7.

In the example above, were our company long of dollars three months away, it might decide, logically according to the implications of the histogram, to sell dollars forward. Thus, the histogramming technique facilitates rational selective hedging. If selective hedging of this kind is undertaken, it is most important to monitor its effectiveness. The recommended post-audit procedure should compare the outturns achieved from selective hedging with those that would have resulted from a policy of hedging everything in the forward market, and it should also compare selective hedging achievements with results based on hedging nothing at all in the forward market. Clearly, one needs to do this kind of post-audit over a fairly lengthy time-span, including periods when the home currency was rising and falling. If selective hedging is to be pursued, the results of post-audits must justify choice of this strategy. Such post-audits need to be undertaken regularly. Individual forecaster weightings may also be changed as a result of this process. It cannot be stressed too much that the post-audit is an essential part of a selective hedging policy.

11.9 | Reinvoicing vehicles

Many multinational companies have turned their treasury department into a separate company. All inter-group trade is then invoiced through this central company. Such companies are known as 'reinvoicing vehicles' or 'netting vehicles' or 'multi-currency management centres'. Practice varies from company to company, but the general outline set out below is reasonably typical.

Group companies invoice exports to other group companies through the reinvoicing company in the currency of the exporter. The reinvoicing company in its turn invoices the importing company in its home currency. This means that neither exporter nor importer has any exchange risk; this is borne by the reinvoicing company, which ultimately takes all covering decisions on a basis which it views as reflecting a balance of future outturns and the extent of its risk aversion.

Exports outside the group are either invoiced in the exporter's currency or, if the importer requires a different currency of sale, the exporter bills the invoicing centre in its own currency and the reinvoicing company bills the customer in the currency agreed between seller and purchaser. Again, all currency risk is concentrated into the reinvoicing centre. Imports are handled in the same manner, enabling all currency risk to be borne by the invoicing company. Of course, the reinvoicing centre does become the legal owner of the goods in these transactions and should therefore have little difficulty in obtaining exchange control permissions to cover its exposure in countries where exchange controls are in place.

This technique concentrates all currency exposure into the reinvoicing centre. It therefore becomes an ideal vehicle for controlling and monitoring the group's foreign exchange exposure. In addition, the reinvoicing centre frequently acts as the banker to the group. In such circumstances cash management is centred in the reinvoicing company as are group borrowings. Such fully fledged, sophisticated and (frequently) costly vehicles are appropriate to large international groups with substantial cross-frontier trade, international borrowings and cash flows – but earlier comments in this chapter about cost effectiveness and its regular review still hold.

Some companies have used reinvoicing centres less than scrupulously in order to lower worldwide tax bills and in cost-plus pricing. However, reinvoicing vehicles need not be part of a less than ethical operation. Indeed, the practice of using the reinvoicing centre for dubious purposes has receded somewhat in recent years because host governments have become suspicious when they are used.

11.10 | Strategies for exposure management

It has been argued that firms should take management action in the foreign exchange markets to counter cash flow exposure. But there is another basic question that top management needs to answer: is its posture one of making as much profit as it can through changes in foreign currency rates? Or is it basically in the business of making and selling goods or services, with a foreign exchange stance designed to minimize losses through changing rates? Is the treasury a profit or a cost centre? There is no universal, clear-cut response to these questions. Different firms will adopt different postures because of their varying degrees of risk aversion. Maybe their postures on foreign exchange risk will vary from time to time. The firm that seeks to maximize profits in the foreign exchange markets is termed an 'aggressive' firm; its counterpart that aims merely to minimize potential losses resulting from changed exchange rates is termed a 'defensive' firm. In reality, judged by their overall strategies and tactics, firms rarely fall neatly into one category or the other but rather lie on a continuum of foreign currency risk between aggressive and defensive – sometimes a particular firm adopts an aggressive policy; at other times the same firm will pursue a defensive policy.

The aggressive posture will involve the firm in deliberately seeking and leaving open foreign exchange positions in currencies in which it expects to make profits. The defensive posture involves the avoidance of foreign exchange exposure by the techniques referred to in the next few chapters. In countries without foreign exchange controls, it is easy for the aggressive firm to back its judgement on future currency movements by opening up exposure unrelated to trade via the forward or swaps markets or the futures or options markets. In countries with exchange controls, the only substantial opportunity open to the firm legally to take currency positions is based on trade transactions. As an example of the aggressive stance in an environment with exchange controls, an exporter might endeavour to invoice a sale in the currency that it expects to be hard relative to its own currency. An aggressive posture would also involve only covering a foreign currency receivable when the forward rate of exchange was more favourable than the expected spot rate on the settlement date. By contrast to these examples, the defensive firm would seek to invoice in its own currency and, where it had a foreign currency receivable or payable, it would cover automatically in the forward market. It should be reiterated that when there are no exchange controls it is far more logical for the firm to take open positions via the forward, swaps, futures or options markets rather than through trade transactions.

With respect to decisions of a long-term nature, the aggressive firm would similarly seek to obtain debt denominated in a soft currency relative to its own, having due regard to interest costs taken together with expected currency depreciation/appreciation. The defensive firm might endeavour to match the currency denomination of cash inflows and outflows, thereby minimizing cash flow exposure, or to match the currency denomination of assets and liabilities.

A firm's posture on foreign exchange risk is usually a function of two key factors. The first is the aggregate risk aversion of the key members of the organization's decision coalition. The second relates to the firm's ability to forecast exchange rates and its ability to beat the forward market. This latter factor takes us back to the whole range of questions concerned with efficiency of foreign exchange markets and the ability of forecasts consistently to yield excess returns.

Were foreign exchange markets efficient and subject to no imperfections, then there would be no systematic biases in rates and management's currency expectations would be synonymous with those of the market as embodied in forward rates. According to this scenario, consistent profit opportunities would not exist. But in a world in which governments create market imperfections by intervening in foreign exchange markets – this is termed 'dirty floating' under the current floating exchange rate regime – and interest rate markets, these actions are likely to create systematic deviations between realized rates and expectations of future rates as embodied in forward rates. Certainly, as we saw in Chapter 7, there have been consistent and persistent biases which have continued for short periods and for substantial periods too, suggesting that recurring profit opportunities do accrue to investors in foreign exchange markets. So the aggressive stance may be justified by two factors. First, market imperfections, such as government intervention in foreign exchange markets, may result in sustained periods when markets fail to demonstrate the features of efficiency. Secondly, and somewhat more doubtful, it may be the case that forecasters have special abilities based on access to information not available to most other participants in the market, or the firm or forecaster may have special expertise in interpreting available information. As pointed out earlier, firms adopting aggressive exposure policies need carefully to monitor the results of pursuing such tactics.

The essence of the defensive strategy varies according to the nature of the company concerned. For the basically domestic company, which occasionally exports or imports, the low-risk policy involves consistent use of the forward markets. For the significant exporter, the defensive policy most frequently used involves forward markets or currency of financing policy. This latter approach is best illustrated with an example. If a firm's operations generate exposed assets or cash inflows, these exposures may be countered by taking on financial liabilities or cash outflows in the same currencies. According to this formula, a company with significant exports denominated in foreign currencies would try to match these by holding part of its liabilities in these currencies.

For the truly multinational company which has interrelated operations in many countries, the defensive financial strategy involves use of forward, swaps and options markets, but it also has a significant further policy at its disposal. This involves protection of expected profit and cash flow levels against changes in foreign exchange markets and financial markets by adjusting operating and financial variables. Operating responses consist of alteration to sourcing, product, plant location, market selection, credit, pricing and currency of invoicing policies – these will be considered in Chapter 12. In passing, we would point out that Jenkins (1995), on the basis of case study evidence, views the first three of the above to be more effective than financial markets in combating competitive disadvantages created by exchange rate disequilibria – although care must be exercised lest long-term operational changes are entered into in order to attack short-term disequilibria. Adjustments of financial variables to protect profit and cash flows generally occur on the liabilities side. A company may finance itself in those currencies with which its operating cash flows are positively correlated. For example, consider a US holding company with a UK subsidiary exporting in euros to Germany. Operating returns of the UK subsidiary are positively correlated with movements in the euro and the subsidiary might therefore decide to raise finance in euros. A movement in the euro against sterling would affect not only operating returns but also financing costs. The change in the one would be countered by changes in the other, thereby reducing foreign exchange risk.

11.11 | Economic exposure revisited

So far in this text, the view has been taken that economic exposure is concerned with the present value of future operating cash flows to be generated by a company's activities and how this present value, expressed in parent currency terms, changes following exchange rate movements. Ideas about hedging economic exposure have been based upon this definition. But nowadays another view of economic exposure is emerging and it is one that may be more useful and powerful from the standpoint of providing information upon which the risk-averse firm may plan a hedging strategy. The term 'macroeconomic exposure' has been coined for it and – as its name implies – it goes far beyond mere exposure to exchange rate changes. Work on this topic is in its infancy; however, the author is firmly of the opinion that the potential for using macroeconomic exposure techniques is not to be underrated. Perhaps in ten or twenty years' time it will be this kind of exposure that is the main focus of the corporate treasurer's job.

11.12 | Macroeconomic exposure

Macroeconomic exposure is concerned with how a firm's cash flows, profit and hence value change as a result of developments in the economic environment as a whole – that is, within the total framework of exchange rates, interest rates, inflation rates, wage levels, commodity price levels and other shocks to the system. All firms are clearly vulnerable to this kind of exposure. The economic shocks may originally emanate from the home economy or abroad – the idea behind managing macroeconomic exposure is first of all to identify the nature of the exposure and then to manage it by hedging techniques. The methodology outlined in this section draws on the work of Oxelheim and Wihlborg (1987, 1989a, b).

The identification of a firm's sensitivity to macroeconomic variables may be established by determining the way in which cash flow, profits and value vary in response to changes in key economic variables, such as interest rates, price levels, exchange rates, commodity prices and so on. The relevant variables would first of all be put forward as a result of deductive reasoning. They would then be fed into a statistical model and recent values would be set against them with the objective of establishing the coefficients of sensitivity using regression analysis techniques. Data must be available for a sufficiently long period of time and it is usual to begin this analysis by breaking down data by product, strategic business unit, country of operations and so on.

Let us assume that an analysis has been undertaken for a UK-based company in terms of estimating, by regression techniques, the percentage rate of change in the firm's real cash flows from unanticipated changes in prices levels abroad and at home, the exchange rate, domestic and foreign interest rates and relative prices of significant inputs. Let us assume that this analysis produces the results, in terms of the exposure coefficients, noted in Table 11.5 (overleaf).

Table 11.5 Effect of a 1 per cent unanticipated change in macroeconomic variables on the firm's real cash flows

Variable	Exposure coefficient	Real effect (£m)	Example of 1% change
Domestic price level	−0.6	−0.45	Retail prices move from 100 to 101
Foreign price level	0	0	
Exchange rate	−0.5	−0.375	$/£ rate moves from 1.80 to 1.7820
Domestic interest rate	−0.8	−0.6	Interest rates move from 10% to 10.1%
Foreign interest rate	0.2	+0.15	US interest rates move from 10% to 10.1%
Commodity prices	−0.2	−0.15	Copper prices move from £1,500 per tonne to £1,515 per tonne
Relative prices	0.6	+0.45	Output price index relative to RPI increases from 1 to 1.01

The figures in the second column of the table indicate, for example, that a 1 per cent unanticipated increase in UK price levels will lead to a fall of 0.6 per cent in real cash flows. The table shows that real UK cash flows are insensitive to changes in foreign price levels. But the table goes on to indicate that, for a 1 per cent unanticipated rise in the exchange rate, real cash flows drop by 0.5 per cent, holding other variables constant. As the table shows, the reference in this case is to the sterling/dollar exchange rate. Depending upon the reality of macroeconomic relationships for the firm concerned, it might be the case that the critical exchange rate to be included in the analysis turned out to be sterling/yen movements or sterling/euro fluctuations. The next exposure coefficient which is highlighted is the domestic interest rate. Here, the indication is that, for a 1 per cent unanticipated rise in interest rates, real cash flow falls by 0.8 per cent. The effect that the domestic interest rate has upon cash flow may ripple through other lead indicators. For example, one of the key lead indicators in the building materials industry is housing starts, but this is predicated, in turn, upon interest rate levels. The next exposure coefficient shown in the table, foreign interest rates, indicates that, for a 1 per cent unanticipated change in their level, real cash flow of the firm rises by 0.2 per cent. Again, it may be the case that only the euro or US interest rate is of any relevance, since it may impinge upon competitors or consumers located in these respective countries. The table goes on to indicate that a 1 per cent unanticipated rise in commodity prices results in a 0.2 per cent fall in real cash flow of the firm. Clearly, what constitutes relevant commodity prices will vary from industry to industry. Cement prices may be critical for one industry but not for another. Steel prices may be significant in one business and not another. And it may be the case that one would wish to allow for more than one critical commodity for a particular strategic business unit. Finally, there is reference in the table to relative prices. This measures the firm's output and/or input prices relative to the general price level. A 1 per cent increase in this ratio results in an increase of 0.6 per cent in the firm's real cash flows.

If the firm's expected real cash flows in the base case are £75m, then by multiplying the exposure coefficient by this amount, we obtain the real effect of changes in the macroeconomic variable detailed in the third column of Table 11.5. We have assumed that the exposure coefficients are partial. This means that they refer to the sensitivity of real cash flows to changes in each variable while other variables are held constant. Thus the domestic interest rate coefficient indicates the effect of a change in domestic interest rates with all other variables held constant.

Once sensitivity measures have been established, financial instruments may be used to hedge exposures. For example, assume that the firm for which data are given in Table 11.5 were concerned only with hedging its dollar/sterling currency exposure. The firm would then deal in the forward market for such an amount that, should there be a 1 per cent strengthening in the dollar against sterling, then the firm would make a profit of £375,000. This would offset the lost £375,000 shown in the table. On the basis of the exchange rate data set out in Table 11.5, the firm would buy twelve-month forward dollars of approximately $67m. Buying this amount of dollars for delivery in twelve months implies that, should there be a depreciation of sterling equivalent to 1 per cent against the dollar, the firm obtains a cash gain of £375,000, which offsets the cash flow loss resulting from the trading depreciation of sterling. Through this means, then, the firm might hedge itself against changes in the sterling/dollar exchange rate.

Other financial contracts, such as interest rate futures, may be used to hedge interest rate exposures. The same can be done in respect of commodity futures. So if the firm wished to hedge exchange rate, interest rate and commodity exposure, it would use foreign exchange forwards, interest rate futures and commodity futures. However, some extra care has to be taken. This arises because of the fact that the value of the forward contract is sensitive to interest rate changes and the value of the interest rate and commodity futures depends upon the exchange rate. The effect of this is that the size of each hedge contract depends upon the size of other hedge contracts.

In connection with the effect upon corporate cash flow of interest rate and exchange rate changes, Oxelheim and Wihlborg (1987, 1989a, b) point out that, on the basis of their practical experience with measures of macroeconomic exposure, they have found that the effects of changes in world interest rate levels have been more statistically pronounced than the effects of exchange rate changes. This evidence would suggest that the traditional method of looking at economic exposure – that is, by focusing upon foreign exchange rate changes – is likely to achieve less good results than the methodology that focuses upon macroeconomic exposure.

Analysis of macroeconomic exposure is very much the leading edge of hedging techniques. Readers interested in pursuing the literature are referred to Oxelheim and Wihlborg's work, of which the content of this chapter so far is a very brief summary. It should be pointed out that they suggest that, in making an analysis of macroeconomic exposure, the analyst should disaggregate cash flows in terms of products, subsidiaries and types of cash flow. While the author would agree that such an analysis would produce a better understanding of the operations of the total corporate entity, it is not necessarily clear why such a breakdown would give us better information with which to undertake a hedging policy. After all, if we are concerned with undertaking a covered strategy designed to eliminate macroeconomic exposure at the group level, it would seem that it is group exposures that are critical rather than exposures at the level of the individual operating companies. Admittedly, if the group has a large number of subsidiary or associated companies which may or may not be wholly owned, then there may be some value in undertaking hedges at the level of the individual companies. However, if this is not so, then there would seem to be no great advantage, beyond that of greater informational content and understanding, to be obtained from carrying out the analysis to the disaggregated level.

Experiments with macroeconomic exposure

It is easy to argue that future developments in corporate hedging policy will take place in the macroeconomic exposure arena. Clearly, assuming that the statistical analysis is undertaken correctly, macroeconomic exposure analysis provides a tool that gets to the very heart of cash flow and profit uncertainty. At the present point in time, there are a number of companies experimenting with the application of this technique. For example, Lighterness (1987) reports that the Rio-Tinto Zinc Corporation plc is using this kind of technique; Maloney (1990) reports that Western Mining is also involved in this kind of analysis; and Garner and Shapiro (1984) report experiments with the technique at Vulcan Materials Co. It is predicted that within the next two decades the major emphasis of exposure management will be in this direction.

11.13 | Value at risk

Value at risk (VAR) is a single number estimate of how much a company can lose due to the price volatility of the instrument it holds for example, a fixed-rate bond or an unhedged currency payable/receivable. More precisely, it defines the likelihood of potential loss not exceeding a particular level, given certain assumptions. These assumptions may involve time horizon, holding period, confidence limits, distribution of probabilities, correlation and the potential for shocks to the system.

VAR is widely used by financial institutions and features strongly in the rules contained in the Capital Adequacy Directives for banks. Its development owes much to bankers J P Morgan whose past chairman demanded a one-page report at the end of business each day summarizing the bank's exposures to losses because of possible market movements in the coming day. J P Morgan's 'Riskmetrics' (a system of measuring VAR) evolved from this request.

VAR's popularity with banks is that it holds out the prospect of aggregating risks across a range of diverse activities and fits well with the banking industry's interest in installing group risk management systems. Corporates, concerned about group risk, seized on VAR as a risk measurement tool. Indeed, the Securities and Exchange Commission (SEC) in the United States has identified VAR as one of several methods which companies might use to summarize market risks in their annual reports.

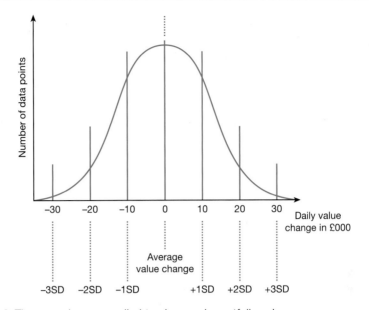

Figure 11.9 The normal curve applied to changes in portfolio value.

VAR is conceptually and practically a powerful tool and needs to be understood by bankers and treasurers alike. However, as we shall see, it falls far short of providing a complete panacea for group risk measurement, particularly for corporates. It does, however, provide a useful estimate of possible losses over a short period under normal market conditions for investments and other instruments which are liquid; in other words, assets and liabilities that can be marked-to-market (valued at objective market prices) and traded freely, for example currency options.

To explain the concept, assume that a financial institution holds a portfolio of fixed interest bonds. The portfolio is unhedged and its value today is therefore based on the current term structure of interest rates – the yield curve today. If we have comparable historic yield data, then we can calculate the value of the portfolio under a wide range of past interest rate scenarios in order to get a distribution of values and of potential changes in value. Most VAR models assume that changes in the value of the portfolio are, on average, random and that their frequency distribution can be estimated using a normal curve – see Figure 11.9. For a normal curve, the standard deviation (σ) is the measure of volatility and data points will be distributed as follows:

$$68.3\% \text{ within} \pm 1\sigma$$
$$95.5\% \text{ within} \pm 2\sigma$$
$$99.7\% \text{ within} \pm 3\sigma$$

If the standard deviation in Figure 11.9 is £10,000, then 95.5% of the time the change in value of the portfolio will be within ±£20,000 (that means, in loss 47.75% of the time and in gain 47.75% of the time). So, the VAR at a 95.5% confidence level is £20,000. If the data are at daily intervals, then this would give the 24-hour VAR. This is what the chairman of J P Morgan wanted.

It is easy to see how the concept can be applied to exchange rate exposure or interest rate exposures that banks may hold. Indeed, bank capital adequacy regulations require measurement of market risk on bank open currency positions as the VAR at 95% confidence limits based on five years' daily data or at 99% confidence limits based on three years' daily data. The bank is then obliged by the regulations to support that VAR by a specific amount of capital – equity and subordinated debt. The bank can calculate the profit it makes by assuming this currency exposure and relate it to the amount of capital used in order to arrive at a return on regulatory capital. If the bank's view of risk differs from the regulators, then the bank is left with a dilemma. It may need to select a portfolio of activities such that, in aggregate, the economic capital requirements and the regulatory capital requirements are equal.

Like most management techniques, there are problems with VAR too. The following are some of the caveats concerning VAR:

■ Changes in value may not be normally distributed. For some instruments, for example options (see Chapters 16 and 17) they are definitely not normally distributed.

■ Shocks to the system may occur with greater frequency than the normal curve implies. So VAR is typically used for normal market conditions and supplemented by stress testing and scenario analysis as modelling devices to quantify the impact of large shocks.

■ For portfolios of risks, some may be correlated, for example, exposures to groups of currencies. Thus, for other than very simple portfolios, one of three calculation methods is normally used. These include:
  (i) the variance/covariance method, involving statistically adjusting data for correlation,
  (ii) historic simulation using historic portfolio returns, and
  (iii) Monte Carlo analysis, which involves a large run of scenarios, say 10,000, to generate a distribution, using one's own assumptions about volatility and correlation. Future volatilities implied by option prices (see Chapters 16 and 17) are sometimes used.

■ The holding period used in the example was 24 hours. An appropriate holding period for each risk type needs to be established and corresponding data captured. One key factor is the degree of liquidity – that is, how fast can the position be liquidated? For holding periods exceeding one month, VAR may not be appropriate because reliability tails off.

For non-bank corporations, there are major additional problems. For example, many corporate assets and risk positions cannot be marked-to-market and neither may they be readily liquidated. Examples are specialized plant, sales revenue risk. In addition, in respect of corporate assets and risk positions, there may not be enough data points for statistical reliability.

For corporates, one way forward is to focus on the volatilities of cash flows for aggregate groups of risk rather than focusing on individual risks themselves and their market values. This approach is called cash flow at risk (CFAR). As an example, assume that the key CFAR relationships for a manufacturing unit are estimated to be the impact of commodity prices, exchange rates and interest rates on sales revenue, cost of goods sold and interest expense. Now, consider a UK corporate exporting to Germany in euros and competing with German imports domestically. Further, assume that both the UK corporate and its German competitors use significant amounts of a US dollar-based commodity.

If the £/euro exchange rate changes, there will be three main exposures for the UK corporate, namely transaction risk on the mark revenue stream, the level of exports to Germany and the level of domestic sales in the face of changed German import prices. Furthermore, £/euro exchange rate adjustments may be part of a wider set of adjustments affecting commodity costs via the £/US dollar rate and the US dollar/euro rate. Interest rates may also be affected. Now, if price elasticities are known, for example the change in German exports for a 1% change in euro exchange rates, then it may be possible to model the impact of currency, commodity and interest price changes on operating cash flow for the manufacturing unit over, say, a quarterly time horizon.

If we were concerned with CFAR for a bank, the regulator would specify the amount of capital required to support a given level of CFAR. However, since our corporate is not a bank, it is only regulated through the market. It can support CFAR risks in a variety of ways – for example, by holding cash reserves, arranging credit lines, postponement of capital expenditure, sale of assets and so on.

The CFAR approach described here melds conventional foreign exchange transaction risk with broader business risk. Conceptually, it is logical. However, in practice, it is complex to implement in a determinate mathematical way. However, this is the sort of approach that group risk management demands and it is the route which is being pursued by companies serious about managing company-wide risk. It is worth noting that VAR and CFAR methodologies are available in treasury software systems.

11.14 | Summary

- Covering exposures is designed to reduce the volatility of a firm's profits and/or cash generation. Presumably, from this it might be deduced that the idea is to reduce the volatility of the value of the firm. And this should lead to enhanced shareholder value. But such a deduction needs to be challenged. While practitioners might accept the virtue of the foregoing argument, financial academics might not. So what is their argument?

- According to the capital asset pricing model (CAPM), well-diversified international investors should not be willing to pay a premium for corporate hedging activities that they, themselves, can readily replicate by adjusting their own portfolios. Hedging to reduce overall variability of cash flow and profits may be important to managers, compensated according to short-term results, but it is irrelevant to diversified shareholders. The ups and downs of individual investments are compensated by holding a well-diversified portfolio.

■ CAPM suggests that what matters in share pricing is systematic risk. If exchange risk and interest rate risk are considered to be unsystematic, then their effect can be diversified away by holding a balanced portfolio. On the other hand, if they are systematic and if forward and interest rate instruments are priced according to CAPM, then all that the firm does by entering into hedging contracts is to move along the security market line. And this adds no value to the firm. In reality, it is arguable that, at the margin, transaction costs in forward contracts actually destroy value.

■ Just as Arsenal and Manchester United are at the apex of English football, so Modigliani and Miller (MM) join CAPM at the top of the first division of corporate finance. (I hope that the aforementioned comment will not cause learning establishments in Liverpool, Leeds or Newcastle to give this text the thumbs down.) And the armoury of MM can also be arrayed against hedging. MM argue, in respect of gearing, that the investor can manufacture home-made leverage which achieves the same result as corporate gearing. The same kind of argument applies in respect of individual hedging versus corporate hedging. In other words, home-made hedging would make corporate hedging irrelevant. But there are counter-arguments here too. Hedging markets are wholesale markets and corporate hedging may, therefore, be cheaper. Furthermore, some hedging techniques are only available to the company – leading and lagging and transfer pricing to name but two. But that is not all. Hedging requires information about current and future exposures and contingent exposures too and it is doubtful whether investors have anything like the wherewithal on this front to achieve optimal hedging – remember that information would be needed for the total portfolio, not just for an individual share. Remember also that data on economic exposure would be embraced by an optimal requirement for information.

■ Hedging may be argued to be a good thing from the standpoint of employees and managers who, clearly, do not have a diversified portfolio of jobs.

■ If the model of corporate valuation is of the form:

$$V_F = \sum \frac{E(\text{NCF}_t)}{(1+k)^t}$$

reflecting that the value of the firm (V_F) is a function of expected net cash flows, $E(\text{NCF})$, discounted at the firm's cost of capital, k, then value can be created by increasing expected net cash flows or lowering the discount rate. If currency risk, interest rate risk and commodity price risk are viewed as diversifiable risks, their hedging cannot lower k – at least, at first sight. But hedging can lower the risk of corporate financial distress – see Figure 11.2. Lowering the risk of bankruptcy enables the firm better to deal with suppliers, customers and employees, to say nothing of bankers. Reducing the risk of financial distress may, from this standpoint, provide significant wherewithal to enhance $E(\text{NCF})$. And it is possible that by lowering the risk of financial distress, debt capacity may be increased with a lowering of the value of k in the above model (assuming an NPV model is used for valuation) or an increase in the value of the tax shield due to debt (should an APV approach be preferred).

- The reader may believe that a more realistic model of valuation conforms to that referred to in the chapter, namely:

$$V_F = \Sigma V_i - P(\sigma)$$

where V_F is the value of the firm, V_i is the net present value of each of the firm's parts and $P(\sigma)$ is a penalty factor that reflects the impact on after tax cash flows of the total risk of the firm. Note that this formula, associated with Adler and Dumas and also Lessard and Shapiro, is not consistent with CAPM ideas – the penalty factor is a function of total risk, not just systematic risk. Anyway, the above proposition of corporate value would obviously suggest that hedging is a good thing for shareholders because, in lowering the penalty factor, corporate value is enhanced.

- Furthermore, this chapter shows that under a tax regime with a convex tax schedule, the firm's net-of-tax cash generation may be increased under an exposure management policy. Again, this is good news for managers, employees, customers, financiers and, in particular, shareholders. Even under a pure CAPM approach, this factor alone would tend to enhance shareholder value.

- The rationale for the centralization of exposure management information can best be seen by virtue of an example. One subsidiary of a UK-based international company may have a C$5m receivable due in six months' time, while another subsidiary has C$5m payable in six months' time. The nature of these two exposures will, at a group level, cancel out. Without an information system that reveals the existence of this kind of internal hedge, divisions may both find themselves covering this kind of exposure.

- To highlight the existence of internal hedges, the chapter suggests a framework for an information system to communicate transaction exposures to head office.

- Like all information systems, it is essential that it should be regularly reviewed to ensure that it is cost effective.

- This chapter makes suggestions as to how a cost-effective system might work. This involves all foreign and home subsidiaries reporting all foreign-currency-denominated transaction exposures and anticipated transaction exposures to the group treasury. The central treasury function then has the information necessary to take decisions designed to optimize at the level of the overall group.

- So far in the text, we have focused upon economic exposure in its guise as the present value of future cash flows expressed in home currency terms and how this present value changes as a result of changed exchange rates. But macroeconomic exposure is broader than this.

- Macroeconomics is concerned with how the firm's cash flows, profits and value change as a result of developments in the economic environment as a whole – that is within the total framework of exchange rates, interest rates, inflation rates, wage levels, key commodity prices and other unexpected shocks to the system.

- The sensitivity of a firm's cash flows, profits, and/or value to changed macro-economic variables may be estimated deductively and measured statistically using regression analysis techniques. The coefficients so obtained can provide the wherewithal for a firm to undertake a logical hedging strategy.

- Macroeconomic exposure management promises to be one of the most powerful tools available to the corporate treasurer. Such techniques are at the leading edge of treasury management. Although not widely encountered at the present point in time, within the next decade or two, their application will become commonplace.

- Value at risk (VAR) estimates the potential pre-tax loss resulting from an adverse movement in interest rates and/or market prices over a defined holding period. It is a measure of sensitivity. It can be used for risks implicit in price movements for equities and commodities, exchange rate and interest rate exposures providing there is a sufficient base of historical data from which to establish the probabilities of future rate changes. There are three popular approaches to developing VAR measures: the tradition correlation method (also called the variance/covariance method), the historic simulation method and the Monte Carlo simulation method. Of these, the correlation method is the simplest and most popular.

- The correlation approach to VAR is built on an assumption that rate changes are, in statistical terms, normally distributed, that is that 68 per cent of changes will fall within ±1 standard deviation of the mean, 95 per cent of changes within ±2 standard deviations and 99 per cent within ±3 standard deviations. By assuming that future changes will follow past changes, it is possible to calculate the maximum adverse change that is likely to occur in, say, $95\frac{1}{2}$ per cent of situations. One of the key decisions for a VAR-based risk management system is the level of statistical confidence to apply. There will always be some risk that a more adverse situation could occur.

- VAR can be calculated for a single instrument, a portfolio of similar instruments or across a bank's entire book. Its application for non-financial institutions is more problematical. But a variant, CFAR (cash flow at risk) has been developed and is being implemented in many corporate treasuries.

11.15 | End of chapter questions

Question 1
Why would an MNC consider examining only its 'net' cash flows in each currency when assessing its transaction exposure?

Question 2
A US-headquartered MNC is assessing its transaction exposures. Its projected cash flows are as follows for the next year:

Currency	Total inflow	Total outflow	Current exchange rate in US$
Ruritanian doppels (RUD)	RUD 4 million	RUD 2 million	$ .15
British pounds (GBP)	GBP 2 million	GBP 1 million	$1.50
Batavian dracs (BTD)	BTD 3 million	BTD 4 million	$ .30

What is your assessment as to the firm's degree of economic exposure? Assume that the RUD and the BTD move in tandem against the US$.

Question 3
Are currency correlations perfectly stable over time? What does your answer imply about using past data on correlations as an indicator for the future?

12 Internal techniques of exposure management

There are a wide range of methods available to minimize foreign exchange risk. This chapter and Chapter 13 focus respectively upon internal and external techniques. Internal techniques use methods of exposure management which are part of a firm's regulatory financial management and do not resort to special contractual relationships outside the group of companies concerned. External techniques use contractual means to insure against potential foreign exchange losses.

Internal techniques of exposure management aim at reducing exposed positions or preventing them from arising. External techniques insure against the possibility that exchange losses will result from an exposed position which internal measures have not been able to eliminate.

Internal techniques embrace netting, matching, leading and lagging, pricing policies and asset/liability management. External techniques include forward contracts, borrowing short term, discounting, factoring, government exchange risk guarantees and currency options. Frequently, some of the above methods are unavailable to the multinational company – netting, matching and leading and lagging are illegal in some countries and restricted in others. It should also be borne in mind that for many less-developed countries there is no forward market in their currencies. We now examine, in turn, netting, matching, leading and lagging, pricing policies and asset/liability management.

12.1 | Netting

Netting involves associated companies which trade with each other. The technique is simple. Group companies merely settle inter-affiliate indebtedness for the net amount owing. Gross intra-group trade receivables and payables are netted out. The simplest scheme is known as bilateral netting. Each pair of associates nets out their own positions with each other and cash flows are reduced by the lower of each company's purchases from or sales to its netting partner. Bilateral netting involves no attempt to bring in the net positions of other group companies.

Bilateral netting is easily illustrated by an example. Assume that the UK subsidiary in a group owes the French subsidiary of the same group the euro equivalent of $6m and at the same time the French company owes the UK company the sterling equivalent of $4m. The actual remittance to clear the inter-company accounts would be

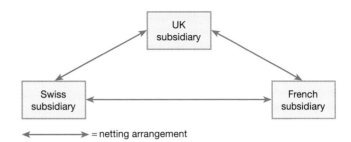

Figure 12.1 Scheme for bilateral netting.

netted down to the equivalent of $2m (in an agreed currency which may be dollars, sterling, euros or any other currency) to be paid by the UK subsidiary to the French counterpart. Between them, the two companies have saved the transfer and exchange costs on the equivalent of $8m. Netting basically reduces the amount of inter-company payments and receipts that pass over the foreign exchanges. Bilateral netting is fairly straightforward to operate, and the main practical problem is usually the decision about what currency to use for settlement.

Multilateral netting is more complicated but in principle is no different from bilateral netting. Multilateral netting involves more than two associated companies' inter-group debt and virtually always involves the services of the group treasury. Bilateral netting involves only two sides and is usually undertaken without the involvement of the corporate centre. Of course, it is true that many subsidiaries may involve themselves in bilateral netting. Figure 12.1 shows how three subsidiaries in a group might be involved in bilateral netting with each other by netting off balances due between pairs of subsidiaries. This scheme involves three lots of bilateral nettings.

Multilateral netting is easily exemplified. Consider a group of companies in which the UK subsidiary buys (during the monthly netting period) $6m worth of goods and services from the Swiss subsidiary and the UK company sells $2m worth of goods to the French subsidiary. During the same month, assume that the Swiss company buys $2m worth of goods and services from the French subsidiary. The potential for multi-lateral netting is shown in the matrix in Table 12.1 (overleaf). It can be seen that settlement of the inter-company debt within the three subsidiaries ends up involving a payment of the equivalent of $4m from the UK company to the Swiss subsidiary.

Unlike the instance referred to in Table 12.1, where bilateral netting could be achieved by a number of subsidiaries netting off balances between each other in pairs, multilateral netting always involves the group treasury as the centre of netting opera-tions (see Figure 12.2 (overleaf)). Participating subsidiaries report all inter-company balances to the group treasury on an agreed date and the treasury subsequently advises all subsidiaries of amounts to be paid to and received from other subsidiaries on a specified date. Multilateral netting yields considerable savings in exchange and transfer costs but it requires a centralized communications system and discipline on the part of subsidiary companies. It should be noted that many countries' exchange controls put restrictions on bilateral and multilateral netting. Exchange control regula-tions need to be investigated carefully before embarking on a policy of netting.

Table 12.1 Multilateral netting matrix ($m)

| | PAYING SUBSIDIARY | | | Total | Net | |
	Swiss	UK	French	receipts	receipts	Eliminated
Receiving Subsidiary						
Swiss	–	6	0	6	4	2
UK	0	–	2	2		2
French	2	0	–	2		2
Total payments	2	6	2	10		
Net payments		4			4	
Eliminated	2	2	2			6

Netting potential: Gross flows $10m
                    Net flows $4m
                    Eliminated flows $6m

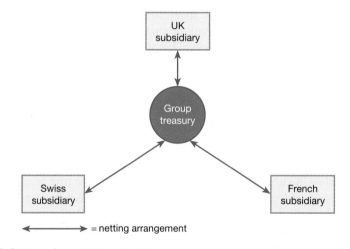

Figure 12.2 Scheme for multilateral netting.

Systems of netting used by international groups of companies involve fairly tight timetables in the period immediately prior to settlement. They usually vary around the following kind of basic schedule:

■ Fix settlement day (e.g. the 6th of every month).

■ Five days before settlement day all participating subsidiaries telex inter-company balances to the centre, stating the currencies of the debt and translating them into a common currency at specified exchange rates.

■ Four days before settlement day inter-company balances are reconciled.

■ Three days before settlement day the group treasury calculates the extent of netting to be used. The centre then issues instructions on payment to subsidiaries.

■ Two days before settlement day subsidiaries instruct their banks to make payments two days hence.

■ Settlement day is when payments and receipts occur.

Netting reduces banking costs and increases central control of inter-company settlements. The reduced number and amount of payments yields savings in terms of buy/sell spreads in the spot and forward markets and reduced bank charges. It is difficult to estimate total benefits but as a guide to the extent of gains flowing from netting techniques McRae and Walker (1980) estimate that savings approximate to one-sixth of 1 per cent of the flows eliminated.

12.2 | Matching

Although netting and matching are terms that are frequently used interchangeably, there are distinctions. Strictly speaking, netting is a term applied to potential flows within a group of companies whereas matching can be applied to both intra-group and third-party balancing.

Matching is a mechanism whereby a company matches its foreign currency inflows with its foreign currency outflows in respect of amount and approximate timing. Receipts in a particular currency are used to make payments in that currency, thereby reducing the need for a group of companies to go through the foreign exchange markets to the unmatched portion of foreign currency cash flows.

The prerequisite for a matching operation is a two-way cash flow in the same foreign currency within a group of companies; this gives rise to a potential for natural matching. This should be distinguished from parallel matching, in which the matching is achieved with receipt and payment in different currencies but these currencies are expected to move closely together, near enough in parallel. An example would be currencies that adhere to a joint currency float. Of course, there is always the chance with parallel matching that the currencies concerned may move away from their previously parallel paths. In this case the expected match fails to be realized.

The practical mechanics of matching are rather like multilateral netting, since it involves the group treasury and gives rise to the need for information centralization with the group finance function just before settlement. Practical problems may arise because of the uncertain timing of third-party receipts and payments. Unexpected delays can create problems for the multinational treasury in its endeavours to match receipts and payments. There are obvious difficulties in the possibility that receipt of a sum due on a certain settlement day is postponed, but payment is nonetheless made on that same date as originally anticipated.

For this reason, success in matching is very much a function of the quality of information coming to the corporate financial centre, including realistic and accurate predictions of settlement dates. Like netting, the extent of matching is constrained by the exchange controls of some countries.

12.3 | Leading and lagging

Leading and lagging refer to the adjustment of credit terms between companies. They are most usually applied with respect to payments between associate companies within a group. Leading means paying an obligation in advance of the due date. Lagging means delaying payment of an obligation beyond its due date. Leading and lagging are aggressive foreign exchange management tactics designed to take advantage of expected devaluations and revaluations of currencies.

An example may help to indicate the processes involved. Suppose that subsidiary b in country B owes money to subsidiary a in country A with payment due in three months' time and with the debt denominated in US$. Suppose further that country B's currency is expected to devalue within three months relative to the US$ and also *vis-à-vis* country A's currency. Obviously, if company B leads – that is, if it pays early – it will have to part with less of country B's currency to buy US$ in order to make payment to company A. So the temptation to lead is attractive.

However, decision takers need to look a little further than this. Should the international Fisher effect be holding in the short term, then the interest rate on deposits in country B's currency should exceed the interest rate on US$ deposits by the amount of the expected devaluation. Decisions on leading and lagging need to take account of relative interest rates as well as expected currency movements. And there is a third relevant dimension, namely the effective tax rates on interest in differing countries. So reverting to our example, we need to compare the net-of-tax cash flow effects after allowing for interest from a group standpoint. Thus, should company b lead, it will save in terms of country B's currency by beating the impending devaluation. But the group will then receive a US$ interest rate rather than an interest rate based on the currency of country B – and this US$ interest rate should be lower than that of country B's currency. All of this has to be taken into account on a net-of-tax basis over the period of the lead.

A similar example could be devised which would suggest lagging. Should country B's currency be expected to revalue or harden against the US$, then lagging would, on the face of things, be suggested. But once again, as is always the case with leading and lagging decisions, we need to consider from a group standpoint the combined impacts of:

■ the expected currency change and its timing;

■ relative interest rates;

■ after-tax effects.

As with matching, the group treasury is usually involved to ensure that the timing of inter-company settlement is functional from a group standpoint rather than merely from a local one. It is also worth mentioning that performance measurement may be affected if some subsidiaries are asked to lead and some to lag. Clearly, the subsidiary that does the leading loses interest receivable and incurs interest charges on the funds led. To overcome this problem, evaluation of performance is frequently done on a pre-interest, pre-tax basis.

The existence of local minority interests gives rise to complications on leading and lagging decisions. Significant local shareholders in the 'losing' subsidiary always raise strong objections because of the added interest costs and lower profitability resulting from the consequent local borrowing. In such cases, the interests of the minority shareholders appear to be subordinated to those of the majority shareholder, the parent company. The existence of strong local minorities frequently results in companies refraining from lead and lag techniques.

Leading and lagging may also be constrained by exchange control regulations. Leading and lagging affect balance of payments figures as well as exchange rates. Because of this, host governments frequently impose allowable bands on credit terms which must be followed in all international trading.

The application of leading and lagging techniques extends beyond the realm of pure risk minimization in exposure management. Opportunities are created for taking aggressive stances on financing. It should be understood that this aggressive strategy is based upon the view, borne out by empirical evidence, that the international Fisher effect does not hold in the short term. Thus an expected devaluation in a host country would probably cause an international company to consider raising local finance to repay borrowings denominated in foreign currency.

12.4 | Pricing policy

In exposure management terms, pricing policy embraces two strategies: price variation and currency of invoicing. Under these headings there are two subsets which are functions of whether trading is with third parties or inside a group of companies. Each of these is now considered.

Price variation

Price variation involves increasing selling prices to counter the adverse effects of exchange rate changes. This tactic raises the question as to why the company has not already raised prices if it is able to do so. In some countries, price increases are the only legally available tactic of exposure management. In most South American countries, for example most other methods are illegal, there is no forward market and local financial markets are so shallow as to make borrowing with the objective of achieving exposure management impossible.

We now turn to price variation on inter-company trade. Transfer pricing is the term used to refer to the pricing of goods and services that change hands within a group of companies. As an exposure management technique, transfer price variation refers to the arbitrary pricing of inter-company sales of goods and services at a higher or lower price than the fair, arm's-length price. This fair price would be the market price if there were an existing market or, if there is not, the price which would be charged to a third-party customer. Taxation authorities, customs and excise departments and exchange control regulations in most countries require that arm's length pricing be used. In virtually all countries in the world, tax authorities have the power to impute a price where transfer price manipulation is suspected, and customs and excise departments base excise duty on an imputed price when the transfer price is not considered to be a fair one.

Having said all this, many multinationals nonetheless attempt to maximize after-tax group cash flows by transfer pricing to minimize tax payable.

Invoicing in foreign currency

Companies engaged in exporting and importing, whether of goods or services, are concerned with decisions relating to the currency in which goods and services are to be invoiced. Trading in a foreign currency gives rise to transaction exposure with its attendant risks and opportunities. Although trading purely in a company's home currency has the advantage of simplicity, it fails to take account of the fact that the currency in which goods are invoiced has become an essential aspect of the overall marketing package given to the customer.

A seller will usually wish to sell in its own currency or the currency in which it incurs cost; this avoids foreign exchange exposure. But buyers' preferences might be for other currencies. Many markets, such as oil or aluminium, effectively require that sales be made in the same currency as that quoted by major competitors, which may not be the seller's own currency. In a buyers' market, sellers increasingly tend to invoice in the buyer's ideal currency. The closer the seller can approximate the buyer's aims, the greater chance it has to make the sale.

Should the seller elect to invoice in foreign currency, perhaps because its prospective customer prefers it that way, or because sellers tend to follow the market leader, then the seller should only choose a major currency in which there is an active forward market for maturities at least as long as the payment period. Currencies that are of limited convertibility, are chronically weak, or have only a limited forward market in London should not be considered.

Where there is the prospect of a major export to a country with a small economy, such that the value of the contract is likely to be a significant factor in that country's balance of payments, then further considerations apply. The seller is advised to avoid the buyer's currency. Where the government or one of its agencies is the customer, it behoves the seller to bear in mind that the customer itself is able to devalue the currency prior to payment, effectively reducing proceeds in the currency of the exporter.

The seller's ideal currency is either its own or one that is stable relative to its own. Often the seller is forced to choose the market leader's currency. Anyway the chosen currency should certainly be one with a deep forward market.

But for the buyer, the ideal currency is usually its own or one that is stable relative to its own, or it may be a currency of which it has reserves or a currency in which it earns reserves.

Strong buyers may be in a position to insist on their own currency being used for pricing; it is often a condition of any deal and quotes in other currencies are simply ignored. An advantage to the seller when selling in the purchaser's currency is that payment is rendered simpler for the buyer; all it must do is make a payment in its own currency. In these circumstances payment is usually much more rapid, and this may constitute good reason for invoicing in the buyer's currency.

Of course, many international traders seek to buy in the same currencies as those in which they receive income, in order to net out exposure at source. This will not necessarily be their home currency. Furthermore, many markets are economically structured in such a way that competitors follow the market leader. In such circumstances it is often the practice of participants to quote in the same currency as that in which the market leader quotes – and this may be the home currency of neither the buyer nor the seller.

Occasionally, it happens that the invoice currency becomes a bone of contention between seller and buyer. Often a proxy currency – that is, one that moves similarly to the buyer's currency – is resorted to as a way of resolving the impasse. Another technique, which was popular in the past although it is less frequently used now, is a currency clause whereby payment is made in one currency but the amount due is fixed by reference to another.

Usually in export contracts at least one party enters into a foreign exchange transaction. It may be the exporter if it is selling in a foreign currency; it may be the importer if it is buying in a currency other than its own. If the currency of the contract is not the home currency of either the importer or the exporter, then both will have to undertake a foreign exchange transaction. Given this background it is eminently sensible to arrange matters such that the cost of doing the foreign exchange contract is minimized. Foreign currency markets within Europe vary widely in their competitiveness and spread or commission structure. For example, French exchange controls used to require that a French company did its foreign exchange deals with a bank in France where costs were high by London standards. The same was true in Scandinavian countries. For those who are able to access it, the London market is the cheapest foreign exchange market to deal in throughout the world. If one of the parties to a trade is based in a country where exchange controls make it relatively expensive to use local foreign exchange markets, it may be wise to structure the deal such that the cheaper London market may be accessed. This is pertinent for intergroup trading. For example, assume that Ruritania (or another fictitious country) has exchange controls. For an Anglo-Ruritanian trade it may be worthwhile to invoice in the Ruritanian currency so that no foreign exchange transaction arises in Ruritania and the foreign exchange deal takes place in London.

The arguments set out above relate to marketing aspects of the question of invoicing in foreign currency. None relates to aspects such as seeking to invoice in strong currencies, which is an issue that seems to concern a great number of companies. Our view is that, in countries without exchange controls, devoting time to seeking to invoice in strong currencies is a waste of effort, since if the company wishes to be long in particular currencies it is free to buy these whether or not there is any underlying trade. Forward markets, futures, currency swaps and currency options all provide scope for the aggressive company to take positions in currencies if its top management so desires. This would seem to be a more direct method of backing one's judgement on currencies without involving directly the basic business operations of the company.

Having said this, there are commercial reasons why a company in a country with or without exchange controls might prefer to use a strong currency as the medium in which it invoices in international trade. The most frequently quoted reason is to enable the firm to maintain stable price lists in circumstances where price lists are expensive to alter. In countries with exchange controls, it is usually the case that trade represents the only mechanism by which a company is able, legally, to take positions in foreign currencies.

Many companies with strong positions in markets where they are under short-term pressure from competitors may decide to invoice in a currency expected to be weak. Thus, as the currency of invoicing depreciates, so the customer receives an increasing discount on the goods without the company formally announcing a price cut. This tactic enables the company to protect market share while market conditions are poor. Conversely, a company in a strong market position in a sellers' market might, in the short term, specify a strong currency for invoicing, thus obtaining the benefit of a continuously rising price in the home currency without formally changing its prices.

In countries where exchange controls limit the taking of positions in foreign currencies, international companies use cross-frontier trade as one of the very few mechanisms available to back their commercial judgement on future exchange rate movements. In these circumstances, and with respect to third-party trade, the defensive strategy is to attempt to invoice all exports and to have all imports invoiced in the home currency irrespective of the strength and weakness of other currencies. By contrast, the aggressive tactic is to seek to invoice export sales in hard currencies and seek to obtain purchases invoiced in relatively soft currencies. When exchange controls are in place and forward markets are expensive to use, the currency of invoicing technique becomes pertinent. Customers frequently seek to buy goods in weak currencies, while the selling company may prefer to invoice in strong currencies. So there is a clear conflict of interests. Marketing executives may prefer to close a sale by whatever means possible and may be functionally influenced to choose the weak currency, while this policy is dysfunctional from a total company standpoint. Evidently, there should be some marketing systems control mechanism which prevents this dysfunctional tactic.

We now turn to currency of invoicing in the context of inter-company trade. Analysed from a pre-tax point of view, the distinction between aggressive and defensive currency of invoicing disappears when looking at inter-company trade between subsidiaries of equal ownership status, but this is not so where there are minority interests. Currency of invoicing is a zero-sum game and therefore the potential benefit to one subsidiary from currency of invoicing equals the potential loss to the other. However, after-tax effects must never be left out of our decision-making criteria and in this context there may be gains to be achieved from currency of invoicing techniques. Consider two subsidiaries, A and B (both in different countries), which trade with each other. Suppose that A pays a higher marginal tax rate than B. In these circumstances, and with all other things being equal, A might logically invoice B in a weak currency while B invoices A in a strong currency. This policy concentrates exchange profits in B and puts losses into A, hence increasing overall after-tax income and cash flow.

12.5 | Asset and liability management

We now consider the final internal technique of exposure management: asset and liability management. This technique can be used to manage balance sheet, income statement or cash flow exposures. As stated earlier, we believe that concentration on cash flow exposure makes economic sense but emphasis on pure translation exposure is misplaced. Hence our focus here is on asset/liability management as a cash flow exposure management technique. However, there are many other texts that take the other and, in our opinion, ill-conceived view that asset/liability management should be applied to non-cash flow exposure management.

In essence, asset/liability management can involve aggressive or defensive postures. In the aggressive attitude, the firm simply increases exposed cash inflows denominated in currencies expected to be stronger and increases exposed cash outflows denominated in weak currencies. By contrast, the defensive approach involves matching cash inflows and outflows according to their currency of denomination, irrespective of whether they are in strong or weak currencies.

Commentators frequently distinguish between operating variables and financing variables. This distinction is useful from an asset/liability standpoint. Manipulation of operating variables to manage cash flow exposure can best be illustrated by an example. Suppose that a UK exporter with an ongoing inflow from sales in US dollars wishes to avoid the dollar exposure. It will most probably use the forward market to do this. However, it might decide to source a significant volume of purchases from the United States, or, at least, denominated in US dollars. By adopting this policy there is a partial match of currency denomination of inflow with currency denomination of outflow.

With respect to financing variables, the international company has considerable discretion in terms of asset/liability management. The aggressive stance will be to increase exposed cash, debtors and loans receivable in strong currencies (taking due consideration of interest impact, potential currency movements and tax effects) and to increase borrowings and trade creditors in weak currencies (again allowing for interest effects, potential currency depreciation and tax impacts). At the same time, policy will involve reducing exposed borrowings and trade creditors in strong currencies and reducing cash, debtors and loans receivable in weak currencies. In the multinational company operating in a country with a weak currency, the aim will be to acquire local debt and remit cash balances as quickly as possible to the hard currency parent either as dividend remittances or as parent loan repayments. The capital structure of subsidiaries based in countries with a weak currency may be organized to facilitate transfer of funds. For example, retained earnings may not be capitalized so that dividend flexibility is maintained by keeping up revenue reserves. Also a high ratio of inter-company debt to parent equity in the subsidiary company's capital structure might help the repatriation of money in circumstances where a high dividend payment might be restricted or discriminated against tax-wise.

However, some of these financial strategies are constrained in many countries by a paucity of local financial sources. Furthermore, host governments often impose limits for debt to equity ratios and restrict dividend repatriation to certain percentages of capital raised outside of the host country. Host governments frequently also penalize, with heavy taxes, dividends in excess of certain stipulated levels.

12.6 ┃ Summary

- Internal techniques of exposure management are those that do not resort to special contractual relationships outside the group of companies concerned. Such techniques include netting, matching, leading and lagging, pricing policies and asset/liability management.

- Netting involves associated companies with debts, possibly as a result of trade with each other. Associate companies simply cancel out amounts owed with amounts due and settle for the difference. At its simplest level, there is bilateral netting; at a more sophisticated level, we have multilateral netting. Either way, the group treasury plays an active part in co-ordinating settlement payments between associated companies. Netting reduces banking costs. It has been estimated that savings of approximately one-sixth of 1 per cent of the flows eliminated are likely to accrue from netting.

- Matching is a term applied to a similar techniques which involves not just affiliates, but also third parties.

- Leading and lagging are techniques that are resorted to in the light of expected devaluations or revaluations. These mechanisms simply involve making an advance payment or delaying payment on amounts due and denominated in foreign currency. The basic idea is to reduce the amount of local currency needed to settle a debt. It should be noted that it is necessary to take into account the effects of interest payments and receipts when considering the implementation of a leading or lagging tactic.

- Pricing policy, used as an exposure management technique, simply involves increasing prices to allow for expected changes in exchange rates or invoicing in a particular currency to reduce the risk associated with invoicing in the host currency when a devaluation is expected.

- Asset and liability management, used in the context of exposure management, involves manipulation of operating or financial variables to balance the currency of payments with the currency of inflows. Thus, a UK subsidiary may raise Canadian dollar finance with a view to offsetting, partially, the fact that its sales are denominated in Canadian dollars. It takes on a Canadian dollar liability to balance the Canadian dollar asset.

12.7 | End of chapter questions

Question 1
What is netting and how can it improve an MNC's performance?

Question 2
How can an MNC implement leading and lagging techniques to help subsidiaries in need of funds?

13 External techniques of exposure management

External techniques of exposure management resort to contractual relationships outside a group of companies to reduce the risk of foreign exchange losses. External techniques include forward exchange contracts, short-term borrowing, financial futures contracts, currency options, discounting bills receivable, factoring receivables, currency overdrafts, currency swaps and government exchange risk guarantees. Each of these, bar currency swaps, financial futures and currency options, is briefly considered in this chapter.

13.1 | Forward markets

Forward markets are available in most, but not all, major currencies of the world. Although in some markets very large sums may be difficult to deal, forward markets for periods out to ten years are available for popular currencies such as the US dollar against sterling, Swiss francs, yen, guilders, Canadian dollars, euros and so on. Generally speaking, the larger the deal, the longer the settlement date is away and the more exotic the currencies involved, the less is the likelihood that a forward contract is obtainable.

A forward foreign exchange contract is an agreement between two parties to exchange one currency for another at some future date. The rate at which the exchange is to be made, the delivery date and the amounts involved are fixed at the time of the agreement. Such a contract must be distinguished from a foreign exchange futures contract and a brief definition is given here. A futures foreign exchange contract is a contract between two parties for the exchange of a standardized amount of foreign currency at a standard future date. On most financial futures exchanges, the sterling/US dollar contract is for £62,500 with delivery dates in most markets fixed for a specified day in the contract month, which may be either March, June, September or December. A forward contract is usually completed by actual delivery of the currency involved. Futures contracts are more usually closed out by completing a deal in the reverse direction before the maturity date – rather than actually taking delivery on the delivery date.

Reference was made in Chapter 5 to the methods by which bankers quote forward rates. It may be worth while briefly revising the content of that chapter.

Table 13.1 Forward cover example

Contract data

Seller	UK exporter
Buyer	Importer in Jansland
Contract date	1 May 2004
Credit term	3 months
Expected payment date	31 July 2004
Invoice value	Geld 5m (the geld is the currency of Jansland)

Exchange rates quotes at 1 May 2004

Spot	$7.92^3/_4$–$7.93^1/_2$ (Geld $7.92^3/_4$–$7.93^1/_2$ to the £)
1 month forward	$3^7/_8$–$3^1/_2$ cpm (100 cents = 1 geld)
2 months forward	$6^3/_4$–$6^1/_8$ cpm
3 months forward	$9^5/_8$–$8^7/_8$ cpm
4 months forward	$12^1/_2$–$11^5/_8$ cpm

Outright exchange rate quotes at 1 May 2004

Spot	$7.92^3/_4$–$7.93^1/_2$
1 month forward	$7.88^7/_8$–7.90
2 months forward	7.86–$7.87^3/_8$
3 months forward	$7.83^1/_8$–$7.84^5/_8$
4 months forward	$7.80^1/_4$–$7.81^7/_8$

Mechanism of forward contract

1 May 2004	UK exporter sells Geld 5m forward 3 months at $7.84^5/_8$
31 July 2004	UK exporter receives Geld 5m from Jansland importer
	UK exporter delivers Geld 5m and receives sterling at the rate of Geld $7.84^5/_8$ equals £1
	For Geld 5m he receives £637,755

13.2 | Trading purpose of the forward market

By entering into a forward foreign exchange contract, a UK importer or exporter is able to fix, at the time of the contract, a price for the purchase or sale of a fixed amount of foreign currency for delivery and payment at a specified future time. By so doing they may eliminate foreign exchange risk through future exchange rate fluctuations. This enables the exact sterling value of an international commercial contract to be calculated despite the fact that payment is to be made in the future in a foreign currency. Table 13.1 indicates the mechanism of forward cover.

If a foreign currency stands at premium in the forward market, it shows that the currency is 'stronger' than the home currency in that forward market. By contrast, if a foreign currency stands at a discount in the forward market, it shows that the currency is 'weaker' than the home currency in that forward market. The words stronger and weaker are put in inverted commas because, in the context of forward markets, strength and weakness merely take account of interest rate differentials as suggested by interest rate parity.

Of course, the reality of the business world is such that one cannot be certain when a customer will pay a bill. He or she may pay before the due date or may pay afterwards. In the example in Table 13.1 it was assumed that the customer in Jansland (a fictitious non-euro zone country) would pay on 31 July 2004, that is three months after invoice date. Let us suppose now that the Jansland purchaser is expected to pay on some uncertain date between 30 June and 31 August 2004.

Forward options

The UK exporter may decide to cover despite an uncertain payment date via a forward option. How does the forward option work? Like all forward contracts, the exchange rate is irrevocably fixed when the contract is made, but with a forward option contract the precise maturity date is left open – it is for the company to decide subsequently. There is a caveat though; the maturity date must fall within a specified option period. Reverting to our numerical example, assume that the UK exporter expects payment between 30 June and 31 August 2004 – that is between two and four months from invoice date. Since the bank giving the option as to timing does not know exactly when exercise of the option will occur, it charges the premium or discount for the most costly of the settlement dates within the customer's option period. In other words, the bank charges its customer the worst rate during the option period. In our example, the forward option is over the third and fourth months. In Table 13.1 it will be seen that the rate is therefore Geld $7.87^3/_8$; in this case (but not always) the rate to the seller of geld is the full two months' discount. This is the worst rate between month 2 and month 4 for selling geld.

It should be clearly understood that the forward option contract, or optional date forward contract as it is sometimes called, is not a currency option. The forward option is optional in terms of the date of delivery – currency must be delivered under the contract. However, under a currency option, currency need not be delivered.

Swap deals

Another method of dealing with unspecified settlement dates is by a swap deal. This method is virtually always cheaper than covering by way of forward options. A swap involves the simultaneous buying and selling of a currency for different maturities. Swap deals used for forward cover are of two basic types: forward/forward and spot/forward. In either case, the exporter begins by covering the foreign currency transaction forward to an arbitrarily selected but fixed date, just as in an ordinary fixed-date forward contract. Then, if the precise settlement date is subsequently agreed before the initial forward contract matures, the original settlement date may be extended to the exact date by a forward/forward swap. Alternatively, if an exact settlement date is not agreed by the date when the initial forward contract matures, the forward cover may be extended by a spot/forward swap. This may sound quite complicated; a closer look shows that it is not all that difficult.

A forward/forward swap, or forward swap as it is sometimes called, is merely a pair of forward exchange contracts involving a forward purchase and a forward sale of a currency, simultaneously entered into but for different maturities. A numerical example may help describe how the forward/forward swap works.

Assume that the details of an export contract from the United Kingdom to Jansland are as set out in Table 13.1 except that the expected settlement date is uncertain (maybe because delivery date is equally uncertain). The UK exporter takes out a forward contract on 1 May 2004 (the date of the sale contract with the Jansland importer). This forward contract is for an arbitrary period, say two months. So he or she sells Geld 5m forward for delivery on 30 June 2004. Now let us suppose that on 20 June 2004, the UK exporter and the Jansland purchaser agree that settlement will take place on 31 July 2004. What the UK exporter needs to do now is to counter the original forward sale of geld for settlement on 30 June and replace it with a contract for delivery on 31 July. This he or she does by buying Geld 5m forward for delivery on 30 June (thereby creating a contra to the original forward sale of geld) and simultaneously selling Geld 5m forward 41 days, thereby extending delivery to 31 July. Let us further assume that on 20 June 2004, the bank gives the UK exporter the following quotes:

Spot	7.94–7.95
10 days forward	$1/_4$c–$1/_2$c discount
1 month forward	$1/_2$c–$3/_4$c discount
41 days forward	$3/_4$c–1c discount

Turning these quotes into full forward data, remembering that the bid/offer spread is wider in the forward market than in the spot market, we obtain:

Spot	7.94–7.95
10 days forward	7.9425–7.9550
1 month forward	7.9450–7.9575
41 days forward	7.9475–7.9600

Thus the overall covering mechanism can be seen to involve the following

1 May 2004	Sell Geld 5m for £ forward 2 months at 7.87$3/_8$	
	(delivery 30 June 2004)	£635,021
20 June 2004	Buy Geld 5m for £ forward 10 days at 7.9425	
	(delivery 30 June 2004)	(629,525)
20 June 2004	Sell Geld 5m for £ forward 41 days at 7.96	
	(delivery 31 July 2004)	628,141
	Net sterling proceeds	£633,637

As can be seen from the above, leg two of the total mechanism reverses leg one. Legs two and three are the opposite sides of the forward swap.

The effect of the above forward swap deal is that the UK exporter has locked in as of 1 May 2004 at the forward rate for two months' cover adjusted for the premium/discount for a further month given by the bid/offer spread incurred on the forward/forward swap. Of course, as at May 2004 the exporter does not know what the premium/discount will be on extending the contract, neither will he or she know what the bid/offer spread will be on the swap. The unknown premium/discount is a function of interest rate differentials prevailing on Eurosterling and Euro-geld at the date when the forward swap is done.

This forward swap deal will mean that on the first two legs the UK exporter makes a profit which will be received from the bank on 30 June 2004. The UK exporter's cash flow on the foreign exchange cover becomes:

30 June 2004	Profit received from bank	£ 5,496
31 July 2004	Sale of receivable at 7.96	628,141
		£633,637

Rather than doing a forward/forward deal the bank would be prepared to roll the contract for their customer. Rolling this old contract forward would work as follows. The market rate for rolling the contract forward by one month is 1.75 centimes (7.96 less 7.9425). So the bank will adjust the original forward deal by 1.75 centimes. For settlement on 31 July 2004, the bank would charge $7.89\frac{1}{8}$ and the sterling proceeds, payable on 31 July 2004 would be:

$$\frac{5,000,000}{7.89125} = £633,613$$

This amount is approximately the same as from the forward/forward swap. Differences are frequently much greater than the small variation in our example. However, the rolling process illustrated above is approximate and it can cost the bank's customer dear at times. The swap mechanism is always cheaper for the customer.

A spot/forward swap is similar to a forward swap. It again involves a simultaneous pair of foreign exchange contracts, one of which is a spot contract while the other is a forward contract. Reverting to our numerical example, the original forward deal would be for the arbitrarily set two-month period. But the exporter would wait until 30 June 2004 to reverse this deal and to extend maturity to the expected settlement date, namely 31 July 2004. The mechanism might then be summarized as:

1 May 2004	Sell Geld 5m for £ forward 2 months	
	at $7.87\frac{3}{8}$ (delivery 30 June)	£635,021
30 June 2004	Buy Geld 5m for £ spot at (say) 8.05	(621,118)
30 June 2004	Sell Geld 5m for £ forward 31 days at	
	(say) 8.0725 (delivery 31 July 2004)	619,387
	Net sterling proceeds	£633,290

The above figuring assumes the spot rate to buy geld as of 30 June 2004 had moved to 8.0500 and the one-month forward rate as of that date had become 8.0725 to sell geld for sterling. Had the customer rolled the old contract forward on 30 June 2004, the proceeds as of 31 July would have been:

$$\frac{5,000,000}{7.89625} = £633,212$$

Again, this is not far out compared with the spot/forward method.

In practice, the forward/forward or spot/forward swap is the preferred method of dealing with uncertain settlement dates. But the option forward contract is a useful mechanism for dealing with a continuing stream of foreign currency payments or receipts. Where a firm's sales include a large number of small transactions denominated in foreign currency terms, it is expensive both in transaction and administrative costs to cover each individual deal. This problem may be overcome by taking out a single, large forward option contract to cover the approximate expected total cash value of the large number of different receivables or payables. Although the large number of small exports would normally have different settlement dates, forward options are ideally suited to this kind of situation. The amount of the forward contract is usually rounded off. Because of this, it is usually necessary to close out bulk forward contracts of this sort by a spot purchase or sale to balance amounts due from or to the bank.

As an example, assume that a UK exporter is sending goods to Koudland (a fictitious non-euro zone country). The exporter is expecting a series of Koudland kas receipts during the course of the six months from 10 January to 10 July. This rough total is estimated at kas 10m. To cover this, the exporter sells kas 10m on a six-month forward option with the option over the whole period. Assume that the rate is kas 15.61 to the pound and that the Koudland kas receipts delivered from proceeds of sales are as follows:

Feb 16	kas 2.4m @ 15.61 = £153,748
Mar 21	kas 2.6m @ 15.61 = 166,560
June 16	kas 3.1m @ 15.61 = 198,591
June 21	kas 1.5m @ 15.61 = 96,092
Sterling proceeds from kas 9.6m @ 15.61 =	£614,991

Thus the exporter has delivered kas 9.6m. If no more kas receipts come in from sales up to 10 July, the exporter must close out the deal by buying in kas 400,000 in the spot market on that date and delivering this against the balance of the forward option contract. If the spot rate on 10 July is kas 15.25, then the receipts for the forward option come out at:

Sterling proceeds from sale of kas 9.6m (as above)	£614,991
Cost of buying in kas 0.4m on 10 July at spot rate of kas 15.25	(26,230)
Sterling proceeds from sale of kas 0.4m at kas 15.61	25,625
Net sterling proceeds	£614,386

Had our exporter actually received in excess of the kas 10m during the forward option period, the excess would be sold spot for sterling.

13.3 | Short-term borrowing

Short-term borrowing provides an alternative way of covering a receivable or payable denominated in a foreign currency. The availability of this technique as a practical tool of exposure management is subject to local credit availability and transactions must conform to exchange controls, which may restrict its use.

The mechanism is best illustrated by a numerical example and for this purpose we return to the data in Table 13.1. Our UK exporter had a three-month exposure of Geld 5m from the contract date of 1 May 2004, through to settlement date on 31 July 2004. Assume that the exporter decides to use short-term borrowing to cover the transaction exposure. Simultaneously with the signing of the contract, he should borrow a sum in Jansland geld such that with interest the expected receipt of Geld 5m in three months' time will repay the principal and accrued interest. This geld sum should be switched immediately to sterling via the spot market. With Jansland geld three-month interest rates equal to $5^3/_{32}$ per cent p.a., the sum to borrow would be Geld 4,937,129 since this would mean that Geld 5m would be payable to clear the loan and interest in three months' time. Converting the borrowing to sterling at the spot rate of Geld 7.935 = £1 would yield £622,196 and if this were immediately put on deposit at the UK investment rate of 10 per cent p.a., this would grow to £637,751 (given by £622,196 × 1.025) at the end of three months. This is approximately the same as the yield on the forward transaction (see Table 13.1).

In practice, it might be the case that our exporter decided to borrow Geld 5m on the signing of the contract and at the same date to buy Geld 63,672 forward (made up as Geld 5m × $5^3/_{32}$ × $^3/_{12}$). He would simultaneously sell the Geld 5m for sterling via the spot market. Thus the UK exporter is completely covered against exchange risk. On 31 July 2004 the UK company receives Geld 5m from its Jansland customer and this is used to repay principal of the Jansland geld borrowing. The exporter simultaneously receives Geld 63,672 from the forward contract and this amount is used to cover accrued interest. All these transactions can be tied in at rates determined on 1 May 2004. Then rates are unaffected by subsequent currency and/or interest rate movements over the exposure period. If the proceeds of the Geld 5m borrowing are switched to sterling at the spot rate on 1 May 2004, the overall proceeds of the deal are as follows:

1 May 2004	Borrow Geld 5m at $5^3/_{32}$% p.a.	
	Buy Geld 63,672 forward 3 months at $7.83^1/_8$	
	Sell Geld 5m spot to give £630,120 at $7.93^1/_2$	
	Invest £630,120 for 3 months at 10% p.a.	
31 July 2004	Receive Geld 5m from customer; use this to repay principal of loan	
	Deliver Geld 63,672 to cover loan interest	
	This comes from forward contract	(£8,131)
	Receive proceeds of sterling loan given by £630,120 at 10% p.a. for 3 months	645,873
	Net sterling proceeds	£637,742

The slightly different proceeds from this transaction arise because the amount borrowed is Geld 5m as opposed to Geld 4.937m.

By this kind of mechanism, any receivable or payable which can be covered by a forward contract may be covered by short-term borrowing, assuming credit is available and that exchange controls do not prohibit any leg of the transaction.

Just as we looked at imprecise settlement dates and how to cover these via a forward option, so we can cover this eventuality by taking an overdraft type of loan.

Rather than doing a forward option for, say, between three and six months, we could arrange an overdraft borrowing for the amount of a receivable for a period of up to six months and remit the proceeds of the borrowing via the spot market to the home country. A complication arises because interest rates on overdraft loans float up and down. Consequently, interest payable cannot be tied in for certain. Interest is usually catered for by a spot transaction, after the event, namely at the date when the borrowing is repaid. But by the same token, the proceeds of the borrowing remitted to the home country via the spot market will earn interest and this will vary according to market conditions in the home country. The interest payable and receivable may both be left to market conditions at floating rates.

Earlier in this chapter we considered briefly how a continuing stream of foreign currency exposures could be covered using the forward market. This kind of situation can also be covered via short-term borrowing. The company in the home country arranges a borrowing facility in the currency of invoicing. This technique can be used simultaneously to handle the problems of continuing foreign currency exposures and uncertain settlement dates. Assume that we have a UK exporter with a continuing stream of Koudland kas export receipts. These can be covered by arranging a fixed rate kas borrowing. When each export contract is finalized, the exporter immediately draws down the kas loan by the amount of the sale and converts the proceeds into sterling. As the receivables are settled, the kas are paid into the exporter's kas account so that the borrowing is reduced. As long as the kas borrowing rate is fixed over the exposure term, the receivable is fully covered against exchange risk.

13.4 | Discounting foreign-currency-denominated bills receivable

Discounting can be used to cover export receivables. Where an export receivable is to be settled by a bill of exchange, the exporter may discount the bill and thereby receive payment before the settlement date. The bill may either be discounted with a bank in the customer's country, in which case the foreign currency proceeds can be repatriated immediately at the current spot rate, or it can be discounted with a bank in the exporter's country so that the exporter may receive settlement direct in home currency. Either way, the exporter is covered against exchange risk, the cost being the discount rate charged by the bank.

13.5 | Factoring foreign-currency-denominated receivables

Like discounting, factoring can be used for covering export receivables. When the export receivable is to be settled on open account, rather than by a bill of exchange, the receivable can be assigned as collateral for bank financing. Normally such a service gives protection against exchange rate changes, though during unsettled periods in the foreign exchange markets appropriate variations in the factoring agreement are usual. Commercial banks and specialized factoring institutions offer factoring services. For the exporter the technique is very straightforward: he simply sells his export receivables to the factor and receives home currency in return. The costs involved include credit risks, the cost of financing, and the cost of covering exchange risk. For these reasons, factoring tends to be an expensive means of covering exposure, although there may be offsetting benefits such as obtaining export finance and reducing sales accounting and credit collection costs.

13.6 | Currency overdrafts

Overdrafts in Eurocurrencies are available in the London money markets in all of the major currencies although banks tend to specialize by currency. The US dollar and the euro are the currencies in which the greatest amounts are advanced.

In terms of avoidance of exposure, all that a company needs to do is to maintain the amount of its foreign currency receivables in a particular currency equal to the balance on the overdraft in that currency. However, if the company uses the proceeds of the receivables to run down the overdraft, then it also needs to draw down the foreign currency loan as sales denominated in foreign currency are made. Some companies find it more convenient to sell the proceeds of foreign-denominated receivables spot rather than to be perpetually adjusting the level of the overdraft. However, if the level of the currency overdraft remains constant, there is an assumption that new sales denominated in foreign currency are exactly offsetting incoming foreign receipts. This may not be realistic. If this is the case then, even with this method, it becomes necessary to refer to the level of foreign currency receivables and increase or run down the overdraft to ensure that exposure is being covered.

The currency overdraft is a particularly useful and economical technique of exposure management where a company carries a large number of small items denominated in foreign currency, all with uncertain payment dates.

In some countries, use of the currency overdraft exposure management technique may be limited by exchange controls which prevent residents from using foreign-currency-denominated bank accounts.

Another similar technique is the currency bank account. This is particularly useful where a company engaged in international trade has receivables in excess of payables in the same currency. The company opens a foreign-currency-denominated deposit account into which receivables in a particular currency are paid and out of which foreign-denominated payments in that currency are made. For example, should a UK company have a US dollar receivable of $2m due on 31 October and should it also have a payment to be made on 30 November of $1.5m, the company might open a dollar-denominated deposit account into which it pays the $2m. Of this, $$^1/_2$$m would be remitted via a previously arranged forward deal for delivery on 31 October and 1^1/_2$$m would remain in the account to meet the payment due on 30 November. In addition, at the end of November some interest would have accrued on the US dollar bank account.

This kind of exercise is designed to save making a large number of forward deals which are priced to the bank's customer on the basis of the worst rate during a future period. In the above example, the trader received US dollar interest on the deposit left in the currency account. Had he or she remitted all proceeds from the initial receivable to the UK, he or she could have obtained a UK interest rate on the proceeds. It can be seen that the essential net saving for the company arises from eliminating the bid/offer spread on amounts left in the currency account to meet future payables. However, a careful comparison should be made of the expected proceeds from the currency account technique with both the outturns from doing a large number of forward deals and the payoff from a forward option since the currency account may not always be the best choice. Remember that the pricing of forward deals is based on interbank Eurocurrency interest differentials, and using markets based on these differentials may give a superior result to the reliance on bank deposit accounts.

13.7 | Exchange risk guarantees

As part of a series of encouragements to exporters, government agencies in many countries offer their businesses insurance against export credit risks and certain export financing schemes. Many of these agencies offer exchange risk insurance to their exporters as well as the usual export credit guarantees. The exporter pays a small premium and in return the government agency absorbs all exchange risk, thereby taking profits and absorbing losses.

The precise details vary from one export finance agency to another and the exact offerings should be checked with such bodies as ECGD in the UK, HERMES in Germany, COFACE in France, Netherlands Credit Insurance Company in the Netherlands, Eximbank in the United States and so on. Nowadays, most countries have export credit and other similar government agencies offering to absorb foreign exchange exposure risk on export and import transactions in return for a fee.

13.8 | Counterparty risk

In providing forward cover for customers, banks take on risk. And just as they do for loans, they evaluate this risk and set credit limits. In this section we consider how a bank might go about this process of risk evaluation. The risk that the bank runs arises from two areas; the risk on unmatured forward contracts and settlement risk. We consider the risk on unmatured contracts first.

When a bank contracts a forward foreign exchange deal with its customer, it will wish at the same time to enter into an opposite transaction so that the net effect is for the bank to have a square position or balanced book.

If the bank's customer should go bankrupt prior to the maturity of the contract, then the bank knows that it will not receive the funds from the customer to satisfy the matching deal done in the market. The bank will enter the market again to buy in the necessary funds to meet the deal at current exchange rates. This will probably be at a different rate from that at which the original deal was done. This difference will cause the bank to incur either a loss or perhaps a profit resulting from the financial failure of its customer.

Because of this, banks set limits on the extent of the risk they are prepared to run on each customer on their books. This credit assessment is done in the normal manner by reference to the company's balance sheet and other indicators of financial health. Setting a limit for foreign exchange deals is exactly similar to setting a limit for the amount and period of an unsecured loan. But it is less easy to establish the extent of the risk represented by an unmatured forward contract. One might set a limit on the total deals outstanding to each counterparty as a gross total. But clearly this implies that all unmatured deals carry an equal degree of risk. An improvement would be an acceptance that deals with a short maturity involve less risk than longer ones and to allow for that in calculating exposure. In fact, banks have computer programs designed to estimate their exposure to each customer allowing for such factors as past exchange rate volatility as between currencies, period to run to maturity and whether the existing contracts would show a profit or a loss if the customer failed and it became necessary to replace them at ruling market rates.

We now turn to settlement risk. This may arise should the customer fail to deliver the currency concerned to the bank on settlement day and then go bankrupt. The bank's problem is that settlement of a foreign exchange contract is simultaneous – the bank pays away the currency due to the customer or its supplier in expectation of simultaneous receipt from the customer of countervalue. Banks are not usually in a position to ensure that countervalue has been received prior to paying away the currency amount. So if the customer fails just after the bank has paid away currency without receipt of countervalue from the customer, the bank has lost this amount. This kind of risk is only present on and immediately after settlement day up to when settlement is made. Most banks operate a system of settlement limits fixing a maximum amount for the settlement to be made on one date for each customer prior to receipt of countervalue.

Having calculated a limit for a customer, the essence of what banks do in terms of estimating whether a limit is breached is to weight contracts that are near to maturity by a small amount and those far from maturity by a larger figure. Thus a bank might adopt a policy of weighting contracts with one month or less to run to maturity by 0.10, contracts with up to three months to run by 0.15, contracts with up to six months to run by 0.20 and contracts with over six months to run by 0.25.

13.9 | Summary

- External techniques of exposure management resort to contractual relationships outside a group of companies to reduce the risk of foreign exchange losses.

- External techniques include forward exchange contracts, short-term borrowing and depositing, financial futures contracts, currency options, discounting bills receivable, factoring receivables, currency overdrafts and currency hold accounts, currency swaps and government exchange risk guarantees. Most of these are considered in this chapter, but swaps, financial futures and currency options are considered in Chapters 14, 15, 16 and 17.

■ The most well-known external method of exposure management involves the forward contract. This may be used to cover receivables and payables, but it also enables a company or high-net-worth individual to speculate on foreign currency movements.

■ Forward markets are available in most major currencies of the world – but by no means all.

■ Forward markets are available for periods beyond five years for such currencies as US dollars, sterling, euros, Swiss francs, yen, Canadian dollars, Danish kroner, Swedish kronor and so on. Ten-year forwards are quoted by some banks for many of the above. The forward market may be used to cover a receipt or payment denominated in a foreign currency when the date of receipt for payment is known. But it can be readily adapted to allow for situations when the exact payment date is not known.

■ Techniques available to deal with imprecise payments dates include the forward option, the forward/forward swap and the spot/forward swap.

■ Note how these three techniques work; a fair amount of space is devoted to them in the main text.

■ Note that it is always cheaper to extend the maturity of a forward contract with a forward/forward swap or a spot/forward swap rather than undertaking a forward option in the first place.

■ Note that a forward option, or option forward, or option dated forward contract, as it is sometimes called, is not a currency option. A forward option involves a right and an obligation to deal in foreign currency – the option is merely as to timing. In the case of a currency option, the holder has a right but not an obligation to deal at a particular price.

■ Short-term, fixed rate borrowing or depositing is another technique for covering foreign-currency-denominated receivables and payables respectively.

■ Currency overdrafts and currency hold accounts simply use floating rate borrowing and depositing, respectively, to achieve the same ends as under short-term borrowing or depositing with a fixed rate. The difference is clearly one of interest rate exposure. Floating rate borrowing or depositing clearly gives rise to an interest rate exposure; fixed rate finance does not.

■ Note that when a forward contract is extended by a forward/forward swap or a spot/forward swap, the overall effect is to lock in the original forward rate plus or minus the effect of interest rate differences for the period by which the original maturity of the forward contract was extended. If this is not clear, check it out with the numerical example in the main text.

13.10 | End of chapter questions

Question 1

Assume that US Co Inc has net receivables of CHF100,000 in 90 days. The spot rate of the franc is $.50, and the Swiss interest rate is 2 per cent over 90 days (not 2 per cent per annum). Suggest how US Co Inc could implement a money market hedge.

Question 2

Assume that US Co Inc has net payables of 200,000 Ballarian watsits (BLW) in 180 days. The BLW interest rate on deposits is 7 per cent over 180 days (not a per annum rate) and the spot rate of the BLW is $.10. Suggest how US Co Inc could implement a money market hedge.

Question 3

If interest rate parity were to prevail, would a forward hedge be more favourable, equally favourable, or less favourable than a money market hedge on BLW payables in the last question?

Test bank 2

Exercises

1. Manana SA is the Coluvian subsidiary of a US manufacturer. Its local currency balance sheet is shown below. The current exchange rate is 20 pesos to the US dollar.

    Figures in million pesos

Shareholders' funds	42	Fixed assets	36
Long-term debt	9	Debtors	12
Current liabilities	3	Cash	6
	54		54

    (a) Translate the peso balance sheet of Manana SA into dollars at the existing exchange rate of 20 pesos to the dollar. All monetary items in Manana's balance sheet are denominated in pesos.
    (b) If Manana's balance sheet remained as above but the peso moved to 25 pesos per dollar, what would be the translation gain or loss if translated by the monetary/non-monetary method? By the current/non-current method? By the all-current rate method?
    (c) If the peso moved to $0.06, what would be the translation gain or loss according to the three accounting translation methods referred to under (b)?
    (d) What is Manana's translation exposure under the three accounting methods?

2. Imagine that you have just been appointed treasurer of a consumer goods company. It manufactures only in the United Kingdom, but exports over 50 per cent of its sales. As the market is an international one, you face the same competitors in each national market, including your domestic market. Your major competitors are Japanese and German.

    (a) How does your foreign exchange exposure arise?
    (b) How would you measure it?
    (c) Could your exposure be reduced by investing in manufacturing facilities abroad?

    (Association of Corporate Treasurers: Part II, September 1985, Paper in Currency Management)

3. Imagine that you work for a company wishing to deal in the foreign exchange markets in Norwegian kroner and US dollars against the pound. The *Financial Times* gives the following quotation $ and NKr against the £:

	US$	NKr
Spot	1.2775–1.2785	11.25–11.26
Forward		
1 month	0.56–0.53 cent pm	$^1/_4$ ore pm–$^3/_8$ dis
2 months	1.03–0.99 pm	$^1/_2$–$1^1/_4$ dis
3 months	1.50–1.45 pm	$^7/_8$–$1^3/_4$ dis

You notice that Eurocurrency interest rates are as following according to the *FT*:

	Sterling	US$
Short-term	$12^7/_8$–$12^5/_8$	$7^7/_8$–$7^1/_4$
1 month	$12^3/_4$–$12^5/_8$	$7^7/_{16}$–$7^5/_{16}$
3 months	$12^1/_2$–$12^3/_8$	$7^9/_{16}$–$7^7/_{16}$

Assuming that your company's bank gives the same quotation as all of those tabulated above, answer the following:

(a) At what rate would your company sell NKr for sterling three months forward, option over the second and third months?

(b) At what rate would the bank sell NKr for sterling three months forward, option running from day 30 to day 90?

(c) At what rate would the bank sell $ for sterling three months forward, option over the third month?

(d) At what rate would your company sell $ for sterling three months forward, option over the third month?

(e) At what rate would the bank buy NKr one month forward?

(f) At what rate would the bank sell NKr one month forward?

Note: There are 100 ore in 1 krone.

4. Imagine that you work for a company wishing to deal in the foreign exchange markets in Danish krone and US dollars against the pound. The *Financial Times* gives the following quotations $ and DKr against the £:

	US$	DKr
Spot	1.3820–1.2830	$13.85^3/_4$–$13.86^3/_4$
Forward		
1 month	0.26–0.29 dis	0.40 ore pm–0.40 ore dis
2 months	0.50–0.54 dis	0.45 ore pm–0.60 ore dis
3 months	0.80–0.85 dis	0.55 ore pm–0.55 ore dis

You notice that Eurocurrency interest rates are as follows according to the *FT*:

	Sterling	US$
Short-term	9 $8^3/_4$	$10^7/_8$–$10^3/_4$
1 month	$9^1/_4$–$9^1/_8$	$11^1/_4$–$11^1/_8$
3 months	$9^1/_2$–$9^3/_8$	$11^{11}/_{16}$–$11^9/_{16}$

Assuming that your company's bank gives the same quotations as all of those tabulated above, answer the following:

(a) At what rate would your company sell DKr three months forward, option over the second and third months?

(b) At what rate would the bank sell $ three months forward?

(c) At what rate would the bank sell $ three months forward, option over the third month?

(d) At what rate would your company sell $ three months forward, option over the third month?

(e) At what rate would the bank buy DKr two months forward?

(f) At what rate would the bank sell DKr spot?

Note: There are 100 ore in 1 krone.

5. A service company with 100 per cent owned subsidiaries in four countries experiences major cash flows between these subsidiaries. The subsidiaries are in Alphaland, Betaland, Gammaland and Deltaland. The respective countries currencies are the ax, the bon, the cop and the drac. The monthly cash flows are as follows:

Alphaland pays	bon 500,000 to Betaland
	drac 40,000,000 to Deltaland
Betaland pays	ax 250,000 to Alphaland
	drac 60,000,000 to Deltaland
	cop 400,000 to Gammaland
Gammaland pays	bon 600,000 to Betaland
	drac 50,000,000 to Deltaland
Deltaland pays	ax 200,000 to Alphaland
	bon 400,000 to Betaland
	cop 500,000 to Gammaland

where ax 1 = cop 4 = bon 4 = drac 200.

How might this system be improved, and what would be the benefits?

▌Multiple choice questions

There is one right answer only to each question.

1. Assume the following information is applicable to the $ and the Swiss franc (CHF) in a particular situation:

Current spot rate of Swiss francs to the US dollar is USD/CHF = 1.70.
Forecast spot rate of Swiss franc one year from now USD/CHF = 1.80.
One year forward rate USD/CHF = 1.76.
Annual interest rate for Swiss franc deposit = 10 per cent.
Annual interest rate for USD = 6 per cent.

Given the above information, the return from covered interest arbitrage by US investors with $500,000 to invest is _____ per cent.

(a) about 3.89 per cent
(b) about 5.31 per cent
(c) about 10.62 per cent
(d) about 6.00 per cent
(e) about 6.25 per cent

2. Assume that Eurosterling interest rates are higher than Eurodollar rates. Assume also that the sterling/dollar spot rate is equal to the forward rate. Covered interest arbitrage puts _____ pressure on the pound's spot rate, and _____ pressure on the pound's forward rate.

    (a) downward; downward
    (b) downward; upward
    (c) upward; downward
    (d) upward; upward

3. Assume that both US and UK investors require a real return of 3 per cent. If the nominal Eurodollar interest rate is 11 per cent and the nominal Eurosterling rate is 9 per cent, then according to the Fisher effect, UK inflation is expected to be about _____ US inflation, and the UK pound is expected to _____.

    (a) 2 percentage points above; depreciate by about 2 per cent
    (b) 3 percentage points above; depreciate by about 3 per cent
    (c) 3 percentage points below; appreciate by about 3 per cent
    (d) 3 percentage points below; depreciate by about 3 per cent
    (e) 2 percentage points below; appreciate by about 2 per cent

4. Translation exposure reflects the exposure of a firm's:

    (a) ongoing international transactions to exchange rate fluctuations;
    (b) local currency value to transactions between foreign exchange traders;
    (c) financial statements to exchange rate fluctuations;
    (d) cash flows to exchange rate fluctuations.

5. The US$ five-year interest rate is 5 per cent annualized, and the Danish krone (DKK) five-year rate is 8 per cent annualized. Today's spot rate is USD/DKK = 5.00. If the international Fisher effect holds, what is the best estimate of the Danish krone spot rate against the US dollar spot rate in five years' time?

    (a) USD0.131
    (b) USD0.226
    (c) USD0.262
    (d) USD0.140
    (e) USD0.174

6. Suppose the spot New York indirect quotes for the Batavian drac and Swedish krona are 1249.25–75 and 5.9925–75, respectively. What is the direct quote for the Swedish krona in Batavia?

    (a) 0.0047969–0.0048008
    (b) 208.30–47
    (c) 208.30–55
    (d) 208.47–55
    (e) none of the above

7. If inflation is expected to be 5 per cent higher in the United Kingdom than in Switzerland:

(a) the theory of purchasing power parity would predict a drop in nominal interest rates in the United Kingdom of approximately 5 per cent;
(b) purchasing power parity would predict that the UK spot rate should decline by about 5 per cent;
(c) expectations theory would suggest that the spot exchange rates between the two countries should remain unchanged over the long run;
(d) the efficient market hypothesis suggests that no predictions can be made under a system of freely floating rates.

8. If inflation in the United States is expected to be 5 per cent annually and the Danish krone is expected to depreciate by 3 per cent per annum relative to the US dollar, Danish krone prices of raw materials imported by a Danish company from the United States and priced in dollars can be expected (*ceteris paribus*) to:

(a) increase by about 8 per cent per annum;
(b) increase by about 2 per cent per annum;
(c) increase by 5 per cent per annum;
(d) increase by 3 per cent per annum.

9. A strong pound sterling places _____ pressure on UK inflation, which in turn places _____ pressure on the pound:

(a) upward; upward
(b) downward; upward
(c) upward; downward
(d) downward; downward

10. What would be the amount of the exchange gain or loss in the following situation? The exchange rate changes from 1 peso = $1.00 to 1 peso = 75c. Translate using the temporal approach. Inventory is valued at cost, this being lower than market value.

	'000 pesos		'000 pesos
Owners' equity	1,000	Fixed assets	1,000
Non-current debt	600	Inventory	200
Current payables	400	Cash	800
	2,000		2,000

(a) $50,000 gain
(b) $150,000 gain
(c) $150,000 loss
(d) $50,000 loss
(e) none of the above

Part D

Derivatives

Derivative instruments comprise financial products that have grown up around securities, currency and commodity trading and whose price is a function of some other underlying security, currency rate or other commodity. The term is usually used to embrace swaps, financial futures, options and a wide range of financially engineered instruments which are hybrids of other financial products. But it also includes, of course, forwards – which have already been discussed in Parts B and C.

14 Swaps

Bankers are in the business of taking deposits in various currencies on the basis of a fixed or floating interest rate. At the same time, banks offer to make loans in various currencies on a fixed or on a floating interest rate basis. The fact that banks are prepared to take deposits on a floating basis and to lend on a fixed basis – and vice versa – in a particular currency gives the essential rationale for the interest rate swap market. The fact that banks will take deposits in one currency on a fixed or floating basis and also make loans to customers in a different currency on a fixed or floating basis provides an underpinning to the currency swap market.

14.1 ▌ Swaps – the basics

In an interest rate swap a company may deposit, for example, €100m with the bank for a three-year period at a floating rate of interest (based, for example on six-month LIBOR) and, at the same time, borrow €100m from the same bank for a three-year period at a fixed rate of interest. Why might the firm wish to do this? Perhaps, because it already has a floating rate borrowing with three years to run to repayment, which it wished to convert to a fixed rate loan. The reader may well ask why did the firm not raise fixed rate funds initially? It is banking practice only to lend at floating rates in a particular set of circumstances – for example in most management buy-outs. The reader might also ask why does the firm not repay the first loan which has been contracted at a floating rate and replace it by a new loan at a fixed rate? It is possible that there would be a penalty for early repayment and the interest rate swap is cheaper than incurring this penalty – this is usually the case.

Note that the interest rate swap exemplified, the amount (€100m) and the term (three years) are the same for each side of the swap. This makes sense and is a key characteristic of an interest rate swap. Note also that since the amount of the swap is the same on each side of the equation (€100m), no money need change hands at the instigation of the swap. The same is true at the end of the interest swap period. The two amounts involved at the end of three years are the same (€100m) so in an interest rate, at maturity no principal changes hands. Each year, though, the two parties to the swap settle interest amounts due (fixed versus floating) usually on a difference basis. The documentation to a swap is standardized and very short. But it incorporates general clauses such that, should the credit standing of the non-bank party deteriorate significantly, the bank may terminate the swap early. Of course, the same thing applies if the non-bank party is in default on an interest payment (or difference) due.

The same kind of logic applies in cross-currency swaps. The interest rate swap described was in one single currency, the euro. What about when two currencies are involved? The underpinning idea remains. Banks are in the business of taking deposits in one currency (A) and lending in another (currency B). Naturally the bank sets interest rates appropriate to currencies A and B for lending or borrowing as the case may be. Such interest rates would be market based and would approximately take account of inflation in the different countries involved plus a real rate of return (usually between 2 and 4 per cent) plus a premium for the credit risk of the borrower (and maybe a premium for political risk in one, or both of the currencies, if appropriate). So, a bank would be happy to take a twelve-month deposit of US$1.6m from a customer, for a twelve-month period, GB£1m. We assume that the exchange rate is GB£1 = US$1.6. Interest rates set as above would apply. It is this possibility that provides the essence of a cross-currency swap.

Let us assume that the company, headquartered in London, in our example has, this time, a borrowing outstanding of US$160m and the loan is at a fixed interest rate. The loan has three years to run to maturity. The reason that the British firm negotiated the loan initially was to hedge a US business that it had bought for US$160m. Now, just for the purpose of our example, assume that the British firm has just sold on this US-based business for exactly GB£100m and that the GB£/US$ exchange rate is 1.6. The proceeds of GB£100m are to be used to finance expansion in operations in Britain. Of course, the UK firm no longer needs the dollar loan to hedge the dollar exposure on the US-based business. But the loan has three years still to run to final maturity – payable in one shot (a bullet repayment, as it is termed). The British firm might repay the loan early – although to do so would incur a penalty – or it might consider a cross-country swap, which would convert the borrowing liability out of dollars and into sterling (or any other currency that the firm desired). How would this work?

Remember that the firm has a US$160m borrowing at a fixed rate with three years to run, but it no longer needs this dollar loan in its books. It wishes to replace it with a sterling borrowing because the proceeds of the US sale have been invested in the UK operations. So, it arranges a cross-currency swap.

Via the swap, the firm effectively borrows GB£100m from the bank and deposits US$160m with the bank, both deposit and borrowing are at a fixed rate and both for a three-year period. At the prevailing exchange rate of GB£/US$ = 1.60, these two amounts are equal when the swap is arranged. Year by year, the balance of interest difference will be paid between the bank and the firm. Effectively, and for balance sheet reporting purposes, the British company now has a sterling liability. At the end of the three-year swap period the company must pay to the bank GB£100m and the bank must pay to the company US$160m. Of course, the company will then use this US$160m to repay the original dollar borrowing. But note that under the swap, at the exchange rate prevailing three years hence the GB£100m that the company pays to the bank will not necessarily equal the US$160m the bank pays to the company. Indeed, at any exchange rate other than 1.60, there will be a balancing payment either from the bank to the company or vice versa, at year 3 to square the books. Note that this was not the case with the one-currency interest rate swap. In three years' time, €100m will equal €100m; but GB£100m will not necessarily equal US$160m. Hence the balancing payment at the end of the cross-currency swap, but not at the end of an interest rate swap.

Once again, the documentation on a cross-currency swap is very short and focused but again there are rules to the effect that the significant deterioration of the credit quality of the non-bank party may result in early termination of the swap. In the cross-currency swap that we have described, we have referred to one involving fixed interest rates on both sides – US$ and GB£ interest were both at fixed rates. This need not be the case, one side of the equation could be fixed while the other was floating. Or, both sides could be floating but using a different floating formula, for example LIBOR versus a specified floating interest base rate.

Before going any further, we would remind readers that in Chapter 13 we introduced forward/forward swaps and spot/forward swaps. It is a little confusing but these are altogether different from currency and interest rate swaps. Basically, swaps involve the exchange of interest or foreign currency exposures or a combination of both by two or more borrowers. They do not necessarily involve the legal swapping of actual debts but an agreement is made to meet certain cash flows under loan or lease agreements. This sounds rather complicated, so what, in practical terms, does it mean? We will approach the problem by focusing upon interest rate swaps first and then moving on to currency swaps.

14.2 | Interest rate swaps

As indicated above, a swap – whether an interest rate swap or a currency swap – can simply be described as the transformation of one stream of future cash flows into another stream of future cash flows with different features. An interest rate swap is an exchange between two counterparties of interest obligations (payments of interest) or receipts (investment income) in the same currency on an agreed amount of notional principal for an agreed period of time. The agreed amount is called notional principal because, since it is not a loan or investment, the principal amount is not initially exchanged or repaid at maturity. An exchange of interest obligations is called a liability swap; an exchange of interest receipts is called an asset swap. Interest streams are exchanged according to predetermined rules and are based upon the underlying notional principal amount.

There are two main types of interest rate swap: the coupon swap and the basis swap. Coupon swaps convert interest flows from a fixed rate to a floating rate basis, or the reverse, in the same currency. A simple example is shown in Figure 14.1 (overleaf). In the figure the arrows refer to interest payment flows.

Basis swaps convert interest flows from a floating rate calculated according to one formula to a floating rate calculated according to another. For example, one set of interest flows might be set against six-month dollar LIBOR (London inter-bank offered rate), while the other set of flows might be based upon another floating rate

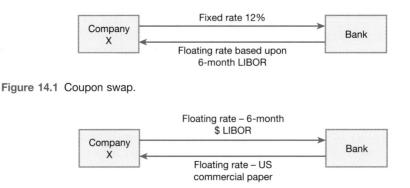

Figure 14.1 Coupon swap.

Figure 14.2 Basis swap.

such as US Commercial Paper, US Treasury Bill Rate or LIBOR based upon one- or three-month maturities. Figure 14.2 gives an example of a basis swap.

To reiterate then, interest rate swaps involve the exchange between two counterparties of interest obligations in the same currency on an agreed amount of notional principal for an agreed period of time. The principal amount applies only for the purpose of calculating the interest to be exchanged under an interest rate swap. At no time is any principal amount physically passed between the parties. The exchange of fixed or floating interest payments is made by reference to prevailing fixed and floating rates available in the market place, due account being taken of credit standing. The counterparties are thus able to convert a fixed rate asset or liability into a floating rate asset or liability and vice versa. Costs savings may be obtained by each party.

When the swap market took off during the early 1980s, these cost savings arose from differentials in the credit standing of the counterparties and other market imperfections. To be more specific, usually investors in fixed rate instruments were more sensitive to credit quality than floating rate lenders. Thus a larger premium was demanded of issuers of lower credit quality in the fixed rate debt market than in the floating rate market. The counterparties to an interest rate swap effectively obtained an arbitrage advantage by drawing down funds in the market where they had the greatest relative cost advantage, subsequently entering into an interest rate swap to convert the cost of the funds so raised from a fixed rate to a floating rate or vice versa.

The methodology of the arbitrage and its cost-saving potential can be seen by reference to an example involving two companies, X and Y. The former has a higher credit rating, as can be seen by the data in Table 14.1. Its superior credit standing gives it a 110 basis point advantage in the fixed rate funding market and a 50 basis point advantage in the floating rate market. Despite the fact that company X can raise funds more cheaply than company Y in both markets, a potential for interest rate arbitrage exists. Company X draws down funds in the fixed rate market, while company Y borrows on a floating basis. Each then enters into an interest rate swap, requiring the payments from one to the other as shown under the heading 'Swap payments' in Table 14.1. It can be seen by comparing the 'All-in cost of funding' line in the table with the 'Cost of direct funding' line that each party has saved 30 basis points on the swap. The interest rate flows are summarized in Figure 14.3, in which the direction of the arrows represents the direction of interest rate flows.

Table 14.1 Example of an interest rate swap

	Company X	Company Y
Credit rating	AAA	BBB
Cost of direct fixed rate funding	10.40%	11.50%
Cost of direct floating rate funding	Six-month LIBOR + 0.25%	Six-month LIBOR + 0.75%
Funds raised directly		
Fixed rate by company X	(10.40%)	
Floating rate by company Y		(Six-month LIBOR + 0.75%)
Swap payments		
Company X pays company Y	(Six-month LIBOR) 10.45%	
Company Y pays company X		Six-month LIBOR (10.45%)
All-in cost of funding	Six-month LIBOR − 0.05%	11.20%
Comparable cost of direct funding	Six-month LIBOR + 0.25%	11.50%
Saving	30 basis points	30 basis points

Figure 14.3 Direction of interest flows.

The ability to transfer relative cost advantages in the manner shown in Table 14.1 and Figure 14.3 has led to many highly creditworthy companies issuing fixed rate Eurobonds solely with the purpose of swapping and frequently obtaining funding at an effective sub-LIBOR cost. In the early phase of the interest rate swap market, a triple A issuer could expect to achieve between 75 and 100 basis points below LIBOR on a swap. Nowadays gains for a comparable borrower might bring the cost of funding down to 25 to 30 basis points below LIBOR. The potential for such big arbitrage gains as exemplified in Table 14.1 has now disappeared as more and more corporates have accessed the market. The effect has been that the disparity between different credit loadings in fixed and floating markets has narrowed very substantially.

Besides providing cost advantages, interest rate swaps enable borrowers effectively to access markets which might otherwise be closed to them – for example, by virtue of credit quality, lack of a familiar name or because of excessive use of a particular capital market segment. Even private companies are able to tap particular markets without the need to comply with disclosure requirements, credit ratings and other formal requirements. Swaps based upon commercial paper as the underlying floating rate instrument are a growing part of the interest rate swap market.

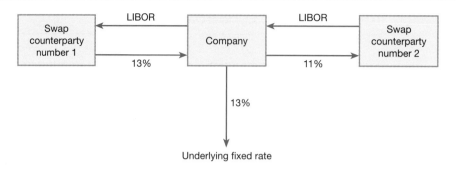

Figure 14.4 Position of company following two swaps.

Interest rate swaps may be used as a means of reducing interest rate exposure or as a pure financing tool. They may also be used to enable a corporate treasurer to back his or her judgement on future trends in interest rates. For example, consider a company with fixed rate debt costing 13 per cent per annum at a time when the treasurer expects a decline in interest rates to occur. The company might enter into a swap to obtain LIBOR-based funding and leave this swap in place during the period when interest rates were falling. At the end of the decline, the company might enter into a second swap to lock into the new lower fixed rate of, say, 11 per cent per annum. The company's position would then be like that summarized in Figure 14.4.

The interest rate swap process has the advantage of utter simplicity. It is often conducted by telephone and confirmed by telex subject to agreement on documentation, which usually incorporates the minimum of restrictive covenants and is now in a standard format. There are both primary and secondary interest rate markets. Many new bond issues are swap driven. Bonds are issued with the express intention of swapping the fixed interest rate obligations into floating interest rate debt at highly competitive rates.

During 1982 the volume of interest rate swaps transacted was estimated to be in the order of $3bn; nowadays the annual volume of such swaps is well in excess of $500bn. Arbitrages like that set out in Table 14.1 originally drove a considerable volume of transactions in the early days of interest rate swaps, particularly in the US domestic market. Nowadays, opportunities tend to be less clear cut as arbitrages have been eroded, but the market has gained a massive momentum nonetheless. Table 14.2 shows the value of interest rate swaps outstanding – that is swaps that are open as they have not yet run to maturity. The table also shows similar data for cross-currency swaps and, also, interest-rate options (although this last topic is not considered until Chapters 16 and 17).

We have so far used the terms 'fixed', 'floating' and 'LIBOR' without exactly defining our meaning. It is proposed to do this now. The term 'fixed' or 'fixed rate' refers to an interest rate which is set at the beginning of a loan or an investment and which holds for the entire life of the loan or investment. For example, a five-year £10m loan with interest rate of 10 per cent requires an annual interest payment of £1m for five years, at the end of which the total principal amount – £10m – would be repayable. By contrast, the term 'floating' or 'floating rate' refers to an interest

Table 14.2 Value of swaps outstanding (US$bn)

	Interest rate swaps	Currency swaps	Interest rate options[a]
1987	683	183	–
1988	1,010	317	327
1989	1,503	435	538
1990	2,312	578	561
1991	3,065	807	577
1992	3,851	860	635
1993	6,117	900	1,398
1994	8,816	915	1,573
1995	12,811	1,197	3,705
1996	19,171	1,560	4,723
1997	22,291	1,824	4,920
1998	36,262	2,253	7,997
1999	43,936	2,444	9,380
2000	48,765	3,194	9,476
2001	51,407	3,832	9,521

[a] Including caps, floors, swaptions and other instruments – see Chapters 16 and 17.

rate on a loan or an investment which is reset on a regular basis. For example, a three-year £10m loan with a six-month floating rate of interest would have the interest rate reset every six months at the then prevailing interest rate for six months. The six-month reference rate used is normally LIBOR.

The term 'LIBOR' is an acronym for London inter-bank offered rate. It is the interest rate at which major banks offer to lend funds to other major banks in the London inter-bank market. The rate at which they bid to borrow funds from other banks is known as 'LIBID', the London inter-bank bid rate. Another rate, known as 'LIMEAN', is simply the midpoint between LIBOR and LIBID. Both LIBOR and LIBID are frequently used as marker rates against which floating payments of interest are calculated. A bank will quote its own LIBOR and LIBID; sometimes interest rate payments under a swap use LIBOR based on an average of several banks' rates. The way in which LIBOR is determined will be clearly stated in the swap agreement.

Also worthy of mention here is the term EURIBOR. This refers to the reference rate for euros. Quotations are posted at 11 a.m. Brussels time on an actual/360 day basis (see later in this chapter). It is proving to be a widely used reference rate in financial circles.

Why, then, should a company use interest rate swaps? They can be employed for a number of reasons – these are the main ones:

- To achieve funding at rates below those otherwise available in bond markets or from banks.

- To obtain fixed rate financing when it is impossible to access the bond markets directly.

- To restructure a debt profile without raising new finance.

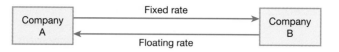

Note: The terms 'receiver' and 'payer' refer to interest flows.
Company A is a payer of fixed; company B is a receiver of fixed.
Company A is a receiver of floating; company B is a payer of floating.

Figure 14.5 Swap payers and receivers.

■   To restructure the profile of interest receipts or investments.

■   To hedge against, or speculate upon, the direction of movement of interest rates.

The first point referred to above is fairly straightforward; it formed the basis of Table 14.1. The second point is more complicated. International bond markets are usually open to companies of the highest quality – well-known and large borrowers. Smaller, top-quality companies may be able to borrow at fixed rates in their domestic markets where they are well known, but the opportunity to do so may arise only infrequently. Companies that cannot raise funds in the bond markets, but which are sufficiently creditworthy for banks to be willing to lend to them, may borrow at a floating rate and swap the proceeds into a fixed rate, thus locking in a fixed rate liability. The third, fourth and fifth points are self-explanatory.

Interest rate swap markets are used by various players – the major ones are set out below:

■   Supra-nationals, such as the World Bank.

■   Sovereign and public sector institutions, such as the Kingdom of Sweden.

■   Multinational corporations.

■   Smaller companies.

■   Banks, either as an intermediary between the two counterparties or as an end counterparty itself to manage its own funding or investment requirements.

It is now necessary to consider a small amount of swap jargon so that the ways in which participants deal can be better understood. The terms 'payer' and 'receiver' are frequently used and their meaning is straightforward (see Figure 14.5).

The market 'talks the fixed rate'. This piece of jargon can best be illustrated by an example. If a swap dealer says that he wants payers in the five years, he means that he wants counterparties who will pay fixed rate on five-year funds. Swap dealers maintain what they call a swap book, which will have positions – that is, exposures to interest, currency and other risks. These positions may be covered or left open. One way to cover a position is to match it with an offsetting swap. This is known as 'squaring the book' or 'running a matched book'.

As market-makers in the swap market, banks quote rates to clients on a regular basis. Like straight interest markets, banks will typically quote two fixed rates on a swap – a rate where the bank is willing to pay the fixed rate and a rate where the bank is willing to receive the fixed rate. In the sterling swap market, the fixed rate is always considered to be quoted against six-month LIBOR as the floating rate – unless specified otherwise. If, therefore, a bank is quoting a five-year swap rate as 10.70–10.85 per cent, then this means that at 10.70 per cent the bank is willing to pay a fixed rate and to receive six-month LIBOR and at 10.85 per cent the bank is willing to receive the fixed rate and to pay six-month LIBOR. Clearly, on the basis set out, the bank stands to make 0.15 per cent on the deal. However, negotiations and competitive pressures may enable the customer to get a better rate from the bank.

Although the sterling market uses six-month LIBOR as its benchmark against which rates are quoted, in the US$ interest rate swap market, the fixed rate is quoted as an amount, or spread, above the equivalent maturity US treasury bond. For example, five-year US treasury swap spreads could be given by a bank as 82–88. This means that the bank is willing to pay the fixed rate in a five-year swap at a rate that is 0.82 per cent, or 82 basis points, above the five-year US Treasury bond rate. If the current US treasury bond rate is 8.08 per cent, then this bank is willing to pay 8.9 per cent (8.08 + 0.82 per cent) on a semi-annual bond basis – both the US treasury bond and the swap spread are considered to have interest calculated on a semi-annual bond basis. The above bank is also willing to receive the fixed rate in a five-year swap at 8.96 per cent (8.08 + 0.88 per cent) on a semi-annual bond basis. Having referred, in the last few sentences, to the semi-annual bond basis, it is perhaps worth while considering methods of calculation of interest. The next section is devoted to this topic.

14.3 | Calculation of interest

There are several ways of calculating interest flows for swaps, especially on the fixed rate. Care has to be taken to ensure that all parties to a transaction are using the same calculation method. The floating rate is usually six-month LIBOR, unless otherwise stated. The fixed rate in a US dollar swap is usually quoted as a semi-annual interest rate, and is calculated on a bond basis. 'Semi-annual' means that interest payments are made twice a year. Thus, if the fixed rate is 10 per cent semi-annual, then every six months 5 per cent would be payable. The term 'bond basis' refers to the manner in which the number of days in a year is treated. In the non-financial world, every year has 365 days – except for leap years. However, financial calculations frequently use a different number of days in a year. The 'bond basis' means that, in calculating interest payments, a year is considered to have twelve months of thirty days each. Hence, calculations would be made on the basis of 360 days in a year – sometimes written as: 360/360. This convention is used in the Eurobond market.

Each currency or interest rate market may have a different approach to calculation, so it is crucial to check that all parties agree the interest calculation basis. Euromarkets use the 360-day year, as do most domestic markets – with the notable exceptions of the sterling and Belgian franc markets. Some bank customers may wish to have the fixed rate quoted on an annual basis – that is, as if interest were paid only once a year at the end of the year. This is frequently required for swaps associated with bonds where the bond pays interest once a year.

There are simple formulae for converting fixed rates from a semi-annual to an annual interest rate basis and vice versa. Two such key formulae are set out below:

- To convert semi-annual to an annual basis:

$$\left[\left(1+\frac{\text{semi-annual}}{200}\right)^2 - 1\right] \times 100 = \text{annual interest}$$

- To convert annual to a semi-annual basis:

$$\left[\left(1+\frac{\text{annual}}{100}\right)^{1/2} - 1\right] \times 200 = \text{semi-annual interest}$$

In the above formulae, one should input the known interest rate and convert as required – for example, 10.4 per cent payable as 5.2 per cent every six months is input to the first equation as 10.4 to arrive at 10.67 per cent if paid annually. Many market professionals notate semi-annual as s.a. and quote annual interest as p.a. It must be borne in mind that an interest rate may look cheaper if quoted on a different basis. So it pays always to check with the counterparty as to the basis being used.

Note that, in swaps, the floating rate will usually be paid or received every six months, while the fixed interest will be received or paid either semi-annually or annually. These payments will generally be netted out when they occur on the same day, so that only one payment between the parties is made.

Bond basis versus money-market basis

The bond basis of calculating interest refers to a year assumed to consist of 360 days (360/360). Another method, the money-market basis, calculates interest on an actual number of days in a year, but by reference to each year being 360 days (365/360). Some swap counterparties may wish to have the fixed rate on the swap quoted on a money-market basis. It is worth mentioning that LIBOR is always quoted and calculated on a money-market basis. Anyway, it may be necessary to convert the standard bond basis swap quote to a money-market basis.

The following formulae allow for bond and money-market conversions. The need to make the conversions for swaps is to ensure that the actual interest basis flow amounts will be equivalent no matter which way the swap is quoted.

- To convert from a bond to a money-market basis:

$$\text{bond rate} \times \frac{360}{365} = \text{money market rate}$$

- To convert from a money market to a bond basis:

$$\text{money-market rate} \times \frac{365}{360} = \text{bond rate}$$

An example will help to illustrate the difference in interest amounts using the two methods:

- 10 per cent interest on a bond basis on $1m for one year:

$$0.10 \times 1{,}000{,}000 \times \frac{360}{360} = \$100{,}000$$

- 10 per cent interest on a money-market basis on $1m for one year:

$$0.10 \times 1{,}000{,}000 \times \frac{365}{360} = \$101{,}389$$

Clearly, since different interest amounts result from using these interest bases, care must be taken to utilize the correct one.

Swap termination

Once an interest rate swap has been transacted, it will normally run to maturity. However, circumstances can arise where a swap counterparty needs to change the nature of existing cash flows or to get out of the swap. There are typically three ways of eliminating an already existing swap: reversal, termination and buy-out. In a reversal, a swap counterparty simply transacts another swap with the opposite flows to the original swap. The net effect is to reverse out the original position. Of course, since interest rates may have changed since the inception, the swap counterparty may have losses to make up or it may be able to realize gains. The swap counterparty need not deal with the same bank on the second swap. In a termination, a swap counterparty can approach the other counterparty to assess whether a termination of an existing swap is possible. Generally, the remaining cash flows are valued at current rates and any gains or losses between the two parties are settled. The swap is then considered terminated. In a buy-out, also sometimes known as a swap sale or assignment, a swap counterparty approaches another bank to buy out the existing swap and take over the swap counterparty's position. The new bank will either pay the swap counterparty if the remaining life of the swap has value, or be paid by the swap counterparty if the swap position is at a loss. The new bank will take over the swap counterparty's position *vis-à-vis* the original bank. Clearly, the original bank must agree to the new counterparty and must be willing to accept its counterparty risk.

Documentation

Interest rate swaps are generally agreed over the telephone by the parties involved. Before the end of the day, written communications are exchanged which detail all aspects of the transaction so that there is no misunderstanding or confusion. After this, an interest rate swap agreement is signed by the counterparties. The International Swap Dealer's Association (ISDA) has co-operated with various other associations to produce standard documentation for swaps. Their documentation runs to about twelve pages and includes sections relating to the following:

- *Payments* – the basis of calculation, amounts and timing.

- *Representations* – the swap counterparties represent that they are authorized to enter into the swap.

- *Events of default* – the conditions under which a party to a swap will be considered to be in default.

- *Termination* – the conditions under which the swap can be terminated. These are normally limited and include taxation or a material change in the circumstances of one of the parties to the swap, for example substantial deterioration of credit quality.

- *Damages* – how these are to be calculated under early termination.

- *Assignability* – swaps are not usually assignable to a new counterparty without the other party's consent.

- *Credit support documents* – these may be required due to the lower credit quality of one counterparty; guarantees and security agreements can then be utilized.

Swaps versus other financial instruments

Although we have not yet considered, in detail, the hedging of interest rate exposure (this is looked at in Chapters 15 and 18), we now compare the use of interest rate swaps with such other mechanisms as caps, floors, collars, swap options and futures. Since these instruments have not yet been covered, we will define them briefly.

We first of all look at the cap. A cap is, in essence, an insurance policy for a company wishing to protect itself against a rise in short-term interest rates (six-month LIBOR, for example) above a certain capped level, but at the same time hoping to take advantage of any future drop in rates. A cap, like an interest rate swap, is independent of a company's underlying floating rate borrowing. But, unlike in the case of a swap, the financial institution writing the cap agrees, in consideration for the payment by the company of a one-off premium, to compensate the company to the extent to which LIBOR on the predetermined roll-over dates exceeds the cap rate. Thus the company continues to pay LIBOR plus any margin on its underlying loan, but with the comfort that it will be reimbursed should LIBOR exceed the capped level, as illustrated in Figure 14.6.

We now examine floors. A floor is similar to a cap, but has the reverse effect. It achieves, for the investor or lender who is receiving floating rate interest, what a cap does for the borrower who pays it. While protecting the investor from a fall in interest rates below the floor, it allows the investor to benefit from any rise, as illustrated in Figure 14.7.

A collar is a cap and floor combined. It gives a company protection against rates rising above a certain level – the cap – and the ability to take advantage of a fall in rates, but only down to a certain level – the floor. Thus a company buying a collar will have a band of tolerance across a minimum and maximum cost of borrowing, as illustrated in Figure 14.8 (overleaf). If rates rise above the cap rate, it is compensated by the counterparty. If rates fall through the floor, it will compensate the

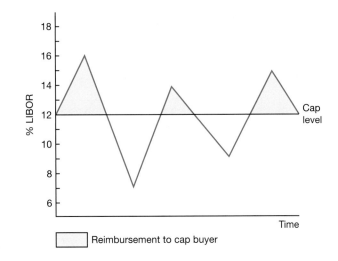

Figure 14.6 Example of a cap.

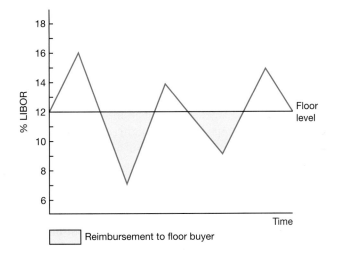

Figure 14.7 Example of a floor.

counterparty. Deals may be structured such that the premium for buying the cap equals the premium at which the writer will buy the floor from the company; in such cases, no up-front payment will be made by either party. Variations in this cap/floor rate will produce a net payment one way or the other.

We now look briefly at swap options or, as they are sometimes called, options on swaps or even swaptions. An option on a swap is an agreement between a company and a financial institution that gives one of the parties the right, but not the obligation, to call upon the other, either on a specified date or during a pre-agreed period, to enter into a swap at a pre-arranged rate. A premium for this facility is paid by the party buying the option.

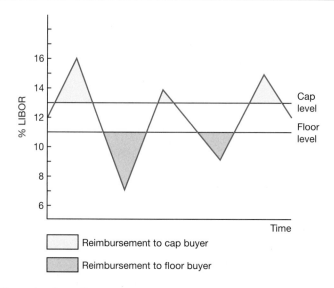

Figure 14.8 Example of a collar.

Financial futures are examined in Chapter 15, but here is a brief definition. A financial futures contract is a legally binding contract to deliver or take delivery on a specified day of a given quality and quantity of a financial commodity at an agreed price and the contract is traded on an organized financial futures exchange.

All the above instruments provide hedging facilities which are widely used in asset and liability management; the suitability of one approach compared with another depends on a company's particular requirements.

Swaps, however, do have several advantages. For example, whenever an up-front payment is required, it appears on a company's accounts. A swap does not normally involve an up-front payment. The avoidance of an up-front cash payment is also a positive advantage for companies with restraints on liquidity. A classic example would be a company that has completed a leveraged buy-out: an interest rate swap is a way for it to switch its debt burden out of floating rate and into fixed rate interest with no cash penalties and no detrimental effect on what might be an already poor gearing ratio.

Swaps do have pitfalls, as any treasurer who has swapped into paying fixed rate interest just before rates began to fall will testify. However, carefully monitored, they can usually be reversed with minimal adverse effect. The substantial depth of the swap market relative to the competing instruments listed above is another advantage. Swaps can be reversed easily because they are generally more widely understood and traded than caps, floors, collars and options. Furthermore, global standardized documentation is now in place for swaps, while documentation for caps, floors and collars tends to be custom-made.

Swaps also have the edge in terms of volume and maturity. Interest rate swaps can last for maturities sometimes in excess of ten years and are commonly transacted for sums in excess of $100m. Caps, floors and collars, by contrast, are typically not written for much beyond five years and cap contracts for amounts of $100m are relatively rare.

14.4 | Currency swaps

We now turn to currency swaps. The most frequently encountered currency swaps have floating rates on both sides, so it might be $ LIBOR against £ LIBOR. However, we begin with fixed rate currency swaps. They are slightly easier to understand. A fixed rate currency swap involves counterparty A exchanging fixed rate interest in one currency with counterparty B in return for fixed rate interest in another currency. Currency swaps usually involve three basic steps:

■ Initial exchange of principal.

■ Ongoing exchange of interest.

■ Re-exchange of principal amounts on maturity.

The initial exchange of principal works as follows. At the outset, the counterparties exchange the principal amounts of the swap at an agreed rate of exchange. This rate is usually based on the spot exchange rate, but a forward rate set in advance of the swap commencement date may also be used. This initial exchange can be on a notional basis – that is, with no physical exchange of principal amounts – or, alternatively, on a physical exchange basis. Whether the initial exchange is on a physical or notional basis, its importance is solely to establish the reference point of the principal amounts for the purpose of calculating, first, the ongoing payments of interest and, secondly, the re-exchange of principal amounts under the swap. The ongoing exchange of interest is the second key step in the currency swap. Having established the principal amounts, the counterparties exchange interest payments on agreed dates based on the outstanding principal amounts at fixed interest rates agreed at the outset of the transaction. The third step in the currency swap involves the ultimate re-exchange of principal amounts at maturity.

This three-step process is standard practice in the currency swap market and it effectively transforms a fixed rate debt raised in one currency into a fixed rate liability in another currency, which may be valuable for hedging purposes. Indeed, the currency swap is similar to a conventional long-date forward foreign exchange contract. Like interest rate swaps, currency swaps are advantageous because they enable borrowers to reduce the cost of borrowing by accessing markets that might otherwise be closed to them. For example, a strong borrower in the Swiss franc market may obtain a finer fixed US dollar rate by raising funds directly in fixed Swiss francs and then swapping them into US dollars. Besides having cost advantages, the currency swap market enables borrowers effectively to access foreign capital markets and obtain funds in currencies that might otherwise be unobtainable except at relatively high cost. The most important currencies in the currency swap market are the US dollar, the Swiss franc, the euro, sterling, the yen and the Canadian dollar. The market is dominated by the US dollar on one side but direct swaps have been frequent in yen/Swiss francs, yen/euro and sterling/euro. The currency swap is one further tool that enables corporate treasurers to manage currency exposure and reap cost benefits at the same time.

We now turn very briefly to the currency coupon swap. Essentially this is a combination of interest rate swap and fixed rate currency swap. The transaction follows the three basic steps described for the fixed rate currency swap except that fixed rate interest in one currency is exchanged for floating rate interest in another currency.

Imagine a borrower that is in a relatively favourable position, for example, to raise long-term fixed rate US dollar funding but in fact wants floating rate yen. The currency swap market enables it to marry its requirements with another borrower of relatively high standing in the yen market but which does not have similar access to long-term fixed rate dollars. The gain accrues by each corporation swapping liabilities raised in those markets which each can readily access; the effect is to broaden the access of borrowers to international lending markets. Clearly, the currency swap enables the treasurer to alter the denomination of his or her liabilities and assets.

Swap transactions may be set up with great speed, and their documentation and formalities are generally much less detailed than in other large financial deals – swap documentation is normally shorter and simpler than that relating to term loan agreements. Transaction costs are relatively low too. And swaps can be unwound easily.

At the beginning of the 1980s, the currency swap market was extremely small; by 1990, the amount of new business being done was in excess of $100bn during the year. A swap has already been defined as the exchange of one stream of future cash flows for another stream of future cash flows with different characteristics. In the currency swap, two currencies are being utilized. The market standard is to quote a fixed rate of interest – an interest rate set for the entire life of the transaction – in one currency against a floating rate of interest, generally reset every six months, for the US dollar.

A rate of exchange between the two currencies must be established at the outset. This will produce principal amounts in the two currencies upon which payments of interest are to be made. At the final maturity of the transaction, along with the final periodic payment of interest, the principal amounts of the two currencies which were fixed at the outset must be exchanged by the swap counterparties. It is possible to have an exchange of the two principal amounts at the beginning of the swap, but this is not a requirement. For example, if the US dollar/sterling exchange rate is 1.80 at the outset of a five-year currency swap, the bank could lend to the corporate customer $18m in exchange for the customer lending the bank £10m – this would create an initial exchange of principal. However, there could be merely a notional exchange. The corporate customer wants $18m and it could get this amount merely by doing a spot deal to sell £10m and buy $18m. If the swap were for fixed rate sterling versus six-month floating rate US dollars, the interest flows would be as in Figure 14.9(a). But there would be a principal payment at maturity – in five years' time – as in Figure 14.9(b). Thus, at final maturity, in addition to the interest flows, each swap counterparty pays the principal amount of that currency on which it had been paying interest over the life of the swap, as one would repay the principal amount of a maturing loan.

Currency swaps are typically arranged for periods ranging from two to ten years, with maturities of five years being most usual. For long maturities, the currency swap market has far greater depth and offers better prices than the forward market and is widely used for covering lengthy exposures. Currency swaps can be executed in most major currencies (fixed rate) against the US dollar (floating rate). Currency swaps between two currencies other than the US dollar are possible, but two separate

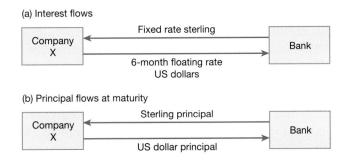

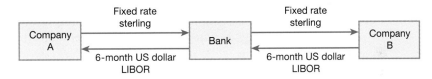

Figure 14.9 Currency swap example: fixed rate sterling versus 6-month floating rate US dollars.

Figure 14.10 Matched currency swap.

swaps may be needed to achieve the desired result. The minimum size for a currency swap is approximately US$3m, or the equivalent in other currencies. Currency swaps attached to bond issues may be as large as $350m. It is possible to have currency swaps where both currencies are calculated on a floating rate basis, but these are rarer than fixed against floating. Generally, banks do not like to arrange only one side of a currency swap, thereby creating a mismatch. Instead they prefer to match their positions by arranging deals with counterparties that have opposite requirements. This matched position reduces the bank's risk. An example of such a matched position is set out in Figure 14.10.

In Figure 14.10, company A is the payer of fixed rate sterling and the receiver of six-month dollar LIBOR. The swap dealer might, using market jargon, say that 'company A is a payer of fixed sterling against US$ LIBOR'. Company B is the receiver of fixed rate sterling and the payer of US dollar six-month LIBOR. The swap dealer might shorten this to 'company B is a receiver of fixed rate sterling against US$ LIBOR'. In dealing in swaps, one must be careful to specify whether interest is to be calculated on an annual or a semi-annual basis and whether it will be calculated on a bond basis or a money-market basis. This has already been referred to earlier in the chapter.

Currency swaps are typically used to achieve one of the following objectives:

■ Hedging a currency exposure, or speculating.

■ Obtaining funds at lower costs.

■ Obtaining access to a restricted market.

■ Altering the currency of a payments stream or investment income.

Each of these objectives is now considered in turn.

Many companies around the world generate cash flows, either receipts or payments, in currencies other than the home currency. One way to minimize the long-term risk of one currency being worth more or less in the future is to offset a particular cash flow stream with an opposite flow in that currency created by a swap against the home currency. The swap also enables the corporate treasurer to transform the currency profile of a company's liabilities relatively quickly. In this respect, the currency swap can easily be used to hedge liabilities or deliberately to take positions in currencies that the treasurer anticipates will soften.

In terms of obtaining lower-cost funds, by raising new borrowings in capital markets in one currency and executing a currency swap into the desired currency, a borrower may reduce the cost of raising funds. This type of swap-driven new issue has been utilized extensively in the Eurobond market. Borrowers have been able to get competitively priced funds by issuing Eurobonds in those segments in which investors' demand is not being met. These funds, when swapped back to the borrower's desired currency, may produce a lower cost of funds than a direct borrowing in the desired currency.

Direct access to a particular segment of the international capital market may be somewhat restricted. In certain countries there are restrictions on the type of borrower that can raise new funds in the bond markets. The currency swap can be used to transform borrowings in one currency into a liability in the desired currency. For example, to issue a yen bond the borrower must qualify for at least a single A credit rating. If a company does not qualify in this respect, it can raise new funds elsewhere – for example, in the US dollar market. And to obtain a yen-denominated liability it might arrange a swap into yen (so long as the bank is willing to accept the company's credit quality).

In terms of altering the currency of investment income for investors, the currency swap can be used to change the currency of cash inflows too. For investors the objective is clearly to change investment receipts from one currency to a more desired currency. This type of currency swap is frequently called an 'asset swap'.

As in the interest rate swap market, the main participants in the currency swap market are supra-nationals, sovereign and public-sector institutions, multinational companies, smaller companies and banks. For currency swaps, the documentation and the closing of a deal by reversal, termination or buy-out are exactly as described in the section relating to interest rate swaps.

Currency swaps – general points

We have referred to the fact that companies may be able, through the currency swap, to raise money cheaply. How can this be achieved if interest rate parity always holds? First of all, windows of opportunity appear only fleetingly, often created by a simultaneous demand in the new issue market and an arbitrage opportunity between domestic and international markets. The fleet-of-foot company may exploit such arbitrage opportunities by raising currency in foreign debt markets where funds are available at below market rates and then swapping the proceeds into the desired currency at a cost lower than might be achieved by accessing the desired denomination money market directly. There are many reasons – psychological as well as technical – why a company can borrow more cheaply in one currency than another. For instance, a company may well need to provide inducements to domestic investors who are over-familiar with its paper, while in a foreign capital market the novelty of its name – or an unusually structured investment opportunity – can be attractive to investors. Similarly, a highly rated company can exploit capital markets where there is a dearth of low-risk investment opportunities. Having borrowed comparatively cheaply, the company can translate some or all of its comparative advantage in that currency into a lower cost on its domestic currency interest payments by use of the currency swap. And, of course, funds at below market rates may be available linked to the purchase, for example of assets from a particular supplier. Yen finance at less than market rates for yen may be on offer to the purchaser of Japanese machinery.

Players in the swap market are aware of each other's prices. So a corporate treasurer shopping around for the cheapest price is likely to receive quotes within a spread of five basis points per annum. Variations within that spread will usually be a measure of how far the market has moved in the direction of each financial institution's swap book. However, differences in price between two rival bids can sometimes be more apparent than real, largely as a result of how they are expressed. So the treasurer comparing two or more prices has to bear a number of factors in mind. These include the following:

- Days basis.

- Payment schedule.

- Delayed start.

- Benchmarks.

- Payment dates.

- Transaction size.

In respect of a day's basis, the two main day-count conventions for interest rate calculations under a swap are the 30-day month/360-day year basis ('Eurobond') and the actual days elapsed/360-day year basis ('money market'). Swaps in sterling are quoted on an actual days elapsed/365-day basis. Another variation is the actual days elapsed/365–6 basis (actual/actual). When comparing prices, it is incumbent upon the treasurer to check that both quotes are expressed using the same basis. A financial institution's quote to receive a fixed rate under a swap expressed using a money-market basis will appear cheaper than the same price expressed using the bond basis. For a proper comparison of two swap prices, they must also be based on the same frequency of payment. Because of the time value of money, a swap price based on quarterly fixed interest payments will appear cheaper than a price based on the semi-annual equivalent of the quarterly interest rate quoted. If there is a delayed start to a swap, there may be value in the 'stub' period for one of the parties, determined by the funding cost of the bank's underlying hedge for the period of carry. This value may represent the apparent difference between two quotes if it is included in one and not the other.

Swap prices for maturities in excess of two to three years are typically quoted as a spread over the semi-annual yield to redemption of an underlying government security or parallel instrument. For a proper comparison of two apparently identical quotes on a spread basis, a corporate treasurer must ensure that both banks are using the same underlying bonds as benchmarks and are pricing them at the same level. The absolute rate is critical to any comparison. In some cases, particularly where a swap is for an odd maturity – say, four and a half years – one financial institution may be quoting a spread over the five-year bond, whereas another could be taking an interpolation of the four- and five-year bond which will produce a different result.

Unless asked to quote on a swap with specific interest payment dates, a financial institution will assume a 'straight run' – that is, equal, semi-annual interest periods from the contract date. Any variation may affect the quotes. Potential corporate users of the swap market also need to bear in mind that there may be a premium for transacting unusually large or small swaps, reflecting the degree of difficulty of placing such a swap in the market place.

14.5 | Assessing risk in swaps

First of all, we consider how one would assess risk in an interest rate swap. Risk in interest rate swaps can be divided into two main types: credit risk and market risk. Credit risk is that the opposite counterparty might default before the end of the swap. If it does, the company will be thrown back with little or no warning into paying an interest rate structure on its liabilities which it deliberately set out to avoid by transacting the swap in the first place. In reality, this scenario rarely happens because the vast majority of swaps are conducted with financial institutions acting as principals to the swap; thereby, credit risk is virtually eliminated.

Market risk can be defined as the cost of reversing a swap before maturity. There are at least two ways to do this. One is to transact an equal but opposite swap. This is perfectly satisfactory but doubles the credit risk exposure. Another way is to request the original counterparty to cancel the initial agreement in consideration for a payment from or to them. This is easily done, especially where the counterparty is a financial institution. The cancellation payment represents the cost to the financial institution of hedging its resulting interest rate exposure by transacting a replacement swap. Its size will depend on how far interest rates have moved since the first swap began. Whether the payment is positive or negative is determined by whether rates have moved up or down.

How it works is shown in Figures 14.11 and 14.12. The shipping corporation is a weak credit and borrows at six-month US dollar LIBOR – say, 9 per cent p.a. – plus a 2 per cent premium. Believing rates are set to rise, it fixes its interest cost by transacting the swap illustrated in Figure 14.11 with a bank for five years. After year 3, however, six-month US dollar LIBOR has fallen – say, to 8 per cent p.a. – and expectations are that further falls are imminent. The shipping company is now paying 2 per cent p.a. above what it would have been paying had it not transacted the swap. It therefore wishes to cancel the swap. The bank may agree to do this in return for a cancellation payment which it calculates from the interest flows it can obtain by transacting a replacement swap as shown in Figure 14.12. The bank will receive the

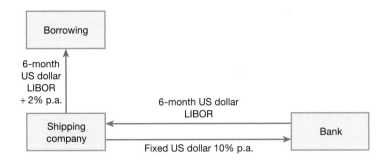

Figure 14.11 Initial swap.

Figure 14.12 Replacement swap.

Table 14.3 Cost of cancelling an interest rate swap

Years left to run	% of notional principal
9	6.00
7	5.03
5	3.89
3	2.53

current two-year fixed rate, which is, say, 8.5 per cent p.a. So in the second swap, the bank is receiving 1.5 per cent less for two years than it was receiving in the first swap. This rate, calculated in present value terms, will be the compensation paid to the bank by the shipping company for cancelling the swap. If cancellation occurs between interest payment dates, then the bank calculates the difference in present value terms between the interest rates it is now paying and receiving compared with what it would have paid and received.

The more exotic the interest rate bases are in swaps, the less liquid they are and so the more difficult they will be to replace. Transacting a swap with 90-day US dollar commercial paper as the index is more difficult than transacting a swap based on six-month US dollar LIBOR. Swaps with US treasury bills as their base are even more unusual, and are consequently more expensive to reverse.

As a rule of thumb, assuming that a ten-year interest rate swap has an initial coupon of 10 per cent p.a., the cost of cancellation, assuming a 1 per cent shift in prevailing rates to 9 per cent p.a., expressed as a percentage of the notional principal, is shown in Table 14.3.

We now turn to risk assessment for a currency swap. The complexity of currency swaps, compared with interest rate swaps, means that they are virtually never transacted by two companies without a financial institution standing between them and

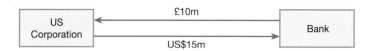

Figure 14.13 Initial exchange of principal.

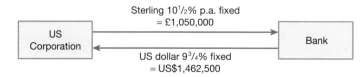

Figure 14.14 Periodic payments.

acting as principal with both counterparties. This means that the risk of default by the opposite counterparty is substantially reduced. The risk remains that a company may wish to cancel a currency swap prior to maturity. Doing so will have a cost, either positive or negative, depending on the direction of movements in interest and foreign exchange rates since the swap first began. The method used to calculate that cost is essentially the same as for assessing risk in an interest rate swap – that is, to calculate the cost to the other counterparty of hedging itself by replacing it at current market rates with another currency swap. However, for currency swaps the calculation is made more complicated by the introduction of an additional variable – foreign currency exchange rates.

Here is an example of how the replacement cost can be calculated. Under the terms of a five-year swap there is an initial exchange of the principal amount as shown in Figure 14.13. The US corporation gives the swap bank $15m in exchange for receiving £10m from the swap bank at the spot foreign exchange rate of $1.5 = £1. Figure 14.14 shows the periodic payments made by both parties throughout the life of the swap. The US corporation agrees to make fixed payments to the swap bank at 10.50 per cent – or £1,050,000 per year. In return, the swap bank makes fixed payments to the US corporation at 9.75 per cent – or $1,462,500 per annum. Now, assume that after four years – that is, one year before maturity – the US corporation wishes to cancel the swap. The swap bank agrees to do so, but must hedge its resulting exposure by transacting another currency swap. However, the interest and exchange rate environment will now be different from that prevailing four years before when the original swap was agreed, meaning that it is not possible to transact an identical swap. Assume that the one-year US dollar fixed interest rate is 9.75 per cent p.a. and that the one year UK sterling fixed interest rate is 10.0 per cent p.a. And the foreign exchange rate has moved to $2.0 = £1. With only one year left until the swap's maturity, the bank expects to make one more interest payment of $1,462,500 and a final exchange of principal of $15,000,000. The one-year US dollar interest rate is 9.75 per cent p.a. – the same as the five-year rate four years ago – so the fixed outflow can remain the same. However, the spot foreign exchange rate has moved. That means the final exchange of principal of $15,000,000 only buys £7,500,000. This, in turn, will yield a fixed inflow of only £750,000 at the new one-year UK sterling swap rate of 10 per cent p.a. as shown in Figure 14.15. Therefore, on the final exchange of

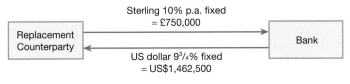

Figure 14.15 Periodic payments in replacement swap.

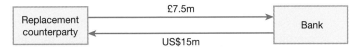

Figure 14.16 Re-exchange of principal in replacement swap.

interest payments the bank loses £300,000, and on the re-exchange of the principal amount (see Figure 14.16) it loses £2,500,000, a total loss of £2,800,000 discounted for one year at 10.0 per cent p.a. to give a present value of £2,545,454. This loss, expressed in terms of US dollars at the new spot rate of $2.0 = £1, is equivalent to a loss of $5,600,000 (discounted for one year at 10 per cent p.a. to a present value of $5,090,909) – or 37.3 per cent of the original $15m principal amount. This sum is the cost to the US corporation of cancelling the currency swap one year before maturity.

14.6 | Summary

- Bankers are in the business of taking deposits in various currencies on the basis of a fixed or floating interest rate. Also, banks offer to make loans in various currencies on a fixed or on a floating interest rate basis.

- That banks are prepared to take deposits on a floating basis and to lend on a fixed basis (and vice versa) in a particular currency gives the essential rationale for the interest rate swap.

- An interest rate swap involves the banker in lending a particular currency on a fixed interest rate basis and receiving a deposit on a floating interest rate basis – or vice versa. In the swap, of course, the amounts lent and borrowed by the banker are the same. Since they are the same, these capital sums cancel out. The interest rate swap simply involves the servicing by one party of the counterparty's interest rate obligation according to the terms of the swap. No principal sum is exchanged. And the fixed/floating rate exchange reflects market rates prevailing at a particular point in time.

- The fact that banks will take deposits in one currency on a fixed or floating basis and also make loans to customers in a different currency on a fixed or floating basis provides the rationale to the currency swap market.

- The essential logic of the currency swap follows the same kind of thinking that applies to the earlier bullet point on the interest rate swap market. The key difference is that principal sums may be exchanged at the initiation of the currency swap. However, this need not be the case. The point is that if a swap is being done involving UK pounds and euros amounting to the equivalent of £2m, if the exchange rate is euro 1.45 to the pound, then the party wanting to obtain a pound liability might give €2.9m and receive £2m. In this circumstance all that has happened is that a principal sum in one currency is exchanged for a principal sum in another – but the amounts are, of course, equal; this might equally well have been achieved by a spot foreign exchange transaction. In short, the currency swap need not kick off by an exchange of principal. The parties concerned can obtain a capital sum in whatever currency they like simply through the spot market. So, in a currency swap with no exchange of principal, the parties to the agreement agree to pay and receive interest in different specified currencies at fixed or floating interest rates depending upon the agreement in respect of an assumed capital amount and also agree to repay notional principal amounts at maturity. Once again the interest rates (whether fixed or floating) will reflect prevailing market conditions.

■ Be sure that you understand how to convert semi-annual to an annual interest rate basis. And also remember how to convert annual interest to a semi-annual basis.

■ In terms of covering exposures, the swap market provides an alternative to forward hedging. For most currencies, the forward marker beyond five years is shallow. This is not so in respect of the swap market, where more competitive rates are generally available compared to long-term forwards, and markets go out to maturities of twenty years or more – if required.

14.7 | End of chapter questions

Question 1
Explain both interest rate swaps and currency swaps. Which instrument has a greater credit risk: an interest rate swap or a currency swap?

Question 2
How can multinational companies utilize a currency swap to reduce borrowing costs?

Question 3
If you expect short-term interest rates to rise more than the yield curve suggests, would you rather pay a fixed long-term rate and receive a floating short-term rate, or receive a fixed long-term rate and pay a floating short-term rate?

15 Financial futures and foreign exchange

A financial futures contract is an agreement to buy or sell a standard quantity of a specific financial instrument at a future date and at a price agreed between the parties through open outcry on the floor of an organized financial futures exchange. With respect to standard quantity, each contract for a given type of financial instrument is for the same standard quantity, for example $100,000. The term 'specific financial instrument' implies that the contract specification lays down the type of financial instrument (for example a twenty-year gilt-edged stock with a stated interest rate, or a foreign currency) with delivery at an explicit maturity. With respect to future date, the delivery of the amounts specified in the contract must take place on one of four specified dates in the forthcoming year. The vast majority of financial futures deals are reversed before delivery date: thus most purchase deals are reversed by matching sale deals, thereby avoiding the need for delivery physically to be effected. Standardization as to quantity and type of instrument enables easy transferability of futures contracts. Financial futures contracts can be sold via the financial futures exchange.

15.1 | Financial futures in general

Someone who buys an interest rate future has the right and obligation to deposit money to the nominal amount contracted for at a specified interest rate for a specified period with the seller. Someone who sells an interest rate future becomes available to take a deposit amounting to the nominal amount contracted at a specific rate of interest for a specific period of time.

Trading in some financial futures markets is still by open outcry but, increasingly, this is being replaced by computers, screen trading, telephones and other telecommunications devices. Under the open outcry system, a principal may give instructions to a broker by telephone but the broker will effect the deal for the client on the financial futures floor (or pit, as it is called). Users, under this system, transact business only through authorized brokers who receive a commission. It is clearly less than ideal, hence its replacement by higher levels of technology.

A clearing house exists to ease the funds flow from the execution of contracts. In financial futures trading, the clearing house evolved to assume the credit risk in futures transactions by guaranteeing the performance of buyer and seller to each other.

While all financial futures transactions must have a buyer and seller, their obligation is not to each other but to a clearing house. After a transaction is recorded, the clearing house substitutes itself for the other party and becomes the seller to every buyer and the buyer to every seller. In this way the clearing house achieves its primary objective which is to guarantee the performance of every transaction done on the floor of the financial futures exchange. Trading on margin is a feature of financial futures. Only a small fraction, called the initial margin, of the underlying instrument's value has to be put up initially by the purchaser or seller as security for performance. This amount varies according to the contract which is being dealt in, but it is typically between 1 and 5 per cent of the instrument's value. Clearly, this produces gearing which may be attractive to market operators. Gearing acts to the advantage of the operator in terms of magnifying his or her gains when markets are moving in that person's favour. But the reverse holds when markets move against the operator. Margin positions are revised daily, accounts are debited or credited according to movements and margin calls are made to cover accrued losses and to top up subsequent margin to the required percentage level. The essential differences between the mechanics of financial futures and forward foreign exchange transactions are summarized in Table 15.1.

Financial futures provide a means of hedging for those who wish to lock in currency exchange rates on future currency transactions. So foreign currency receivables and payables may be hedged via financial futures if a market exists in the foreign and home currency. In fact, financial futures markets in foreign currencies exist for only a small spectrum of currencies; these are listed later in this chapter.

Financial futures may be traded by those who are willing to assume risk and wish to profit from the rises or falls they expect to occur in interest rates or exchange rates. This enables users to take a view about trends in rates without actually having to purchase or sell the underlying currency or financial instrument. They may sell a contract which they do not already own (going short) when they feel that it is likely that interest rates will rise or a currency's value will decline. The operator hopes to buy the contract in after a fall in its price prior to the delivery date, thereby making a profit.

Hedgers and speculators each have an important role to play in creating efficient operations in financial futures markets. Traders (or speculators) provide liquidity to the market, enabling hedgers to buy or sell in volume without difficulty. Only a small percentage of futures contracts is held until delivery. The reason for this is that most hedgers have no further need for the hedge once they have traded out of their position in the cash market. Traders usually close their position once they have achieved their profit objectives or decided to cut their losses. A buyer closes his or her position by making an offsetting sale of the same contract; a seller makes an offsetting purchase.

There are two key elements of cost involved in dealing in financial futures. These are direct costs and margin costs. Members charge a negotiated commission for executing orders for a customer. Commission is charged for a round trip. This covers both the opening and the closing of a position and is normally payable either when the position is closed or when delivery takes place. This is the direct cost element.

Margin works differently. When a deal has been done, both buyer and seller have to put up margin to the clearing house (either cash or collateral) to provide against

Table 15.1 Comparison of forward and futures markets in foreign exchange

	Financial futures	Forward markets
Location	Futures exchanges for some countries. But increasingly banks without a specific physical exchange location	Banks and other traders – no single location
Trading medium	Screen trading/computers/ telephone/other telecommunications devices. Where futures exchanges have a specific physical location, trading via open outcry	Screen trading/computers/ telephone/other telecommunications devices
Contract size	Standardized	As required by customer
Maturity/delivery date	Standardized	As required by customer
Counterparty	Clearing house	Known bank or other trader
Credit risk	Clearing house	Individual counterparty
Commissions	Always payable – flat rate for small deals; otherwise negotiable	Negotiable or implied in dealer's spread when no specific commission is payable
Security	Margin required	Counterparty credit risk; banks set this against credit limits according to their own house rules
Liquidity	Provided by margin payments	Provided by credit limits
Leverage	Very high	No formal gearing, but since payment is not required until delivery, although credit limits are used, gearing may in effect be achieved
Settlement	Via clearing house	Via arrangements with banks

adverse price movements of the futures contract. The minimum level of this margin, the initial margin, is set by the clearing house and reflects the volatility of the under-lying instrument. Typically, margin may range from 1 to 5 per cent of the face value of the contract. As prices fluctuate daily, the value of outstanding contracts (open positions) will change. The amount of each day's gain or loss (called variation margin) is added to or subtracted from the margin account. Daily profits may be drawn by the investor. However, in order to maintain the initial margin intact, any losses have to be paid to the broker. Because the initial margin is greater than the likely daily movement of the underlying cash instruments, losses on a given day will not generally exceed the amount in a customer's margin account. If a contract is held until delivery, the buyer has to pay the seller the full value of the contract.

Table 15.2 An example of currency futures contracts*

Currency against US dollar	Sterling	Euros	Swiss franc	Japanese yen
Unit of trading	£62,500	€125,000	Sfr 125,000	¥12,500,000
Delivery months	For all contracts, delivery months are March, June, September and December			
Delivery date	For all contracts, delivery is on a specified day of the above delivery months			
Quotation	US$ per £	US$ per €	US$ per Sfr	US$ per ¥100
Minimum price movement	0.01 cent per £	0.01 cent per €	0.01 cent per Sfr	0.01 cent per ¥100
Tick size and value	$6.25	$12.50	$12.50	$12.50
Initial margin	$1,000	$1,000	$1,000	$1,000

* The contract sizes are based on Chicago Mercantile Exchange contracts.

15.2 | Currency contracts

We are concerned here with currency contracts traded on financial futures exchanges. For purposes of illustration we use as an example contracts for the dollar against sterling, the euro, the Swiss franc and the Japanese yen. Sizes and key data for such currency future contracts, based on Chicago Mercantile Exchange data, appear in Table 15.2.

Financial futures contracts in currencies are priced in terms of the underlying exchange rate. The sterling futures contract (that is, sterling against the US dollar) might be quoted one day at 1.6800 and at 1.6950 on the next day. The pricing system is similar to that in the foreign exchange market. Other forms of currency contracts in yen, euros and Swiss francs were quoted in terms of the number of dollars per unit of foreign currency, that is, equivalent to the direct quote as in New York. As shown in Table 15.2, the tick value is 0.01 cent per unit of foreign currency. The term 'tick' refers to the minimum price movement in a contract – it is the last decimal place quoted by dealers. With this background, let us consider a simple example. A trader buys three sterling currency contracts at a price of \$1.6800; he may find that within a week the position is closable at a price of \$1.7300. This would yield a profit of \$9,375 as calculated below:

$$3 \text{ contracts} \times 500 \text{ ticks}$$

Or, put another way, profit equals:

$$\$ \frac{(1.7300 - 1.6800)}{0.0001} \times 6.25 \, (\$ \text{ per tick}) \times 3 \text{ contracts} = \$9,375 \text{ (total profit)}$$

The trader calculates the overall profit or loss by multiplying the number of contracts by the number of ticks of price change by the tick value. These three contracts would require initial margin of \$3,000 and this would be outstanding for one week.

It should be noted that rates of initial margin quoted in Table 15.2 would only apply between clearing members of the financial futures exchange and the clearing house. Margin arrangements for others may vary. A member may insist on being paid higher initial margins than those stated; the effect of this is to provide a cushion to cover variation margin calls and obviate the need for frequent charges or payments for small price changes on futures contracts. The key factor regarding margin is to know exactly how much cash will be needed to take up the desired futures position, and to relate interest forgone on financing the deal to potential trading profits.

The financial futures markets do not claim to be superior to forward markets in terms of covering foreign exchange risk. However, they may be used to enable a company respectively to cover a receivable or payable by selling or buying the appropriate foreign currency. Clearly there are disadvantages compared with forward markets. Financial futures markets have only four delivery dates per year; deals are done for standard quantities of currency; and only a small number of currencies are dealt. The problem of specific delivery dates can be overcome by trading a number of contracts for the next delivery date immediately beyond the exposure, and selling on such contracts when the receivable or payable is met.

Arbitraging between financial futures currency quotations and forward markets tends to lead to equality of quotations. So it should be the case that the profit or loss on the financial futures currency contract used to cover an exposure should approximate the profit or loss accruing where cover is achieved through the forward markets. Normally the proceeds from covering via forwards and futures are similar, but forward contracts use up credit lines negotiated with a bank whereas futures contracts do not.

Standardization of size of financial futures contracts is a problem for the corporate treasurer seeking cover for foreign exchange exposure via financial futures. This is easily overcome by taking that number of contracts which approximates the value of the desired exposed amount – but of course this method cannot yield an exact hedge.

The Chicago Mercantile Exchange deals with a vast range of currencies against the US dollar: for example, Mexican peso, Swiss franc, sterling, euros, Canadian dollar, Japanese yen, and more. UK-based brokers will readily arrange Chicago contracts for clients wishing to do business in these markets. The range of contracts offered is expanding all the time as new financial futures centres open all around the world.

The financial futures markets are frequently used for currency trading and speculation. Trading may involve taking an uncovered position in a financial futures contract. This occurs when the trader backs his opinion that exchange rates are going to move in a particular direction and when he believes that the general expectations of rates which are reflected in the current level of futures prices do not fully, or even correctly, discount likely events enabling a position to be taken that will show a profit should rates move in the way the trader predicts.

15.3 | Hedging a borrowing

One of the most useful features of hedging via financial futures concerns the rolling over of floating rate borrowings. The financial futures markets enable an investor or borrower to tie in to a fixed rate; the way in which futures may be used to achieve this with respect to a borrowing is best explained with the help of a numerical example. Suppose that it is 1 February. A borrower has a three-month Eurodollar loan of $1m at a rate of 8 per cent per annum, which is due to be rolled over on 31 May. The borrower suspects that by that date rates will have risen. By using a three-month Eurodollar interest rate contract the borrower may cover the risk of higher interest rates. The contract is for a three-month deposit of 1m Eurodollars beginning in March, June, September or December. Since the March contract will have matured before the 31 May roll-over date, the borrower selects the June delivery month for covering. The contract is priced in the normal way by deducting the deposit interest rate from 100. On 1 February the interest rate is 8 per cent, giving a contract price of 92.00. Assume that the contract tick size is 0.01 cents and the value of one tick is $25. Being concerned that interest rates will rise, the borrower sells one June contract at 92.00. By 31 May, when the borrowing is due to be rolled over, assume that

Eurodollar interest rates for the month deposits have risen to 10 per cent per annum. The result of the hedge is as follows:

> 1 February   Sells one June contract at 92.00
> 31 May   Buys one June contract at 90.00
> Profit on deal = 200 ticks at $25
>   = $5,000

The profit on the financial futures deal exactly offsets the extra cost of interest amounting to $5,000, given by:

$$\text{Additional interest paid} = 2\% \times \frac{3 \text{ months}}{12 \text{ months}} \times \$1,000,000$$

$$= \$5,000$$

The hedge has worked perfectly because the cash market interest rates have moved exactly in line with financial futures prices. In practice such perfect matching is rare – futures prices and cash market rates do not move exactly in line.

15.4 | Basis risk

Hedging via financial futures is not always exactly achievable. Standardization of contract size means that precise hedges may not be possible. Remember that it is only possible to deal whole contracts. But the main reason why perfect hedges are not always achievable is the existence of basis risk. So what is basis risk? It simply arises because the rates that the cash market (for example, the foreign exchange forward market) and the futures market quote may be different and the amount of the difference varies over time. For example, to cover an interest rate exposure in the futures market, a company will have to buy at one time and to sell before the expiry of the contract concerned. The difference between the futures market price and the cash market interest rate may be 40 basis points (0.40 per cent p.a.) at the time of the purchase and 20 basis points at the time of sale. Clearly, the hedge may make a profit or incur a loss as a result of the changing basis risk in the above example. The relationship between yields in the cash and futures markets may arise in part due to the different cash flows required – remember that futures contracts require margin payments whereas currency forward contracts require no up-front payment (except for relatively weak credits – and very poor credits cannot access the forward market). This source of basis risk is termed the 'carrying cost' element.

The second source of basis risk is different expectations in the two markets, largely brought about by the relative risk aversion of the participants in the different markets. Of course, there is a ceiling to the extent of basis risk inasmuch as arbitrageurs will whittle it away should it become excessive. Diagrammatically, the sources of basis risk can be summarized as shown in Figure 15.1 (overleaf).

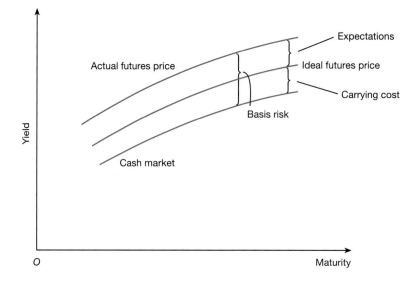

Figure 15.1 Sources of basis risk.

15.5 | Use of currency futures market

Companies are comparatively small users of the currency futures markets. They can invariably achieve cover more easily, more cheaply and more effectively via the forward market. As we have mentioned earlier, the forward market does not require – for the reasonably strong company – any up-front payment; banks set forward deals against negotiated credit lines. Weak credits may be asked for an up-front payment for forward deals based upon a percentage of the size of the contract. And very weak companies, financially speaking, may be denied access to the forward market because commercial banks may not wish to carry the risk that the firm may default on its obligations under any contract granted. For such companies, the futures market may be an ideal alternative. Their brokers will, remember, require initial and variation margin and, to the extent that this is not forthcoming as requested, the futures contracts will be closed out at the prevailing market price. This mechanism reduces the credit risk attached to the financially weak corporation in its dealings in futures markets.

15.6 | Summary

■ Cover against foreign exchange exposures may be obtained through the forward or swap markets. Financial futures on foreign currency provide another means of covering currency exposures. Forward rates, swap rates and financial futures quotations on currency are based upon interest rate differentials.

- The pricing of financial futures contracts on foreign exchanges varies slightly from forward quotations by virtue of the different timing of cash flows. Note that financial futures requires an initial margin; this contrasts to the forward contract which, for corporations with an acceptable credit standing, involves exchange of cash only at maturity. It is this difference in cash flow configuration that gives rise to quotation differences.

- It is worth noting that the forward market provides a far better way of achieving cover than financial futures on foreign currency.

- The futures market may be resorted to by corporations whose inferior credit standing precludes them from access to the forward market. It is a relatively cumbersome market to monitor positions in and is a more expensive market to deal in compared with the forward market. Futures markets are used by individuals for speculative purposes.

15.7 | End of chapter questions

Question 1
Explain how a US corporation could hedge net receivables in British pounds with futures contracts.

Question 2
What is basis risk? How does a cross-hedge (where the cash flow exposure being hedged has different characteristics to the future used as a hedge – hence the expression across markets – hence the expression cross-hedge) create basis risk? How does a mismatch in maturities between the asset being hedged and the futures contract in the hedge create basis risk?

Question 3
Assume that, on 1 November, the spot rate of the £/US$ was $1.58 and the price on a December futures contract was $1.59. Assume that the pound depreciates over November, so that by 30 November it is worth $1.51.

(a) What do you think would happen to the futures price over the month of November? Why?

(b) If you expected this to occur, would you have purchased or sold a December futures contract on GBP on 1 November? Explain.

16 Options

Options are contractual arrangements giving the owner the right to buy or sell an asset at a fixed price anytime on or before a given date. Share options are options to buy and sell shares. Share options are frequently referred to as stock options. Both terms have the same meaning. Share options are traded on stock exchanges. This chapter contains a description of different types of options. We identify and discuss factors that determine option values.

An option is a contract giving its owner the right to buy or sell an asset at a fixed price on or before a given date. For example, an option on a building might give the buyer the right to buy the building for £1m on or any time before the Saturday prior to the third Wednesday in January 2010. Options are a singular type of financial contract because they give the buyer the right, but not the obligation, to do something. The buyer uses the option only if it is a sensible thing to do so. Otherwise, the option can be simply discarded.

There is a vocabulary associated with options. Some of the most important definitions are as follows:

- *Exercising the option.* The act of buying or selling the underlying asset via the option contract is referred to as exercising the option.

- *Strike or exercise price.* The fixed price in the option contract at which the holder of the option can buy or sell the underlying asset is called the strike price or exercise price.

- *Expiration date.* The maturity date of the option is termed the expiration date. After this date, the option is dead.

- *American and European options.* An American option may be exercised at any time up to the expiration date. A European option differs from an American option in that it can only be exercised on the expiration date.

16.1 | Call options

The most frequently encountered option is a call option. It gives the owner the right to buy an asset at a fixed price during a particular time period. The most common options traded on exchanges are options on shares and bonds. Usually the assets involved are ordinary shares.

For example, call options on XYZ plc shares can be purchased on the London Stock Exchange. XYZ itself does not issue (that is, sell) call options on its ordinary shares. In fact, individual investors or banks are the original sellers and buyers of call options on XYZ ordinary shares. A call option on XYZ enables an investor to buy 1,000 shares of XYZ on or before, say, 15 July, 2000, at an exercise price of £12. This is a valuable option if there is some probability that the price of XYZ ordinary shares will exceed £12 on or before 15 July, 2000.

Virtually all option contracts on shares specify that the exercise price and the number of shares are adjusted for stock splits and stock dividends. Suppose that XYZ shares were selling for £18 on the day the option was purchased. Suppose that the next day it split 6 for 1. Each share would drop in price to £3, and the probability that the share would rise over £12 per share in the near future becomes very remote. To protect the option holder from such an occurrence, call options are typically adjusted for stock splits and stock dividends. In the case of a 6-for-1 split, the exercise price would become £2 (£12 divided by 6). Furthermore, the option contract would now cover 6,000 shares, rather than the original 1,000 shares. Note that no adjustment is made for the payment by XYZ of cash dividends to shareholders. This failure to adjust clearly hurts holders of call options, though, of course, they should know the terms of option contracts and the proximity of dividends before buying.

The value of a call option at expiration

The value of a call option contract on ordinary shares at expiration depends on the value of the underlying shares at expiration. We use S_T as the market price of the underlying shares on the expiration date, T. This price is not known prior to expiration. Suppose that a particular call option could be exercised one year from now at the exercise price of £50. If the value of the ordinary shares at expiration, S_T, is greater than the exercise price of £50, the option will be worth the difference, $S_T - £50$. When $S_T > £50$, the call is said to be in the money.

Suppose the share price on expiration day is £60. The option holder has the right to buy the share from the option seller for £50.[1] Because the share is selling in the market for £60, the option holder would exercise the option, that is, buy the share for £50. If he were to wish to do so, he could then sell the share for £60 and keep the difference of £10 (£60 – £50). Options are not usually on just one share. More usually the option might be on 1,000 shares or 10,000 shares.

Of course, it is possible that the value of the share will turn out to be less than the exercise price. If $S_T < £50$, the call is said to be out of the money. The holder would not exercise in this case. If the share price at the expiration date were £40, no rational investor would exercise. Why pay £50 (by exercising the option) for a share worth only £40? Since the option holder has no obligation to exercise the call, he can walk away from the option. Thus, if $S_T < £50$ on the expiration date, the value of the call option will be zero. In this case the value of the call option is not $S_T - £50$, as it would be if the holder of the call option had the an obligation to exercise the call. The *payoff of a call option at expiration* is

	if $S_T \leq £50$	if $S_T > £50$
Call-option value:	0	$S_T - £50$

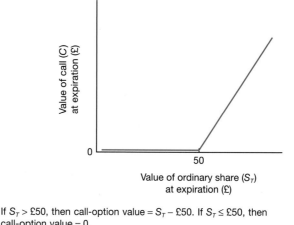

If $S_T > £50$, then call-option value $= S_T - £50$. If $S_T \le £50$, then call-option value $= 0$.

A call option gives the owner the right to *buy* an asset at a fixed price during a particular time period.

Figure 16.1 The value of a call option on the expiration date.

Figure 16.1 plots the value of the call option at expiration against the value of the share. It is often referred to as the hockey-stick diagram of call-option values. If $S_T < £50$, the call is out of the money and worthless. If $S_T > £50$, the call is in the money and rises one-for-one with increases in share price. Note that the call can never have a negative value. A call is a limited liability instrument; the maximum amount that the holder can lose on a call option is the initial amount he or she paid for it.

Consider an example. Suppose that Henry Hope holds a one year call option for 1,000 shares of ABC plc. It is a European call option and can be exercised at £15 per share. Assume that the expiration date has arrived. What is the value of the ABC call option at the expiration date? If ABC is selling for £20 per share, Henry Hope can exercise the option-purchase 1,000 shares of ABC at £15 per share – and then immediately sell the shares at £20. Henry Hope will have made £5,000 (1,000 shares × £5). Instead, assume that ABC is selling for £10 per share on the expiration date. If Henry Hope were still to hold the call option, he would tear it up. The value of the ABC call on the expiration date would, in this case, be zero.

16.2 | Put options

A put option is really the opposite of a call option. Just as a call gives the holder the right to buy shares at a fixed price, so a put gives the holder the right to sell shares for a fixed exercise price.

The value of a put option at expiration

Circumstances that determine the value of a put option are the opposite of those for a call option, because a put option gives the holder the right to sell shares. Assume

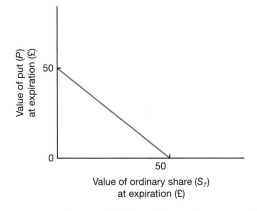

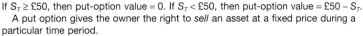

If $S_T \geq £50$, then put-option value = 0. If $S_T < £50$, then put-option value = $£50 - S_T$.
A put option gives the owner the right to *sell* an asset at a fixed price during a
particular time period.

Figure 16.2 The value of a put option on the expiration date.

that the exercise price of the put is £50. If the price, S_T, of the underlying ordinary
shares at expiration is greater than the exercise price, it would be foolish to exercise
the option and sell shares for £50 each. The put option is worthless if $S_T > £50$. In
this case, the put is out-of-the-money. However, if $S_T < £50$, the put is in-the-money.
It will pay to buy shares at S_T and use the option to sell shares at the exercise price
of £50. So, if the share price at expiration is £40, the holder should buy the shares in
the open market at £40. By immediately exercising, he receives £50 for the sale. His
profit is £10 per share (£50 – £40).

The *payoff of a put option at expiration* is given by:

	if $S_T < £50$	if $S_T \geq £50$
Put-option value:	$£50 - S_T$	0

Figure 16.2 plots the values of a put option for all values of the underlying shares.
It is instructive to compare Figure 16.2 with Figure 16.1 for the call-option value.
The call option is valuable whenever the stock is above the exercise price. The put is
valuable when the stock price is below the exercise price.

Take an example. Felicity Fear is quite certain that ABC plc will fall from its
current £16 per share price. So she buys a put on 1,000 ABC shares. Her put option
contract gives her the right to sell 1,000 shares of ABC at £15 per share one year
from now. If the price of ABC is £20 on the expiration date, she will tear up the put
option contract because it is worthless. She will not want to sell shares worth £20 for
the exercise price of £15. On the other hand, if ABC is selling for £10 on the expiration date, she would exercise the option. Felicity Fear has the right to sell 1,000
shares of ABC for £15 per share. In this case, she could buy 1,000 shares of ABC in
the market for £10 per share and turn around and sell the shares at the exercise price
of £15 per share. Her profit would be £5,000 (1,000 shares × £5). The value of the
put option on the expiration date would be £5,000.

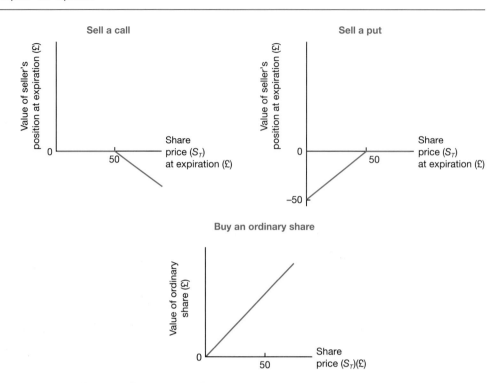

Figure 16.3 The payoffs to sellers of calls and puts, and to buyers of ordinary shares.

16.3 | Writing options

An investor who writes a call on ordinary shares promises to deliver shares of the company concerned if required to do so by the call-option holder. Note that the seller is obligated to do so. The option writer is the original seller of the option. The seller of a call option obtains a cash payment from the holder, or buyer, at the time the option is bought. If, at the expiration date, the price of the ordinary share is below the exercise price, the call option will not be exercised and the seller's liability will be zero.

If, at expiration date, the price of the ordinary share is greater than the exercise price, the holder will exercise the call and the writer or seller must give the holder shares in exchange for the exercise price. The seller loses the difference between the share price and the exercise price. Assume that the share price is £60 and the exercise price is £50. Knowing that exercise is imminent, the option seller buys shares in the open market at £60. Because he is obligated to sell at £50, he loses £10 (£50 – £60) per share.

By a reverse logic, an investor who sells a put option on ordinary shares agrees to purchase shares if the put holder should so request. The seller loses on this deal if the share price falls below the strike price and the holder puts the shares to the seller. For example, assume that the share price is £40 and the exercise price is £50. In this case, the holder of the put will exercise. So he will sell the underlying shares at the exercise price of £50. This means that the seller of the put must buy the underlying shares

Table 16.1 Information on the options of mmO$_2$

Option & London close	Strike price	LIFFE Calls			Puts		
		April	July	Oct.	April	July	Oct.
48.50	45	6.75	9.00	11.00	3.00	5.00	6.50
48.50	50	4.00	6.75	8.75	5.25	7.50	9.00

Source: Data from *Financial Times*, 14 February 2003.

at the strike price of £50. Because the share is only worth £40, the loss here is £10 (£40 − £50) per share under option.

The 'sell-a-call' and 'sell-a-put' positions are depicted in Figure 16.3. The chart on the left-hand side of the figure shows that the seller of a call loses nothing when the share price at expiration date is below £50. However, the seller loses £1 for every £1 that the share price rises above £50. The chart in the centre shows that the seller of a put loses nothing when the share price at expiration date is above £50. However, the seller loses £1 for every £1 that the share falls below £50. The third chart also shows the value at expiration of simply buying ordinary shares.

16.4 | Reading the *Financial Times*

Now that we understand the definitions for calls and puts, let us see how options are quoted. Table 16.1 presents information on the options of mmO$_2$ from the Friday, 14 February 2003 issue of the *Financial Times* (FT). The options are traded on the London International Financial Futures Exchange (LIFFE), one of a number of options exchanges. The first column tells us that the shares of mmO$_2$ closed at $48^{1}/_{2}$ pence per share on the previous day (Thursday, 13 February 2003). Now consider the second and third columns. Thursday's closing price for an option maturing at the end of April 2003 with a strike price of 45 pence was 6.75 pence. Because the option is sold as a 1,000-share contract, the cost of the contract is £67.50 (1,000 × 6.75p) before commissions. The call maturing in April 2003 with an exercise price of 50p closed at 4.00p.

The last three columns display quotes on puts. For example, a put maturing in April 2003 with an exercise price of 45p sells at 3.00p.

16.5 | Combinations of options

Puts and calls may serve as building blocks for more complex option contracts. For example, Figure 16.4 (overleaf) illustrates the payoff from buying a put option on a share and simultaneously buying the share.

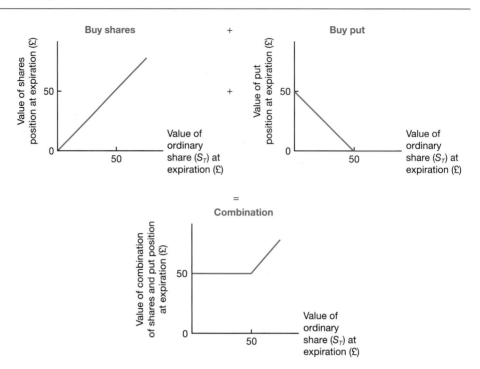

Figure 16.4 Payoffs to the combination of buying puts and buying stock.

If the share price is above the exercise price, the put option is worthless and the value of the combined position is equal to the value of the ordinary share. If, instead, the exercise price is above the share price, the decline in the value of the shares will be exactly offset by the rise in value of the put.

The combination of buying a put and buying the underlying share has the same shape in Figure 16.4 as the call purchase in Figure 16.1. Furthermore, the shape of the combination strategy in Figure 16.4 is the mirror image of the shape of the call sale in the upper left-hand corner of Figure 16.3. This suggests that a strategy in the options market may offset another strategy, resulting in a riskless return.

This possibility is in fact true, as shown in the following example. Assume that both the exercise price of the call and the exercise price of the put on Breitner GmbH are €55. Both options are European. Thus, they cannot be exercised prior to expiration. The expiration date is one year from today. The share price is currently €44. At the expiration date, the stock will be priced, say, at either €58 or €34.

The *offsetting strategy*: suppose you pursue the following strategy:

■ Buy the stock.

■ Buy the put.

■ Sell the call.

The *payoffs at expiration* are:

Initial transaction	Share price rises to €58	Share price falls to €34
Buy an ordinary share	€58	€34
Buy a put	0 (You let put expire)	€21 = €55 – €34
Sell a call	–€3 = –(€58 – €55)	0 (Holder lets call expire)
Total	€55	€55

Note that, when the share price falls, the put is in the money and the call expires without being exercised. When the share price rises, the call is in the money and you let the put expire. The major point is that you end up with €55 in either case.

There is no risk in this strategy. While this result may bother students – or even shock some – it is actually quite intuitive. As pointed out earlier, the graph of the strategy of buying both a put and the underlying shares is the mirror image of the graph from the strategy of selling the call. Thus, combining both strategies, as we did in the example, should eliminate all risk.

The above payoff diagram separately valued each asset at the expiration date. Actually, a discussion of the actual exercise process may simplify things, because here the share is always linked with an option. Consider the following *strategy* tabulation:

Share price rises to €58		Share price falls to €34	
You let put expire.	0	Call expires.	0
Call is exercised against you, obligating you to sell the share you own and receive the exercise price of	€55	You choose to exercise put. That is, you sell the share you own at the exercise price of	€55
Total	€55	Total	€55

Again, we see the riskless nature of the strategy. Regardless of the price movement of the share, exercise entails surrendering the share for €55.

Though we have specified the payoffs at expiration, we have ignored the earlier investment that you made. To remedy this, suppose that you originally pay €44 for the share and €7 for the put and receive €1 for selling the call.[2] In addition, the riskless interest rate is 10 per cent.

You have paid

–€50 = –€44   –€7   +€1

Share purchase   Purchase of put   Sale of call

Because you pay €50 today and are guaranteed €55 in one year, you are just earning the interest rate of 10 per cent. Thus, the prices in this example allow no possibility of arbitrage or easy money. Conversely, if the put sold for only €6, your initial investment would be €49. You would then have a non-equilibrium return of 12.2 per cent (€55/€49 – 1) over the year.

It can be proved that, in order to prevent arbitrage, the prices at the time you take on your original position must conform to the following fundamental relationship:

$$
\underset{\substack{\text{share} \\ €44}}{\text{Value of}} + \underset{\substack{\text{put} \\ +€7}}{\text{Value of}} - \underset{\substack{\text{call} \\ -€1}}{\text{Value of}} = \underset{\substack{\text{exercise price} \\ =€50}}{\text{Present value of}} = €55/1.10
$$

This result is called *put–call parity*. It shows that the values of a put and a call with the same exercise price and same expiration date are precisely related to each other. It holds generally, not just in the specific example we have chosen.[3]

16.6 | Valuing options

In the last section, we determined what options are worth on the expiration date. Now we wish to determine the value of options when we buy them well before expiration. We begin by considering the upper and lower bounds on the value of a call.

Bounding the value of a call

Consider an American call that is in the money prior to expiration. For example, assume that the share price is €60 and the exercise price is €50. In this case, the option cannot sell below €10. To see this, note the simple strategy if the option sells at, say, €9.

Date	Transaction	
Today	(1) Buy call	−€9
Today	(2) Exercise call, that is, buy underlying share at exercise price	−€50
Today	(3) Sell stock at current market price	+€60
Arbitrage profit		+€1

The type of profit that is described in this transaction is an arbitrage profit. Arbitrage profits come from transactions that have no risk or cost and cannot occur regularly in normal, well-functioning financial markets. The excess demand for these options would quickly force the option price up[4] to at least €10 (€60 − €50).

Of course, the price of the option is likely to sell above €10. Investors will rationally pay more than €10 given the possibility that the share price will rise above €60 before expiration. Is there also an upper boundary for the option price? It turns out that the upper boundary is the price of the underlying share. Thus, an option to buy ordinary shares cannot have a greater value than the ordinary share itself. A call option can be used to buy ordinary shares with a payment of an exercise price. It

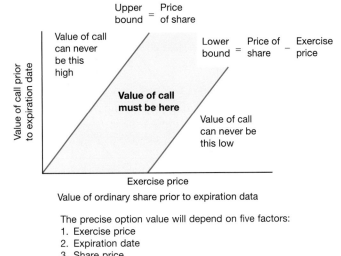

The precise option value will depend on five factors:
1. Exercise price
2. Expiration date
3. Share price
4. Risk-free interest rate
5. Variance of the share

Figure 16.5 The upper and lower boundaries of call-option values.

would not be sensible to buy shares this way if the shares could be purchased directly at a lower price. The upper and lower bounds are represented in Figure 16.5.

The factors determining call-option values

The previous discussion indicated that the price of a call option must fall somewhere in the shaded region of Figure 16.5. Now, we can determine more precisely where in the shaded region it should be. The factors that determine a call's value can be broken into two sets. The first set contains the features of the option contract. The two basic contractual features are the expiration price and the exercise date. The second set of factors affecting the call price concerns characteristics of the share and the market.

Exercise price

It should be obvious that if all other things are held constant, the higher the exercise price, the lower the value of a call option. However, the value of a call option cannot be negative, no matter how high we set the exercise price. Furthermore, as long as there is some possibility that the price of the underlying asset will exceed the exercise price before the expiration date, the option will have value.

Expiration date

The value of an American call option must be at least as great as the value of an otherwise identical option with a shorter term to expiration. Consider two American

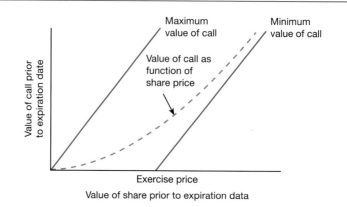

The call price is positively related to the share price. In addition, the change in the call price for a given change in the share price is greater when the share price is high than when it is low.

Figure 16.6 Value of a call as a function of share price.

calls. One has a maturity of nine month's and the other expires in six months' time. Clearly, the nine-month call has the same rights as the six-month call but it also has an additional three months within which these rights can be exercised. It cannot be worth less and will generally be more valuable.[5]

Share price

Other things being equal, the higher the share price, the more valuable the call option will be. This is obvious and is illustrated in any of the figures that plot the call price against the share price at expiration.

Now consider Figure 16.6, which shows the relationship between the call price and the share price prior to expiration. The curve indicates that the call price increases as the share price increases. Furthermore, it can be shown that the relationship is represented, not by a straight line, but by a convex curve. That is, the increase in the call price for a given change in the share price is greater when the share price is high than when the share price is low.

The variability of the underlying asset

The greater the variability of the underlying asset, the more valuable the call option will be. Consider the following example. Suppose that just before the call expires, the share price will be either €100 with probability 0.5 or €80 with probability 0.5. What will be the value of a call with an exercise price of €110? Clearly, it will be worthless because no matter what happens to the share, its price will always be below the exercise price.

Now let us see what happens if the share is more variable. Suppose that we add €20 to the best case and take €20 away from the worst case. Now the share has a one-half chance of being worth €60 and a one-half chance of being worth €120. We have spread the share returns, but, of course, the expected value of the share has stayed the same:

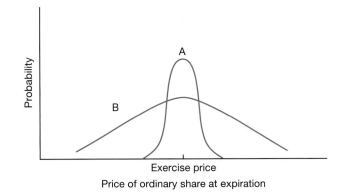

The call on share B is worth more than the call on share A because share B is more volatile. At expiration, a call that is way in the money is more valuable than a call that is way out of the money. However, at expiration, a call way out of the money is worth zero, just as is a call slightly out of the money.

Figure 16.7 Distribution of ordinary share price at expiration for both security A and security B. Options on the two securities have the same exercise price.

$$(^1/_2 \times €80) + (^1/_2 \times €100) = €90 = (^1/_2 \times €60) + (^1/_2 \times €120)$$

Notice that the call option has value now because there is a one-half chance that the share price will be €120, or €10 above the exercise price of €110. This illustrates an important point. There is a fundamental distinction between holding an option on an underlying asset and holding the underlying asset. If investors in the market place are risk-averse, a rise in the variability of the share will decrease its market value. However, the holder of a call receives payoffs from the positive tail of the probability distribution. As a consequence, a rise in the variability in the underlying share increases the market value of the call.

This result can also be seen from Figure 16.7. Consider two shares, A and B, each of which is distributed differently. For each security, the figure illustrates the probability of different share prices on the expiration date.[6] As can be seen from the figures, share B has more volatility than does share A. This means that share B has higher probability of both abnormally high returns and abnormally low returns. Let us assume that options on each of the two securities have the same exercise price. To option holders, a return much below average on stock B is no worse than a return only moderately below average on share A. In either situation, the option expires out of the money. However, to option holders, a return much above average on share B is better than a return only moderately above average on share A. Because a call's price at the expiration date is the difference between the share price and the exercise price, the value of the call on B at expiration will be higher in this case.

The interest rate

Call prices are also a function of the level of interest rates. Buyers of calls do not pay the exercise price until they exercise the option, if they do so at all. The delayed payment is more valuable when interest rates are high and less valuable when interest rates are low. Thus, the value of a call is positively related to interest rates.

Table 16.2 Factors affecting US option values

	Call option	Put option
Value of underlying asset (share price)	+	−
Exercise price	−	+
Share volatility	+	+
Interest rate	+	−
Time to exercise date	+	+

The signs (+, −) indicate the effect of the variables on the value of the option. For example, the two +s for share volatility indicate that an increase in volatility will increase both the value of a call and the value of a put.

Factors determining put-option values

Given our extended discussion of the factors influencing a call's value, we can examine the effect of these factors on puts very easily. Table 16.2 summarizes the five factors influencing the prices of both American calls and American puts. The effect of three factors on puts are the opposite of the effect of these three factors on calls:

■ The put's market price *decreases* as the share price increases because puts are in the money when the share sells below the exercise price.

■ The market value of a put with a high exercise price is *greater* than the value of an otherwise-identical put with a low exercise price for the reason given above.

■ A high interest rate *adversely* affects the value of a put. The ability to sell a share at a fixed exercise price sometime in the future is worth less if the present value of the exercise price is diminished by a high interest rate.

The effect of the other two factors on puts is the same as the effect of these factors on calls:

■ The value of an American put with a distant expiration date is greater than an otherwise identical put with an earlier expiration.[7] The longer time to maturity gives the put holder more flexibility, just as it did in the case of a call.

■ Volatility of the underlying share increases the value of the put. The reasoning is analogous to that for a call. At expiration, a put that is way in the money is more valuable than a put only slightly in the money. However, at expiration, a put way out of the money is worth zero, just as is a put only slightly out of the money.

16.7 | An option-pricing formula

We have explained qualitatively that the value of a call option is a function of five variables:

■ The current price of the underlying asset, which for share options is the price of the ordinary shares.

■ The exercise price.

■   The time to expiration date.

■   The variance of the underlying asset.

■   The risk-free interest rate.

We now replace the qualitative model with a precise option-valuation model. The model we use is the well-known Black and Scholes (1972, 1973) option-pricing model. One can put numbers into the Black and Scholes model and get values back. The Black and Scholes model is represented by a rather imposing formula. A derivation of the formula is not presented in this textbook since it is fairly complicated.

Black and Scholes argue that a strategy of borrowing to finance a share purchase duplicates the risk of a call. Then, knowing the price of a share already, one can determine the price of a call such that its return is identical to that of the share-with borrowing alternative.

The intuition behind the Black and Scholes approach in illustrated by considering a simple example where a combination of a call and a share eliminates all risk. This example works because we let the future share price be one of only two values. Hence, the example is called a two-state option model. By eliminating the possibility that the share price can take on other values, we are able to duplicate the call exactly.

A two-state option model

To find the option price, we assume a market where an arbitrage possibility can never be created. To see how the model works, consider the following example. Suppose the market price of a share is €50 and it will be either €60 or €40 at the end of the year. Further suppose that there exists a call option for 100 shares with a one-year expiration date and a €50 exercise price. Investors can borrow at 10 per cent.

There are two possible trading strategies that we shall examine. The first is to buy a call on the share, and the second is to buy 50 shares and borrow a duplicating amount. The duplicating amount is the amount of borrowing necessary to make the future payoffs from buying stock and borrowing the same as the future payoffs from buying a call on the stock. In our example, the duplicating amount of borrowing is €1,818. With a 10 per cent interest rate, principal and interest at the end of the year total €2,000 (€1,818 × 1.10). At the end of one year, the *future payoffs* are set out as follows:

Initial transactions	If share price is €60	If share price is €40
1. Buy a call (100-share contract)	$100 \times (€60 - €50) =$ €1,000	0
2. Buy 50 shares	$50 \times €60$ = €3,000	$50 \times €40 =$ €2,000
Borrow €1,818	$-(€1,818 \times 1.10)$ = −€2,000	−€2,000
Total from strategy 2	€1,000	0

Note that the future payoff structure of 'buy a call' is duplicated by the strategy of 'buy shares' and 'borrow'. These two trading strategies are equivalent as far as market traders are concerned. As a consequence, the two strategies must have the same cost. The cost of purchasing 50 shares while borrowing €1,818 is €682, given by:

Buy 50 shares	50 × €50 =	€2,500
Borrow €1,818 at 10%		−€1,818
		€682

Because the call option gives the same return, the call must be priced at €682. This is the value of the call option in a market where arbitrage profits do not exist.

Before leaving this simple example, we should comment on a remarkable feature. We found the exact value of the option without even knowing the probability that the share would go up or down! If an optimist thought the probability of an up move was very high and a pessimist thought it was very low, they would still agree on the option value. How could that be? The answer is that the current €50 share price already balances the views of the optimists and the pessimists. The option reflects that balance because its value depends on the share price.

The Black and Scholes model

The above example illustrates the duplicating strategy. Unfortunately, a strategy such as this will not work in the real world because there are many more than two possibilities for next year's share price. However, the number of possibilities is reduced as the time period is shortened. In fact, the assumption that there are only two possibilities for the share price over the next infinitesimal instant is plausible.[8]

In our opinion, the fundamental insight of Black and Scholes is to shorten the time period. They show that a specific combination of shares and borrowing can indeed duplicate a call over an infinitesimal time horizon. Because the price of the share will change over the first instant, another combination of shares and borrowing is needed to duplicate the call over the second instant and so on. By adjusting the combination from moment to moment, it is possible continually to duplicate the call. It may seem difficult to comprehend but an appropriate formula can, firstly, determine the duplicating combination at any moment and, secondly, value the option based on this duplicating strategy. Suffice to say that the Black and Scholes dynamic strategy allows one to value a call in the real world just as we showed how to value the call in the two-state model.

This is the basic intuition behind the Black and Scholes model. Because the actual derivation of their formula is far beyond the scope of this text, we simply present the formula itself. The formula is

$$C = SN(d_1) - E\,e^{-rt}N(d_2)$$

where

$$d_1 = \frac{\ln(S/E) + (r + {}^1\!/_2\sigma^2)t}{\sqrt{\sigma^2 t}}$$

$$d_2 = d_1 - \sqrt{\sigma^2 t}$$

This formula for the value of a call, C, is one of the most complex in finance. However, it involves only five parameters:

- ■ S = current share price.

- ■ E = exercise price of call (some instructors and some textbooks use the notation X, not E).

- ■ r = continuous risk-free rate of return (annualized).

- ■ σ^2 = variance (per year) of the continuous return on the stock.

- ■ t = time (in years) to expiration date.

In addition, there is the statistical concept:

- ■ $N(d)$ = probability that a standardized, normally distributed, random variable will be less than or equal to d.

Rather than discuss the formula in its algebraic state, we illustrate the formula with an example. Consider the German company, PEC GmbH. On 4 October 2004, the PEC April call option with an exercise price at €49 had a closing value of €4. The share itself is selling at €50. On 4 October, the option had 199 days to expiration (maturity date = 21 April, 2005). The annual risk-free interest rate is 7 per cent.

The above information determines three variables directly:

- ■ The share price, S, is €50.

- ■ The exercise price, E, is €49.

- ■ The risk-free rate, r, is 0.07.

In addition, the time to maturity, t, can be calculated quickly: The formula calls for t to be expressed in years.

- ■ We express the 199-day interval in years as $t = 199/365$.

In the real world, an option trader would know S and E exactly. Traders generally view government bills as riskless, so a current quote from a financial newspaper would be obtained for the interest rate. The trader would also know (or could count) the number of days to expiration exactly. Thus, the fraction of a year to expiration, t, could be calculated quickly. The problem comes in determining the variance of the share's return. The formula calls for the variance in operation between the purchase date of 4 October and the expiration date. Unfortunately, this represents the future and the future value for variance is not available. Instead, traders frequently estimate variance from past data. In addition, some traders may use intuition to adjust their estimate. For example, if anticipation of an upcoming event is currently increasing the volatility of the share, the trader might adjust his or her estimate of variance upward to reflect this. This problem was really severe immediately after the stock market crash of 19 October 1987. The stock market was viewed as risky in the immediate aftermath. Consequently, estimates using pre-crash data were reckoned to be too low.

The above discussion is intended merely to spotlight the difficulties in variance estimation – not to present a solution. For our purposes, we assume that a trader has come up with an estimate of variance:

■ The variance of PEC has been estimated to be 0.09 per year.

Using the above five parameters, we calculate the Black and Scholes value of the PEC option in three steps.

Step 1: calculate d_1 and d_2.

These values can be determined by a straightforward, but rather tedious, insertion of our parameters into the basic formula. We have

$$d_1 = \frac{\ln(S/E) + (r + \frac{1}{2}\sigma^2)t}{\sqrt{\sigma^2 t}}$$

$$= \frac{\ln(50/49) + (0.07 + \frac{1}{2} \times 0.09) \times 199/365}{\sqrt{0.09 \times 199/365}}$$

$$= \frac{0.0202 + 0.0627}{\sqrt{0.2215}} = 0.3743$$

$$d_2 = d_1 - \sqrt{\sigma^2 t}$$

$$= 0.1528$$

Step 2: calculate $N(d_1)$ and $N(d_2)$.

The values $N(d_1)$ and $N(d_2)$ can best be understood by examining Figure 16.8. The figure shows the normal distribution with an expected value of 0 and a standard deviation of 1. This is frequently called the standardized normal distribution. The probability that a drawing from this distribution will be within one standard deviation of its mean is 68.26 per cent.

Now, we ask a different question. What is the probability that a drawing from the standardized normal distribution will be below a particular value? For example, the probability that a drawing will be below 0 is clearly 50 per cent because the normal distribution is symmetrical. Using statistical terminology, we say that the cumulative probability of 0 is 50 per cent. Statisticians say $N(0) = 50\%$. It turns out that

$$N(d_1) = N(0.3743) = 0.6459$$

$$N(d_2) = N(0.1528) = 0.5607$$

The first value indicates that there is a 64.59 per cent probability that a drawing from the standardized normal distribution will be below 0.3743. The second value tells us that there is a 56.07 per cent probability that a drawing from the standardized normal distribution will be below 0.1528. More generally, $N(d)$ is the notation that a drawing from the standardized normal distribution will be below d. In other

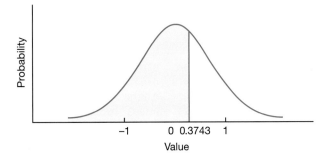

Shaded area represents cumulative probability. Because the probability is 0.6459 that a drawing from the standard normal distribution will be below 0.3743, we say that $N(0.3743) = 0.6459$. That is, the cumulative probability of 0.3743 is 0.6459.

Figure 16.8 Graph of cumulative probability.

words, $N(d)$ is the cumulative probability of d. Note that d_1 and d_2 in our example are slightly positive, so $N(d_1)$ and $N(d_2)$ are slightly greater than 0.50.

We can determine the cumulative probability from Table 16.3 (overleaf). For example, consider $d = 0.37$. This can be found in the table as 0.3 on the vertical and 0.07 on the horizontal. The value in the table for $d = 0.37$ is 0.1443. This value is not the cumulative probability of 0.37. One must first make an adjustment to determine cumulative probability. That is,

$$N(0.37) = 0.50 + 0.1443 = 0.6443$$

$$N(-0.37) = 0.50 - 0.1443 = 0.3557$$

Unfortunately, our table only handles two significant digits, whereas our value of 0.3743 has four significant digits. Hence, we must interpolate to find $N(0.3743)$. Because $N(0.37) = 0.6443$ and $N(0.38) = 0.6480$, the difference between the two values is 0.0037 ($0.6480 - 0.6443$). Because 0.3743 is 43 per cent of the way between 0.37 and 0.38, we interpolate, using linear interpolation, as

$$N(0.3743) = 0.6443 + 0.43 \times 0.0037 = 0.6459$$

Step 3: *Calculate C. We have*

$$C = S \times [N(d_1)] - E\,e^{-rt} \times [N(d_2)]$$
$$= €50 \times [N(d_1)] - €49 \times [e^{-0.07 \times (199/365)}] \times N(d_2)$$
$$= (€50 \times 0.6459) - (€49 \times 0.9626 \times 0.5607)$$
$$= €32.295 - €26.447$$
$$= €5.85$$

Table 16.3 Cumulative probabilities of the standard normal distribution function

d	00.00	0.01	0.02	0.03	0.04	0.05	0.06	0.07	0.08	0.09
0.0	0.0000	0.0040	0.0080	0.0120	0.0160	0.0199	0.0239	0.0279	0.0319	0.0359
0.1	0.0398	0.0438	0.0478	0.0517	0.0557	0.0596	0.0636	0.0675	0.0714	0.0753
0.2	0.0793	0.0832	0.0871	0.0910	0.0948	0.0987	0.1026	0.1064	0.1103	0.1141
0.3	0.1179	0.1217	0.1255	0.1293	0.1331	0.1368	0.1406	0.1443	0.1480	0.1517
0.4	0.1554	0.1591	0.1628	0.1664	0.1700	0.1736	0.1772	0.1808	0.1844	0.1879
0.5	0.1915	0.1950	0.1985	0.2019	0.2054	0.2088	0.2123	0.2157	0.2190	0.2224
0.6	0.2257	0.2291	0.2324	0.2357	0.2389	0.2422	0.2454	0.2486	0.2517	0.2549
0.7	0.2580	0.2611	0.2642	0.2673	0.2704	0.2734	0.2764	0.2794	0.2823	0.2852
0.8	0.2881	0.2910	0.2939	0.2967	0.2995	0.3023	0.3051	0.3078	0.3106	0.3133
0.9	0.3159	0.3186	0.3212	0.3238	0.3264	0.3289	0.3315	0.3240	0.3365	0.3389
1.0	0.3413	0.3438	0.3461	0.3485	0.3508	0.3531	0.3554	0.3577	0.3599	0.3621
1.1	0.3643	0.3665	0.3686	0.3708	0.3729	0.3749	0.3770	0.3790	0.3810	0.3830
1.2	0.3849	0.3869	0.3888	0.3907	0.3925	0.3944	0.3962	0.3980	0.3997	0.4015
1.3	0.4032	0.4049	0.4066	0.4082	0.4099	0.4115	0.4131	0.4147	0.4162	0.4177
1.4	0.4192	0.4207	0.4222	0.4236	0.4251	0.4265	0.4279	0.4292	0.4306	0.4319
1.5	0.4332	0.4345	0.4357	0.4370	0.4382	0.4394	0.4406	0.4418	0.4429	0.4441
1.6	0.4452	0.4463	0.4474	0.4484	0.4495	0.4505	0.4515	0.4525	0.4535	0.4545
1.7	0.4554	0.4564	0.4573	0.4582	0.4591	0.4599	0.4608	0.4616	0.4625	0.4633
1.8	0.4641	0.4649	0.4656	0.4664	0.4671	0.4678	0.4686	0.4693	0.4699	0.4706
1.9	0.4713	0.4719	0.4726	0.4732	0.4738	0.4744	0.4750	0.4756	0.4761	0.4767
2.0	0.4773	0.4778	0.4783	0.4788	0.4793	0.4798	0.4803	0.4808	0.4812	0.4817
2.1	0.4821	0.4826	0.4830	0.4834	0.4838	0.4842	0.4846	0.4850	0.4854	0.4857
2.2	0.4861	0.4866	0.4830	0.4871	0.4875	0.4878	0.4881	0.4884	0.4887	0.4890
2.3	0.4893	0.4896	0.4898	0.4901	0.4904	0.4906	0.4909	0.4911	0.4913	0.4916
2.4	0.4918	0.4920	0.4922	0.4925	0.4927	0.4929	0.4931	0.4932	0.4934	0.4936
2.5	0.4938	0.4940	0.4941	0.4943	0.4945	0.4946	0.4948	0.4949	0.4951	0.4952
2.6	0.4953	0.4955	0.4956	0.4957	0.4959	0.4960	0.4961	0.4962	0.4963	0.4964
2.7	0.4965	0.4966	0.4967	0.4968	0.4969	0.4970	0.4971	0.4972	0.4973	0.4974
2.8	0.4974	0.4975	0.4976	0.4977	0.4977	0.4978	0.4979	0.4979	0.4980	0.4981
2.9	0.4981	0.4982	0.4982	0.4982	0.4984	0.4984	0.4985	0.4985	0.4986	0.4986
3.0	0.4987	0.4987	0.4987	0.4988	0.4988	0.4989	0.4989	0.4989	0.4990	0.4990

$N(d)$ represents areas under the standard normal distribution function. Suppose that $d_1 = 0.24$. This table implies a cumulative probability of $0.5000 + 0.0948 = 0.5948$. If d_1 is equal to 0.2452, we must estimate the probability by interpolating between $N(0.25)$ and $N(0.24)$.

The estimated price of €5.85 is greater than the €4 actual price, implying that the call option is underpriced. A trader, believing in the Black and Scholes model, would buy a call.

The Black and Scholes formula is among the most important contributions in finance. It allows anyone to calculate the value of an option given a few parameters. The attraction of the formula is that four of the parameters are observable – the current price of the stock, S, the exercise price, E, the interest rate, r, and the time to expiration date, t. Only one of the parameters must be estimated: the variance of return, σ^2.

Think of the formula another way. Note what parameters are not needed. First, the investor's risk aversion does not affect value. The formula can be used by anyone, regardless of willingness to bear risk. Second, it does not depend on the expected return on the share. Investors with different assessments of the share's expected return should agree on the call price. As in the two-state example, this is because the call depends on the stock price and that price already balances investors' divergent views.

The assumptions of the Black and Scholes model are worth mentioning:

■ There are no penalties for or restrictions on short selling.

■ Transaction costs and taxes are zero.

■ The option is European.

■ The share pays no dividends.

■ There are no jumps in share price. Prices move continuously.

■ The market operates continuously.

■ The short-term interest rate is known and constant.

■ The share price is log-normally distributed.

These assumptions are the sufficient conditions for the Black and Scholes model to be correct.

We now refer to certain pieces of option market jargon. Where a call option on a share has an exercise price below the underlying share price, the holder of such a call is obviously in a profitable position. The fact that the exercise price of the call is below the share price is referred to in terms of the option being in-the-money. The same would be the case where the exercise price of a put option is above the underlying share price. When an option is in-the-money, it is said to have intrinsic value. In such circumstances, intrinsic value refers to the amount given, either, by the exercise price less the share price (if positive) for a put option, or, the share price less the exercise price (if positive) for a call option. Options that have intrinsic value are said to be in-the-money. It is easy to remember: each begins with 'in'.

By contrast, when a call option has an exercise price above the underlying share price, it is said to be out-of-the-money. Similarly, a put option on a share with an exercise price below the underlying share price would be out-of-the-money. Options that are out-of-the-money have no intrinsic value. Note, of course, that such options cannot have negative intrinsic value since a European option that was out-of-the-money at maturity would simply not be exercised. The option holder would not incur a loss in the sense that he would simply not exercise the option but let it lapse (of course, allowing for the option premium already paid, a loss could be said to have been incurred – but the option premium is clearly a sunk cost).

Where an option has time to run to maturity, the value of the option (assuming it is a call and the exercise price is below the underlying share price) will be more than $(S - E)$. The amount by which the option value exceeds $(S - E)$ is what the Black and Scholes model is all about. In all such circumstances, the amount by which the option premium exceeds intrinsic value is termed time value. Captured within the general expression, time value, will be the effects of time to run to maturity, volatility and the risk-free interest rate – that is, t, σ and r, respectively. An option with zero intrinsic value but with time to run to maturity will have time value only.

Where the exercise price of an option is equal to the underlying share price, whether it is a call option or a put, it is said to be at-the-money. Such options will have zero intrinsic value but will have time value. Time value plus intrinsic value will always give the value of an option.

In circumstances where some of the eight assumptions, referred to earlier in this section, of the Black and Scholes model do not hold, then a variation of the model often works. For example, the formula can be fine-tuned to account for dividends – see the last paragraph of this section. Empirical studies suggest that the model, particularly when fine-tuned, does a very good job in computing call-option value.

Note that the Black and Scholes option-pricing model applies to European options. It is worth mentioning that, where a share pays no dividends, an American call should be equal in terms of option premium to a European call with all other characteristics similar. The rationale for this is as follows. The value of a call option increases as the time to maturity increases. Thus, if exercised early, an American call option would lose its time value – if exercised early it would have intrinsic value only. Early exercise of an American call would seem pointless. Since an American call option should not be exercised early, its value should be the same as a European call option and the Black and Scholes model would be applicable to each.

As regards American puts, equality of price with a European put is not the case. On occasions, it can pay to exercise an American put before maturity. For example, imagine that, immediately after purchase of an American put, the share price falls to zero. In this case there is no advantage to continuing to hold the option. It has reached its maximum value. It is better to exercise the option and invest the proceeds. This kind of situation applies, too, where the underlying share moves towards zero – it becomes 'bombed out'. This feature means that an American put will always be worth more than a European put with characteristics otherwise the same. Depending upon the situation, the difference may be significant, as in our extreme example. In other cases than this extreme, the difference is less marked. However, it remains the case that an American put might be exercised early where interest rates have moved sufficiently high to justify early exercise with reinvestment of the proceeds. This occurs where the interest rate effect exceeds the volatility effect. Since the Black and Scholes formula does not allow for early exercise, it cannot be used to value an American put option. Note, of course, that put–call parity would not therefore apply to American options.

It is worth mentioning, too, that there are cases where an otherwise identical European put option with a short time to maturity is worth more than one with a long time to maturity. This occurs where a European put is deep in-the-money (the exercise price is a long way above the share price): maybe again the share has become 'bombed out'. The long time to expiry may have a negative influence on the premium value compared with the shorter maturity put because the longer maturity provides greater opportunity for the share to revive from being 'bombed out'.

In the case of European options on dividend paying shares, the existing share price includes the present value of dividends during the period to maturity, to which the option holder is not entitled. Thus to value a European option on a dividend-paying stock, one must disaggregate from the share price (S) the present value of dividends accruing before the maturity of the option.

16.8 | An option-pricing table

Earlier sections of this chapter have indicated that, for a share which pays no dividend, the five factors affecting an option's value are the exercise price, the under-lying share price, the time to expiration of the option, the variance (σ^2) – or the standard deviation (σ), sometimes termed volatility – of returns on the share, and the risk-free rate of return. It is possible to bring all these factors together to produce a table for pricing European call options (and hence put option value via put–call parity). The variability, per unit of time, of returns on a share is measured by the variance of returns, σ^2. Multiplying the variance per unit of time by the amount of time remaining gives cumulative variance, $\sigma^2 t$. Cumulative variance is a measure of how much things could change before time runs out and a decision must be made in relation to the option. $\sigma\sqrt{t}$ is simply the square root of cumulative variance. Of course, options for which either σ or t is zero have no cumulative variance. Were we to plot the share price dividend by the present value of the exercise price – that is, the exercise price discounted at the risk-free rate of interest – against the square root of cumulative variance, given by $\sigma\sqrt{t}$, we would capture all five critical factors.

The tabulation headed 'Black and Scholes value of a call option expressed as a percentage of the share price' (see Appendix 4) at the end of this book plots $S/PV(E)$ on one axis against $\sigma\sqrt{t}$ on the other. The figure found in the appropriate part of the matrix represents a percentage of the underlying share price. This percentage multiplied by the share price gives the call option value. Take an example. Digital Couplets plc is quoted on the London stock market at a current price of £9.00. The problem is to value a twelve-month European call option with an exercise price of £9.20. The estimated volatility (σ) is estimated at 12 per cent per annum and the risk-free rate is 5 per cent per annum on a continuously compounded basis.

The value of $S/PV(E)$ can be calculated as:

$$\frac{9.00}{9.20 \times 0.9512} = 1.02845$$

Note that the tablulation has been used to calculate the one-year continuous dis-count factor at the risk-free rate of 5 per cent. The value of $\sigma\sqrt{t}$ is simply equal to:

$$0.12\sqrt{1} = 0.12$$

Since the exact value of $S/PV(E)$ at 1.02845 does not appear in Appendix 4, we have to use interpolation to value the option. The same goes for the value of $\sigma\sqrt{t}$ at 0.12. The relevant parts of the matrix, taken from Appendix 4, for the purpose of inter-polation, are:

| | $S/PV(E)$ | |
	1.02	1.04
0.10	5.0	6.1
0.15	7.0	8.0

(with $\sigma\sqrt{t}$ labelling the rows 0.10 and 0.15)

Interpolating downwards would give figures of 5.80 and 6.86 for a value of $\sigma\sqrt{t}$ of 0.12 against values of $S/PV(E)$ of 1.02 and 1.04, respectively. Further interpolation between 1.02 and 1.04 to 1.02845 as a value for $S/PV(E)$ gives a figure of 6.25 as the appropriate figure in the matrix. This figure is a percentage of the underlying share price. Thus, the value of the call option is simply:

$$£9.00 \ (6.25\%) = £0.56$$

Were one to wish to value a twelve-month European put option with a strike price at £9.20, with all other factors identical, the put–call parity formula would enable us to do so. This is shown below:

$$\begin{aligned} \text{Put} &= \text{Call} + PV(E) - S \\ &= 0.56 + 9.20(0.9512) - 9.00 \\ &= 0.56 + 8.75 - 9.00 \\ &= £0.31 \end{aligned}$$

Note that it is also possible to determine the market's implied volatility (and implied variance) from Appendix 4. Implied volatility relates to what the market is building into the Black and Scholes valuation for an option as a volatility factor. If the values of S, E, r, t and the amount of the option premium are known, as would typically be the case for an exchange-quoted option, the volatility that option traders are building into the option premium can be determined. In such a situation, the value of $S/PV(E)$ can be calculated. The percentage given by the option premium divided by S can be calculated. Now, it is easy to read down the matrix table in Appendix 4 for the value of $S/PV(E)$ which has already been determined until one arrives at the figure calculated for the option premium divided by S. Reading across the matrix, this will enable a figure for $\sigma\sqrt{t}$ to be read off. Since t, the time the option has to run to maturity, is known, the value of σ, implied volatility, can be calculated.

Of course, if the data one has relate to a European put option, and if the matrix table in Appendix 4 is to be used to determine implied volatility, then it is necessary to convert the put premium into a call price via the put–call parity formula. Appendix 5 presents tables of the factor for calculating the present value of £1 with a continuous discount rate r for T periods.

For an outstanding and challenging coverage of options, interested readers are referred to Wilmott (1998).

16.9 | Summary

■ The most familiar options are puts and calls. These options give the holder the right to sell or buy ordinary shares at a given exercise price. American options can be exercised any time up to and including the expiration date. European options can be exercised only on the expiration date.

■ Options can either be held in isolation or in combination. We focused on the strategy of:
(i)   buying the put,
(ii) buying the stock,
(iii) selling the call.
where the put and call have both the same exercise price and the same expiration date. This strategy yields a riskless return because the gain or loss on the call precisely offsets the gain or loss on the stock-and-put combination. In equilibrium, the return on this strategy must be exactly equal to the riskless rate. From this, the put–call parity relationship was established:

Value of stock + Value of put – Value of call = Present value of exercise price.

■ The value of an option depends on five factors:
(i)   the price of the underlying asset,
(ii) the exercise price,
(iii) the expiration date,
(iv) the variability of the underlying asset,
(v)   the interest rate on risk-free bonds.

The Black and Scholes model can determine the intrinsic price of an option from these five factors. An option-pricing table (Appendix 4) is available to ease calculation.

16.10 | End of chapter questions

Question 1
What are the components of an option premium?

Question 2
Why is the price of an option always greater than its intrinsic value?

Question 3
What is an in-the-money option? When is a call versus a put in the money?

Notes

1.   The terms *buyer*, *owner* and *holder* are used interchangeably.

2.   Note that the options are both European. An American put must sell for more than €11 (€55 – €44). That is, if the price of an American put is only €7, one would buy the put, buy the share and exercise immediately, generating arbitrage profit of €4 (–€7 – €44 + €55).

3.   However, the formula is applicable only when both the put and the call have the same expiration date and the same exercise price.

4.   It should be noted that this lower bound is strictly true for an American option, but not for a European one.

5.   This relationship need not hold for a European call option. Consider a firm with two otherwise identical European call options, one expiring at the end of May and the other expiring a few months later. Further assume that a *huge* dividend is paid in early June. If the first call is exercised at the end of May, its holder will receive the underlying share. If he or she does not sell the share, he would receive the large dividend shortly thereafter. However, the holder of the second call will receive the share through exercise after the dividend is paid. Because the market knows that the holder of this option will miss the dividend, the value of the second call option could be less than the value of the first.

6.   This graph assumes that, for each security, the exercise price is equal to the expected share price. This assumption is employed merely to facilitate the discussion. It is not needed to show the relationship between a call's value and the volatility of the underlying share.

7.   Though this result must hold in the case of an American put, it need not hold for a European put.

8.   A full treatment of this assumption can be found in Chapter 5 of Cox and Rubinstein (1985).

17 Currency options

Currency options provide the right, but not the obligation, to buy or sell a specific currency at a specific price at any time prior to a specified date. That options provide 'the right but not the obligation' means that commercial users of the market are able to obtain insurance against an adverse movement in the exchange rate while still retaining the opportunity to benefit from favourable exchange movements. At the same time, the maximum risk to the buyer of an option is the actual up-front premium cost of the option. Currency options have not been designed as a substitute for forward markets but as a new, distinct financial vehicle that offers significant opportunities and advantages to those seeking either protection or profit from changes in exchange rates.

Since December 1982, the Philadelphia Stock Exchange has been trading standardized foreign currency option contracts. Philadelphia offers a competitive market place in which to buy and sell options against US dollars on numerous currencies. Philadelphia was the first trading centre to deal in currency options and it remains the world market leader although it has been joined by other centres such as the Chicago International Monetary Market, the Montreal Stock Exchange, the Amsterdam Stock Exchange and the London International Financial Futures Exchange (LIFFE), to name but a few. They provide the means to deal currency options for a vast range of currencies.

In this chapter we focus upon Philadelphia options. It begins with a description of how currency option markets work. This is linked with a discussion of currency option terminology and is followed by a discussion relating to currency option pricing. A section is devoted to use of currency options as risk-reducing instruments available to the corporate treasurer.

17.1 | How currency option markets work

Philadelphia currency options are similar to options on ordinary shares. The buyer of an option cannot lose more than the cost of the option and is not subject to any margin calls. The Philadelphia Stock Exchange offers investors an organized market place in which to buy and sell options on sterling, euros, Canadian dollars, Swiss francs, Japanese yen, Australian dollars and others too, all against the US dollar. Options are traded on three-, six- and nine-month cycles.

Currency option markets have a jargon of their own, although this language has much in common with that of traded options on shares. Because we shall frequently use the jargon in this chapter, a short list of currency options terms and definitions follows. Readers of the previous chapter should be familiar with their meanings already, but here we apply them to currency options.

- *American option.* A currency option that can be exercised on any business day within the option period.

- *European option.* A currency option that can only be exercised on the expiry date.

- *A call option.* An option to purchase a stated number of units of the underlying foreign currency at a specific price per unit during a specific period of time. By 'underlying foreign currency' we refer to the currency that is not the US dollar. Thus the term 'underlying foreign currency' could refer to sterling in the context of a US dollar/sterling currency option.

- *A put option.* An option to sell a stated number of units of the underlying foreign currency at a specific price per unit during a specific period of time.

- *Option buyer.* The party who obtains the benefit under a currency option by paying a premium. These benefits are the right, but not the obligation, to buy the currency if the option is a call or to sell the currency if the option is a put. The option buyer is known as the option holder.

- *Option seller.* The party who has the obligation to perform if the currency option is exercised. This person will have to sell the foreign currency at a stated price if a call is exercised or buy the foreign currency at a stated price if a put is exercised. The original option seller is known as the option writer.

- *Exercise price, exercise rate or strike price.* The price at which the currency option holder has the right to purchase or sell the underlying currency. Except for the Japanese yen, exercise prices are stated in US cents. Thus a CHF75 (CHF is the code for Swiss francs) call would be an option to buy Swiss francs at USD0.75 per Swiss franc, that is CHF1.33 = USD1. The Japanese yen option exercise prices are stated in hundredths of a cent, so a JPY67 call entitles the holder to purchase the underlying yen at USD0.0067 per yen.

- *Expiration months.* The expiration months for currency options are usually March, June, September and December. At any given time trading is available in the nearest three of these months.

- *Option premium.* The option premium is the price of a currency option, that is the sum of money that the buyer of an option pays when an option is purchased or the sum that the writer of an option receives when an option is written.

- *Intrinsic value.* The extent to which a currency option would currently be profitable to exercise. In the case of a call, if the spot price of the underlying currency is above the option exercise price, this difference is its intrinsic value. In the case of a put, if the spot price is below the option exercise price, this is its intrinsic value. Options with intrinsic value are said to be in-the-money. If the spot Swiss franc price is USD0.75, a CHF72 call would have an intrinsic value of USD0.03 per CHF, but a CHF72 put would have no intrinsic value.

- *Time value.* That part of the premium representing the length of time that the currency option has to run. In other words, the premium less the intrinsic value.

- *Notice of exercise.* Notice given by a currency option holder to the option writer that an option is being exercised. Only an option holder may exercise an option. The option holder may exercise the option and the option writer may be assigned a notice of exercise at any time prior to expiration of the option. But only an American option will result in immediate delivery.

- *Opening transaction.* A purchase or sale transaction that establishes a currency option's position.

- *Closing transaction.* A transaction that liquidates or offsets an existing currency option's position. Option holders may liquidate their positions by an offsetting sale. An option writer may liquidate his or her position by an offsetting purchase.

- *At-the-money.* An option whose exercise price is the same as the spot price or the forward price. To distinguish the two, the jargon used is, respectively, at-the-money and at-the-money forward.

- *Out-of-the-money.* A call whose exercise price is above the current spot price of the underlying currency or a put option whose exercise price is below the current spot price of the underlying currency. Out-of-the-money options have no intrinsic value.

- *In-the-money.* A call whose exercise price is below the current spot price of the underlying currency or a put whose exercise price is above the current spot price of the underlying currency. In-the-money options have intrinsic value.

Traded currency option contracts are standardized. When trading is introduced in an option with a new expiration month, the practice is for one option to be introduced with an exercise price above the current spot price and one to be introduced with an exercise price below the current spot price. As the spot price of a currency changes over time, additional options are introduced with the same expiration month but higher or lower exercise prices. The exercise price intervals are USD0.01 for euros, sterling and Swiss francs; and USD0.0001 for Japanese yen.

If Swiss franc options with a September expiration are introduced when the spot price is USD0.75, exercise prices would normally be established at 74, 75 and 76. If the spot price were to change to USD0.76, a new series of options, having the same expiration date, would be introduced with an exercise price of 77.

Prices, or premia, for foreign exchange options are arrived at through competition between buyers and sellers on the floor of the Philadelphia Stock Exchange. The premium quoted represents a consensus opinion of the option's current value and will comprise intrinsic value and time value. Option premium quotations have bid and offer rates like most financial exchange contracts. We would expect Philadelphia option prices to be in equilibrium with other markets' option quotations. Otherwise, riskless arbitrage profits would be available. Table 17.1 (overleaf) shows contract sizes for a selection of Philadelphia currency option contracts. It is worth noting that

Table 17.1 Philadelphia Stock Exchange – selected currency option specification. US$ versus foreign currency.

	British pound	Euro	Swiss franc	Japanese yen
Contract size	£31,250	€62,500	CHF62,500	JPY6,250,000
Exercise price intervals	2¢*	1¢	1¢*	0.01¢*
Expiration months	March, June, September and December			
Expiration date	Friday before third Wednesday of the expiring month (Friday is also the last trading day)			
Expiration settlement date	Third Wednesday of month			

*In the three near-term months only, exercise price intervals for £ (1¢), CHF (0.5¢) and JPY (0.005¢).

contract sizes on the Chicago Mercantile Exchange for currency options are twice as much as for Philadelphia. For example, the euro contract is for EUR125,000 when dealt on Chicago versus EUR62,500 for Philadelphia.

Intrinsic value is the amount, if any, by which an option is currently in the money. Time value is that sum of money which buyers are willing to pay over and above any intrinsic value. Such buyers hope that, before expiration, the option will increase in value and may be sold or exchanged at a profit. If an option has no intrinsic value, its premium will be entirely a reflection of its time value.

The price or premium of an option reflects changes in the spot price of the underlying currency and the length of time remaining until expiration. Thus, with the spot Swiss franc price at US$0.75, a CHF73 call option with three months until expiration may command a premium US$1,600. Of this, US$1,250, given by US$0.02 × CHF62,500, is intrinsic value and the remaining US$350 is time value. One Swiss franc contract is for CHF62,500. It should be borne in mind that an option is a wasting asset. Its sole value (if any) at expiration will be its intrinsic value. Without intrinsic value, it will expire worthless. Thus, if the Swiss franc spot price in the previous example were still US$0.75 when the Swiss franc call expired, the value of the option would be its intrinsic value of US$1,250; it can no longer have time value. Of course, if the spot price had fallen by expiration to US$0.73 or below, the CHF73 call option would expire as worthless. Key readings on factors influencing option premia and their behaviours are briefly considered in section 17.5.

It should be noted that option premia are quoted in US cents per unit of the underlying currency with the exception of the Japanese yen. Thus an option premium quotation of 1.00 for a Swiss franc option is 1 cent per Swiss franc. Each option is for a standardized value CHF62,500, so the total option premium would be US$625 given by 62,500 × US$0.01. An option premium quotation for the Swiss franc contract of 0.76 would represent US$0.0076 per Swiss franc. The option premium would be US$475, given by 62,500 × US$0.0076.

Similarly, if the premium quoted for an option on sterling is 8.4, the total premium amount would be US$2,625, given by 31,250 × US$0.084 (£31,250 is the contract size of one Philadelphia sterling option). For a Japanese yen contract a premium quotation of 2.0 would be two-hundredths of a cent ($0.0002). The premium would thus be US$1,250, given by 6,250,000 × US$0.0002. It seems a little complicated at first, but the simple arithmetic for translating these quotations into the cost per option contract becomes second nature to investors trading in options.

Currency option markets aim to provide a continuously active and liquid market in put and call options on foreign currencies. Orders to buy and sell options on foreign currencies are transmitted through brokers to the trading floor of the exchange in the same way as transactions involving shares, but currency options, like other types of option, are investments not backed with a certificate of any sort.

17.2 | Currency option strategies

This section outlines some strategies for buying and writing options on foreign currencies. First we consider a situation in which there is a profit potential in buying call options to exploit a foreign currency's strength or the dollar's weakness. A call option entitles the holder to purchase units of the foreign currency at the option price stated in US dollars. The option holder will make a profit if the value of the option at expiration is greater than the premium paid to acquire the option. Put another way, profit will accrue if the spot market price of the currency is above the option exercise price plus the initial option premium. As an example, assume that in March an investor pays USD750 to buy a Swiss franc September 75 call and by the expiration date in September, the Swiss franc spot prices has risen to 78, that is USD0.78. The call option with an exercise price of 75, that is USD0.75, gives the investor the right to purchase Swiss francs at 3 cents below their current market value; thus the option is in the money by 3 cents. Consequently, through selling or exercising the option, the investor will realize USD1,875 given by USD0.03 × 62,500. This amount less the USD750 originally paid for the option produces a profit of USD1.125 over a six-month period. If the Swiss franc spot price at expiration had been USD0.75 or below, the option would have expired worthless. The investor would have lost all of the USD750 premium. But in no circumstance could his or her loss have exceeded the USD750 paid for the option.

If the initial premium cost of a CHF75 call is USD750, the following tabulation indicates the investor's profit or loss depending upon the Swiss franc spot price at the time the option expires.

CHF spot rate at expiration	Profit or (loss) in USD
USD0.75 or below	(750)
0.76	(125)
0.77	500
0.78	1,125
0.79	1,750
0.80	2,375
0.81	3,000
0.82	3,625
0.83	4,250

The presence of high gearing for relatively low risk is evident from the above figures. The call-option buyer has an unlimited profit potential, whereas his potential loss is fixed at the cost of the option itself.

Of course, even when purchase of a call option is indicated, the investor seeking to profit from the currency change must still decide which call option to invest in. Options differ in the length of time remaining until expiration and in their exercise price. On a given date in April, there will be trading in Swiss franc options expiring in June, September and December. Assuming a Swiss franc spot price of USD0.75, options may be available with exercise prices ranging from USD0.73 to USD0.77.

Options with more distant expiration months command a higher premium because they provide more time for the investor's expectations to be realized – that is, greater time value. Thus, an at-the-money CHF75 call with three months to expiration may command a premium of USD750. A CHF75 option with six months to expiration may be priced at USD1,150 and a similar option with nine months to expiration may cost USD1,500.

In-the-money options always cost more than at-the-money options which in turn cost more than out-of-the-money options. Although the in-the-money option costs most in terms of investment, it also yields the greatest profit potential for any given increase of a foreign currency against the dollar.

There is no formula for arriving at an answer to the question of which option to select. The key thing to bear in mind is that for a call option buyer to make a net profit at expiration, the spot currency price must be above the option exercise price by an amount greater than the premium paid for the option.

Just as call options provide profit opportunities, so put options can do the same. Thus, investors expecting a particular currency to decline in value relative to the US dollar may seek to profit by the purchase of put options. These options convey the right, but not the obligation, to sell the foreign currency at an agreed price. Assume that at a time when the Swiss franc spot rate is USD0.75, an investor expecting the Swiss franc to weaken relative to the US dollar pays USD450 to purchase an at-the-money CHF75 put option with six months to run. Should the Swiss franc have dropped by expiration to, say, USD0.72, the option may be sold or exercised at its intrinsic value of USD1,875 and the investor's profit will be USD1,425.

Assuming the investor pays a premium of USD450 to purchase a Swiss franc put option with an exercise price of 75, the table below indicates his or her profit potential at various expiration spot prices:

CHF spot rate at expiration	Profit or (loss) in USD
0.75 or above	(450)
0.74	175
0.73	800
0.72	1,425
0.71	2,050
0.70	2,675
0.69	3,300
0.68	3,925
0.67	4,550

Considerations involved in buying put options are the inverse of those applicable to call options. Again, an option with a long period of time until expiry normally commands a higher premium than an otherwise identical option soon to expire. It is worth bearing in mind that the premium for an out-of-the-money option is low because such an option is less likely to become profitable to exercise.

Like traded options on shares, it is possible to write currency options for investment income. The writer of an option is obligated, if the option is exercised, to perform according to the terms of the option contract. Thus, the writer must sell and deliver the required number of units of the underlying currency at the option exercise price, if the option is a call, or purchase the required number of units at the option exercise price if the option is a put. Investors considering writing options must remember that holders of an option may exercise their rights under the option at any time (for an American option). Of course, option writing (unless covered) involves substantial and potentially unlimited risk. The limited risk of option trading applies only to the option buyer, not to the option writer. However, the terms of an option can make option writing a potentially attractive source of profit.

The currency option, despite giving the holder the effective opportunity to deal at either the strike price or the spot price, will always come out, on an *ex-post* basis, second best. If this is not intuitively obvious, consider the following example. A UK company has a $5 million receivable, with payment in three months' time, which it is considering covering via either:

- the forward market at 1.65, or

- the currency option market at a strike price of $1.65, involving a premium of 5 cents per pound.

Using the forward market will ensure that the UK company obtains sterling proceeds of exactly £3,030,303. Under the currency option, the guaranteed minimum proceeds are £3,030,303 but a premium has to be paid amounting to $151,515 – or approximately £91,827. But if the dollar should strengthen sufficiently, then the sterling proceeds will be greater because the receivable will be closed out via the spot market. The results in Figure 17.1 (overleaf) summarize the payoff. Clearly, by reference to the crossed line in the figure – this refers to the net receipts under the currency option – it can be seen that, for strong dollar outturns at maturity, the currency option proceeds are inferior to the spot payoff (the latter avoids the upfront premium); and for a weak dollar scenario in three months' time, the currency option proceeds are inferior to the forward, although ahead of the spot. Evidently the currency option net outturn is always second best.

17.3 | Average rate option

In Chapter 13 we referred to the option dated forward contract, which, we concluded, was ideal for covering a continuing stream of small exposures in a particular currency. Remember, though, that the option dated forward contract is basically a forward contract. Parties to such a contract have a right and an obligation to

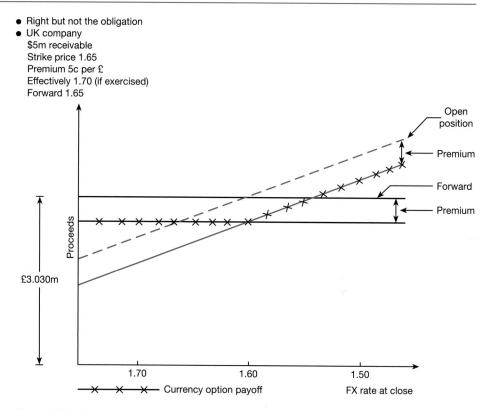

- Right but not the obligation
- UK company
  $5m receivable
  Strike price 1.65
  Premium 5c per £
  Effectively 1.70 (if exercised)
  Forward 1.65

Figure 17.1 Currency options: always second best.

perform according to its conditions. The optional feature relates to timing of delivery of currency.

On the true option front, there is a contract which is similarly ideal in terms of covering a continuing stream of small exposures. This is the average rate option, or Asro or even Asian option, as it is sometimes called.

An average rate option is an option whose strike price is compared not to the exchange rate at maturity, but to the average exchange rate over the period of the option. This sounds a bit complicated. Let us see whether an example can make things easier. Consider a company with a US dollar/yen exposure. It might have entered into an option giving it the right to buy USD20m against Japanese yen over a three-month period at a rate of JPY135 = USD1. In terms of calculating the payment to the option buyer, assume that the exchange rate at the option's maturity is JPY137.50. But also assume that the average exchange rate during the whole of the term of the option is JPY141.21. Now the payment to the option buyer can be calculated under the standard currency option and under the average rate option – this is shown in Table 17.2.

The example in the table shows the average rate option with a higher return than the standard option. But depending upon the spot price at maturity, the standard option could offer a better return. The average rate option may be 35–50 per cent

Table 17.2 Standard and average rate options compared

	Standard option	*Average rate option*
Strike	135.00	135.00
Exchange rate at expiry (e)	137.50	137.50
Average exchange rate over period	–	141.21
Payment to option buyer	20m (137.50–135)e	20m (141.21–135.00)e
	$363,636	$903,273
Premium (% of US$ principal)	0.61	0.52

cheaper than the standard option depending on the frequency of sampling to obtain the average rate. Why this is so has everything to do with volatility. The more volatile an underlying instrument, the greater the cost of the option. Average rates are more stable than the spot rate itself, hence their lower volatility. If the average is computed by taking daily spot rate fixings, then it will turn out to be cheaper than if the average is computed every month. Beyond twenty periodic fixings in one year, the premium does not fall very much.

The average rate option gives the buyer two advantages compared with typical straight options:

- Standard options may be very effective when covering single cash flows at a known future maturity. Standard options and forwards are less effective when hedging a large number of smallish cash flows distributed uncertainly over time. Many firms with foreign exchange exposures have just this type of fluctuating cash flow configuration. Average rate options are ideal instruments to cover this kind of exposure.

- Although only traded over-the-counter (OTC), they are relatively cheap. The hedging institution is concerned about the average exchange rate, not the exchange rate when each separate cash flow comes due. The average rate option costs less than the sum of the separate options for each period – by some 40 per cent or so.

How does a potential user set about hedging with an average rate option? The trader not only decides the principal amount, strike price and period for the option, but also agrees the data source to compute the average and the time period between samples. For example, Reuters daily, weekly or monthly figures might be used.

The option settles net cash. At the end of the option's life, the average exchange rate is computed and compared with the strike price. A cash payment is made to the buyer of the option equal to the face amount of the option multiplied by the difference between these two rates, assuming that the option is in the money. Otherwise the option expires worthless. For an in-the-money expiry, this approach was set out in the numerical example above. For a good exposition on this instrument and other derivatives, see Duker (1989).

Finally in this section, we outline its application to hedging on profit and loss account denominated in foreign currency – assuming, of course, that this is deemed to be a valid goal of currency management. A multinational corporation has an exposure in respect of its foreign subsidiaries' budgeted profits. The average rate option may be used to hedge this. Dealing an Asro for the budgeted after-tax foreign profit at a strike rate equivalent to the budgeted average exchange rate effectively locks in such an exchange rate. Take an example. Assume that a UK-based international group expects its US subsidiary to make $60m after tax and anticipates an average exchange rate of $1.70, giving sterling-denominated profits of £35.3m. By dealing an average rate sterling call (dollar put) for $60m at a strike price of $1.70, this will be achieved – assuming that the budget is also at least achieved. Arranging the deal through a tax haven will avoid problems of tax asymmetry. Should the subsidiary make its budget of $60m and if the average exchange rate is, say, $2, then this will give sterling profits of £30m. But the profit on the option will amount to £5.3m. Of course, the company has to achieve – or beat – its budget in dollar terms for the hedge to work. The reporting anomaly referred to in discussing Table 10.2 is avoided by the hedge described here. Of course, if the exchange rate averages 1.50, the option lapses but the sterling value of translated profit comes out at £40m.

By arranging an average rate option with the same frequency of fixings as for the measurement of the average exchange rate for translation purposes, the hedge is readily achieved. Remember that this is possible given the lack of direction under SSAP20 as to how to work out the average exchange rate. Remember also that the hedge achieved will, substantially, cover exchange risk on dividends paid out of profits. Care must be taken on this point to avoid double hedging.

17.4 | Hedging a currency option

There are ways in which writers of currency options can cover themselves. The detail of covering strategies is outside the scope of this book but it is worth while spending a little time on the generalities of covering option writing.

Assume that, at the time a call option is written, the pound spot rate is $1.70, the exercise price of the call option is $1.70 and the price of the call is 4 cents per dollar. A UK exporter expects to receive $1,000,000 in six months' time. It can guarantee a minimum rate of exchange by buying a six-month call on sterling. At the maturity of the option, if the spot rate is above $1.70, the option will logically be exercised and the $1,000,000 will be converted to sterling at $1.70 rather than at the spot rate. This guarantees that the net proceeds of the trade will be at least £588,235 minus the £23,529 paid for the call.

In this example, at the time the call is written, sterling is trading at $1.70 and the value of the call is 4 cents. If sterling were to rise to $1.72, the call premium might rise to 5 cents; if sterling were to fall to $1.68, the call premium might fall to 3 cents. So, for every 2 cents move in the spot price there is a 1 cent move in the option value. The call is behaving like a spot position equal to half the currency on which the call is written. The ratio of the move in the call value to the move in the spot price is known as the 'hedge ratio' or 'delta' of the position. In our example, the delta is 0.5.

The importance of the delta is that it tells the writer of the option how much spot currency to hold in order to eliminate the risk of the option. In this example, if the writer of the option had held sterling of an amount equal to £294,117.50, half the face value of the call, the writer would not have been exposed to the change in the value of the currency option. Over a particular period, if the spot rate had risen to $1.72, the call value would have risen in value by $10,000 and the spot sterling position would also have changed by the same amount, offsetting the loss on the written call.

It must be stated that, as the spot price moves, so the delta may change and the spot position that is equivalent to the option changes accordingly. To construct a spot position that is equivalent to the option over its entire life, the amount of spot currency held to hedge the option must therefore change in response to the spot price. As a result, if a call is written and a spot position in delta is taken, and delta is revised frequently enough, the net position will be riskless over the entire life of the option. This forms the basis of one approach to covering for banks that write options.

To recapitulate, the hedge ratio, or the delta, is the amount that should be held in the currency in order to hedge the option position. It is the rate of change in the premium given a change in the underlying currency (see Figure 17.2).

Thus, if a call option on sterling with a strike at $1.60 costs 3 cents and has a delta of 0.4, an instantaneous move of 1 cent in the spot rate will result in an immediate increase or decrease in the option premium of 0.4 cents. With the spot at $1.61 the premium will increase to 3.4 cents, and with the spot at $1.59 the premium will fall to 2.6 cents. With a delta of 1, which would apply only to very deep in-the-money options, a 1 cent move in the spot would result in a 1 cent move in the premium. With a delta of 0.1 for far out-of-the-money options, a 1 cent move in the spot would see the premium change by only 0.1 cent.

Delta can never be below zero and never, in normal circumstances, above 1. In other words, an option can move one for one with the underlying currency but, all things being equal, never more than the change in the spot rate. Whereas the delta for an at-the-money option is always about 0.5, the delta for an out- or in-the-money option varies according to the intrinsic value of the option, the time left to expiry,

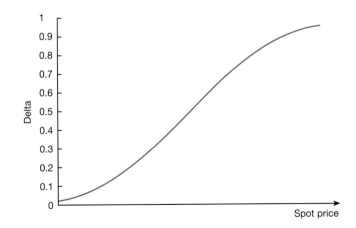

Figure 17.2 Call option delta (30-day option).

the volatility of the underlying currency, and even the level of interest rate differentials. Another way of using delta is as a probability measure: the higher the delta, the greater the probability of the option being exercised. Delta is important for option traders because it provides a key to the gearing of the option position. Traders who buy far out-of-the-money options because they appear 'cheap' are often disappointed when the anticipated move in the spot market occurs and the option itself hardly moves. Option writers should be aware of the increasing sensitivity of their short positions as the delta picks up from 0.25 through 0.35 and eventually moves above 0.5.

The delta, the first derivative of the option-pricing model, is a dynamic concept. It changes as the market changes. The 'gamma', the second derivative of the model, describes the change in the delta given a change in the underlying price. Gamma measures the sensitivity of the delta – it is the delta of the delta. The higher the gamma, the higher the delta sensitivity. Gamma is at its highest for short-dated at-the-money options. This can be explained using the following example.

If the spot sterling rate is at $1.51, the $1.50 sterling call expiring in a few minutes' time has a delta of 1. In the statistical sense, the option will certainly be exercised, which means that the option writer should hold 100 per cent of the currency as a hedge against the short options position. But if the spot rate suddenly falls to $1.49, the option delta falls to zero because the option, statistically, now has a virtually zero chance of being exercised. Therefore no hedge is required. By contrast, consider a one-year at-the-money call on sterling which has a delta of 0.47; an instantaneous move up or down in the spot rate of 1 cent will result in the delta moving up to 0.49 or down to 0.45 respectively. Thus:

At-the-money call deltas expiry	A few minutes' time	One year
Delta	0.5	0.47
Delta as a result of 1 cent increase in spot rate	1	0.49
Delta as a result of 1 cent decrease in spot rate	0	0.45

Option buyers are attracted to high gamma options because of the gearing in such a position. Conversely, writers of high gamma options are taking considerable risks because of the large potential fluctuations in the premium caused by relatively small movements in the spot rate.

The trade-off of high delta sensitivity – gamma – is high time decay. Short-dated, at-the-money options are highly leveraged and subject to sharp premium loss in stable conditions. Low gamma options, such as longer-dated options, are less sensitive to market movement and experience only minor losses in premium on a day-to-day basis. The technical term for the rate of time decay is 'theta'. A theta of 0.01 means that the premium will decline by 0.01 over a one-day period, all other factors remaining the same. High gamma and high theta options go hand in hand with each other. To return to the sterling option expiring in a few minutes, if the strike is at the money, the delta is about 0.5 and the option is worth only time value; in a few minutes' time – that is, on the expiry of the option – the premium will be zero, assuming that the spot rate is at the same level. This is an extreme example of high time decay loss, or high theta. We also know that such an option has a very high gamma. Conversely, a very long-dated option has very little gamma or theta risk. In other words, the delta hardly changes even given comparatively large spot movements and, day to day, the time decay loss on the premium is virtually nil.

If long-dated options are insensitive to spot or time decay effects, they are very vulnerable to shifts in volatility. 'Vega' is the technical term used to describe the effect on the premium of a change in volatility. A vega of 0.1 means that the premium will change by 0.1 per cent given a 1 per cent change in volatility. Whereas the time decay effect (namely theta) and the change in the delta (namely gamma) are low for long-dated options, the volatility sensitivity – vega – is at its highest. This is another example of the trade-off effect in option markets. Currency traders may well decide to buy options rather than spot because their view of the market is that a substantial move is likely, but over a longer time-scale rather than a short duration. The trader feels that, because implied volatility is at a relatively high level, the shorter-dated options are too expensive. In other words, the trader is well aware of the possibility of high time decay loss – the high theta effect – in shorter maturity options. Thus, the trader buys a one-year sterling at-the-money call option. But, in high volatility conditions, buying long-dated options may result in larger than expected losses, not through time decay loss, which is negligible day to day, but because of the option's sensitivity to declines in implied volatility – vega.

For example, consider the data shown in Table 17.3 for an at-the-money sterling call at 1.60. Although the absolute loss through a fall in volatility is much higher with the longer-dated option, namely 1.5 cents against only 0.5 cent for the one-month option, the percentage fall in the one-month option premium is actually slightly greater at 20 per cent as against 19.7 per cent. The shorter and further out of money the option, the more pronounced is this effect.

Using the same situation but with a $1.65 sterling call option – that is, 5 cents out of the money, our tabulation might be as shown in Table 17.4 (overleaf). Again, the absolute loss is much larger for the twelve-month call than for the one-month option – that is, 1.4 cents as against 0.4 cent. And the percentage loss is 24 per cent compared with 44 per cent for the one-month option. The percentage loss due to a decline in volatility is known as 'vega elasticity'. The option writer who anticipates a fall in implied volatility will make more dollars by writing a long-dated, at-the-money, high vega option, but he will make more in percentage terms by writing out of-the-money, short-dated options.

Table 17.3 Effect of a fall in volatility on premium: at-the-money call option

Expiry	Volatility	Premium
1 month	15%	2.5 cents
1 month	12.5%	2.0 cents
12 months	15%	7.6 cents
12 months	12.5%	6.1 cents

Table 17.4 Effect of a fall in volatility on premium: out-of-the-money call option

Expiry	Volatility	Premium
1 month	15%	0.9 cent
1 month	12.5%	0.5 cent
12 months	15%	5.8 cents
12 months	12.5%	4.4 cents

17.5 | Option pricing models

A mathematical model for pricing stock market options was referred to in detail in Chapter 16. Their model has been adapted by Garman and Kohlhagen (1983) for pricing currency options. The Garman and Kohlhagen model for pricing currency options is an adaptation of the Black and Scholes model applied to a slightly different environment. Their model for the valuation of a currency call option at an exercise price of E is given by:

$$C = \frac{FN(\text{dist 1}) - EN(\text{dist 2})}{e^{pt}}$$

In this case the notation (where different from Black and Scholes) is as follows:

C = price of the currency option
F = the forward exchange rate
E = the exercise price
p = the risk-free interest rate differential (that is, domestic rate less foreign rate for comparable deposits) expressed on a continually compounded basis

$$\text{dist 1} = \frac{\ln(F/E) + (r + \tfrac{1}{2}\sigma^2)t}{\sigma\sqrt{t}}$$

$$\text{dist 2} = \text{dist 1} - \sigma\sqrt{t}$$

σ^2 = the variance of the continuously compounded annual rate of change of the exchange rate

There are many other models for pricing currency options. One of these, the Leland (1984) model, is interesting – it is a Black and Scholes variant which incorporates transaction costs. The formula developed by Leland allows direct comparison of the effects of changes in transaction costs or in the 'revision interval' – that is, the frequency with which a position is rehedged. One of the features of option management is that a hedged portfolio of options and currencies (or shares) must be rehedged every time the exchange rate (or share price) moves. In the Black and Scholes model, continuous rehedging is implicit. Clearly, in reality, transaction costs preclude such a policy. Traders generally hedge their position only at certain regular

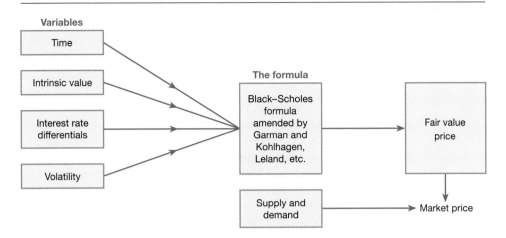

Figure 17.3 How a currency option is priced.

intervals when the original hedged position is seen to be imperfect. Leland's model allows for this with a revision interval term (Δt).

Nowadays most banks use computer models based on formulations similar to the above for pricing currency options. Some institutions are using their own in-house formulae for valuing currency options but these are similar to the Black and Scholes, Garman and Kohlhagen, or Leland models summarized above.

What all of the models have in common is the logic they apply to the problem of pricing a currency option. Effectively, it follows the routine set out in Figure 17.3. As we mentioned in Chapter 16, what is most interesting is not the variables that are used in the formulations but those that were left out. No mention has been made of market direction or bias as an appropriate input. An implicit assumption of the models is that the market moves in a random fashion. In other words, while prices will change, the chances of a positive return are the same as the chances of a negative one. In fact, plots of currency price movements are usually found to be skewed, or log-normal (see Figure 17.4). This arises partly because, while currency prices can rise without limit, they cannot fall below zero. Remember, too, it is possible that when there is government intervention in foreign exchange markets, a bias is introduced into currency movements – as noted in Chapter 7.

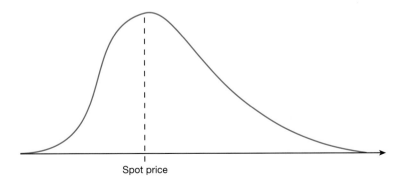

Figure 17.4 Log-normal distribution of currency movements from spot.

The Black and Scholes model explains well the option premium for a European call on equities. Garman and Kohlhagen's extension of the formula to cover currency options allows for the fact that currency pricing involves two interest rates, not one, and that a currency can trade at a premium or discount forward depending upon the interest rate differential.

Cox, Ross and Rubinstein (1979) and Cox and Rubinstein (1985) have developed a variant of the currency-pricing model which accounts for the early exercise provisions of American-style options. Using the same approach as Black and Scholes, they incorporated a binomial method, to evaluate the call premium. This same binomial model is now used alongside the Garman and Kolhagen version of Black and Scholes to price currency options. Assuming that early exercise will take place only if the advantage of holding the currency is greater than the time value of the option, the binomial method involves making a series of trial estimates over the life of the option, each estimate being a probability analysis of early exercise for each successive day. Thus, for a one-year option the probability of a rise or fall in the currency is estimated for every day until expiry. The theoretical premium for the option, given various probabilities over time, is compared with the cost of holding the cash hedge position. Once the time value of the option is worth less than the forward points of the currency hedge, the position becomes too expensive to carry and the option should be exercised. In practice, the computation of 360 trials (one for each day of the year) would take too long, even for most computers. Most binomial-pricing models therefore reduce the number of iterations to a compromise level where the calculation process is reasonably fast and the approximation is not too great.

A less complex version has been developed by Barone-Adesi and Whaley (1987) using a simple quadratic approximation to value American-style currency options. Its essential mathematics are summarized in Tucker, Madura and Chiang (1991).

The early exercise provision in American options can make a significant difference to the premium value of some options, namely calls on higher interest rate currencies and puts on lower interest rate currencies. When early exercise is unlikely, however, as possibly with sterling puts or Swiss franc calls, the Black and Scholes and the binomial models give identical results.

There is a danger in taking the premium derived from the option-pricing model too literally. The market price and the fair-value price may well differ considerably, and while it is always possible for an arbitrageur to sell what is believed to be an overpriced option, or to buy an option that is underpriced compared to the theoretical value according to the pricing model, this will not necessarily guarantee profits. The main reason is that the key inputs to the model are by no means certain. Consider the following:

- Known and constant volatility.
- Constant interest rates.
- No transaction costs and/or taxation effects.
- Continuous trading.
- No dividends.
- No early exercise.

Interest rate differentials may vary over the life of an option – and sometimes erratically so. The foreign exchange market does have transaction costs in the bid/ask spread, and when conditions become thin or volatile the spreads widen. And *ex-ante* volatility estimates may vary from one trade to another and will presumably be different from past volatility. The big unknown, is, of course, by how much. Also, the assumption of normal or even log-normal distribution of such movements is questionable as far as the foreign exchange markets are concerned. We have seen that researchers of behaviour in currency markets have identified biased price movements – they have observed frequent occasions when prices do not behave in a neat distribution. Central bank intervention is often the cause of this bias.

Before moving on to consider how well the Black and Scholes formula stands up in practice, we briefly take the concept of volatility a little further. Consider an option that is held entirely for insurance purposes. The value of the option depends upon the chance that the spot price will be above or below the exercise price of the option at the maturity date. In turn, this probability depends upon the uncertainty about the spot rate at the time the option matures. The standard deviation of the distribution of possible levels of the spot rate at the maturity date describes this uncertainty – and this is what volatility is all about. There is a simple relationship between volatility over a short period and over a long period. The standard deviation over t days is equal to the square root of t times the daily standard deviation. The standard deviation over three months is equal to approximately eight times the standard deviation over 1 day, since there are about 63 trading days in a quarter and the square root of 63 is approximately 8. Table 17.5 sets out standard deviations over different time periods. All of these are equivalent to a standard deviation of 10 per cent per annum. The market has adopted the convention of always quoting volatilities on an annalistic basis, just as interest rates and forward premiums are always quoted on an annual basis.

Volatility does not increase in a linear way with time. Over three months there is half as much volatility as over one year. Table 17.6 (overleaf) illustrates why this is so. Assume that a currency rate can move up or down by 1 per cent or stay the same over a single day. The standard deviation is 0.82 per cent. Over two days the standard deviation is 1.15 per cent, equal to $\sqrt{2} \times 0.82$ per cent. The two-day moves are not twice as scattered as the one-day moves, since sometimes when the currency moves up on the first day it moves back down on the second day and vice versa. This offsets part of the volatility contributed by the first day, resulting in the two-day

Table 17.5 Volatility over different time periods

	Standard deviation (%)
1 year	10.0
9 months	8.7
6 months	7.1
3 months	5.0
1 day	0.6

Table 17.6 Volatility over 1 and 2 days

Over 1 day		Over 2 days	
Move (%)	*Probability*	*Move (%)*	*Probability*
+1	1/3	+2	1/9
0	1/3	+1	2/9
−1	1/3	0	3/9
		−1	2/9
		−2	1/9
Standard deviation 0.82%		Standard deviation 1.15%	

standard deviation being less than twice the one-day standard deviation. Having said this, if both are annalist, they will give the same number.

Most currency options are hedged by some party. It may be that the bank writing the option takes cover; it may be that the market-maker in the option market carries out the delta hedging strategy. In theory, the company could, instead of buying an option, perform these trades itself and thereby replicate the option. Potential competition from company synthesizers of their own options forces prices towards the option model prices. This means that the spread of the market price over the model price is limited by the possibility of corporations and others synthesizing their own options. The actual price paid by a corporation in the currency option market is likely therefore to be equal to the model price plus transactions costs of hedging by the option writer, plus a premium for risk of volatility changing plus a pure profit spread.

Companies synthesizing their own currency options would save on the pure profit spread. Their cost would be based upon the model price plus transactions costs of replication by the corporation plus a premium for the risk of volatility changing.

17.6 | Option pricing models for stocks and currencies: the empirical evidence

There are problems in carrying out empirical research to test the Black and Scholes model and other option-pricing models. First, any statistical hypothesis about how options are priced has to be a joint hypothesis to the effect that (1) the option-pricing formula is correct, and that (2) markets price financial instruments efficiently. If the hypothesis is rejected, it may be the case that (1) is untrue, that (2) is untrue, or that both (1) and (2) are untrue. A second problem is that future stock price volatility is an unobservable variable. One might estimate volatility from historical stock price data. Alternatively, implied volatilities can be used in some way – although this may result in circular reasoning. Another problem is to ensure that data on stock price and option price are obtained at the same time. Thus, if the option is thinly traded, it may be unacceptable to compare closing options prices with closing stock prices. For example, if the last option trade were at 11 a.m. while the closing stock price corresponded to a trade at 4.30 p.m., we would have something of a data problem.

Black and Scholes (1972) and Galai (1977) have tested whether it is possible to make excess returns above the risk-free rate of interest by buying options that are undervalued by the market, relative to the theoretical price, and selling options that are overvalued by the market, relative to the theoretical price. A riskless delta-neutral portfolio is assumed to be maintained at all times by trading the underlying stocks as described earlier in section 17.4 under the heading of 'Hedging a currency option'. Black and Scholes used data from the over-the-counter options market and Galai used data from the Chicago Board Options Exchange (CBOE). Both of these studies found that, in the absence of transactions costs, significant excess returns over the risk-free rate could be obtained by buying undervalued options and selling overvalued options. But some caution is needed. It is possible that these excess returns are available only to market-makers; when transactions costs are considered, they tend to vanish.

A number of researchers, for example Garman (1976), have sought to identify arbitrage strategies which may be followed in order to earn riskless profits in options markets. A study by Klemkosky and Resnick (1979) concludes that small arbitrage profits are available, mainly because of the overpricing of American calls.

Chiras and Manaster (1978) carried out a study of CBOE data investigating the weighted implied standard deviation from options on a share with the standard deviation calculated from historic data. The former provided a better forecast of the volatility of the stock price during the life of an option. Replications by other researchers have confirmed this conclusion. Apparently, option traders are using more than just historical data when estimating future volatilities. Chiras and Manaster also tested whether it was possible to earn above-average returns by buying options with low implied standard deviations and selling options with high implied standard deviations. This strategy showed a profit of 10 per cent per month. This finding suggests that option-pricing models are great sources of potential profit and that the CBOE was far from an efficient market.

MacBeth and Merville (1979) have tested the Black and Scholes model by looking at prices of call options on a small number of blue-chip shares and comparing the volatilities implied. They looked at AT&T, Avon, Kodak, Exxon, IBM and Xerox during 1976. They found that implied volatilities tended to be relatively high for in-the-money options and relatively low for out-of-the-money options. A relatively high implied volatility is indicative of a relatively high option price; a relatively low implied volatility is indicative of a relatively low option price. If it is assumed that the Black and Scholes model prices at-the-money options correctly, it can be concluded that out-of-the-money call options are overpriced by the model and in-the-money call options are underpriced by Black and Scholes. These effects become more pronounced as the time to maturity increases and the degree to which the option is in or out of the money increases.

Rubinstein (1985) carried out a study similar to that of MacBeth and Merville, using evidence from option trades on the most frequently traded options on the CBOE during 1976 and 1978. He found differing results for different sub-periods.

For the first half of the period studied, his results were consistent with those of MacBeth and Merville. But for the second half, the opposite result was obtained – that is, implied volatilities were relatively high for out-of-the-money options and relatively low for in-the-money options. Through the whole period, Rubinstein found that, for out-of-the-money options, short-maturity options had significantly higher implied volatilities than long-maturity options. Results for at-the-money and in-the-money options were mixed. Possibly Rubinstein's reversing results reflect some interaction of macroeconomic variables which is not yet fully understood or incorporated in the Black and Scholes model.

Later work by Rubinstein (1994) concludes that out-of-the-money puts, and hence in-the-money calls (by put–call parity) become valued much more highly, eventually leading to the 1990–92 situation where low strike price options had significantly higher implied volatilities than high strike price options. Rubinstein speculated that one reason for this might have been investors' fear of a repeat of the crash of 1987. But he also suggests other reasons to do with departures from log-normality.

What do we mean by this? The Black and Scholes model assumes that the distribution of the asset price at some future time, conditional on its value today, is log-normal. Some tests of option pricing indicated that in-the-money and out-of-the-money options appear to be mispriced relative to at-the-money options. In other words, the volatility for which the Black and Scholes equation correctly prices at-the-money options causes it to misprice in-the-money and out-of-the-money options. These pricing errors can be explained by differences between the log-normal distribution assumed by Black and Scholes and the true distribution.

Thus, Figure 17.5 shows four ways in which the true asset price distribution may be different from the log-normal distribution but still give the same mean and standard deviation for the asset price return. The features of these distributions are summarized in Table 17.7. For Figure 17.5(a), both tails of the true distribution are thinner than those of the log-normal distribution. For Figure 17.5(b), the right tail is thinner and the left tail is fatter. For Figure 17.5(c), the right tail is fatter and the left tail is thinner. In Figure 17.5(d) both tails are fatter. The true distributions in Figure 17.5 are derived from the log-normal distribution by removing probability mass from some areas and adding it to other areas in such a way that the overall mean and standard deviation of asset returns remain as before. Thus, in Figure 17.5(d) probability mass has been added to both tails of the distribution and to the central part of the distribution. This has been balanced by the removal of probability mass from those versions of the distribution that are between around one and two standard deviations from the mean.

So, what would be the difference between correct option price and the Black and Scholes model price that would be observed in these four situations? This difference is sometimes termed bias. Consider a call option that is significantly out of the money. It will have a positive intrinsic value only if there is a large increase in the asset price. Therefore, its value critically depends only on the right tail of the terminal asset price distribution. The fatter this tail, the more valuable the option. Consequently, the Black and Scholes model will tend to underprice out-of-the-money calls when the asset price distribution is as illustrated in Figure 17.5(c) and (d), and it will overprice out-of-the-money calls in the cases shown in Figure 17.5(a)

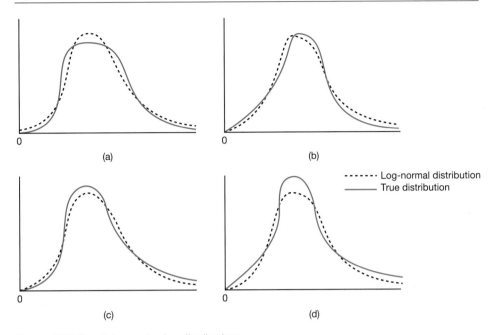

Figure 17.5 Possible asset price distributions.

Table 17.7 Bias created by possible stock price distributions in Figure 17.5

Distribution in Figure 17.5	Features	Bias created
(a)	Both tails thinner	The Black and Scholes model overprices both out-of-the-money and in-the-money calls and puts.
(b)	Left tail fatter, right tail thinner	The Black and Scholes model overprices out-of-the-money calls and in-the-money puts. It underprices out-of-the-money puts and in-the-money calls.
(c)	Left tail thinner, right tail fatter	The Black and Scholes model overprices out-of-the-money puts and in-the-money calls. It underprices in-the-money puts and out-of-the-money calls.
(d)	Both tails fatter	The Black and Scholes model underprices both out-of-the-money and in-the-money calls and puts.

and (b). We now turn to a put option that is significantly out of the money. It will have a positive intrinsic value only if there is a large decrease in the asset price. Therefore, its value critically depends only on the left tail of the terminal asset price distribution. The fatter this tail, the more valuable the option. Thus, the Black and

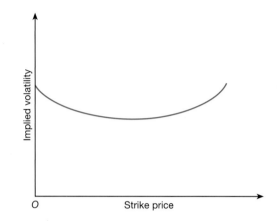

Figure 17.6 Volatility smile for foreign exchange options.

Scholes model will tend to underprice out-of-the-money puts when the asset distribution is as illustrated in Figure 17.5(b) and (d), and it will overprice out-of-the-money puts in the cases of Figure 17.5(a) and (c). The findings of Rubinstein (1994) tend to conform to the asset price distribution shown in Figure 17.5(b).

A number of researchers have investigated the behaviour of other options. Shastri and Tandon (1986a) and Bodurtha and Courtadon (1987) have examined the market prices of currency options. Elsewhere, Shastri and Tandon (1986b) have examined the market prices of futures options and Chance (1986) has examined the market prices of index options. These authors' studies tend to find that the Black and Scholes model misprices some options. But the mispricing is not sufficient, in most cases, to present profitable opportunities to investors when transaction costs and bid/offer spreads are taken into account.

It is worth noting that Tucker and Pond (1988) and Tucker (1990) found that a currency option-pricing model which incorporates discrete jumps in exchange rates outperforms the Black and Scholes model in pricing Philadelphia-traded currency options. The source of such jumps might be central bank intervention or realignments within a currency float group.

Volatility smile is a plot of the implied volatility of an option as a function of its strike price. For options on foreign exchange, a typical volatility smile is shown in Figure 17.6. Out-of-the-money and in-the-money options both tend to have higher implied volatilities than at-the-money options. Here, we define an at-the-money option as an option whose strike price equals the forward price of the asset. Figure 17.6 is therefore consistent with Figure 17.5(d).

17.7 | Corporate use of currency options

If a company wishes to leave open the possibility of making a currency gain on a receivable or payable, while protecting itself against adverse movements in the exchange rate, it can do so via the currency option market. Currency options are of particular interest to the treasurer where a future currency cash flow is uncertain, as in the case of putting in a contract tender or issuing a foreign currency price list. In the case of a tender, if the contract is not awarded, the company merely lets the currency option lapse – or, if it pays it to do otherwise, it sells it on at a profit. If the company obtains the contract tendered for, it will exchange the currency option for a forward option running out to the payment dates under the contract.

But treasurers may also use currency options to hedge a contractually agreed deal in order to protect the downside exchange risk on a receivable or payable, while leaving open the upside potential. Currency options have become particularly attractive to corporate treasurers in times when there is substantial volatility in the foreign exchange markets. In 1984 the dollar was strengthening rapidly against most currencies, although many corporate treasurers felt that it was clearly overvalued in terms of purchasing power parity criteria. Given that trends in the market and purchasing power parity considerations pointed in opposite directions, it might have been an apposite time to use currency options. Of course, it would have been better not to hedge dollar receivables at all, but this view only emerges with the benefit of hindsight.

A price has to be paid to secure the benefit of an option. This is the front-end non-returnable premium which the option writer receives whether or not the company exercises its option. The decision to use currency options needs to be assessed carefully, taking into account the likelihood of the currency flow occurring, the volatility of the exchange rate until the funds are received and the cost of the premium. The answer to the criticism made by some treasurers to the effect that currency options are expensive comes back loud and clear. Why not write options yourself then?

Of course, one of the major problems with currency options traded on the Philadelphia, London or Amsterdam Stock Exchanges is that they have specific expiration dates which will usually differ from the date up to which cover is required. Because of this there has developed an over-the-counter (OTC) market in which tailor-made options are bought and sold privately between banks and their customers. The growth of exchange-traded and of OTC currency options are really complementary. The exchange-traded markets are used most frequently by banks hedging OTC positions. The OTC currency option business is largely made up of corporate activity. Increased volume in one market supports increased activity in the other. There are obvious reasons why a large volume of corporate currency option business has been channelled through the OTC market rather than directly through exchange markets. First and foremost is the fact that OTC options are tailor-made to meet a company's specific needs. A company may therefore ask a bank to quote a price on a currency option which exactly matches its hedge requirements with respect to the currency to be bought and sold, the amount, the price and the time period to be covered. The option specifications of exchange-traded products are standardized, so that a company's precise needs will not easily be met through this market place.

Corporate treasurers are also attracted by the fact that OTC transactions are operationally straightforward and are rather similar to forward foreign exchange dealing procedures. It should be noted that there is no formal secondary market in OTC currency options, which makes them less flexible than exchange-traded options. But the

Table 17.8 Exchange-traded and OTC options compared

	Exchange traded	OTC
Contract terms, including amounts	Standardized	Fixed to suit circumstances; terms are not standard
Expiration	Standardized	Determined by requirements of customer
Transaction method	Stock exchange type medium	Bank-to-client or bank-to-bank
Secondary market	Continuous secondary market	No formal secondary market
Commissions	Negotiable	Negotiable, but usually built into the premium
Participants	Exchange members and clients	Banks, corporations and financial institutions

company may sell its OTC option back to the bank writing it, or enter into an OTC option with exactly the reverse characteristics of the original one. OTC options do have far greater flexibility for companies in terms of expiry dates, amounts involved and the possibility of dealing in currencies not quoted on the traded exchanges. Banks may be prepared to tailor options in a range of currencies wider than that quoted on the currency options markets. In Table 17.8, a comparison between exchange-traded and OTC options is tabulated.

The currency option market is an innovative one. A variant of the basic option contract which has been introduced is the cylinder option, or zero-cost option as it is sometimes called. Its interest to corporate treasurers arises because, in times of high volatility, it enables the treasurer to lock into a narrow band in the exchange rate range. The workings of the cylinder option will become apparent with the help of a numerical example.

Assume that a UK company has a dollar receivable. The treasurer has a range of possible options in respect of the asset. The treasurer may, among other actions:

- leave the dollars uncovered;

- sell the dollars forward;

- buy a sterling call option;[1]

- buy a sterling option cylinder.

Assume that the spot rate at the date when the treasurer is considering taking action amounts to $1.86 and the forward rate for the maturity of the receivable is $1.85. Assume also that the premium for an option to sell dollars at $1.90 for the appropriate period is 4.50 cents. Having been informed of the premium by the bank, the treasurer expresses the opinion that it is expensive, to which the bank replies that it will write a zero-cost option. What this involves is as follows. To counter the premium payable on the $1.90 option bought, the client writes an option to sell dollars to the bank at $1.80 with a premium of 4.50 cents payable by the bank to the client.

The two premia set off against each other, giving rise to the zero cost. If the client takes the zero-cost option, then the client will be in a position:

- To carry the profit or loss for exchange rate movements between $1.80 and $1.90. If the rate moves to $1.82 on maturity, the client takes the profit from the dollar strengthening from $1.86 to $1.82. Should the maturity rate be $1.88, the client takes the loss.

- To limit profit or loss should the exchange rate on maturity move outside the cylinder $1.90 to $1.80. So should the rate on maturity go to $1.92, the client bears a limited loss based on $1.90 less $1.86 and the bank bears the remainder of the loss from $1.92 to $1.90. In a reverse direction, if the rate on maturity is $1.76, the client makes a gain based on $1.86 less $1.80 and the bank takes the remaining profit based on the dollar strengthening from $1.80 to $1.76.

Effectively the cylinder option in the example provides the treasurer with total cover against the dollar weakening beyond $1.90 and gives a gain to the company from the dollar strengthening to $1.80: but the company limits its gain should the dollar strengthen beyond $1.80.

Ignoring interest rate considerations, Table 17.9 (overleaf) shows comparative results from leaving the dollars uncovered versus taking forward cover versus buying a sterling option cylinder. Gains and losses shown in the table are in US cents against a base rate of $1.86. What the option cylinder hedge does is to allow the corporate treasurer to fix an exchange rate within a narrow band for a nil net front-end premium. This is achieved by the treasurer writing an option in the opposite direction to that in which cover is desired. The rate at which the option is written is such that its premium is equal to the premium on the option to be bought or sold to give cover for the receivable or payable.

Before leaving the topic of corporate use of currency options, it is worth mentioning that there are some treasurers who are of the opinion that currency options have one basic use: to protect profitability. Consider an example. Assume that a company imports wine from the United States, priced in dollars, into the United Kingdom. It has only one direct competitor importing US wine, although a host of importers deal in French, German, Italian and other wines. Against its immediate competitor it may suffer a disadvantage if it hedges via the forward market and its competitor does not and the dollar weakens. Obviously, the competitor might now gain market share by pricing down. It is just to avoid this competitive disadvantage, so the argument goes, that the currency option is designed. If the importer were covered by a currency option, its competitor would not be put at an advantage by exchange rate changes, since, whether the dollar hardened or weakened, the importer covered by the option can match whatever tactic its competitor employs without incurring loss – except of the currency option premium, of course. Given the above scenario, the covered wine competitor will, should the dollar harden, be in a position to gain at its uncovered competitor's expense. By carefully planning its tactics, the company might, through an aggressive competitive stance at such times, more than recoup the cost of the total currency premium paid out in the past.

Currency options may also, at least in theory, be employed to hedge economic exposure. Again consider an example. Imagine a UK exporter competing with a

Table 17.9 Comparative results of option cylinder (data as given in text)

Maturity exchange rate	Dollar uncovered gain (+) or loss (–)*	Forward sale: profit forgone (–) or loss saved (+)*	Buy sterling cylinder option: gain (+) or loss (–)*
1.92	–6	+7	–4
1.91	–5	+6	–4
1.90	–4	+5	–4
1.89	–3	+4	–3
1.88	–2	+3	–2
1.87	–1	+2	–1
1.86	0	+1	0
1.85	+1	0	+1
1.84	+2	–1	+2
1.83	+3	–2	+3
1.82	+4	–3	+4
1.81	+5	–4	+5
1.80	+6	–5	+6
1.79	+7	–6	+6
1.78	+8	–7	+6

* Gains and losses shown in US cents versus spots of $1.86.

Japanese company for US market share. It has a transaction exposure against the dollar, and an economic exposure against the yen. It could hedge against the dollar exposure by selling dollars forward for sterling. But it could also hedge against its Japanese rival by buying yen put options. If the yen falls, the UK firm can use its option profits to match the Japanese firm's price cuts in the Unites States. If the yen rises, the options expire worthless, but the UK firm has the price advantage anyway.

In the above example, the hedging of the transaction exposure requires the existence of long-term forward contracts – these are available up to ten years for major currencies against the dollar. But the hedging of economic exposure in the above example requires an availability of long-term currency options. At the time of writing, OTC options are available for a few currencies against the US dollar up to a maturity of ten years or more. Not all banks are prepared to quote them and because of this lack of competitiveness many corporate treasurers reckon them to be expensive. The long and short is, therefore, that exposures for only a limited period can currently be hedged with currency options. Clearly, in the example above, the UK firm has a long-run exposure against the yen which cannot be covered via options.

Of course, there are other ways of hedging economic exposures, such as seeking overseas sourcing or even relocating to the same countries as one's competitors. But care has to be taken that short-term exchange rate movements are not interpreted as long-run changes – as the US manufacturer of earth-moving equipment, Caterpillar, did. In the early 1980s Caterpillar moved some of its manufacture abroad to offset the impact of the strong dollar on its costs, compared with those of its Japanese competitor, Komatsu. Overseas production went from 19 per cent of total sales in 1982 to 25 per cent in 1986; overseas sourcing rose fourfold. Then the dollar started to fall. Caterpillar lost out. It might have been better to stay put and hedge its exposure via currency options.

17.8 | Summary

- Currency options provide the right, but not the obligation, to buy or sell a specific currency at a specific price at a time prior to a specified date or on a particular date.

- Users of currency options obtain insurance against adverse movements in the exchange rate while still retaining the opportunity to benefit from a favourable exchange rate movement. The maximum risk that is incurred by the buyer of an option is the premium cost of the said option.

- Currency options come in two forms. There are traded currency options and over-the-counter options. Be sure that you know the distinction between these two.

- Currency options may be classified as American or European options. Be sure that you know the difference. It is made clear in the text.

- Should a company wish to leave open the possibility of making a currency gain on a receivable or payable while protecting itself against adverse movements in the exchange rate, it may do so via the currency option market.

- Currency options are of particular interest where a future currency cash flow is uncertain as in the case of a tender on a contract or an overseas takeover bid.

- Currency options provide an easy way for a company to take positions and to speculate in foreign currency with limited downside risk.

- In competitive terms, currency options can provide valuable benefits. Take an example. Company A buys imports from overseas in foreign currency and sells in the home market for home currency. Its biggest competitor – indeed the market leader – has the same cash input and output profile. If the market leader decides not to hedge its foreign currency payables while company A does hedge, a problem arises. Company A may gain in competitive terms if the foreign currency strengthens but it may lose out should it weaken. The currency option provides the wherewithal to back both horses. But it can be expensive. At the time of writing, sterling/dollar twelve-month at-the-money American options were costing 5 per cent or so, while similar but European options were running at 4 per cent.

- Make sure you understand what in-the-money, at-the-money and out-of-the-money mean. If you have difficulty remembering, try this mnemonic. In the money options have intrinsic value. Do you see? 'In' the money = 'in'-trinsic value.

■ Also make sure you understand what the Black and Scholes formula is saying. Remember the essence of Figure 17.3. If you are going to become an *aficionado* of option pricing you will need to be able to manipulate Black and Scholes. If not, merely understanding how it works will be enough. But do not be afraid of it. Remember the relatively user-friendly table for pricing options in Chapter 16.

■ It is worth spending a little time ensuring that you know how to use an average rate option in order to hedge a foreign currency profit and loss account exposure.

17.9 | End of chapter questions

Question 1
When should a firm consider purchasing a call option for foreign currency hedging?

Question 2
When should a firm consider purchasing a put option for foreign currency hedging?

Question 3
Why should a firm consider hedging net payables or net receivables with currency options rather than forward contracts? What are the disadvantages of hedging with currency options as opposed to forward contracts?

18 Interest rate risk

Interest rate risk is concerned with the sensitivity of profit, cash flows or valuation of the firm to changes in interest rates. Viewed from the perspective of this definition, the firm should analyse how its profit, cash outturns and value change in response to changes in interest rate levels. Should its profits and cash flow fall when interest rates rise, then the risk-averse company, seeking to stabilize profit trends, will finance itself with fixed rate funds. A speculative housebuilder might be a company falling into this category. However, some companies' profits and cash flows move directly with interest rates – this is true of many financial institutions. Such firms might, if they were risk averse, fund themselves with floating rate finance. Having said all this, firms may back their view of the market by funding themselves in a particular way. Thus the housebuilder which anticipates a fall in interest rates might source from floating rate funds. Interest rate exposure arises from two sources. There is macro-economic exposure – the kind that the housebuilder in the example faced. And there is the exposure that the lender faces in respect of interest receivable on its deposit and, similarly, that the borrower faces relating to interest to be paid on loans drawn down.

We take interest rate risk much further later in this chapter, but first of all it is necessary to consider the term structure of interest rates because this topic is at the centre of so much of our analysis.

18.1 | The term structure of interest rates

The term structure of interest rates can be thought of as a graph of interest rates on securities of a particular risk class at a particular time, in which the interest rate is plotted on the vertical axis and time to maturity on the horizontal axis. Term structure theory is concerned with why the term structure has a particular shape at a particular time. Analysts sometimes refer to the term structure as being flat (same interest for all maturities), upward sloping (long-term interest rates higher than short-term interest rates) or downward sloping (short-term interest rates higher than long-term rates). Figure 18.1 (overleaf) illustrates these three situations.

The best-known explanation of the term structure is the expectations theory. According to this hypothesis, expectations of future interest rates constitute the key determinant of the yield/maturity relationship. Each investor can either buy

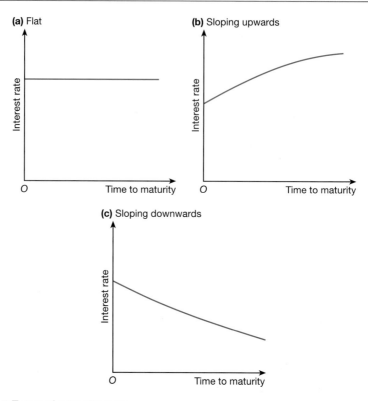

Figure 18.1 Types of term structure.

long-term securities and hold them or buy short-term securities and continually reinvest in shorts at each maturity over the holding period. In equilibrium, the expected return for each holding period will tend to be the same, whatever alternative or combination of alternatives was chosen. As a result, the return on a long-term bond will tend to equal an unbiased average of the current short-term rates and future short-term rates expected to prevail to maturity of the long-term bond. With this background, one can calculate the implicit or expected short-term rate for any future period based upon actual rates of interest prevailing in the market at a specific time. Expectations theory contends that the term structure of interest rates is entirely a function of investors' expectations about future interest rates.

Most evidence underpins the importance of interest rate expectations in the term structure of interest rates. However, Hicks and others have argued that long-term rates in fact tend to differ from the average of expected short-term rates because market participants prefer to lend short unless offered a premium sufficient to offset the risk of lending long. Hicks (1946) argues that these liquidity premiums tend to be greater, the longer the maturity of the bond. His findings support the liquidity preference theory of the term structure of interest rates. Advocates of this theory believe that for the most part investors wish to lend short, and organizations aim to borrow long, so that liquidity premiums are positive – that is, the forward rate exceeds the expected future spot interest rate. If liquidity preference theory is right, the term structure should be upward sloping more often than not. A positive liquidity pre-mium rewards investors for lending long. The reward manifests itself in high long-term rates of interest. Of course, if future spot rates were expected to fall, the term structure could still be downward sloping – but liquidity preference theory would predict a less dramatic downward slope than expectations theory.

A third theory, the preferred habitat hypothesis of Modigliani and Sutch (1966), argues that bond markets are segmented by maturity, and that the maturity prefer-ences of market participants are so strong that investors tend to borrow and lend only in a particular range of maturities. Therefore, in each different credit market, interest rates tend to be determined by supply and demand rather than by interest rate expectations. This explanation is sometimes called the market segmentation theory, or the hedging pressure theory.

Finally, there is the inflation premium theory. Like the liquidity preference explana-tion, this theory argues that long-term interest rates reflect investors' expectations about future short-term interest rates plus a premium for risk. However, advocates of the theory contend that the principal source of risk is the rate of inflation. They argue that investors are interested in real returns and that the primary determin-ant in the term structure of interest rates is investors' expectations of inflation over different holding periods, which is the critical factor by which investors translate nominal interest rates into real expected returns.

Whichever theory of term structure seems to predominate in the domestic market should hold for the Euromarket. In the absence of capital controls, arbitrage would ensure the virtual equality of internal and external rates at each maturity, and what-ever holds for the domestic market would also hold for Eurorates. In other words, there is normally no independent Eurodollar term structure of interest rates.

If capital controls are in place and they affect all maturities equally, the internal term structure might not be identical to the external one, but since Eurorates should tend to be at the same position relative to internal rates for each maturity, a nearly identical term structure should hold. As in the domestic market, if Eurocurrency investors think interest rates will drop, they will try to lock into long-term deposits; this will tend to lower the long-term yield to maturity.

The term structure of Eurocurrency interest rates will be consonant with the mar-ket's interest rate forecasts if, and only if, the yield on a long-term deposit equals the expected yield obtained from investing in short-term securities and reinvesting the proceeds successively in short-term deposits at the interest rate expected to prevail during each future period.

The above point can be observed easily by reference to a numerical example. Assume that a firm has money to invest for, say, six months. It might invest now for the whole six-month period. Or it might invest now for only three months and then reinvest for a further three later on. Clearly, if the interest is for six months now, the firm will receive a quotation for a fixed rate for the whole six-month period, with interest being credited at the end of the period. Also, if the firm invests for three months expecting to extend the investment by reinvesting at the end of that period for a further three months, it can expect to receive an offer of a fixed rate for three months with interest credited at the end of the period. But the firm could also obtain a forward/forward fixed interest rate for the period from the beginning of month 4 to the end of month 6. By pursuing this latter policy, the firm would have manufactured exactly the same investment as locking in for the whole six months – so the proceeds should, in present value terms, be the same. After all, the two investments are exactly equal in terms of risk, so they should yield the same returns.

If the firm invests for six months in accordance with the first scenario above, the proceeds of investing £1 now will be:

$$£1\left[1 + r_6\left(\frac{6}{12}\right)\right]$$

(18.1)

where r_6 is the annual (as bankers quote it) interest rate for six months. Investing according to the second scenario, the terminal proceeds of investing £1 now would be:

$$£1\left[1 + r_3\left(\frac{3}{12}\right)\right]\left[1 + r_{3/6}\left(\frac{3}{12}\right)\right]$$

(18.2)

where r_3 is the annual interest rate for the first three months and $r_{3/6}$ is the annual interest rate from the beginning of month 4 to the end of month 6.

Generalizing from equation (18.1), we could say that the terminal proceeds for the former scenario amounted to:

$$1 + \left(r_{t_2} \times \frac{t_2}{12}\right)$$

(18.3)

where r is the interest rate and t_2 is the far term in months. Similarly, the terminal value of the latter scenario can be said to be equal to:

$$\left[1 + \left(r_{t_1} \times \frac{t_2}{12}\right)\right]\left[\left(r_{t_1 \to 2} \times \frac{t_{1\to 2}}{12}\right) + 1\right]$$

(18.4)

where t_1 is the near term in months and $t_{1\to 2}$ is the difference between the near and far terms in months.

Since the proceeds from the two investments should be the same, it follows logically that:

$$\frac{1 + \left(r_{t_2} \times \dfrac{t_2}{12}\right)}{1 + \left(r_{t_1} \times \dfrac{t_1}{12}\right)} = 1 + r_{t_{1\to 2}}$$

(18.5)

The figure obtained from the above additions for $r_{t_{1\to 2}}$ may be annualized to put it into terms used by bankers.

This forward rate is, of course, essentially the market's best estimate of a future interest rate based upon the term structure of interest rates, from which both forward quotes of interest rates are derived. An understanding of these very basic ideas is useful because it is the underpinning of various quotations to do with interest rates – for example, forward rate agreements and some other instruments which we will encounter in this chapter.

18.2 | Interest rate exposure

Besides the exposure of the firm's operating income stream to changes in interest rate, there are at least two other types of interest rate exposure: these are called basis risk and gap exposure. Basis risk occurs when the basis upon which interest rates are determined for assets and liabilities is different. Consider a bank that has lent £5m to a corporate customer for three months based on LIBOR, but assume that the bank has funded itself with three-month certificates of deposit (CDs). In three months, the bank itself anticipates rolling over both the assets and the liabilities. The bank is exposed to interest rate changes, inasmuch as the basis on which interest is determined on the bank's asset and liability is different. A 1 per cent change in LIBOR need not necessarily lead to an exactly equal change in CD rates.

By contrast, gap exposure arises from timing differences in the repricing of assets and liabilities that are sensitive to interest rates. Consider a bank that has invested heavily in six-month CDs issued by other banks. It has funded itself by issuing its own three-month CDs, thus creating a gap exposure. The basis on which interest is calculated on both assets and liabilities is similar – CD rates. But the timing of repricing is different. The bank will have to roll over its borrowings in three months' time. Should rates have increased, then the cost of financing will increase but the bank's income stream will not change for a further three months. Its profit on this transaction will be affected. Should the bank have had a greater proportion of liabilities being repriced before assets, it would presumably have been expecting rates to fall.

Managing interest rate exposure begins with its measurement. Gap management techniques focus upon just this problem. They are concerned with the exposure of net income to changes in interest rates during a period. If fixed rate liabilities exceed fixed rate assets, there is a positive gap. With a positive gap, a rise in short-term rates increases margins, while declining rates reduce margins. By contrast, if fixed rate liabilities are less than fixed rate assets, there is a negative gap. With such a gap, net interest margins decline if short-term interest rates rise and margins increase if rates fall. There are three widely used techniques of gap management: maturity gap modelling, duration analysis and simulation techniques. These are briefly considered in order.

The essential approach of maturity gap modelling is best illustrated by an example. Assume that for a particular gap period, interest-rate-sensitive assets are £6m while interest-rate-sensitive liabilities are £10m. At first sight, the analysis suggests a gap of £4m. While this is correct, it might be misleading. For example, assume that the firm is financing itself via 90-day CDs and that the assets in which it has invested are 90-day commercial paper. If it is the case that the historic volatilities of these two instruments vary – say, CDs are 110 per cent as volatile as the 90-day financial future while commercial paper is 85 per cent as volatile as the same financial future – then the interest rate exposure (volatility adjusted) can be estimated as £5.9m (see Table 18.1).

Table 18.1 Maturity gap modelling

	Cash flow (£m)	Volatility (% v. financial futures)	Financial futures equivalent (£m)
Assets	6	85	5.1
Liabilities	10	110	11.0
Gap	4		5.9

In this kind of analysis, the choice of financial futures as a standard is preferred for two reasons – first of all, their rates are market determined and, secondly, they can be used to adjust the gap in the desired direction by hedging without further correlation calculations being necessary – although, of course, volatilities can change.

Duration analysis is different and is again best explained by means of an example. Consider a bond. Its final maturity is often considered – erroneously – to be its key component. This concentrates simply on the final cash flow, rather than the whole configuration of cash flows throughout the bond's life. A 10 per cent bond with a ten-year life is not the same as a 5 per cent bond with a ten-year life, but both have the same final maturity. The concept of duration is designed to encapsulate all of the cash flows accruing under a bond, duly allowing for the incidence of their timing.

Assume two bonds. Each has a fifteen-year term to maturity and each sells to yield 10 per cent to maturity. The first bond is priced at par while the second sells at a substantial discount because its coupon is only 5 per cent. Much more of the first bond's total present value is received during the earlier years to maturity. This bond has a shorter maturity in a present value sense. Deep discount bonds are much more price sensitive to rate movements than regular bonds. Also, on questions of default, the expected value of any loss on the second bond is greater because a larger proportion of the investors' outlay is riding on the more distant payments.

The concept of duration explicitly takes account of the timing of the return of value to a bondholder. Essentially, duration is the weighted average maturity stated in present value terms. The number of years into the future when a cash flow is received is weighted by the proportion which that cash flow contributes to the total present value of the bond.

If a bond has one coupon payment a year, then duration, D, may be defined, in algebraic terms, as:

$$D = \frac{\sum_{t=1}^{n} \dfrac{tC}{(1+r)^t}}{p}$$

where

n = the life of the bond,

C = the cash receipt at end of year t – this will be equal to the annual coupon, except for the last year, which is equal to the annual coupon and the repayment amount,

r = the yield to maturity as a percentage,

t = the number of years from now in respect of which each cash receipt, C, is receivable,

p = price of bond.

The top half of the expression is the present value of a single year's cash receipt weighted according to the year in which it is received. The denominator is the price of the bond or the sum of all of those cash flows that make the present value of the bond. Table 18.2 shows the calculation of the duration of a £1m bond with a 10 per cent coupon bond priced at par with five years to maturity.

The duration of a bond is less than the life of the bond. The duration can never exceed the term to maturity. A zero-coupon bond will have a duration equal to its maturity. The difference between duration and term to maturity increases as the term to maturity increases.

The notion of duration can be applied to a portfolio of assets too. By multiplying the duration of the individual asset in the portfolio by its weight in the value of the portfolio, an average duration can be calculated. This is valuable because it may be shown that a change in bond price with respect to a change in discount factor is approximately equal to its duration with the sign reversed. So, if a bond's duration is known, then it is possible to calculate how much the price will change as the yield of the bond changes. If the yield increases by, say, 1 per cent, for a bond with a duration of 4.73 years, the price should decrease by 4.73 per cent. For a portfolio of bonds with a duration of 6.38 years, every 1 per cent change in interest rates will lead to a change in the market value of the portfolio by approximately 6.38 per cent.

The final technique of gap management is simulation analysis. This merely consists of building a mathematical model of the financial flows of the corporation, incorporating the assets and liabilities from the current and projected balance sheets, given changes in interest rates. Clearly, for simulation models to be effective, the assumptions and data analysis need to be accurate and realistic.

Having identified and quantified interest rate exposure, the next step is to hedge the risk. This involves transferring risk from one party to a counterparty. The

Table 18.2 Duration of a 10 per cent five-year bond priced at par (face value of bond £1m)

Year	Cash flow (£000)	Discount at 10%	Present value of ($000)	Proportion of PV	Duration (years)*
1	100	0.909	90.9	0.0909	0.0909
2	100	0.826	82.6	0.0826	0.1652
3	100	0.751	75.1	0.0751	0.2253
4	100	0.683	68.3	0.0683	0.2732
5	1,100	0.621	683.1	0.6831	3.4155
			1,000.0	1.0000	4.1701

Duration of bond = 4.17 years

* Each year, proportion of PV is multiplied by number of years, i.e. column (5) is multiplied by column (1).

counterparty may have an opposite exposure to one's own or be willing to take on that position. Many interest rate instruments are available to do this. These include forward rate agreements, financial futures, interest rate swaps, options and options on interest rate swaps. Although some of these have already been briefly discussed in this book, they are now looked at in more detail.

18.3 ┃ Forward rate agreements

Forward rate agreements (FRAs) allow borrowers or investors to lock in today a LIBOR rate accruing from a forward start date for a given period – for example, for month 3 in the future to month 6. The FRA is currently an off-balance-sheet instrument. It is widely used to cover short-term interest rate exposures for periods up to two or three years. It is a contract between two parties to agree an interest rate on a notional loan or deposit of a specified amount and maturity at a specific future date and to make payments between counterparties computed by reference to changes in the interest rate. FRAs involve no exchange of the principal amount. They are concerned only with the interest element. To hedge an interest rate exposure, the notional amount of the FRA contract is made equal to the principal amount of the underlying asset or liability.

A borrower desirous of hedging an interest rate exposure in three months' time for a period of three months would purchase a three-month FRA starting in three months. This is known as purchasing a '3s *v.* 6s' FRA (or 'threes' against 'sixes'). An investor with floating rate assets wishing to lock in an investment rate for a similar period would sell an FRA contract. To see how FRAs work, assume that a borrower has a one-year floating rate loan that has to be rolled over every three months based on three months' LIBOR. For the first three months, LIBOR has already been fixed. The borrower is concerned about a short-term increase in interest rates and wishes to hedge this exposure for the following three months. This can be achieved by purchasing an FRA in respect of the next interest period and for a notional amount identical to the underlying loan transaction.

In three months' time, the borrower continues to borrow from the original source of finance. The FRA contract that the borrower has entered into will have the same start date as the next interest rate repricing date. On that day, the three-month LIBOR rate is compared with the rate agreed under the FRA contract. If the FRA rate is greater than LIBOR, then the borrower will pay the seller of the FRA contract the difference between the two rates. The borrower's cost of borrowing will be equal to the market LIBOR rate plus the difference paid to the FRA as counterparty. The all-in rate will be the same as the rate agreed under the FRA contract. If the FRA rate is less than LIBOR, then the FRA counterparty will pay the borrower the difference between the two rates. This time the cost of borrowing will be the three-month LIBOR rate less the difference received from the FRA counterparty. Similarly, the net cost to the borrower will be the same rate as agreed under the FRA contract.

In the FRA market it is common practice to discount the net interest amount and settle at the beginning of an interest period. The discount factor used is the prevailing LIBOR rate. By dealing an FRA contract, the borrower can fix the borrowing costs for, say, the next six months. The borrowing cost can be fixed for the rest of the year by purchasing a strip of FRAs – a borrower will purchase not only a '3s *v.* 6s' but also a '6s *v.* 9s' and a '9s *v.* 12s' contract.

As an example, assume that a corporate borrower deals a $10m 3s *v.* 6s FRA on 10 September 2004 for settlement on 10 December 2004 based on a maturity date of 10 March 2005. The contract rate is 9.65 per cent and the contract period is 90 days. If, on 10 December 2004, the three-month LIBOR fixing is at $10^{1}/_{8}$ per cent, the settlement amount payable on that date would be:

$$\frac{(0.10125 - 0.0965) \times 10,000,000 \times 90/360}{1 + (0.10125 \times 90/360)}$$

$$= \$11,581.83 \text{ payable to the buyer of the FRA}$$

The above settlement formula is virtually standard in the business nowadays.

The price of each FRA contract is a function of the yield curve. It will be priced in the manner explained by reference to forward/forward interest rates earlier in this chapter.

18.4 | Interest rate futures

Chapter 15 on financial futures explained how futures contracts could be used to hedge exposures. They are traded on exchanges and are standardized. Such standardized features include a set contract size, a specific settlement date and a specific interest period. These standard features make them less than utterly appealing to corporations as hedging tools because they do not allow for specific exposures. However, they are widely used by banks and financial institutions for hedging their portfolios. These institutions are not generally concerned with matching, with 100 per cent exactitude, their underlying exposures.

As we have mentioned in earlier chapters, financial futures contracts are for standardized amounts and delivery dates. The number of instruments traded is limited and they are traded off-balance sheet. All futures contracts are registered with the clearing house, which becomes the counterparty to any deal, and there are obligatory initial and variation margin requirements for all futures contracts.

18.5 | Interest rate swaps

Interest rate swaps provide another means of eliminating interest rate exposure. Swaps were the topic of Chapter 14, where they were dealt with extensively. To spend more time on them here would be repetitious.

18.6 | Interest rate options

Interest rate options include caps, floors and collars. Their mechanism, theory, advantages and disadvantages are just like those of currency options, which were discussed in Chapters 16 and 17. Such instruments as caps, floors and collars were covered in Chapter 14 on swaps.

Swaps, futures and FRAs lock in an interest rate. The company is protected against any adverse movements of interest rates, but it cannot take advantage of favourable movements of interest rates.

Interest rate options overcome this. They provide the right but not the obligation to fix a rate of interest, on a notional loan or deposit, for an agreed amount, for a fixed term, on a specific forward date. The buyer of the option has the right but not the obligation to deal at the agreed rate. The buyer is protected against adverse rate movements but is able to take advantage of a favourable movement in interest rates. The seller guarantees an interest rate if the option is exercised. The seller receives a fee – the premium – for providing this guarantee. The factors that determine the price of interest rate options are similar to those that determine currency option prices. Remember Black and Scholes, volatilities and all that? If not, refer again to Chapters 16 and 17.

The most common type of interest rate option available to borrowers as a hedge against rising interest rates is the interest rate cap. Interest rate floors protect investors against falling interest rates.

An interest rate cap is an arrangement where, in return for a premium, the seller of the cap undertakes, over an agreed period, to compensate the buyer of the cap whenever a reference interest rate (for example, three- or six-month LIBOR) exceeds a pre-agreed maximum interest rate (the cap rate). In addition to having this protection whenever the reference rate exceeds the cap rate, the buyer of the cap can benefit when the reference rate is below the cap rate. This is because, at such times, the borrower is not locked into a fixed rate and can take advantage of the lower market rates.

If an investor purchases a floor, he or she will be compensated by the seller whenever, say, three-month LIBOR falls below a pre-agreed minimum rate. The buyer will exercise the option only if rates fall below the agreed level and is therefore able to enjoy the benefits if interest rates remain at levels above the agreed rate.

Interest settlement procedures for a cap or floor transaction are straightforward. A borrower is compensated by the seller of the cap whenever the reference rate exceeds the cap rate. A floor investor is compensated whenever the reference rate falls below the floor rate.

Just as we mentioned in Chapter 17 that there are zero-cost options, so there are similar interest rate instruments – collars. Effectively, the simultaneous purchase and sale of a cap and a floor is known as a 'collar'. To illustrate how collars work, assume that a treasurer wishes to protect his or her interest income by buying a floor struck at 10 per cent. But he or she does not wish to pay the full premium and therefore sells a cap struck at, for example, 13 per cent. In this case, the cost of buying the floor exactly matches the premium received from selling the cap. So we have a zero-cost collar. By undertaking these transactions, the company has an investment that pays a minimum of 10 per cent if the floating rate is at or below 10 per cent and a maximum of 13 per cent when the floating rate is at or above 13 per cent on the interest determination date. If the floating rate is between 10 per cent and 13 per cent, then the return equals the reference rate.

Dealing an interest rate collar is always cheaper than buying the straight interest rate cap or floor, since the buyer is forgoing some of the upside benefit if rates move favourably. This is exactly the same as the zero-cost currency option.

Another interest rate exposure instrument is worth mentioning: this is the option on an interest rate swap, often called a swaption. It allows a company to protect itself against unfavourable interest rate movements but at the same time to benefit from favourable interest rate movements by initiating a swap transaction during a specific period at a predetermined rate. Interest rate swaps are similar to caps and floors although less flexible – the rate of borrowing or investing in the future is fixed once a swaption is exercised. With a cap or floor transaction, the buyer would continue to enjoy any benefits of favourable movements in interest rates during the period of the hedge. Swaptions are cheaper than interest rate caps or floors. The swaption premium is a function of market volatility together with factors such as the period of the option, the period of the underlying swap and the rate on the underlying swap. Like currency options, a swaption may be European style, where the buyer may exercise the option only on a specific day, or American style, where the buyer can exercise the swaption at any time during the option period.

18.7 | Summary

- Interest rate risk is concerned with the sensitivity of profit, cash flows or valuation of the firm to changes in interest rates.

- Given this definition, the firm should analyse how its profits, cash outturns and value alter in response to movements in interest rate levels.

- If a firm's profits and cash flows are likely to fall when interest rates rise, the risk-averse firm will finance itself with fixed-rate funds. A speculative housebuilder, for example would fall into this category.

- For some companies, profits and cash flows move directly with interest rates. This is true of many financial institutions. Risk-averse firms that fall into this category might be more attracted to floating rate interest in terms of funding themselves.

- The term structure of interest rates can be thought of as a graph of interest rates on securities of a particular risk class at a particular time. Interest rate is plotted on the vertical axis and time to maturity on the horizontal.

- Note that the term structure of interest rates may be flat, upwards sloping or downwards sloping. There are various explanations of the term structure.

- Expectations theory suggests that anticipation of future interest rates by market players constitutes the key determinant of the term structure.

- According to the liquidity preference theory of the term structure of interest rates, market participants prefer to lend short rather than for longer periods. This merely reflects a view about risk. It means that liquidity premiums tend to be greater the longer the maturity of a bond, and this tends to suggest an upward-sloping term structure more often than not, all other things being equal.

- According to the preferred habitat theory of the term structure of interest rates, bond markets are segmented according to maturity. Within the various segments, a bargaining process takes place between lenders and borrowers and the piecing together of these mini-term structures for each segment by maturity gives us the overall shape of the term structure.

- According to the inflation premium theory of the term structure of interest rates, it is argued that investors are interested in real returns. This means that in order to get to, for example a twelve-month interest rate, investors look to the real return and adjust in line with expected inflation for the next twelve months. A similar kind of process would operate in respect of interest rates over a two-year period. Investors would look for a real return and adjust this in accordance with expected inflation over a twenty-four-month period. Thus the nominal interest rate for a particular period reflects the real return adjusted for expectations of inflation over that period.

- Note how equation (18.5) in the chapter works. It is underpinned by the notion that an investor can buy either long-term securities and hold them or buy short-term securities and continually reinvest in shorts at each maturity over the holding period. In equilibrium, the expected return for each holding period will tend to be the same whichever alternative or combination of alternatives is chosen. As a result of this, the return on a long-term bond will tend to equal the average of the current short-term rates and future short-term rates expected to prevail to maturity of the long-term bond. Equation (18.5) is important because it underpins the pricing of FRAs and forward/forward interest instruments.

- Note the definition of duration. It is the weighted average maturity of all payments on a security, coupons and principal, where the weights are the discounted present value of the payments. This means that the duration of a bond is shorter than the stated term to maturity on all securities except for zero-coupon bonds, where they are equal.

- Choices between fixed and floating rate funding should be based upon a careful analysis of the firm's interest rate exposure and a view of future rate movements given the level of risk aversion of the management.

- FRAs, interest rate futures and interest rate swaps may all be used to lock in interest rates for the firm.

- There are also interest rate options. These give the firm the right but not the obligation to fix a rate of interest on a notional loan or deposit, for an agreed amount, for a fixed term, on a specific forward date. Caps, collars and floors are all examples of interest rate options. As one would expect, they are priced according to the Black and Scholes model of option valuation.

18.8 | End of chapter questions

Question 1

(a) How does a company become exposed to interest rate risk?

(b) How does a bank become exposed to interest rate risk?

Question 2
How might a company attempt to reduce interest rate risk?

Question 3
How might a bank attempt to reduce interest rate risk?

19 Financial engineering

The term 'financial engineering' sounds complicated. Engineers are generally good at understanding the complexities of finance – they are numerate and logical, which financial management requires. But most finance people make poor engineers. Perhaps this is why financial engineering sounds esoteric. But, as Smithson (1987) points out, financial engineering is 'usually nothing more difficult than using the box of financial LEGOs'. What he means is that the essence of financial engineering involves simple building blocks which can be bolted together to make a complex financial construction. And Smithson also points out that using an approach that derives from simple financial ideas to analyse complex financial instruments has a timelessness about it. The techniques of financial engineering will not get out of date even though many of the products built by the financial engineer may. Even though banks introduce innovative instruments, all that it is necessary to do to understand them is to break them down from their complicated financial construction into simple Lego components. Using this methodology, the analyst cannot get out of date and he or she does not have to learn new tricks – the analyst simply disaggregates the complicated new financial edifices into simple old ones. So what are the simple tools necessary to analyse the most complex financial instrument? The answer is easy – merely forwards and options and an idea of the risk profile which they create. Let us see whether we can make financial engineering easy then. We begin by looking at forwards.

19.1 Forward contracts

Eliminating a foreign exchange receivable exposure can be achieved, using on-balance sheet methods, by borrowing in the foreign currency concerned. Chapter 13 suggested various ways of doing this. Or a forward contract could be used – this involves off-balance sheet cover.

To analyse the effect of a forward contract, the resulting payoff from buying the forward may be superimposed upon the original risk profile. So, let us first of all look at the original risk profile without forward cover. If the actual exchange rate movement is adverse, the inherent risk will lead to a decline in profit, cash flow and hence the value of the firm. But with forward cover, this decline is exactly offset by the profit on the forward contract. Hence, from the risk profile illustrated in Figure 19.1

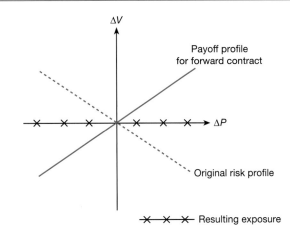

Figure 19.1 Payoff profile for a forward contract.

it can be seen that the forward contract provides the perfect hedge. In the figure, ΔV refers to the resulting change in the value of the firm and ΔP measures the difference between the actual price and the expected price.

As we know from earlier chapters, the forward contract is entered into and is subsequently closed out and settled at its maturity. A futures contract is really very similar. Yes, there is an initial margin requirement and top-up, or variation, margins may be called for during the course of the contract's life as it is marked to market daily. It is this feature that led Black (1976) to liken a futures contract to 'a series of forward contracts. Each day, yesterday's contract is settled, and today's contract is written.' Certainly, a futures contract is really just like a sequence of forwards. The forward written on day 1 is settled on day 2 and is replaced, in essence, by a new forward reflecting day 2 expectations. The new contract is itself settled on day 3 and replaced, and so on until the day the contract ends at its ultimate maturity.

Just as a futures contract is very similar to a forward, so is a swap. Each is priced off interest rate differentials and, at least in theory, what can be achieved by a swap can be achieved by a forward. There may be occasions when one is more appropriate than the other, but essentially futures, forwards and swaps are very close relatives – not quite identical, but not far off. Admittedly, on the question of default risk, there are differences – the futures contract has the clearing house guaranteeing performance whereas the swap involves colateralization of one loan against the other rather in the manner that the forward contract does. But the point is that the essential mechanics of futures, forwards and swaps are the same and the idea behind covering using forwards which was summarized in Figure 19.1 works similarly for futures and swaps. For forwards, swaps and futures contracts, the original risk profile is exactly offset by the payoff profile of the contract assumed. In short, the rationale of Figure 19.1 is equally applicable to futures and swaps as it is to forwards.

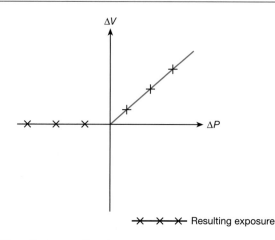

Figure 19.2 Payoff profile for a call option.

19.2 | Option contracts

Option contracts are different. An option gives its owner the right, but not the obligation, to purchase or sell an asset. A generalized model of the payoff profile for an option is provided in Figure 19.2. Here, as in Figure 19.1, the financial price, P, might be an interest rate, a foreign exchange rate, a commodity price or the price of another financial asset (e.g. a share) – in short, whatever it is that the option relates to. The owner of the contract illustrated has the right to purchase the asset at a price agreed upon today. So, if P rises, the value of the option goes up. But the option contract holder is not obligated to purchase the asset if P goes down – so the value of the option remains unchanged, at zero, if P declines.

The option whose payoff profile is illustrated in Figure 19.2 and repeated in case (i) of Figure 19.3 is referred to as a call option; the option holder has bought the right to buy the asset at a specified price – the exercise, or strike, price. The payoff profile for the party selling the call option, known as the call writer, is shown in case (ii) of Figure 19.3. In contrast to the buyer of the call option, the writer of the call option has the obligation to perform. Thus, if the owner of the option decides to exercise his or her option, the seller of the option is required to sell the asset. Note that the buyer of a call has limited downside – the premium, which in any case is a sunk cost – but unlimited upside. The payoff profile for the unhedged option writer is exactly opposite. He or she has limited upside – the receipt of the premium – and unlimited downside risk.

There are also options to sell an asset at a specified price – this is the put option. The payoff to the buyer of a put is shown in case (iii) of Figure 19.3 and the payoff for the writer of the put is shown in case (iv). The points referred to in the previous paragraph about unlimited upside and downside continue to apply in the case of the put option.

All too often, one encounters confusion about the terminology used in option markets and in ways of achieving cover. Always remember that there is more than one

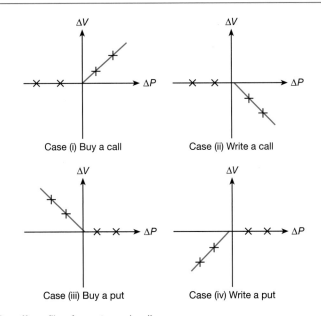

Figure 19.3 Payoff profiles for puts and calls.

way of skinning a cat (with apologies to cat lovers). Back to terminology first. The reader must remember that, for a dollar/sterling option, a call on dollars is equivalent to a put on sterling. And the same kind of idea applies to interest rates and bond prices. Remember too that when interest rates go up, bond prices go down. The problem about terminology here is best explained by way of an example. Suppose that a firm carries an interest rate exposure – a rise in interest rates adversely affects profit and value. As illustrated in case (i) of Figure 19.4, this downside risk might be eliminated by buying a call on the interest rate – commonly termed an interest rate 'cap'. In the figure, Δi represents a change in the interest rate and ΔV represents a change in the value of the firm. The same hedge effect could be achieved by buying a put on bonds. Remember that bond prices move in the opposite direction to interest rates. Case (ii) of Figure 19.4 (overleaf) illustrates the point. In these diagrams ΔP_{bond} represents a change in the bond price.

In the payoff profiles for options considered so far, we have not taken account of the premium paid by the buyer to the seller. In Figure 19.5 (overleaf) we remedy this. Case (i) in the figure shows the payoff profile for an at-the-money call option with the premium taken into account. In other words, the strike price is at the prevailing expected price as implied by the market. If the risk profile of this option is superimposed upon the underlying exposure, we obtain case (ii) in Figure 19.5. Note the shape of this new resulting exposure – this is obtained by merely combining the original exposure with the option inclusive of the premium. The premium for a call option falls as the strike price increases relative to the prevailing price of the asset. An option buyer seeking to lower the premium cost may do so by using an out-of-the-money option. As case (iv) of Figure 19.5 indicates, the buyer will incur larger potential losses. This simply reflects the fact that the buyer has paid a lower

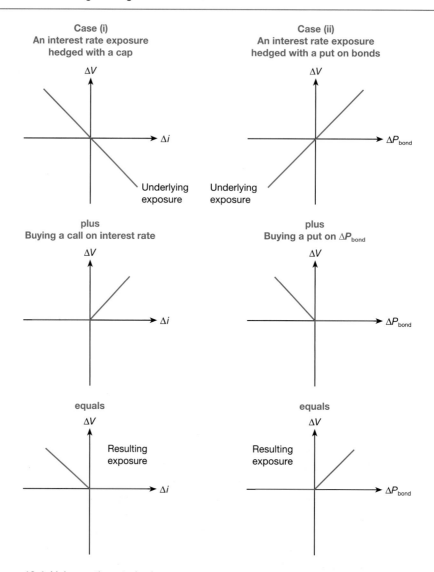

Figure 19.4 Using options to hedge exposures.

premium – has bought less insurance. The diagrammatic representation in case (iii) of Figure 19.5 shows the out-of-the-money option with the premium cost built in and case (iv) of the figure shows the underlying exposure and how the resulting exposure appears after allowing for the option's effects. The out-of-the-money option gives less downside protection, but the premium is significantly less. In other words, the option buyer can alter the payoff profile simply by changing the strike price; this will alter the premium cost too.

Clearly, options have a payoff profile which differs significantly from forwards, futures or swaps. However, an option's payoff profile may be replicated by a combination of forwards and risk-free securities. This point was tellingly made by Black

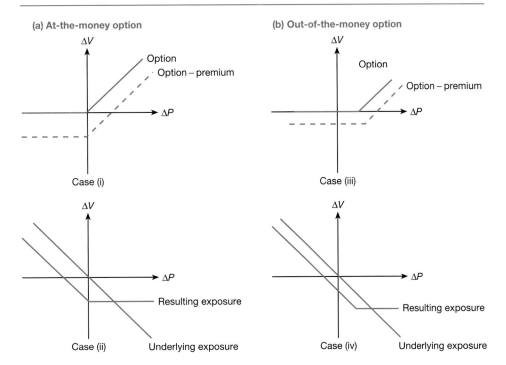

Figure 19.5 Hedging with an at-the-money call option and an out-of-the-money call option.

and Scholes (1973); their argument may be summarized by reference to Figure 19.2, which describes the payoff profile for a call option. For increases with financial price P, the payoff profile for the option is that of a forward contract. For decreases in P, the value of the option is constant – this part of the payoff profile for the option is akin to a riskless security such as a treasury bill. Black and Scholes go on to demonstrate that a call option could be replicated by a continuously adjusting portfolio of two securities – forward contracts on the underlying asset and riskless securities. As the financial price P rises, the call option equivalent portfolio contains an increasing proportion of forward contracts; it contains a decreasing proportion when P falls. Arbitrage activity should ensure that the value of the portfolio is close to the market price of the exchange-traded option. Effectively, then, the value of a call option is determined by the value of its option equivalent portfolio of forwards and riskless securities.

From this, it should be evident that options do have more in common with the other instruments than was immediately apparent. As discussed earlier, futures are effectively nothing more than portfolios of forward contracts. And options are akin to portfolios of forward contracts and risk-free securities.

This is further borne out when we consider ways in which options may be combined. Take a portfolio constructed by buying a call and selling a put with a common strike price. As case (i) in Figure 19.6 (overleaf) shows, the resulting portfolio – long a call, short a put – has a payoff profile equivalent (assuming premiums are disregarded) to that of buying a forward contract on the asset. And case (ii) of Figure 19.6

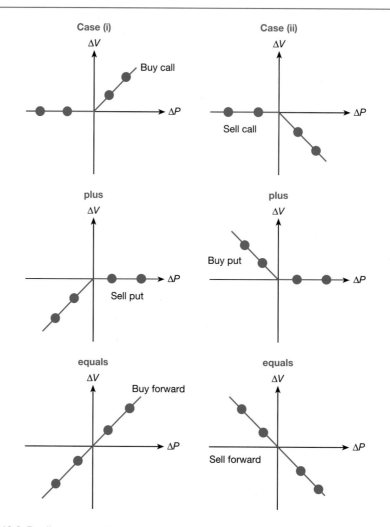

Figure 19.6 Dealing puts and calls can be like forwards.

shows that a portfolio created by selling a call and buying a put – that is, short a call, long a put – is equivalent to selling a forward contract.

The relationship summarized by Figure 19.6 is known more formally as the 'put–call parity' of the option parity theorem. According to this theorem, buying a European call and selling a European put is equivalent to being long forward. In other words:

$$\text{Buy call} + \text{Sell put} = \text{Long forward}$$

If the foreign currency appreciates relative to the strike price, it is profitable to exercise the call. By contrast, if the foreign currency depreciates relative to the exercise price, the buyer of the put exercises the option, forcing the seller of the put to buy in the foreign currency at the strike price. In effect, then, the simultaneous purchase of a call and sale of a put at the same exercise price is similar to the purchase of a forward contract at that exercise price. Note that this equivalence is only perfect for European options, which, it will be recalled, may only be exercised at maturity – not before. This equivalence does not hold for American options, which may be exercised before maturity and can consequently result in a position in the foreign currency prior to the maturity of the forward contract.

Going back to the option parity equation, it can be shown, by rearranging the terms, that:

$$\text{Buy call} + \text{Short forward} = \text{Buy put}$$

Remember that, algebraically, minus sell put would equal plus buy put. And minus long forward equals plus short forward.

As Smithson (1987) states, 'we discovered two LEGO-like relations between options and the other three instruments: (1) Options can be replicated by snapping together a forward, futures, or swap contract together with a position in risk-free securities; (2) Calls and puts can be snapped together to become forwards.'

Caps and floors are, of course, nothing but fancy names for options. The collar, sometimes called the zero-cost option or cylinder, is simply manufactured by snapping together a put and a call at different strike prices such that the premium on the put and the premium on the call equal each other. Banks are perpetually introducing new financially engineered products to corporations – their understanding, and indeed their replication, is not difficult with the tools summarized in this chapter. To quote Smithson again, 'financial engineering is hard. Building innovative financial products with LEGOs is not'.

19.3 | Some financial instruments

In the past, commercial banks have made a lot of money from slightly differentiated financial products which were made up from the simple snapping together of financial LEGOs. Different banks made it difficult for treasurers immediately to identify how one bank's product differed from another's by calling the same instrument different names. Salomon's 'range forward' is almost exactly the same as Citibank's 'cylinder option'.

Although their financial instruments are much less profitable now than heretofore, banks continue to produce their financially engineered products to meet the perceived needs of corporate customers. The corporate treasurer, in turn, tries to analyse the product in terms of its basic LEGOs in order to establish a fair price for the engineered product. We consider some of these products in turn.

Non-deliverable forward (NDF)

A non-deliverable forward is a foreign exchange forward outright where, instead of each party delivering the full amount of currency at settlement, there is a single net cash payment to reflect the change in value between the forward rate transacted and the spot rate two working days before settlement.

Imagine that one party wished to transact a forward outright but one of the currencies was not fully convertible or had no forward market. It is not possible for that currency to be delivered to, or by, a non-resident of that country. The need to deal an outright forward might arise because of the required precaution of a hedge for a commercial transaction or because of the apparent attractiveness of a speculation in that currency.

In the case of non-convertibility, normal outright forwards are either not permitted or highly government-regulated. If the purpose of the deal were speculation, the NDF would be sufficient. It provides a cash settlement yielding the same economic effect as if a normal forward outright had been dealt and then closed out two days before maturity by an offsetting spot deal. If the purpose of the deal were to hedge a commercial transaction, the same economic effect as a normal outright forward may be achieved by first transacting and settling the NDF, and buying or selling the non-convertible currency for spot value at the same time as the NDF is settled.

An NDF also has the effect of reducing counterparty risk, as the risk is limited to the settlement amount and does not involve the usual settlement risk on the whole nominal amount of the deal. Consequently, the rationale for NDFs is not limited just to non-convertible currencies.

Any contract for differences (CFD) resembles the NDF in that it comprises any transaction which is cash settled against a reference rate, rather than delivered in full. In other words, a net cash payment is made from one party to the other to reflect the difference between a price or rate agreed at the time of transaction and a reference price or rate determined later, or between two such reference prices or rates.

Banks are able to hedge net NDF positions that they have entered into either via their positions with their appropriate associated overseas bank, or by laying off their net exposure to another bank, or by undertaking money market hedges – see section 13.3.

Barrier options: knock-out option and knock-in option

A barrier option is a class of options (including knock-out and knock-in options) which are either cancelled or activated if the underlying price reaches a predetermined barrier or trigger level. A knock-out option is an option which is cancelled if the trigger level is reached. A knock-in option is an option which is activated if the trigger level is reached.

Barrier options are straightforward European options until, or from, the time the underlying reaches the trigger level. With a knock-out option, the option exists in the usual way (and either it is exercised at expiry or it expires worthless, depending upon the underlying price at that time) unless the underlying price reaches an agreed trigger level before then. If it does, the option is immediately cancelled.

With a knock-in option, the option cannot be exercised at expiry, regardless of the underlying rate at that time, unless an agreed trigger level has been reached at some time during the life of the option. If the trigger level has been reached, the option becomes a standard European option from that time onwards.

Due to these cancelling or activating features, barrier options are usually cheaper than ordinary options. This is because there are some situations under which a normal option would be exercised, but with a knock-in or knock-out option, exercise is not possible in these circumstances. There is less probability of the seller of the option paying out on the option; hence the lower value attaching to it. Consequently, barrier options can provide a hedge at a lower cost than a straightforward option, while still providing adequate protection. For example, the trigger level may be set by the buyer so that, if the trigger point is reached, the purchaser is then happy not to be protected, because the underlying provides a better bet.

Also, because of the lower premium, barrier options provide a more leveraged speculative instrument than a straightforward call or put. If the underlying moves as anticipated, the buyer achieves the same profit for lower initial cost.

Barrier options have an extensive jargon associated with them. They are also known as trigger options, exploding options and extinguishing options – four terms for the same instrument. The trigger level in a knock-out option is also known as an outstrike. The trigger level in a knock-in option is also known as an instrike.

An up-and-in option and a down-and-in option are knock-in options where the trigger is respectively higher than, or lower than, the underlying rate at the inception of the option. An up-and-out option and a down-and-out option are knock-out options where the trigger is respectively higher than, or lower than, the underlying rate at the birth of the option.

A reverse knock-out option (or kick-out option) and a reverse knock-in option (or kick-in option) are types of knock-out and knock-in option, where the trigger level is such that, at the point of its being triggered, the option would be in-the-money rather than out-of-the-money.

A double knock-out option and a double knock-in option refer to a knock-out option and a knock-in option with two trigger levels – one above and one below the underlying rate at the start – either of which will trigger the cancellation or activation of the option.

A path-dependent option is a general term for options such as barrier options, American options and average options, where the decision or ability to exercise them, and hence their value, depends not only on the underlying price at expiry, but also on the path that the price of the underlying has taken during the life of the option. Finally, the term exotic option refers to any complex option, including barrier options.

The financial engineering of barrier options basically derives from combining puts and calls at difference strike prices with forwards. Clearly, the precise nature of the engineering will vary depending on the nature of the barrier option involved.

The cylinder or zero-cost option

First of all, we consider the zero-cost option – sometimes called a cylinder option. On interest rates, the term 'collar' is used. Cylinders offer cover at reduced cost in return for the customer forgoing part of the profit potential if rates move favourably.

A cylinder enables the corporate treasurer to reduce the premium payable on the purchase of an option by simultaneously writing a second option to the bank for the same premium amount and tenor but at a different strike price. The treasurer selects the degree of risk to be taken, or the profit potential to be forgone, by choosing the strike prices of the two options that form the ceiling and the floor of the cylinder. By so doing, the treasurer can eliminate the premium altogether.

As an example, assume that a UK company is due to receive dollars from export sales in three months' time. The spot rate is $1.85, although the treasurer had budgeted for sales at $1.90. The premium to buy a normal currency option with a strike price of $1.90, matching the budget rate, is 1 per cent of the transaction amount. This is a low premium already, as the option is five cents 'out of the money' – that is, less favourable than the current spot. The treasurer still considers the hedge expensive and decides to negotiate a cylinder under which:

■ the company buys an out-of-the-money option to sell (put) dollars at $1.90;

■ the company simultaneously writes an out-of-the-money option to the bank, for the bank to buy (call) the same amount of dollars at a strike price such that the net premium the treasurer pays comes out at zero (or whatever amount the treasurer wants).

The range forward

Next, let us look briefly at the range forward. Like a zero-cost option, no up-front premium is payable. The contract specifies the top and bottom of a range of exchange rates. Within this range, the hedger can benefit from positive movements while having a limit to the downside. If, when the contract ends, the exchange rate falls within the range, the contract to buy or sell is effected at the spot exchange rate.

Getting into the range forward, the hedger chooses one of the two ends of the range plus the expiry date of the contract. It is left to the bank to choose the other end of the range, depending on the level of put and call premiums. Part of the calculation will include a small spread.

For example, assume that a US corporate needs to purchase sterling three months forward. The spot rate is $1.8200 to the pound and the three-month forward rate is $1.8085. The company is worried that rates may go against it, and it is looking for downside cover. The bank offering the range forward allows the company to pick the dollar rate above which it cannot afford to go. So one end of the range is fixed at $1.8700 to the pound. The bank decides it can offer $1.7520 at the other end. It could work the other way round, with the company setting the rate on the upside and the bank working out the downside. Either way, if in three months' time the exchange rate is between the two rates, the hedger deals spot. If the rates push outside the range agreed upon, the hedger deals at the top or bottom rate.

Obviously, the range forward, like the cylinder, is engineered via a put and call contract at differing strike premiums.

The participating forward contract

Next we consider the participating forward contract. Like the range forward, the participating forward requires no up-front payment. The contract represents a commitment to buy or sell foreign currency above an agreed floor exchange rate without setting any limit on potential movements in the buyer's favour. In the event of a positive movement, the buyer pays for the downside protection by taking less than 100 per cent of the favourable currency move.

The instrument is appropriate to hedgers who think their currency exposure has positive potential but who would like to buy downside protection. In volatile markets, the instrument comes into its own: participation in large movements, even if not 100 per cent, can render handsome returns. The participating forward is engineered via the currency option. The premium forgone by the bank is simply made good by its participation in resulting profits.

The break forward or fox (forward with optional exit)

The break forward, or fox, is a forward foreign exchange contract which can be unwound at a predetermined rate. It therefore combines many of the features of the conventional forward contract and the currency option. Like conventional forwards, break forwards allow the buyer, usually a corporate customer, to hedge against adverse exchange rate movements by locking in a fixed rate. Unlike conventional forwards, the customer can benefit from favourable exchange rate movements by breaking the deal at any time with only limited loss and then dealing at the more favourable spot or forward rate. As with currency options, the customer may take advantage of upside potential. But unlike currency options, the break forward does not require the payment of an up-front premium – this is rolled forward to settlement. A further advantage is that the tax treatment is more favourable than for currency options.

Under the break forward, the customer chooses the fixed rate, below which full downside protection is received, by agreeing to a loading – in effect the option premium of, say, 2 per cent – on the normal outright forward rate. The bank then calculates the rate at which the forward deal can be unwound – the break rate. Alternatively, the customer can nominate the break rate and the bank then calculates the fixed rate. Once entered into, the customer can unwind the break forward at any time if the current spot or forward rate looks better. In addition, if the funds being hedged are to be paid or received early, they can be bought/sold spot and the break forward then unwound at the break rate or the prevailing spot rate, whichever is more advantageous to the customer.

The break forward or fox is engineered through an American option with the premium compounded and taken by the bank in ultimate settlement.

The forward spread agreement (FSA)

Engineered via the forward rate agreement (FRA), but closer in function to the forward/forward currency swap, the FSA allows two counterparties to come to an agreement on the spread or interest rate differential between two currencies. Unlike the forward/forward currency swap, or back-to-back FRAs, the FSA involves no currency risk.

A banker funding, for example, a yen asset with a dollar liability, might want to insure against a widening of the interest rate differential in three-month deposits in the respective currencies. If the interest rate on the dollar liability rises, or the rate on the yen asset falls, opening the spread, the banker suffers. With an FSA, one contract covers exposure in two currencies where it would previously have required two FRAs, each FRA guaranteeing a forward rate in either the yen or dollar deposit. Another advantage is that bankers covering a yen exposure do not have to worry about illiquidity in the non-dollar FRA market. FSAs are dual currency instruments. While one side of the deal must be in US dollars, the other can, in principle, be for any other currency.

19.4 | Summary

- Financial engineering involves the coupling of two or more simple financial instruments to create a more complex one.

- Financial engineering involves simple building blocks which can be bolted together to create complex financial constructions.

- Even though banks may introduce innovative, complex financial instruments, they can easily be analysed by breaking them down into their more simple components. The analyst simply disaggregates the complicated new financial edifice into the simple old ones.

- The simple tools that are necessary to analyse the most complex financial instruments merely involve forwards and options. It is these that are bolted together to create the complex instrument.

- The text shows how this process can be used to produce some of the banker's most complicated new financial instruments to a simple combination. And, of course, their pricing should reflect the simple underlying components that make up the complex new product.

19.5 | End of chapter questions

Question 1
Describe the essentials of financial engineering.

Question 2
Some companies have come unstuck dealing financially engineered instruments. Why do you suppose this is?

Question 3
Banks pay big salaries to financial engineers. What traits do the financial engineers need to succeed?

Test bank 3

Exercises

1. Your company has made a number of long-term borrowings in various foreign currencies over the past decade. Your new chairman questions the policy of foreign currency borrowing. Suggest ways in which such a policy might be justified *ex ante* and *ex post*.

   (Association of Corporate Treasurers: Part II, September 1988, Paper in Currency Management)

2. A substantial part of Prestige Cars Ltd's sales are to North America where it operates through a wholly owned subsidiary. Its principal competitors are German.

   It has been reported widely that Prestige Cars Ltd hedges its US$ exposure, using the foreign exchange markets, by covering future expected US$ sales revenue. In March 1988 its 1987 results were announced showing a reduction in profit from the previous year. This reduction was attributed partly to the decline in the sterling value of the US dollar. On this announcement Prestige Cars Ltd's share price fell by about 5 per cent, relative to the market.

   (a) How would you expect hedging of future sales revenue to be implemented?
   (b) Given that sales revenue has been hedged, why are current earnings affected by the £/$ exchange rate?
   (c) What impact would you expect the covering of future sales revenue to have on Prestige Cars Ltd's share price?

   (Association of Corporate Treasurers: Part II, September 1988, Paper in Currency Management)

3. A UK-based multinational company has sold an overseas chemical plant, the price for the plant being determined by an earn-out agreement. The amount of the receipt under the agreement is likely to be $10m, with a maximum of $12m. The receipt is expected in eleven months' time; the exact amount will be known in eight months' time.

   A policy decision has been taken that the expected receipt should be fully covered.

   (a) What are the alternatives available to cover the expected receipt?
   (b) What factors could influence your choice between these alternatives?

   (Association of Corporate Treasurers: Part II, September 1989, Paper in Currency Management)

4. You are Group Treasurer of Sun and Sand plc, a UK package tour operator offering holidays in many parts of the world but specializing in Morocco, Spain and the United States. Sun and Sand is one of the major operators in the market, which is very price competitive. All competitors operate on margins less than 5 per cent.

The group contracts to purchase air travel and hotel accommodation up to one year ahead, air travel being ultimately invoiced in US$ and hotel accommodation being invoiced in the relevant local currency. Revenue is exclusively in sterling.

The basis of competition in the industry is price which must be set one year ahead, for inclusion in the brochures. The impact of one competitor being slightly out of line on price produces a disproportionate change in that competitor's market share.

(a) If the biggest competitor decides not to hedge any of its exposures, what risks does this create for Sun and Sand plc?

(b) How would you manage these risks?

(Association of Corporate Treasurers Part II, September 1991, Paper in Currency Management)

▌ Multiple choice questions

There is one right answer only to each question.

1. Which of the following is the most logical policy for a US firm that will be receiving Swiss francs in the future and desires to avoid exchange rate risk assuming the firm has no offsetting position in Swiss francs?

    (a) Buy a call option on Swiss francs.
    (b) Sell a futures contract on Swiss francs.
    (c) Enter into a forward contract to buy Swiss francs.
    (d) Buy Swiss francs now and put them on deposit to meet the payment when it falls due.

2. If one anticipates that the pound sterling is going to appreciate against the US dollar, one might speculate by _____ pound call options or _____ pound put options.

    (a) buying; selling
    (b) buying; buying
    (c) selling; selling
    (d) selling; buying

3. You purchase a put option on Swiss francs for a premium of 2 cents with an exercise price of $0.61. The option will not be exercised until the expiration date, if then. Should the spot rate on the expiration date be $0.58, your net profit or loss per unit is likely to be:

    (a) 3¢ loss;
    (b) 1¢ loss;
    (c) 2¢ loss;
    (d) 2¢ profit;
    (e) none of the above.

4. A US firm is bidding for a contract required by the Swiss government. The firm will not know until three months from now, whether the bid is accepted. The firm will need Swiss francs to cover expenses but will be paid by the Swiss government in dollars if it

is awarded the contract. The US firm can best insulate itself against exchange rate exposure by:

(a)   selling Swiss franc futures;
(b)   buying Swiss franc futures;
(c)   buying Swiss franc put options;
(d)   buying Swiss franc call options.

5.   A US firm has CHF10 million receivables due in sixty days. The firm's management is certain that the Swiss franc will depreciate substantially over this period. Assuming the firm's expectation turns out to be correct, it will make the greatest gain by:

(a)   selling Swiss francs forward;
(b)   buying Swiss franc put options;
(c)   buying Swiss franc call options;
(d)   buying Swiss francs forward;
(e)   doing nothing.

6.   Netting achieves all but one of the following:

(a)   Foreign exchange movements between subsidiaries are reduced;
(b)   Transactions costs are lowered;
(c)   Currency conversion costs are reduced;
(d)   Transaction exposure is reduced.

7.   Which of the following statements is true about designing a good reporting system on foreign exchange exposure?

(a)   Central control with virtually no input from the local level is essential;
(b)   Reports should be generated by currency as well as by subsidiary;
(c)   Reports should concentrate on translation exposure because this will affect earnings per share which is the key to corporate valuation;
(d)   Routine reports should concentrate upon economic exposure, rather than translation or transaction exposure, because this represents the present value of future cash flows which is the key to corporate valuation.

8.   On a Tuesday in January an operator contacts his financial futures broker. He wishes to speculate on the £/$ exchange rate. He sells seven March Sterling contracts at $1.7200. On the Thursday of that week he buys seven March Sterling contracts at 1.7100. Given that the tick size is 0.01 cent and the value of the tick is $2.50, what is the net of commission gain or loss achieved by the operator? Commission on the round trip is $120 per contract. In your answer ignore all aspects of interest (including interest on margin) and opportunity cost.

(a) $230 profit.
(b) $1,610 profit.
(c) $1,750 profit.
(d)   We cannot say because we are not told the contract size.
(e)   None of the above is correct.

9. Which of the following is true of foreign exchange markets?

    (a) The futures market is mainly used by speculators while the forward market is mainly used for hedging.
    (b) The futures market is mainly used by hedgers while the forward market is mainly used for speculating.
    (c) The futures market and the forward market are mainly used for speculating.
    (d) The futures market and the forward market are mainly used for hedging.

10. Which of the following is not a logical tactic for a US firm that will have to pay for a machine in euros in the future and desires to avoid exchange rate risk assuming the firm has no offsetting position in euros?

    (a) Buy a call option on euros.
    (b) Enter into a forward contract to buy euros.
    (c) Sell a futures contract on euros.
    (d) Buy euros now and put them on deposit to meet the payment when it falls due.
    (e) None is illogical; (a), (b), (c) and (d) are all logical.

Part E

International capital budgeting

Analysing capital investment decisions involves comparing cash inflows with cash outflows from a project. Investment appraisal systems are frequently collectively termed capital budgeting, and this focuses upon expected incremental cash flows associated with a project. The specification of these flows for the overseas project creates the usual difficulties found in a domestic capital project, but international project analysis is much more complex. Although the basic pattern follows the same model as that suggested by corporate financial theory, the multinational firm must consider factors peculiar to international operations. These differences are very considerable and are focused upon in this section.

20 The internationalization process

Multinational finance is really a financial subset of international business strategy – but it is a critically important one. Just as domestic financial management should be set within the context of domestic corporate strategy, cross-frontier financial management should be looked upon as a function within international business. Given this background, this chapter attempts to summarize views on the rationale of international corporate expansion.

20.1 | Foreign direct investment

Foreign direct investment (FDI) is a term used to denote the acquisition abroad of physical assets, such as plant and equipment, with operational control ultimately residing with the parent company in the home country. It may take a number of different forms including:

- the establishment of a new enterprise in an overseas country – either as a branch or as a subsidiary;

- the expansion of an existing overseas branch or subsidiary;

- the acquisition of an overseas business enterprise or its assets.

It contrasts with foreign portfolio investment where a stake is taken in an overseas business without operational control, but with the view to acquiring an investment income stream through dividends, capital gains or, maybe, through enhanced business links. Without making foreign direct investment commitments, firms may engage in international business via exporting and importing, licensing, sale of technology, foreign management contracts, selling turnkey projects or undertaking portfolio investment.

The world economy is internationalizing. Between 1980 and 1991, according to the International Monetary Fund (1992), annual world exports doubled to a total value of $3,500bn. Foreign direct investment by the twelve leading OECD countries quadrupled over the ten years to 1990, reaching $193.55bn – see OECD (1992). Since then, figures have more than doubled. The driving forces impelling this rapidly growing internationalization process are varied and often disputed.

United Nations research (1993) has put the number of multinational corporations as high as 35,000 with control over 170,000 affiliate companies. It was estimated that the largest 100 multinationals, excluding those in banking and finance, accounted for over $3,000bn of worldwide assets in 1990 of which $1,200bn was outside the home country of the multinational concerned. The former total of assets probably represents some 16 per cent of worldwide, private non-residential, non-banking and financial assets with only 6 per cent being outside of the 100 largest multinationals' home country. This may be significant but it hardly represents massive domination by any standards.

Internationalization, in the form of FDI, began in the late nineteenth century. The Victorian and Edwardian eras saw the creation of many of the great vertically integrated multinationals that we would recognize today – colonial plantation companies such as Lever Brothers (now Unilever) investing in West African vegetable oil plantations, Cadbury's in cocoa, Dunlop in rubber. The United Kingdom, as the great imperial power of the time, dominated world international business, with over 45 per cent of the world's total stock of FDI in 1914. Following the Second World War, the FDI league leadership passed to the USA, with US companies such as General Motors, IBM and ITT developing manufacturing bases around the world. By 1960, the United States accounted for over 48 per cent of world FDI. Since then, we have witnessed the re-emergence of European multinationals; however, the most significant entrant in the international scene has been Japan. In 1960, Japanese firms accounted for less than 1 per cent of the world's accumulated FDI. By 1989, the Japanese share was over 12 per cent, against 29.5 per cent for the United States and 15.2 per cent for the United Kingdom.

A significant component of FDI in the 1990s was in terms of flows to developing countries with Western European countries and North America the main recipients. But more recent trends have emerged. Whereas in the late 1980s investment flows to developing countries had been 15–18 per cent of the total recorded, in the middle 1990s investment flowing to developing countries surged to 30–40 per cent. The majority of FDI went to the countries of the Asia–Pacific region. This surge continued beyond 1996, the last year in Figure 20.1 showing FDI flows by recipient areas. The effect of this on the Asian economic crisis of 1997 is interesting. It is probably the case that the massive inflows into South East Asia created an inflation which caused significant problems for so many host countries' exchange rate systems which were tied to the US dollar rather than being freely floating. Had purchasing power parity been allowed to rule, a major portion of the Asian crisis might well have been averted. Since the turn of the century up to 2003, FDI flows have abated. Also, since then, China has become one of the main country recipients of FDI.

Five home countries account for the bulk of outward investment. The United States still had the largest involvement, followed at a distance by the United Kingdom and Japan, which, in turn, were followed by Germany and France. Corporations from the Netherlands, Switzerland and Sweden had a disproportionate percentage of their assets held abroad. Actual stocks of FDI (as opposed to flows) are summarized in the appendices to this chapter.

But the great puzzle about FDI remains. Why do companies do it? As opposed to going to the trouble, risk and expense of setting up and managing manufacturing

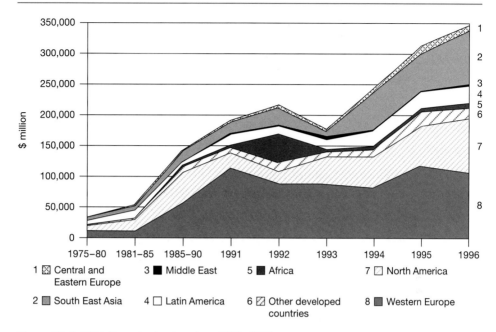

1 ⊠ Central and   3 ■ Middle East   5 ■ Africa   7 □ North America
  Eastern Europe

2 ▨ South East Asia   4 □ Latin America   6 ▨ Other developed   8 ■ Western Europe
                                                countries

Figure 20.1 FDI inflows by host region, 1975–1996.

Source: World Investment Report, 1997.

operations in a foreign country, why not export? If transport costs are prohibitive, why not license? Or sell technology and/or brands to an overseas firm which knows the territory well, and can manage and adapt to local conditions?

Any theory of FDI must, as Root (1978) observes, address the following key questions:

■ Why do firms move abroad as direct investors?

■ How can direct-investing overseas firms compete successfully with local firms in the host country, given the disadvantage of operating in an unfamiliar foreign territory?

■ Why do firms choose to enter a foreign country via FDI instead of exporting or licensing?

Before we move on to look at theories of the evolution of international business, we focus upon the sequential nature of the development of corporate international involvement.

20.2 | The sequential process

The dynamic view of corporate internationalization as involving a sequential process was identified by Johanson and Vahlne (1977) and Luostarinen (1977). It normally moves through exporting to the setting up of a foreign sales subsidiary,

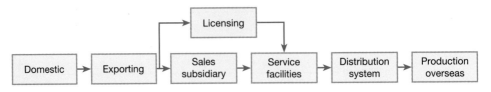

Figure 20.2 Typical foreign expansion sequence.

to licensing agreements and similar contracts before actual investment in foreign production facilities takes place. This evolutionary approach may act as a risk-minimizing process given the relative uncertainty associated with operating in a foreign environment. By internationalizing in stages, the firm gradually moves from a relatively low risk, but easily reversible export-oriented policy, to a higher risk, but less reversible strategy involving production in other countries; at the same time, the profit payoff should multiply. The typical sequence of overseas expansion is depicted in Figure 20.2.

The firm with international ambitions typically makes its initial moves in this direction by exporting to a foreign market. Exporting has significant advantages over more fully fledged involvement. Capital requirements are minimal, risk is low, the decision is easily reversed and profits are immediate. Exporting provides a steep learning curve effect about the ways and business culture of the foreign country concerned. This is especially so in the areas of supply and demand conditions, competition, channels of distribution, payment conventions and the methods of foreign financial institutions. Building on export success, the firm may expand its marketing organization abroad. It may switch from using export agents and similar intermediaries to dealing direct with foreign agents and distributors. As knowledge is built through increased communication with customers, the firm may establish its own sales subsidiary and service facilities. The culmination of this marketing expansion is often control of its own foreign distribution system.

As Figure 20.2 indicates, another route towards foreign expansion involves licensing as opposed to the overseas sales subsidiary. Licensing involves a local firm in the manufacture of another company's products in return for royalties and/or other forms of payment. For the home-based company, the main advantage of licensing is the minimal investment required. However, the corresponding cash flow may also be relatively low. There are sometimes problems in maintaining quality standards and it may be difficult to control exports by a foreign licensee. Indeed, a licensing agreement may create a competitor in some markets, with a resultant loss of future revenues to the licensing firm. Despite the risks, it appears very frequently that licensing, on its own, is the preferred method of penetrating foreign markets.

Some firms follow a policy of selling technology for equity in foreign joint ventures plus royalty payments. This kind of route towards internationalization is really somewhere between licensing and developing overseas production facilities on one's own. It often results in a network of associate companies around the world. Other firms evolve to become fully fledged multinationals with production facilities overseas without passing through the licensing (or quasi-licensing), phase – hence the mode of evolution summarized in Figure 20.2.

One of the disadvantages with both exporting and licensing is their inability to realize the full potential of a product in a foreign market. And licensing may create a significant competitor in some markets unless carefully controlled. Setting up a firm's own production facility overseas overcomes these drawbacks and enables the firm to keep up to date with local market developments and adapt its products and production and marketing methods to meet changing local tastes and conditions while also providing better after-sales service. At the same time, establishing local production facilities demonstrates a greater commitment to the local market and an increased assurance of supply stability. This is important for firms that produce intermediate goods for sale to other companies, rather than for the end-user. Tied in to the firm's decision to produce abroad is the question of whether to create its own subsidiaries and associates organically or to acquire going concerns. An advantage of the acquisitive route is the greater capacity to effect a speedy transfer overseas of parent skills, such as innovative production technology. And, the inorganically acquired local firm may provide ready-made marketing networks. This could be important if the parent is a late entrant to the market. Many firms use the acquisition route to gain knowledge about the local market or about a particular technology. The disincentive to use of this route is, of course, the cost of the acquisition.

The incremental model set out in Figure 20.2 proves a useful pedagogic approach to internationalization and is undergoing continuous empirical investigation. It has a number of shortcomings. The dynamics of progress from one stage to another are not necessarily fully understood. The model is unidirectional and, as such, cannot explain divestment or strategic reorientation. Also, the sequential nature of the process denies the leapfrogging of stages, which has, in fact, been observed by Welch and Luostarinen (1988). The model has also been criticized for representing a process of great complexity in too simple a format – see Dichtl, Liebold, Koglmayr and Muller (1983). And the unidirectional orientation of the model assumes, or at least suggests, a cause and effect relationship that may be less than justified. The complexity of the process, plus the possibility of feedback loops representing reorientations, aggravates the neat ordering of the variables. Clearly, empirical testing in the area is difficult. In short, the model is by no means proven. Export seems, certainly, to be first step in the process of internationalization. Like many of our models in the social sciences, the sequential route to full FDI illustrated in Figure 20.2 is not an immutable picture of a complex process. Nonetheless, it should not be given short shrift; it deserves healthy respect – and also a certain amount of suspicion.

Certainly empirical work underpins the deductive hypothesis that the initial move towards internationalization is via the export route. And, according to Johanson and Wiedersheim-Paul (1975), Bilkey and Tesar (1977), Cavusgil and Nevin (1980) and Cavusgil (1982), internationalization as a process follows an incremental or sequential route. This may be seen as a learning process – an attempt to overcome the problems of information, language, culture, education, business practice and legislation, that constitute, for many organizations, a 'psychic distance' from strange foreign markets. Incremental development provides the cautious route that tends to overcome any lack of experience, knowledge or market information that would otherwise create strong barriers to international development; see Johanson and Vahlne (1977).

We now turn to the next of our key theories of multinational strategy – it is the market imperfections approach.

20.3 | Market imperfections

The most important idea in developing theories of FDI is that firms engaging in international production are at a disadvantage compared with local firms. This is generally assumed to be so because of their unfamiliarity with local market conditions. The operation of a subsidiary in a foreign market probably requires a greater commitment of time, attention and control compared with operating a subsidiary in the home market. Additional costs are incurred in terms, for example of communication, administration and transportation. For FDI to be successful, multinationals must, therefore, possess certain advantages not available to existing or potential local competitors.

The conditions required for multinationals to compete successfully with local firms in host country environments are discussed by Hymer (1960). He observes that foreign firms must possess advantages over local firms to make such investment viable and, usually, the market for the sale of the product or service is imperfect. FDI is motivated by market imperfections which permit the multinational to exploit its monopolistic advantages in foreign markets.

This view is elaborated further by Kindleberger (1969), who suggests that market imperfections offer multinationals compensating advantages of a magnitude that exceeds the disadvantages due to their lack of origins within a host environment, and it is the financial effects of this that underpin FDI. Again, FDI is a direct outcome of imperfect markets.

Market imperfections may arise in one or more of several areas – for example, product differentiation, marketing skills, proprietary technology, managerial skills, better access to capital, economies of scale and government-imposed market distortions, to name but a few. Such advantages give multinationals an edge over their competitors in foreign locations and thus serve to compensate for the additional costs of operating at a distance.

The suggestion, therefore, is that FDI may take place once the multinational has secured internally transferable advantages. These enable it to overcome its lack of knowledge of local conditions in host environments and to compete with local firms successfully. Market imperfections, created by the existence of an oligopolistic advantage for the multinational, may become a driving force for FDI.

Multinational firms are typically oligopolists. Virtually all multinationals enjoy considerable market power. The market in which they operate is usually one of international oligopoly with shades of monopolistic competition. Maybe this is because of the sizeable set-up costs involved in establishing an overseas plant. Only large firms may be willing to incur this entry cost. In a UK study, Dunning (1985) identified oligopoly as a distinguishing feature of markets in which multinationals operate, confirming many other investigators' findings.

Establishing overseas subsidiaries is not compatible with perfect competition. In a perfectly competitive industry there are many small firms enjoying common access to knowledge and earning normal returns. Oligopoly power provides an insight as to why certain firms establish cross-border plants. Entry barriers are critical in maintaining high profits. As these are eroded in the domestic market, the firm may find it expedient and profitable to set up plants overseas. Of course, the firm need not be under pressure of eroding margins in the home market to stimulate scanning the world environment to seek to replicate its domestic market imperfections overseas. This may be a natural part of corporate strategy. It is merely an observation that expected adverse trends in home profits, owing to increased competition from rivals, may goad a firm into analysing its options elsewhere in the world carefully – something it is less likely to do under tranquil competitive conditions.

Logically, the question that follows concerns the whereabouts of any planned overseas plant. Considerations of locational efficiency concern market demand and comparative production and distribution costs; these obviously help to explain where production occurs. But they may not be the only factors at work. The multinational must have some firm-specific advantage – the source of market imperfection – giving it an edge over would-be indigenous producers. Michalet and Chevalier (1985) cite over thirty reasons given by French multinationals for setting up overseas plants. Prominent were the importance of access to a particular market, the desire to spread risks, and adverse trends in the home market, although there seemed to be no single overriding factor at work. However, most of those cited related to some form of market imperfection.

Giddy (1978b) neatly summarized the situation saying that 'the maintenance of an oligopoly depends on the existence of barriers to competitive entry'. Hence, if domestic oligopolists are to become global ones, the sources of their domestic advantage must be transferable abroad. In addition, these advantages must be monopolistically held, for without such market imperfections foreign direct investment would be unlikely to occur. National firms would be better placed to meet the market need. The incentive for foreign investment is based, in part, on the advantages of internalizing markets across national boundaries. So, what exactly do we mean by internalizing?

Market imperfections arise from imperfect competition or imperfect information. If the supplier of a critical factor input to a firm's production process has some monopoly power, then the supplied firm may be faced with the possibility of having to pay a higher price for the input than it would under conditions of perfect competition. In such circumstances, it may pay the firm to internalize supply by buying up the supply source. This is sometimes termed 'integration backwards'. It simply makes the supplying firm part of the buying firm's production process. If the firm supplying the internalized goods or services happens to be located in another country, then the firm that undertakes the internalization automatically moves along the path towards becoming a multinational business.

Multinationals obviously have intangible capital in the form of trade marks, patents, general marketing know-how and other organizational skills. These create market imperfections too. But it may be argued that local firms have an inherent cost advantage over foreign investors. After all, the multinational must bear the costs of operating in an unfamiliar environment. The multinational can, theoretically, only succeed abroad if its monopolistic advantages cannot be purchased or duplicated by local competitors. Of course, in the fullness of time, all barriers to entry erode. Then, the multinational firm must find new sources of competitive advantage. To survive as a multinational enterprise, the firm must create and preserve effective barriers to direct competition in product and factor markets worldwide.

Another market imperfection in financial markets has been called into play in explaining the growth of the multinational. This argument uses some of the capital asset pricing model concepts and takes the following form. Systematic risk affecting the firm is related to the business environment in that firm's national economy. By diversifying across frontiers, the variance in the firm's overall earnings and cash flows can be reduced to some extent. As its results become less tied to its home national economy, so the multinational's beta should fall.

Let us return to the pioneering work of Hymer (1960), in terms of explaining the application of market imperfections to FDI. He suggested that the decision of a multinational to invest in an overseas market can only be explained if the company has, and can utilize, certain advantages not possessed by its local competitors. These advantages may derive from skills in management, marketing, production, finance or technology. They may refer to preferential access to raw materials or other inputs. Whatever the source, the market for the sale of these advantages must be imperfect. Kindleberger (1969) went further when he suggested that market imperfections are the reason for FDI.

Another requirement is that the specific advantages possessed by the multinational must be easily transferable within the firm, often over long distances. The facts that such firm-specific advantages exist, are transferable, and cannot easily be marketed, is not a sufficient explanation for the firm's decision to locate manufacturing facilities overseas. It might, alternatively, produce at home and export, or license production to an overseas partner. Other location-specific advantages – for example, input prices, transport and communication availability and costs, existence of trade barriers, sophistication of infrastructure – are said to be required in order to evolve necessary and sufficient conditions for the decision to locate production in foreign countries. Most theories of FDI flow from this premise.

Many of the insights into the role of market imperfections in impelling foreign direct investment derive from the work of Hymer (1960). In pursuing foreign direct investment, it would seem that an organization must possess a specific advantage to such an extent that this outweighs its fear, in terms of language, culture, physical distance and so on, of doing business in an environment where local practices are different from the home market. The argument goes that this advantage must be sufficient to offset the presumed potential of competition from locally situated organizations in order for foreign investment to occur. Such specific advantages may reside in barriers to entry. Caves (1982) makes the point that the most powerful source of specific advantage is product differentiation through, for example, a patented product or via production technology or marketing investment in branding, styling, distribution and/or service. But other sources are significant in creating competitive advantage – for example, economies of scale, access to capital and raw materials, integration backwards or forwards, skills such as managerial know-how, research and development and so on.

Market imperfections may be created in a number of ways:

■ Internal or external economies of scale often exist, possibly because of privileged access to raw materials or to final markets, possibly from the exploitation of firm-specific knowledge assets, possibly from increases in physical production. The oligopolies which may result do not react as would firms in perfectly competitive markets. For example, Knickerbocker (1973) has shown that oligopolistic competitors tend to follow one another into individual foreign markets – behaviour that may not always be justified by pure profit potential.

■ Effective differentiation – not only to products and processes but also to marketing and organizational skills – may create substantial imperfections.

■ Government policies have an impact on fiscal and monetary matters, on trade barriers and so on. Multinationals are often able to borrow at lower rates than indigenous firms. Due to their stronger credit ratings, multinationals may often borrow funds in international markets at favourable rates when host government policies make domestic capital expensive or unavailable for indigenous firms. And multinationals are able to build efficient portfolios of FDI – thus reducing the risk involved in any one host's intervention. This may not be available to more regional competitors.

Market imperfections enable firms to use the power of their specific advantage to close markets and obtain superior rents on their activities. To quote Hymer (1960), multinationals are propelled for monopolistic reasons 'to separate markets and prevent competition between units'. Clearly, if markets were open and efficient, organizations would not be able to sustain monopolistic advantages and, perhaps, the amount of FDI would be less.

Essentially, then, theories of international investment, based on the existence of market imperfections, suggest that foreign investment is undertaken by those firms that enjoy some monopolistic or oligopolistic advantage. This is because, under perfect market conditions, foreign firms would be non-competitive due to the cost of operating from a distance, both geographically and culturally. Presumably, the firm that invests abroad has some unique advantage, whether it be in terms of product differentiation, marketing or managerial skills, proprietary technology, favourable access to finance or other critical inputs. Oligopoly theory may also explain the phenomenon of defensive investment, which may occur in concentrated industries to prevent competitors from gaining or enlarging advantages that could then be exploited globally – see McClain (1983).

The more modern ideas expounded by Porter (1980, 1985) on strategic management, which emphasize the role of building generic strategies on sustainable competitive advantages behind entry barriers, can be traced, partially, to Hymer's work, which in turn has been substantially influenced by Bain (1956) and, further back, by Coase (1937).

It may be worth mentioning, in passing, that organizations operating in oligopoly but with a relatively undifferentiated product, for example, timber, tend to be involved in vertical-type foreign investments, while oligopolists with differentiated products are more generally involved in horizontal-type FDI.

Other important insights of Hymer's work have been observed by Dunning and Rugman (1985). First of all, there is the emphasis on market structure and the dynamic nature of the specific advantage of the multinational. This fits in neatly with the product life cycle models of Vernon (1966, 1977), which are examined later in this chapter, and the nature of competitive reactions to innovations. The competitive advantage which the multinational possesses is continuously threatened by competitors who launch new products and seek new technology. This is designed to ensure that new specific advantages accrue to them. Hymer's theory, like Vernon's product life cycle model, implies that a specific advantage may be wrested over time by rivals.

Also, Hymer tells us that 'profits in one country may be negatively correlated with profits of another . . . an investor may be able to achieve greater stability in his profitability by diversifying his portfolio and investing part in each country'. Hymer recognized diversification as a motivating force in international investment, enabling risk to be spread in the portfolio of an individual or a corporation. The point is of particular importance where costs of carrying out the transactions internationally for individuals are greater than those for organizations. In strategic management terminology, companies balance their portfolios of strategic business units internationally so as to reduce the risk component of their returns by investing in economies at different stages of the business cycle, ultimately to prevent overexposure to recessions in individual economies. Given that Hymer's contribution was published in 1960, before the advent of the capital asset pricing model with its relatively similar focus, his insight is remarkable and significant.

At this point it is worth referring to another theory of the multinational which is based on diversification in order to smooth earnings. Products are diversified geographically and income is thereby earned in a variety of different currencies. As a result of constraints which may exist in capital markets through exchange controls, a company may undertake international diversification that cannot be replicated by shareholders. Whether the multinational achieves superior results through this policy is an empirical question but there is some weak evidence that it may – see Rugman (1981). Multinationals' policies of diversification by product and by region in their attempt to stabilize earnings look reasonable in this light.

Hymer might also have been influential in another direction. His comparison of multinational business strategy as 'contractual collusion' among oligopolists may, partially, have steered host governments to increase regulation and to perceive multinationals as creaming profits, a view which was prevalent in the 1960s and 1970s. The opinion was then rife that the multinational was a huge, terrifying, ruthless, stateless organization capable of exploiting the poor, manipulating governments and flouting popular opinion. Vernon (1977) observed that 'the multinational enterprise has come to be seen as the embodiment of almost anything disconcerting about modern industrial society'.

Nowadays it is only a slight exaggeration to say that the multinational is seen as the reverse – the embodiment of modernity, the prospect of wealth, full of technology, rich in capital, replete with skilled jobs. Governments around the world, and particularly in developing countries, are queuing up to attract multinationals.

Departments within the United Nations spent years fretting about these firms and drawing up codes of conduct to control them; now they commit much of their time to advising countries how best to seduce them.

Hymer's significant contribution to our understanding of multinational strategy failed, though, to address the geographic and spatial dimensions of internationalization. It went some way to explaining why FDI occurs, but not where.

Moreover, Hymer's insights do not extend to the question of why FDI is the chosen route towards internationalization. Why not licensing? To some extent the answer advanced turns around transaction costs (examined in more detail in the next section). What do we mean by this? Essentially it is concerned with the costs of doing transactions in a particular way. Take a general example. We have seen that it is the possession of a specific advantage that enables international organizations to overcome the home advantage of local firms and thereby, partially, influences them to enter foreign markets. If the specific advantage is knowledge-based, for example if it is related to research and development, there is an obvious problem, namely retaining control of this intangible asset. Might an unscrupulous licensee steal it and exploit the advantage itself? How does the organization provide sufficient information on such an asset without revealing its critical formula for success? The predicament is resolved if the organization continues to exploit the underlying asset itself by retaining control over it. As Hennart (1988) argues, in these circumstances FDI can be expected to be more frequent among technologically intensive companies, intent on sheltering trade secrets.

These considerations also impinge upon our views relating to internalization. In circumstances where there is an exchange relationship, matters would be easy if all parties to a transaction were honest, reliable, fair, would abide by their word, and did business 'our way'. In reality, this is hardly immutably the case. Thus costs are incurred to minimize risks on these fronts whenever business is done with third parties. The intent is to reduce uncertainty. Will a monopoly supplier of raw materials hike the price? Can a supplier be depended upon to move heaven and earth to get the goods to us? These transaction costs can be minimized through internalization – getting processes done within the group rather than by third parties, or external agents. These ideas about internalization may help organizations select between different routes when it comes to expansion overseas – the choice between exporting, licensing and FDI. The decision between licensing and FDI may depend on such factors as the risk of knowledge dissipation, enforcement costs, the state of proprietary technology, probabilities of substitute products and so on. If there is a low risk of dissipation, licensing may be preferred over FDI, all other things being equal.

The choice between exports and FDI may be influenced by expectations of changes in tariff and non-tariff barriers. If tariff barriers are low, exports may be preferred over licensing and FDI. And it may make sense for the organization to substitute internal markets (FDI) for licensing or for export, if exporting is ruled out on the grounds of transportation and/or tariff factors and if licensing is unattractive because of knowledge dissipation possibilities.

This approach has its critics. They tend to focus on whether internalization is a general and predictive theory. Buckley (1983) suggests that it is a 'concept in search of a theory'. He contends that it is tautological inasmuch as firms automatically internalize imperfect markets until the cost of so doing outweighs any benefits. Casson (1982) states that 'internalization is, in fact, a general theory of why firms exist'. And Kay (1983) observes that 'internalization does not satisfy the condition of refutability that is required for theory'. In defence of internalization as an approach, rather than as a theory, Rugman (1986) argues in its favour because of its potentially explanatory power as to when organizations internalize markets or otherwise. This, he claims, is a big contribution to our insights and understandings of FDI. So, let us look a little more closely at the ideas surrounding internalization. But before we do, an overview of a closely related theory – that of transaction costs – is presented.

20.4 | Transaction cost theory

Most theories of multinational enterprise attempt to identify and explain the conditions conducive to the multinational firm's existence. They seek to answer the question as to why the international organization of economic activity within a multinational firm might be preferred to a network of arm's-length contractual arrangements with third parties.

Coase (1937) argues from the starting point that the firm carries on various activities to achieve the end result of profitable production of goods and services. These activities, encompassing, for example, marketing and research and development, are related through flows of intermediate products – mostly, according to Buckley and Casson (1976), in the form of knowledge and expertise. Because of imperfections in intermediate product markets, there will be an incentive to bypass them and create internal markets. Activities that were previously linked by the market mechanism are brought under common ownership and control in a market (if market is the right word) internal to the firm. As Buckley and Casson (1979) observe, where markets are internalized in this way across international boundaries, multinational firms are created.

According to transaction cost theory, as conceived by Coase (1937) and further developed by McManus (1972), Williamson (1975, 1979) and Teece (1976), the firm (termed the 'hierarchy' in their theories) and the market are alternative methods of organizing exchange. The choice between intra-firm and arm's-length market exchange with third parties is based upon relative costs. Coase's view is that the main reason for a firm to exist as a hierarchy of interrelated transactions is that it is more costly for the market to handle a transaction. The firm may therefore bypass the regular market and use internal prices to overcome the excessive transaction costs of an outside market. Coase goes on to suggest that, given transaction costs, firms will tend to expand until the marginal cost of organizing an extra transaction within the firm becomes equal to the marginal cost of carrying out the same transaction by means of an exchange in the open market.

In perfect markets – that is, by definition, with zero transaction costs – prices convey information about the consequences of actions and provide agents with the information necessary to reach optimal decisions. The large number of buyers and sellers makes prices exogenous and eliminates incentives for bargaining. Thus, market outcomes tend to be efficient when competition is strong. Competitive pressures drive parties to perform effectively at low cost and to deal with others fairly and honestly. Consequently, the firm will not internalize whenever the supplier market is competitive.

Of course, in the real world, markets are seldom perfectly competitive. Thus transaction costs are positive. When the number of potential buyers and/or sellers falls, prices are no longer exogenous and bargaining becomes possible. Consequently, given imperfect markets, internalization is likely to have compelling efficiency properties.

To undertake a market transaction, it is necessary to research who to deal with and on what terms. It is also necessary to consider competing deals, to conduct negotiations leading up to the bargain, to draw up a contract and to undertake the inspection necessary to ensure that the terms of the contract are being observed. Market exchanges of information will therefore be costly relative to intra-firm exchange. In many circumstances, therefore, firms are efficient alternatives to markets. The most important efficiency property of the multinational arises from an organizational mode that is capable of transforming knowledge abroad in a relatively efficient fashion. As Teece (1976) observes, it is less costly to monitor activities and enforce proprietary rights over information within an internal organizational hierarchy than it is to enforce such rights in contractual market relationships with third parties. In short, the choice of arm's length and open market exchanges depends upon relative transaction costs.

20.5 | Internalization and firm-specific advantages

Internalization theory and transaction cost theory are closely related. Internalization theory suggests that a firm internalizes a transaction whenever the cost of using markets or contractual agreements is higher than that of organizing it internally. Applied to multinationals, the suggestion is that international markets may be difficult to organize, monitor and control. Multinationals will tend to develop and use their own internal organizational hierarchy whenever intra-firm transactions are less costly than market transactions. The internal market within the firm therefore substitutes for the external market.

Perhaps we now have the wherewithal to answer the key question. Why go to all the lengths of FDI when exporting, licensing or selling technology and/or brands can be less risky and promise very fair returns? As mentioned earlier in this chapter, Pilkington pursued this route with float glass and General Foods followed it in exploiting the Birds Eye frozen food brand. Coase (1937) gave us a hypothesis which he originally applied to the multiplant indigenous firm, but which may be applied equally to multinational activity. He suggested that the external market mechanism inflicts high transaction costs in areas such as defining and accepting contractual obligations, fixing the contract price, taxes to be paid on market transactions, and so on. He argued that these activities might be internalized by the firm wherever this is more effective in cost terms than using the external market mechanism. Obviously, internalization is as much a feature of a multiplant domestic firm as of a multinational.

Buckley and Casson (1976) developed this into an explanation of multinational activity, arguing the influence of market imperfections as a causative factor leading to internalization. They emphasized the importance of imperfections in intermediate product markets, particularly those of patented technical knowledge and human capital. Such imperfections provide an incentive for the firm to internalize, for example, the knowledge market. The incentive to internalize depends upon the four key groups of factors:

- Industry-specific factors, for example, economies of scale, external market structure, and so on.

- Region-specific factors, for example, geographical distance and cultural differences.

- Nation-specific factors, for example, political and fiscal conditions.

- Firm-specific factors, for example, management expertise and technical know-how.

The multinational may realize valuable cost savings via the process of internalization. According to Giddy (1978b), such economies may arise through bypassing any of the following:

- Concentrated markets for raw materials and arm's-length supply which may be both expensive and risky.

- Imperfect markets for the firm's resources, for example as created by brand names.

- Imperfect markets for outputs due to monopolistic control over distribution channels – a significant factor in many small countries.

- Imperfect markets for product resources, perhaps because of government-imposed barriers to entry, such as tariffs.

Of course, internalizing markets through FDI also imposes further costs, for example:

- Additional communication costs which will vary with geographical and cultural distance.

- The cost of operating in an unfamiliar environment.

- The cost of overcoming political and social preferences for domestically owned firms.

- The administrative cost of managing an internal market.

The significance of the work of Buckley and Casson, and others who have developed the internalization approach, is that it extends and deepens the market imperfections analysis by focusing upon intermediate product markets rather than on final product markets. Effectively, their key hypothesis is that when the costs of internalization are outweighed by the benefits, FDI aimed at harvesting this potential may follow. Magee (1981), writing on the theory of FDI, closely echoes the views of Buckley and Casson, and Hymer too. For example, he claims that 'many of the reasons for choosing not to license arose from the imperfect nature of the market for the advantage. These imperfections prevented the appropriation of all the returns to the advantage.'

Perhaps internalization provides answers to some aspects of the FDI puzzle. Rugman (1980) points out that firms may prefer to co-ordinate their international transactions by hierarchy because of the specific problems of overseas trade. A lack of legal and managerial control, with associated uncertainty about the flow of goods and services, together with possible distortions and problems created by tariffs and customs delays, make international markets much less efficient and predictable than domestic ones. Teece (1986) argues that research and development and branded assets are particularly difficult to trade internationally, being especially hard to value. He suggests, therefore, that knowledge-intensive industries are particularly likely to set up their own operations overseas and he actually finds that the extent of multinational operations by US corporations is positively correlated with the importance of advertising and research and development expenditures – although there may be a spurious correlation here deriving from size.

From the internalization point of view, multinationals are merely searchers after efficiency, ready to substitute hierarchies for markets (and, possibly, vice versa too) as the balance of transaction costs changes. The internalization argument does not assume a precise, risk-adjusted analysis of markets against hierarchies – in practice, such an analysis would be difficult and complex, if not impossible. The assumption is that the competitive forces of the market will normally render extinct, rather like evolution, those multinationals which do not get the balance right. This line of argument is suggested by Hennart (1988, 1991).

20.6 | Location-specific advantages

Hood and Young (1979) advance four factors that are relevant to the location-specific theory of FDI, which involves the multinational in seeking locations such that the differences between benefits and costs are maximized. Their four key factors are follows:

- *Labour costs*. Real wage costs vary, not only between developing and industrialized countries, but also within these groupings. Thus low-technology international industries may logically locate in low-wage economies. A similar movement is observed in other industries as technology becomes standardized.

- *Marketing factors*. FDI decisions may be affected by host-country characteristics such as market size, market growth, stage of development and the presence of local competition.

- *Trade barriers*. Such impositions are used by many host countries trying to encourage inward investment. Often multinationals set up local production facilities to protect an already developed export market when trade barriers are erected or mooted.

■ *Government policy*. This may have a significant effect on the investment climate in a particular host country, either directly through fiscal investives, monetary policies or the regulatory regime, or indirectly through the prevailing social environment.

Hood and Young's analysis is mainly couched in terms of cost advantages. Work by Ronstadt (1977) and Lall (1979) into the location of international R&D facilities has indicated that non-price benefits may arise from foreign dispersal of research and development.

20.7 | The product life cycle

One of the theories advanced to explain foreign direct investment is associated with product life cycle ideas. It is based on the concept that most products go through a number of clearly defined stages from birth to eventual old age. Much of the work in this area has been developed by Vernon (1966, 1977) and modified by Wells (1972). The essence of Vernon's ideas is presented first, then the ideas are looked at in more detail. Vernon's early work (1966) suggested that research and development of new products are undertaken in the most advanced countries whose population has sufficient income to demand the new product. Once developed, the product is introduced to the home market. As demand increases, it enters the growth stage in which the product is improved, standardized and economies of scale gained. As production increases, new export markets are opened. The success of exports may encourage firms in host countries to enter the market. This tends to result in the firm from the advanced country considering the setting up of local production facilities to maintain its advantage. The motive for foreign direct investment at this stage is defensive. The product eventually moves into the maturity stage when growth levels off. Competition from new products occurs, competition for market share heightens and margins are squeezed. Price competition may be so severe that the labour-intensive stages of production are actually undertaken, via foreign direct investment, in less-developed countries where labour is cheap. The multinational's decision to invest abroad depends on both the desire to protect and prolong an innovation lead and on relative labour and transportation costs, economies of scale, currency changes and legal/tax factors. Competitive multinationals do not wait for the product cycle to run its course; instead they have learnt to anticipate and accelerate it. Figure 20.3 summarizes the typical product life cycle according to this view of the world of multinational business.

The product life cycle theory is based on four key assumptions, which set it apart from traditional trade theory. These are summarized below:

■ Tastes differ in different countries.

■ The production process is characterized by economies of scale.

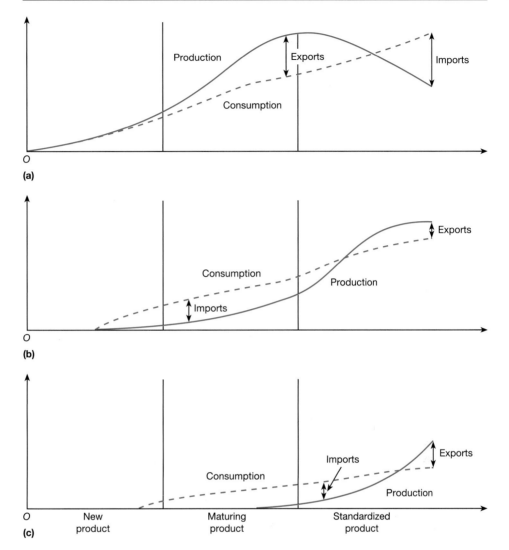

Figure 20.3 The product cycle in international trade and production: (a) home country, (b) other advanced nations, (c) less-developed countries.

■ Information flows across national borders are restricted.

■ Products undergo changes in their production techniques and marketing characteristics over time. The pattern of these changes is largely predictable.

The above represents merely a summary of some of the main aspects of the theory. It certainly deserves more detailed consideration and this now follows. According to product life cycle theory, the stimulus to innovation in the development of new products or processes is typically provided by a perceived opportunity or threat in the firm's major, generally the home, market. This market provides both the source of stimulus for the innovation and the preferred location for the product development. Various reasons account for this. The expense of research and development precludes duplication in numerous locations. Such activities are generally centralized near to the organization's headquarters owing to their long-run strategic importance and to the necessity of keeping major breakthroughs in-house. There are other benefits to be gained by central location of R&D activities. These include maintenance of close links and communications among scientists and engineers and tight co-ordination between R&D activities and such functions as planning, production, marketing and finance. It is necessary to keep close to prospective customers and to monitor competitive developments. The nature of product development also influences the decision to begin production first in the home market. Vernon suggests that the transitions from development project to pilot plant to first commercial production are generally incremental in nature – they are bolted on. Specifications are frequently changed until the proper process and designs are established before the prototype for volume production is prepared. If this view is correct, close physical proximity between R&D and production is beneficial.

One corollary from conducting R&D within the home territory may be, as Vernon suggests, that innovations tend to reflect the characteristics of the home market. Perhaps this is why US firms have tended to develop and manufacture products that are both labour-saving and respond to relatively high-income needs. This line of argument would tend to suggest, as is possibly the case, that European firms would develop and manufacture products that are raw material-saving and labour-saving. And Japanese and European firms might take the lead in energy-saving innovations.

Product life cycle theory in international business recognizes four phases. During the first of these, the innovating firm produces and markets solely in the home market. On commercial introduction, costs and prices tend to be high. If the product is sufficiently differentiated from other existing products, the innovating firm may benefit from monopolistic advantages with initial buyers relatively insensitive to price. If the product succeeds, there is a rapid expansion of the market, eventually providing increasing economies of scale, lower unit costs and possibly a further expansion of the market. Such success encourages the entry of competitors, especially as production becomes more standardized. Eventually the home market will tend to become saturated and profits will decline. Phase two is then looming.

In phase two, bigger markets and greater economies may be available through exporting. An underpinning assumption is that there is an imperfect market for knowledge and technology and that the original advantage held by the innovator in the home market may be applied abroad. Firms in the United States have typically sought markets in Canada and Europe first of all. These markets are frequently large enough to be attractive, and the demand patterns of many industrialized countries are relatively similar; this avoids the requirement to adapt the product substantially for the foreign market. Success in exporting prolongs the life of the product. In time, competition emerges from domestic firms in the targeted export market. At first it tends to be weak owing to the normal start-up problems and to the lack of economies of scale. But eventually this new competition tends to strengthen sufficiently to pose a real threat, given its lesser transport costs and nil import tariff. Phase three is at hand.

Phase three is typified by overseas producers gaining a substantial market share by honing their production techniques and by gaining economies of scale sufficient to cause a challenge to the original exporter, who incurs the added costs of transportation, tariffs and communication. Cultural distance may also become a factor for exporting firms less familiar with the market. Foreign governments often undertake protectionist actions to facilitate development and/or to enhance the competitiveness of local producers. In phase three, these factors become serious; they adversely affect exports. The exporting firm starts to consider shifting its strategy towards the location of production facilities abroad in the market that has heretofore been served by exports. This seemed to be the pattern applicable to the two decades following the Second World War, but its relevance now seems much less pronounced.

For very labour-intensive products for which mass manufacturing technologies are feasible, a fourth stage in the life cycle is apparent. This final phase involves the original innovating firm ceasing production in parts of the world with high labour costs. In this phase, the home market is serviced through imports from foreign subsidiaries located in low-wage countries abroad. These production locations will tend to be in rapidly developing countries, such as the currently emerging dragons of South East Asia – South Korea, China, Vietnam, the Philippines, Indonesia and Thailand – where low labour costs are combined with sufficient infrastructure and potentially high productivity levels.

A modified version of the original product life cycle model was advanced by Vernon (1977) in which he categorized multinationals within various stages of the development cycle. He distinguished three types of multinational oligopoly as follows:

■ *Innovation-based oligopolies.* These firms create barriers to entry through continuous introduction of new products and aggressive differentiation of existing ones, both at home and abroad. Such firms tend to have a high ratio of R&D expenditure to sales and a low ratio of direct employees to sales. Firms in this category behave very much in accordance with product life cycle theory. However, the most aggressive of these firms are observed to exploit foreign markets without waiting for the product life cycle to run its course.

■ *Mature oligopolies.* These firms tend to share markets in the traditional oligopolistic way long after their products have become standardized, through the maintenance of entry barriers via experience curve effects and economies of scale in marketing, production and/or transportation. These oligopolies may rely on high fixed costs as a barrier to entry, and adopt stabilizing strategies including:
   (i)   follow-the-leader behaviour in entering new countries or product lines,
   (ii) pricing conventions,
   (iii) mutual alliances, including joint subsidiaries and joint contracts.

■ *Senescent oligopolies.* These tend to occur when existing barriers to entry erode. Multinationals either drop out of the particular market to concentrate on newer products or move production to low-cost locations.

The product life cycle theory is not fully accepted by economists. Some see it as a concept that has outgrown its usefulness. Amusingly, Giddy (1978b) feels that the theory has experienced growth, maturity and decline as a concept in explaining international investment patterns. He points to some of the shortcomings of the model, as follows:

- It is unable to predict correctly international patterns in many manufactured goods – for example, new products including digital watches and disposable razors, and mature products such as processed foods and toiletries.

- Raw materials trade cannot be predicted by the model.

- The model does not address the question of why multinationals do not license or export, but prefer to pursue an FDI strategy.

- The model does not examine the systematic advantages that foreign firms possess to enable them to overcome inherent disadvantages versus local firms.

Giddy acknowledges that the theory still has a degree of explanatory power in some cases, but, to him, it is not a fully blown theory of FDI.

The product life cycle now

By no means completely discredited, the product life cycle theory seems to have less relevance now compared with its heyday two or three decades ago. Certainly the theory represents an attempt at explaining trade in manufactured products that require some degree of technical sophistication in their invention, design and development. In some cases, the theory seems to fit the facts. Colour television was invented in the United States. In the early days of the product, the United States produced and exported these goods. Over time, the production of colour televisions shifted almost entirely to countries such as Japan, Taiwan, Korea and elsewhere in the Far East. And the product life cycle model has also been suggested as an explanation for the relative decline of the US semiconductor industry. But for other sophisticated products – for example, aircraft – the model seems to fit less well. The United States, which took the lead in their development, still retains comparative advantage despite the fact that aircraft are now a relatively mature product. The fundamental weakness of the product life cycle model is its inability to generalize its predictions in terms of industry or the timing of the changes in the location of comparative advantage.

Why have the predictive powers of the theory waned in recent years? There are possible explanations. First of all, there has been an undoubted increase in the geographical reach of many of the enterprises involved in the innovation process due to their having established subsidiaries abroad already. Secondly, the national markets of advanced industrialized countries now are far more homogeneous.

During the thirty or so years immediately following the Second World War, there was a rapid growth in foreign investment. For all of this period, the process of innovation, export and foreign investment probably ran full tilt, as predicted by the theory. One consequence is that one now rarely finds major innovative firms that do not already have extensive overseas operations. This has had at least two significant effects. First, the time interval between the introduction of a new product in the home market and its first production in a foreign location has substantially decreased. New facilities are easily bolted on to hasten the transfer of new technoogy abroad. Secondly, there is now a significant reverse flow of technology through innovations, by subsidiaries abroad, which are subsequently introduced into the original home market. This has, in part, been a consequence of the narrowing of differences between the markets of the industrialized countries.

Even if it is less applicable now than in the past, the product life cycle theory has not utterly passed its 'sell-by' date. It certainly continues to provide numerous insights. The model links the demand side to the theory of comparative advantage, and presents the argument that the pattern of many exports and imports is better explained by competitive factors at the firm level rather than at the national level. It suggests that international trade follows markets, and that international investment responds to potential and real threats to export markets. In short, product life cycle ideas attempt to describe how the export, import and location of manufacture of a product changes through time as firms respond to changing competitive conditions and as domestic and foreign markets for the product grow, mature and decline.

So, product life cycle theory has been important because it explained international investment. The theory recognized the mobility of capital across countries in contrast to traditional assumptions of factor immobility and it shifted the focus from the country to the product. This meant that it was important to match the product by its maturity stage with its production location in order to examine competitiveness.

But product life cycle theory has limitations. It is clearly most appropriate for technology-based products. These products are likely to experience changes in production process as they grow and mature. Others, for example resource-based products, such as minerals and other commodities, and services, which mainly employ human capital, are not so easily characterized by stages of maturity. Product life cycle theory is most relevant to products that involve mass production and cheap labour costs. However, product life cycle theory has bridged a wide gap between older trade theories and the newer, with more globally competitive markets in which capital, technology, information and firms themselves are more internationally mobile.

20.8 | The eclectic theory

The ideas summarized above about firm-specific advantages, location-specific advantages and internalization have been melded by Dunning (1977, 1988a, b) in his eclectic theory of international production. For him, these sources of profit are competitive advantages to the multinational and are defined in the following terms:

- *Firm-specific advantages.* The multinational possesses ownership advantages which may be held temporarily or permanently and are held exclusively. They promise superior returns over competitors in foreign markets. Firm-specific advantages include intangible assets such as expertise or patents.

- *Location-specific advantages.* These include factors specific to a particular place and have to be used in that place. They would embrace trade barriers that restrict imports, labour advantages, natural resources, proximity to final markets, conditions of transportation and communication, favourable government intervention and cultural factors.

- *Internalization advantages*. These include factors for which a company gains by using its ownership internally instead of buying or selling on the market from or to third parties, respectively. These factors include possession of raw material sources and downstream consumption within the company, the ability to cross-subsidize products, the ability to avoid transaction and negotiation costs, avoiding uncertainty about buying and selling, the ability to control supplies of inputs and their conditions of sale, and so on.

Dunning formulated his main hypothesis in the following way. Given the possession of net ownership advantages over local firms, the most profitable development for the multinational is to internalize them by extending its own activities. It must then be beneficial for the multinational to combine these internalized advantages with some factor inputs in some foreign countries – otherwise foreign markets would be served entirely by exports and home markets by home production.

This model has received support from various empirical studies and it has survived criticisms that throw some doubt on its universality as a general theory of international operations. For example, Kojima (1978) suggested that the eclectic model is built on the experience of US multinationals and has less relevance to non-US firms – for example, the Japanese. This suggestion is refuted, in part at least, by work by Dunning and Archer (1987). In a study of fifteen UK-based multinationals active between 1914 and 1983, they found that the eclectic model fairly adequately explained sources of competitive advantage enjoyed by these firms and explained the geographical orientation of their FDI.

Also, the eclectic theory seems more appropriate to greenfield operations than to acquisitions, which seem to be motivated more by reason of strategic development than by economic advantage – for example, the follow-the-leader oligopolistic reaction referred to earlier. Furthermore, a growing proportion of FDI is carried out to acquire technology – the eclectic theory has little to offer in this respect. However, in an appraisal of the empirical work carried out in testing the eclectic theory, Hood and Young (1979) refer to difficulties of data deficiency, problems in devising empirical tests for internalization factors and numerous statistical problems. They concluded that a satisfactory test of the eclectic theory had yet to be devised. But that was in 1979, and more recent work has cast some doubt on the immutability of the eclectic model. Perhaps that is almost inevitable in the social sciences where our models are rarely valid 100 per cent of the time.

Even if we are not wholly satisfied with the eclectic model, it cannot be denied that it has given us great insights into the logic and process of FDI. The first question on FDI is: why does the firm extend its activities to other countries? Dunning's theory suggests that there are location-specific advantages available in the host country. The question that follows is: how do foreign firms compete with domestic firms of the host country? The eclectic theory points to firm-specific advantages. Then there is a further question to be answered: why should the firm choose FDI instead of exporting or licensing? The response lies in internalization. These three advantages may be sufficient to explain FDI, but are they necessary? The answer seems to be in the negative since location-specific advantages and internalization advantages seem to be sufficient to explain multinational activity – thus rendering firm-specific advantages redundant. Some economists go so far as to claim that the concept of internalization alone is sufficient to explain multinational activity, and that the theory of internalization is the theory of FDI – see, for example, Casson (1982).

Porter (1986) provides insights into the FDI conundrum. He argues that, in seeking competitive advantage, multinationals should seek either a low-cost strategy or one concentrating upon product differentiation. Internationally, these two generic strategies may be operated within four strategic contexts; Porter refers to these as follows:

- *Country-focused strategy.* Here the full range of the value adding activities is located in each country with little or no co-ordination between the various subsidiaries – for example, as in food manufacturing, retailing, and service industries such as insurance, advertising, banking, management consultancy.

- *High foreign investment with extensive co-ordination among subsidiaries.* This route is often followed with a view to protecting intangible, but strategically important, rights – for example, research and development, technology, etc. In the pharmaceutical industry, for instance, research and development activities may be spread across a number of countries. Such dispersion calls for global co-ordination of research and development to maximize its utility and minimize overlap and waste.

- *Export-based strategy with decentralized marketing.* This is surely the simplest form of international strategy and is widely used by companies new to the international arena.

- *Purest global strategy.* Here a high degree of co-ordination and concentration of activities is aimed at producing standardized products for a global market. For example, well into the 1980s, Toyota concentrated manufacturing in Japan, with activities such as advertising, servicing and spare parts decentralized. Many of these activities could be standardized, but they all had to be closer to the final buyer than was the case for manufacturing.

Porter's focus reflects current trends in international investment and strategy, for example:

- FDI is expanding with more players from more countries.

- Products sold around the world are becoming more homogeneous in nature and/or appearance, although local markets in some sectors are simultaneously becoming more highly segmented.

- There is a distinct trend for service industries to become more globalized.

- In a growing number of industries, concentration of activities is becoming less attractive as economies of scale begin to reach their limits.

- The historic year-by-year drop in unit transport costs is beginning to flatten out.

- As telecommunications technology and costs drop quickly, the ability of firms to improve the efficiency of co-ordination grows.

These trends militate in favour of high foreign investment with extensive co-ordination among subsidiaries, which was undoubtedly the trend of the 1980s and 1990s.

Over recent years there has also been a plethora of international joint ventures. Indeed it is fair to say that one of the most common FDI routes in the 1980s was joint ventures with a local partner. As an alternative to outright ownership and control over foreign assets, such ventures have interesting properties. Sharing ownership rights spreads the risks of ownership and provides incentives for trading partners to invest in specific assets or to dedicate them to specific uses in a way that they might be unwilling to do if transacting on a purely arm's-length basis. But such ventures also pose hazards for either or both of the partners and these should always be borne in mind when entering a joint venture or considering the qualities of a partner. The hazard is that one party to the venture may behave opportunistically once the investment has been made and attempt to appropriate value for itself at the expense of the joint venture partner. This temptation often looms large in international joint ventures, making them a potentially unstable form of long-term investment which may provide one of the partners with an incentive to assume complete control.

20.9 | Globalization

No overview of international business strategy would be complete without reference to globalization. Levitt (1983) comments upon

> the emergence of global markets for standardized consumer products on a previously unimagined scale of magnitude. Corporations geared to this new reality benefit from enormous economies of scale in production, distribution, marketing, and management. By translating these benefits into reduced world prices, they can decimate competitors that still live in the disabling grip of old assumptions about how the world works.

Stopford and Turner (1985) have given us a model summarizing forces which may influence global positioning. Their model is reproduced as Figure 20.4. Each factor specified in the figure can be a driver towards or away from global operations.

Analysis by Cvar (1986) suggests that industries which become global have a series of characteristics. The opportunity exists for high levels of economies of scale given a market or markets demanding standardized products. Globalization is anything but a naturally occurring state. It is purpose-made. It is triggered by the identification of market segments in different countries that enable a product to be defined globally; this, in turn, enables supply sources to be consolidated, yielding competitive cost advantages. Cvar's study indicated that successful global companies had five themes in common. They had all developed a pre-emptive strategy. They all managed their companies on a global concept and measured their performance this way. They all had higher than average R&D compared with their industry and were striving single-mindedly to overcome obstacles to globalization. Cvar's findings are summarized in Figure 20.5.

Ohmae (1985) adds a further – if somewhat contentious and by no means universally accepted – dimension to observations about the need to become global. He

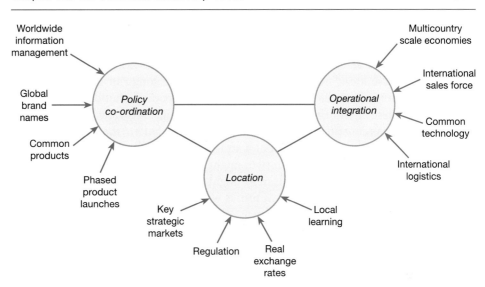

Figure 20.4 Factors influencing global positioning.

Source: Stopford and Turner, 1985.

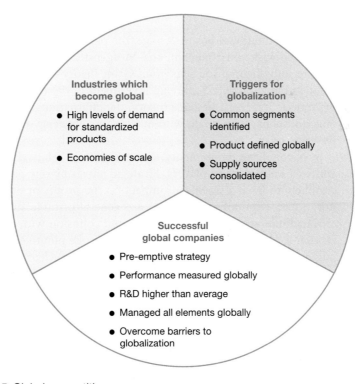

Figure 20.5 Global competition.

Source: Cvar, 1986.

argues that industries that have the right characteristics to become global will succeed if they operate in the three geographic centres of the world – the United States,
Japan and Europe. Ohmae suggests that those firms that stay in only one or two of
these areas are less likely to succeed in the long run since their volumes of production will probably be below those of competitors that do cover the total triad, giving
these latter firms an immense cost advantage. His view is based on the fact that these
areas contain some 600 million people in what are the largest and most sophisticated
markets of the world. But a strategy that sought to establish dominance in just one
of these markets, or in two, might yield costs at levels just as low as competitors in
all three and such a strategy might be just as profitable. The cost of building a presence in a market where a firm is weak can be astronomical, as many have discovered
in Japan. The triad strategy could easily be so costly that it endangers a firm's
strengths elsewhere. One reason for adopting it could well be to counter competitors'
moves. A presence in a rival's home market might distract the rival or might lower
the rival's profits and it might also yield valuable information about tactics and/or
technology.

20.10 | Game theory and international strategy

On the multinational business stage, the players are oligopolists. And game theory,
associated with von Neumann and Morgenstern (1944) and Oster (1990), gives us
insights into oligopolistic behaviour. Game theory focuses upon interactions between
competitors and explains foreign investment in these terms rather than by comparing transaction costs. In game theory, the international moves and countermoves of
oligopolists have less to do with maximizing efficiency than with defence of market
position.

In oligopolistic game theory, competitors are relatively few and are identifiable
and well known by all players. Strategic moves by one party are highly visible and
are likely to have a significant impact on the profits of other players. The competitors in an oligopolistic industry are generally stable over time. They engage in
repeated interactions and negotiation and collusion with a fairly stable equilibrium
becoming possible. Aggression tends to provoke punitive responses. Competition in
oligopoly is not unlike the restraint observed by nuclear powers. The peace depends
upon all parties knowing that disturbance of the equilibrium can set off a mutually
disastrous course of events.

Game theory provides significant insights on FDI decisions. FDI may give one
player the competitive advantage that would enable it to make a more menacing
attack upon fellow oligopolists. In other words, it may create a change in the league
table of competitive power – see Knickerbocker (1973). The first venture abroad in
a particular market may enable the prime mover to gain market knowledge, economies of scale and other advantages over its rivals that have remained at home. In
consequence, other players in the home oligopoly may tend to match each other's
moves abroad to reduce this risk. By shadowing rivals' moves, they may not be left
behind – no single player then gains a possibly destabilizing competitive advantage

versus the others. A matching of moves of this kind is precisely what Knickerbocker (1973) found in a study of FDI by US corporations between 1948 and 1967. He observed that FDI activity tended to concentrate in relatively clear and short time-spans. Some 47 per cent of all FDI by 197 US corporations was clustered in particular three-year periods. He concluded that moves by one company into a particular country sector prompted a rush by its domestic rivals into that same country group. Bunching of FDI was marked in oligopolistic industries. Game theory may also illuminate international strategies of rivals from different countries. For Graham (1990), FDI in different countries can be seen as an exchange of threats between oligopolistic players in the same industry. A move by a foreign multinational into the home market may then be matched by home-based multinationals responding in kind.

The greater the extent of multinationality, the greater the ability of the multinational to exchange threats. A proliferation of country investment improves the ability to retaliate against competitors. The firm may fire warning shots in minor markets first of all and build up to a battle in major markets if the aggressor fails to back down. Additionally, a spread of markets makes it possible to cross-subsidize such battles. Networks of international joint ventures and alliances also improve information sources on competitor moves.

Underpinning game theory explanations of international competition is the premise that all players are acting according to the same rules. The expected outcome is a kind of collusive equilibrium, in which exchange of threats ensures an equilibrium, where established multinationals continue to enjoy oligopolistic profits. Multinationals become, to use the term coined by Porter (1985), 'good competitors'. They offer sufficient threat to prevent complacency but never enough to disrupt the equilibrium. According to Porter (1985), powerful players should offer gentle competition as opposed to striving for complete dominance. Others might shelter under the umbrella of the market leader rather than offering all-out attack. If competitors perceive these as the rules, destructive battles may be avoided.

In global competition 'good competitors' may be thinner on the ground than in the domestic market place. Competitors from different countries may well have different philosophies of business and different objectives, particularly if backed by their government. According to Brouthers and Werner (1990), US firms tend to see Japanese competitors as (to use Porter's term) bad competitors. This is because Japanese firms play according to different rules – often because of the extensive, long-run support given by their banks and the preferential industrial policies of MITI (Ministry for International Trade and Industry) plus the virtual absence of hostile takeovers in Japan. These factors tend to support the expansionist strategy of long-term investment in market share that has been so typical of Japanese companies as part of their attack upon Western markets.

From a study of strategies of a matched sample of Japanese, US and UK competitors in the UK market, Doyle, Saunders and Wong (1992) note that four out of five Japanese managers point to aggressive growth or market domination as their key strategic objective. Only half of the US managers and one-fifth of the UK managers put this top. Twenty-five per cent of the Japanese companies put good short-term profits as their objective – 80 per cent of their US and UK competitors were so oriented. These different goals might suggest that UK and US companies are likely to retire before their Japanese counterparts in a cut-throat battle. Given their different views and time-scales, Japanese companies may be less likely to accede to the tacit collusion common in Western oligopolies. Threats may be ignored and wars fought to the death.

In the international arena, game theory provides insights into oligopolistic behaviour as long as all competitors follow the same set of rules. On the international scene this is not so likely – especially when some competitors are state-owned. Government-influenced policies are not just associated with Far Eastern competition. About a quarter of French-based multinationals were state-owned in the early 1990s.

The game theory school might view international strategy, including FDI, as a chess game of pre-empting and countering competitors; others would perceive international moves as seeking to internalize activities to obtain competitive advantage, while others still would be sceptical, favouring behavioural and imperialistic goals. Perhaps the major lesson is to point out that not all players in multinational business have the same rule book.

20.11 | The new trade theory

World trade developments in the 1980s led to criticism of existing theories. Although there was rapid growth in trade, much of it was not explained by prevailing theories. Two new contributions to trade theory emerged. Helpman and Krugman (1985) developed a theory of how trade is altered when production of specific products possess economies of scale. A second development was associated with Porter (1990) who examined the global competitiveness of industries rather than relying on country-specific factors.

Economies of scale and imperfect competition

Krugman's major contribution focused on costs of production and how costs and prices drive international trade. He highlighted two types of economics of scale: internal economies of scale and external economies of scale.

When there are economies of scale that accrue to the individual firm, we talk of internal economies of scale. The larger the firm the greater the scale of benefits and the lower the cost per unit. A firm possessing internal economies of scale could potentially monopolize an industry both domestically and internationally by lowering the market price. Such a firm would be using its internal economies of scale to create, first, imperfect competition and, potentially, a monopoly.

The link between the domination of domestic industry and influencing international trade comes from taking the assumption of imperfect markets back to the concept of comparative advantage. For the firm to expand sufficiently fully to enjoy its economies of scale, it must divert resources from other domestic business units in order to expand. Conflated to a country level, a nation's range of products in which it specializes narrows, providing an opportunity for other countries to specialize in these abandoned product ranges. Countries again search out and exploit comparative advantage. An implication of internal economies of scale is that it provides an explanation of intra-industry trade, an area in which traditional trade theory failed to provide an explanation. Intra-industry trade occurs when a country apparently imports and exports the same product, an idea inconsistent with traditional trade theory. According to Krugman, internal economies of scale lead a firm to specialize in a narrow product line. Firms in other countries may then produce products that are similar but were relinquished by the former firm. If consumers in either country wish to buy both products, they will be importing and exporting products that are, for purposes of national statistics, the same.

Turning briefly to external economies of scale, these are said to derive when the cost per unit of output depends on the size of an industry, not the size of the individual firm. Thus, an industry in one country may produce at lower costs than the same industry that is smaller in other countries. A country might dominate world markets in a particular product, not because it has one massive firm producing enormous quantities, but rather because it has many small firms that interact to create significant, competitive, critical mass – for example, crystal glassware in Germany. No one firm may be large, but all small firms in total create such a competitive industry that firms in other countries cannot break into the industry.

Unlike internal economies of scale, external economies of scale do not necessarily lead to imperfect markets, but they tend to result in an industry dominating its field in world markets. This provides an explanation as to why all industries do not necessarily move to the country with the lowest cost energy, resources or labour. What gives rise to this critical mass of small firms and their interrelationships is a complex question. Porter's work provides a partial explanation as to how these critical masses are sustained.

The competitive advantage of nations

The focus of early trade theory was on the country or nation and its inherent, natural endowment that might give rise to increasing competitiveness. As trade theory evolved, its focus moved to the industry and product level, leaving the question of national competitiveness behind. More recently, attention has moved to the question of how countries, governments and private industry can alter the conditions within a country and aid the competitiveness of its firms.

The prime mover in this area has been Porter (1990). He observes that national prosperity is created, not inherited. It does not merely grow out of a country's natural endowments, as classical economics suggests. To Porter, a nation's competitiveness depends on the capacity of its industry to innovate and upgrade. Thus, companies gain advantage against world competitors because of pressure and challenge. They benefit from having strong rivals domestically, aggressive local suppliers and demanding customers in the home market. Porter concludes that, ultimately, nations succeed in particular industries because their home environment is most forward-looking, dynamic and challenging.

Porter argues that innovation drives and sustains competitiveness. A firm must avail itself of all dimensions of competition which he categorizes into the four components of the diamond of national advantage:

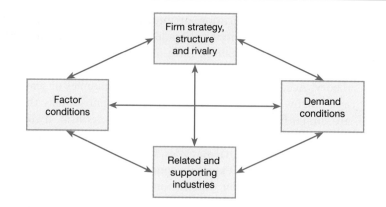

Figure 20.6 The diamond of national advantage.
Source: Porter, 1990.

- *Factor conditions.* Most important, for Porter, is the ability of a nation continually to create, upgrade and deploy its factors of production, such as resources and skilled labour, rather than the initial endowment.

- *Demand conditions.* This embraces the spirit of competition that the firm faces in its domestic market. Highly competitive and demanding local markets are most likely to give rise to competitive edge. The character of the market, rather than its size, is paramount in promoting and maintaining the competitiveness of the firm. For Porter, character of the market translates into demanding customers.

- *Related and supporting industries.* This refers to the competitiveness of related industries and suppliers to the firm. The firm that is operating within a mass of related firms and industries gains and maintains advantages through close working relationships, proximity to suppliers and timeliness of product and information flows.

- *Firm strategy, structure and rivalry.* The conditions in the home market influence the ability to compete internationally. But no single operating strategy, form of ownership or management style can be said to be universally appropriate – flexibility becomes of essence.

These four components (see Figure 20.6) constitute what nations and firms must create and sustain locally as a forerunner to international success.

20.12 | Summary

- Although many multinational firms appear to pursue a haphazard approach to overseas expansion, there is invariably an underlying rationale.

- Generally, this involves understanding and then capitalizing on those factors that led to success in the past – and this usually involves a variety of market imperfections.

- These imperfections include barriers to entry, product differentiation, control of raw materials, patents, know-how, trademarks, marketing and organizational skills and so on.

- Theories of international business and foreign direct investment are summarized in this chapter.

20.13 | End of chapter questions

Question1

King Company and President Inc. are automobile manufacturers that desire to benefit from economies of scale. King Company has decided to establish distributorship subsidiaries in various countries, while President Inc. has decided to establish manufacturing in various countries. Which firm is more likely to benefit from economies of scale?

Question 2

Why do you suppose that foreign governments provide MNCs with incentives to undertake FDI in their countries?

Question 3

Explain the theory of comparative advantage as a motive for foreign trade.

20.14 | *Appendix 1* Inward stock of world foreign direct investment

Regions/countries	1990 (in billions of US$)	% of total	1999 (in billion of US$)	% of total
Developed countries	1,380,827	78.4	3,230,800	67.7
North America	507,780	28.8	1,253,555	26.3
United States	394,911	22.4	1,087,289	22.8
Canada	112,872	6.4	166,266	3.5
Western Europe	770,434	43.7	1,757,208	36.8
European Union	723,455	41.1	1,652,322	34.6
Austria	9,884	0.6	23,363	0.5
Belgium/Luxembourg	58,388	3.3	181,184	3.8
Denmark	9,192	0.5	37,830	0.8
Finland	5,132	0.3	16,540	0.3
France	86,508	4.9	181,974	3.8
Germany	111,232	6.3	225,595	4.7
Greece	14,016	0.8	22,948	0.5
Ireland	5,502	0.3	43,969	0.9
Italy	57,985	3.3	107,995	2.3
Netherlands	73,564	4.2	215,234	4.5
Portugal	9,769	0.6	20,513	0.4
Spain	65,916	3.7	112,582	2.4
Sweden	12,461	0.7	68,035	1.4
United Kingdom	203,905	11.6	394,560	8.3
Other western Europe	46,979	2.7	104,886	2.2
Switzerland	34,245	1.9	73,099	1.5
Norway	12,391	0.7	30,885	0.6
Others	343	0.0	902	0.0
Other developed countries	102,609	5.8	220,037	4.6
Australia and New Zealand	81,549	4.6	151,817	3.2
Japan	9,850	0.6	38,806	0.8
Israel	2,012	0.1	12,366	0.3
South Africa	9,198	0.5	17,048	0.4
Developing countries	377,380	21.4	1,438,484	30.1
Africa	44,104	2.5	93,066	2.0
Asia	211,632	12.0	846,677	17.7
Latin America and the Caribbean	118,300	6.7	485,604	10.2
Developing Europe	1,131	0.1	9,773	0.2
Central and eastern Europe	2,991	0.2	102,697	2.2
Least developed countries	7,092	0.4	28,602	0.6
Total	1,761,198	100.0	4,771,981	100.0
Addenda:				
Outward stock	1,716,364		4,759,333	
Inward stock	1,761,198		4,771,981	
Difference	−44,834		−12,648	

Note: Numbers might not add up due to rounding.
Developing Europe refers to Bosnia and Herzegovina, Croatia, Malta, Slovenia and TFYR Macedonia.
Source: Rugman and Hodgetts (2003).

20.15 | *Appendix 2* Outward stock of world foreign direct investment

Regions/countries	1990 (in billions of US$)	% of total	1999 (in billion of US$)	% of total
Developed countries	1,634,099	95.2	4,276,961	89.9
North America	515,350	30.0	1,309,813	27.5
United States	430,521	25.1	1,131,466	23.8
Canada	84,829	4.9	178,347	3.7
Western Europe	866,450	50.5	2,574,926	54.1
European Union	789,401	46.0	2,336,631	49.1
Austria	4,273	0.2	17,522	0.4
Belgium/Luxembourg	40,636	2.4	159,461	3.4
Denmark	7,342	0.4	42,035	0.9
Finland	11,227	0.7	31,803	0.7
France	110,119	6.4	298,012	6.3
Germany	151,581	8.8	420,908	8.8
Greece	853	0.0	783	0.0
Ireland	2,150	0.1	15,096	0.3
Italy	57,261	3.3	168,370	3.5
Netherlands	109,005	6.4	306,396	6.4
Portugal	504	0.0	9,605	0.2
Spain	15,652	0.9	97,553	2.0
Sweden	49,491	2.9	104,985	2.2
United Kingdom	229,307	13.4	664,103	14.0
Other western Europe	77,049	4.5	238,295	5.0
Switzerland	66,086	3.9	199,452	4.2
Norway	10,888	0.6	38,423	0.8
Others	75	0.0	420	0.0
Other developed countries	252,299	14.7	392,222	8.2
Australia and New Zealand	34,680	2.0	62,453	1.3
Japan	201,440	11.7	292,781	6.2
Israel	1,169	0.1	6,873	0.1
South Africa	15,010	0.9	30,115	0.6
Developing countries	81,907	4.8	468,744	9.8
Africa	12,249	0.7	16,974	0.4
Asia	48,929	2.9	345,206	7.3
Latin America and the Caribbean	20,378	1.2	104,580	2.2
Developing Europe	258	0.0	607	0.0
Central and eastern Europe	358	0.0	13,628	0.3
Least developed countries	533	0.0	1,653	0.0
Total	1,716,364	100.0	4,759,333	100.0

Note: Numbers might not add up due to rounding.
Developing Europe refers to Bosnia and Herzegovina, Croatia, Malta, Slovenia and TFYR Macedonia.
Source: Rugman and Hodgetts (2003).

21 Exchange controls and corporate tax in international investment

Two of the major distorting features of international investment appraisal, which are absent in the domestic counterpart, are exchange controls and international corporation tax. In this chapter, a summary of the potential problems that they create is set out. So, as a prerequisite to arriving at a logical model for international capital budgeting, we present an overview that is highly specific to the task of analysing and appraising international investment opportunities.

21.1 | Exchange controls

One of the major differences between domestic and international capital budgeting is the possible distorting effect of exchange controls. Not all host countries impose exchange controls but a significant number do – hence the overview of this topic in this chapter. Exchange controls refer to regulations that forbid or restrict the holding of assets denominated in foreign currency and foreign exchange transactions of residents insofar as they affect the earning, holding and spending of foreign currencies or the acquisition, retention or disposal of assets and liabilities situated abroad and/or denominated in foreign currency; exchange controls may also circumscribe the actions of non-residents in the host country. In connection with controls, currency is said to be convertible if the authorities of the country allow it to be exchanged without restriction or the need for permission into currencies of other countries. Complete freedom for all residents of a country and for all holders of a national currency to buy foreign currency or foreign-currency-denominated assets is termed full convertibility or free convertibility. It exists in a significant number of Western economies and for a number of developing countries.

When faced with problems such as recurring deficits on balance of payments, governments frequently resort to various controls. Exchange control is one such form. Confronted with inadequate reserves to finance deficits, or faced with increasing liquid liabilities to foreigners on a scale that threatens to create future difficulties if redemption of these liabilities is requested, exchange controls are often invoked in an effort to prevent problems becoming worse. Exchange rate movements affect such broad segments of the economy that governments, faced with financial difficulties, often resort to supporting exchange rates within some range or band. Exchange controls take many forms and they affect international transactions. In balance of

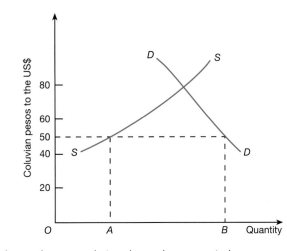

Figure 21.1 Foreign exchange market under exchange controls.

payments terms, they are intended to have positive effects – or perhaps less negative effects than would otherwise be the case – upon current account and capital account outturns.

The imposition of exchange controls usually follows a consistent pattern. Payments to foreigners exceed receipts from foreign countries. Depreciation of the value of the country's currency is anticipated and in an effort to strengthen the home currency, exchange controls are invoked. The government legislates that those who obtain foreign exchange through exports and other transactions must sell their foreign exchange to the government or designated banks. The government must allocate this foreign exchange to importers and other purchasers of foreign goods and services. The host government usually keeps its exchange rate at a level at which it is overvalued, even though this means that demand for imports increases and exporting becomes less profitable and more difficult. In turn, this means that demand for foreign currency is greater than its supply. Hence some of those who wish to buy foreign exchange cannot be permitted to do so.

The situation is illustrated in Figure 21.1 in which it is assumed that the Coluvian government attempts to keep the exchange rate of the Coluvian peso equivalent to 50 pesos to the dollar. Demand and supply in a free market would result in an equilibrium rate of 80 pesos to the dollar. At the exchange rate of 50 pesos, holders of foreign exchange would be reluctant to surrender it since they know that the equilibrium rate is 80 pesos. So the government must force the sale of the supply of foreign exchange, *OA*, to it or to designated banks, and it must allocate that supply to those who wish to buy it. At the official rate of 50 pesos to the dollar, rather than the equilibrium rate of 80, demand for dollars and indeed goods priced in foreign currency will be greater than at the equilibrium rate. The government has therefore created a problem which it must solve by dictate. It has to nominate who may purchase foreign exchange or it must simply restrict purposes for which foreign currency may be purchased. At 50 pesos to the dollar, the quantity *OB* would be purchased, but this is legally prevented since the country only has *OA*. Hardly surprisingly, significant black markets begin to develop in foreign currency with the black market price reflecting that rate which would hold in equilibrium rather than the official rate.

Exchange controls restrict imports to a level less than under free-market conditions. When a country maintaining exchange controls devalues its currency, imports increase – if permitted. In Figure 21.1, if Coluvia were to devalue its currency from 50 pesos per dollar to 80 pesos per dollar, the supply of foreign exchange would tend to increase and therefore the purchase of foreign exchange for imports would also tend to increase.

Typically, exchange controls apply to residents of a country. The nature of the transaction for which foreign exchange is required is invariably important as is the location to which foreign currency is to be transferred and the location of the party with whom the transaction is being carried out. All companies operating in a given country are usually treated, for exchange control purposes, as resident in that country. That the head office or controlling staff reside in another country does not affect residence for exchange control purposes. Where financial institutions import and export large amounts of foreign currency, special rules usually apply. Residence for exchange control purposes is determined by a different set of rules from that which determines residence for tax purposes.

The applicability of exchange control rules is governed by the type of transaction involved, but such rules normally embrace:

- imports, including obtaining the foreign currency required and licences, if any;

- exports and the disposition of foreign exchange proceeds;

- invisibles;

- investment abroad, including direct and portfolio investment;

- operation of multiple currency rates (this would include different exchange rates for different purposes);

- borrowing abroad by residents;

- permissions for non-residents to open bank accounts in the host country;

- permissions for residents to hold foreign currency accounts;

- limitations on the use of some foreign exchange management techniques;

- profit repatriation out of the host country.

It is the last bullet point that is particularly relevant for international capital budgeting. It is especially worthy of separate focus, and this now follows.

21.2 | Profits repatriation

This is a critically important and complex topic. Profits made and cash flows earned in a foreign country are of no value to the international corporation if they cannot ultimately be repatriated to the home country for distribution to shareholders.

Many developed countries allow free repatriation of all profits and capital at any time. Normally under exchange control regulations, capital put into a country may be repatriated but the return of profits is strictly limited. Given that international companies have sought to circumvent the profits repatriation constraint by the use of billings for royalties, research and development, consultancy fees and the use of transfer pricing distortions and so on, it is hardly surprising that countries with exchange controls have responded by drawing up tough regulations and limiting repatriations in general. Many countries with exchange controls limit the amount to be returned to a given percentage of total capital invested and/or to a proportion of retained profit. This has the effect of forcing reinvestment of some of the profit in the host country. Frequently, profits that cannot be repatriated for a specified time – blocked profits – have to be invested in specified government bonds; upon maturity of the bond, they may be sent abroad. Since such government bonds attract low interest rates and since they are frequently used in high-inflation countries, their effect is hardly advantageous to the multinational corporation.

Sometimes countries with exchange controls segregate investments according to whether they are of an approved or of an ordinary status. Approved status projects have a privileged profits repatriation position or they may attract advantageous exchange rates on repatriation. From the international company's point of view such stipulations are critical in evaluating overseas investment projects.

Rules on profit distribution are so complex and varied and subject to such frequent change that investing international companies make it a policy to scrutinize carefully local regulations and they often negotiate a specific watertight agreement with the host nation in respect of capital and profit repatriation. But even this may not be sufficient. Such agreements have been renounced by existing governments. And new incoming governments may also disregard agreements made by their predecessors. Compensation guarantees from home governments are available for some countries – however there is, inevitably, a cost involved.

21.3 | Circumventing profit repatriation restrictions

Various means are available to the international company for moving funds and profits from one country to another. These include:

- transfer pricing;
- fees and royalty agreements;
- leading and lagging;
- dividends;
- loans;
- equity versus debt considerations;
- currency invoicing;
- reinvoicing centres.

Exchange control authorities have become well aware that multinational companies use transfer pricing, royalties and leading and lagging to move funds and have consequently put impediments in the way of these techniques. Tight controls on invisibles, validation of import and export prices and constraints on leading and lagging are all examples of ways in which host governments have attacked this problem.

The making and repaying of inter-company loans which originally involved the input of foreign finance into the host country is often one of the few legitimate ways to transfer funds from a country with tight exchange controls. But, because foreign debt capital is subject to political risk and because funds may become blocked in foreign countries, multinationals have resorted to the use of parallel loans, back-to-back loans and currency swaps. Parallel loans are effectively a pair of loans made simultaneously in two countries. A parallel loan transaction involves two parties, who simultaneously make loans of the same value to one another's foreign subsidiaries. The parent, company A, will extend a loan in its home country and currency to a subsidiary of company B, whose foreign parent will lend the local currency equivalent in its country to the subsidiary of company A. Drawdown of the loan, repayment of principal and payments of interest are arranged to occur simultaneously. It should be noted that such transactions involve two separate loans but no cross-border movement of funds. Normally, there is some arrangement whereby, legally, the loans may be set off one against the other. But loans cannot be offset in the respective consolidated balance sheets. Such loans appear as both assets and liabilities. Payment of interest is made by both parties. This is based upon the cost of money in each country.

Back-to-back loans are often employed to finance associates located in countries with high interest rates or restricted capital markets – particularly when there is a danger of currency controls, or where different rates of withholding tax are applied to loans from a financial institution. As an example, assume that the parent company deposits funds with a bank in country A which in turn lends the money to a subsidiary in country B. In this sense, the back-to-back loan is an inter-corporate loan channelled through a bank. The bank simply acts as an intermediary and from the bank's point of view the loan is risk-free because the parent's deposit provides collateral for the loan. Back-to-back loans of this sort create advantages where countries apply different withholding tax rates to interest paid to a foreign parent and interest paid to a financial institution. Furthermore, should currency controls be imposed, governments usually permit the local subsidiary to honour the repayment schedule of a loan from a major multinational bank. However, host government monetary authorities may have few reservations about placing impediments in the way of repayment of a straight inter-company loan. Back-to-back financing therefore provides better protection than an inter-company loan against exchange controls or expropriation.

Currency swaps achieve similar objectives to parallel loans but they are somewhat simpler. They involve two parties and one agreement. The two companies involved may sell currencies to each other at the spot rate and undertake to reverse the exchange after a specified term. Currency swaps have one or two advantages over parallel loans: they are reported off balance sheet, they have simpler documentation and they afford greater protection in the event of a default.

We now turn to considerations of debt versus equity in financing an overseas subsidiary. Generally speaking, financing an overseas subsidiary with debt from the parent company, as opposed to equity, provides greater flexibility. It is usually the case that a firm has greater latitude to repatriate funds in the form of interest and loan repayments than as dividends or reductions in equity. Furthermore, reductions in equity may be frowned upon by the host government. In addition, the use of loans as opposed to equity investment confers possibilities for reducing taxes. This arises on two fronts. Interest paid on a loan is usually tax deductible in the host nation, whereas dividend payments are not. Also, unlike dividends, loan repayments do not normally constitute taxable income to the parent company. To counter this, host countries' exchange controls may incorporate thin capitalization rules whereby debt maximum levels are assumed and imposed in terms of interpreting exchange control regulations.

Capital controls may be circumvented by the judicious use of currency invoicing. The choice of currency in which an invoice is billed may enable a firm to remove blocked funds from a country that has exchange controls. Assume that a subsidiary is located within a country which restricts profit repatriation. If a devaluation of the host currency is forecast, this may provide the firm with an opportunity to move excess blocked funds elsewhere. This may be achieved by invoicing exports from that subsidiary to the rest of the corporation in the local currency of the devaluing country at a contracted price. As the local currency depreciates, profit margins are reduced in that subsidiary as opposed to what they would have been had billing been in a hard currency. But elsewhere within the corporation, they are improved. Effectively, cash from the devaluing country is shifted to another part of the group.

Multinationals also consider the use of reinvoicing centres. They are mainly used by multinationals as part of the exposure management function but they are sometimes used to disguise profitability, avoid government scrutiny and co-ordinate transfer pricing policy for tax purposes. The reinvoicing centre may be used to counter exchange controls by setting it in low-tax countries. These centres take title to all goods sold across frontiers, whether by one subsidiary to another or by sale to a third-party customer, although the goods themselves move directly from the factory to the purchaser. The centre pays the seller and the centre receives payment from the purchaser. While reinvoicing centres create obvious opportunities for using transfer pricing to the best advantage, they also give the international company considerable flexibility to utilize currency invoicing techniques. Needless to say, tax authorities and exchange control authorities are very suspicious of transactions which move through reinvoicing centres, especially when they are located in a tax haven.

It is also worth mentioning four other techniques that are used for circumventing exchange controls. These involve:

■ purchase of capital goods with blocked currency where the equipment is for corporate-wide use;

■ purchase of local services with blocked funds when such services are for use throughout the group;

- conducting and paying for research and development in the host country when the benefits accrue throughout the group;

- hosting corporate conventions, vacations and other expenses in the host country and paying for them with blocked currency.

The above techniques all involve purchasing goods or services locally which may aid the firm in other countries, thus achieving some measure of unblocking.

We now turn to a series of other techniques which can be categorized as countertrade but embrace barter, counterpurchase, industrial offset, buy-back and switch trading. All may be used by multinationals with the objective of unblocking funds which would otherwise be trapped in a host country by virtue of its exchange control regulations.

Countertrade

One method of profit remittance frequently used involves countertrade deals. Countertrade involves a reciprocal agreement for the exchange of goods or services. The parties involved may be firms or governments, and the reciprocal agreements can take a number of forms – for example, barter, counterpurchase, industrial offset, buy-back and switch trading. So what distinguishes the different types of countertrade?

Barter is the simplest form of countertrade. It involves the direct exchange of goods and services from one country for the goods or services of another. No money crosses frontiers, so there is no need for letters of credit or drafts, or trade financing or credit insurance. Frequently, one of the parties in a barter deal does not want the goods that are received, and so a third party that specializes in brokering arranges to sell them on for a fee. An oft-quoted example of a barter deal was the transfer in 1978 of the Polish international footballer, Kazimierz Deyna, for photocopiers and French lingerie.

Barter requires a mutual coincidence of wants. The ultimate parties in the transaction must each want what the other party has to offer, and want it at the same time. Such complete coincidence is unlikely, and to account for this, a different form of countertrade, called counterpurchase, has evolved and is now more common than barter. Under counterpurchase, the seller agrees with the buyer either:

- to make purchases from a company nominated by the buyer (the buyer then settles up with the company it has nominated); or

- to take products from the buyer in the future.

Counterpurchase may involve a combination of the above two possibilities. Counterpurchase may involve partial compensation with products and the balance in cash. Such types of countertrade deals are, strictly speaking, called compensation agreements.

Another form of countertrade involves industrial offset. A large part of countertrade involves reciprocal agreements to buy materials or components from the buying company or country. Thus, an aircraft manufacturer might agree to buy engines from a buyer of its aircraft. Or the deal might involve the aircraft manufacturer buying aircraft engines from a foreign producer with the engine manufacturer's country buying a large number of the aircraft.

Buy-back is a frequently encountered form of countertrade: it is common with capital equipment. In a buy-back agreement, the seller of the capital equipment agrees to buy the products made with the equipment it supplies. Thus a maker of mining equipment might agree to buy the output of the mine for a given period, maybe ten to fifteen years. Sometimes the equipment buyer pays partly in terms of its own product and partly in cash. Again, buy-back agreements of this latter kind are correctly called compensation agreements.

Switch trading is different. It occurs when the importer has received credit for selling goods or services to another country at a previous time, and where this credit cannot be converted into financial payment, but has to be used for purchases in the country where the credit is held. The owner of the credit switches title to its credit to the company or country from which it is making a purchase. Thus, a UK firm might have a credit in blocking country X for manufacturing equipment it has delivered. If a UK firm finds a product in France that it wishes to purchase, the UK firm might pay the French firm with its credit in country X. The French firm might agree to this if it wished to buy goods from country X. Most switch deals are arranged through brokers.

21.4 | Other techniques of unblocking funds

A checklist and skeleton explanation of thirty methods used by international companies to enable profit remittance in the presence of exchange controls can be found in Buckley (1992). The whole point about the techniques referred to, including countertrade in all of its forms, is that they are relevant to international capital budgeting because they may provide the wherewithal to convert blocked cash generation in an overseas project into parent cash flows – but, of course, at a cost. Dependent upon the foreign country concerned, fees may range from 5 to 35 per cent – or even more.

Having completed a quick overview of exchange controls, we now move on to consider the essentials of international corporate taxation as it impacts upon cross-border investment appraisal.

21.5 | International corporate taxation

One of the essential steps in domestic capital budgeting is the allowance for corporate taxation in order to arrive at incremental net of tax cash flows. Of course, domestic capital budgeting essentially involves only home country taxation. A similar step applies to international capital budgeting, but it is of greater complexity since it may involve tax outflows at both host and home country levels.

Clearly, every aspect of corporate tax in every country cannot possibly be covered here – even briefly. However, there are certain common themes that do recur in the domain of international taxation and it is upon these that we focus. For the purposes of this overview for international capital budgeting purposes, the focus is upon key aspects of international corporate tax – namely, withholding taxes, branch versus subsidiary and taxation of dividend remittances. But the topic is really a vast one and has far more facets than these. What follows in the next three sections in this chapter is an essential simplification. It is necessary to understand this before embarking upon the analysis of international capital projects.

Withholding taxes

Withholding taxes are collected from foreign individuals and/or corporations on income they have received from sources within a country. If a UK resident earns dividends in Canada, taxes will be withheld and paid to the Canadian revenue authorities. Credit is generally received at home for taxes withheld overseas. So the level of withholding primarily affects the amount of taxes received by the respective tax authorities. If the UK resident in the example above has 15 per cent withheld in Canada and is in a 20 per cent marginal tax bracket in the United Kingdom (assuming the tax rate on dividends to be 20 per cent, which is not precisely the case at the time of writing), the UK tax payable will be reduced to 5 per cent after credit for the 15 per cent is given. Higher withholding rates therefore generally mean that more tax is collected by the foreign authorities and a smaller amount by the home government. This is the essence of a particular topic that is extremely complicated in reality and is, of course, subject to regular change.

Branch versus subsidiary

A key aspect of corporate tax planning concerns whether to operate abroad via a branch or through a subsidiary. A branch is a foreign operation that is incorporated at home – not in the host territory. A subsidiary is incorporated in the host country.

If a foreign activity is not expected to be profitable for a number of years, there may be an advantage to starting out with a branch so that negative earnings abroad may be used to offset profits at home. The tax laws of some countries allow branch income to be consolidated in this way. If a company expects positive foreign income, and this income is not to be repatriated, there may be tax advantages to a foreign subsidiary. Foreign branches pay home taxes on income as it is earned. Foreign subsidiaries do not pay home taxes until the income is repatriated to the home country.

Dividends

The description in this section relates specifically to the holding company based in the United Kingdom. But since US and many European countries' tax rules relating to overseas dividends apply in a similar manner to that in the United Kingdom, the exposition is equally applicable to many other countries. But whenever one is dealing with tax regulations the advice that one examines local tax rules carefully applies. They are not always logical. For example, for dividends from an EU host to an EU parent, dividends may be (but not for all EU countries) exempt from withholding taxes.

If a UK-resident company makes investments abroad, the company is liable to corporation tax on income received before deduction of foreign taxes. This rule applies

Table 21.1 Tax position of UK company with overseas income

Holding company in UK owns 100% of the Ruritanian business.
Columns 1 and 3 assume that the UK corporation tax rate is 50%.
Columns 2 and 4 assume that UK corporation tax is only 35% (this is not exactly true, of course).
Columns 1 and 2 assume that the Ruritanian business is a subsidiary.
Columns 3 and 4 assume that the Ruritanian business is a branch of the UK.
Ruritanian profits are, in sterling terms, £2m pre-tax. In Ruritania, businesses are subject to a 30% tax. Where the local business is a subsidiary, the Ruritanian company pays a dividend of £500,000 and this is subject to a local withholding tax on dividends of 10%. In the case of the branch, there is no distribution.

Ruritania as a subsidiary (£000)			Ruritania as a branch (£000)	
50%	35%	UK corporation tax rate	50%	35%
2,000	2,000	Pre-tax profits	2,000	2,000
600	600	Foreign profits tax	600	600
1,400	1,400	Profit available for distribution	1,400	1,400
500	500	Paid out as dividend	–	–
900	900	Profit retained	1,400	1,400
450	450	UK net receipt of dividend	–	–
50	50	Withholding tax thereon	–	–
500	500	Distribution gross of dividend tax	–	–
714	714	Grossed up for UK tax purposes (multiply by 100/70)	–	–
714	714	Subject to tax	2,000	2,000
357	250	UK tax rate applied	1,000	700
		Foreign tax credit		
(214)	(214)	Profits tax	(600)	(600)
(50)	(50)	Withholding tax	–	–
93	nil	Additional UK tax payable	400	100
–	14	Excess taxes paid	–	–

to foreign subsidiaries and also to the chargeable fraction of any capital gains on the disposal of foreign assets.

Where a business is carried on through a foreign subsidiary, the UK company's liability arises on actual amounts received from the subsidiary by way of interest or dividend. Double tax relief is available in respect of the foreign tax suffered on both income and other gains.

Normally, only direct foreign taxes are taken into account for double tax relief, but if a UK company receives dividends from a foreign company in which it owns 10 per cent or more of the voting power, underlying taxes on the profits out of which the dividends are paid are taken into account as well. In this case, the amount included in UK profits is the dividend plus both the direct and underlying foreign taxes. Double tax relief is given, but it should be noted that the relief on overseas income cannot exceed the UK corporation tax payable on overseas income. Table 21.1 is included to show how this treatment works in numerical terms for a UK group that owns 100 per cent of a business in Ruritania, a fictional foreign country.

The assumptions at the head of Table 21.1 are important. They indicate the underlying position of the Ruritanian business relative to its UK parent and they set out UK and Ruritanian rates of corporate tax. In particular, it should be noted that when the Ruritanian business is a subsidiary of the UK parent, the distribution before overseas dividend tax is grossed up to obtain the amount subject to UK tax (see halfway down columns 1 and 2 in the table). This sum is taxed at the UK corporate tax rate but a foreign tax credit is available. This is given in respect of all the dividend withholding tax borne and for a proportion of foreign profits tax paid. In the example, the foreign profits tax credit, amounting to £214,000, is obtained by taking the amount of foreign profits tax paid (the equivalent of £600,000) and multiplying it by the amount paid out as dividend (the equivalent of £500,000) divided by the profit available for distribution (the equivalent of £1,400,000).

Note also that if there are excess taxes paid, as in column 2 of Table 21.1, the United Kingdom will impose additional taxes but will, in fact, allow the use of these excess taxes paid as an offset against UK taxes due on other income arising from that country. In other words, credit for foreign taxes is given on a source by source basis.

An overseas holding company (or dividend cleaning company) may be interposed between a foreign operating company and group head office with the function of bringing together foreign dividends paid out of profits that have suffered tax at high and low effective rates. The resulting dividends from the overseas holding company will be regarded as a single source and as having suffered foreign tax at the weighted average of the effective rates attaching to the dividends that it has received from subsidiaries. The proportion of dividend income into the mixer company may be planned to produce the best underlying rate on dividend flows to the parent – see Figure 21.2.

For UK companies, with effect from 31 March 2001, it is no longer possible (under the legislation in the Finance Act 2000) to mix high and low tax dividends within an intermediate offshore holding company. However, following representations from British companies, it remains the case that the illogical effects of double taxation as exemplified in the pre-mixing situation in Figure 21.2 may be dealt with under new holding company, mixer company and double taxation rules. The complexity of the regulations makes them inappropriate for discussion in this text.

The position where the foreign business is a branch of the UK company is exemplified in the right-hand columns of Table 21.1. Note that all foreign profit, whether remitted to the United Kingdom or not, is liable to UK tax with a credit for overseas tax already paid. This kind of tax treatment is applicable for many countries other than the United Kingdom.

Foreign tax credits are not available in all jurisdictions and some countries operate an exemption rather than a credit system, in which case dividend planning needs will be different.

Another important feature of dividend planning is the operation of intermediate holding companies to accumulate investment income. For example, a holding company might be formed and dividends received from lower-tier subsidiaries are retained there, rather than sending them by dividend to the parent company. Such treasury planning is, however, subject to anti-avoidance tax legislation in many

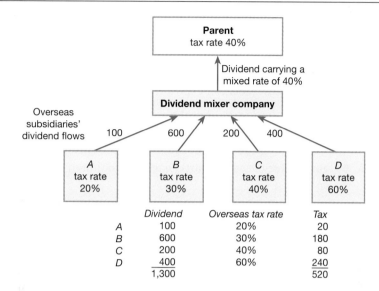

Figure 21.2 Operation of a dividend mixer company.

countries. Intermediate holding companies are also used to take advantage of tax treaties in order to reduce withholding taxes. It may be possible, by correct choice of the intermediate company, to reduce a withholding tax rate to zero.

Evidently, the process is so complex that corporate treasury executives and tax experts need to get together to consider the possibilities before them created by non-symmetrical tax treatment of dividends – and of other features as well. The whole point of this section is, of course, to present the sinews of international taxation given its relevance in international capital budgeting.

21.6 | Taxation of UK multinationals

We now turn to the tax regime facing UK-based multinationals with respect to the tax position on foreign exchange positions. In essence, the legislation sets down two acceptable accounting methods for foreign exchange taxation purposes – accruals or mark to market. Under the tax rules, foreign exchange differences arising on most monetary assets and liabilities will be taxed or relieved as income. Assets within the scope of the regime include cash, foreign currency and debts. Liabilities include debts and tax-deductible trading provisions; foreign currency contracts are also included.

The basic rule is that monetary items denominated in foreign currency will be translated into sterling at the end of each accounting period and the difference taken into account in computing taxable profit or loss. Complications arise where accounting rules allow a different result. In some cases, there may be an accounting versus tax mismatch. In other cases there are special rules – which require elections to be made within tight time limits – under which an alternative tax treatment is applied to reflect more closely the accounting treatment. Examples of cases where special rules may apply include:

■ taxation of foreign branch operations;

■ hedging of translation exposure;

■ taxation of unrealized exchange profits.

Complications are likely to arise in relation to:

■ anticipatory hedging, particularly in relation to gains realized on rolling forward contracts;

■ hedging of transactions or exposures of one company by another company.

The tax regime requires annual recognition of exchange differences arising on translation of foreign currency monetary assets and liabilities. Accordingly, companies will be taxed on unrealized foreign exchange gains, but at the same time will benefit from any unrealized foreign exchange losses. But there are special rules which allow, in certain circumstances, for deferral of part of the taxation of unrealized exchange gains on long-term assets or liabilities. The deferral is available only to the extent that this amount exceeds 10 per cent of the company's profits. This deferral provision should affect only the tax payable – not the tax charge in the accounts. Thus a deferred tax provision will normally be needed.

As with the rules for foreign exchange, the rule for the taxation of financial instruments is that payments and receipts under the instruments covered by the legislation, including most interest rate and currency swaps, floors, caps, collars, futures and FRAs, will be taxed as income or allowed as deductions from profits. Where the lifetime of the instrument spans more than one accounting period, income or expense is to be recognized each year according to either mark-to-market criteria or on an accruals basis.

21.7 | Multicurrency management centres

Multinational corporations frequently set up currency management centres to focus and control currency management. Foreign exchange deals and covering by subsidiaries are usually routed through such centres. The mere existence of such centres often creates suspicion in the minds of local tax authorities. There may be problems in persuading tax authorities to accept such centres as legitimate business ventures rather than as tax avoidance vehicles. Nonetheless, where a multicurrency management centre has been created, it can provide possibilities for tax minimization.

The centre is likely to be the focus of foreign exchange transactions and will probably carry the currency exposure risk of the total corporation. Clearly, the tax implications of the location of such a centre need to be carefully studied. A tax haven may reduce the tax charge on foreign exchange gains but will not provide relief for any losses or the cost of administrating the centre itself. The centre should be set in a location that has tax treaties with other countries and in which there are advantages for the corporation as a whole. Tax on interest or dividends withheld should be available to reduce local taxes, and foreign tax credits should be similarly available. An extremely careful assessment of the worldwide tax burden of the corporation must precede choice of centre.

Should the multinational corporation wish to charge foreign exchange losses and administration costs of the centre to its various subsidiaries, it will probably have to prove the need for the centre other than as a tax avoidance device. The charging of a fee for the use of the centre's services to subsidiaries at a rate, for example of $1/_2$ per cent of the value of each deal helps in this context. Such charges should be in line with fees charged by independent consultancy services. However, tax authorities view with great suspicion fees paid to offshore multicurrency management centres located in areas where the corporation tax rate is very low.

Multicurrency management centres may be the focus of inter-company pricing. A company has scope in choosing the currencies in which it will undertake its inter-company transactions. This choice may be neutral before tax but far from neutral after tax. Take an international company that manufactures in a low-tax area with a strong currency and sells to an affiliate in a high-tax area with a weak currency. It is preferable to invoice in the strong currency and have the exchange loss realized in the high-tax area. This is preferable to invoicing in the weak currency and recognizing the exchange loss in the low-tax territory.

21.8 | Co-ordination centres

The Netherlands, Luxembourg, Belgium, Dublin Docks and Switzerland have become popular domiciles among European companies for the location of financial subsidiaries designed to reduce tax payments. A checklist for where to locate a financial subsidiary would include the following criteria:

■ political and economic stability;

■ favourable tax laws;

■ hard currency;

■ no exchange controls;

■ low stamp duty rates;

■ low capital taxes;

■ good banking and other financial infrastructure;

■ no withholding taxes on interest payments and dividends;

■ no (or low) taxes on interest income;

- good tax treaty network;

- no securities turnover tax;

- no (or low) taxes on foreign participation.

Belgium has become very popular among companies in the United States and Europe for siting co-ordination centres. Co-ordination centre legislation, enacted in Belgium, provides tax incentives for international groups which centralize their co-ordination activities in Belgium. The legislation permits the multinational, in agreement with the Belgian government, to construct a tailor-made centre to meet its needs. Such centres may carry out a wide variety of financial and managerial services on a virtually tax-free basis. The following activities are permitted for co-ordination centres:

- To establish in-house banks which can engage in inter-group lending, netting, reinvoicing, factoring, leasing and centralizing foreign exchange management.

- To raise external loans and issue Euronotes and Eurobonds.

- To centralize marketing, research and development and other group support activities.

Legislation can provide the following cash advantages to co-ordination centres:

- Ten-year tax exemption.

- No capital registration tax.

- No tax on real estate used by the company.

- Tax withholding credits, exemption from withholding taxes and from foreign exchange regulation, and tax and social security exemptions for expatriate employees.

Two sorts of business activity are permitted under co-ordination centre rules. The first includes advertising, information collection and dissemination, insurance and reinsurance, research, government relations, accounting and data processing and centralized purchasing. The second group covers inter-company financial transactions whose objective is to centralize treasury management.

To qualify, the co-ordination centre must be part of an international group with a specified level of aggregate capital and annual turnover. Financial institutions are excluded from obtaining the tax benefits of co-ordination centres in Belgium. The co-ordination centre must have at least ten full-time employees by the end of the second year of operations with no restriction on their nationality – although it is probably prudent to have some Belgian nationals. If legislation designed to attack these facilities were introduced, they would not disappear but merely relocate to a territory outside any newly enacted rules.

The effect of taking advantage of co-ordination centre legislation is that the multinational can readily centralize treasury and other cross-border activities in a low-tax environment while creating tax-deductible inter-company costs for subsidiaries in high-tax countries.

21.9 | Foreign exchange rate strategy

The range of local tax rules on foreign exchange gains and losses makes the achievement of an optimal foreign exchange tax strategy difficult. Complexity is compounded by frequent changes in tax legislation.

The objective of tax strategy is to maximize distributable net-of-tax profit. As such, tax planning is part of the overall corporate strategy. But tax strategy may have important behavioural implications. If the multinational decides to devolve maximum autonomy to its foreign subsidiaries, it is not likely to permit a tax tactic of repaying loans to obtain tax credits to compromise its style of decentralized management. Low profits in certain foreign subsidiaries, created and manipulated for tax reasons, may lower morale of key staff in a foreign subsidiary.

Nonetheless, tax treatment of exchange gains and losses provides a rich and broad seam for the skills of the corporate treasurer. In this area, particular attention must be paid to the lack of symmetry in tax laws.

Devising a tax strategy involves tabulating tax rules, exchange controls and tax rates in each territory in which the multinational corporation operates. This represents the framework within which tax strategy operates. Another important step towards the specification of a fruitful tax strategy is the tabulation of expected cash flows and assets and liabilities held in each currency. This may already have been done as a stage in normal foreign exchange exposure management. Examination of tax effects of future transactions – in particular, loans in foreign currencies, forward cover and translation gains or losses, plus a schedule of the benefits and costs of channelling such transactions through an offshore tax haven – should also be considered. Treatment of individual transactions will depend upon the local tax laws and exchange control regulations existing. Hodder and Senbet (1990) note the key role that tax arbitrage plays in developing an international capital structure and they set out a number of mechanisms for tax arbitrage transactions.

Examples abound of policies designed to maximize distributable post-tax cash flows. Financial assets may be moved between subsidiaries so that gains occur in countries where the tax on gains is nil or very low. Inter-company debt repayment may be accelerated (or retarded) to achieve optimal tax treatment. Subsidiaries may borrow from one another in weak foreign currencies if the exchange gain on the loan devaluation is not taxed in one centre but the loss is tax allowable elsewhere. And they might borrow in strong currencies if the loss on loan revaluation is allowable in one centre while the profit is not taxable in the other. The tax effect in either case may be a key factor in the decision as to where and in which currency to borrow. If the unrealized loss on a foreign loan is not allowed against tax until the loan is repaid, it may be tax efficient to repay it and refinance. Allowable exchange losses should be located in those countries where tax rates are highest. Subsidiaries in weak currency countries may be funded by foreign loans if the exchange loss can be set against local profits. Ensuring that debt is concentrated in countries where operations are profitable and where the tax rate is high is tax efficient. Financing a venture with short-term roll-over funds which are exchange loss allowable against tax, rather than with a long-term loan which is allowable only on termination of the loan, may be tax efficient. Making all currency contracts assignable may also be a useful tactic. Schemes of this sort have to conform to local exchange control regulations, but within such constraints there is plenty of scope to maximize post-tax profits.

We now have the wherewithal to examine the topic of international capital budgeting in more depth; we do so starting in the next chapter.

21.10 ▌ Summary

- The tax treatment of foreign exchange gains and losses varies from one country to another. Great care must be taken to ensure that local tax regulations are properly and comprehensively understood if optimal tax treatment is to be obtained for a multinational group.

- Within the confines of a general text, it is only possible to describe a series of general principles.

- Under the UK tax rules, foreign exchange differences arising on most monetary assets and liabilities denominated in foreign currency will be taxed or relieved as income, usually in line with accounting treatments. The same idea applies to revenues and expenses on financial instruments. By and large, this puts the UK tax treatment on a similar footing to that in the United States.

- Exchange control regulations forbid or restrict the holding of assets denominated in foreign currency and foreign exchange transactions of residents of the country which has instituted the control. Exchange controls also circumscribe the actions of non-residents in the host country.

- Currency is said to be convertible if the authorities of the home country allow it to be exchanged, without restriction or the need for permission, into currencies of other countries.

- Exchange controls take many forms which range from requirements that residents surrender all holdings of foreign currency to restrictions on the acquisition of foreign-currency-denominated assets and liabilities, from the stipulation that foreign companies meet certain requirements for setting up businesses in the host country to restrictions on remittances out of the host country.

- In response to exchange controls, multinational companies have developed techniques to mitigate some of their adverse impacts. These include the use of transfer pricing, royalty payments, leading and lagging, matching, reinvoicing centres, parallel loans and many others.

- Living with exchange controls clearly presupposes a detailed knowledge of the actual regulations. Resort to a local consultant is often the wisest course because of complexities and unwritten interpretations of regulations and because of the scope for arranging individual agreements with host governments – and, not to put too fine a point on it, the availability of corruption when implementing regulations.

21.11 | End of chapter questions

Question 1
Why do you suppose countries impose foreign exchange controls?

Question 2
Do you think that, long-term, foreign exchange controls will encourage or discourage inward foreign investment?

22 The international capital budgeting framework

Like domestic capital investment decisions, international capital budgeting focuses upon expected incremental cash flows associated with a project. The specification of these flows for the international project creates the usual difficulties found in a domestic capital project, but international project analysis is more complex. Although the basic pattern follows the same model as that suggested by corporate financial theory, the multinational firm must consider factors peculiar to international operations.

A project may be estimated to produce very considerable cash flows in a foreign territory but, because of exchange control restrictions, the bulk of these foreign cash flows may not be distributable to the parent company. In these circumstances, looking at the project purely in terms of cash flows accruing in the foreign territory may indicate that it is worth investing. But is this good enough? Surely the present value to the parent company is a function of future cash flows accruing to it which are distributable to the parent company's investors. If the bulk of foreign territory cash flows were blocked by exchange controls, it would only be incremental cash flows which are remittable back to the parent company that add value for its investors. International capital projects may be looked at from at least two standpoints: incremental project cash flows and incremental parent cash flows. To the international company it is only incremental parent cash flows that can add shareholder value.

Complexities often arise in multinational companies because overseas investment projects have substantial knock-on effects on other operations elsewhere within the group. For example, an international engineering company, contemplating the establishment of a plant in Spain, may find that the proposed investment will affect the operations of other units within the multinational group. This may arise, in part, through the new project's effect on sales of other parts of the group within Europe – for example, sales deriving from the UK and Danish plants. But it may also arise through vertical integration by, for example, affecting the output of a mining operation in South America that it owns. It could be the case that the new plant is expected to absorb output from the mine. Where such knock-on effects exist, the firm needs to evaluate the project by aggregating all incremental cash flows accruing. Thus, while cash flows in Spain are clearly relevant, so are reduced cash flows accruing to the UK and Danish operations, and so are increased flows accruing to the South American mine. To get to grips with the difficulties of multinational capital budgeting, it is necessary to take cognizance of such effects.

This chapter gives a simplified overview of international capital budgeting. This is accompanied by a summary of the findings of various surveys of international project appraisal techniques used by US-based multinationals. That these tend to fall short of normative theory will become apparent. The development of a full spectrum of preferred practices in international capital budgeting follows in the chapters immediately following.

22.1 | The international complications

There is a handful of complexities in international capital budgeting. These embrace situations where:

- project cash flows and parent cash flows differ;

- part of the parent input is via equipment;

- exchange rates are not expected to be constant throughout the project's life;

- different rates of tax apply in the country of the project and in the parent's country;

- royalties and management fees are involved;

- full remittance of cash flows arising from a project are restricted in terms of payment to the parent.

In international capital budgeting, a significant difference usually exists between the cash flow of a project and the amount that is remittable to the parent. The main reason for this may be the existence of exchange controls in the host nation. Management in an overseas subsidiary can be excused for focusing only upon project cash flows accruing locally. Overseas managers often ignore the consequences of an investment upon the rest of the corporation – in particular the impact of the project at the level of distributable cash flows of the parent company. At the level of the project itself, the appropriate incremental cash inflows are those additional cash outturns resulting from new operations after adjustment for local corporate taxes. From the parent's view, the critical incremental cash flow figures are the additional remittable funds to the parent treasury in London or New York or Amsterdam or wherever. From the central treasury's point of view, the important cash flows relating to a new investment are incremental cash flows that are distributable to the multinational's headquarters. This means that management fees (net of the costs of providing supervision), royalties, interest, dividend remittances, loan inputs and repayments and equity inputs are all key cash flows.

According to corporate financial theory, the value of a project is determined by the net present value of future cash flows available for the investor. Generally, the parent multinational values only those cash flows that are available for repatriation. Valuation would logically be done net of any transfer costs, since it is only these remaining funds that can be used to pay interest at home and corporate dividends.

Table 22.1 Parent cash flows for an international investment in a country with exchange controls

---

Equity put into overseas project
Dividends remittable back from overseas project
Equity capital remitted back to parent
Loans put into overseas project
Loan interest
Loan repayments
Management fees received from overseas project net of supervision costs
Royalties
Equipment or inventory contributed to overseas project (here the opportunity cost is the relevant figure)
Contribution accruing to the parent or to a subsidiary within the group on incremental sales to the project. This effect may be positive or negative
Appropriate tax effects on remittance
Remittable value of real operating options
Terminal value of remittable dividends
Terminal value of remittable royalties, management fees, contribution from intra-group sales, etc.
Terminal value of blocked funds multiplied by factor to allow for probability of unblocking by the terminal value date

---

The estimation of parent cash flows involves us in focusing upon incremental remittable cash flows. Whether they are actually remitted or not is immaterial – we need to home in on flows that may be remitted.

International project evaluation might embrace two key stages of analysis. First, project cash flows might be computed from the overseas subsidiary's standpoint, as if it were a separate free-standing entity, that is as if it were being evaluated by a resident of the host country. Focus in the second stage of analysis moves to the parent. Here analysis requires forecasts of the amounts and timing of distributable cash flows. It also requires information about taxes payable. The cash flow projections to the parent may be checked in terms of logic by considering what the parent distributable cash flows would be without the investment and then considering the parent distributable post-investment cash flows and subtracting the former from the latter. It is distributable parent cash flows that matter from the standpoint of the multinational.

For an overseas investment in a country where there are no restrictions on remittance, incremental cash flows accruing to the multinational corporation might be forecast in local currency and then converted into the multinational corporation's home currency in accordance with expected exchange rates prevailing when such cash flows accrue. Where a project is in a country from which cash flow repatriation is restricted, the relevant focus should be upon remittable incremental parent cash flows. Analysis might embrace the cash flows set out in Table 22.1. The simplification described in the table is expanded upon in later chapters of this text.

Theoretically, the arguments in favour of considering only distributable parent cash flows in international capital budgeting decisions are overwhelming. However, one influential text, that by Rodriguez and Carter (1984), casts doubt upon this mode of analysis in respect of what its authors call the 'true multinational'. To use their own words:

> to the extent that the corporation views itself as a true multinational, the effect of restrictions on repatriation may not be severe. If the firm anticipates continued investment in a country which is in a growing market, the restriction is not even an issue to be addressed in a good-citizen or bad-citizen framework. Rather, the commitment is made for long-term continuing investments in the country and the restriction on repatriation is generally irrelevant.

Surely such a view is less than acceptable. Even the true multinational would be well advised to focus upon remittable cash flows from a project although this may include some subjective probabilities being applied to blocked cash flows to allow for their probability of becoming unblocked. In respect of reinvestment in the host country 'in a growing market', surely the potential of such investment might be taken into account by a valuation of the remittable cash flow implications to include a value put upon real operating options – see later on in this text.

In practice, surveys have shown that firms give distributable parent cash flows far too little weight in evaluating international investments. Most surveys indicate that leading multinationals focus upon income measures other than distributable parent cash flows as often as homing in on remittable parent cash flow. Furthermore, they indicate an amazing lack of sophistication – between 10 and 20 per cent of large US multinationals are reported as using accounting rate of return as their primary evaluation technique. Estimates of the use of payback as a first-choice decision criterion are variously reported as high in frequency as 28 per cent. Given the apparently regular use of these basic techniques as primary evaluation screens, which is far away from what normative theory would suggest, the topic is probably worthy of a closer scrutiny. To this end, the last section of this chapter is devoted to the empirical findings of the most important of these surveys.

Another major complication in international capital budgeting arises in situations where the headquarters company puts up part of its equity or loan capital in an overseas subsidiary by way of equipment or inventory. Clearly the project should be debited with this input for the purpose of calculating project returns. But parent returns are of paramount importance, so how should we treat this factor at the level of parent incremental cash flows?

The home territory company has surrendered value – in the form of equipment or inventory – in the expectation of obtaining greater value later on in terms of remittable, incremental parent cash flows. The problem that the financial analyst has is to put a value on the equipment or inventory surrendered. There is an ideally suited technique for valuing the property put in by the home territory company – and this involves the use of the concept of deprival value. This was defined by Bonbright (1937) as the 'adverse value of the entire loss, direct or indirect, that the owner might expect to suffer if he were to be deprived of the property'. Effectively, in subscribing equipment or inventory, the home territory company is voluntarily being deprived of assets in favour of the foreign business. Bonbright advances three meaningful bases for valuation of an asset:

- The current purchase price of an asset in a comparable state of wear and tear. This is replacement cost (RC).

- The net realizable value (NRV) of the asset. This is the current net disposable value.

- The present value of the expected future earnings stream flowing from the asset (PV).

An individual asset may be valued on each of these three alternative bases. But there are six ways in which values may be ranked in order of magnitude:

1. NRV > PV > RC
2. NRV > RC > PV
3. PV > RC > NRV
4. PV > NRV > RC
5. RC > PV > NRV
6. RC > NRV > PV

It should be noted that replacement cost in all of these circumstances would be the cost of replacing the asset in a condition and location similar to that deprived – this means in a comparable state of wear and tear, of comparable output and cash-generating capacity and in the same place as before deprival.

In cases 1 and 2, the firm would be best advised to dispose of the asset concerned. However the maximum loss suffered on disposal of the asset in these two cases is not NRV but RC. By purchasing another asset of the same type, the firm would restore the opportunity to obtain NRV. Thus, the correct basis for valuation would be replacement cost.

In cases 3 and 4, the firm would be advised to use the asset in the business, thus realizing its present value, which is the greatest payoff. However, if the firm were deprived of the asset concerned, it could simply replace it and thereby achieve the PV, which is the most advantageous outturn. In cases 3 and 4, the replacement cost is evidently the relevant deprival value involved.

In case 5, if the firm were deprived of the asset, the amount forgone would be the PV. Evidently what the firm has forgone is the asset with which to earn future cash flow. Since the PV of future cash flows exceeds the NRV, the amount lost by the firm would be the PV. Note that in this case if the firm were deprived of the asset there would be no point in replacing it – hence the amount of RC is irrelevant here.

Likewise in case 6, if the firm were deprived of the asset, there would be no logical reason to replace it because RC exceeds both PV and NRV. This time, if deprived of the asset, the firm has surrendered the NRV rather than the PV. It would have paid the firm to obtain the NRV by selling it off rather than to concentrate upon PV by working the asset.

This approach was, in fact, the recommended method of asset valuation in Sandilands Committee report on Inflation Accounting (1975) in the United Kingdom. Although inflation accounting is not the focus of this chapter, the Bonbright approach seems the relevant and logical way to assess the value forgone by the home territory company in surrendering assets to an overseas venture. The correct basis of valuation is summarized in Table 22.2.

Table 22.2 Basis of asset valuation

Case	Circumstances	Correct basis
1	NRV > PV > RC	RC
2	NRV > RC > PV	RC
3	PV > RC > NRV	RC
4	PV > NRV > RC	RC
5	RC > PV > NRV	PV
6	RC > NRV > PV	NRV

Cases 1, 2 and 4, where NRV exceeds RC, are likely to be relevant where inventory is input to a project.[1] These cases are much less likely to apply to fixed assets. The most common basis for equipment valuation is likely to derive from case 3, where the purpose for which the equipment is used in the home territory is likely to be ongoing. But cases 5 and 6 might also be encountered. Case 5 implies that the purpose to which the asset is put has a limited life since presumably when it was worn out it would pay to cease operations. Case 6 clearly implies that, rationally, the asset should be sold off immediately anyway.

Obviously when an asset subscribed to an overseas venture is completely unnecessary to the home operations, then the relevant valuation basis would be NRV. Having identified the appropriate valuation method in respect of the asset subscribed to an overseas project, this becomes the initial minus item in the parent cash flow projections against which subsequent estimated inflows are set. It is worth noting that, whether in a domestic or international situation, were one company to subscribe equipment and inventory to another company in return for a share of its equity, deprival value would provide the correct basis for valuing the input as part of the process of investment appraisal.

We now turn to the third area of complication – exchange rates. If exchange rates are in equilibrium at the time the project commences and if future exchange rates move in line with inflation differentials and if, further, project cash inflows and outflows move in line with general inflation in the overseas territory, then, assuming that there are no exchange control restrictions and assuming that host territory and home country taxes are at similar rates, project cash flow analysis will give exactly the same indication about investment viability as parent cash flow analysis. Rarely, if ever, will all these conditions hold. Because of this, it is recommended that estimated future project cash flows (net of local tax) are shown in money terms (that is, gross of expected host country inflation) and that the project net present value is calculated by following the application of a money terms host country discount rate.

Parent cash flows should be estimated by applying the expected future exchange rate to host country net cash flows if there are no exchange controls, or to remittable net cash flows if exchange controls are in place or are expected to be introduced. Due allowance must be made for host and home country taxation impacts and a parent net present value would be estimated following the application of a risk-adjusted parent discount rate, which might be based upon a weighted average cost of capital where the NPV method is used or upon the ungeared cost of equity in adjusted present values (APV) calculations – see the next section in this chapter.

Estimation of future exchange rates might follow projections of inflation rates. In reality, movement of rates in this way tends to hold in the long term; in the short term, movements in exchange rates often follow discontinuous paths with governments supporting currencies for long periods before giving in and letting the economics of inflation rate differentials have their full effect. Thus, exchange rate movements are often discontinuous and financial analysts may wish to reflect this in their forecasts – although the time at which the full effect of inflation differentials is likely to reassert itself is incredibly difficult to predict. Perhaps this problem is best handled via sensitivity analysis, with various sets of figures being prepared for different timings of purchasing power parity re-establishing equilibrium. More detail on these points appears in the next chapter.

The fourth area of complication concerns taxation. Clearly, project cash flows should be estimated net of local taxation and parent cash flows should be calculated net of host and parent taxation. On this point, reference should be made to Chapter 21 on relevant aspects of international corporate taxation. Also, if royalties and management fees are charged by a home-based company to an overseas operating subsidiary, then these should be shown as a debit to the project cash flow and as a credit in the parent cash flow analysis. Strictly speaking, of course, income to be forgone and/or incremental costs to be incurred in deploying management in pursuit of the project should be set against parent cash inflows.

To reiterate, situations where full remittance of net cash flow from project to parent is restricted are the major source of difficulty in international capital budgeting.

22.2 | NPV or APV?

Under the net present value method, all cash flows are discounted to present value at the required rate of return (sometimes called the criterion rate or cut-off rate or hurdle rate). The net present value of an investment proposal is given by:

$$\text{NPV} = \sum_{t=0}^{n} \frac{A_t}{(1+k)^t} \tag{22.1}$$

where k is the required rate of return and A_t is the cash flow in year t.

The NPV approach is not the only one available. Another line of attack is through the adjusted present value. Its pedigree is undoubted. Sired by Modigliani and Miller (1958, 1963), this thoroughbred has been trained by Myers (1974).

Remember Modigliani and Miller's proposition that the total market value of the firm and its cost of capital are independent of its capital structure. Thus, the total market value of a firm is given by capitalizing the expected stream of operating earnings at a discount rate appropriate to its risk class. It follows that this cut-off rate for investment purposes is completely independent of the way in which investment is financed. Remember too that their original propositions (1958) were developed with assumptions of a world without taxes, among other things. Relaxing this assumption, as they did in their 1963 article, they conceded that because the payment of interest is deductible for corporate tax purposes, leverage lowers the cost of capital – but only to this extent. Their valuation model assumes that after-tax operating flows are capitalized at the appropriate capitalization rate for a firm with no debt in the risk class specified plus a further increment to value resulting from the present value of lower tax payments consequent upon the use of debt and hence the deduction of interest. Myers' APV approach (1974) to discounting cash flows from an investment opportunity, which gives rise to debt capacity, disaggregates sources of value accruing to the project into:

■ the capitalized value of the unleveraged project's operating cash flows, plus

■ the capitalized value of the tax shield associated with the debt capacity of the project itself.

These cash flows are logically discounted at different rates, a function of their different risks. Naturally, the former are viewed as being more risky. The adjusted present value of a project is given by:

$$APV = \sum_{t=0}^{n} \frac{OCF_t}{(1+k^*)^t} + \sum_{t=0}^{n} \frac{k_d DT_c}{(1+k_d)^t} - \text{initial investment} \qquad (22.2)$$

where OCF_t is the after-tax operating cash flow in period t. The required rate of return in the absence of leverage – that means all-equity financing – is k^*. The cost of debt financing is given by k_d. The value of debt financing sustainable by the project is D and T_c is the corporate tax rate. The discount rate applied to unlevered cash flows, k^*, does not, of course, include any allowance for the impact of debt financing. The notion is simply to disaggregate the financing effect of a project from its operating cash flow effect. The discount rate applied to the tax shield is that applicable to the source of this effect – namely the cost of debt funds. The affinity between Modigliani and Miller's tax adjustments approach and Myers' APV should be self-evident. It should be mentioned that the relationship in equation (22.2) is better expressed as the sum of the present value of operational cash flows and the value of the tax shield less initial investment assuming a constant debt ratio through time. By using a constant amount of debt, D, in the above formulation, the implication is that the outstanding debt in future periods is determined by initially expected market values inclusive of the value created by the project under consideration itself. To model this might involve an approach similar to that presented in Franks, Broyles and Carleton (1985). Their methodology involves an iterative procedure. First of all the adjusted present value is found given as estimated debt capacity for the project based on initial capital invested. Of course, if one were to assume a constant debt/equity ratio for the project, the absolute level of debt would change as the project earned further present value – and this would, in turn, enhance the tax shield on debt. What Franks, Broyles and Carleton suggest is that, following the initial calculation of an adjusted present value, this value increase is the source of further debt and thus further tax shield. A form of multiplier is therefore applied to the tax shield. However, this is certainly not the only way to model the value of the tax shield – see Miles and Ezzell (1980) and Ezzell and Miles (1983).

It is also worth mentioning that there is scope for debate about the discount rate to be applied to tax savings due to the deductibility of interest from profit for corporation tax purposes. In developing the argument here, one of the key assumptions is that the firm has sufficient profit to cover interest payments and thus render the effective cost of debt to the firm as equal to the net of tax cost.

But should the discount rate applied to the tax savings in equation (22.2) in order to quantify the present value of the tax shield be k_d before tax or $k_d (1 - T)$, that is, after tax? The appropriate tax rate is represented by T. While we prefer the post-tax rate, the answer comes out the same whether the pre-tax approach is adopted and correctly applied.

22.3 | Foreign investment and the cost of capital

A reasonable question is whether foreign investment justifies a higher rate of return than does comparable domestic investment. Intuitively, managers often feel that a higher real return is justified for overseas investment given that the company is moving outside a geographical market which its executives know and in which it is presumably already successful. However, one might argue that international diversification lowers a firm's beta. This topic is discussed in Chapter 24 where it is pointed out that there is conflicting and rather weak statistical evidence as to whether multinationality affects beta. A fairly simple routine is also presented for computing the cost of equity capital (in home country terms and therefore in a manner suitable for application to remittable cash flows) for emerging market investments – see the end of section 24.10.

22.4 | The basic model

There is sometimes confusion about the order of calculation necessary to arrive at a home country net present value for a project where a multinational corporation is contemplating investment in a country that puts no restrictions on remittance of cash and profit flows. At least four methods may be followed to arrive at the present value. The methods themselves and the stages of evaluation involved in each are summarized in Table 22.3. They all give the same result as long as purchasing power parity holds throughout the period of analysis and as long as taxes are ignored.

Corporate tax is an important issue in international capital budgeting. Free cash flows in the overseas territory are obviously critical in analysing potential profitability. These must be stated net of local taxation. Assuming that no exchange controls exist, all incremental foreign cash flows should (notionally) be treated as if they were remitted to the parent. In turn, this means that overseas free cash flows net of local taxes have to be subjected (again notionally) to overseas withholding tax, then converted to home currency where they will (probably) bear further tax. Before proceeding to the detailed model for international capital budgeting model, it is

Table 22.3 Framework for international investment decision evaluation

Stage	Method 1	Method 2	Method 3	Method 4
1	Estimate future cash flows in local currency and in money terms	Estimate future cash flows in local currency and in money terms	Estimate future cash flows in local currency and in money terms	Estimate future cash flows in local currency and in money terms
2	Convert to home currency using forecast exchange rates	Calculate present value using local currency money terms discount rate	Reduce to real terms flows in local currency by discounting for local inflation	Reduce to real terms flows in local currency by discounting for local inflation
3	Calculate present value using home currency money terms discount rates	Convert to home currency present value using spot rate	Convert to home currency using spot exchange rate	Calculate real terms present value in local cash using real terms discount rate
4		Convert to home currency present value using real terms discount rate	Calculate present value using real terms discount rate	Convert to home currency present value using spot rate

obviously necessary to be aware of the problems posed by international corporate taxation; this was the subject matter of Chapter 21.

Of course, the firm might hold foreign free cash flow either in the host country or in a tax haven prior to passing it on, perhaps, to another investment elsewhere in the world, rather than back to the parent. In such circumstances, does it make more sense to focus upon incremental cash flows without subjecting them to home territory taxes? This is one of many problems that needs to be addressed. In fact, it receives further attention in later chapters.

Returning to Table 22.3 it is suggested that the superior approach to capital budgeting in countries with no regulations preventing the repatriation of funds would be to use method number 1, duly adjusted for taxation, and might involve the following steps:

■ Forecasting local currency, money terms, free cash flows after local taxes. Given the existence of inflation, this better simulates reality than does calculation in real terms.

■ Converting these to home currency, money terms, free cash flows net of all taxes – host and home. Conversion would involve forecasts of exchange rates, whether using an allowance for inflation differentials for all years of the project, or a correction for disequilibrium followed by a trajectory reflecting inflation differentials.

■ Discounting of home currency, money terms, free cash flows net of all taxes to net present value using a home currency, money terms, risk-adjusted, net of tax discount rate.

■ If the project's assumptions are reasonable and if it promises a positive NPV under these most stringent tax assumptions, the project is likely to be attractive.

Even where exchange controls are an impediment to full distribution of project cash flows, the same order of routine as that suggested in the bullet points above is the preferred method since it takes account of host inflation which may have a big effect on a project. But, clearly the analysis has to be restricted to remittable flows only. This creates some problems in terms of cash flow analysis – but consideration of these is best deferred until the next chapter. The discount rate applied would logically be a risk-adjusted weighted average cost of capital in NPV calculations or the ungeared cost of equity in APV calculations.

22.5 | Empirical studies of international investment appraisal

As mentioned earlier in this chapter, a number of surveys of US multinationals' practices of international capital budgeting have been published and they seem to indicate that actual procedures are far from what theory would suggest. The surveys focused upon here embrace all the major investigations that could be found in the literature – they have not been selected because they prove a point. The essence of their findings is presented here. Major published investigations have been associated with Stonehill and Nathanson (1968), Oblak and Helm (1980), Bavishi (1981), Wicks Kelly and Philippatos (1982), Stanley and Block (1983), Kim, Farragher and Crick (1984), Shao and Shao (1993) and Buckley, Buckley, Langevin and Tse (1996). All have used questionnaire survey methods and drawn their samples from large US businesses, with the exception of Buckley, Buckley, Langevin and Tse, whose data derived from large UK firms. An attempt is made in Tables 22.4 and 22.5 to summarize the findings of these surveys. Of course, any tabulation of comparisons of findings from diverse surveys is fraught with problems because the questions asked by different researchers are different, to say nothing of problems of occasional lack of clarity in presentation of results. Having said this, Tables 22.4 and 22.5 are intended to be instructive but not necessarily definitive. The former tabulation focuses upon techniques of appraisal used and income measures applied in assessing potential foreign investment opportunities. The latter table looks at the computation of the discount rate used and methods of undertaking risk adjustments. For each study, Table 22.4 shows the date of publication, sample size and response rate.

The first indicative finding that is apparent from Table 22.4 is that there has not necessarily been a continuing increase in terms of sophistication of techniques used over the recent past. In Oblak and Helm's 1980 survey, 76 per cent of multinational firms surveyed seemed to be using discounting techniques as their primary evaluation method; Stanley and Block's 1983 survey found the use of these techniques as high as 81 per cent. However, the three most recent studies in our overview of surveys show that discounting techniques are used as the foremost decision method by between 52 per cent, 58 per cent and well over 70 per cent. Similarly, with respect to the use of either accounting rate of return or payback as primary decision criteria, Oblak and Helm found that 24 per cent of their respondents rated these criteria first. The more recent investigations of Kim, Farragher and Crick, Shao and Shao, and Buckley, Buckley, Langevin and Tse put this figure at 36 per cent, 45 per cent and over 40 per cent respectively.

Equally disturbing are the reported practices on income measurement. According to our ideas of what income measures should be used in international capital budgeting, deductive theory would suggest the use of cash flow to the parent after foreign and home taxes. However, for the surveys reported which were published in or after 1980, the highest percentage of multinationals reporting this as their key income measure was found to be only 51 per cent – see Oblak and Helm (1980). The conclusion that multinationals have not really thought through sufficiently their international investment decision criteria is reinforced (see Table 22.5) by the fact that such a high proportion seem to be basing their hurdle rate on the cost of debt – frequently reported as the source of the discount rate by up to 17 per cent of firms in most surveys. But, quite remarkably, the survey of Shao and Shao (1993) found that the cost of debt was the single most frequently used source of the discount rate by as many as 41 per cent of respondents. Certainly it seems that the real world methodology in respect of the evaluation of international investments by multinationals leaves a significant amount to be desired.

Only three of the studies summarized in Tables 22.4 and 22.5 (overleaf) applied significance tests to their data. Wicks Kelly and Philippatos (1982) tested various demographic and behavioural variables for statistical significance using

Table 22.4 Summary of findings of major empirical studies of multinationals' investment appraisal: techniques and income measures

	Stonehill and Nathanson (1968)	Oblak and Helm (1980) Primary	Oblak and Helm (1980) Ancillary	Bavishi (1981) Used by	Wicks, Kelly and Philippatos (1982) Rated as important by	Stanley and Block (1983) Primary	Stanley and Block (1983) Secondary	Kim, Farragher and Crick (1984) Primary	Shao and Shao (1993) Primary	Shao and Shao (1993) Secondary	Buckley, Buckley, Langevin and Tse (1996) Primary / Without exchange controls	Buckley, Buckley, Langevin and Tse (1996) Secondary / With exchange controls
Survey data from	92 + 18*	58		156	105	121		186	90†		90	
Questionnaires sent to	219 + 100*	226		306	225	339		500	274†		217	
Response rate	34%	26%		51%	47%	36%		37%	33%		40%	
Technique												
Accounting rate of return	15%	14%	33%	63%	31%	11%	15%	15%	17%	6%	20%	25%
Internal rate of return	17%	60%	21%	69%	47%	65%	15%	48%	38%	14%	41%	10%
Net present value		14%	36%	40%	13%	16%	30%	10%	14%	41%‡	38%	19%
Payback		10%	62%	76%	22%	5%	38%	21%	28%	30%	27%	26%
Other present value technique		2%	12%	10%								
Income measure												
Earnings based	15%	31%		N	53%	N	N	24%	N	N	43%	27%
Book value ROI	17%	14%		N	N	N	N	14%	N	N	N	N
Cash flow to parent after domestic and foreign taxes	29%	51%		N	44%**	N		48%	N		26%	41%
Cash flow to parent after foreign taxes only	14%	3%		N	7%	N	N	13%	N	N	12%	28%
Discounted cash flow	11%	N		N	N	N	N	N	N	N	N	N
Cash flow to foreign subsidiary	N	N		42%	N	N	N	N	N	N	37%	3%
Cash flow to parent	N	N		21%	N	N	N	N	N	N	N	N
Cash flow to both foreign subsidiary and to parent	N	N		37%	N	N	N	N	N	N	N	N

Notes: N This idea was not prompted or this question was not asked.
* Stonehill and Nathanson's data were drawn from a large population of US multinationals and a smaller sample of foreign multinationals.
† Shao and Shao drew their responses from European affiliates of US-based transnational companies.
‡ Includes 2% and 5% for primary and secondary ranking respectively using adjusted present value.
** Includes some double counting. But in excess of 44% may be more realistic.

Table 22.5 Summary of findings of major empirical studies of multinationals' investment appraisal: computation of discount rate and risk adjustments

	Stonehill and Nathanson (1968)	Oblak and Helm (1980)	Bavishi (1981)	Wicks Kelly and Philippatos (1982)	Kim, Ferragher and Crick, (1984)	Shao and Shao (1993)	Buckley, Buckley, Langevin and Tse (1996)
Discount rate derived from							
Weighted average cost of capital	60%	54%	70%[†]	73%[‡]	45%	30%	N
Risk-free rate plus premium	N	9%	N	N	10%	10%	N
Experience/subjective	5%	5%	30%	N	10%	9%	N
Cost of equity	N	N	N	14%[§]	N	5%	N
Cost of debt	5%**	13%	N	14%[‡‡]	17%	41%	N
Actual funding used	7%	N	N	N	N		N
Risk adjusted for by						Ranking[§§]	
Subjectivity	45%	N	N	84%	N	2	
Varying rate of return requirement	42%	33%	N	N	31%	4/5	44%
Via payback requirement	5%	13%	N	N	19%	1	10%
Insurance for risk	8%	9%	N	N	12%		
Borrowing locally	6%	22%	N	N	21%		
Certainty equivalents	N	7%	N	N	8%	6	8%[††]
Sensitivity analysis	N	N	N	48%	N		29%
Probability analysis	N	N	N	26%	N		

Notes: Stanley and Block (1983) contained relatively little data on derivation of discount rate and risk adjustments but there was a lot of information on techniques and income measure used.

N This idea was not prompted or this question was not asked.

* Includes 9% using local weighted average cost of capital.

** This 5% used local cost of debt.

[†] Includes 27% using local weighted average cost of capital.

[‡] Includes 22% using local weighted average cost of capital.

[§] Includes 6% using local cost of equity.

[‡‡] Includes 8% using local cost of debt.

[§§] Shao and Shao's number 3 ranking was 'no adjustment is made'.

[††] Essentially by adjusting inflows.

cross-tabulations and chi-square analysis. They tested investment evaluation practices against such factors as firm size, commitment to foreign operations, geographic
dispersion, period of time involved in multinational operations and a number of
other variables. The investigators found their most interesting results when looking
at evaluation practices versus firm size. However, here only four significant relationships were found out of a possible ninety-three, with size cross-tabulated against
investment evaluation practices. These were that:

■ smaller firms tended to use accounting rate of return as their evaluation method;

■ larger firms dominated in using the local cost of debt as their discount rate;

■ smaller firms dominated in the use of cash flows to adjust for political risk;

■ smaller firms dominated in varying the required rate of return to adjust for political risk.

Buckley, Buckley, Langevin and Tse (1996) also found four significant relationships. Here the findings related to involvement in foreign business:

■ Firms with a smaller involvement in international business tended to use the
income measure of pre-tax net cash inflow to the foreign business in local currency terms in their international investment appraisals in countries without
exchange controls.

■ Firms with a smaller involvement in international business tended to evaluate
international investment decisions using an income measure of profit before tax
in home currency terms when they are investing in territories without exchange
controls.

■ Firms with a smaller involvement in international business tended to evaluate
cross-border involvement decisions using an accounting rate of return criterion.

■ Firms with a larger involvement in international business tended to evaluate
international investment decisions incorporating an allowance for consequential
cross-border cash flow impacts – the international cannibalization effect.

It is interesting to note that of the six other studies quoted here, the only one that
used statistical tests, namely Stanley and Block (1983), also found a significant relationship in terms of sophistication of evaluation technique versus firm size. It must,
of course, be remembered that, usually, samples were drawn from the largest of companies anyway. Smaller firms within such a source as the Fortune 500, for example,
would be large firms in absolute terms.

Although not as detailed as the surveys referred to in Tables 22.4 and 22.5, Baker
and Beardsley (1973) found, in a survey of 62 responding US multinationals out
of 134 to whom questionnaires were sent, that some of the key risk influences in
international investment were prospects of remittance of profits to the United States,
ability to repatriate capital to the United States, convertibility of currency and stability of exchange rate. These were respectively rated as being substantial risk factors
influencing international capital investment by 92 per cent, 76 per cent, 84 per cent
and 63 per cent of respondents. Also briefly worthy of mention is a study of US and

Japanese practices in evaluating investments undertaken by Hodder (1986). The most interesting finding is that 'although most Japanese firms are not formally using discounted cash flow (DCF) techniques, they all seem to be incorporating the time value of money in their analysis'. Finally, in a questionnaire survey of the international capital budgeting practices of 59 out of a sample of 729 companies in the UK Times 1,000 (an extremely low response rate), Wilson (1990) found that almost all respondent companies used at least two evaluation techniques. Payback was cited most frequently by 73 per cent of respondents, contribution to earnings per share was mentioned by 67 per cent and accounting rate of return by 60 per cent. Internal rate of return and net present value were used, respectively, by 54 per cent and 31 per cent. The most common method of arriving at a discount rate was via a group-weighted average cost of capital.

Reverting to Stonehill and Nathanson's 1968 paper, it is worthy of note that they began their paper with the observation that 'a better conceptual framework for evaluating foreign investments is needed'. Judging from the findings of this brief summary of surveys, this sadly seems to remain the case.

In this chapter, we only touched the tip of the iceberg that is the preferred model for appraising international investments. We develop the ideas specified here into a far fuller approach in the remaining chapters in the international capital budgeting part of the text.

22.6 | Summary

- Analysing capital investment decisions involves comparing cash inflows with cash outflows from a project.

- Investment appraisal focuses upon expected incremental cash flows associated with a project.

- Overseas projects possess the usual difficulties found with respect to domestic capital projects but international project analysis is much more complex.

- The same basic model as that suggested by corporate financial theory is used in international capital budgeting, but the multinational firm must consider factors peculiar to international operations.

- A project may be estimated to produce considerable cash flows in a foreign territory but, because of exchange control restrictions, the bulk of these foreign cash flows may not be distributable to the parent company.

- In the circumstances above, looking at a project purely in terms of cash flows accruing in the foreign territory may indicate that it is worth investing – but is this good enough?

- The present value to the parent company of a multinational is a function of future cash flows accruing to it which are distributable to the parent company's investors.

- Remember that for an overseas project some cash flows may be blocked by exchange controls.

- Only incremental cash flows are remittable back to the parent company which add value for its shareholders. Where there are no exchange controls, such problems are minimized – but note that they still exist. It is always possible that a host government may impose exchange controls sometime in the future.

- An overseas capital project may be looked at from at least two standpoints. The first of these is incremental project cash flows. This angle is concerned with foreign currency cash flows. The second angle is incremental parent cash flows. This means cash flows that may find their way back to the parent. To the multinational company, it is only incremental parent cash flows that matter.

- There are six key categories of complexity in international capital budgeting. In reality, of course, at least one of these is equally applicable to domestic capital budgeting. The six categories embrace situations where:
  - (i)   full remittance of cash flows arising from a project is restricted in terms of payment to the parent;
  - (ii)   part of the parent input is via equipment;
  - (iii) exchange rates are not expected to be constant throughout the project's life;
  - (iv) different rates of tax apply in the country of the project and in the parent's country;
  - (v)   royalties and management fees are involved;
  - (vi) there are knock-on effects impinging upon group operations elsewhere in the world.

  Difficulties raised by these six points are considered in more detail in Chapter 23. Be fully conversant with the problem.

- Many poor international investment decisions have been made because of the failure of the management of the multinational company fully to comprehend that it is distributable parent cash flows that matter rather than mere project cash flows.

22.7 | End of chapter questions

Question 1
Why should capital budgeting for projects in an overseas subsidiary be assessed from the parent's perspective rather than just the subsidiary's cash flow perspective?

Question 2
What additional factors deserve consideration in multinational capital budgeting that may not normally be relevant for a purely domestic project?

Note

1. The assumption is that the input of inventory does not affect corporate sales at home. This would presumably be achieved by building up production prior to the shipment of inventory to the overseas project. It is reasonable to believe that companies would wish to pursue this kind of production pattern. Likewise, with respect to case 3 (which is most likely to apply to fixed assets), the choice of RC as the appropriate valuation method presupposes that the home company would purchase a replacement asset before shipping the old one to the overseas territory, thereby avoiding disruption to home production and sales.

23 The international capital budgeting model

Analysing capital investment decisions involves comparing cash inflows with cash outflows from a project. Investment appraisal focuses upon expected incremental cash flows associated with a project. As we pointed out in Chapter 22, overseas projects possess the usual difficulties found with respect to domestic capital projects plus a few more which makes international project analysis more complex. The same basic model as that suggested by corporate financial theory is used in international capital budgeting, but the multinational firm must consider factors peculiar to international operations.

A project may be estimated to produce considerable cash flows in a foreign territory but, because of exchange control restrictions, the bulk of these foreign cash flows may not be distributable to the parent company. In these circumstances, looking at a project purely in terms of cash flows accruing in the foreign territory may indicate that it is worth investing – but this level of analysis may not be good enough.

The present value to the parent company of an international investment is a function of future cash flows accruing to it which are distributable to the parent company. But, for an overseas project, there may be some cash flows that are blocked in the host territory by exchange controls. It is only incremental cash flows which are remittable back to the parent company that add value for its shareholders. Where there are no exchange controls, such problems are minimized – but many of the complexities referred to in Chapter 22 still exist. And it is always possible that a host government may impose exchange controls sometime in the future.

An overseas capital project may be looked at from at least two standpoints. The first of these is incremental project cash flows. This angle is concerned with foreign currency cash flows. It would be the relevant angle from which a local partner would look at an overseas project. The second perspective is incremental parent cash flows. This means that focus is upon cash flows that may find their way back to the parent. To the multinational company, it is only incremental parent cash flows that matter. So this would be the right focus for a multinational in appraising overseas projects.

In Chapter 22, a handful of sources of complexity in international capital budgeting were pointed out – in fact, there were six. In reality, of course, at least one of these is equally applicable to domestic capital budgeting. The categories embrace situations where:

■ full remittance of cash flows arising from a project are restricted in terms of payment to the parent;

■ part of the parent input is via equipment;

- exchange rates are not expected to be constant throughout the project's life;

- different rates of tax apply in the country of the project and in the parent's country;

- royalties and management fees are involved;

- there are knock-on effects impinging upon group operations elsewhere in the world.

Various texts – such as Abdullah (1987), Clark, Levasseur and Rousseau (1993), Demirag and Goddard (1994), Buckley (1996), Levi (1996), Eiteman, Stonehill and Moffett (2001), Madura (2003) and Shapiro (2003) – point out the source of difference between project cash flows and parent cash flows. This may, in the main, be due to:

- exchange rate movements not reflecting purchasing power parity;

- different rates of host and home corporate taxation;

- full remittances of overseas cash flows being restricted.

Note that enabling blocked cash flows to become remittable – for example, through countertrade – may reverse the original categorization of a project as inferior, on the basis of apparent parent cash flows, to acceptability while still using the same set of decision criteria.

23.1 | International project appraisal

Domestic and international investment appraisal may be similar in some respects but there are very significant differences. The essential message is that, while domestic project appraisal is concerned with establishing the present value of future cash flows at home, international capital budgeting focuses upon the present value of remittable future cash flows.

The six problem areas highlighted earlier impinge upon international investment such that any overseas opportunity possesses Janus-like qualities. Its two-facedness becomes manifest in that, viewed from the project standpoint, its appearance is unlike the image presented when seen from the parent's angle. The argument has been advanced that it is remittable cash generation that matters in terms of adding value for the corporation. When there are no exchange controls creating an impediment, project cash flows should all be remittable – although changing exchange rates and parent taxation will present difficulties to be borne in mind. When there are exchange controls, a further complexity is in place. In these circumstances, remittable parent cash flows may be achieved by:

- dividends;

- royalties and management fees;

- loan repayments;

■ countertrade;

■ other means of unblocking.

Such remittable flows must, of course, take account of changing exchange rates and parent tax rates, as would be the case if cash generated by a project were not fettered by exchange control regulations. Note that loan repayments are specified as a means of hastening remittance when exchange controls are in place – the whys and wherefores are discussed later in this chapter. It follows that, where there are remittance constraints, the role of financing international investment may be critical in terms of parent NPV. In these circumstances, financing can affect the present value of investments – and significantly.

In short, international project appraisal needs to take account, in home currency parent cash flow terms, of capital outlays (allowing for equipment transfer effects), maximum remittable cash flows (including royalty and management fee flows and loan repayments), and tax and exchange rate effects, and these flows have to be discounted at the appropriate risk-adjusted opportunity cost of capital. One of these problem areas is taxation – it is to this topic that we now turn.

23.2 | Taxation

It will be noted that the approach advocated here involves investment appraisal from the parent standpoint, with profit flows arising in the host territory first of all falling into the local tax net. Then, on distribution (or assumed distribution) they may be subjected to a withholding tax and, finally, in the home territory they may fall into the tax net again.

Assume that a company with a proposed project in an overseas territory expects to earn the foreign currency equivalent of $1m in both pre-tax profit and cash generation terms. With an overseas tax rate of 15 per cent, a withholding tax of 10 per cent and a home corporation tax rate of 33 per cent, the figures that go into the project appraisal would be as shown in Table 23.1.

Of course, it may be the case that the multinational decides to reinvest all of the profit post-foreign tax in the host country – this would involve a reinvestment of the equivalent of $850,000. In other words, no withholding tax or home tax would be paid. Equally, it may be the case that the multinational decides to pay out profits to an intermediate holding company. And the cash so distributed would be onward re-routed for reinvestment elsewhere in the worldwide operations of the multinational. Under this scenario, the amount available for reinvestment would equal $765,000 (that is, the amount before home country tax but after foreign and withholding taxes – see Table 23.1). Evidently, by taking credit for only $670,000, we are applying a scenario that is the harshest possible in tax terms. If the investment exhibits a positive NPV in parent cash flow terms under this scenario, then clearly, assuming monies generated by the investment are either reinvested in the host country or routed elsewhere in the multinational's global operations, the effect will be to enhance the anticipated outturn.

Table 23.1 Project appraisal: parent cash flows net of taxes

	$	$
Profit and cash generated before tax		1,000,000
Foreign tax equivalent of		150,000
Withholding tax equivalent of $850,000 @ 10%		85,000
Home country tax		
$1m @ 33%	330,000	
Less foreign tax credit	235,000	
		95,000
Giving net of tax profit flow of		670,000

If the project fails to promise a positive NPV in parent terms under this harshest scenario but does look acceptable if these assumptions are relaxed on the basis of re-routeing funds around the world without their being returned to the home country, then top management has further information upon which to make a decision. Whether it gives such a project the green light or not is a matter of judgement. At least the project appraisal is producing data that would be valuable in reaching that goal for which management is paid – a wise decision based upon informed judgement.

In any case, using the harshest tax scenario could be said to take cognizance of the corporation tax rules in various countries applying to controlled foreign companies (CFCs). Legislation on CFCs has been introduced to counter the following two perceived abuses that inland revenue authorities believed had resulted in tax avoidance:

■ The accumulation of income by subsidiaries in low-tax areas.

■ The artificial diversion of business profits away from the home country when otherwise those profits would have been subject to home country tax.

CFC legislation seeks to impose home country tax on home country companies in respect of the unremitted profits of certain types of companies located in low-tax countries. The legislation is complex and varies from country to country.

The essential point is that the application of host and home taxation in terms of arriving at cash generation in home country currency is the harshest tax treatment. But does it best take account of the real world of the multinational? To answer the question, consider an example. Imagine a multinational based in the United States but with no home operations – all of its businesses are overseas. Suppose that dividends to group shareholders and amounts to cover head office costs are paid out of dividends remitted from the European subsidiaries. Assume further that the group has interests in the Far East, Australasia and Africa. These are profitable but pay no dividend to the headquarters in the United States. Surely, given such a scenario, it would be illogical to apply home and host tax to new investments in Europe only, but debit Far Eastern, Australasian and African projects with host country taxation only – in other words to allow them to avoid home tax for evaluation purposes.

If the illogicality is not immediately apparent, we could take as an example an otherwise similar group except that this second multinational pays for group dividend and head office costs out of profit remittances from the Far East, Australasia and Africa – in other words, the European subsidiaries would remit no dividends in this instance. Clearly, it would not be sensible for the first multinational to give investments in the Far East, Australasia and Africa a free ride as far as US tax is concerned and for the latter to exempt European project proposals from US tax.

The author of this text has come across evidence of more than one multinational charging all of its overseas projects (for investment appraisal purposes) with a hypothetical average home tax rate based on evening out the above anomaly. Perhaps the best approach is to look at overseas projects with the harshest tax treatment in a base case and run sensitivity analysis scenarios assuming zero home tax and with an average home tax rate (see the previous sentence). This should give group directors the wherewithal to exercise informed judgement.

We now turn to the analysis of international capital budgeting decisions where there are no exchange controls in force.

23.3 | Project evaluation with no exchange controls

Whether a project is subject to exchange controls or not, the initial appraisal invariably begins with an analysis in host country currency. Such an appraisal involves the basic cash flow techniques of domestic capital budgeting incorporating the computation of a net present value or internal rate of return. The methodology might incorporate NPV or APV figuring, using the logic of the respective frameworks as summarized in Chapter 22 with discount rates reflecting required returns in local currency terms. Clearly this would indicate how a local partner might view a particular project. But it would not be this perspective from which the multinational should evaluate a foreign capital investment decision. To the international corporation, the relevant focus is upon remittable cash flows. In terms of adding value, it does not matter whether the flows are actually remitted; the fact that there is no impediment to remittance should, logically, create value for the corporation. Thus, it is assumed that all available incremental free cash flow (normally profit before interest and tax, add back depreciation, less fixed capital inputs, less working capital inputs, less tax payable) is paid out and remitted to the multinational headquarters. The parent will, for project evaluation purposes, convert to home currency at the anticipated exchange rate and also allow for notional home territory corporate tax.

In the analysis which follows, we approach the problem of international project evaluation without exchange controls on the assumption that the parent company owns all of the equity in the foreign subsidiary. This assumption is relaxed later on. Although Shapiro (1978) points out that 'incremental cash flows to the parent can be found by subtracting world-wide parent company cash flows (without the investment) from post-investment parent company cash flows', the more usual approach is to concentrate from the very beginning upon incremental cash flows to the parent, focusing substantially upon the project rather than the entire company. This latter method usually involves less computation, but where there are knock-on effects, great care has to be exercised. By this is meant those kinds of situation where, for example, investment in a new plant in Spain affects output and cash generation in, say, the French and Belgian subsidiaries. This kind of situation is encompassed by the third bullet point in the next paragraph. Of course, whether the route to incremental cash flows is via worldwide remittable cash flows or through remittable cash generation at the level of the project itself, the final decision should be the same.

Where a multinational company contemplates an overseas investment on the basis of 100 per cent ownership, as is frequently the case, and when there are no exchange controls, the present value calculation, from the parent's viewpoint, should include:

■ The multinational's incremental free cash flow year by year (net of host and home tax).

■ Royalties, management fees and the like, if any (net of home tax).

■ Any cannibalization effects must be allowed for in the evaluation. For example, if the multinational were exporting direct to the host country prior to implementation of the project and subsequently it is to be locally sourced, the loss of contribution, net of tax, must be built into the calculation.

■ If any subsidized interest is involved, the present value of the subsidy must be incorporated. For example, use of purchased US equipment by a European-based multinational, undertaking investment in the Far East, may attract a lower than market interest rate for dollars based on Exim Bank finance. The subsidy, net of tax, should be discounted year by year at the market rate for dollar finance, net of tax, to arrive at a present value. Of course, where such subsidized finance is available in a foreign currency, the question of covering the exposure must be considered and appropriate action taken.

■ Where part of the parent's contribution to the overseas project is via equipment input, this must be allowed for. If the equipment input is without actual cost passing, but would otherwise be used within the parent's ongoing business, Table 22.2 in Chapter 22 sets out an appropriate basis of valuation. If the circumstances are as above, except that cash is paid, the consideration, net of any tax effects, must be incorporated.

■ The multinational's opportunity to exploit any growth opportunities over and above the base case valuation of incremental cash flows. These kind of opportunities are frequently called real operating options. How any such options might be valued is also considered later in this chapter.

■ If incremental free cash flows are forecast over a finite time period only, the question of a terminal value has to be addressed. Various approaches to calculating this are considered later in this chapter.

Table 23.2 (overleaf) provides a summary of generally encountered incremental cash flows as sources of value in international capital budgeting without exchange controls. Table 23.3 (overleaf) shows this information in a slightly different format. The items in Table 23.3 are considered in turn.

The value of investment inputs embraces fixed capital and working capital required to undertake the project. This might be thought of as a gross amount, in local currency terms as at year of the project. In our initial scenario there are no

Table 23.2 Summary of relevant incremental cash flows: international investment with no exchange controls

	Approach used	
Value	NPV	APV
Value of investment inputs	✓	✓
Value of incremental free cash flow of overseas investment	✓	✓
Value of management fees and royalties	✓	✓
Value of any cannibalization effects to the group	✓	✓
Value of any subsidized interest involved	✓	✓
Value of any growth opportunities in excess of value of incremental free cash flows	✓	✓
Allowance for terminal values	✓	✓
Value of tax shield due to debt; the amount will vary from classical to imputation tax system		✓

Table 23.3 Valuation of overseas project from parent's perspective: no exchange controls

Value of overseas project	=	−	Value of investment inputs
		+	Value of incremental free cash flows of investment
		+	Value of management fees and royalties back to parent
		−	Value of any cannibalization effects to the group
		+	Value of any subsidized interest
		+	Value of growth opportunities in excess of value of incremental free cash flows
		+	Allowance for terminal values
		+	Value of tax shield due to debt capacity created by project in cases where the APV method is used

minority interests, but we should nonetheless focus upon the present value of this amount, converted to home currency at the time-zero exchange rate less any allowances for the opportunity cost of any parent equipment input along the lines suggested in Table 22.2.

The next item in Table 23.3 is the value of incremental free cash flows. The specification of this item is relatively straightforward, with flows converted to home currency net of taxes using expected exchange rates for each year of cash generation. Of course, if free cash flow is forecast for a finite period only, it will be necessary to incorporate a terminal value – see Table 23.3. Where the valuation of free cash flow is based on forecasting to infinity, this would not be necessary.

Table 23.3 next specifies the value of management fees and royalties. These should be specified net of host country withholding taxes and home currency corporate taxes. It is suggested that, to avoid double-counting, incremental free cash flows of investment should be calculated net of management fees and royalties.

Again, assessing forecasts for a finite period, it would logically follow that a terminal value of royalties and management fees should be incorporated in the valuation exercise. Where the forecast is done on a simplified assumption of being to infinity, this would not be necessary. The same kind of idea also applies in respect of cannibalization effects, the next of our valuation parts in Table 23.3.

In international capital budgeting, it is often the case that a new investment may have knock-on effects. For example, a new plant in a host country may mean lost exports to the host country from elsewhere in the group, or it may mean a new scheduling of production and sales with the new facility taking output from elsewhere in the group. The contribution on such lost turnover (net of taxes) should be allowed for in the capital budgeting proposal if accurate simulation of reality is to be achieved. Of course, for an integrated group of companies, there may be positive upstream and/or downstream effects, the contribution from which should be included in the analysis.

Referring back to Table 23.3, we next look at subsidized interest. As mentioned earlier, this frequently arises as a result of equipment purchase involving the equivalent of the Exim Bank in the country of supply. So, the subsidy may be in a currency other than that of host or parent, in which case forward cover or swapping has to be considered. For example, a Dutch parent company considering investment in Malaysia but purchasing Japanese equipment may find that it can access yen at below the market rate. The amount of the interest subsidy would be given by the annual interest payment in yen versus the market rate annual interest payment in yen – less costs of forward cover assuming the company wishes to avoid foreign exchange risk on such interest payments. Usually such subsidized finance is only available for relatively short periods. The discount rate used to value this item is the market rate for the currency in which the subsidy is denominated. This contrasts with earlier value calculations where the discount rate is the appropriate rate representing either a risk-adjusted weighted average cost of capital for the project concerned or the ungeared cost of equity, dependent upon whether the calculation is based upon NPV or APV methods respectively.

A different approach is adopted in this case because we would normally discount at a rate reflecting the riskiness of the cash flow stream concerned. To apply the weighted average rate to our interest rate stream is not an acceptable practice. The riskiness of the interest-related stream of cash flows should be taken into account by discounting at the market interest rate – and this is clearly very different from the weighted average cost of capital. If this is accepted, the next question concerns whether the discount rate should be pre-tax or post-tax. In capital budgeting exercises we are always concerned with post-tax incremental cash generation so it follows that the logical discount rate should be an after-tax rate. Since we are concerned with home country value creation, the relevant tax rate to apply to both the interest subsidy and to the discount rate would logically be the home country corporate tax rate. Note that this tax rate should be applied to both numerator and denominator to ensure consistency.

If we revert to Table 23.3, it will be noted that our next source of value creation is growth opportunities. Since this topic is moderately complicated, we return to it under a separate heading (see the next section).

According to the order of considering topics in Table 23.3, terminal values come next. When we forecast incremental cash generation for a project out to year n and this is a finite period, we may or may not expect the project to cease at that time. If we do expect it to cease, we should get back the value of invested working capital and something for fixed capital too. This must be allowed for as a terminal value.

If we do not expect the project to cease but are merely truncating it at some finite number of years for analysis purposes, then we should allow for a terminal value to take account of operations beyond the conveniently assumed truncation date. In such cases the terminal value should embrace the value of:

- free cash flows from the investment converted to home currency and net of host, withholding and home taxes;

- royalty and management fees, net of all taxes;

- cannibalization effects beyond the truncation date, net of all taxes.

While the former is usually allowed for in calculations, the latter two are frequently forgotten in international investment appraisal.

The suggested methodology for estimating the value of an international investment to the multinational corporation in a situation where there are no exchange controls has so far been approached on the assumption that the project does not have minority interests. Where there are minorities in the overseas investment, the valuation process needs to be changed marginally, since the minorities will participate in some cash flow streams, but not all. Note that, normally, of the cash flow categories listed in Table 23.2, the minority partners will participate pro rata in:

- value of incremental free cash flows of the overseas investment;

- value of subsidized interest;

- value of growth opportunities accruing in the host country.

The minority might not share pro rata in the investment inputs. Remember that the parent may sell, or transfer for value, equipment to the overseas venture; clearly such effects have to be allowed for in investment appraisal from the home-based parent company's standpoint. Management fees, royalties and cannibalization effects also have to be allowed for but these are invariably exclusively for the parent – the minority does not participate in such effects at all. Similarly, when it comes to calculating a terminal value and this is based on future free cash flows of the project, future royalties and future cannibalization effects, clearly the minority interests would only be participants in the first of these values – and adjustment needs to be made appropriately.

23.4 ▌ Growth opportunities – aka real operating options

Real options analysis is one way of looking at, and attempting to value, growth opportunities. Indeed, real options are often referred to as reflecting the present value of growth opportunities (PVGO). Valuing projects with growth opportunities may readily be undertaken by:

■ Making cash flow projections for a base case scenario, perhaps with a fairly modest growth assumption, for example in line with the growth of the economy. The point is that this base case scenario might be written around most likely outturns.

■ On top of the base case cash flow projections, the analyst might superimpose further projections based on more optimistic outturns with the firm pursuing a more growth-orientated strategy, if this is compatible within the market place.

■ The net present value of the base gives a good idea of most likely outturns.

■ The net present value of the superimposed expansionary situation (assuming that it is supported by reasonable assumptions) gives an idea of PVGO.

■ With sensitivity analysis logically applied to the base case outturns and to the PVGO scenario, a realistic view of the project's expectations may be obtained.

This kind of methodology is a perfectly good way to look at valuing growth opportunities. Indeed, discounted cash flow analysis is the gold standard of valuation and, as such, is necessarily the cornerstone of any valuation process.

Real options analysis may provide a raincheck on the magnitude attached to the value of growth opportunities. But we would stress that the valuation by discounted cash flow comes top of the league of valuation techniques. Real options analysis is something of a reinforcement. So, how does it work?

The central argument for a real options approach is that the standard discounting process adopts a static analysis. While this is true, using sensitivity analysis stops the analysis being too static. The standard discounting process is static in the sense that operating decisions are viewed as being fixed in advance and, as such, give rise to the base case set of incremental cash flows. This feature is at the heart of why the pure discounted cash flow techniques, used by so many companies, may be less than perfect in simulating the business world.

In reality, good managers are frequently good because they pursue policies that maintain flexibility on as many fronts as possible and maintain options that promise upside potential. For investment decision making, this means keeping open the opportunity to make decisions contingent upon information that may become available in the future. For example, dependent upon actual levels of demand, or competition, or cost, the rate of output of a new product may be accelerated, existing facilities may be extended or, should outturns be less attractive than expected, they may be closed temporarily or even abandoned altogether.

Research and development is an obvious case in point. Testing a new market via a pilot operation is clearly another. Oil exploration obviously falls into this category, levels of exploration and investment being highly contingent upon oil prices prevailing. Mining and quarrying are similar kinds of investment – extraction, temporary closure or even abandonment being obvious courses of action that will depend on actual prices of and/or demand for the product concerned. International investment is another example. Invariably it begins with a small commitment which may be scaled upwards should the environment prove profitable, or it may be curtailed should the host country appear to offer less attractive cash flows than anticipated. Of course, many purely domestic investments are rather like this, having scale-up possibilities.

All of these examples have one key feature in common: the firm has flexibility in terms of its course of action depending upon outcomes and factors that are unknown at the time of the project's inception. Qualitatively, the idea is fairly straightforward, and we can take it further by incorporating numerical data.

23.5 | Valuing real operating options

Let us look at a very simple numerical example and consider how the decision tree approach can be used to value real operating options. Following on from this example, we will show how further complexity can be built into the model as necessary.

Imagine a European firm, United Chemicals and Colloids plc (UCC), confronted with a foreign investment which is likely to absorb €9.5m and promises a best estimate of remittable future net cash flows, in real terms, amounting to:

| Years 1 and 2 | €1.1m p.a. |
| Years 3 to 12 inclusive | €1.45m p.a. |

The firm forecasts remittable cash flow for twelve years only and uses a 10 per cent discount rate to evaluate the project. As shown in Table 23.4, the investment promises a best estimate net present value of €0.23m (negative).

However, note the probability distribution of potential remittable cash flows. This is summarized in Table 23.5 and it shows that there is a 5 per cent chance (based on subjective probability estimates) of the project yielding annual remittable cash generation equal to €4m per annum from year 3 through to year 12. But if this level of outturn were achieved, the firm would, most likely, scale up and invest the equivalent of a further €30m in year 4 and would, according to best estimates, achieve very creditable returns reflecting the potential buoyancy which would translate into remittable cash flows of foreign currency giving €16m per annum from year 5 to year 12 inclusive.

What should be apparent is that, with the scale-up decision incorporated into the analysis, the NPV of the project will now be different. As shown by Table 23.6

Table 23.4 UCC case: best estimate net present value (euro million)

	Years		
	0	*1–2*	*3–12*
Investment	−9.50		
Remittable net cash flow		+1.10 p.a.	+1.45 p.a.
Discount at 10%	−9.50	+1.91	+7.36
Net present value = euro 0.23m (negative)			

Table 23.5 UCC case: expected remittable cash flows (and their probabilities)
(euro million)

	Years				
	0	1–2		3–12	
		Probability	Amount	Probability	Amount
Investment	−9.50				
Remittable cash flow		0.4	+2	0.05	+4*
		0.4	+1	0.50	+2
		0.1	0	0.30	+1
		0.1	−1	0.10	0
				0.05	−1

* At this level of outturn, UCC would invest a further €30m in year 4 with best estimate remittable cash generation for years 5 to 12 inclusive of €16m per annum.

(overleaf), the new NPV of the project comes out at €0.94m positive. In other words, the value of the call option embedded in the project may be said to approximate €1.17m.

Clearly the project referred to is simplistic. This is deliberately so to illustrate the basic routine required. Obviously the €16m forecast beyond year 4 with the scale-up option is a single number estimate and fails to incorporate probabilities.

To pursue the problem of evaluating real options further, we now consider a single project that requires a capital outlay of £10m. In return, the company receives an asset with present value of net inflows of £9m. Assume that both of these figures, and all others in this example, are in real terms. Assume also that the asset is risky and its value is likely to change. Returns on the asset have a standard deviation of about 40 per cent per year and the company can wait for up to three years before deciding to invest or not. The appropriate discount rate is 5 per cent. Viewed conventionally, this project's NPV is £9m minus £10m. That is £1m negative. But having the opportunity to wait three years and see what happens is a valuable option. In effect, the company owns a three-year American call with an exercise price of £10m on underlying assets worth £9m. With an American call option on a stock which pays no dividend, it is not optimal prematurely to exercise it. In this case, an American option is valued as a European call option. Now, if we use the Black and Scholes approach and the notation of Chapter 16, NPV_q for this option is £9m ÷ [£10m/(1.05)^3]. This equals 1.04. The option has a cumulative variance of 0.40 times $\sqrt{3}$, or 0.69. The Black and Scholes matrix table, which was introduced in Chapter 16, shows that an option with these characteristics is worth 28.4 per cent of the value of the underlying asset, or 0.284 (£9m). This equals £2.556m positive. Compare £2.556m positive with £1m negative.

The simple project just examined had an NPV, traditionally measured, of minus £1m. But valued inclusive of option value, its worth is around £2.5m positive. Is this contradictory? What should the company do? In fact, the traditional NPV and the option value do not contradict one another. The company should not invest in the

Table 23.6 UCC case: calculation of net present value with scale-up option (euro million)

	Years									
	0	1 and 2		3 and 4		4		5–12		
		Probability	Amount	Probability	Amount	Probability	Amount	Probability	Amount	
Investment	−9.50					0.05	−30			
Remittable cash flow		0.4	+2	0.05	+4			0.05	+16	
		0.4	+1	0.50	+2			0.50	+2	
		0.1	0	0.30	+1			0.30	+1	
		0.1	−1	0.10	0			0.10	0	
				0.05	−1			0.05	−1	
Expected PV at 10% discount rate	−9.50		+1.91		+2.08		−1.02		+7.47	
Expected NPV = euro 0.94m (positive)										

project now. If it does, it will forfeit the option and waste £1m. But neither should it discard the project. It should wait, watch and actively cultivate the project over the next three years. Although the project's traditional NPV is less than 0, the project is very promising because NPV_q is greater than 1. Although $E > S$, these two variables are relatively close to one another and $S > PV(E)$. By the end of three years, there is a good chance that the NPV will exceed zero and the option will be exercised. In the meantime, the option on the project really is worth over £2.5m, not minus £1m, provided the company does not, suboptimally, exercise it now.

This example could be likened to a biotechnology project which a firm is thinking of selling off because it is not part of its core research and development focus. The project may not promise a positive net present value if developed now, but if the firm were to dispose of it, what price should it ask? Naturally, the asking price would be based upon jam tomorrow. One way to put a value on this might be via real options analysis. Incidentally, another approach would be to use discounted cash flow valuation of various possible outturns plus subjective probabilities attached to these scenarios.

In the example of UCC, valuation of the growth option was approached via subjective probabilities. The solution to the valuation problem in this case could have been achieved by specifying volatilities, a time factor relating to the exercise period and, finally, an exercise price.

A question that the reader is likely to ask, in connection with the valuation of real options, concerns estimating the volatility of a project. There is not one single guaranteed approach here but there are at least three possible routes to putting a figure on volatility:

■ *One might take a guess*. What is a high standard deviation? Returns on leading US stocks have a standard deviation of about 21 per cent per year. For the United Kingdom, the figure is nearer 26 per cent per year. For small US companies, the figure is 36 per cent per year. Individual projects will have higher volatilities than a diversified portfolio like a company. Volatility of 20–30 per cent per year is not remarkably high for a single project.

■ *One might gather some data*. Volatility can be estimated for some businesses using historical data on investment returns in certain industries. Alternatively, implied volatilities can be computed from quoted option prices for a very large number of traded equities.

■ *One might do a simulation*. Spreadsheet-based projections of a project's future cash flows, together with a probability distribution for project returns, might be helpful.

The question of the magnitude of t in real options valuation is also critical. The big issue here is how long the firm is likely to maintain a profitable, value-enhancing competitive advantage. This is a matter of judgement but there are major concerns that might be raised in attempting to quantify this competitive advantage period (CAP). They relate to barriers to entry, patent positions and ferocity of competition, among others – for a considered view on this topic, see Buckley, Tse, Rijken and Eijgenhuijsen (2002).

Sometimes multinationals pursue an almost scatter-gun pre-empting strategy which creates numerous minor real operating options. For example, the firm might make a number of small investments in a few Eastern European countries with the expectation that at least one will be highly successful and, maybe, provide the location for a scale-up in that country and for export to other nearby buoyant economies too. The point is that the physical presence in a multiplicity of countries may deter competition and provide a portfolio of question marks (to use Boston box jargon), of which at least one is expected to be very successful. In the above kind of instance, the evaluation might be undertaken to reflect the strategy of pre-emption with cash outflows for the various different countries in year zero aggregated and with inflows expected for a small number of years from all of these locations also aggregated, followed by the expected scale-up allowed for in the quantitative analysis using real operating option valuation methods as above. Of course, this type of scatter-gun strategy would be likely to be the exception rather than the rule. On such occasions, evaluation using this approach truly reflects the firm's strategic choice of intended pre-emptive action.

The message should be apparent. A strategy that adds corporate value is to maintain flexibility through structuring investments in a manner paralleling options. Investments of this kind, which includes most international commitments, should be analysed beyond the traditional DCF model. This means evaluating them to embrace the option characteristic. Structuring investment decisions in such a way as to confer an option element enhances shareholder value over and above the base case present value scenario. Failure to evaluate investments of this kind to allow for this option aspect may, at best, result in an understatement of the potential shareholder value created and may, at worst, mean that firms fail to undertake growth strategies and ultimately pack their product portfolios with yesterday's winners but today's dogs.

23.6 | Project evaluation with exchange controls

Rather like project analysis where no exchange controls are operative, investment appraisal with controls normally begins by focusing upon the host country currency cash flows. This would be the perspective from which a local partner would appraise the investment – but it would not be the angle that the multinational would find most relevant. Again, as in the case where no exchange controls were assumed to exist, the focus of the international group would be upon remittable cash generation. And, of course, the existence of exchange controls create a significant barrier to such remittability.

When exchange controls exist, it is very frequently the case that investment is undertaken in conjunction with a local partner – sometimes this is a legal requirement in the host country, sometimes it is of the multinational manager's own volition. Given this tendency, the analysis here assumes the involvement of a local partner.

Where a multinational firm contemplates an overseas investment and where there are exchange controls impacting upon potential remittances to the parent, then the present value calculation, from the parent company's standpoint, would include the following:

■ The multinational's investment input. There are complications here since such subscription may be via equity or parent debt. Subscribing by the debt route may allow cash generated by the project to be returned to the home country by debt repayment and interest whereas, were subscription to be via equity, such flows might be blocked by controls.

■ Remittances of cash generated back to the parent, primarily, through dividend payment. Of course, not all cash generated would be remittable because of exchange control constraints. Thus, forecasts of annual profit and loss accounts and balance sheets – not just cash generation details – will be critical to the evaluation since, when exchange controls exist, remittance is invariably based upon a proportion of profit or some formula related to profit in conjunction with capital employed (or capital originally subscribed from outside the host country plus retained earnings).

■ Remittances back to the parent by way of parent debt service – capital plus interest – and management fees and royalties, although these are invariably subject to very careful scrutiny and to ceilings set by exchange control authorities and regulations.

■ Allowance for investment from local debt raised as part of the initial financing. Against this, one should logically include debt repayment and interest thereon. The virtue of an analysis which embraces investment financed by third-party debt and its service is that it ensures that all capital required is accounted for in the project appraisal. Some analysts, by contrast, leave these items out of the analysis altogether. If the project generates sufficient blocked cash flows to repay debt and accrued interest, this latter approach is entirely acceptable (it will, incidentally, achieve the same bottom-line result as the approach recommended). If this is not the case, then the more conservative approach is to reduce the dividends assumed to be distributed to take account of the repayment schedule. The data for this more conservative approach are less readily available if local debt raising and its service are left out of the cash flow equation – see Buckley (1996) for further detail on this point.

■ As in the earlier example, where no relevant exchange controls were in existence, cannibalization effects must be built into the equation.

■ When we are confronted with exchange controls on an overseas project and where finance with a subsidized interest rate is raised by the overseas venture, we do not need to take account of any subsidized interest as a separate item in the cash flow analysis – as was the case where no exchange controls were present. Remember that when there were no exchange controls, we would undertake our cash flow appraisal by applying a discount rate to cash generation before interest. So the worth of the interest subsidy must be calculated separately. By contrast, where exchange controls are present, the bottom line of the forecast profit and loss account will already have taken into account interest charges – including the effect of the subsidy itself. However, when host country exchange controls are present but the multinational raises soft debt, specifically and unequivocally tied to the project, in a company outside the host country, then the case for including the value of the subsidy as a parent cash flow is clear. Indeed, the multinational may structure the financing deal to ensure that it receives the full benefit of the subsidized interest itself.

- Allowances, as in the case where there are no exchange controls, for parent contribution of equipment as part of its input. The cash flow analysis, of course, may well have different values for the equipment compared with the local balance sheet figure for initial input.

- Any real operating option effects.

- Invariably, in international capital budgeting with exchange controls, blocked cash flows remain after allowing for dividend distribution (whether expected or notional) and debt service. There are a number of approaches to valuing these. But, first of all, let it be said that if such cash were permanently blocked with no means available to get cash back to the parent then the value of such blocked funds must be zero. In reality, this is rarely the case. First, countertrade and such techniques present ways of unblocking. And, second, there is usually some expectation of existing controls being relaxed or removed altogether. A probability factor may be applied to model such expectations. Care has to be taken to avoid double counting: we refer to this later on in this section.

- An allowance for any terminal values.

Table 23.7 provides a summary of the generally encountered sources of value in international investment appraisal with exchange controls. Table 23.8 shows the same information along slightly different lines. We now examine the items in the tables in more detail and in turn.

The value of the parent's share of investment inputs may cover fixed and working capital required to undertake the project, with equipment inputs valued in accordance with the asset value concept referred to in Table 22.2. The parent's share of capital inputs would logically be valued in home currency terms and the split between equity and debt input would be a question of the particular contractual agreements between parent and overseas operating business.

The next item in Table 23.8 concerns locally raised debt. There are two approaches available with respect to this item. First of all, we might leave this out of the analysis entirely and we might compensate for this by disregarding local debt service. This is entirely acceptable as long as it is remembered that there may be cash effects in terms of reduction in assumed dividend where insufficient cash is generated to service debt and dividend in an individual year. Thus, for evaluation purposes, payment of dividend may be constrained by shortages of cash in particular years. The alternative approach is to include investment financed by local debt and, to compensate, to allow for debt service in the cash flow analysis. This latter approach ensures the full control of cash flow, and this may be valuable when it comes to undertaking sensitivity analysis with lower than expected outturns.

Table 23.7 Summary of relevant incremental cash flows: international investment with exchange controls

	Approach used	
	NPV	APV
Share of equity inputs allowing for subscription via equipment, etc.	✓	✓
Share of input as parent debt	✓	✓
Share of input as local debt*	✓	✓
Value of remittable dividend stream	✓	✓
Value of management fees and royalties	✓	✓
Value of cannibalization effects to the group	✓	✓
Value of any subsidized interest involved only if it is raised and serviced outside the host country and, presumably, in a territory without exchange controls	✓	✓
Repayments of parent debt and interest thereon	✓	✓
Repayment of local debt and interest thereon*	✓	✓
Value of any real operating options	✓	✓
Share of blocked cash flows allowing for:	✓	✓
• countertrade remittability, or		
• multiplying by factor for discontinuance of exchange controls		
Allowance for terminal value	✓	✓
Value of tax shield due to debt: the amount will vary from classical to imputation tax system		✓

* Some analysts exclude both of these items – see text for an overview and commentary on this problem.

Table 23.8 Valuation of overseas project from parent's perspective but with exchange controls

Value of project = − Value of share of equity input allowing for subscription via equipment, etc.
            − Value of input as parent debt
            − Value of input as local debt*
            + Value of remittable dividend stream
            + Value of management fees and royalty stream
            − Value of any cannibalization effects to the group
            + Value of any subsidized interest only if it is raised and serviced outside the host country and, presumably, in a territory without exchange controls
            + Value of parent debt repayment and interest thereon
            + Value of local debt repayment and interest thereon*
            + Share of value of any real operating options
            + Value of blocked cash flows assuming either unblocking via countertrade and similar means or multiplying by a factor representing the probability of discontinuance of exchange controls
            + Allowance for terminal values
            + Value of tax shield due to debt capacity created by project in cases where the APV method is used

* Some analysts exclude both of these two items – see text for further details on this problem.

The next item is the value of the parent's share of remittable dividend stream. Of course, in order to determine the estimated level of remittable dividend to the parent, forecast profit and loss accounts and balance sheets for the overseas venture will have to be prepared. Any dividend remittance will only be payable out of the balance on profit and loss account after taking off such items as royalties and interest payments.

The value of management fees and royalties is, in fact, the next item listed in Table 23.8. This value should be stated net of host country withholding taxes and net of home currency taxes too.

As we mentioned earlier in this chapter, cannibalization effects in international capital budgeting have to be taken into account in terms of the present value of the lost margin, net of taxes, in home currency terms arising from knock-on effects.

Next we turn to subsidized interest. Note that Tables 23.7 and 23.8 state that its value would only, logically, be included if it were raised and serviced outside the host country's exchange controls – indeed, presumably, in a country without exchange controls thus enabling the multinational to acquire the full value of the subsidy. The whole point here is that if the debt is raised in the host country, by the operating company there, its financial effects will already be felt in profit and loss account terms before determining dividends remittable. By contrast, if raised outside the host country, the subsidy will not have been built into the equation. Essentially, the earlier remarks under the sixth bullet point at the start of this section should make the point clear. If such subsidized funding is outside the host territory, its value should be determined in exactly the same manner as suggested in the section on subsidized debt in cases where there are no exchange controls.

When we refer back to Table 23.8, we see that the next items are parent and local loan repayments and interest. Clearly, the inclusion of local debt service will be a function of whether or not it has been allowed for in the initial cost of the investment. (This was discussed earlier in this section.) There is no such problem with parent debt – this should unequivocally be included in our cash flow analysis. The objective of the multinational putting in some of its subscription as parent debt is to enable payments to the parent to occur in the presence of host country exchange controls. Of course, host governments respond by restricting debt levels, for exchange control purposes, through thin capitalization rules, which allow the host to refer to notional leverage levels for parent debt service purposes. Aside from such problems, the cash flow implications for the parent in the home country are clear. Capital and interest would normally be denominated in home currency terms. This would ensure that debt service was in parent currency terms and would result in relatively straightforward cash flow implications from the parent's standpoint.

The next item to be referred to in Table 23.8 relates to real operating options. Calculations on this front should accord with the methodology suggested earlier in this chapter – but it should be noted that, where there is a local partner, the effect will be to share the value of such options which are within the host territory operating company.

We next turn to the value of blocked cash flows. Clearly, if blocked for ever, with no possibility of unblocking, the value of such cash to the parent can only, logically, be zero. Usually, in the real world, there are possibilities of unblocking based on:

- such devices as countertrade;

- the probability of the host country relaxing exchange controls.

Both of the above bullet points mean that we might put a value on blocked cash which is 'unblockable'. For capital budgeting purposes, this might involve estimating the amount of blocked cash to be built each year, taking the multinational's share, allowing for countertrade costs and then estimating the net of tax value in parent currency terms.

Another approach, in terms of valuing blocked cash flows, is to assume that they build up within the company in the host country, earning appropriate interest up to some terminal value date and then to apply a probability factor to take account of potential unblocking as of that date.

Of course, it should be mentioned that these ideas apply also to the value of real operating options. A portion of the value of the multinational's share might be blocked and must be valued in a manner approximately consistent with the approach suggested immediately above.

In Table 23.8, terminal value comes next. When we focus upon cash flows over a finite period, we might or might not expect cash flows to cease then. If we do expect them to cease, we should get back a share of invested capital in terms of working capital released, any residual values of fixed capital and any blocked cash. Clearly the multinational's share of this represents a terminal value in the project – although care may have to be exercised to ensure that no double-counting of blocked cash occurs and it is also necessary to allow for the impact of controls to be in place at the end of the project's life.

If it is not expected that the project will cease but it is merely being truncated after a finite period for ease of analysis, then a terminal value should be allowed for on the basis of expected operations and their cash flow implications beyond the assumed truncation date. In such a case, the terminal value should embrace the value of:

- dividend flows in home currency terms net of all taxes;

- blocked cash generation beyond the truncation date capitalized as suggested above; this might include, of course, blocked real operating options;

- royalties and management fees net of all taxes;

- cannibalization effects beyond the truncation period net of all taxes.

Of course, it is assumed that all loans (especially to the parent) have been repaid by the truncation date; if not, then appropriate amounts with their specific timing should be duly taken into account.

Finally, in terms of items listed in Table 23.8, there is the question of whether the NPV or APV criterion is being used to estimate value. Where the APV route is adopted, the appropriate tax shield calculations must be made – the coverage given to this topic in Chapter 22 applies equally in the case of international investment appraisal with exchange controlling.

Timing: international investment with exchange controls

It will be recalled that, in an earlier section in this chapter, we briefly referred to the timing of international investments in an environment without exchange controls. It must be mentioned that exactly the same set of ideas applies under a regime with exchange controls.

23.7 | Debt–equity swaps

Debt–equity swaps are becoming popular with corporations as a means of reducing the cost of investment in less-developed countries (LDCs). Debt–equity swaps are financial transactions in which LDCs exchange part of their debt with foreign commercial banks for equity rights which are sold to an interested party. The purchasers of these equity rights may be either the same lenders – the foreign banks – or firms that pay the lenders for these rights. Debt–equity swaps can be a profitable source of advantage for firms that exploit their key benefit – access to local currency at exchange rates more favourable than the official rate.

Debt–equity swaps have their roots in the international debt crisis and the resultant difficulties suffered by debtor nations, banks and the international financial community. Commercial banks have been swapping their problem loans into equity investments because the debtors have insufficient hard currency to make interest payments, let alone to pay back principal. They make the swaps either directly, as an exchange for other loans with which the bank invests abroad, or indirectly, by selling the loan in the secondary market.

The commercial bank which has lent to the LDC has an asset. Since there is some possibility of rescheduling and even default, the asset may be worth less than $100 for a face value debt of $100. The bank will evaluate this worth and also what might be paid for it in the secondary market. If the bank decides to sell, it may negotiate (in discount terms) a level that will satisfy its financial requirements. When the bank's discounted loan is matched by an offer from a corporate investor, the loan may be sold. In some cases, the investor may be a domestic corporation in the LDC which has access to hard currency, perhaps as a result of previous capital flight. The debtor country then redeems the debt in local currency. The first of the above transactions is a debt sale in hard currency. Lending banks sell debt obligations in hard currency in the US secondary loan market, at a price lower than their nominal (or face) value.

Next in the debt–equity swap process, a currency exchange takes place. The acquired hard currency debt is presented by the purchaser to the country's central bank, which redeems it for local currency. The redemption rate is roughly equal to the debt's original dollar face value but converted at the official exchange rate minus a transaction fee. The debt–equity swap is concluded when the corporate investor purchases, in local currency, equity rights to existing ventures or invests in the start-up of new ones.

Clearly, from the standpoint of the corporate investor, entry into a developing country via the debt–equity swap market is achieved at a cost lower than would otherwise be the case. In capital budgeting terms, then, the initial capital cost is lowered. From the point of view of the Third World country, debt is redeemed and increased investment is encouraged. Obviously this topic is one that is particularly relevant in the case of international capital budgeting with exchange controls since most of the LDCs with the potential for undertaking attractive debt–equity swaps are nations with significant exchange controls.

23.8 | Sensitivity analysis

So far, both under the heading of international capital budgeting with and without exchange controls, a route has been suggested towards the estimation of value. Naturally, the usual capital budgeting considerations as regards beginning the analysis with a best estimate picture of cash flows and then adjusting outturns to allow for the effects of a number of 'what if?' scenarios would apply. In addition to the usual changes to market share, lower demand, late commissioning of plant and so on, one might allow for variations from the harshest tax treatment, using different exchange rates, estimating terminal values using different methodologies, and assessing the sensitivity of outturns to varying levels of political risk (see Chapter 25) and to varying assumptions about real operating options.

23.9 | Summary

■ When analysing international capital budgeting propositions it is necessary to distinguish two very different kinds of situation. The first of these is where there are no exchange controls in the host country. The second is where there is partial blockage of overseas cash generation. Distinguishing which category a particular project falls into is necessary because the recommended methodology of analysis varies from one to the other.

■ We look, first of all, at the situation where there are no exchange controls in the host country. In this kind of situation, we may do our analysis in terms of project cash flows or in terms of parent cash flows. Really, though, it is the result of the parent analysis that matters. Project cash flow forecasts, duly discounted, usually give the same indication as to attractiveness of an investment opportunity as parent cash flow analysis – but this is not necessarily the case. To reiterate, it is parent cash flows that matter from the standpoint of the investors in the multinational company.

■ Project cash flows, of course, involve the comparison of cash outflows and cash inflows in local currency terms. Such an analysis will lead to the calculation of an internal rate of return or a present value for the project under consideration. Calculation may involve the APV or NPV techniques. Be sure that you are clear as to how the APV and NPV methods differ.

- Since we are dealing, first of all, with a situation where there is no restriction on remittances of bottom-line cash generation from a territory without exchange controls, cash generation in the host country is just as good as cash generated in the United Kingdom or in the United States or in Germany. In situations where there are no exchange controls, there is no point in restricting the analysis in parent cash flow terms merely to the dividend remitted.

- Calculations in terms of parent cash flows should begin by undertaking an analysis of overseas cash flows in local currency terms, at local rates of inflation and then converting them to home currency flows by using expected future exchange rates, allowing for home taxes and then discounting at a risk-adjusted rate which allows for anticipated inflation in the home country. Exchange rate movements should be consistent with these different inflation levels except for corrections of previously prevailing disequilibria.

- The valuation of growth opportunities is a recommended step in valuing overseas investments, whether with or without exchange controls.

- It is usual, in undertaking analysis of an overseas project in terms of home parent cash flows, to subject potential cash generation available for remittance to withholding taxes and home taxes. Since not all overseas cash generation will be remitted to the parent company, this is really the harshest tax treatment possible. If the project stands up on this severest set of tax assumptions, it must also stand up assuming a less strict tax burden. And it may, of course, be possible to engineer a less tough tax impact through the use of tax havens and other devices.

- In terms of converting host currency cash generation into home currency terms, we have suggested that exchange rates prevailing in future years should be estimated. Note that this may be done simply by using the forward rate or through a purchasing power parity analysis. We believe that it is useful to undertake the analysis in home currency terms using both methodologies.

- We now have the wherewithal to undertake a full analysis of the potential of the project in home currency terms. We have details of capital outflows and capital inflows translated back into home currency terms. In addition, where there is subsidized finance, we need to calculate the present value of this subsidy in home currency terms and, if we are using the APV approach, we will need to estimate the value of the tax shield of the debt capacity of the project in home currency terms. All of this can readily be done and the summation will give us full present value details of the project in home currency terms.

- We now turn to the situation where there is some blockage of cash flows in the host country. This usually arises because of exchange controls. The bullet points from here onwards relate to the situation where there is some constraint upon remittance of cash generated in the host country.

- Only remittable cash flows out of an overseas territory create added shareholder value. Cash permanently blocked in an overseas territory adds no value.

- The multinational may remit monies to the parent company in a number of ways. This may include dividend payments, but, in addition, it may involve royalty payments and interest payments on parent loans. This represents a departure from the rules which students have learned in respect of domestic capital budgeting, but debt repayment is a genuine technique by which multinationals hasten the transfer of monies out of a blocking host territory and this needs to be reflected in international capital budgeting analysis. It reinforces the idea that financing does affect parent cash flows in capital appraisal when exchange controls create constraints on remittances. This is a very important point.

■ If it is possible to hasten repayment through parent loans, a pertinent question follows. Why not finance all overseas projects by parent loans? In fact, host countries rarely allow it – their exchange controls frequently require a substantial equity input from the parent company. Often, exchange controls stipulate that if an overseas company has an excessively high debt level, then thin capitalization rules may be invoked under which part of the debt is reclassified for exchange control purposes as equity. Secondly, excessive use of parent debt closes one route by which political risk is minimized, namely the use of local funding. This technique is dealt with in Chapter 25.

■ One route towards avoiding remittance constraints involves royalties and loan interest and capital repayments on parent loans. In international capital budgeting terms, these are converted into home currency terms. To these are added allowable dividend remittances to the extent that they are covered by profit earned overseas. To specify this allowable level of dividend, it is necessary to make projections of profit after tax in the host territory. The summation of royalties, loan interest and dividend payments plus parent loan repayments, when converted into home currency terms, gives us the wherewithal to calculate parent cash flows and hence a present value. To this it is necessary to add the effect of the tax shield on debt if the APV approach is being used.

■ Note that where there are exchange controls, a different approach is used in respect of subsidized interest. Effectively subsidized interest is taken into account in arriving at the profit after tax in the host territory. Dividend remittances are based upon this profit after tax, so the specification of dividends receivable from the host territory already takes into account the effect of subsidized interest. To add in the effect of subsidized interest in the manner specified where there are no exchange controls would have the effect of double counting.

■ We charge as a capital cost in overseas project evaluation, even when there are exchange controls, the full capital cost irrespective of whether it involves funding from the United Kingdom or whether local funds are used. However, a difficulty arises where exchange controls are in force and an overseas project is funded (or partially financed) from local capital markets. In normal domestic capital budgeting we estimate future cash flows generated from a project which are available to repay interest, dividend, debt repayment or whatever. Logically in the overseas project, then, we should include as a notional parent cash flow cash generation available for local debt interest and principal repayment. Consequently, in this circumstance we credit as a parent cash inflow the project's cash generation that repays interest and capital on the foreign loan.

■ Just as we may include an estimate of terminal value for a project in domestic capital budgeting, we must do the same for overseas capital budgeting projects. This terminal value, calculated in overseas currency terms, will be converted back to home currency values at the estimated ongoing exchange rate at the terminal value date. Terminal value calculations are an inexact science and we often use such methods as asset value, a price to earnings ratio or capitalization of ongoing cash flows over a very long period (this may involve the use of the perpetuity valuation formula).

23.10 | End of chapter questions

Question 1
Explain debt-equity swaps and how they increase activity in the secondary loan market.

Question 2
List additional factors that deserve consideration in a foreign project analysis but are not relevant for a purely domestic project.

24 International investment: what discount rate?

This chapter focuses on international investment. If we are to use the capital asset pricing model as an aid to establish the value of the cost of equity capital through the formula

$$k_e = R_F + \beta(R_M - R_F)$$

we need to specify the value of $(R_M - R_F)$. Of course, if we are looking into the future, as is the case in investment appraisal, we would ideally wish to be using a future-oriented value for the excess return (that is, $R_M - R_F$). We would be in a position to make a fortune were we to have this knowledge of the future for certain for every year. In its absence, we are able to lay our hands on past outturns. If there was a good chance that history would repeat itself, past data would provide a reasonable proxy for future returns. In the long run, this may be the best approximation that we have. But the underpinning caveat that it is based upon history repeating itself has to be borne in mind.

It has to be admitted that vast differences in international real, risk-adjusted returns should not be evident because the potential for arbitrage would eliminate substantial divergences. As Copeland, Koller and Murrin (2000) state:

> our point of view is that there is no difference in the costs of capital among developed countries after adjusting nominal costs of capital for differences in expected rates of inflation, risk, and taxation. If the cost of capital is really lower in Japan, for example, then the world would rush to borrow from Japanese lenders until supply and demand imbalance was eliminated and the cost of capital was the same across borders.

These authors subsequently state that 'government regulations or taxes could serve as barriers to the flow of capital and lead to differences'. Of course, the above quotes are deductively derived. The question of relative magnitudes of international return is an empirical one.

When examining the evidence from various economies, we will ask whether there is any consistent pattern of realized excess return from one country to another. We commence our analysis by examining the evidence from US equity markets given that they are undoubtedly more widely researched than any other.

24.1 | The original US evidence

There are some classic studies of US equity returns and an annual update of such out-turns. Fisher and Lorie (1968) analysed common stock returns for the period from 1926 to 1965. The before-tax return, including dividends and capital gains over the whole period was 9.3 per cent using annual compounding. The real before-tax rate of return was about 7.7 per cent per annum over the forty-year period. For an investor in a relatively high tax bracket, nominal post-tax returns fell to 7.1 per cent compounded annually and to 5.6 per cent per annum after adjusting for inflation. Note that the above data relate to total shareholder returns and not to the excess return.

Of course, the base year and the end year can have a critical impact on realized returns. Indeed Ritter and Urich (1984), measuring equity yields over the period 1968 to 1983, obtained starkly different results. US equities yielded a real return of only 1 per cent per annum in their study.

Given the need to take a long-term view in measuring equity investor returns, Ibbotson and Sinquefield publish annual data in their *Stocks, Bonds, Bills and Inflation Yearbook*. They use 1926 as a base year and produce figures for US returns since then in respect of:

- common stocks (that is, ordinary shares);

- small company stocks;

- long-term corporate bonds;

- long-term government bonds;

- intermediate-term government bonds;

- US treasury bills (that is, three-month government securities);

- inflation rates.

They present their findings in terms of an arithmetic average and a geometric average of returns. Determining the former involves the calculation of annual returns based on the end of year value of the portfolio plus dividends versus the beginning year value. Over a long period, the arithmetic mean is given by the average of such returns based on the formulation:

$$\text{Arithmetic mean } \overline{R}_a = \frac{1}{n}\sum_{t=1}^{n} R_t$$

where R_t is the annual rate of return in year t and n is the number of annual return observations. Also, the standard deviation of returns can be calculated according to the formula:

$$\text{Standard deviation} = \sqrt{\frac{1}{n-1}\sum_{t=1}^{n}(R_t - \overline{R}_a)^2}$$

Table 24.1 Total annual returns from US investment over long run from 1926

	Geometric mean (%)	Arithmetic mean (%)	Standard deviation (%)
Ordinary shares	9.75–10.0	12.0–12.5	21.0
Small company ordinary shares	12.0–12.25	17.5–18.0	35.5
Long-term corporate bonds	4.9–5.1	5.2–5.7	8.5
Long-term government bonds	4.3–4.5	4.6–5.1	8.5
Intermediate-term government bonds	4.6–4.8	4.9–5.4	5.5
US treasury bills	3.5–3.9	3.5–3.9	3.4
Inflation	2.8–3.0	3.0–3.2	4.75
$R_M - R_F$ (R_F based on long-term government bonds)	5.5	7.4	
$R_M - R_F$ (R_F based on US treasury bills)	6.2	8.5	

Source: Ibbotson and Sinquefield.

The geometric mean is calculated differently. Like the arithmetic mean, its practical calculation involves annual returns – but, unlike the arithmetic mean, such returns are compounded. Using the notation referred to above, the formulation for the geometric mean is:

$$\text{Geometric mean } \overline{R}_g = \left[\prod_{t=1}^{n} (1 + R_t) \right]^{\frac{1}{n}} - 1$$

Written another way, this is equal to:

$$\overline{R}_g = \sqrt[n]{(1 + R_1)(1 + R_2)(1 + R_3) \dots (1 + R_n)} - 1$$

Of course, returns, whether measured by arithmetic or geometric means, will be affected by start and end periods used in measurement. A discussion on the relative merits of the two means follows later.

So what is the evidence from the Ibbotson and Sinquefield research? As observed, the achieved returns, calculated according to the above definitions of arithmetic and geometric mean, vary according to which year is chosen as an end year. Immediately following the 1987 stock market crash would yield a lower return than immediately prior. Remember that Ibbotson and Sinquefield always start their calculations from 1926. Interestingly enough, whether the end of the period is chosen as 1986, 1988, 1990 or whatever, there is a fairly persistent outturn – see recent publications of the Ibbotson Associates Yearbooks. Their results are summarized in Table 24.1. This exhibit shows a range of returns for the simple reason that returns vary over the period. Note that the US data reproduced show returns based on capital gains plus dividends – but such dividends are expressed gross of shareholder dividend taxes.

According to Ibbotson and Sinquefield, long-term returns accruing from investment in a broad range of US equities over the last 70 years or so amount to real returns of around 9 to $9\frac{1}{4}$ per cent per annum on an arithmetic mean basis and 7 per cent per annum on a geometric basis (gross of shareholder taxes on dividends). The value of $(R_M - R_F)$ is around $8^1/_2$ per cent per annum if an arithmetic mean is used and about 6.2 per cent per annum if a geometric mean is used – in this instance R_F is based on three-month government securities. If R_F were measured in terms of the yield on long-term government securities, the value of $(R_M - R_F)$ would approximate 7.4 per cent per annum and 5.5 per cent per annum respectively measured by arithmetic and geometric means. Note from Table 24.1 that the standard deviation of equity returns is substantial. Given this fact, the use of our evidence in *ex-ante* estimates of the equity risk premium needs to be treated with caution.

24.2 | The new international evidence

New evidence suggests that the figures in Table 24.1 should be revised. This emerges from in-depth work by Dimson, Marsh and Staunton (2002), who set out to eliminate some of the biases contained in previously published data. Because returns had been derived from index figures, there was a bias towards successful firms – weakly performing companies, perhaps affected by financial distress and falling market capitalization, tend to be demoted from indexes of top stocks. Correcting for this kind of bias and others relating, for example to small index sizes and incorrect rights issue adjustments, among others, enabled Dimson, Marsh and Staunton to focus upon international equity, bond and bill returns over the period from 1900 to 2000. As they say:

> Good indexes follow an investment strategy that could be followed in real life. Apart from dealing costs, an investor should in principle have been able to replicate index performance. Indexes, especially when they are constructed retrospectively, must therefore be free from any look-ahead bias. They must be constructed solely from information that would have been available at the time of investment. Serious bias can arise if index constituents are tilted towards companies that subsequently survived or became large, or towards sectors that later became important.

Having corrected for various biases, Dimson, Marsh and Staunton produced key tables of returns. These are brought together in our composite Table 24.2 (overleaf). This shows returns accruing to capital gains and dividends, or interest, on a per annum basis from equities, government bonds or government bills (three-month bills) for sixteen Western economies over the last century. The figures here show lower returns than the Ibbotson and Sinquefield data because of the elimination of various biases. It is our opinion that the new data carries greater authority than that quantified earlier.

On the topic of the equity risk premium (that is, $R_M - R_F$), data on past worldwide returns allow us to put a figure upon this key piece of information, country by country. Statistics are reproduced in Table 24.3 (overleaf).

The data shown in Table 24.3 may be helpful when applying the capital asset pricing model (see the equation at the start of this chapter) approach in estimating a firm's cost of equity capital in various parts of the world. However there are pitfalls. Note for example, the very low figures for Denmark, Spain, Belgium and Switzerland.

We would suspect that future returns for these countries would be close to leading international equity markets, like the United States. We are of this opinion because international returns on equities have demonstrated an increasing convergence. Table 24.4 – see page 464 – shows correlation coefficients between world equity markets. The correlations in the lower left-hand triangle in Table 24.4 (in bold) are based on a century of real, common currency (US$) returns while those in the top right-hand triangle in Table 24.4 are derived from the return data over 60 months from 1996 to 2000 in real common currency (US$) terms. Note the general picture of increasing correlation coefficients. This is reinforced by the evidence of Goetzmann, Li and Rouwenhorst (2001) who provide evidence of increasing market integration over the recent past – see Figure 24.1 (on page 464).

As a further warning against the use of the actual figures in Table 24.3 in respect of, for example, Belgium, Denmark, Spain and Switzerland, we would refer readers to the quote from Copeland, Koller and Murrin in the second paragraph of this chapter.

24.3 | Arithmetic or geometric mean?

The question of whether an arithmetic or geometric mean should be used in *ex-ante* estimates is another issue demanding caution. Leading financial texts differ in their prescription. Early editions of Brealey and Myers (1996) seem to err on the side of the arithmetic mean; Levy and Sarnat (1994) propose a geometric mean. As Brigham and Gapenski (1997) point out, the arithmetic average is more consistent with CAPM theory as one of its key underpinning assumptions is that investors are supposed to focus, in their portfolio decisions, upon returns in the next period and the standard deviation of this return. Is this 'next period' one year? If so, the preference for the arithmetic mean which derives from a set of single one-year period returns follows. Investors probably use single periods to assess performance, but are such single periods of twelve months' duration? That investors patently hold shares for longer periods may cast some doubt upon this assumption. This conclusion is reinforced in a paper by Blume (1974) who proposes that the arithmetic average should be applied in discounting one year cash flows, while the geometric mean is an unbiased estimate for very long periods for which it is more appropriate.

One of the arguments favouring the arithmetic mean flows from looking at the outturn, year by year, as annual independent draws for a stable distribution of returns. Thus, suppose that a two-period investment has equally likely outcomes of a 40 per cent return and a minus 20 per cent return. Average returns might be computed thus:

$$\text{Arithmetic mean} \quad \frac{40\% + (-20\%)}{2} = 10\%$$

$$\text{Geometric mean} \quad \sqrt{(1.4)(0.8)} - 1 = 5.8\%$$

But which is the more realistic measure?

Table 24.2 Real (inflation-adjusted) equity, bond and bill returns around the world, 1900–2000

Country	Equities (% pa)			Bonds (% pa)			Bills (% pa)		
	Geometric mean %	Arithmetic mean %	Standard deviation %	Geometric mean %	Arithmetic mean %	Standard deviation %	Geometric mean %	Arithmetic mean %	Standard deviation %
Australia	7.5	9.0	17.7	1.1	1.9	13.0	0.4	0.6	5.6
Belgium	2.5	4.8	22.8	-0.4	0.3	12.1	-0.3	0.0	8.2
Canada	6.4	7.7	16.8	1.8	2.4	10.6	1.7	1.8	5.1
Denmark	4.6	6.2	20.1	2.5	3.3	12.5	2.8	3.0	6.4
France	3.8	6.3	23.1	-1.0	0.1	14.4	-3.3	-2.6	11.4
Germany*	3.6	8.8	32.3	-2.2	0.3	15.9	-0.6	0.1	10.6
Ireland	4.8	7.0	22.2	1.5	2.4	13.3	1.3	1.4	6.0
Italy	2.7	6.8	29.4	-2.2	-0.8	14.4	-4.1	-2.9	12.0
Japan	4.5	9.3	30.3	-1.6	1.3	20.9	-2.0	-0.3	14.5
The Netherlands	5.8	7.7	21.0	1.1	1.5	9.4	0.7	0.8	5.2
South Africa	6.8	9.1	22.8	1.4	1.9	10.6	0.8	1.0	6.4
Spain	3.6	5.8	22.0	1.2	1.9	12.0	0.4	0.6	6.1
Sweden	7.6	9.9	22.8	2.4	3.1	12.7	2.0	2.2	6.8
Switzerland[†]	5.0	6.9	20.4	2.8	3.1	8.0	1.1	1.2	6.2
United Kingdom	5.8	7.6	20.0	1.3	2.3	14.5	1.0	1.2	6.6
United States	6.7	8.7	20.2	1.6	2.1	10.0	0.9	1.0	4.7

* Bond and bill statistics for Germany exclude the years 1922–23. [†] Swiss equities are from 1911.
Source: Dimson, Marsh and Staunton (2002).

Table 24.3 Worldwide equity risk premia relative to long-term government bonds and treasury bills, 1900–2000

Country	Annual equity risk premium relative to long-term government bonds			Annual equity risk premium relative to three-month treasury bills		
	Geometric mean %	*Arithmetic mean %*	*Standard deviation %*	*Geometric mean %*	*Arithmetic mean %*	*Standard deviation %*
Australia	6.3	8.0	18.9	7.1	8.5	17.2
Belgium	2.9	4.8	20.7	2.9	5.1	23.5
Canada	4.5	6.0	17.8	4.6	5.9	16.7
Denmark	2.0	3.3	16.9	1.8	3.4	19.4
France	4.9	7.0	21.6	7.4	9.8	23.8
Germany*	6.7	9.9	28.4	4.9	10.3	35.3
Ireland	3.2	4.6	17.4	3.5	5.4	20.6
Italy	5.0	8.4	30.0	7.0	11.0	32.5
Japan	6.2	10.3	33.2	6.7	9.9	27.9
The Netherlands	4.7	6.7	21.4	5.1	7.1	22.2
South Africa	5.4	7.1	19.7	6.0	8.1	22.5
Spain	2.3	4.2	20.3	3.2	5.3	21.5
Sweden	5.2	7.4	22.1	5.5	7.7	21.9
Switzerland[†]	2.7	4.2	17.9	4.3	6.1	19.4
United Kingdom	4.4	5.6	16.7	4.8	6.5	19.9
United States	5.0	7.0	20.0	5.8	7.7	19.6
World	4.6	5.6	14.5	4.9	6.2	16.4

* All statistics for Germany exclude 1922–23. [†] Premia for Switzerland are from 1911.
Source: Dimson, Marsh and Staunton (2002).

Table 24.4 Correlation coefficients between world equity markets*

	Wld	US	UK	Swi	Swe	Spa	SAf	Neth	Jap	Ita	Ire	Ger	Fra	Den	Can	Bel	Aus
Wld		.93	.77	.59	.62	.67	.54	.73	.68	.52	.69	.69	.73	.57	.82	.54	.69
US	.85		.67	.44	.46	.53	.46	.57	.49	.40	.66	.56	.56	.46	.78	.45	.57
UK	.70	.55		.58	.44	.63	.31	.71	.42	.39	.73	.58	.59	.57	.57	.59	.56
Swi	.68	.50	.62		.39	.60	.19	.72	.36	.45	.57	.53	.64	.58	.35	.63	.37
Swe	.62	.44	.42	.54		.63	.38	.63	.34	.49	.27	.76	.76	.44	.61	.29	.44
Spa	.41	.25	.25	.36	.37		.35	.63	.32	.64	.50	.64	.75	.56	.51	.55	.54
SAf	.55	.43	.49	.39	.34	.26		.30	.44	.24	.31	.42	.37	.25	.62	.10	.66
Neth	.57	.39	.42	.51	.43	.28	.29		.39	.59	.63	.74	.77	.64	.55	.70	.46
Jap	.45	.21	.33	.29	.39	.40	.31	.25		.18	.33	.25	.36	.24	.50	.17	.59
Ita	.54	.37	.43	.52	.39	.41	.41	.32	.34		.33	.55	.71	.50	.40	.51	.38
Ire	.58	.38	.73	.70	.42	.35	.42	.46	.29	.43		.42	.45	.49	.54	.57	.50
Ger	.30	.12	−.01	.22	.09	−.03	.05	.27	.06	.16	.03		.83	.61	.57	.59	.46
Fra	.62	.36	.45	.54	.44	.47	.38	.48	.25	.52	.53	.19		.63	.60	.66	.48
Den	.57	.38	.40	.51	.56	.34	.31	.50	.46	.38	.55	.22	.45		.55	.54	.30
Can	.80	.80	.55	.48	.53	.27	.54	.34	.30	.37	.41	.13	.35	.46		.30	.65
Bel	.58	.38	.40	.57	.43	.40	.29	.60	.25	.47	.49	.26	.68	.42	.35		.30
Aus	.66	.47	.66	.51	.50	.28	.56	.41	.28	.43	.62	.04	.47	.42	.62	.35	

Abbreviations are for World, USA, UK, Switzerland, Sweden, Spain, South Africa, Netherlands, Japan, Italy, Ireland, Germany, France, Denmark, Canada, Belgium and Australia, respectively.
* Correlations in bold (lower left-hand triangle) are based on 101 years of real dollar returns, 1900–2000. Correlations not in bold (top right-hand triangle) are based on 60 months of real dollar returns, 1996–2000.
Source: Dimson, Marsh and Staunton (2002).

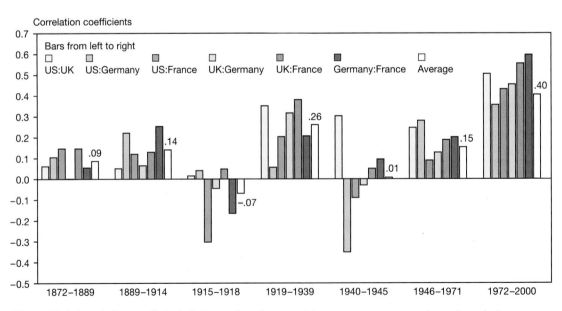

Figure 24.1 Correlation coefficients between four key countries over seven successive sub-periods.
Source: Goetzmann, Li, and Rouwenhorst, 2001.

The expected result at the end of the two-year period can be computed thus. Assume $1,000 is invested and that the returns conform to the expected frequency distribution below:

$$
\begin{aligned}
\$1,000 \times (1.4) \times (1.4) \times (0.25) &= \quad\$490 \\
\$1,000 \times (1.4) \times (0.8) \times (0.25) &= \quad\$280 \\
\$1,000 \times (0.8) \times (1.4) \times (0.25) &= \quad\$280 \\
\$1,000 \times (0.8) \times (0.8) \times (0.25) &= \quad\underline{\$160} \\
\text{Expected value} \qquad\qquad &= \underline{\underline{\$1,210}}
\end{aligned}
$$

Clearly we are looking at an expected outturn at the end of year 2 of $1,210. This expected return is the arithmetic average return given by:

$$\$1,000 \times (1.10)^2 = \$1,210$$

The incorrect argument is that the expected outturn at the end of the investment period is given by:

$$\$1,000 \times (1.4) \times (0.8) = \$1,120$$

To be sure, the latter figure of $1,120 may accrue but, as shown above, it only has a 50 per cent probability of occurrence. What is ignored is the *ex-ante* possibility of outturns amounting to $1,960 (given by $1,000 \times 1.4 \times 1.4$) and $640 (given by $1,000 \times 0.8 \times 0.8$). Each of these has a 25 per cent probability of occurrence. Allowing for these probabilities, we obtain an expected value at the end of two years amounting to $1,210. Note that, according to this argument, the false return conforms to the geometric return. In the context here, its falsity relates to the fact that it does not take into account the binomial-type distribution of potential outturns.

Viewed from a standpoint before the event, by undertaking a risky investment, we are exposed to a broad spread of potential results. We require a higher return on this risky investment, compared with an investment with a certain return, to compensate for the spread of possible outturns. The arithmetic mean takes into account the full distribution of potential results. The question that follows is what is the appropriate time interval to use? Is it one year? Or are investors single period expected utility of terminal wealth maximizers, given a two-year period? Or a three-year period? Lengthening the time interval increases the precision of the estimate of the mean return. But lengthening the time interval also strains the plausibility of the assumption that returns are drawn from a stable distribution.

On the topic of arithmetic versus geometric mean, Cooper (1993) focuses upon correction of estimation errors in US data from 1926 to 1992 by measuring real returns and adjusting to allow for serial correlation in returns. The unbiased estimates of discount rates at which he tentatively arrives are far closer to the arithmetic than the geometric mean.

One of the arguments favouring the geometric mean is also one of the simplest. If a share falls by 50 per cent in the first year and then doubles – that is, it increases by 100 per cent – in the second, the investor breaks even. The total return is zero. The geometric return conveys this precisely:

$$\sqrt{(1-0.5)(1+1)} - 1 = 0$$

However, the arithmetic mean return comes out at 25 per cent per annum, given by:

$$\frac{-0.5 + 1}{2} = 0.25$$

But investors can really only be expected to realize geometric returns over the long time frame. Indeed, the compound rate of return to a buy and hold strategy would tend to be measured by the geometric, rather than the arithmetic, mean. The geometric mean return is always less then the arithmetic mean return, except when all yearly returns are exactly equal. There is an approximate relationship between the two means such that the geometric mean is roughly equal to the arithmetic mean minus one half of the variance, σ^2, of yearly returns. Thus:

$$\overline{R}_g \approx \overline{R}_a - {}^1\!/_2\sigma^2$$

Another idea occasionally quoted as suggesting the use of a geometric mean flows from the view that both it and the internal rate of return (IRR) are essentially based on compound interest arithmetic. The argument that one should compare like with like would militate in favour of comparing a geometrically derived IRR with a geometrically derived mean in capital budgeting (similar to the point about a buy and hold strategy mentioned earlier).

There is other evidence favouring the use of a geometric mean. In essence, it derives from ideas of mean reversion of share returns to a trend. If share returns were expected to revert to a trend, then this would suggest the use of a geometric mean since the geometric mean is, by definition, an estimate of a smoothed long run trend. Referring back to the example of the investment offering an equal chance of a 40 per cent return and a minus 20 per cent return period by period, mean reversion would tend to chop off the more extreme outturns in the distribution of potential payoffs. Of course, it is these less likely outturns that give the pattern of potential payoffs its binomial distribution. It is the likelihood of achieving this kind of distribution that is at the heart of the argument preferring the arithmetic mean over the geometric counterpart. With mean reversion, and hence a more narrow range of outturns than the full binomial distribution, this line of argument breaks down. The fact is that there is now a substantial body of evidence identifying mean reverting behaviours in stock returns – see section 24.5. This empirical observation is one of the strongest arguments supporting the use of the geometric mean[1] in estimating the cost of equity capital for the firm. Given this background, we will be returning to the topic of mean reversion later on.

24.4 | The equity premium puzzle

However, the story so far is only the tip of the iceberg of evidence. For example, Mehra and Prescott (1985) suggested that the historical returns from common stocks were excessive when compared with the rates of return on bonds. They termed this excessive return on equities the equity premium puzzle. The arguments here pre-date the corrective work of Dimson, Marsh and Staunton (2002). However, the puzzle of

Table 24.5 US returns since 1802 (Figures in percentages per annum)

	1802–1870	*1871–1925*	*1926–2001*	*1802–2001*
Common stocks (nominal)				
arithmetic return	8.1	8.4	12.2	9.7
geometric return	7.1	7.2	10.2	8.3
Common stocks (real)				
arithmetic return	8.3	7.9	8.9	8.4
geometric return	7.0	6.6	6.9	6.9
Short-term government securities (nominal)				
arithmetic return	5.2	3.8	3.9	4.3
geometric return	5.2	3.8	3.9	4.3
Long-term government securities (nominal)				
arithmetic return	4.9	4.4	5.7	5.1
geometric return	4.9	4.3	5.3	4.9
$R_M - R_F$ (R_F based on short-term government securities)				
arithmetic return	2.9	4.6	8.3	5.4
geometric return	1.9	3.4	6.3	4.0
$R_M - R_F$ (R_F based on long-term government securities)				
arithmetic returns	3.2	4.0	6.5	4.6
geometric returns	2.2	2.9	4.9	3.4
Consumer price inflation	0.1	0.6	3.1	1.4

Source: Siegel (2002).

the equity premium remains. Mehra and Prescott point out that the difference in returns implies a high degree of risk aversion on the part of investors. The high historical equity risk premium is intriguing compared with the low historical rate of return on Treasury securities – see Table 24.1. On this very topic, Siegel (2002) has estimated excess returns since 1802 – see Table 24.5. He points out that the real geometric excess return has risen dramatically over the period analysed. But this is nothing to do with the returns from investment in common stocks showing an increase – indeed the returns have barely changed – but it has everything to do with a falling real returns from bonds, with investors having been caught out in times of rising inflation. The risk premium from 1926 onwards arrived at by Siegel differs slightly from the Ibbotson and Sinquefield data in the earlier table in this paper because Table 24.5 uses a single finishing date of 2001 whereas Table 24.1 figures are based upon a range using various terminating dates.

Rising inflation rates tend to increase long-term interest rates and lower bond prices, resulting in realized real yields on long-term bonds (to the extent that rising inflation exceeded expectations) at a level below the *ex-ante* expected yield. If realized bond yields were below expected yields, then the risk premium (RP) as measured by

$$k_{\text{shares}} - k_{\text{bonds}} = \text{RP}_{\text{market}}$$

would overstate the risk premium. If this were correct, then the excess return of stocks over government bonds on an arithmetic or a geometric mean basis as reported in Table 24.1 would be too large for use in the CAPM unless inflation were to continue in the long run to exceed expectations.

But there are even stranger things afoot in our story of returns on stocks and bonds. One way to describe risk is via a worst case/best case picture. Table 24.6, adapted from Siegel (2002), shows the best and worst real returns for US stocks, bonds and treasury bills from 1802 for holding periods ranging from 1 to 30 years. Stocks are clearly riskier than bonds or bills in the short run. But, for every five-year holding period, the worst performance in stocks, at minus 11 per cent per year, has been only a little inferior to the worst performance in bonds and bills. But, and this is startling, over ten-year holding periods, the worst stock performance has been better than the worst outturns for bonds or bills. Furthermore, over twenty-year holding periods, stocks have never fallen behind inflation. The worst outturns for both bonds and bills over this time period have been 3 per cent per year below the rate of inflation. Finally, for thirty-year holding periods, the worst annual stock performance remained comfortably ahead of inflation by 2.6 per cent per year, while the worst inflation-adjusted outturns for bonds and bills were well into negative territory.

Stocks, in contrast to bonds or bills, have never yielded a negative real return over holding periods of 17 years or more. It is riskier to hold stocks than bonds in the short term, as one would expect. But unlike theoretical expectations, the opposite has been true for the long term. Of course, unexpected inflation may be partially responsible for this *ex-post* phenomenon.

In fairness, as Siegel (2002) shows, although the dominance of stocks over bonds is clear in the long run, it is important to note that over one-year and two-year periods, stocks outperform bonds or bills only in three years out of five. Thus, in two out of every five years, a shareholder's return is likely to be below the return on government securities.

Table 24.6 Maximum and minimum real holding period compound annual returns in the USA from 1802 to 2001

Holding period	Stocks (%)		Government long bonds (%)		Government bills (%)	
	Max.	Min.	Max.	Min.	Max.	Min.
1 year	+66.6	−38.6	+35.1	−21.9	+23.7	−15.6
2 years	+41.0	−31.6	+24.7	−15.9	+21.6	−15.1
5 years	+26.7	−11.0	+17.7	−10.1	+14.9	−8.2
10 years	+16.9	−4.1	+12.4	−5.4	+11.6	−5.1
20 years	+12.6	+1.0	+8.8	−3.1	+8.3	−3.0
30 years	+10.6	+2.6	+7.4	−2.0	+7.6	−1.8

Source: Siegel (2002).

Siegel (2002) also indicates that the same picture is arrived at if we use standard deviation as our measure of risk. Once the holding period increases to between fifteen and twenty years, the standard deviation of average annual returns for stocks become lower than the standard deviation of average bond and bill returns. Over thirty-year holding periods, the equity standard deviation is only two-thirds that of bonds or bills. Of course, we should be wary about using data from as long ago as 1802, and the methodology used by Siegel to construct his dataset can be criticized. But, as Siegel (1996) shows, these findings seem to have persisted over the whole period relatively consistently. Mathematically, it can be determined how fast the risk of average annual returns should decline as the holding period lengthens if returns follow a random walk. Under a random walk process, future returns are completely independent of past returns. The data suggest that the random walk hypothesis is decidedly suspect; the risk of stocks declines far faster than predicted as the holding period increases. This may be an indication of mean reversion of equity returns.

The whole point is that if returns follow a random walk, then the period over which risk and return are measured is irrelevant. To be more precise, risk and return increase linearly as time increases. Hence relative risks between assets remain unchanged and the length of the period chosen to measure risk is not relevant.

If asset returns do not follow a random walk, the period chosen to measure risk matters. The examination of longer-term return data shows important deviations from a random walk. The standard deviation of average annual returns in Siegel's work declines almost twice as fast as the holding period increases for stocks compared with that predicted by random walk theory. This looks like evidence of mean reversion of real stock returns.

The standard deviation of the average annual real return on government bonds declines more slowly then theory would predict as the holding period increases. This is mean aversion, a behaviour in which a variable tends to wander from its mean value, rather than moving towards it, as is the case for stocks.

24.5 | Mean reversion

There is now a significant body of research which has sought to identify mean reversion in stock returns. While some studies have found evidence of mean reversion in stock returns, it is relatively weak. Furthermore, the findings of many of these studies have been criticized on statistical or methodological grounds in follow-up papers. Two well-known articles indicating some mean reversion are by Fama and French (1988) and Poterba and Summers (1988). But they have their critics. For example, Kim, Nelson and Startz (1991) pointed out that the Fama and French study does not show mean reversion estimates in the post-war period which differ significantly from zero. And Poterba and Summers' study only finds evidence of mean reversion by relaxing the statistical significance test from 5 per cent to 40 per cent, which casts doubt on its findings. If mean reversion were shown to exist, then the arithmetic mean would be an upward biased estimator of the market risk premium. In a subsequent paper, Fama and French (1992) reported finding that beta has little power in explaining US stock returns from 1941 to 1990 while size by market capitalization and the ratio of market value to book value were far better predictors displaying significant negative relationships with realized returns. This negative relationship between the ratio of market value to book value and realized return is also found by Capaul, Rowley and Sharpe (1993) in a study of French, German, Swiss, UK, Japanese and US equity markets (as well as European and global markets) over the relatively short period from January 1981 to June 1992. The Fama and French (1992) study continued to find weak evidence of mean reversion and Haugen (1999), in summarizing and commenting (certainly without due criticism) upon various papers in this area, seems convinced of the evidence of mean reversion. Whether the evidence of mean reversion is strong enough categorically to point towards the use of a geometric mean, as opposed to an arithmetic mean, in equity risk premium estimation remains an uncertainty. But we feel that the empirical evidence is strong enough to justify the geometric mean.

Lo and MacKinlay (1988) strongly reject the random walk model according to the evidence of their tests of US stocks over the period 1962 to 1985. But they are careful not to conclude that this implies, with absolute certainty, mean reverting behaviour. However, de Bondt and Thaler (1985) found that stocks that had behaved very badly over the past three to five years subsequently outperformed the market whereas stocks that had outperformed over the past subsequently underperformed. They concluded that stocks overreact. Subsequently research by Lakonishok, Shleifer and Vishny (1994), among others, has shown that value stocks – stocks with low price/earnings (P/E) ratios or low market value to book value ratios – achieve higher returns than glamour, or growth, stocks. Haugen and Baker (1996) and Haugen (2002) also found that US value stocks (distinguished by lower P/E ratios, lower cash flow to price and higher dividend yield – but not market value to book value) achieved superior performance than US growth stocks over the period from 1979 to 1993. According to Thaler (1998), value stocks yield high returns because they are mispriced, investors having become bearish about their recent performance and having driven their prices down too low. When earnings improve – partly, according to Thaler, due to natural mean reversion – their prices rebound. By contrast, glamour stocks are bid up too high by excessive expectations and underperform when earnings fail to meet these optimistic projections. Does this lead to mean reversion in stock prices? Is there some long-run predictable component that causes prices temporarily to swing away from but return gradually to fundamental values?

Many financial economists (but not all) believe that there is good evidence of mean reversion in stock returns. This means, for example that a poor year for stock market returns is slightly more likely to be followed by a good year, rather than by another poor year. Similarly, good returns are more likely to lead to weak subsequent returns rather than another good year. Thus, bad years would cancel out good years and vice versa. Over long periods of time, the risk of equities is reduced and if there is more mean reversion with stocks than with bonds, stocks eventually become less risky than bonds. Of course, it is possible to argue that the mean reverting behaviour of stocks versus the mean averting behaviour of bonds has a lot to do with unexpectedly large inflation levels after the Second World War and this is merely a fleeting phenomenon – at least, the mean averting behaviour of bonds might be.

The problem with data on mean reversion is that they go back only a few decades and we do not have very many independent and non-overlapping twenty-year periods from which to draw inferences. Formal statistical tests have been unable to establish convincingly that there is absolutely certain mean reversion in stock returns, even though the raw numbers suggest it. If there were no mean reversion in stock returns, there would be no reason to believe that stocks would become less risky than bonds over long horizons – unless bonds themselves were to exhibit mean aversion.

But there are psychological hypotheses underpinning mean reversion. According to behavioural finance (see, for example, Thaler, 1998), if investors become overly optimistic about economic prospects and push stock markets to levels that are unreasonably high, then sobering news may lead investors to correct this error, forcing markets back down. Bubble correction phases of this type generate mean reversion in returns.

Mean reversion is frequently viewed with scepticism because it seems to imply a conflict with the idea that markets are efficient and prices tend to be right. It is a misconception that if prices reflect fundamental value they should move randomly. Mean reversion can be consistent with a world where prices are rational. All that is needed is that the risk perception for stocks, in general, changes over time. Following a big market setback, investors may find stocks more risky. Higher risk should be compensated by a higher expected return. So, after a stock market setback, we might see higher average returns and we would call this mean reversion.

Another view of the risk/return paradox is that by looking at stock returns on existing stock markets, we miss the risk of collapse of a particular stock market. Advocates of this idea are quick to point out that of all of the stock exchanges that existed in 1900, half have since then experienced significant interruptions or have been completely abolished. Looking only at data for the United States and a handful of Western-type markets misses this kind of risk because these markets have never experienced collapse. However, the risk of future collapse is always there. Perhaps high return on stocks relative to bonds simply reflects the possibility of a complete market collapse. This is, really, a rather frail argument because this kind of risk might not just limit itself to the stock market. A shock that could bring down stock markets would surely also affect bond markets. Indeed, this is usually the way things have happened.

24.6 | The equity risk premium

So where does all this leave us in terms of estimating the value of the equity risk premium, that is (R_M minus R_F)? We use data from the United States. We have to confront the significant problem of the use of a geometric or an arithmetic mean. According to the new evidence, a figure of 5.8 per cent to 7.7 per cent, depending upon which of the respective means is used, looks like the appropriate amount, given that R_F is measured by reference to treasury bills. The figure is 5 per cent to 7 per cent if R_F is measured against long-term government bonds. But are these returns sustainable in the future? Humbly, we have to admit that we cannot be sure. Perhaps a way around this problem is simply to take the real return achieved from stocks in the past and use this as an estimate for a firm with a CAPM beta of 1. Given a geometric mean basis, this would imply a real return from equities of 6.7 per cent for the United States. If bonds were expected not to be outmanoeuvred by inflation and to yield a real return of between 2 and 4 per cent, this would suggest an equity premium of around 3 to 5 per cent.

It is also worth mentioning that mean reversion in stock returns is not the same as mean reversion in corporate investment project returns. However, Fuller, Huberts and Levinson (1993) find that earnings per share growth numbers for corporations seem to revert to the mean after seven years or so.

Furthermore, we cannot be completely certain as to whether arithmetic or geometric means should be used in valuation exercises. Perhaps the evidence of mean reversion is sufficient to make a strong case for the geometric[1] mean – but the jury is still deliberating. So, vendor and purchaser, regulator and regulated can continue their discussions. Certainly, using more than a single discount rate in valuation is realistic. Of course, such a methodology would result in a range of value. Once again, this is surely realistic.

24.7 | The international risk premium

The issue of whether we should add in a country risk premium in non-domestic investment appraisal is, with practitioners at least, a vexing one. The answer depends upon an assessment of whether country risk is systematic or unsystematic. If the risk is unsystematic, it should, according to CAPM theory, not be included in the cost of equity.

For a company operating primarily in an advanced European country or the United States, it may be argued that investment in less-developed countries would provide greater diversification benefits than investment in developed countries because the economies of less-developed countries are less closely linked to those of industrialized nations. However, the systematic risk of projects in less developed countries is unlikely to be too far below the average for all projects, since such countries are still ultimately tied in to the world economy. According to this view, the systematic risk of projects in less-developed countries might be only marginally below that of comparable projects in industrialized countries. A Zambian copper mine may represent a capital project in a less-developed country but its systematic risk will be near to that in industrialized countries because the world demand and the world price of copper are functions of the state of economies in industrialized countries.

If stock markets take cognizance and are influenced by domestic and international operations of firms, then it follows, according to CAPM, that it is reasonable for foreign operations to be set required rates of return based upon systematic risk. Many investigations have attempted to test the hypothesis that investors take account of the foreign involvement of multinational firms. Severn (1974) found that the greater the foreign involvement of a firm, the lower the covariance of its earnings per share with the earnings of the Standard and Poor's index. But multinationals are larger than most domestic corporations and the reduction in earnings variability found by Severn might have been due to size and greater product diversification rather than to foreign earnings. Consistent with this view, Haegele (1974) showed that, while multinationals' systematic risk is lower than for domestic corporations, these differences disappear once the results are adjusted for firm size. In this area, Agmon and Lessard (1977) examined the stock market behaviour of US multinational corporations. If investors recognize and reward international diversification, they argued, price movements of multinational shares should be more closely related to a world market factor and less to a domestic US market factor, and this should be more pronounced the greater the degree of international operations. While their regression analysis, based on portfolios of US multinationals with an increasing proportion of their sales outside the United States, weakly supports this hypothesis, their results are very low on statistical significance. Similarly, Aggarwal (1977) failed to locate any statistical relationship between multinationality and the cost of equity capital.

Perhaps, then, investors do not recognize the portfolio effects of a multinational corporation's foreign activities. Perhaps international diversification by companies has an insignificant effect upon systematic risk. But, according to Hughes, Logue and Sweeney (1975), who developed indices using portfolios of solely domestic and multinational firms, their results suggest that the performance of the multinational is clearly superior to that of its purely domestic counterpart.

Of course, there are also the well-known pieces of work on portfolio diversification undertaken by Solnik (1974) and Jacquillat and Solnik (1978). Comparing the results achieved in terms of reduction of variance by an international portfolio versus a portfolio of internationally diversified companies, they concluded that, while multinational firms do provide diversification for investors, international portfolio diversification is a far superior source of elimination of variance. Furthermore, investors are able, in the absence of restrictions on portfolio investment, to action this superior diversification on their own. The lower the co-movement between the returns on securities in a portfolio, the better the diversification – see Table 24.4 and Figure 21.1. These show some evidence of increasing integration of leading stock markets of the world over time.

There is now a wealth of literature to the effect that international portfolio diversification can increase returns without increasing the standard deviation of returns. Solnik (1974) and Lessard (1976) both presented evidence that national factors have a significant impact upon security returns relative to that of any world factor. Solnik's 1974 study demonstrated the potential benefits from international portfolio diversification following inclusion of foreign securities therein. Other studies tend to confirm this point. Looking at data from the period 1970 to 1986, Hunter and Coggin (1990) found in favour of risk reduction via international portfolio diversification. Bailey and Stulz (1990) found that, for the period 1977 to 1985, a US investor could have achieved similar returns, while lowering the standard deviation of his portfolio by a third, through the optimal use of Pacific Basin plus US equities. Also, according to a number of empirical studies, diversification gains are not just limited to risk reduction. For example, Solnik (1988) reported that from 1971 to 1985, the average annual returns of the world stock index in US dollars outperformed the US stock index by 13 per cent to 9.95 per cent with a volatility of only 13.85 per cent versus 15.41 per cent for the US index and the Morgan Stanley Capital International EAFE (Europe, Australia, Far East) stock index outperformed the US stock index by 17.09 per cent to 9.95 per cent and its rate of return per unit of risk – or return/standard deviation – was 0.99 versus only 0.65 for the US index.

On the bond front too, Barnett and Rosenberg (1983) showed that, based on 1973 to 1983 evidence, investing in an internationally diversified bond portfolio lowered risk and increased return. Similar findings have been supplied by work by Cholerton, Pieraerts and Solnik (1986) drawing evidence from the period 1971 to 1984 and by Thomas (1989) whose database covered the years from 1975 to 1988.

The combination of equity shares and bonds, in an appropriate portfolio-optimizing manner so that return is maximized for any given level of risk, was investigated by Solnik and Noetzlin (1982) in the context of international diversification effects. They concluded that international stock diversification yielded an improved risk–return pay-off and international diversification involving stock and bond investments resulted in substantially less risk than international stock diversification alone. Furthermore, substantial improvement in the risk–return trade-off may be realized by investing in internationally diversified stock and bond portfolios whose weights do not conform to relative market capitalizations. This would be consistent with the various market indices used to measure world stock and bond portfolios not lying on the efficient frontier. Certainly, it has to be said that Solnik and Noetzlin had the advantage of hindsight in constructing their model. But they concluded that the potential for increased risk-adjusted returns are very large indeed.

The surprise for French and Poterba (1991) was that, based upon aggregated equity data, US investors held less than 5 per cent of their equity portfolios in the ordinary stock of UK and Japanese companies. Similar data were reported by Cooper and Kaplanis (1994).

There is, then, conflicting evidence as to whether we should use different required rates of return for comparable international and domestic projects, given ultimate measurement in home currency terms. The empirical evidence gives us little more than a partial answer.

If country risk were unsystematic it would not, in the context of a CAPM approach, be included in the cost of equity. Exploratory work by Roll (1993) suggests, in an arbitrage pricing theory (APT) framework, that the systematic country factor is significant in the case of many emerging, as opposed to industrialized country, equity markets.

Rather than attempting an adjustment to beta, some firms, including some City of London and Wall Street bankers, add on a risk premium derived from adjusting for the basis points spread of the country's bonds against UK government bonds or US Treasuries of similar maturity and other terms. We give an example of this approach in section 24.10 on emerging markets. A more explicit way of dealing with country risk is to make adjustment in the numerator of the present value calculation, that is in the cash flow forecast for the project itself. Clearly, using both of these approaches in a particular case would be double counting.

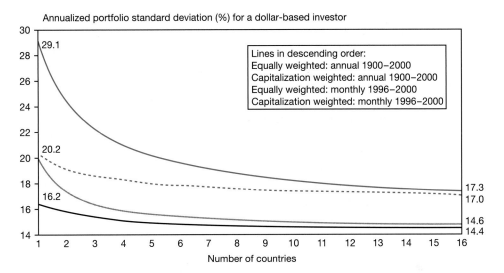

Figure 24.2 Historical risk reduction from international diversification of equity portfolios.

24.8 | Gains from international diversification

By adopting an international approach to stock market investment, it is possible to maintain returns while lowering risk (measured by standard deviation of returns). Figure 24.2, derived from data in Dimson, Marsh and Staunton (2002) shows this effect. The top line shows the risk reduction that might have been achieved by a dollar-based investor over the last century. It assumes equal equity holdings in each of the sixteen countries listed in Table 24.2 and assumes that cross-border investment was possible and costless throughout the period. The standard deviation of 29.1 per cent for the single-country investment falls off to 17.3 per cent for an equally weighted sixteen-country portfolio – a dramatic fall in risk. If we were to use market capitalization weightings, the above process reduces the standard deviation of returns from 20.2 per cent to 17.0 per cent.

We should anticipate less risk reduction nowadays, as world equity markets are more integrated than was the case over the whole of the period from 1900 to 2000. The third line (moving downwards) in Figure 24.2 is based on standard deviations estimated from sixty recent monthly return data from 1996 to 2000, showing late twentieth century risk reduction. These data derive from equally weighted investments and show risk reduction moving from around 20 per cent to 14.6 per cent. Using market capitalization data, risk is reduced from 16.2 per cent to 14.4 per cent.

Equally weighted results may be misleading. It is unrealistic to assume that investors hold the same amount in small markets as in large ones. Hence, the data relating to market capitalization weightings – see lines 2 and 4 (reading from the top) in Figure 24.2 – is probably more meaningful.

24.9 ▌ The international capital asset pricing model

We now turn to another approach in terms of looking at excess returns achieved from equity investment around the globe. Let it be stated clearly, at the outset, that the findings here are by no means conclusive – indicative is certainly the best that can be said. They concern evidence of an international capital asset pricing model (ICAPM). Essentially what we are looking at concerns the nature of international capital markets. Two extreme views are possible:

■ International capital markets are integrated and risky assets are priced according to their undiversifiable world risk, that is, a world (or international) CAPM applies. The relevant risk measure would be a beta measured against the world market portfolio.

■ International capital markets are segmented and risky assets are priced relative to domestic assets only – that is, domestic systematic risk is the basis of asset pricing. The relevant risk measure in pricing assets is the beta measured against the domestic market portfolio.

No single national capital market has been found to be fully segmented or fully integrated with world markets at all times. The capital markets of most industrial countries are much more integrated today than they were a decade ago. A second tier seems to be moving towards integration with industrial countries' capital markets.

Capital market segmentation is a financial market imperfection driven either by government constraints or investor perceptions and regulations – or both. The most important imperfections are information barriers (including accounting and regulatory disclosure quality), transactions costs, foreign exchange regulations, the nature of the market for corporate control, small country bias (due, often, to illiquidity factors), political risk, regulatory barriers (including remittance restrictions and a number of other controls) and, finally, equity market controls, regulations and lack of transparency.

The extent to which capital markets are segmented is likely to have a significant input on the cost of capital. In a fully segmented market, it is likely to be higher than in other capital markets. This means, all other things being equal, lower security prices, as Stapleton and Subrahmanyam (1977) point out. However, to a limited extent, firms may be able to overcome this disadvantage by arranging financing tactics that access more sophisticated and integrated capital markets – see Stonehill and Dullum (1982) and Oxelheim, Stonehill, Randøy, Vikkula, Dullum and Modén (1998).

On the issues of integrated versus segmented capital markets, there have been numerous empirical studies. Solnik (1973) tested an ICAPM and found that national factors were of importance. But when these were diversified with an international portfolio, a strong relationship existed between actual returns and international systematic risk. Stehle (1977) sought to establish whether international capital markets were integrated or separated by testing the hypothesis that US capital markets are isolated against the null hypothesis of integration. The findings suggested that neither hypothesis could be rejected in favour of the other. But some empirical support was found for an ICAPM.

Cumby (1990) tested whether real stock returns were consistent with a model of international asset pricing. Equity markets indices for the United States, the United Kingdom, Japan and Germany were investigated. Cumby's tests of integration required that the conditional covariance of real stock returns and the rate of change of real consumption should move together over time. This was rejected for the 1970s but could not be rejected for the 1980s. These results do not necessarily demonstrate integration in these four key equity markets, but they are consistent with increasing integration of international capital markets during the period concerned.

Howe and Madura (1990) assessed international capital market integration in a study of international listings. They showed that Euroequity listings by US corporations do not yield shifts on various risk-related measures. Companies' domestic betas did not seem to alter with international listings and there was no evidence that the overseas listing affected a security's sensitivity to the overseas security market. This, they claim, is evidence that the markets concerned were integrated and that listing had no risk-related impact on the firm's securities. This evidence points in the opposite direction to that suggested in a study by Alexander, Eun and Janakiramanan (1988) who hypothesized that if markets were segmented, the foreign listing of a security would increase demand for that security, hence raising its price and reducing its expected rate of return. They found evidence of a lower expected return (thus, a higher price) for firms obtaining a foreign listing, which indicates some market segmentation. In a study by Mittoo (1992) of integration of US and Canadian stock markets, it was found that Canadian stocks cross-listed on US exchanges were priced in an integrated market but segmentation was predominantly the case for Canadian stocks that were not cross-listed.

A study by Cochran and Mansur (1991) examined the interrelationship between yields on the US and foreign equity markets over the period 1980–89. They identified the existence of significant unidirectional and bidirectional causality, suggesting that international equity markets were not completely integrated. These causality effects seemed to vary from time to time, indicating that market integration may be unstable and vary over time. Our earlier discussion suggests some evidence of increasing integration of leading stock markets of the world. In a highly pragmatic paper designed to calculate costs of equity capital in emerging markets, Godfrey and Espinosa (1996) present data suggestive of some market integration for developed countries' stock markets but with a sharply contrasting picture for emerging markets.

However, lest it be thought that increased integration in developed countries' stock markets is an established fact, it should be noted that Artis and Taylor (1990) found no significant shifts in the correlation of monthly stock returns after 1979 and they found little to suggest that the European stock markets of Germany, the Netherlands and the United Kingdom were converging. Fraser, Helliar and Power (1994), using data from 1974 to 1990 for France, Germany, Italy, the United Kingdom and the United States, found greater convergence of excess returns on shares traded in London and New York as opposed to those in the United Kingdom and their European neighbours. Reporting on European stock returns, Drummen and Zimmermann (1992) analysed local currency returns for 105 stocks in 11 European countries over the period 1986 to 1989. They found that the country factor explained 19 per cent of the average stock variance, world stock market movements accounted for 11 per cent, while European market trends explained 8 per cent, industry factors accounted for 9 per cent and currency movements accounted for 2 per cent. These factors appeared to explain 49 per cent of the risk of European stocks, leaving over 50 per cent of the variance as specific.

If, overall, the evidence tends to suggest increasing integration of world capital markets, it is certainly not an issue that has been resolved. Having said this, the next part of this section, which is based upon ideas of equity market integration, is essentially consistent with an ICAPM.

Despite evidence for and against, if it is accepted that major stock markets around the globe have some tendency to move in sympathy with one another, we might think of a world excess return relationship in which the monthly excess returns for a particular market, for example the UK equity market, might be related to the monthly excess return on the world index. In algebraic terms, we might be thinking of a relationship of the following kind:

$$(R_C - R_F) = \alpha_C + \beta_C(R_W - R_F) \qquad (24.1)$$

In the above equation, R_C represents the monthly return in, for example, US dollar terms for the equity market in country C, R_F represents the monthly riskless rate of return, again to ensure consistency, expressed in US dollar terms, proxied by the return on US treasury bills, α_C is the monthly risk premium for country C, β_C is the beta for country C and R_W represents the monthly return, expressed in US dollar terms, from equity investment in the world index.

24.10 | Emerging markets

There then remains the perplexing problem of the appropriate discount rate for corporate investment in emerging markets. On this topic, there is a polarization of views which is exemplified by the recommendations of Lessard (1996) and Godfrey and Espinosa (1996). So what are their contrasting standpoints?

All other things being equal, it is generally agreed that projects in emerging markets are more risky than similar projects in domestic and developed markets. To take account of these higher risks and, also, greater unfamiliarity, many companies build an extra premium into the discount rate to be applied to projects in emerging markets. But, usually, the basis for these adjustments is arbitrary. Consequently, companies often over-discount projected cash flows and, in so doing, unduly penalize projects.

The view that the extra premium required is modest is the stance taken by Lessard. He suggests other assets, its information advantage and its ability to manage these risks. Although more volatile in themselves, investments in emerging economies generally contribute relatively little to the volatility of a company's cash flows and its shareholders' portfolios compared with domestic projects, which would probably have less diversification effect. Furthermore, political risks, such as the threat of expropriation, shifts in policy and exchange inconvertibility, can be roughly allowed for by incorporating a premium reflecting the risk of non-payment on government bonds. This is represented by the credit spread on government bonds above the cost of similar term US government bonds and it is Lessard's view that this should be added as a risk premium to the normal required return in evaluating the return on remittable home currency cash flows. Finally, Lessard suggests that unfamiliarity with an emerging market host country should not be factored into the discount rate. The effects of unfamiliarity should decrease over time, as opposed to increasing at a compound rate as would be implied by adjusting the discount rate.

Having developed the idea of country betas in the previous section, one of the first ideas that might occur to the reader is the use of country betas for emerging market projects. Immediately, a problem arises. In their estimates of costs of equity capital by country, Godfrey and Espinosa (1996) found that all developed countries had betas in excess of 0.5. But, by contrast, for emerging markets, calculation of country betas (for the period from 1989 for some countries, 1991 and 1993 for others, up to 1996) revealed that 15 out of 26 major emerging markets in the world had betas below 0.5 and four of these countries had betas that were negative, thus implying, via the CAPM equation, discount rates below the risk-free rate. The reason for the low betas for emerging markets is the low correlations between returns from equity investment in these countries and returns from the world equity portfolio. In fact, the correlation between developed market returns, on average (unweighted), and world market returns was 0.6; for emerging market versus the world market, the correlation was 0.2. This low correlation essentially suggests that emerging markets are not integrated with developed capital markets and, as such, it implies that an ICAPM is not totally applicable.

Like Godfrey and Espinosa, Lessard reports similar findings on low – and some negative – correlations. This led him to suggest an approach other than one that is based on country betas. In terms of specifying a premium, Lessard agrees that bond risk premia reflect the market's assessment of potential losses due to rescheduling or default. These events do not exactly match the events that would jeopardize the generation or the remittance of cash flows from an overseas investment. For example, in the case of Argentina, despite repeated negotiations and non-payment of interest on sovereign debt in the 1980s – to the point where the secondary market price of Argentine government debt fell to 15 per cent of its face value – dividends from businesses were fully convertible.

On the other hand, adverse factors may impact the direct foreign investor without the event of rescheduling or default on government debt. Despite these reservations, bond risk premia provide objective measures of potential payments difficulties that may be closely correlated with problems that a direct investor would encounter. Therefore, government bond spreads on US Treasuries do provide fair measures of the impact of downside country risks.

Godfrey and Espinosa argue for an even greater premium. Their first step is to suggest a premium on the US risk-free rate for country credit quality, as above. However, to this they add a further premium – the premium for business volatility. They argue as follows. The measure of an asset's systematic risk, or beta, is calculated as:

$$\text{Beta} = \frac{\text{cov}(r_i, r_m)}{\sigma_m^2} = \rho_{i,m}(\sigma_i/\sigma_m)$$

where σ_i and σ_m are, respectively, the volatilities of the asset and the market. $\text{Cov}(r_i, r_m)$ is the covariance between the asset and the market portfolio of all risky assets and, finally, $\rho_{i,m}$ is the correlation between the asset and the market portfolio. So, beta is the product of the correlation between the investment and the market and the ratio of the asset's volatility to the volatility of the market. The latter ratio is an indication of the relative risk of the asset versus the market. If this ratio is greater than 1, the asset is more volatile than the market. If it is less than 1, it is less volatile than the market. The correlation coefficient, ρ, measures the degree of co-movement between the asset and the market. Beta thus adjusts the individual stand-alone risk (that is the ratio-of-volatilities term) to reflect only the non-diversifiable (that is the correlation term) aspects of the risk.

Accepting that empirically determined country betas for emerging markets are less than reliable, their argument continues thus. In calculating the premium for business volatility they use an adjusted beta that is equal to the ratio of an individual country's equity volatility to that of the US market. In essence, in the equation for beta above, this assumes that the correlation coefficient is equal to one. In short, their adjusted beta is equal to:

$$\sigma_i/\sigma_{US}$$

For the purpose of generating their business risk premium, they simply multiply this adjusted beta by the US equity market risk premium. This approach to calculating emerging market discount rates focuses on total risk – not just systematic risk as in CAPM.

Godfrey and Espinosa concede that by allowing for a country's credit quality and the volatility of the local equity market, there is an element of double counting. Yes, but how much? For developed countries, this problem of double counting is likely to be trivial. For emerging countries, however, both the credit spreads and business volatility premia are larger and there is undoubtedly a greater risk of double counting. They cite a research study by Erb, Harvey and Viskanta (1995) which found that 40 per cent of the variation in equity volatility could be explained by variation in credit quality. Godfrey and Espinosa argue that this suggests that, for emerging countries, their business volatility premium may be overstated by about 40 per cent. In light of this, they suggest reducing their second premium by 40 per cent.

Reducing the adjusted beta by 40 per cent could also, they claim, be interpreted as using traditional betas in which the correlation coefficients are equal to 0.60. However, as they point out, the average correlation for developed countries is around 60 per cent. Since it is much less for emerging markets, there may be a case for a greater reduction. On the basis of a 40 per cent reduction, they estimate the cost of equity capital for a number of emerging markets. Compared with 11.5 per cent for the United States, Godfrey and Espinosa arrived at costs of equity of between 29 per cent and 27 per cent for Argentina, Turkey, Brazil, Poland and Hungary, around 23 per cent for the Czech Republic and Mexico and between 19 per cent and 14 per cent for the Philippines, India, Thailand, Indonesia, South Korea, Malaysia and South Africa. Interested readers are referred to the original paper.

This approach is less then perfect for a number of reasons. First of all, in applying the premium for business volatility, it will be recalled that the premium derives from:

$$\text{Beta} = \rho_{i,m} \times (\sigma_i / \sigma_m)$$

Essentially, by using a correlation figure based on $\rho_{i,m}$ as equal to 0.6, there is an assumption of substantial market integration between emerging markets and world markets. According to our calculations, this is not the case. Indeed, the correlation between the emerging markets in the Godfrey and Espinosa study and the world markets is estimated at around 0.2, on average. This implies very weak integration of emerging markets in world markets. Given this background, the author is doubtful of this methodology. However, the ranges of magnitude seem to conform to those often used by investment banks. Hooke (1998), for example, reckons that the cost of equity capital for emerging markets can be conceptualized as being equal to a comparable domestic return plus a foreign risk premium ranging between 5 per cent and 15 per cent. Thus, he recommends target returns for low-risk emerging markets, for example Poland, the Czech Republic and Chile, at 18–20 per cent. For medium-risk markets, such as Brazil, India, Indonesia, Mexico, Thailand and Turkey, he reports a recommended return of 20–25 per cent. And for high-risk countries, his cost of equity is between 25 and 30 per cent. Into this group, he categorizes China, Peru and Russia.

A similar, and widely-used approach, involves adding an appropriate premium to the equity risk premium for a mature equity market to obtain an equity premium for the emerging market concerned. The 'appropriate premium' is given by:

$$\text{Risk premium for country} = \text{Default spread for country} \times \frac{\sigma \text{ for country's equity market}}{\sigma \text{ for country's government bonds}}$$

Thus, assume a country rating for Ruritania's debt equal to Standard and Poor's B rating. Assume that the default spread for Ruritanian government bonds of the investment's maturity versus the US treasury bond for a similar maturity is 3 per cent per annum. Assume further that the annualized standard deviation of returns from the Ruritanian equity market is 32 per cent and the standard deviation for Ruritanian government bonds is 15 per cent. The country premium for Ruritania would come out at:

$$\text{Risk premium for Ruritania} = 3\% \times \frac{32\%}{15\%}$$
$$= 6.4\%$$

Assuming that the US equity risk premium is 5 per cent per annum (in geometric mean terms) this would imply a figure for the equity risk premium from Ruritanian investment of 11.4 per cent (in US$ terms).

To round off this section, it is emphasized that while capital markets exhibit a wide disparity in degrees of segmentation and integration – see Figure 24.3 (overleaf), which adapts a model proposed by Jacque and Hawawini (1993) – asset markets (which is what capital budgeting is all about) may not do so.

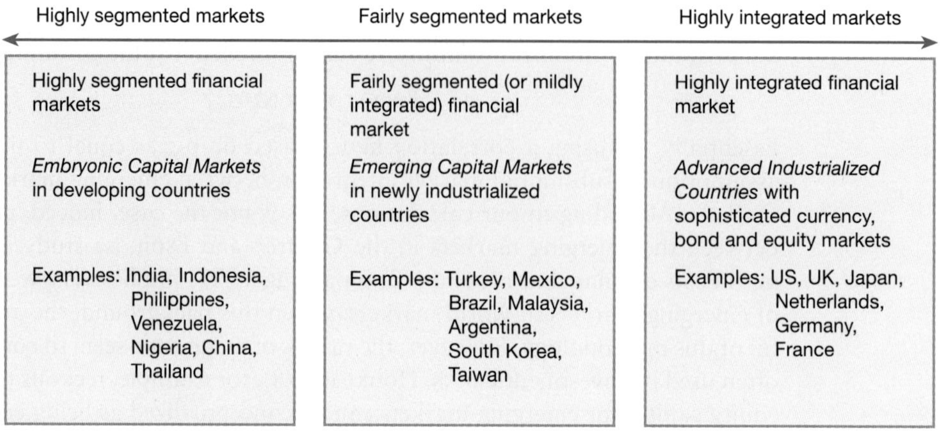

Highly segmented markets	Fairly segmented markets	Highly integrated markets
Highly segmented financial markets *Embryonic Capital Markets* in developing countries Examples: India, Indonesia, Philippines, Venezuela, Nigeria, China, Thailand	Fairly segmented (or mildly integrated) financial market *Emerging Capital Markets* in newly industrialized countries Examples: Turkey, Mexico, Brazil, Malaysia, Argentina, South Korea, Taiwan	Highly integrated financial market *Advanced Industrialized Countries* with sophisticated currency, bond and equity markets Examples: US, UK, Japan, Netherlands, Germany, France

Figure 24.3 The capital market segmentation/integration continuum.

Source: Adapted from Jacque and Hawawini (1993).

24.11 | Summary

- The capital asset pricing model derives a method of estimating the cost of equity using a formula which adds to the risk-free rate of return the product of the appropriate beta and the excess return. This excess return is given by the difference between the return expected to be earned by a market portfolio of equity shares minus the risk-free rate of return.

- This chapter is intended to act as an aid in estimating the value of the excess return around the world.

- We prefer to use the geometric mean measure of returns.

- Evidence is presented from various countries and this is followed by an overview of the international capital asset pricing model.

- A method of estimating the cost of equity capital for emerging markets is presented.

24.12 | End of chapter questions

Question 1
Explain how characteristics of MNCs can affect the cost of capital.

Question 2
From an investor's standpoint, have small companies, in general over the past, been more profitable than their larger brethren?

Note

1. Your author's view that there is now strong enough evidence to opt for the geometric mean is in contrast to the personal opinion expressed in the first three editions of this text. The fact is that new evidence is always appearing and it would be very short-sighted to ignore it.

25 Country risk analysis and political risk

Multinational firms constantly assess the business environments of the countries in which they are operating as well as those that they are considering for investment. Likewise, investors are interested in assessing which countries offer the best prospects for sound investment. This is what country risk analysis is about – the assessment of potential risks and rewards associated with making investments and doing business in a country. Essentially, we are interested in whether reasonable economic policies are likely to be pursued because this creates a business environment in which firms may flourish. But political factors may lead countries to pursue economic policies that are adverse to business and to their own economic wellbeing. Because of this, the focus of country risk analysis cannot be purely economic in its approach. It must also study political factors that give rise to economic policies.

The international economic environment is dependent upon the policies that individual nations pursue. Given the linkage between a country's economic policies and the degree of exchange risk, inflation risk and interest rate risk that multinational companies and investors face, it is vital to study these areas and attempt to forecast them. One cannot assess a country's risk profile without an insight into its economic and political policies and how these policies affect the country's prospects for economic growth. Forecasts at exchange rates, inflation rates and interest rates are enhanced by understanding the economic factors affecting national policies.

25.1 Country risk analysis

Country risk analysis took off in the 1960s and 1970s in response to the banking sector's attempts to define and measure its exposure to cross-border lending. At one time, before widespread international lending, country risk was often called transfer risk – that is, the risk that a government might impose restrictions on debt service payments abroad. When governments themselves became major bank borrowers, the concept of sovereign risk emerged. Sovereign risk is wider than transfer risk. It embraces the idea that even if the government is willing to honour its external obligations, it might not be able to do so if the economy cannot generate sufficient foreign exchange. Country risk began to include transfer risk and sovereign risk.

Political risk came to be used by industrial firms to describe adverse foreign events of a macroeconomic, social, political or strategic nature that might affect their business.

The globalization of financial markets and the growth of portfolio investment brought further demand for country risk analysis since a significant part was viewed, in capital asset pricing model terms, as unsystemic risk that could be diversified away. Nowadays, the term country risk is synonymous with cross-border risk or international business risk, terms which have recently gained currency. These terms are widely used and are used interchangeably.

25.2 | Sources of country risk

The sources of country risk are numerous. They embrace all aspects of a country's economic, financial, social and political organization as well as its geographic location and strategic importance. A comprehensive checklist of risk sources specified by Nagy (1984) includes the following:

- war;

- occupation by a foreign power;

- civil war, revolution, riots, disorders;

- takeover by an extremist government;

- politically motivated debt default, renegotiation or rescheduling;

- unilateral change in debt service terms;

- state takeover of an enterprise;

- indigenization (forced relinquishment of control by foreign owners of enterprises);

- natural calamities;

- depression or severe recession;

- mismanagement of the economy;

- credit squeeze;

- long-term slowdown in real GNP growth;

- strikes;

- rapid rise in production costs;

- fall in export earnings;

- sudden increase in food and/or energy imports;

- over-extension in external borrowing;

- devaluation or depreciation of the currency.

All of the above headings, according to Nagy, include a set of sub-headings, sometimes extending to over two dozen such subsidiary events. Country risk analysis usually begins by specifying a country's position in accordance with Nagy's list and placing the country on a five (or seven) point scale depending on its likelihood to suffer the risk sources detailed above.

25.3 | Measuring country risk

In terms of measuring country risk, it is possible to use a form of ratio analysis to allow us to augment the qualitative approach described above. In corporate finance, financial gearing or leverage plays a major role in determining financial risk. Financial gearing is measured by the extent to which the assets of the firm are financed with debt. It shows up in the income statement, as an interest expense, causing variability in net income over and above the variability in operating income caused by operating risk.

With macroeconomic risk, the same type of effect is present. But, in the absence of a macroeconomic balance sheet, we are forced to look at other proxies. In standard economic risk assessment, analysts combine variables to generate ratios considered to be significant indicators of the ongoing and prospective economic situation. One set of ratios aims at assessing the prospects for long-term growth in GDP or GNP. It includes:

- gross domestic fixed investment/GDP (or GNP);

- gross domestic savings/GDP (or GNP);

- marginal capital/output (the number of dollars of increase in investment necessary to increase output by one dollar);

- net capital imports/gross domestic fixed investment;

- gross domestic savings/gross domestic fixed investment.

The ratio of gross domestic fixed investment to GDP measures the economy's propensity to invest. Usually, a higher rate of investment leads to increased output and higher rates of growth of GDP. The extent to which this applies depends on the marginal capital to output ratio. This ratio claims to measure the marginal productivity of capital. It is usually calculated by dividing gross fixed domestic investment in one period by the increase to GDP in one or two periods later. A lower ratio signifies a higher productivity of capital and the higher the productivity of capital, the better the outlook for growth in GDP. The net capital imports over gross domestic fixed investment ratio indicates the extent to which GDP growth is dependent on goods from abroad. The higher the ratio, the more dependent the economy is upon overseas imports. Through the gross domestic savings to gross domestic fixed investment ratio, one obtains an insight into how dependent the economy is on foreign resources. The lower the domestic savings to domestic investment ratio, the more dependent is the economy. Usually, dependence on foreign resources is interpreted as a negative factor in economic risk assessment. Whether or not this is true is a moot point. For example, the resource gap may be large due to profitable investment opportunities and the willingness of foreigners to lend. This is hardly a negative. However, in the absence of profitable investment opportunities, the resource gap may be large due to a high propensity to consume. This is a negative because it signals that current consumption is being financed with foreign borrowing and that the rate of return on domestic investment is lower than the cost of the foreign resources.

Other ratios are used to indicate price stability – these are:

■ government budget deficit/GDP (or GNP);

■ percentage increase in the money supply.

As high inflation is generally considered to be undesirable, the outlook for price stability and economic performance should be more favourable when both the government budget deficit and the growth in the money supply are, relatively speaking, low.

The main ratios for assessing potential changes in the balance of payments are:

■ percentage change in exports/percentage change in world GDP, or the GDP charge for the main customer countries (this represents the income elasticity of demand for exports);

■ percentage change in imports/percentage change in GDP (this is, of course, equal to the income elasticity of demand for imports);

■ imports/GDP;

■ commodity exports/total exports;

■ official reserves/imports.

A high income elasticity of demand for exports (first bullet point) and a low income elasticity of demand for imports (second bullet point) is usually considered to be favourable for the balance of payments. A high ratio of imports to GDP is usually considered unfavourably. Because of the possible volatility of commodity prices, a high ratio of commodity exports to total exports is usually viewed unfavourably, while a high ratio of reserves to imports is viewed as a plus.

A country's financial risk refers to its ability to generate enough foreign exchange to meet payments of interest and principal (together this is termed debt service) on its foreign debt. The debt crisis of many developing countries in the 1980s provides a well-known example of financial risk. Because of over-borrowing and the unproductive use of borrowed resources, the countries in crisis were unable to honour their debts to the banks that had lent to them, causing big losses for the banks and economic sacrifices from defaulting countries.

Financial risk analysis for a country involves an assessment of the country's foreign obligations compared to its current and prospective economic situation. The variables used in assessing cross-border financial risk include those already cited plus ratios concerned with the country's foreign debt and interest, for example:

■ total external debt (EDT), which may be broken down into:
  – long-term public and publicly guaranteed debt outstanding and disbursed (DOD)
  – long-term private non-guaranteed outstanding debt
  – short-term debt
  – use of IMF credit;

- total debt service (TDS) which can be broken down into:
  - interest payments (INT)
  - principal payments.

Information on a country's external debt can be combined with the economic and balance of payments data to generate a number of significant ratios on the ongoing and prospective financial situation. The most common of these include:

- total external debt/exports (EDT/X);

- total external debt/GNP (EDT/GNP);

- official reserves/total external debt (RES/EDT);

- official reserves/imports (RES/M);

- long-term public and publicly guaranteed debt outstanding and disbursed/exports (DOD/X);

- long-term public and publicly guaranteed debt outstanding and disbursed/GNP (DOD/GNP);

- total debt service/exports (TDS/X);

- total debt service/GNP (TDS/GNP);

- interest payments/exports (INT/X);

- interest payments/GNP (INT/GNP);

- official reserves/long-term public and publicly guaranteed debt outstanding and disbursed (RES/DOD).

As mentioned earlier, financial leverage plays a major role in determining financial risk in the corporate finance arena. This is also the case with assessment of a country's financial risk. Here financial leverage shows up as an interest expense, affecting the variability of GDP less interest paid and exports net of debt service. Given this background, analysts often look at such ratios as EDT/X, EDT /GNP, DOD/X and DOD/GNP as measures of the company's financial leverage. The lower these ratios are, the better the country's financial position. As with a company's financial ratios, these country ratios should be used with caution – their measurement may be less than 100 per cent accurate, especially for developing countries.

Other ratios used in corporate finance, like times interest earned and cash flow coverage are used to determine the extent to which current obligations are covered by current income. The interest cover ratio relates earnings before interest and taxes to interest charges and the cash flow cover ratio relates earnings before interest and taxes to total annual debt service including payments for interest and principal. So, INT/X and INT/GNP are akin to a times interest earned ratio. TDS/X and TDS/GNP are like cash flow coverage ratios. Again, lower ratios indicate a stronger financial position, all other things being equal.

Note that these ratios use exports and GNP, which are gross of costs and do not reflect the net flows such as earnings or net exports $(X - M)$ that the country generates to honour its external financial obligations.

Finally, the ratio RES/M resembles a liquidity ratio in corporate finance. Liquidity ratios measure the firm's ability to meet maturing short-term liabilities. The RES/M ratio measures a country's ability to maintain import levels out of gold and foreign exchange reserves.

Clearly, just as ratio analysis is available to help assess the financial strength of a company, so it has a place in country analysis in quantifying the strength of national economies. In the hands of skilled analysts, both are potent forces in determining financial and economic strength. But neither form of ratio analysis is a simple black box that throws up an answer. Their interpretation is an art – but a potentially valuable and telling one.

25.4 | Political risk

In most countries, governments intervene in their national economies. This increases the political risk that multinational firms face. Political risk takes various forms, from changes in tax regulations to exchange controls, from stipulations about local production to expropriation, from commercial discrimination against foreign-controlled businesses to restrictions on access to local borrowings. Political risk can be defined as the exposure to a change in value of an investment or cash position resultant upon government actions. When viewed from the multinational corporation's standpoint, the effect of changes in government policies may be positive as well as negative.

Although political risk poses severe threats and may create profitable opportunities for multinational companies, firms have been found to view and to react to political risk without formal planning or systematic analysis. This is naive; a formal assessment of political risk and its implications for the multinational firm is important for decision making and it is towards the specification of such a framework that this chapter is aimed.

Formal assessment of political risk usually involves three key steps:

- The recognition of the existence of political risk and its likely consequence; this stage is concerned with measuring political risk.

- The development of policies to cope with political risk; this stage is concerned with managing political risk.

- Should expropriation occur, the development of tactics to maximize compensation; this stage is concerned with developing post-expropriation policies.

25.5 | The measurement of political risk

There are two ways to approach the measurement of political risk. First of all there is the country-specific route (this is also called the macro approach) and there is also the firm-specific route (this is frequently called the micro approach).

Various political risk-forecasting services are available. These services normally develop models leading to country risk indices which purport to quantify the level of political risk for each nation analysed. These indices generally reflect the stability of the local political environment. Such measures generally take cognizance of changes of government, levels of violence in the country, internal and external conflicts, and so on. Indices of this sort are intended to assess whether the government in power at a particular point in time will be there in the future and hence the extent to which the existing political status quo can be expected to continue.

The rating method developed by Haner (1979) is worth mentioning because its approach is systematic and its rationale is not dissimilar to many others. Haner rates, on a scale from 0 to 7, a number of factors that cause internal political stress. These include:

■ fractionalization of the political spectrum and the power of resulting factions;

■ fractionalization by language, ethnic or religious groups and the power of resulting factions;

■ restrictive measures required to retain power;

■ xenophobia, nationalism, inclination to compromise;

■ social conditions, including extremes in population density and the distribution of wealth;

■ organization and strength of a radical left government.

To these scores are added ratings arising from external factors. These include:

■ dependence on or importance to a hostile major power;

■ negative influence of regional political forces, possibilities of border wars and disruptions arising from such sources of conflict.

Finally, additional ratings relating to estimated symptoms of problems are computed and aggregated. These include:

■ societal conflict;

■ political instability.

Scores are aggregated and updated regularly as the world political environment changes. Countries are then rated as to:

■ minimal risk – 0 to 19 rating points;

■ acceptable risk – 20 to 34 rating points;

■ high risk – 35 to 44 rating points;

■ prohibitive risk – 45 rating points and over.

A not-dissimilar method of country risk evaluation is prepared regularly by the monthly financial magazine, *Euromoney*. Its rating draws on the weighting implied in Table 25.1. *Euromoney* polls a cross-section of experts. These specialists are asked

Table 25.1 Country risk evaluation system used by *Euromoney*

	Weighting (%)
Analytical indicators	
Economic indicators	15
Debt service to export ratio	
Balance of payments to GNP	
External debt to GNP	
Political risk	15
Economic risk	10
Credit indicators	
Debt service record	15
Ease of rescheduling	5
Market indicators	
Access to bond markets	15
Selldown of short-term paper	10
Access to forfaiting market	15
	100

to give their opinions on each country with regard to one or more of the factors in the scheme. Three broad categories are considered: analytical indicators (40 per cent), credit indicators (20 per cent) and market indicators (40 per cent). Each of these is further subdivided into more detailed components as shown in Table 25.1.

The analytical indicators include economic factors, a political risk evaluation and an economic risk view. The economic indicators included reflect the ability to service debt and are obtained from currently available data involving the ratio of external debt to GNP, the ratio of the balance of payments to GNP, and the ratio of debt-service payments to exports – see 25.3 above. The economic risk evaluation is provided by a panel of expert economists who are asked to take a forward look. Likewise, a political risk evaluation is obtained by polling specialists in assessing political risk.

Credit indicators are based on how easily a country is viewed as being able to reschedule debt payments, and how well the country has performed in meeting payments in the past. As can be seen from Table 25.1, the payments record carries more weight than the rescheduling ability.

Market indicators are based on the risk premia that financial markets are placing on a country's bonds, its short-term securities and the non-recourse loans made to its exporters. Large premia are a sign of high market-perceived risk. Of course, the market does consider factors already included elsewhere in Euromoney's rating scheme in pricing country debt, so there is an element of double counting.

Another financial monthly, *Institutional Investor*, also publishes country risk ratings based on a panel of banks' scores for creditworthiness. A number of similar systems are available for subscription; however, their approaches vary only slightly and most rely on a combination of objective data and subjective estimates. Frequently, their input data are different – for example, inflation rates, balance of payment deficits and surpluses, and other macroeconomic factors are used. The objective is always to assess whether there is a high risk of adverse changes resulting from government intervention. The development of political risk models is becoming more sophisticated and the ability of political risk models to forecast the timing of changes in the environment is important. However, research in this area is at too rudimentary a stage to be anything like conclusive. As a rule, the models used by rating agencies have not been consistently successful. It is worth mentioning that most models have not evolved out of discriminant analysis techniques, which would, perhaps, be the most scientific approach to the rating of country-specific political risk.

One exception to this comes from recent research by Morgan (1986) who did use discriminant analysis to assess the influence of variables on the likelihood that a country would need to reschedule loan repayments. Morgan found the following characteristics of rescheduling countries:

- A relatively high ratio of total debt to exports.

- A relatively high proportion of floating rate loans to total loans.

- A relatively low rate of growth in GDP.

Work in the area of the use of data drawn from statistical analysis as an aid to forecasting political risk is in its infancy, but it seems set to experience considerable growth.

It needs to be stressed that some firms may gain by the same event that harms other firms. A firm relying on imports will be adversely affected by trade restrictions, but an import-competing firm may well be the beneficiary of such regulations.

Political risk has a different impact on different firms. Generalized political risk indices must be used cautiously and subjected to careful analysis to assess the full impact upon a particular company. Governments rarely expropriate foreign investments indiscriminately. The greater the benefits of a foreign operation to the host country and the more expensive the replacement of such facilities by a purely local operation, the lower the degree of political risk to the firm. Governments select expropriation targets according to criteria other than purely political ones.

Firms frequently incorporate the consequences of political risk into investment decisions via the following:

- Shortening the minimum payback period.

- Raising the required discount rate for the investment.

- Adjusting cash flows for the cost of risk reduction – for example, by charging a premium for overseas political risk insurance.

- Adjusting cash flows to reflect the impact of a particular risk.

- Using certainty equivalents in place of expected cash flows.

Of the above methods, the last is the least fraught with theoretical objections, but it is probably the least used.

25.6 | Managing political risk

A firm may take action to control its exposure to political risk. Having analysed the political environment of a country and assessed its implications for corporate operations, it has to decide whether or not to invest there. If it decides to go ahead, it should structure the investment so as to minimize political risk. It needs to be reiterated that the impact of political risk is a function of the firm's activities. The firm's overseas investments determine its susceptibility to political risk. Political risk may be controlled at the pre-investment stage or in the course of operations – or both. There are four approaches aimed at minimizing risk in the pre-investment period. These can be classified as avoidance, insurance, negotiating the environment and structuring the environment.

The simplest approach to the management of political risk is to avoid it. Many firms do this by simply deciding against going ahead with investments in politically uncertain countries. If the international firm does decide to go ahead, the key question is the extent of political risk which a company is prepared to tolerate and whether the investment promises an appropriate return to compensate for it. Avoiding countries likely to be politically unstable ignores the possible high returns available from investment there. Business is all about taking risks and ensuring that sufficient returns are earned to compensate for them.

The second approach to pre-investment planning for political risk is insurance. Having insured assets in politically risky areas against expropriation and lesser risks of a political kind, the international firm can concentrate upon managing the business rather than worrying about political risk. Specific government departments of most developed countries sell political risk insurance to cover the foreign assets of domestic companies. In the United Kingdom, ECGD offers a confiscation cover scheme for new overseas investments only. Lloyd's of London also offers the company opportunities to insure against political risk, including expropriation. Its cover applies to new and existing investments on a comprehensive, non-selective policy. Lloyd's is, in fact, the only private insurer against expropriation. Fees vary according to country and the type of risk insured, with cover usually limited to 90 per cent of equity participation.

In addition to insurance, many firms try to reach an agreement with the host government before making an investment. This 'concession agreement' defines rights and responsibilities on the parts of both parties. Effectively, it specifies the rules under which the firm can operate locally. Such agreements have frequently been resorted to by multinationals operating in less-developed countries. They are often negotiated with weak governments. However, they have frequently been repudiated following a change in government and cannot therefore guarantee the international company avoidance of political risk. Concession agreements have carried less weight in the Third World as time has gone on; nonetheless they are usually observed in developed countries.

Having decided to invest in a country, a firm may minimize its exposure to political risk by structuring its operating and financial policies to make its posture acceptable and to ensure that the multinational remains in charge of events. A strategy of keeping the foreign company dependent upon group companies for markets and/or supplies is one such tactic. With virtually integrated production in different countries, there is little point in a government in a host country expropriating assets, since it would continue to be dependent upon the multinational corporation for supplies. This policy is one of the approaches used by international motor companies.

For companies that depend heavily upon research and development facilities and proprietary technology, concentrating these facilities in the home country enables a firm to lower the probability of expropriation. Similarly, establishing a single global trademark that cannot legally be duplicated can be effective. Sourcing from various plants reduces the host nation's ability to hurt the worldwide firm by seizing a single plant. And encouraging external local shareholders is another risk-reducing policy. This may involve raising capital from the host government, international financial institutions and customers, rather than employing funds supplied or guaranteed by the parent company. But it may not necessarily be the cheapest way of raising capital.

Obtaining unconditional host government guarantees is another way of minimizing financial aspects of political risk. Such guarantees enable creditors to initiate legal action in foreign courts against any commercial transactions between the host country and third parties should a subsequent government repudiate the original obligations. Such guarantees provide the international company with sanctions against a foreign nation without relying upon the support of its home government.

Operating policies may also be resorted to as a ploy to avoid political risk. In such a category we would put planned divestment, short-term profit maximization, creating benefits for the host nation, developing local shareholders and adaptation. Each of these is now briefly considered.

Planned divestment speaks for itself and is a policy commonly used to minimize political risk. Under short-term profit maximization, we include policies of withdrawing the maximum amount of cash from the local operation. Cutting reinvestment to the bare minimum, deferring maintenance expenditures, cutting marketing expenditures and eliminating training programmes are all tactics aimed at short-term cash generation. These policies are not unusual in the light of clear expropriation threats as they ensure that the company will have a short life locally. However, this behaviour is likely to hasten expropriation. International firms also try to manage political risk by changing the benefit/cost split between the multinational and the host country. If a local government's objectives are concerned with economic benefits and costs, then the international firm may attempt to reduce the perceived advantages of nationalization or expropriation. Policies include ensuring that benefits accrue locally. Such approaches embrace training local workers and managers, developing export markets for the host nation and manufacturing a wide range of products locally as substitutes for imports. Another common strategy is the encouragement of local stakeholders, including customers, suppliers, employees, bankers and so on, all based in the host nation. This policy includes concentrating operations upon joint venture partnerships with local firms. Another tactic for political risk management involves adaptation to potential expropriation and the development of policies to earn profits following expropriation. Many oil companies whose properties have been nationalized or expropriated receive management contracts to continue exploration, refining and marketing. Such multinationals recognize that they do not have to own or control an asset to earn profits and create cash flow.

Financial tactics designed to minimize political risk embrace a whole spectrum. Threats exist because of the possibility of confiscation of assets and the possibility that a foreign currency will become less convertible. If funds are not convertible, it is best to borrow locally as much as possible rather than risk funds becoming permanently blocked overseas. Methods by which multinationals reduce political risk through financing tactics include the use of a very high proportion of local gearing, minimizing intra-group sources of finance and avoiding parent or group guarantees. It also pays the multinational to try to ensure that profit arises in the United Kingdom, through such devices as royalty payments, transfer pricing and so on, rather than leaving surplus funds in a country where political risk may be perceived to be high. No medals should be won for building up blocked funds overseas.

25.7 | Post-expropriation policies

Expropriation does not come out of the blue. Generally, there are cues and signals that precede expropriation. Recognition of these gives the international firm opportunities to open discussions with the host government. In anticipated expropriation situations, the international firm frequently moves from rational negotiation, to applying power, to legal remedies and then to management surrender. When expropriation occurs, the aim of negotiation changes. Trying to persuade the host government of its folly comes first. The multinational corporation often quotes the future economic benefits that it will provide, but presumably the host government has already assessed these and its own actions have already taken them into account. If confiscation was merely a bargaining ploy on the part of the host nation to gain concessions, then this approach is likely to be successful. The multinational that perceives host government sabre-rattling to be of this kind may resort to a policy of retreat aimed at profitably keeping in the battle.

The firm may bargain with the government in an attempt to persuade it to reconsider. Mutual concessions may be suggested with the intention of the firm continuing its operations. Such concessions may include the following:

■ Hiring national managers.

■ Raising transfer prices charged from the locally based firm to other parts of the group.

■ Accepting local partners.

■ Changing expatriate management.

■ Investing more capital.

- Contributing to political campaigns.

- Releasing the host government from concessionary agreements.

- Supporting government programmes.

- Suspending payment of dividends.

- Surrendering majority control.

- Removing all home-country personnel.

- Reorganizing to give greater benefit to the local company.

Of the above concessions, the first four are the most attractive to the international firm. As a rule, the second four are the next most attractive and the final four are the least attractive.

If the above concessions do not work, then the firm begins to apply negative sanctions. These may take the form of supporting an opposition political party or invoking home government support for the firm's position. But these political tactics rarely work. By contrast, the international firm may agree at this stage to relinquish control in return for compensation, thereby saving the host government and the firm itself a considerable investment in negotiating time.

While rational negotiation and applying power continue, the firm may also begin to seek legal redress. It is a rule of law that legal remedy must first be sought in the courts of the host country. After this route has been exhausted, the international firm may proceed to put its case in the home country and in international courts. Where host courts are impartial, seeking local redress is likely to be moderately effective. But where the judiciary is subservient to the government, the international firm can expect little payoff here and it may be most expeditious to seek judgments against the host country's property in the home or third countries.

Efforts to sue national governments are frustrated by the doctrine of sovereign immunity and the act of state doctrine. The former says that a sovereign state may not be tried in the courts of another state without its consent. And the latter doctrine implies that a nation is sovereign within its own borders and that its domestic actions may not be questioned in the courts of another nation, even if those actions violate international law. However, the doctrine of sovereign immunity is normally waived when it comes to a foreign country's commercial activities.

Another route is to lobby in the home country in an attempt to restrict the import of raw materials and other products from the host country. Arbitration of investment disputes is another alternative; this is now moderately effective since the establishment of the International Centre for Settlements of Investment Disputes, set up in 1966 by the World Bank. Created to encourage foreign direct investment by providing a forum for settling international investment disputes, the centre provides binding arbitration, although in practice its influence is small.

Should the firm have experienced a lack of success during the phases of negotiation, applying power and seeking legal redress, eventual surrender follows and attempts at salvaging some of the investment ensue. This usually involves settling for whatever insurance and other payments may be obtained.

25.8 | Political risk analysis in international capital budgeting

Companies undertaking overseas projects explicitly take on an element of political risk which is related to host government actions. Shapiro (2003) details a series of models designed to quantify, in an interesting way, whether that risk is acceptable or not. One route is via a break-even probability analysis for a particular government action. The sinews of his approach are summarized in this chapter. Essentially, the aim is to develop a generalized formula for assessment of political risk in investment appraisal. This approach enables analysts to assess the impact of various political risk factors, one by one.

The basic argument is developed by looking at the effects on project outturns of a number of political risk events. Here we consider, in turn, expropriation, blocked funds and increased taxes. And following on from this we develop our generalized model.

So, first of all, we consider expropriation. The base case net present value of a project in a foreign territory can be written as:

$$-I + \sum_{i=1}^{n} \frac{X_i}{(1+k)^i}$$

where I represents the present value of the capital investment inputs, X_i refers to the remittable net cash flow generated by the project in year i, and k represents the appropriate discount rate. Now, should expropriation occur in year h, the net present value of the project will fall, to:

$$-I + \sum_{i=1}^{h-1} \frac{X_i}{(1+k)^i} + \frac{G_h}{(1+k)^h}$$

The notation above remains as before except that the amount represented by G would embrace not only direct compensation paid by the host government, political risk insurance and so on, but also the effect of tax deductibility (if any) and capital repayment of obligations which might be avoided resultant upon the expropriation. We have allowed for G being paid in year h in the equation above. In the real world it may not be the case that payment is so prompt – but the sentiment remains, and the effect of timing of payment of the sum, G, must be incorporated into the equation.

We now take things a little further. Suppose that the probability of expropriation in year h is p_h and zero in all other years, then the project's net present value becomes:

$$-I + \sum_{i=1}^{h-1} \frac{X_i}{(1+k)^i} + p_h \frac{G_h}{(1+k)^h} + (1-p_h)\sum_{i=h}^{n} \frac{X_i}{(1+k)^i}$$

If the project exactly breaks even under expropriation, its net present value will be zero. So, if we set the above equation equal to zero, we can find the break-even value of p_h. Doing this and rearranging terms, it can be seen that:

$$p_h\left[\sum_{i=h}^{n} \frac{X_i}{(1+k)^i} - \frac{G_h}{(1+k)^h}\right] = -I + \sum_{i=1}^{n} \frac{X_i}{(1+k)^i}$$

And rearranging the above terms further, the break-even value of p_b can be found thus:

$$p_b = \frac{\displaystyle\sum_{i=1}^{n} \frac{X_i}{(1+k)^i} - I}{\displaystyle\sum_{i=b}^{n} \frac{X_i}{(1+k)^i} - \frac{G_b}{(1+k)^b}}$$

In a particular expropriation case, if we find that the break-even value of p is, for example, 0.25, we need not spend time worrying about whether the likely value is 0.10 or 0.15 – suffice it to say that, being less than 0.25, the project is acceptable. By a similar line of argument, if the probability of expropriation is somewhere between 0.40 and 0.50, clearly the project is not acceptable.

As an example of the use of the above formula, consider an investment with a capital cost of £1m, a project life of five years, an annual net remittable cash flow of £500,000 and a discount rate of 20 per cent per annum. The project's net present value can be calculated as £495,305. Expropriation data involve a possible nationalization of the project at the end of year 2 with compensation from the host government estimated at £200,000. Using the break-even formula above it can be shown that this value comes out at:

$$\frac{495,305}{731,416 - 138,889} = 0.84$$

If, incidentally, compensation were zero, the break-even probability would be:

$$\frac{495,305}{731,416} = 0.68$$

The same series of arguments leads to a similar kind of proposition with respect to blocked funds. Our deductions begin with the base case net present value of the project at:

$$-I + \sum_{i=1}^{n} \frac{X_i}{(1+k)^i}$$

If we assume that funds become blocked in year j and beyond, the project's net present value can be stated as:

$$-I + \sum_{i=1}^{j-1} \frac{X_i}{(1+k)^i} + \sum_{j}^{n} \frac{X_i(1+r)^{n-i}}{(1+k)^n}$$

The above formulation assumes a reinvestment rate of r per cent per annum in the blocking territory, with all blocked proceeds ultimately remitted in year n; otherwise all notation is as earlier.

If the probability of blocking in year j is q_j and zero in all other years, then the net present value of the project becomes:

$$-I + \sum_{i=1}^{j-1} \frac{X_i}{(1+k)^i} + q_j \sum_{i=j}^{n} \frac{X_i(1+r)^{n-i}}{(1+k)^n} + (1-q_j) \sum_{i=j}^{n} \frac{X_i}{(1+k)^i}$$

The break-even value of q is obtained when the value of the above equation is zero. In this circumstance it can be shown that:

$$q_j \left[\sum_{i=j}^{n} \frac{X_i}{(1+k)^i} + \sum_{i=j}^{n} \frac{X_i(1+r)^{n-i}}{(1+k)^n} \right] = \sum_{i=1}^{n} \frac{X_i}{(1+k)^i} - I$$

And the above formulation can be rearranged to give the break-even probability as:

$$q_j = \frac{\displaystyle\sum_{i=1}^{n} \frac{X_i}{(1+k)^i} - I}{\displaystyle\sum_{i=j}^{n} \frac{X_i}{(1+k)^i} + \sum_{i=j}^{n} \frac{X_i(1+r)^{n-i}}{(1+k)^n}}$$

Again, take a simple example. Assume that a project involves a capital investment of £1m, has a project life of five years and creates annual remittable cash generation, net of taxes, of £375,000 per annum. With a 20 per cent per annum discount rate, the project's net present value comes out at £121,625. On the question of blocking, it is considered that this is likely immediately after year 1 and the host government is expected to insist on a reinvestment rate of 5 per cent per annum. The break-even blocking probability comes out, using the above formula, as:

$$\frac{121,625}{808,975 - 649,555} = 0.76$$

Turning now to the political risk of increased taxes, an almost exactly similar line of argument can enable us to identify a break-even probability which may be useful in assessing political risk in international project appraisal. The base case net present value, as before, is given by:

$$-I + \sum_{i=1}^{n} \frac{X_i}{(1+k)^i}$$

With a tax increase coming in year m, and where π represents taxable profit and Δt is the change in the tax rate, the project's net present value falls to:

$$-I + \sum_{i=1}^{m-1} \frac{X_i}{(1+k)^i} + \sum_{i=m}^{n} \frac{X_i - \pi_i \Delta t}{(1+k)^i}$$

If the probability of a tax increase in year m is p_m and zero in all other years, then the net present value of the project becomes:

$$-I + \sum_{i=1}^{m-1} \frac{X_i}{(1+k)^i} + p_m \sum_{i=m}^{n} \frac{X_i - \pi_i \Delta t}{(1+k)^i} + (1-p_m) \sum_{i=m}^{n} \frac{X_i}{(1+k)^i}$$

Using the normal methodology developed in the immediately preceding section, the break-even value of p_m is where the net present value of the project becomes zero:

$$0 = -I + \sum_{i=1}^{n} \frac{X_i}{(1+k)^i} + p_m \sum_{i=m}^{n} \frac{X_i - \pi_i \Delta t}{(1+k)^i} + (1 - p_m) \sum_{i=m}^{n} \frac{X_i}{(1+k)^i}$$

And this simplifies to give:

$$0 = -I + \sum_{i=1}^{n} \frac{X_i}{(1+k)^i} - p_m \sum_{i=m}^{n} \frac{\pi_i \Delta t}{(1+k)^i}$$

Rearranging, we can establish that the break-even value of p_m is given by:

$$p_m = \frac{\displaystyle\sum_{i=1}^{n} \frac{X_i}{(1+k)^i} - I}{\displaystyle\sum_{i=m}^{n} \frac{\pi_i \Delta t}{(1+k)^i}}$$

Again, let us take a numerical example. Assume, as before, that the base case data are as follows. The investment has a cost of £1m and a project life of five years, it generates £375,000 per annum of remittable cash flow, net of tax, and the relevant discount rate is 20 per cent per annum. As before, the base case net present value comes out at £121,625. If there is a possibility of an increase in the tax rate from, say, 25 per cent to 50 per cent, immediately after year 2, then the break-even probability comes out as:

$$p_m = \frac{121{,}625}{\displaystyle\sum_{i=3}^{5} \frac{500{,}000 \times 25\%}{(1.20)^i}}$$

$$= \frac{121{,}625}{182{,}695}$$

$$= 0.67$$

So far, we have developed three models to analyse political risk in international capital investment appraisal; in turn these have been concerned with expropriation, blocked funds and tax increases. But we can generalize. The base case net present value, in all instances, is:

$$-I + \sum_{i=1}^{n} \frac{X_i}{(1+k)^i}$$

With political risk built in, the base case is reduced by the probability of the political risk occurrence multiplied by the present value of the forgone cash flows resultant upon the occurrence. So the net present value becomes:

$$-I + \sum_{i=1}^{n} \frac{X_i}{(1+k)^i} - p \text{ (PV of forgone cash flow)}$$

where p is the break-even probability of occurrence of the political risk event. Rearranging the above equation, we can establish that the generalized formula is:

$$p = \frac{-I + \sum_{i=1}^{n} \frac{X_i}{(1+k)^i}}{\text{PV of forgone cash flows}}$$

Or, to present it another way, the break-even probability always equals:

$$\frac{\text{NPV of investment (base case)}}{\text{PV of forgone cash flows following implementation of political risk factor}}$$

We believe that this formula provides a most useful way of analysing political risk in capital investment appraisal.

The method advocated here is not dissimilar to that put forward by Levi (1990, pp. 389–390). He arrives at the conclusion that political risk can be allowed for by multiplying the cash flow in any year of operations by the probability of survival and dividing this by the sum of the discount rate and the probability of confiscation. By summing such terms for each year of operations, and allowing for the initial capital input, a net present value can be arrived at for the project.

25.9 | Summary

- Political risk can be defined as the exposure to a change in the value of an investment of cash position resultant upon government actions.

- Governments intervene in their national economies and, in so doing, increase the level of political risk that the multinational firm faces. Political risk ranges from exposure to changes in tax legislation, through the impacts of exchange controls to restrictions affecting operations and financing in a host currency.

- Multinationals are concerned with the measurement and management of political risk. There are various approaches to the measurement of political risk – most of them are subjective in nature.

- In terms of managing political risk, one way is clearly to avoid it by deciding against going ahead with investments in political uncertain countries.

- Another approach is through insurance. Assets may be insured in politically risky areas against expropriation and other risks of a political kind. Fees vary according to the country concerned and the type of risk insured and cover is usually limited to 90 per cent of equity participation.

- The multinational may reach an agreement with the host government prior to investment – although subsequent governments may renege on such concessions.

- Keeping the foreign subsidiary dependent upon group companies for supplies and markets – the integrated operations approach – is a useful means of management of political risk.

- Financing a local subsidiary with a high level of local debt is another tactic. If expropriated, the host government takes over the assets and liabilities of the local business. Liabilities of the subsidiary include the high level of local debt.

- Political risk in international capital budgeting is best taken into account at the *ex-ante* stage by the break-even probability approach. This involves estimating the probability of occurrence of a particular political risk factor such that the present value of the project moves from being positive to being zero. The generalized formula for the break-even probability always equals:

$$\frac{\text{NPV of investment (base case)}}{\text{PV of forgone cash flows following implementation of political risk factor}}$$

Follow through some of the numeric calculations in the main text, rather than the algebraic. If you do this, it is relatively straightforward.

25.10 | End of chapter questions

Question 1
Explain an MNC's strategy of diversifying projects internationally to maintain a low level of overall country risk.

Question 2
Once a project is accepted, country risk analysis for the foreign country involved is no longer necessary, assuming that no other proposed projects are being evaluated for that country. Do you agree with this statement? Why or why not?

Question 3
Do you think that a full country risk analysis can replace a capital budgeting analysis of a project in a foreign country? Why?

26 International capital budgeting: the practicalities

Having homed in on the underlying theory of international capital budgeting in Chapters 22 and 23, we now apply this knowledge in the real world of business.

In this chapter we provide a fairly straightforward case study of international capital budgeting. It should be easily assimilated by students who have progressed this far in the text. The case is designed to illustrate, in a practical way, how the proposed method should be used to evaluate financially projects which involve overseas spending. The case is concerned with the situation where the host country constrains multinational freedom by restricting the flow of cash back to the parent or elsewhere in the world by the imposition of exchange controls. In this set of circumstances, the potential flow of moneys back to the parent may be hastened by, for example financial engineering. It follows that the role of financial ingenuity in international investment may be critical in terms of parent net present value; its importance is outstandingly marked where there are remittance constraints. In other words, in these circumstances, financial creativity can affect the present value of investments – and significantly. The calculations in the worked example in this chapter should bring out this point.

26.1 | Net present value and adjusted present value

The calculation of the present value of a project may be approached by way of the net present value method or via the adjusted present value technique. Both have the backing of a sound theoretical underpinning. The net present value has its roots in the traditional theory of finance, which was well expounded by Solomon (1963). The adjusted present value draws on the Modigliani and Miller (1958, 1963) approach to the cost of capital and has been developed by Myers (1974). The rationale and detail relating to both techniques are well covered in any of the thorough texts on financial management.

In practical terms, the prescriptions of the two methods were summarized in Chapter 23. Correctly applied, they should give similar answers. For a good discussion see Ross, Westerfield and Jaffe (1999).

We now turn to a worked example on international capital appraisal. It involves problems with partial blockage of overseas cash generation.

26.2 | Overseas project appraisal: Alpha NV

Alpha NV (Alpha) is a multinational company headquartered in a eurozone country. It is engaged in the manufacture and distribution of electrical motors that find a broad spectrum of end uses in commercial and industrial applications in various parts of the world. So far, it has not made any sales in Olifa, a republic which is experiencing lift-off as a result of newly-found mineral reserves which are planned to come on-stream in some two or three years' time. This is one of the main drivers of Olifa's attractiveness to Alpha. Olifa has a right-wing government which has been in power for 20 years (but with so-called democratic elections) but its citizens have a feeling of well-being in a country where success and upward mobility are highly rated. Olifa is encouraging industrialization but also seeks to push multinationals entering the country to privatize their investments after five years. The government has specified a price earnings multiple around four times historic profits after tax for this purpose. Because of a 25 per cent industrialization impost (which is not tax deductible) on all new inward investment, as opposed to a 50 per cent duty on other imports to Olifa, Alpha's project analysis team has concluded that direct investment appears to be the preferred mode of entry to Olifa. For this purpose, a wholly-owned Olifa subsidiary (Olifa Alpha Limited) is to be formed. This subsidiary is referred to as OAL.

The base case

Key financial data relating to the Olifan project is as follows:

- The local currency is the Olifan dollar (OLD). Olifa is currently experiencing inflation of around 15 per cent per annum and this is likely to continue into the foreseeable future. The exchange rate now (year 0) is 5 Olifan dollars to the euro. Inflation in the euro area, for the purposes of this example, is put at 3 per cent per annum over the next five years or so.

- The capital cost of the project is OLD200m plus an import duty of OLD50m. Under Olifan regulations, this capital must be subscribed from the overseas investor as equity capital in the Olifan subsidiary.

- Olifa has implemented fairly tough foreign exchange control regulations but they seem relatively transparent and honest (although some readers might say that an honest foreign exchange control was an oxymoron – a figure of speech which involves contradictory terms used in conjunction, like Hannibal Lecter being a beautiful killer). These involve a remittance of profits based on 10 per cent of profit after tax. When arriving at this profit level, initial entry costs (exclusive of the industrialization impost) are to be depreciated on an historic cost basis, straight line over five years – that is, 20 per cent per annum. However, the profit on realization at the end of year 5 – that is, the proceeds less the initial input (exclusive of industrialization impost) – is to be taxed at 50 per cent. Furthermore, these realization proceeds are not remittable to the parent until year 8. During this period, from year 5 to year 8, such proceeds must be deposited in a bank approved by the Olifan government at a zero interest rate. On remittance, these proceeds will attract an exchange rate (this is guaranteed by the Olifan government) of OLD12.0744 equals EUR1. This exchange rate is based upon inflation differences of 15 per cent per annum for Olifa and 3 per cent per annum for the eurozone. This guaranteed rate will prevail whatever the market level for the EUR/OLD. Despite exchange controls, the OLD is a freely floating currency. In fact, in recent years, the OLD has followed, very closely, a purchasing power parity path.

■ Under exchange controls, non-Olifan owned companies are precluded from earning interest on deposits in banks in Olifa.

■ On selling out at the end of year 5, the retained profit within OAL may also be remitted to the multinational without any further imposition of Olifan tax but, otherwise, on the same conditions as those summarized in the last but one bullet point – that is deferment until year 8.

■ These are the allowable remittances under Olifan foreign exchange regulations:
  – the tax rate on corporate profits in Olifa is 20 per cent, and this is guaranteed up to year 5 for multinationals investing in Olifa
  – no withholding tax will be encountered on remittances of dividends and terminal value from Olifa to the eurozone
  – remittances of profit will be assumed to have borne a tax rate of 20 per cent as a foreign tax credit for purposes of taxation in the home eurozone country of Alpha NV. This regulation applies for remittances of profit and the terminal value part of the year 8 remittance for retained profit
  – the home country corporate tax rate is to be taken as 41 per cent. This means that the net amount of profit remittances in home country terms are to be grossed up at 20 per cent to allow for Olifan tax paid. This grossed up amount attracts a 41 per cent home tax rate but from this is deducted a 20 per cent foreign tax credit. So, if the taxed remittance were EUR5 million, the following home tax treatment would apply:

Remittance	EUR5m
Grossed up (multiply by 100 over 80)	6.25m
Total tax (41%)	2.56m
Less Olifan tax credit (6.25 – 5)	1.25m
Home tax payable	1.31m

  Note that there is a more straightforward way of calculating the home tax and this is simply to take the foreign tax rate (20 per cent) away from the home tax rate (41 per cent) giving home tax payable of 21 per cent of the grossed up remittance.

■ To attract its investment, the Olifan government has guaranteed Alpha a monopoly of its market out to year 5. This is a normal procedure in Olifa.

■ This has enabled Alpha's analysts to come up comfortably with estimates of best estimate outturns which are summarized in Table 26.1 (overleaf).

■ Alpha uses a real rate of return expectation of 8 per cent to screen investments. Based upon the risk premium attaching to Olifa and to Oifan government

Table 26.1 Alpha Olifa best estimates of project cash inflows based on an Olifan inflation rate of 15 per cent per annum

Year	Units sold thousands	Sales price OLD	Sales revenue OLDm	Variable costs at 50% of sales revenue OLDm	Fixed costs OLDm	Depreciation OLDm	Operating profit OLDm	Olifan tax at 20% OLDm	Profit after tax OLDm	Additional working capital* OLDm	Free cash flows† OLDm
1	160	2000	320	160	40	40	80	16	64	(48)	56
2	200	2300	460	230	46	40	144	29	115	(21)	134
3	250	2645	661	330	53	40	238	38	190	(30)	200
4	300	3042	913	456	61	40	356	71	285	(38)	287
5	360	3498	1259	629	70	40	520	104	416	(52)	404
6	Terminal value based upon P/E ratio of 4 times										1664

* Working capital is based on 15 per cent of sales.

† Free cash flow equals profit after tax, add back depreciation, less additional working capital. No new capital expenditure is assumed. Initial investment is reckoned to have a twelve-year life, even though the depreciation write off gives a five-year life – consistent with Olifan tax rules.

Table 26.2 Alpha Olifa calculation of net present value from a project standpoint

Step 1	The approximate discount rate					
	Real terms requirement + Inflation + Risk premium for Olifa					
	8% + 15% + 3% = 26%					
Step 2	The more precise discount rate					
	(1 + Real terms requirement) (1 + Inflation) (1 + Risk premium for Olifa) – 1					
	(1.08) (1.15) (1.03) – 1 = 0.279					
	say 28%					
Step 3	Calculation of the project standpoint net present value					
	Free cash flow for year	0	1	2	3	4	5
	Flow – see Table 26.1 (OLDm)	(250)	56	134	200	287	404
	– terminal value* (OLDm)						1664
	Discounted to present value at 28% (OLDm)	(250)	44	82	95	107	602
	Net present value (OLDm)	680					

* No tax has been applied to the terminal value. In the Olifan information bullet points, the terminal value was assumed to attract tax on remittance. The cash flow analysis in Table 26.2 is from a project standpoint – that is, without remittance.

securities, an additional 3 per cent is required to compensate for Olifan risk (the calculation of this is not shown). Remember, too, that Olifan inflation is estimated at 15 per cent per annum while eurozone inflation is estimated at 3 per cent per annum – and this is the inflation rate to be used for the home country concerned within the eurozone.

Although it is not of absolute interest (because the preferred angle of analysis in international capital budgeting is the parent viewpoint with parent cash flows as the appropriate input), we can calculate the net present value of the investment from a project viewpoint. This is done in Table 26.2. Note that we use the more correct 28 per cent discount rate based on multiplying up risk premiums rather than the approximate rate of 26 per cent based upon their addition. This approach becomes a most relevant precaution when dealing with very high inflation economies.

As can be seen from Table 26.2, the investment in Olifa shows a fairly substantial net present value from a project standpoint – equal to OLD680m, that is EUR136m (OLD680m ÷ 5). But it is the parent standpoint return we are focusing upon, and this means further analysis. The project net present value may not be good enough for a eurozone investor because of remittance restrictions.

The next steps that we need to take to estimate the net present value of the Olifan project from a parent standpoint are as follows:

■ We must estimate remittable profits to the eurozone country. To do this, we must look at the profit after tax as per Table 26.1 and build in a 10 per cent dividend which is sent back to the home country.

■ To convert these remittances to euros, we must estimate future exchange rates. To do this, we assume a purchasing power parity trajectory. Of course, exchange rates rarely follow a PPP trend year in year out. But, past evidence points in this direction for the OLD versus the EUR. And, in any case, analysis with different scenarios is possible and these may prove useful for managerial judgement.

Table 26.3 Purchasing power parity forecast of the OLD against the EUR

- Note that the PPP equation (see Figure 4.1) is used. Subscript E represents the euro and subscript O represents the Olifan dollar, we use the equation:

$$\frac{p_E - p_O}{1 + p_O} = \frac{s_t - s_O}{s_O}$$

Otherwise the notation used in Figure 4.1 applies. In dealing with data in the equation, given our notation, we should use a direct eurozone quotation for currencies – again see Figure 4.1.

- Calculations below follow PPP

Year	Opening exchange rate	Euro inflation	Olifan inflation	Closing exchange rate
0	€0.2			
1		3%	15%	€0.17913 (OLD5.5825)
2		3%	15%	€0.16044 (OLD6.2329)
3		3%	15%	€0.14370 (OLD6.9589)
4		3%	15%	€0.12870 (OLD7.7700)
5		3%	15%	€0.11527 (OLD8.6753)
6		3%	15%	€0.10324 (OLD9.6862)
7		3%	15%	€0.09247 (OLD10.8143)
8		3%	15%	€0.08282 (OLD12.0744)

- We must also forecast the terminal value in terms of the estimated P/E multiple of 4 times; the capital profit arising here will be subject to Olifan tax at 50%. Additionally, retained profits within OAL may be remitted too. Both of these final remittances must be deferred to year 8. The former will be subject to a home capital gains tax of 41 per cent and the latter will be treated like any other profit remittance.

- Home remittances are discounted at the appropriate euro discount rate.

Covering all of these calculations, we have presented Tables 26.3–Table 26.7. Their content is explained below:

- Table 26.3 – a PPP forecast for the OLD versus the EUR.

- Table 26.4 – dividend remittances from Olifa to the home country showing tax payable on their arrival in the home territory.

- Table 26.5 – terminal value and retained profit remittances in year 8 from Olifa to the home country with Olifan and home taxes shown.

- Table 26.6 – tabulation summarizing the appropriate home country discount rate to be applied to flows from Olifa.

- Table 26.7 (overleaf) – an overarching table bringing together data from Tables 26.3–26.6 into a summary of home country cash flows which are then discounted to net present value.

Table 26.4 Dividend remittances from Olifa to the home country

Year	Profit after taxes as per Table 26.1 in OLDm	Dividend at 10% of PAT OLDm	Exchange rates as per Table 26.3 OLD to one €	Dividend in €m	Dividend grossed up €m	Additional home tax at 21% €m	Net of tax dividends to home country €m
1	64	6.4	5.5825	1.15	1.44	(0.30)	0.85
2	115	11.5	6.2329	1.85	2.31	(0.48)	1.37
3	190	19.0	6.9589	2.73	3.41	(0.72)	2.01
4	285	28.5	7.7700	3.67	4.59	(0.96)	2.71
5	416	41.6	8.6753	4.80	6.00	(1.26)	3.54

Table 26.5 Net remittance of terminal value (based on P/E of 4) and retained profit

- Terminal value based on P/E 4

PAT year 5	OLD416m
Value (PAT × 4)	OLD1664m
Cost of investment (excl import duty)	OLD200m
Taxable amount	OLD1464m
Olifan tax at 50%	OLD732m
Net amount remitted	OLD932m (Value 1664 minus tax 732)

- Retained profit is given by total PAT (see Table 26.1) of OLD1070m less dividends paid of OLD107m to give OLD963m

- Remittances deferred until year 8

	Remittance based on 4 P/E OLDm	Remittance of retained profit OLDm	Year 8 exchange rate (contractual)	Euro amount remitted €m	Remitted profit grossed up €m	Home country capital gains tax* €m	Home tax @21% €m	Net cash flow €m
Cash flows (1)	932		12.0744	77.19		(11.15)		66.04
(2)		963	12.0744	79.76	99.70		(20.94)	58.82

* Based on 41% of amount remitted less cost of EUR50m, assuming no indexation for capital gains tax purposes.

Table 26.6 Appropriate discount rate to be applied to cash flows back to parent

- The approximate discount rate
  - Real return requirement + Home inflation + Risk premium for Olifan project
  - 8% + 3% + 3% = 14%

- More precise calculation
  - (1 + Real terms requirement) (1 + Inflation) (1 + Risk premium) − 1
  - (1.08) (1.03) (1.03) − 1 = 14.58%
  - (say) 15%

Table 26.7 Parent net cash flows from Olifan project leading to parent net present value

Year	Outflow EURm	Dividends to home country EURm (see Table 26.4)	Final remittance deferred to year 8 EURm (see Table 26.5)	Parent net cash flow EURm	Present value of cash flows discounted at 15% EURm
0	(50)			(50)	(50)
1		0.85		0.85	0.74
2		1.37		1.37	1.04
3		2.01		2.01	1.32
4		2.71		2.71	1.55
5		3.54		3.54	1.76
8			124.86	124.86	40.83
Net present value					(2.76)

Evidently, as Table 26.7 shows, the net present value in home currency parent cash flow terms is in negative territory to the extent of EUR2.76m.

Financially engineering the project

Is it possible to use financial engineering to improve parent cash flows? Perhaps there are three areas where this is feasible. The first concerns the possibility of overcoming the foreign exchange restriction relating to foreign companies earning zero interest from banks in Olifa. Could Alpha Olifa deposit surplus funds with, say, a European bank in Olifa at zero interest with the condition that the European bank would credit interest to Alpha in its home country? Obviously this would be subject to negotiation as to rates – but perhaps it might involve receiving an amount in euros based on:

$$\text{(Real rate)} + \text{(Inflation)}$$

This might amount to around 6 per cent – probably, in reality, something less than this because the bank is accommodating Alpha. Under Olifan exchange controls, OAL probably loses an OLD interest rate of around 22 per cent given by:

$$\text{(1 + Real interest rate) (1 + Inflation) (1 + Risk premium)} - 1$$
$$(1.03)\,(1.15)\,(1.03) - 1$$

The second possibility of financial engineering is to hasten the year 8 terminal value to year 5. Could this be achieved by some financially engineered device, such as countertrade? For more on this issue, see section 21.3.

There is also a third route, again involving financial engineering via a commercial bank. The essential feature here is to hasten the final payments from year 8 to year 5. How might this be achieved?

It is apparent that by year 5, if all goes according to plan, Alpha NV can expect to receive €156.95m (77.19 + 79.76, see Table 26.5) in year 8 and it can expect to pay home taxes of €32.09m (again see Table 26.5, €11.15 + €20.94) on this remittance in year 8. Alpha might approach its commercial bank with a view to securitizing the

Table 26.8 Parent net cash flows from Olifan project plus securitization of terminal payment

Year	Parent net cash flow as per Table 26.7 EURm	Securitization effect EURm	Parent net cash flows after securitization EURm	Present value of cash flows discounted at 15% EURm
0	(50)		(50)	(50)
1	0.85		0.85	0.74
2	1.37		1.37	1.04
3	2.01		2.01	1.32
4	2.71		2.71	1.55
5	3.54	124.62	128.16	63.69
8	124.86	(156.95)	(32.09)	(10.49)
Net present value				7.85

receipt of €156.95m from year 8 to year 5. If the bank were to decide to charge Alpha a 2 per cent credit spread, the cost of such a financial transaction could be around 8 per cent per annum (given by real return; 3%, plus euroland inflation, 3%, plus credit spread 2%). So the bank would advance to Alpha NV at the end of year 5 the sum of:

$$\frac{EUR156.95m}{(1.08)^3} = EUR124.62m$$

and Alpha NV would repay the bank EUR156.95m, out of the proceeds of the remittance from Olifa, in year 8. The effect of this would be an alteration of the parent net cash flow schedule shown in Table 26.7 to the more favourable pattern shown in Table 26.8. This latter table shows a new net present value of parent cash flows amounting to EUR7.85m. Note that we are now in positive territory. In fact, this net present value understates the true figure because the discount on the 'securitization' amount to EUR32.33m (156.95 − 124.62) would, in all probability, be tax deductible as interest payable.

So, our project which originally showed a positive net present value from a project cash flow standpoint but a negative net present value in terms of parent cash flows (base case) has been transformed. By financial engineering, we have turned the Olifan project into positive territory in terms of parent cash flows. In real life, these kinds of situation are frequently encountered.

Note that what we have presented here is, of course, a base case for the Olifan project. In the real world, it would be useful to run various pieces of sensitivity analysis or scenarios for the project. Testing underpinning project assumptions is a critical piece of analysis here. In truth, it is rarely the case that we home in on one immutable value for a project. What we arrive at is, rather, a range of values that might be useful in aiding management judgement about whether to go ahead with a project or not.

Note also that the case example has focused on a situation where remittances are constrained. Where one is dealing with a host country without any exchange controls, the total amount of free cash flow generated normally becomes remittable.

Thus, with no exchange controls, complexities are far fewer than in the Alpha NV case.

Overall, what we are concerned with here is the methodology. More complicated examples of international capital budgeting are available in the fourth edition of this text. Readers desirous of taking matters to a more complex level are referred to that edition.

26.3 | Summary

- International capital budgeting and its domestic counterpart are different.

- It is hoped that, with the help of the case study in this chapter, it has become apparent that, under the general heading of international project appraisal, there are many complications.

- The financial analyst has to be more aware and more alert when confronted with international project appraisal than with its domestic cousin.

- You have been warned in this chapter of some of the pitfalls in cross-frontier investment analysis. There are undoubtedly more. Take care.

26.4 | End of chapter questions

Question 1
What is the limitation of using point estimates of exchange rates within the capital budgeting analysis?

Question 2
Explain how simulation can be used in multinational capital budgeting.

Test bank 4

▌Exercises

1. The Inter-Continental Company is considering investing in a new chalet hotel at Verbier in Switzerland. The initial investment required is for $2m, or CHF4m at the current exchange rate of $1 = CHF2. Profits for the first ten years will be reinvested, at which time Inter-Continental expects to sell out. Inter-Continental estimates that its interest in the hotel will realise CHF6.5m in six years' time.

   (a) Indicate what factors you would regard as relevant in evaluating this investment.
   (b) How will changes in the value of the Swiss franc affect the investment?
   (c) Indicate possible ways of forecasting the $: CHF exchange rate ten years ahead.

2. Compare and contrast international investment and financing decisions with their domestic counterparts.

3. One of the UK divisions of Global Enterprises plc wishes to set up a new manufacturing plant in Indonesia, because this would give it an important foothold in one of the fast growing parts of the world market, and would to a large extent deny this market to its main world competitors. The investment would amount to some £60m, of which the process plant would represent £40m.

   The total effort of studying this proposal will be considerable and you, as treasurer, are asked to write a memorandum outlining the issues that you regard as critical to the decision to invest, other than purely commercial ones about product costs, markets and prices, and competition.

   (Association of Corporate Treasurers: Part II, Specimen paper in Treasury Management)

4. You are the treasurer of Development Properties Ltd and are considering the funding of a project due for completion over the next six months. At the end of the six months payment will be received from the client for the total costs and the profit element, although a progress payment of £2m will be received in one month's time.

   The funding of the project is maintained separately from the remainder of the funding of Development Properties and a special loan facility has been arranged at a cost of LIBOR + $^1/_2$ per cent p.a. £4m of costs require to be funded immediately and a further £5m in three months' time.

Interest rates quoted are:

LIBOR	%
1 month	$14-13^{7}/_{8}$
2 months	$13^{7}/_{8}-13^{3}/_{4}$
3 months	$13^{7}/_{8}-13^{5}/_{8}$
6 months	$13^{1}/_{2}-13^{1}/_{4}$

FRA quotes have also been obtained:

1 v 3 13.70–13.50
3 v 6 12.70–12.50

(a) Identify the cheapest method of borrowing overall for the project for the next six months.

(b) What factors would you consider if you believed interest rates would fall by $^{1}/_{4}$ per cent within the next month?

(c) What other mechanisms would you consider to manage the interest rate if you believed that interest rates might increase sharply over the next few weeks?

(Association of Corporate Treasurers: Part II, September 1989, Paper in Liquidity Management)

Multiple choice questions

1. A US multinational is setting up a subsidiary in France with local operations only and French competition only. Funds from the subsidiary will be regularly sent to the parent. *Ceteris paribus*, the ideal situation from the parent's standpoint is:

   (a) a stable euro after the subsidiary is established;
   (b) a weak euro after the subsidiary is established;
   (c) a decision by the French government to leave the euro because this would be congruent with free market economics so beloved of American capitalists;
   (d) a strengthening euro after the subsidiary is established.

2. A Japanese-based multinational has a German subsidiary that annually remits DM20 million to Japan. If the mark _____ against the yen, the yen amount of remitted funds _____.

   (a) appreciates; decreases
   (b) depreciates; is unaffected
   (c) appreciates; is unaffected
   (d) depreciates; decreases

3. The degree of political risk faced by a European company operating in an Asian country:

   (a) may be specified objectively by using a political risk index;
   (b) depends on the benefits provided by the firm;
   (c) depends on how the firm has structured and financed its Asian operations;
   (d) is given by the net present value of the Asian investment divided by the present value of cash flows relating to the political risk factor.

4. A Belgian multinational anticipates cash flows of EUR10m, EUR12m and EUR16m, respectively, for the first three years of a project in Ruritania. The initial investment is EUR79m. The firm expects a perpetuity of EUR20m in years 4 and beyond. If the required return on the investment is 17 per cent, how large does the probability of expropriation in year 5 have to be before the investment breaks even in NPV terms? Assume that the total cash flow in year 5 in the event of expropriation is equal to EUR36m.

(a) 22 per cent
(b) 31 per cent
(c) 40 per cent
(d) 47 per cent
(e) 79 per cent

5. When trying to establish whether to go ahead or not with an international capital project, which of the following factors is not relevant?

(a) Future inflation.
(b) Exchange control blockages.
(c) Remittance provisions.
(d) Sales cannibalization.
(e) Home and host country taxation.
(f) Expenditures already made in the host country.

6. A multinational company based in Switzerland is considering establishing a two-year venture in Malaysia with an initial investment equal to CHF30m. The firm's weighted average cost of capital is 10 per cent and the required rate of return on this project is 12 per cent. The project is expected to generate cash flows of M$12m at the end of year 1 and M$30m at the end of year 2, excluding salvage value. Assume no taxes, and a stable exchange rate of M$1.35 per Swiss franc over the next two years. And further assume that all cash flows are remitted to the parent. What is the approximate break-even salvage value? Note that M$ represents the Malaysian ringitt.

(a) M$1.39m
(b) M$1.88m
(c) M$5.45m
(d) M$7.36m

7. The cost of capital for a project in Australia but evaluated in home currency on the basis of converted remittable cash flows, should theoretically:

(a) equal the parent's weighted average cost of capital;
(b) equal the minimum rate of return necessary to induce investors to buy or hold the multinational firm's shares;
(c) equal the average rate used by Australian investors to capitalize corporate cash flows;
(d) be a function of the riskiness of the project itself.

8. From the viewpoint of a foreign subsidiary, the required nominal rate of return on a project (i.e. the discount rate used to find the NPV):

(a)   is usually lower than the rate of inflation in that country;

(b)   should be equal to the required money terms rate of return used in the parent country for a project of the type being analysed;

(c)   should be equal to $(1 + p)(1 + r) - 1$, where p is the expected inflation rate in the foreign country and r is the required nominal return used in the parent country for a project of the type being analysed;

(d)   should be the local required nominal rate of return for a project of the type being analysed;

(e)   should always be higher than that in the home country to allow for the additional risk;

(f)   two of the above are correct.

9.   An international firm preparing to site production facilities in the Far East has been offered direct investment incentives worth US$25m from Thailand and US$15m from Malaysia but Singapore has offered no investment incentives. According to this scenario:

(a)   it will definitely cost $10m less to build the plant in Thailand than in Malaysia;

(b)   it will definitely cost $15m less to build the plant in Malaysia than in Singapore;

(c)   the incentives may be available to offset higher costs of production in Thailand and Malaysia;

(d)   all of the above.

10.   The government of a host country with no exchange controls offers a multinational a ten-year $50m loan at 12 per cent to set up a local production facility. The principal is due for repayment in a bullet at the end of six years. The market interest rate on such a loan is 18 per cent. With a marginal tax rate of $33^{1}/_{3}$ per cent, how much is this loan worth to the multinational? Assume that tax is paid in the year that profit on which it is assessed is earned. Assume that the multinational is in a tax-paying situation.

(a) $3.50m

(b) $4.11m

(c) $8.22m

(d) $10.49m

(e)   None of the above

Part F

International financing

Companies – whether they operate within national boundaries alone, or beyond – may borrow in their own domestic capital markets or they may move further afield and tap international markets to finance their operations. International borrowing enables companies to lower their average cost of finance and it may be an important part of the funding equation for companies whose base is within countries with shallow capital markets, as well as for major multinational companies. This section is concerned with international financing, project finance and finance for international trade.

27 International debt instruments

Debt management, whether at the domestic or international level, is part of the company's armoury of techniques which is designed to maximize the present value of shareholder wealth. Most practitioners and academics take the view that judicious debt strategy can play a part, through the achievement of an optimal gearing level, in reaching towards value maximization for equity investors. The firm's exact optimal debt to equity ratio may, in percentage terms, be a subject for fruitful debate, but it is doubtful whether it can be identified for certain *ex ante*. It is often speculated that the key determining factors are as follows:

■ The amount of business risk affecting the firm. This is really all to do with the volatility of profit before interest and tax – or, to be more precise, operating income.

■ The ability of the firm to service debt, in terms of interest payments and capital repayments, under varying scenarios regarding future outturns. Clearly, the essential point is that recessionary cash generation should be sufficient to cover debt service.

■ The former two points are central in influencing the third key point, namely the limits imposed by financiers' lending policies and practices.

■ The perceived norm for the sector.

■ The firm's historic track record in terms of debt raised and the volatility of its earnings.

Beyond the debt/equity ratio, there are a number of other fundamental issues that need to be addressed by the corporate treasurer in considering and implementing debt policy. These factors include maturity profile, fixed/floating interest mix, interest rate sensitivity and currency mix. Interest rate sensitivity was considered in detail in Chapter 18, but the other three topics are analysed here.

The conservative approach to raising funds is to match the maturity of finance to the maturity of assets. On this criterion, long-term assets should be funded by long-term finance; short-term assets would logically be backed by short-term funds. In terms of maturity profits of debt, the treasurer is well advised to ensure that repayments of borrowings are evenly spread. This reduces exposure to repayment vulnerabilities, which may be magnified due to unforeseen recession.

From the standpoint of the company, short-term debt is riskier than long-term debt. Why? There are two main reasons. First of all, long-term interest rates are generally more stable over time than short-term rates. The firm that borrows predominantly on a short-term basis may experience widely fluctuating interest rate payments. Short-term borrowings have to be renewed regularly. Thus, not only has the firm to pay the going rate at the time, but if the renewal comes at a point when either the firm or the banker is experiencing financial difficulties, then the rate may be raised or the bank may refuse to renew the loan. It is clearly important to ensure that the right balance is struck between short-term and long-term debt and that the maturity profile of debt does not introduce repayment difficulties. The business environment can change very rapidly, hence the treasurer is advised to ensure that an excessive amount of debt does not fall due in any one year. Corporate debt policy also involves the mix between the fixed and floating rate loans. The interest rate on a fixed rate loan is fixed for the entire life of the loan regardless of changes in market conditions. A floating rate loan is one where the interest rate varies in line with the market. The loans are usually made at an agreed margin over a published marker rate. This may be a clearing bank's base rate for sterling or prime rate for US dollars, or LIBOR (London inter-bank offered rate) for term loans whether in sterling, dollars or Eurocurrency, and so on. On the question of the mix between fixed and floating interest rates, the treasurer needs to bear in mind the following points:

■ The sensitivity of profit and cash flows to changes in interest rates. The company whose operating profits fall when interest rates rise – for example, a housebuilder – will show less variability in profit after tax if it finances itself fixed rate. Floating rate finance may be appropriate to a financial institution whose income before interest increases, *ceteris paribus*, as general interest rates rise.

■ A high proportion of fixed rate debt creates an exposure if interest rates fall.

■ If the treasurer has not agreed with the lender the margin over market rates for floating rate loans, then the treasurer may be forced to pay larger margins when business conditions deteriorate.

■ Long-term fixed rate loans are not the only means of ensuring that a secure source of funds is available at all times. A committed borrowing facility (see later) may be preferable in many cases.

On the question of currency mix of loans, matching the currency of liabilities with assets is widely recommended on the grounds that currency movements affect asset and liability value equally. As we have seen in earlier chapters, the key problem is one of interpretation of exposure.

In managing debt, there are certain key axioms that should affect the treasurer's course of action. Two of the most important are liquidity and profitability. Liquidity is critical for any company. The treasurer should ensure that borrowing facilities are arranged for all foreseen needs plus a realistic margin for contingencies. During periods of financial strength, many companies take it for granted that funds will be available indefinitely. They continue to operate with only the minimum of facilities in the expectation that their past success will make an increase in borrowing

Table 27.1 True interest rates

Period	Eurodollar interest rates	
	Quoted rate (%) (360 days)	True rate (%) (365 days)*
Overnight	9.250–9.375	9.68–9.82
7 days	9.375–9.500	9.81–9.95
1 month (30 days)	9.375–9.500	9.79–9.92
3 months (90 days)	9.375–9.500	9.74–9.87
6 months (180 days)	9.375–9.500	9.66–9.79
1 year:		
Annual interest	9.500–9.625	9.63–9.76
Semi-annual interest	9.500–9.625	9.79–9.92
Sterling overdraft at base rate (12%) plus 1%		
Interest charged:		
Monthly	13%	13.67
Quarterly	13%	13.54
Half-yearly	13%	13.35

* True rate equals IRR.

facilities a mere formality. This is not a wise approach. Increasing facilities when the company is riding high makes a lot of sense. Many a financially sound firm has exploited its successful position by turning it into a strong bargaining position with banks and other lenders rather than waiting until times are hard or the banks or the company itself is facing liquidity problems.

Subject to the need for liquidity, the treasurer aims to borrow at the lowest overall cost after tax. Borrowing at the lowest possible cost sounds simple but there are complications. Besides the points already referred to in this chapter, the treasurer needs to ensure that comparisons of borrowing sources are computed on a common basis. It is suggested that the true cost of borrowing under various loans is computed – this is best done by looking at the IRR of a loan, sometimes called the true rate or the annual percentage rate (APR). An example of how true interest rates vary from those quoted is summarized in Table 27.1.

27.1 | Short-term borrowing

Short-term debt is defined as borrowings originally scheduled for repayment within one year. A wide range of short-term debt finance is available. The treasurer needs to assess the advantages and disadvantages of each. We now consider the major sources of short-term finance.

Trade credit is undoubtedly the major source. In its normal transactions, the firm buys raw materials on credit from other firms. The debt is recorded as trade creditors in its books of account. This is a customary aspect of doing business in most industries. It is a convenient and important source of financing for most non-financial companies.

The next most frequent form of short-term finance, at least in the United Kingdom, is the overdraft. An overdraft is a credit arrangement whereby a bank permits a customer to run its current account into deficit up to an agreed limit. The overdraft is flexible and is particularly appropriate for providing ongoing and especially seasonal working capital. Bankers like to see overdrafts run down to zero at some point during the year. Nowadays companies tend to finance some of their core borrowing needs by overdraft. The overdraft borrower is at liberty to operate within the established limit and to repay and redraw any amount at any time without advance notice or penalty. The interest charged is usually on an agreed formula, such as between one and four or five percentage points above the bank's base rate. The size of this spread depends on the credit rating of the borrower. For large first-line companies, it is normally 1 per cent; for small weak firms it is frequently up to 5 per cent. Interest is based on the daily cleared debit balance and is usually payable quarterly in arrears. Overdrafts are contractually repayable on demand. But in practice they may be available for a stated period – for example, one year. Although flexible, the overdraft may be more expensive than other sources of short-term debt.

Turning now to money-market sources of short-term debt, the domestic sterling inter-bank market provides a source of corporate borrowing. In this market, the corporate customer obtains very competitive borrowing and deposit rates. The interest rate is usually based on a margin over LIBOR. Large companies may obtain funds at LIBOR or at a very small spread over LIBOR. Transactions are for fixed terms, which can be anything from overnight to twelve months. The treasurer may obtain best rates by talking directly to banks with which the company has credit lines or by using a money broker.

Interest is paid at the end of the loan period. For overnight funds, this means that it is paid daily. It is imperative that cash flow timing differences are taken into account when comparing costs of different borrowings. The true cost of each borrowing ought to be calculated before a borrowing source is actually selected.

We now turn to sterling eligible bills – or bankers' acceptances as they are sometimes called. These are bills of exchange and they are the oldest instrument in the UK money market. The purpose of the UK bill market is to provide trade finance. Acceptances are issued on a discounted basis. As such, the interest and acceptance commissions are paid at the time of drawing the bill. Clearly, the true cost of borrowing is higher than the nominal discount rate. If the discount rate plus commission is quoted as $15^1/_2$ per cent, this amounts to a true rate of interest of well over $16^1/_4$ per cent. The procedure for companies wishing to use this market is to discount the bills with an accepting bank. The bill will be discounted at the eligible bill rate. The accepting bank receives an acceptance commission for discounting the bill. The bank pays the proceeds of the discounted bill to the company's bank account. Once the accepting bank receives the bill, it will endorse it. The bank may either hold it for its own trading purposes or rediscount it with a discount house. On maturity, the company – or its agent – pays the face value of the bill to the holder at that firm.

Another source of short-term funds is borrowing via commercial paper – basically an IOU. Since April 1986 there has been a market in sterling commercial paper. This paper is in the form of unsecured promissory notes. Its duration is from 7 to 364 days. There are strict rules about which corporations can, and cannot, issue sterling commercial paper. The virtue of this market to the company is endorsed by the fact that a top-rate corporation may raise money at around five basis points below LIBID, the London inter-bank bid rate, which is, of course, always less than LIBOR. Unlike US commercial paper, credit rating is not a prerequisite of issue in the UK. In deciding whether to have an issue rated, a treasurer has to consider the following factors:

■ The rating process is fairly complex and management has to spend a fair amount of time with the rating agencies.

■ Rating improves the chances of selling the paper if the programme has been rated A1/P1, the highest possible rating.

■ The cost of rating exceeds £25,000 annually. If a company were to have an average level of commercial paper outstanding through a year amounting to £15m, the rating process would only be cost effective if ratings could lower the cost of funding by twenty basis points per annum. The main rating agencies are Standard and Poor's, and Moody's.

Leaving aside the cost of rating, the up-front cost of establishing a sterling commercial paper programme is about £10,000. Thereafter, the cost is around £5,000 per annum. The US commercial paper market is deep, active and liquid. It is far larger than its sterling counterpart. There are many similarities between the US and UK markets, but the overriding difference is that, in the United States, all commercial paper programmes have to be credit rated. Corporate use of commercial paper and credit rating is considered further in Chapter 32.

Finally, on the topic of short-term financing, it is worth mentioning that overdrafts are still relatively unknown in the United States despite their wide use throughout the rest of the Western world. The greatest source of short-term funding in the United States is commercial paper.

27.2 | Medium-term borrowing

Medium-term debt is defined as borrowings originally scheduled for repayment in more than one year but less than ten years. Until about fifteen years ago, European corporate treasurers had few options when seeking to raise debt – the opportunities included overdraft or short-term bill discounting and long-term debentures and mortgages. This range of choice was poor compared with that confronting the treasurer in the United States, where there has always been an array of medium-term finance available. The expansion of US banks in the international arena aided by the colossal expansion of the Euromarkets and the widespread demise of exchange controls have meant that these financing techniques have been exported to European companies.

Nowadays, medium-term borrowing facilities are widely available. Repayment schedules are negotiable but the usual practice is to require periodic repayments (amortization) over the life of the loan. The rationale of amortization is to ensure that the loan is repaid gradually over its life in equal instalments commensurate with corporate cash generation rather than falling due all at once. In some cases, there may be a moratorium on repayments during the early stages of a loan. This is particularly the case when the project being financed has a long gestation period. Medium-term loans are normally priced on a basis related to LIBOR. The spread over LIBOR depends on the credit standing of the borrower and the maturity of the facility. They normally vary between 0.25 and 2 per cent. But prime credits may pay even less. Drawings under medium-term borrowings are normally for three, six or twelve months and are rolled over as specified in the loan agreement. Interest is usually paid at the end of this three-, six- or twelve-month period.

There are two types of fee associated with medium-term facilities. First, there is the commitment fee. The bank is usually committed to lend once the loan agreement is signed, even though the loan is not drawn down instantly. To compensate for this reduced flexibility, the bank charges a fee. This commitment fee is usually payable for the portion of the loan which is undrawn. The size of the fee may be ten to fifteen basis points.

When the facility is arranged via a syndication of banks, it is normal for the borrower to pay a management fee. The fee is similar to underwriting fees associated with public issues. Other costs to be paid by the borrower may include the legal fees of the lender for organizing the loan and, the cost of publishing a 'tombstone' advertising the name or names of the banks involved in arranging the facility. There may also be a penalty payable for early repayment.

27.3 | Euromarkets

We now turn to some of the most interesting financial markets in the world – the Euromarkets. So what are these markets? The Euromarkets are usually defined to include the markets for Eurocurrency, Eurocredits and Eurobonds. Each of these markets is described in this chapter. The Eurocurrency market is that market in which Eurobanks accept deposits and make loans denominated in currencies other than that of the country in which the banks are located. This whole area is not to be confused with the relatively new currency, the euro.

The traditional definition of Eurodollars is that they are dollars held in the form of time deposits in banks outside the United States. However, since 3 December 1981, US banks have been allowed to open international banking facilities (IBFs) within the United States which can transact international business free from most Federal Reserve Bank regulations. In essence, dollars deposited in an IBF become Eurodollars for all practical purposes. The IBF itself is a set of segregated asset and liability accounts maintained on the books of a banking organization. IBF deposits must be for a minimum amount of $100,000 and for a minimum time of two days. Depositors and customers of IBFs must be foreign residents or other IBFs.

Euro-yen are yen deposited in banks outside Japan. The prefix 'Euro' really means external and refers to funds that are intermediated outside the country of the currency in which the funds are denominated. The Eurocurrency market is made up of financial institutions that compete for dollar time deposits and make dollar loans outside the United States, plus IBFs, institutions outside the eurozone that bid for eurodeposits and make euro loans, financial institutions outside the United Kingdom that bid for sterling deposits and loan sterling, and so on. The Eurocurrency market is by no means the same as the Eurobond market. The latter is defined later in this chapter. There are a number of key Euromarket terms and concepts which need to be clarified before moving on to the complexities of Eurofinance; the following section aims to provide this clarification.

27.4 | Definitions of key Eurocurrency terms

The Euromarkets are banking markets for deposits and loans. They are located outside the country of the currency in which the claims are denominated. These markets are prefixed as 'Euro-' to indicate that they are not part of the domestic system, although they are closely linked to domestic systems through international transactions.

The term 'Eurodollar market' is sometimes used in the widest sense to encompass not only the market for dollars outside the United States but also the market for Euro-yen, Eurosterling, etc. In this kind of usage, the term 'Eurodollar market' becomes synonymous with the Eurocurrency market.

The gross size of the Eurocurrency market is the sum of all Eurocurrency liabilities, including the many inter-bank deposits on the books of Eurobanks. The total amount of credit extended to end-users is best measured by the net figure, which excludes inter-bank deposits and considers only deposits or loan transactions between Eurobanks and non-bank users of funds.

Eurobonds are bonds denominated in currencies other than that of the country in which the bonds are sold – for example, dollar-denominated bonds in London or sterling-denominated bonds in Luxembourg. Although the Eurobond market achieves the same ends as the Eurodollar market, it is distinctly different. In the Eurodollar market, financial institutions have traditionally played an intermediate role by bearing the risk of lending; in the Eurobond market this risk is borne directly by the lender.

Eurobanks are financial intermediaries that bid for time deposits and make loans in currencies other than that of the country in which they are located.

LIBOR, the London inter-bank offered rate, is the interest rate at which London Euromarket banks offer funds for deposit in the inter-bank market. It is the most usually quoted base for Eurocurrency transactions. The interest cost to the borrower is set as a spread over the LIBOR rate. Spreads over LIBOR have ranged from around 0.25 per cent to 2 per cent. There is, of course, a separate LIBOR for each of the many currencies in which inter-bank loans are made in London. Similarly, EURIBOR (a reference rate for euros) is becoming very widely used in international financial markets.

We now consider reserve asset requirements. Domestic and foreign banks taking deposits and lending in the currency of the country in which they operate are, in most financially sophisticated countries, required to hold asset reserves equal to a specified percentage of their deposit liabilities. These assets are usually required to be held in minimal interest-bearing forms. This situation contrasts with that relating to Eurocurrency deposits. Eurocurrency holdings are not subject to reserve asset requirements. Eurobanks are therefore able to lend at more competitive rates than their domestic counterparts, since part of their portfolio of assets is not tied up in low-interest-bearing reserve assets.

The term 'currency swap' also needs definition. A currency swap is an agreement to exchange specified amounts of two different currencies immediately on a spot basis and to reverse the transaction at an agreed exchange rate at a stated time in the future. In a swap transaction, the swap rate is all important. This is the difference between the price at which a currency is bought and the price at which it is sold. The difference reflects the interest rate differential between the two currencies.

Market operators frequently talk of the Asian dollar market. This is simply that segment of the Eurocurrency market which is operated in the Far East and is centred primarily on Singapore and to a lesser extent on Hong Kong.

Finally in this section on definitions, we look briefly at syndicated Eurocredits. Eurocredit lending is the medium-term (and occasionally long-term) market for Eurocurrency loans provided by an organized group of financial institutions. Through grouping, with lenders each taking a small share of a loan, diversification can be achieved. The currencies lent need not be those of either borrower or lender. However, loans are made on a one-to-one basis and this has become more common in the bank lending to the corporate-sector market.

27.5 | Eurodollar deposits and loans

The most important distinction between the Eurodollar banking market and domestic banking is that Eurocurrency markets are not subject to domestic banking regulations. Because of the absence of this constraint on profitability, Eurobanks may obtain the same profit levels as domestic banks even though they achieve lower spreads on lending depositors' funds than their domestic counterparts. This is, in fact, what happens in the market. The absence of reserve requirements and regulations enables Eurobanks to offer slightly better terms to both borrowers and lenders. Eurodollar deposit rates are somewhat higher, and effective lending rates a little lower, than they are in domestic money markets. The absence of regulations is the key to the success of the Eurocurrency markets.

Deep Euromarkets exist only in those currencies, such as the US dollar, and sterling, that are relatively freely convertible into other currencies. Eurobanks are located in those centres that refrain from regulating foreign currency banking activities.

A Eurodollar deposit may be created and lent on in the manner set out below. A US corporation with $2m surplus funds decides to take advantage of the more attractive Eurodollar rates on deposits relative to domestic dollars. The company's surplus funds were held originally in a time deposit in a local branch of a US bank. On maturing of this deposit the company replaces its time deposit with a demand deposit in the local US bank. The company transfers ownership, by payment, of the demand deposit in the local US bank to the US bank in London, where a time deposit is made. This process creates a Eurodollar deposit, substituting for an equivalent domestic time deposit in a US bank. The London branch of the US bank deposits the cheque in its account in a US bank. The US company holds a dollar deposit in a bank in London rather than in the United States. The total deposits of the banks in the United States remains unchanged. However, investors hold smaller deposits in the United States and larger deposits in London. The London bank now has a larger deposit in the United States. The increase in the London bank's deposits in the US bank is matched by the increase in dollar deposits for the world as a whole. The volume of dollar deposits in the United States remains unchanged, while the volume in London increases.

The London bank will not leave the newly acquired $2 million idle. If the bank does not have a commercial borrower or government to which it can lend the funds, it will place the $2m in the Eurodollar inter-bank market. In other words, it will deposit the funds in some other Eurobank.

If this second Eurobank cannot immediately use the funds to make a loan, it will redeposit them again in the inter-bank market. This process of redepositing might proceed through several Eurobanks before the $2m finds its way to a final borrower. At each stage the next bank will pay a slightly higher rate than the previous bank paid. But the margins involved in the inter-bank market are very small – of the order of $^1/_8$ per cent. As a rule, larger, better-known banks will receive initial deposits while smaller banks will have to bid for deposits in the inter-bank market.

This inter-bank redepositing of an original Eurodollar deposit merely involves the passing on of funds from bank to bank. It does not, of course, add to the final extension of credit in the financial markets. Only when the $2m is lent on to a corporation or a government or other non-bank borrower is credit eventually and effectively extended. To evaluate the true credit-creation capacity of the Eurodollar market, inter-bank deposits have to be netted out. The ultimate stage in the credit-creating process occurs when a Eurobank lends funds to a non-bank borrower.

Loans made in the Euromarket are similar to those made domestically by UK and US banks and so on. More lending is done on a corporate reputation or name basis, as it is sometimes called, to well-known entities, with less credit investigation and documentation being involved than in domestic lending. When the amount needed is greater than one Eurobank is prepared to provide, borrowers obtain funds by tapping a syndicate of banks from different countries. Borrowers often have the option of borrowing in any of several currencies. Eurocurrency loans may be for short-term working capital or trade finance, or they may have maturities up to ten years. The latter would be called medium-term Eurocredits, although they are basically no different from their short-term counterparts. When a Eurocurrency loan or commitment has a maturity of more than six months, the interest rate is usually set on a roll-over basis – that is, at the start of each three- or six-month period, it is reset at a fixed amount (e.g. 1 per cent) above the prevailing London inter-bank offered rate.

Eurocurrency deposits often carry interest rates of $\frac{1}{2}$ per cent higher than domestic deposits (since they avoid domestic interest rate ceilings where they exist) and borrowers can obtain cheaper money in Euromarkets as opposed to domestic ones. So why do not all depositors and borrowers shift their business into the Eurocurrency market? One reason is the existence of exchange controls. Many governments make it difficult for depositors to invest abroad, and many restrict foreign borrowing by domestic companies. Another reason is the inconvenience and cost involved with maintaining balances or borrowing in a foreign country. Furthermore, the market is largely a wholesale one, and deals in sums of under $1m are not available. Euro-banks also prefer to lend to large, well-known corporations, banks or governments. But the most important difference is that Eurodeposits, because they are located in a different country, are in some respects subject to the jurisdiction of that country. This is referred to as the 'sovereign risk' characteristic of Eurocurrency markets and is discussed later in the chapter.

27.6 | Historical underpinnings of the Eurocurrency market

Ironically, the initial stimulus to the world's largest and least regulated international market for credit – the Eurocurrency market – was provided allegedly by the actions of the world's main socialist states. Shortly after the Second World War, the Soviet Union and its satellites and the Republic of China decided to hold their dollar assets in banks in Paris and London, rather than banks in the United States. These communist countries feared, first, that their deposits in the United States might be blocked and, secondly, that their funds might be attacked by US residents with claims against communist country governments.

Growth of this rather small Eurocurrency market was stimulated in the late 1950s. In 1957 the United Kingdom placed restrictions on the use of sterling for financing third-country trade. This policy followed the Suez crisis and one of the recurrent weaknesses of sterling. Encouraged to do so by the Bank of England, UK bankers turned to the dollar to finance trade – hence their interest in tapping the Eurodollar market. Also during the late 1950s, many European countries relaxed their exchange controls for the first time since the war. Dollar convertibility was widely restored and the US domestic money market was reopened for the first time since the early 1930s. These features led investors to move their funds more freely and gave lenders and borrowers more options.

But the take-off stage for the Euromarket did not come until the middle to late 1960s when the net size of the market tripled. Three restrictions in the United States played a substantial part in this growth. The interest equalization tax, which was brought in during 1963, imposed a penalty on US residents buying securities issued by foreigners. This encouraged the creation of alternative sources of medium- and long-term financing and the Eurocurrency and newly emerging Eurobond markets grew in response to this demand. Furthermore, voluntary restrictions on direct foreign investment, which were set up in 1965 and made mandatory in 1968, forced US multinationals to raise funds for their overseas operations outside the United States.

Also the Federal Reserve Bank's foreign credit restraint programme closed off the opportunity for foreign borrowers, including foreign-based affiliates of US companies, to borrow medium-term debt in the United States.

These regulations had the effect of encouraging the use of the Euromarkets. Growth continued at a rapid pace even after the removal of the US restrictions in 1974. A further key influence in the market's growth was Regulation Q. This was first implemented in 1966 and limited the amount of interest that commercial banks in the United States were allowed to pay on time deposits. It resulted in very large shifts of corporate moneys into non-bank financial assets and into the Eurodollar market. This gave an enormous boost to the Eurocurrency market in 1966, and again in 1969 and 1970, when regulations intensified. US banks began to set up foreign branches to have easier access to the Eurocurrency market. The liabilities of US banks to their foreign branches increased from $2bn to $15bn between 1967 and 1969. Subsequently, larger certificates of deposit – those over £100,000 – were exempted from Regulation Q. Nevertheless the Eurocurrency market, with its obvious attractiveness of higher rates for depositors and lower rates for borrowers than domestic markets, continued to grow. Regulation Q was finally phased out in 1986. But the growth of the Eurocurrency market has continued strongly – nowadays its size is vast.

Growth of the Eurodollar market has also been influenced by the US balance of payments deficits and the redistribution of international wealth away from the United States. The recurrent US balance of payments deficit is not, however, viewed as itself being a reason for the growth of the Eurodollar market. Certainly repeated and substantial deficits have transferred wealth from the United States to other countries. But this does not mean that the dollars moving away from the United States should necessarily find their way into the Eurodollar market. Were domestic US dollar rates on deposits superior to offshore rates, then these dollars would probably find their way on to deposits within the United States. The fact is that, because the lower regulatory levels have meant that deposit rates are higher in the Eurodollar market, funds have found their way into the Eurocurrency arena. But why should these monies be allocated to the dollar-denominated segment of the Euromarket rather than to Euro-Deutschmarks or Euro-yen and so on? First, political risk is viewed as being lower on dollar assets than on most others. Secondly, the market is much larger. Hence it is possible to move more funds in and out of US dollars without affecting rates than is the case for any other currency in the world. The United States ran a repeated and substantial balance of payments deficit during the 1980s, financed by attracting funds from overseas via high real interest rates.

Some idea of the growth and size of the Eurocurrency market can be obtained from Table 27.2 (overleaf) which summarizes its development from 1980 to 1996. By 1999, the market had reached a total of $5.5 trillion (one trillion equals one thousand billion).

27.7 | The players in the market

The Eurocurrency market is entirely a wholesale market. Transactions are rarely for less than $1m and sometimes they are for $100m. Like the foreign exchange markets,

Table 27.2 Eurocurrency market 1980–1996

Year	Market turnover ($bn)	Year	Market turnover ($bn)
1980	755	1989	3,530
1981	1,155	1990	3,350
1982	1,285	1991	3,610
1983	1,382	1992	3,660
1984	1,430	1993	3,780
1985	1,678	1994	4,240
1986	2,076	1995	4,645
1987	2,584	1996	5,015
1988	3,200		

Source: Bank for International Settlements, *Annual Reports* (various years).

the vast bulk is confined to inter-bank operations. The largest non-banking companies have to deal via banks. Borrowers are the very highest pedigree corporate names carrying the lowest credit risks. The market is telephone linked or telecommunications linked and is focused on London, which has a share of around one-third of the Eurocurrency market. All Eurocurrency transactions are unsecured credits, hence the fact that lenders pay particular attention to borrowers' status and name.

Commercial banks form the institutional core of the market. Banks enter the Eurocurrency market both as depositors and as lenders. Around twenty of the world's biggest banks play a dominant role in the Euromarket. They attract a disproportionate volume of primary deposits, which are then re-lent to other Eurobanks. These banks link the external with the domestic market, taking funds from one and placing them in other markets. The breadth and depth of the inter-bank market enable banks to adjust liquidity positions with great ease.

Corporations borrowing Eurocurrencies are mainly those whose name, size and good standing enable banks to make loans to them with little more than a superficial analysis of creditworthiness. But more recently the range of corporate and government borrowers has widened to embrace less good names. The main reason for this is the vast amount of funds available for lending. In the last decade the market has also seen an expansion in government and government-related borrowers. This is especially true of the medium-term Eurocredit market, which has become widely tapped for infrastructure projects and for financing balance of payments deficits. Governments and central banks are also lenders in the Eurocurrency markets. In addition, international institutions such as the World Bank and various regional development banks, and institutions associated with the EU, have been regular borrowers. Private individuals are minor participants in the Eurodollar markets. High-net-worth people have, however, always been significant participants as investors in the Eurobond market, where the fact that payment of interest is gross of tax and securities are bearer securities gives the market anonymity and an obvious attractiveness from a tax point of view.

27.8 | Euromarket deposits and borrowings

Most deposits in the Eurocurrency market are time deposits at fixed interest rates, usually of short maturity. Around three-quarters of deposits in London Eurobanks have maturities of less than three months. Many of these deposits are on call; thus they can be withdrawn without notice. Most of the time deposits are made by other banks, but many are made by governments and their central banks as well as multinational corporations. A few are made by wealthy individuals, often through a Swiss bank.

Deposits come in many forms. Besides negotiable Eurodollar certificates of deposit (sometimes termed London dollar CDs), there are various similar certificates of deposit. Floating rate notes (FRNs) have become popular for longer maturity deposits, including floating rate CDs.

Many Eurodollar loans are direct, bank-to-customer credits on the basis of formal lines of credit or customer relationships. However, the market has developed the technique of loan syndication for very large currencies. The Eurocurrency syndication technique arose principally because of the large size of credits required by some government borrowers and multinational firms. The syndication procedure allows banks to diversify some of the unique sovereign risks that arise in international lending. Syndicated Euroloans involve formal arrangements in which competitively selected lead banks assemble a management group of other banks to underwrite the loan and to market participation in it to other banks.

Interest on syndicated loans is usually computed by adding a spread to LIBOR, although the US prime rate is also used as a basis for interest pricing. LIBOR interest rates change continuously, of course. The rate on any particular loan is usually readjusted every three or six months on to the prevailing LIBOR rate – this method of pricing is known as a roll-over basis.

27.9 | The Eurocredit market

The Eurocredit market, sometimes called the medium-term Eurocredit market, or the medium-term Eurocurrency market, is defined as the market for loans in currencies which are not native to the country in which the bank office making the loans is located. The Eurocredit market is concerned with medium- and long-term loans. Banks are the major lenders, with major borrowers being large multinational companies, international organizations and governments (frequently in developing countries). Generally, Eurocredits are extended by a large group of banks from many countries. The risk of loan default is spread among many banks.

27.10 | Loan syndication

There are usually three categories of bank in a loan syndicate. There are lead banks, managing banks and participating banks. In large credits, there is a separate group called co-managers. This group comprises participating banks providing more than a specified amount of funds. Most loans are led by one or two major banks which negotiate to obtain a mandate from the borrower to raise funds. After the preliminary stages of negotiation with a borrower, the lead bank begins to assemble the management group, which commits itself to provide the entire amount of the loan, if necessary. Portions of the loan are then marketed to participating banks.

In the early stages of negotiation with a borrower, the lead bank assembles a management group to assure the borrower that the entire amount of the loan will be taken up. The management group may be in place before the mandate is received or may be assembled immediately afterwards. During this phase, the lead bank may renegotiate the terms and conditions of the loan if it cannot assemble a managing group on the initial terms. But, rather than renegotiate, many lead banks are willing to take more of the credit into their own portfolio than they had originally planned. The lead bank is normally expected to provide a share at least as large as any other bank. Once the lead bank has established the group of managing banks, it then commits the group to raise funds for the borrower on specified terms and conditions.

When the management group is established and the lead bank has received a mandate from the borrower, a placement memorandum is prepared by the lead bank and the loan is marketed to other banks which may be interested in taking up shares. Such lenders are termed the participating banks. The placement memorandum describes the transaction and gives information regarding the financial health of the borrower. The statistical information given in the memorandum is usually provided by the borrower.

The lead bank emphasizes that the placement memorandum is not a substitute for an independent credit review by participating banks, and such participating banks generally sign a statement that they have performed an independent analysis of the credit. However, smaller banks tend to rely heavily on the judgement of the lead and managing banks.

The lead bank bears the chief responsibility for marketing the loan, although other members of the managing group assist in this respect. There are three main methods used to find participants for syndicated credits. The borrower may specify that a certain bank should be given the opportunity to participate because the borrower wishes to establish a relationship with that bank. Often banks contact the borrower expressing an interest in participating in a given credit. But the bulk of participants are banks invited by the lead bank to join the syndication. Each major bank maintains files on the syndicated lending activities of other banks. The files contain lists of banks that have joined various syndications. This information enables the loan syndication officers at the lead bank to estimate which banks might be interested in which borrowers. Once a first list of potential participants has been assembled, the lead bank, operating through informal contacts in London and elsewhere, will try to determine which of the banks are interested in expanding their portfolio to particular borrowers and on what terms, and which banks are unwilling to increase their credit exposure to particular countries. From this analysis the list is finalized.

When a bank is invited to participate in a syndication, the amount and the terms and conditions it is being asked to accept are set out in a telex sent by the lead bank. This short-cuts the negotiation process and expedites the credit.

The lead bank usually offers to sell off more of the credit than it really wishes, since some of the banks that receive invitations will opt not to participate. An experienced lead bank can usually gauge the appropriate number of participation invitations to be extended. If the credit is attractive, fewer banks will be contacted. If the credit (based on terms and conditions) appears hard to place, a greater number of invitations will be sent out. If the loan is oversubscribed, the borrower is usually given the opportunity to borrow more money than initially negotiated on the same terms. If the borrower does not choose to take advantage of this, the amounts assigned to each bank are scaled down pro rata.

In a successful loan syndication, once the marketing to participants is completed, the lead and managing banks usually keep 50–75 per cent of their initial underwritten share. The lead bank is generally expected to take into its portfolio about 10 per cent of the total credit. This rule of thumb does not apply to very large credits, where a 10 per cent commitment to a single borrower may, when taken with credits to the borrower already in the bank's portfolio, give the bank an excess exposure in relation to its capital. It is not acceptable market practice for a bank to lead and arrange a credit and not take any portion of the credit into its own portfolio. It takes from two weeks to three months to arrange a syndication, with six weeks as the norm – the more familiar the borrower, the quicker the terms can be set and the placement memorandum prepared.

The most common type of syndicated loan is a term loan, where funds can be drawn down by the borrower within a specified time of the loan being signed – this is called the 'drawdown period'. Repayments are subsequently made in accordance with an amortization schedule. Sometimes amortization of loans commences almost immediately following drawdown. For other loans, amortization may not commence until five or six years after drawing down the loan. Sometimes term loans have no amortization over the life of the loan and all repayment is due on maturity – this kind of loan is termed a 'bullet loan'. Loans that require repayment according to an amortization schedule and include a larger final payment on maturity are termed 'balloon repayment loans'. The period prior to the commencement of repayment is termed the 'grace period'. The extent of the grace period is usually a major negotiating point between borrower and lead bank. Borrowers are usually willing to pay a wider spread in order to obtain a longer grace period.

Syndicated loans of the revolving credit type are occasionally encountered. In these, the borrower is given a line of credit which it may draw down and repay with greater flexibility than under a term loan. Borrowers pay a fee on the undrawn amount of the credit line.

Additional to interest costs on a loan, there are also front-end fees, commitment fees and occasionally an annual agent's fee. Front-end management fees are one-off charges negotiated in advance and imposed when the loan agreement is signed. These fees are usually in the range of 0.5 to 1 per cent of the value of the loan. The fees may be higher if a particular borrower insists upon obtaining funds at a lower spread than is warranted by market conditions and creditworthiness.

The relationship between spreads and fees is hard to quantify, as data on all fees are usually unobtainable. But there is some evidence to suggest that banks will accept lower spreads if compensated by higher fees, since they are interested in the total return on the loan. Some borrowers prefer to pay a higher fee, which is not published, while going on record as paying a low spread. Over time, demand and supply conditions determine both spreads and fees. During periods of easy market conditions, borrowers can command low fees and low spreads. During periods when banks are reluctant to extend credit, high spreads and high fees are the norm.

Front-end fees consist of participation fees and management fees. Each of these typically amounts to between 0.25 and 0.5 per cent of the entire amount of the loan. Participation fees are divided among all banks in relation to their share of the loan. The management fees are divided between the underwriting banks and the lead bank. The lead bank usually takes a *praecipium* – an overall fee – on the entire loan. The rest of the management fee is divided among the managing banks in proportion to the amount each agrees to underwrite prior to syndication.

In addition to front-end fees, borrowers may pay commitment fees. These fees are charged to the borrower as a percentage of the undrawn portion of the credit in return for the bank tying up part of its credit capacity on behalf of the borrower, even though the loan has not yet been drawn down and does not earn any interest for the bank. Commitment fees of 0.375 to 0.5 per cent per annum are typically imposed on both term loans and revolving credits.

The agent's fee, if applicable, is usually a yearly charge but may occasionally be paid at the outset. The agent's fee is relatively small; on a large credit it may amount to $10,000 annually and is meant to cover administrative and minor incidental expenses related to the syndication.

To protect their margins, banks usually require all payments of principal and interest to be made after taxes imposed have been paid. If those taxes are not creditable against the banks' home country taxes, the borrower must adjust payments so that the banks receive the same net repayment. The decision as to whether the borrower or lender absorbs any additional taxes imposed by the country in which the loan is booked is negotiated between the parties. Additionally, a reserve requirement clause is generally inserted, stipulating that an adjustment will be made if the cost of funds increases because reserve requirements are imposed or increased.

There is generally no prepayment penalty on Eurocredits. The charges on syndicated loans may be summarized as follows:

Annual payments = (LIBOR + spread)
  × amount of loan drawn down and outstanding
  + commitment fee × amount of loan undrawn
  + annual agent's fee (if any)
  + tax adjustment (if any)
  + reserve requirement adjustment (if any)

Front-end charges = lead bank *praecipium* × total amount of loan
  + participation fee × face amount of loan
  + management fee × face amount of loan
  + initial agent's fee (if any)

27.11 | Securitization

During the mid-1980s, a number of influences affected the syndicated lending market and changed its nature. The volume of funds intermediated through international capital markets remained firm but there was a switch away from the syndicated loan. Why should this have been so?

The underpinning reason is to be found in the fact that international banks' ratios were showing a sharp decline as they increasingly reported bad loans and provided for other doubtful debts. The key ratios of capital to assets deteriorated for a wide spectrum of banks towards levels which regulating central banks regard as imprudent. In syndicated lending, banks take a deposit and re-lend. The effect of this flows through to banks' ratios. The banks themselves therefore increasingly sought ways to make profit off balance sheet. They looked for ways to transfer money from lenders to borrowers while collecting a fee for so doing, but without affecting their own balance sheets, and they came up with the formula of securitization, or disintermediation as it is sometimes called. Their approach involved the increasing use of the Eurobond and the Euronote issuance facility. Eurobonds are looked at later in this chapter but Euronotes are considered here.

The Euronote technique involves a reallocation of roles within the international capital market, the impact of which is to allow borrowers to raise what is effectively medium-term, say five- to seven-year, money at very low rates available traditionally only in the short-term money markets. A borrower which raises money in the Euronote market does so by the issue of short-term notes, with maturities of three and six months, that are negotiable like certificates of deposit and can be placed with non-bank investors such as large companies and central banks. As one issue of notes matures after three or six months, the borrower issues some more, so that, while the holders of the debt change over time, the total amount outstanding in the market can be maintained in the medium term. But borrowers have to be sure that they will always be able to find buyers for their notes in the market. If they could not, they might find that they had to pay down the debt before the planned maturity. Because of this, a Euronote facility is normally backed up or underwritten by a group of commercial banks which stands ready to buy the paper at a specified price or to provide credit should the appetite of short-term investors wane.

The traditional function of commercial banks, which was to lend money over the medium term, has been split. Instead of lending money, commercial banks simply commit their resources, under Euronote issuance facilities, to guaranteeing that it will be available over the medium term. The actual funds are provided from elsewhere in the market – for example, by non-bank investors looking for a short-term home for their surplus cash.

Linked to the deterioration of banks' capital ratios and the success of the Euronote issuance facility is the fact that prime companies and developed country governments have appeared as more attractive propositions to lenders than placing money with bankers. So much so that some have been borrowing in the Euronote markets at between five and ten basis points (between one-twentieth and one-tenth of a percentage point) below LIBOR.

Lead banks, in attempts at product differentiation in this market, have packaged Euronote deals in marginally different ways, giving rise to numerous acronyms which include NIFs (note issuance facilities), RUFs (revolving underwriting facilities), MOFFs (multiple option funding facilities), TRUFs (transferable revolving underwriting facilities) and BONUS (borrower's option for notes and underwritten standby) – and there are more appearing all the time.

27.12 | Eurocurrency interest rates and their linkage with domestic rates

Each Eurocurrency market, whether it be Eurodollars, Eurosterling or whatever, is linked through arbitrage to its domestic counterpart. Hence Eurocurrency rates are strongly influenced by domestic rates. Because there is no regulating authority to set interest rates in the Euromarkets and no one set of banks enforces administered rates, Eurocurrency interest rates are determined by the forces of competition.

Furthermore, domestic and external markets compete for funds. The essential starting point to the analysis of the relationship between domestic and external interest rates is a clear understanding of what the Eurocurrency market is. Using the United States and the US dollar for illustration, the Eurodollar market (external) and the domestic market (internal) are merely competing segments of the total market for dollar-denominated credit, intermediated by financial institutions operating either internally (domestic banks) or externally (Eurobanks). The Eurodollar market competes with the domestic US credit market for deposits and for the making of loans. Within this competitive arena, the Eurocurrency segment possesses certain unique characteristics:

- Eurobanks are not required to maintain reserves against their deposit liabilities.

- Eurobanks are less subject to regulation.

- Eurobanks are not subject to interest rate ceilings, whether imposed by government or by cartel.

- Eurobanks can take better advantage of low-tax locations.

- High degrees of competitiveness, and virtually unrestricted entry, force Eurobanks to keep margins small and overhead costs low.

- Eurobanks are less subject than domestic markets to pressure to allocate credit for socially valued but unprofitable purposes.

- Eurobanks are subject to greater risk than domestic banks (see later in this section).

Given that the Eurodollar market and the domestic dollar money markets deal in the same currency and that there is very considerable freedom for capital to move between these markets in response to interest rate differentials, it is no coincidence that interest rate structures are closely linked. In the absence of specific obstacles and barriers (such as exchange controls), arbitrage between the domestic and external segments of the dollar-denominated money markets ensures close correspondence both in terms of rate levels and in terms of timing and magnitude of rate changes. This close cleavage of rates has regularly been demonstrated in empirical work; but where exchange controls or the like are in place, the tendency for the close movement of rates in domestic and external markets is found to be much weaker. Indeed, an indication of the efficacy of capital controls can be seen in the degree of divergence of interest rates in the two markets. Wide divergences are associated with tight capital controls, and vice versa.

In our earlier discussions on the four-way equivalence model, we found that the major influences upon Eurocurrency interest rates, currency expectations and forward exchange rates might be summarized as follows:

- Eurocurrency interest rate differential = forward premium or discount (this is known as interest rate parity).

- Forward premium or discount = expected change in exchange rate (expectations theory).

- Expected change in exchange rate = Eurocurrency interest rate differential (international Fisher effect).

- Eurocurrency interest rate differential = difference in expected inflation rates (Fisher effect).

It should be recalled – and this is most important – that when using the four-way equivalence model, interest rate differentials must be based upon Eurocurrency interest rates. It should also be recalled that, empirically, interest rate parity is the only one of the above equivalences which is found to hold in the short term.

That Eurocurrency rates do not exactly equal domestic interest rates is explained in the main by regulatory factors such as reserve requirements affecting one market but not the other. The extent to which reserve requirements impinge upon rates can be demonstrated by a simplified numerical example. Assume that a US bank receives $10m in domestic deposits and that the reserve requirement (which has to be deposited with the central bank and does not earn any interest) is 5 per cent. The effective funds received, then, amount to only $9.5m – that is, 95 per cent of the deposit. Assume further that the bank pays 15 per cent per annum on the full $10m. The effective cost of the funds in the domestic deposit is therefore given by:

$$\text{Effective cost of domestic deposit} = \frac{\text{Interest rate paid}}{1 - \text{Reserve requirement}}$$

$$= \frac{15\%}{1 - 0.05}$$

$$= 15.79\%$$

The additional cost of the reserve requirement is therefore 79 basis points. This is the extra amount that the bank can afford to pay on Eurodollar deposits (which avoid reserve requirements) to achieve the same true cost of funds.

Another major reason for different interest rate levels in domestic and external markets arises because of perceived differences in risk. These risk differences can best be explained with the help of an example. A US depositor in the Eurodollar market holds a claim in one location – for example, London – but may ultimately receive payment in the United States. The depositor might be deprived of its funds at maturity by an action of either the UK or the US government. In the case of a domestic deposit, it is only the actions of one government that can affect the deposit.

Of course, it is also possible to argue that Euromarkets may actually reduce risk. In countries where new capital controls upon disposition of residents' funds are feared, external deposits might well be considered less risky by residents than leaving funds on domestic deposits. As well as indirect interference through government regulations, depositors may be concerned with direct government intervention. The government of the country in which the Eurobank operates may seize the assets of the bank and block repayment of liabilities or otherwise restrict its activities through political action. The scenario might be as follows. In a fit of nationalism or in an attempt to alleviate foreign exchange difficulties, the government of a country where Eurocurrency deposits and loans are made intervenes in the operations of branches of foreign banks within its territory. This is the kind of risk termed 'sovereign risk' in Eurobanking. And, by definition, it is always present in the Eurocurrency business. Eurobanking involves attracting funds from non-residents and making loans to other non-residents. If very few of the Eurobank's assets are directly subject to the host country's jurisdiction, then offshore operations are at risk only if that government is able to press its claims in the jurisdictions of the borrowers against the competing claims of the parent bank. Another fear is that, while the central banks of various countries are often perceived as being ready to bail out any major bank whose domestic operations get into trouble, they might not do so for offshore branches. After all, who is the lender of last resort when difficulties originate from loans on the books of foreign affiliates?

In short, the risks associated with external dollar deposits and loans are usually greater than those associated with their domestic counterparts. These greater risks stem from the possibility of government intervention of not just one, but two or more countries, and from the possibility that central banks might not function as lenders of last resort for Eurobanks.

Just as there is a relationship between domestic and external interest rates, so Eurodollar interest rates of different maturities follow similar term structures to domestic rates. Interest rates of the same maturity move in tandem in the two markets. Generally, long-term rates are less volatile than short-term rates. This is because short-term rates are very sensitive to the near-term outlook for credit conditions, whereas long-term rates are affected to a greater degree by long-term inflationary expectations.

The relationship between domestic and eurocurrency credit markets is summarized in Figure 27.1.

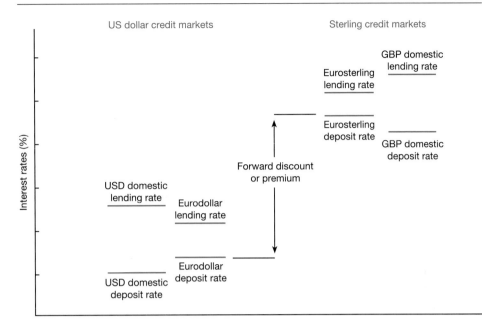

Figure 27.1 Interest relationships in domestic and eurocurrency credit markets.

27.13 | The international bond market

Money may be raised internationally by bond issues and by bank loans. This is done in domestic as well as international markets. The difference is that in international markets the money may come in a currency which is different from that normally used by the borrower. The characteristic feature of the international bond market is that bonds are always sold outside the country of the borrower. There are three main types of bond, of which two are international bonds. A domestic bond is a bond issued in a country by a resident of that country. A foreign bond is a bond issued in a particular country by a foreign borrower. Eurobonds are bonds underwritten and sold in more than one country.

A foreign bond may be defined as an international bond sold by a foreign borrower but denominated in the currency of the country in which it is placed. It is underwritten and sold by a national underwriting syndicate in the lending country. Thus, a US company might float a bond issue in the London capital market, underwritten by a British syndicate and denominated in sterling. The foreign bond issue would be sold to investors in the UK capital market, where it would be quoted and traded. It would be called a Bulldog bond. Foreign bonds issued within the United States are called Yankee bonds, while foreign bonds issued in Japan are called Samurai bonds. Canadian entities are the major floaters of foreign bonds in the United States.

A Eurobond may be defined as an international bond underwritten by an international syndicate and sold in countries other than the country of the currency in

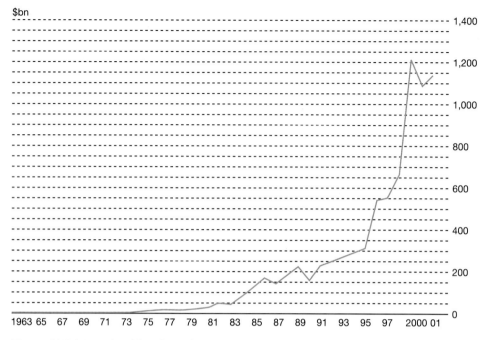

Figure 27.2 International bond new issue value.

Source: IFR; Bank for International Settlements.

which the issue is denominated. An example of a Eurobond transaction would be an issue by a German company of dollar-denominated bonds through a consortium of UK merchant banks, a large German bank and the overseas affiliate of an American investment bank.

US government restrictions introduced in 1964 gave the Eurobond market a considerable boost. Faced with a rising balance of payments deficit, the US authorities introduced the interest equalization tax. The objective of this was to close the New York capital market to borrowers from abroad. At the same time, restrictions were placed on the amount of funds that US multinationals could raise in the United States for overseas operations. These restrictions, which have since been lifted, caused borrowers and lenders to shift their activities from New York to Europe. This set the stage for the rapid growth of the Eurobond market.

Some idea of the growth of issues of international bonds, from the sixties to the current time may be obtained from Figure 27.2. When the euro was created in 1999, it immediately became an important currency for bond denomination – see Table 27.3.

In the Eurobond market, the investor holds a claim directly on the borrower rather than on a financial institution. Eurobonds are generally issued by corporations and governments needing secure, long-term funds and are sold through a geographically diverse group of banks to investors around the world.

Eurobonds are similar to domestic bonds in that they may be issued with fixed or floating interest rates. But they possess a number of distinctive features:

Table 27.3 Net international bond and note issues, by currency ($bn)

	1995	1997	1998	1999	2000	2001
US dollar	74.1	321.4	404.3	525.8	554.1	547.6
Euro	–	–	–	508.9	406.0	473.8
D-mark	55.1	43.0	69.1	–	–	–
Pound sterling	10.1	46.8	55.3	77.8	91.9	65.9
French franc	5.2	34.0	27.1	–	–	–
Hong Kong dollar	4.0	1.7	6.9	6.0	4.9	–
Swiss franc	4.4	−0.2	7.0	3.9	3.5	−2.8
Australian dollar	14.3	2.1	−4.5	0.8	−1.0	–
Canadian dollar	−2.1	−6.3	−7.8	−2.3	−2.6	−2.1
Yen	108.4	31.7	−24.7	−23.1	11.2	13.3

Source: Bank for International Settlements.

- The issuing technique takes the form of a placing rather than formal issuing; this avoids national regulations on new issues.

- Eurobonds are placed simultaneously in many countries through syndicates of underwriting banks which sell them to their investment clientele throughout the world.

- Unlike foreign bonds, Eurobonds are sold in countries other than that of the currency of denomination; thus dollar-denominated Eurobonds are sold outside the United States.

- The interest on Eurobonds is not subject to withholding tax.

Bonds are usually issued through a special financing subsidiary, often in a tax haven, thus ensuring the absence of withholding tax. The subsidiary issuing the bonds, usually in the form of bearer bonds, has a parent company guarantee. Threats of governments to impose withholding taxes on Eurobond interest would be likely, were they to crystallize, to result merely in relocation to ensure the non-impact of such taxes.

There are a number of different types of Eurobond. A straight bond is one having a specified interest coupon and a specified maturity date. Straight bonds may be issued with a floating rate of interest. Such bonds may have their interest rate fixed at six-month intervals at a stated margin over the LIBOR for deposits in the currency of the bond. So, in the case of a Eurodollar bond, the interest rate may be based upon LIBOR for Eurodollar deposits. In the case of bonds based on euros, the interest rate will be related to EURIBOR. Floating rate notes have come to represent an increasing proportion of new issues on the Eurobond market. Interest on these bonds is paid at the end of each six-month period. Such bonds usually carry guaranteed minimum interest. If a bond has an interest rate of LIBOR plus 1 per cent with a minimum of 6 per cent and if LIBOR were to fall below 5 per cent, the interest would remain at 6 per cent. Floating rate notes (FRNs) help to eliminate risk for investors by keeping long-term interest receipts in line with prevailing short-term interest rates.

Table 27.4 Eurobond issues classified by type 1980–1996 (%)

	1980	*1982*	*1984*	*1986*	*1988*	*1990*	*1992*	*1994*	*1996*
Straight	68	70	52	65	72	69	80	70	68
Floating-rate note	22	22	39	25	11	18	13	21	25
Equity related	9	9	8	8	17	14	7	9	7

Source: BIS, annual reports, various.

Table 27.5 Euronotes: amounts outstanding at year end 1986–1996 ($bn)

	1986	*1988*	*1990*	*1992*	*1994*	*1996*
Euronotes	29.4	72.3	111.3	177.1	378.7	834.1
of which:						
short-term notes*	29.0	66.7	89.4	115.7	119.3	172.0
medium-term notes	0.4	5.6	21.9	61.4	259.4	662.1

* Combines eurocommercial paper and other short-term notes.
Source: BIS, annual report, various years.

A convertible Eurobond is a bond having a specified interest coupon and maturity date, but it includes an option for the holder to convert its bonds into an equity share of the company at a conversion price set at the time of issue.

An indication of the breakdown of Eurobonds by type, over the period 1980 to 1996, is given in Table 27.4.

Medium-term Euronotes are shorter-term Eurobonds with maturities ranging from three to eight years. Their issuing procedure is less formal than for large bonds. Interest rates on Euronotes can be fixed or variable. Medium-term Euronotes are similar to medium-term roll-over Eurodollar credits. The difference is that in the Eurodollar market lenders hold a claim on a bank and not directly on the borrower. The amount of Euronotes outstanding is shown in Table 27.5.

The issue of Eurobonds is normally undertaken by a consortium of international banks. The procedures for placing are similar to those for syndicated loans detailed earlier in this chapter. The borrower may be a large corporation or a government. The borrower normally asks a major international bank to arrange the issue. A managing syndicate, including at least four or five leading banks, plus a bank from the borrowing country, is then organized. Eurobonds are placed, rather than formally issued, with the banks' clientele of international investors. In the past, Eurobond underwriting and fee costs have come out at between 2 and $2\frac{1}{2}$ per cent, divided between the following parts:

Management fee	0.375–0.5 per cent
Underwriting fee	0.375–0.5 per cent
Selling concession	1.250–1.5 per cent
Total gross spread	2.000–2.5 per cent

A record of the transaction called a 'tombstone' is subsequently published in the financial press. Those banks whose names appear at the top of the tombstone have agreed to subscribe to the issue. At a second level, a much larger underwriting syndicate is mentioned. The banks in the managing syndicate will have made arrangements with a worldwide group of underwriters, mainly banks and security dealers. After arranging the participation of a number of underwriters, the managing syndicate will have made a firm offer to the borrower, which obtains the funds from the loan immediately. At a third level, the underwriting group usually arranges for the sale of the issue through an even larger selling group of banks, brokers and dealers.

Eurobond issues have been made in a wide variety of currencies and composite currencies. These include US dollars, sterling, euros (and the predecessor currencies of the euro), Swiss francs, SDRs and so on. Issues generally have been for $10m upwards, towards $1bn and often beyond this figure.

In addition, there is the US domestic debt market. Over six times as large as its UK counterpart, it is, with the exception of the Euromarket, the largest in the world. It is also the most technically complicated in which to borrow. This means that only the largest foreign companies are able to justify the investment in set-up costs necessary to tap the market.

The US Securities and Exchange Commission (SEC) is responsible for setting standards and reviewing the content of all issue prospectuses. It also sets the standard for certain routine reports that companies must comply with if they are listed on one of the US stock markets or have public bonds in issue. As a result of this involvement, the documentation associated directly and indirectly with a money-raising operation in the United States is much greater than in any comparable market. Although the amount of compulsory disclosure is high, it is not really significantly higher than that usually met voluntarily by most major UK companies.

Another novelty for the first-time borrower in the US domestic debt market is the requirement that it must be rated by the two rating agencies. It is from this rating procedure that the term 'triple A' for the very highest quality of credit comes. Moody's writes Aaa, while Standard and Poor's writes AAA. After triple A comes double A and then three gradations of single A: A+, A and A–. Then comes triple B, which is the lowest rating acceptable in the bond market for a domestic credit. A foreign borrower would have to be rated single A to borrow, but if it were an initial borrowing it would probably have to be A+. The rating largely determines the coupon rate, although foreign borrowers can usually expect to pay around 50 basis points more than an equivalent rated and otherwise comparable domestic offer. It should be noted that it is the bond issue that is rated rather than the company; a company's whole spectrum of bond issues will usually carry the same rating but need not necessarily do so because of the varying quality of security. Each bond floated is rated prior to issue and the agencies monitor the rating, and may change it, through its life. This normally involves an annual review with occasional changes in rating.

The representatives of each rating agency require a comprehensive statement of affairs from the intending borrower. The data required will be greatly reduced if the borrower has already had bonds rated in the market. The statement is usually as strong on business strategy as on finance. It is reinforced by a number of senior executives submitting to a detailed interrogation. A new borrower would certainly

Table 27.6 Spreads between corporate bonds and
US Treasury bonds 1973–1987 (averages)

Rating	Basis points
AAA	43
AA	73
A	99
BBB	166
BB	299
B	404
CCC	724

Source: Cantor and Packer (1994).

be expected to field its chief executive and finance director. During this process, borrowers need the support of their investment bankers. Rating agency staff are extremely bright and sharp in debate. They specialize by industry. Given that they are being exposed to a great deal of confidential information, they have a very good insight into the strategies, structures and shares in market segments. The rating agencies give their rating decision to the borrower in confidence so that the company may withdraw the issue should the ratings be unacceptably low. The borrower may make representations at this stage, but the depth of analysis carried out makes it improbable that an agency will alter its rating. Agencies do not necessarily agree and split ratings are by no means unusual, but they persist only if they are one place apart. Should the gap be wider, a compromise will be reached with one or both agencies adjusting their rating. Where agreed, ratings are announced publicly and stand until they are adjusted on review. An idea of how bond ratings have been reflected in borrowing costs is given in Table 27.6. Comparisons of what is meant by various bond-rating agencies' categorizations is summarized in Table 27.7.

The scale of the US domestic bond market makes it attractive to large borrowers, but a significant sales effort is usually necessary, especially for first-time borrowers. Meetings to address investors are arranged, with a roadshow visiting financial centres; the quality of such presentations is a significant factor in the success of an issue.

It always has to be remembered that the United States is a highly litigious society. It is not expensive to lose a lawsuit in the United States because costs are not awarded in favour of the successful litigant. This means that it is always possible to find an attorney prepared to fight any fairly reasonable case on an opportunistic basis. If the attorney wins, he or she takes a percentage of the damages, but no basic fee is claimed, whether the case is won or lost. The managers of companies entering the US financial markets should not forget this. It means that they are exposed to the risk of action for damages from any investor which can demonstrate that it was misled by a prospectus. Consequently, documentation is intensively studied by the issue managers, their solicitors and the senior executives of the borrowing company to ensure its accuracy.

Table 27.7 What bond ratings mean*

	Moody's	Standard & Poor's	Fitch IBCA
Highest credit quality; issuer has strong ability to meet obligations	Aaa	AAA	AAA
Very high credit quality; low risk of default	Aa1 Aa2 Aa3	AA+ AA AA–	AA
High credit quality, but more vulnerable to changes in economy or business	A1 A2 A3	A+ A A–	A
Adequate credit quality for now, but more likely to be impaired if conditions worsen	Baa1 Baa2 Baa3	BBB+ BBB BBB–	BBB
Below investment grade, but good chance that issuer can meet commitments	Ba1 Ba2 Ba3	BB+ BB BB–	BB
Significant credit risk, but issuer is presently able to meet obligations	B1 B2 B3	B+ B B–	B
High default risk	Caa1 Caa2 Caa3	CCC+ CCC CCC–	CCC CC C
Issuer failed to meet scheduled interest or principal payments	C	D	DDD DD D

* Firms' precise definition of ratings vary.

Before leaving this brief review of the US domestic market, reference must be made to the US commercial paper market. The term 'commercial paper' simply means an unsecured promissory note usually issued by corporations for maturities from 1 to 270 days. This market is open to foreigners and has been tapped at extremely fine rates by UK and continental European companies. The market's size can be assessed by the figure of some $300bn outstanding at any one time, with an average life of twenty-two days. The market works rather like acceptance credits, with paper held largely by non-bank investors, although there is no secondary market in US commercial paper. Rates are usually lower than US banks' prime rates. To tap the commercial paper market, credit rating is required and this is again carried out by Moody's and Standard and Poor's, though the evaluation scale is a broader one and the investigation carried out is less penetrating. This market has been tapped by a wider range of non-US companies than the bond market and it is substantially less demanding in terms of cost and, since the SEC is not involved, of disclosure. We return to the topic of credit rating of bonds and commercial paper in Chapter 32.

Table 27.8 Breakdown of international financing 1980–1996 ($bn)

	1980	1982	1984	1986	1988	1990	1992	1994	1996
Net international bank lending*	160	95	90	206	260	465	195	190	410
Net international bond financing[†]	28	59	84	158	139	132	119	145	275
Net euronote placement[‡]			5	13	20	33	40	140	224
Total international financing	188	154	179	377	419	630	354	475	909
minus double counting[§]	8	9	24	82	69	80	75	60	196
Total net international financing	180	145	155	295	350	550	279	415	713
Bank lending as % of total financing	89	66	58	70	74	85	68	45	56

* Net figure excludes inter-bank lending but allows for banks' own use of external funds for domestic lending.
[†] Completed international bond issues (as distinct from announced bond issues) minus redemptions and repurchases.
[‡] Completed euronote placements (as distinct from announced issues recorded).
[§] Purchases of bonds by banks and bonds issued by banks to underpin international lending activities.
Source: BIS annual reports, various issues.

27.14 | Disintermediation

Borrowers can raise funds in the international markets by borrowing from the banking system, issuing equities, or issuing debt instruments, such as bonds or notes.

During the 1980s, international banks were beset by problems, such as bank failures in the United States and the sovereign debt crisis. This reduced the credit standing of many banks and, thus, the competitiveness of their lending rates. Consequently, many large borrowers with good credit ratings found that they could raise funds more cheaply directly themselves than through international banks. During some periods in the 1980s, corporates preferred direct financing rather than indirect financing through a bank intermediary. This is partially borne out by Table 27.8. Net international bank lending was a declining proportion of total net international financing over the period 1980 to 1985. This was because of the switch from bank financing to indirect financing through the capital markets, a process known as disintermediation. Eurobonds were the main alternative long-term funding security to bank intermediation in the early 1980s. In the mid-1980s, short-term and medium-term direct financing through the issue of Euronotes also emerged to compete with sydicated bank lending. This process tended to slacken in the latter half of the 1980s. The reason for this was principally the renewed growth in bank lending following improvement to bank balance sheets.

It would be wrong to link disintermediation with a decline in the role of banks. Banks are involved in this market by arranging the issue of disintermediating securities and underwriting or providing guarantees of liquidity in the Euronote markets.

It may be argued that disintermediation did not lead to an exclusion of banks from the international financing processes but merely transferred intermediation business that appeared on their balance sheet to a fee-earning business conducted off the balance sheet.

27.15 | The advantages of the Eurobond market to borrowers

The Eurobond markets possess a number of advantages for borrowers. These include the following:

- The size and depth of the market are such that it has the capacity to absorb large and frequent issues.

- The Eurobond market has a freedom and flexibility not found in domestic markets. The issuing techniques make it possible to bypass restrictions, such as requirements of official authorization, queuing arrangements, formal disclosure, exchange listing obligations and so forth, which govern the issue of securities by domestic as well as foreign borrowers in the individual national markets. All the financial institutions involved in Eurobond issues are subject to at least one national jurisdiction. National authorities can, and sometimes do, make their influence felt, especially when their own currency is used to denominate the issue.

- The cost of issue of Eurobonds, at on average less than 2.5 per cent of the face value of the issue, is relatively low.

- Interest costs on dollar Eurobonds are competitive with those in New York. Often US multinationals have been able to raise funds at a slightly lower cost in the Eurobond market than in the US domestic market.

- Maturities in the Eurobond market are suited to long-term funding requirements. Maturities may reach thirty years, but fifteen-year Eurobonds are more common. In the medium-term range, five- to ten-year Eurobonds run into competition with medium-term Eurodollar loans. But the longer maturities provide the assurance of funds availability at a known rate.

- A key feature of the Eurobond market is the development of a sound institutional framework for underwriting, distribution and placing of securities.

27.16 | The advantages of Eurobonds to investors

There are a number of special characteristics of the Eurobond market which make it particularly attractive to investors. These include the following:

- Eurobonds are issued in such a form that interest can be paid free of income or withholding taxes of the borrowing countries. Also, the bonds are issued in bearer form and are held outside the country of the investor, enabling the investor to evade domestic income tax. But some countries' exchange control regulations limit an investor's ability to purchase Eurobonds.

- Issuers of Eurobonds have, on the whole, an excellent reputation for creditworthiness. Most of the borrowers – governments, international organizations or large multinational companies – have first-class reputations. The market is very much a name market.

- A special advantage to borrowers as well as lenders is provided by convertible Eurobonds. Holders of convertible debentures are given an option to exchange their bonds at a fixed price and within a specified period for the stock of the parent company of the financing subsidiary. A bond with a warrant gives the bondholder an option to buy a certain number of shares of common stock at a stated price. The more the price of the underlying stock rises, the more valuable the warrant becomes. Since warrants are usually detachable, the bondholder may retain the bond but sell the warrants.

- The Eurobond market is active both as a primary and as a secondary market. The secondary market expanded in the late 1960s and early 1970s. Eurobonds are traded over the counter both locally and internationally by financial institutions that are ready to buy or sell Eurobonds for their own accounts or on behalf of their clients. Just as telecommunications linkages have integrated foreign exchange markets, so they have integrated the secondary market in Eurobonds. Since 1968 international trading in Eurobonds has been greatly facilitated by a clearing house arrangement formed by Morgan Guaranty Trust Company in Brussels and called Euroclear. Participants in Euroclear can complete transactions by means of book entries rather than physical movements of the securities. This has removed the main barrier to secondary market trading, which had been the inability to deliver bonds on time. There are now various other clearing arrangements in the market.

27.17 | Summary

- Through the achievement of an optimal gearing level, judicious debt strategy has a role to play in terms of maximization of shareholder value.

- In arriving at an optimal debt to equity level, a number of key factors are taken into consideration. These include the amount of business risk affecting the firm, the ability of the firm to service debt – especially in recessionary conditions – the perceived norm for the sector, the firm's track record and its future projections, its asset backing and financiers' lending policies and practices.

- Implementation of debt strategy includes a consideration of maturity profile, fixed/floating interest mix, interest rate sensitivity and currency mix. The conservative approach to debt raising is to match the maturity of borrowing to the maturity of assets. To tap long-term borrowing markets, the firm needs to demonstrate long-run profit- and cash-generating ability. In respect of the level of floating rate interest, the key consideration is the ability of the firm to service debt repayments and interest. The essential point is that recessionary cash generation should be sufficient to cover debt service. Remember that the obligation imposed by floating rate interest payments will be such that they will probably rise in recessionary conditions – especially at the start of the recession.

■ The correct balance between long-term and short-term debt needs to be struck in such a way that the maturity profile of debt does not introduce repayment difficulties for the firm. Debt maturities are usually overlapped or phased therefore.

■ The financial manager should ensure that borrowing facilities are available to cover all foreseen needs plus a realistic margin for contingencies.

■ Debt policy should be aimed at rising finance at the lowest overall cost after tax. It is suggested that all debt propositions should be compared in terms of the IRR of the financing. Note how true interest rates vary from those quoted by bankers; this is summarized in Table 27.1 in the text.

■ The largest international debt market is in Eurocurrency. The Eurocurrency market is that market in which Eurobanks accept deposits and make loans denominated in currencies other than that of the country in which the bank is located.

■ Remember that the prefix 'Euro' essentially means external and refers to funds that are intermediated outside the country of the currency in which the funds are denominated. It should not be confused with the European currency, the euro.

■ This chapter essentially described the institutions of the Euromarkets – their growth, the players and the way in which the market operates.

27.18 | End of chapter questions

Question 1
Why might a US-based MNC issue bonds denominated in euros?

Question 2
What is syndicated lending? Why do banks sometimes prefer this form of lending?

Question 3
What is the difference between Eurobonds and foreign bonds?

28

Financing the multinational and its overseas subsidiaries

In addition to the general issues of financing which apply to any business, there are special factors which impinge upon the funding of a multinational company and its overseas subsidiaries. With respect to the financing of any business, management needs to consider exactly what is being financed, the extent to which the problem can be solved by more efficient operation of the assets owned (for example, better working capital management can reduce the needs for funds), the extent of debt, the blend of short-term and long-term funds, the maturity structure and evaluation of the true relative costs of different sources of capital. But on the multinational financial stage there are more considerations that have to be borne in mind. In this chapter we present an analysis of these features peculiar to the financing of overseas operations. An approach to the problems of domestic financing can be found in any of the good standard texts on financial management.

In terms of global financing considerations, this chapter first of all sets out a framework designed to minimize taxes, manage currency and political risk and exploit financial market distortions. It then moves on to look at special features of financing overseas subsidiaries. Here we shall cover factors that impinge on overseas subsidiary financing, such as the presence of political risk, exchange control risk, currency risk, losses earned by subsidiaries, inter-company credit, taxation effects, dividend policy, other methods of profit transfer, parent company guarantees and the problem of partly owned subsidiaries. It is our contention that rational recommendations on the financing of an overseas subsidiary can flow only from a careful study of all the special features above and an evaluation of how they are likely to impact upon a company confronted with an overseas opportunity which it wishes to finance. But first of all we attempt to develop a series of guidelines for global financing. In this section, a debt is acknowledged to an excellent article by Lessard and Shapiro (1983).

28.1 | The international financing choice

At least three factors play a major part in multinational financing choices – the opportunities to minimize global taxes paid, the possibilities to manage currency risk and political risk, and the windows of opportunity that may be available to exploit financial market distortions to raise money at rates below the normal market rate.

Financial theory has long discussed whether there is an optimal capital structure for the corporation which maximizes the value of the firm. In a world where taxes play a major part in the financial equation, it now seems pretty clear that the search for this holy grail is justified.

As discussed earlier, we believe that hedging of currency and other risks does have a value. We would agree that the capital asset pricing model suggests that reducing corporate risks that are diversifiable at the portfolio level should not benefit shareholders. But we would also agree that diversifiable risks, if left unmanaged, may have significant effects on the expected spread of outturns in respect of the firm's profits and cash flow. Excessive earnings variability may affect a number of issues which would be detrimental to shareholder interests. For example:

- Excess earnings volatility may lower a firm's credit rating, resulting in higher interest costs. It may also adversely affect access to bank credit and thereby prevent the firm from taking advantage of interest tax shields.

- Earnings volatility, with the increased risk of financial distress may adversely influence the willingness of suppliers, customers and employees to enter into relationships with the firm.

- Excess earnings volatility may hinder management in taking a long-run view which would be in the best interests of investors.

The contention is, therefore, that the objective function of the firm might be postulated in the following form:

$$\text{Maximize } V_F = \sum V_i - P(\sigma)$$

where V_F is the value of the firm, V_i is the present value of each of the firm's divisions, strategic business units or projects, and $P(\sigma)$ is a penalty factor that reflects the impact on expected after-tax cash flows of the total risk of the firm. According to this formulation, the value of the firm is adversely affected by expected variability of cash flow. This form of objective function has been proposed by Adler and Dumas (1977a, b) and is reinforced by Lessard and Shapiro (1983).

The inclusion of a penalty cost in the above formulation reflects the possibility that the firm may wish to hedge those unsystematic risks which might contribute significantly to the expected variability of its cash and profit flows. Admittedly, such hedging transactions will have a zero present value in their own right. We nonetheless feel that they can be justified because of their effect in reducing the penalty factor specified in the above objective function. We now turn to the three major issues briefly referred to earlier: taxes, hedging and financial market imperfections.

28.2 | Minimization of global taxes

Non-symmetrical tax treatment of various components of financial cost means that equality of before-tax costs may lead to inequality at the after-tax level. The fear of countries imposing withholding taxes on dividends and interest paid to foreign investors by entities operating in the host country has led to a multiplicity of foreign finance subsidiaries designed to avoid this additional tax inconvenience. Financing choices designed to minimize corporate taxes are frequently concerned with:

- selecting the tax-minimizing currency, jurisdiction and vehicle for issue;

- selecting the tax-minimizing mode of internal transfer of currency and/or profit.

Interest payments on debt are tax deductible; dividends are not. It follows that, all other things being equal, there is an incentive to increase the firm's gearing. Also, because inter-group dividend payments may lead to tax consequences different from those of interest and principal payments, parent company financing of its affiliates in the form of debt rather than equity may have frequent tax advantages.

Furthermore, where there is asymmetrical tax treatment of foreign exchange gains and losses, or where interest expenses are subject to one tax treatment and dividend payments are subject to another, the expected after-tax cost of financing will differ across countries even if their expected before-tax costs are the same. Clearly, the firm will wish to structure its international borrowings in such a way as to minimize global tax deductions. This may favour very high debt levels in certain territories – but there are problems. Limits to the extent to which debt may be substituted for equity may be set by the regulations in a number of countries concerning thin capitalization rules. These set a limit on the gearing ratio. Beyond this specified debt level, capital is simply treated by the tax authorities as equity. The implication of this is that interest on debt above the acceptable maximum is not tax deductible and payments may be subject to dividend withholding tax. The United States is the most notable example of a country concerned about thin capitalization. Although no formal statement has been made by the US tax authorities, a commonly used rule of thumb is that a debt to equity ratio in a range between 2.5 to 1 and 4 to 1 is the maximum acceptable.

Tax arbitrage is clearly a source of reduction in the total tax burden. It basically involves moving revenues and/or expenses from one tax jurisdiction to another with the specific objective of lowering the global tax bill. Of course, in terms of assessing underlying management performance, the distorting effect of such movements should be eliminated.

28.3 | Managing risk

Financing to manage foreign exchange risk essentially involves offsetting unanticipated changes in the currency value of operating cash flows with identical changes in the same currency in terms of the cost of servicing liabilities. Perfect hedging is difficult because of the uncertainty in estimating the expected effects of currency changes on operating flows. Thus, a firm with a sizeable export market might hold a portion of its liabilities in the currency of determination of the export revenues – this might be the currency of competitors or it might be the currency of the buying country. Any reduction in operating cash inflows due to an exchange rate change would be offset by a reduction in the debt service cash outflows.

In using financing hedges to offset exchange risks, the firm seeks to finance in such a way that it balances the currency risks inherent in the operation. In using financing to reduce political risk, the idea is that, as political risk increases, the mode of financing reduces potential adverse effects overall. For example, firms may reduce the risk of currency inconvertibility by appropriate inter-affiliate financing. Parent funds may be invested as debt rather than as equity. Back-to-back and parallel loans may be arranged. As much local financing as possible may be sought.

Another approach to managing political risk draws upon project finance techniques (see Chapter 30). Instead of supplying subsidiaries with direct or guaranteed capital, the sponsoring company raises project finance for a foreign investment from (perhaps) the host and other governments, international development agencies, overseas banks – or even from customers. Repayment is tied to the project's success. For the sponsoring firm or consortium, the project finance creates an international network of banks, government agencies and customers with a vested interest in the fulfilment of the host government's contract with the consortium. An expropriation threat is likely to upset relations with customers, banks and governments worldwide. As reported by Moran (1974), this tactic was pursued by Kennecott, the minerals company, in financing a major copper mine expansion in Chile. In spite of the subsequent rise to power of the Allende regime, which promised to expropriate all foreign holdings in Chile with zero compensation, Allende was forced to honour commitments to Kennecott.

28.4 | Financial market distortions

One of the most important aspects of global financing strategy is to gain access to a broad range of fixed sources to lessen dependence on any one single source. At the same time, the multinational is concerned with minimizing the cost of funds so raised. The hypothesis is that the cost of international borrowing is below the cost of pure domestic funding. The corporate treasurer accessing international capital markets hopes to ensure that this hypothesis works for his or her firm by exploiting financial market imperfections, distortions and inefficiencies. Subsidized finance is often the source of such potential saving.

Government credit and capital controls may lead to deviations from equilibrium in capital markets. Governments frequently intervene in domestic financial markets to achieve goals other than economic ones. A government might limit corporate borrowing in an effort to hold down interest rates, thus providing its finance ministry with a lower-cost source of funds to meet a budget deficit. Where governments do restrict access to local credit markets, local interest rates are usually at a level below equilibrium on a risk-adjusted basis. If there is a viable offshore market for the currency, the controls will result in a difference between domestic and offshore rates, giving rise to arbitrage opportunities. Firms might borrow in domestic markets and, to the extent that it is feasible, on-lend in offshore markets. In fact, the firm should borrow as much as possible, *ceteris paribus*, in the subsidized market.

Other financial market distortions may be available because many governments offer incentives to multinationals to influence their production and export-sourcing decisions. Direct investment incentives include interest rate subsidies, very long loan maturities, loan guarantees, official repatriation guarantees, direct grants related to project size, favourable prices for land and favourable terms for the building of plants, to say nothing of favourable tax incentives. All of these – and a great many further variants – create possibilities for drawing down finance at a cost below the fair market rate.

Also, governments of developed nations have export finance agencies whose purpose is to boost local exports by providing long repayment periods, low interest rates and low-cost political and economic risk insurance. These export credit agencies may frequently be used to advantage by multinationals, depending on whether the firm is seeking to export or import goods or services. Firms engaged in projects with sizeable import requirements may also be able to finance their purchases on attractive financial terms via the appropriate export-financing agency. The basic tactic remains. Shopping around among the various export credit agencies for the best possible financing arrangement can pay dividends. As an example, in connection with the financing of the Russian gas pipeline to Western Europe, Russia played off various European and Japanese suppliers and their export-financing agencies against each other and managed to get quite extraordinarily favourable credit and pricing terms.

28.5 | The multinational's capital structure

Should the multinational obtain finance in such a way that its debt structure conforms to parent company norms? Or should it operate throughout the world conforming to the debt/equity capitalization norms for each country in which it operates? Or should it vary its subsidiaries' capital structures to take advantage of opportunities to minimize taxes, offset risks and exploit distortions in capital markets? Students of international financial management often ask these questions. The answer surely flows from the view that, when deciding on a wholly owned subsidiary's funding, any accounting version of a separate capital structure for the subsidiary is illusory unless the parent is willing to allow its affiliate to default on its debt. As long as the multinational group has a legal or moral obligation to prevent the affiliate from defaulting, the individual unit truly has no independent capital structure. Its true debt/equity ratio is equal to that of the consolidated group.

Evidence on parent willingness to guarantee their affiliates' debts is provided by two surveys – one by Stobaugh (1970) and the other by Business International (1979). In the survey by Stobaugh, not one of a sample of twenty medium and large multinationals said that they would allow their subsidiaries to default on debt – even though it did not have a parent company guarantee attached. And of the small multinationals reporting, only one out of seventeen indicated that it would allow a subsidiary to default on its obligations. The Business International survey of eight US-based multinationals had similar findings. The majority of firms interviewed said that they would make good the non-guaranteed debt of a subsidiary that defaulted on its borrowings. These surveys appear to indicate that most multinationals view subsidiary financial structures as having little relevance. Perhaps the third option above, namely to vary subsidiary financial structure to take advantage of local financing opportunities, appears to be the best course of action.

In spite of the argument that a subsidiary's capital structure is relevant only in so far as it affects the parent's consolidated worldwide debt ratio, some firms still follow a policy of not providing parent financing and guarantees beyond the initial investment. Why should this be so? Their rationale for this policy may be understood in the context of agency theory. Forcing the foreign affiliate to stand on its own feet means that the parent firm is, by implication, admitting that its power of surveillance over foreign subsidiaries and associates is limited. In effect, the parent is turning over some of its monitoring responsibilities to local financial institutions. At the same time, affiliate managers are presumably working to improve local operations, thereby generating the internal flows that will negate the need for parent financing. The existence of agency costs also affects corporate policy regarding parent guarantees. When a parent provides an affiliate with a loan guarantee, it explicitly loses the bank as a partner in the risk, with an attendant reduction in the need to monitor and control the loan – since the bank will probably be repaid irrespective of whether it monitors the affiliate loan or not. On the other side of the equation, of course, the bank will doubtless insist on inserting tougher covenants when there is no loan guarantee from the parent.

28.6 | Political risk

Chapter 25 of this book was devoted to the topic of country risk and political risk. In the context of financing an overseas subsidiary, we need to consider confiscation risk, commercial political risk and financial political risk.

Subsidiaries operating in most stable, industrialized countries might consider themselves free from confiscation risk. However, even countries such as the United Kingdom and Canada have shown, for example in their postures on oil exploration, that US multinational companies run risk in this area. Obviously, exposure in advanced industrialized countries is less than in, say, Nicaragua or Iran, but it nonetheless exists. The parent company may partially counter such risk by the way in which it finances its overseas subsidiaries. It may also resort to confiscation insurance. Many government-aided agencies, such as the ECGD in Britain, offer confiscation cover for new overseas investments, and Lloyd's offers cover for existing and new investments in a comprehensive, non-selective form. Financial tactics designed to minimize this risk embrace the use of high levels of gearing (preferably local gearing), maximum use of local sources of funds, including local debt and equity where a partly owned subsidiary is deemed acceptable, minimizing the use of inter-group sources of finance and avoiding parent company guarantees. The essential idea is that, should the subsidiary be confiscated, the host government takes over the liabilities as well as the assets of the multinational's local operations.

The second class of political risk considered here is commercial political risk, which is best explained by an example. Consider that an overseas country is taken over by a left-wing government which imposes regulations of high minimum wages and freezes price levels, resulting in falling profit margins. This kind of exposure may affect all businesses in the country or it may be designed specifically to attack foreign-owned operations. Exposure to discrimination against foreign-owned businesses may take various guises, such as not awarding government contracts to them, giving advantages and subsidies to local-owned competitors, restricting import licences for key raw materials, refusing to grant work permits to non-indigenous staff and so on. By taking in local shareholders, it may be possible to create an influential body of opinion which would result in avoidance of some of the worst aspects of commercial political risk.

Financial political risk takes such forms as restricting access to local capital markets, restricting the repatriation of capital and dividends, imposing heavy interest-free import deposits and so on. Financing tactics designed to beat such impediments are not always easy to access. If the problem is merely the non-availability of cheap local capital markets, then the company must weigh up the relative merits of funds from outside the country versus the more expensive version of local funds. Restrictions on dividend remittance favour financing using parent debt or other debt borrowed from outside the host country. Interest and capital repayments will, in all probability, be remittable. If dividend remittances are severely restricted, analysis of parent cash flows as recommended in Chapter 23 may show a lack of economic viability for the whole operation.

28.7 | Exchange control risk

Frequently, exchange controls affect the multinational company because an overseas subsidiary has accumulated surplus cash in the country in which it operates and this may not be remitted out of the overseas territory. This surplus cash may arise from profits earned or as sums owed for imports into the overseas country. As an example of how this latter constraint works, France used to have a regulation that stipulated that inter-group trade debts of a French subsidiary to an associated company, if not paid within one year of import, became blocked as an unremittable sum of capital invested in the subsidiary.

Goods shipped to some countries, notably Nigeria and India, which were denominated in the local currency became blocked since the host country's currencies were virtually totally inconvertible. The rule of thumb for the international company, irrespective of whether it is shipping to a subsidiary or to a third party, is not to ship goods without guaranteed clearance from exchange control and licensing authorities.

Where blocked funds are likely to accrue, the logical financing tactic for the international group is to finance overseas subsidiaries with as high a proportion of local borrowings as is possible; blocked funds resulting from earning non-remittable profits may subsequently be used to repay these borrowings.

28.8 | Currency risk

Currency risk needs to be managed for the group as a whole and it is preferable if it is managed for the subsidiary too – even if this be by way of hedging with the group treasury. For the risk-averse company, the preferred policy is to match assets and liabilities in the same currencies both at group and at subsidiary level. In the overseas subsidiary, this would probably be assisted by drawing down as much local debt as is feasible. If local debt cannot be obtained by the overseas subsidiary because of its foreign ownership, the group treasurer may seek to borrow offshore the currency of the overseas subsidiary. If this cannot be drawn by the local company because of exchange controls, it may be logical for the parent to do the borrowing.

If the only source of finance for the risk-averse overseas subsidiary is hard currency debt – for example, US dollars or Swiss francs – then, if available, forward cover should be arranged for principal and interest payments. In evaluating competing sources of hard currency finance, if such has to be resorted to, it is assumed that the treasurer will not fall into the interest rate trap. Take the example of 'cheap' Swiss franc finance versus 'more expensive' US dollar funds. If the respective interest costs are 3 per cent per annum and 6 per cent per annum, the market is expecting the dollar to weaken over the borrowing period to eliminate this difference – this is what the international Fisher effect would be predicting. But remember that all this is on a pre-tax basis. To allow for tax effects, we have to take cognizance of the tax system under which the borrower is liable to pay tax on its income. According to most tax systems in the world, the total amount of interest (including any foreign exchange losses due to currency depreciation in the territory of operations relative to the currency of borrowing) is tax deductible. But in some countries, currency losses on principal repayment are not. The conclusion is that in such circumstances, all other things being equal, it is cheaper and safer to pay the higher interest rate rather than to incur relatively large unrelieved losses on repayment of principal.

28.9 | Losses earned by subsidiaries

Although there may be no currency exposure position for the group as a whole, it could be the case that local exchange controls mean that an overseas subsidiary carries an exposed position which could make the subsidiary insolvent should adverse currency movements materialize. This may result in trading becoming illegal.

The parent company may overcome this problem (and, for that matter, the general problem occasioned by local losses leading to insolvency) by injecting further capital or by advancing new loans and subordinating them to the other creditors. Alternatively, the parent may subordinate any existing inter-company debt to the other creditors, or it may guarantee all debts of the subsidiary, provided that these courses of action are acceptable under local legal rules. However, such policies leave any resultant losses unrelieved for tax purposes.

When trading losses have a high probability, it is perhaps better that the overseas business should be set up as a branch of the home operation – in which case losses would be tax allowable against the home territory tax liability. Alternatively, an agreement may be made between a home territory exporting subsidiary, which is liable to tax, and the overseas operation to which it sells products, whereby it agrees to guarantee each year to meet the shortfall should overseas expenses exceed revenues. To be effective, this kind of revenue subvention must be defensible in the sense that the expense legitimately belongs in the home country. There is a defensible case where a substantial volume of goods is shipped from the home subsidiary to the overseas counterpart. It would not, of course, be a defensible argument were there no inter-company trade.

28.10 | Inter-company credit

The reader of this chapter so far is probably convinced that a very low parent input plus substantial local borrowing represents the ideal solution to the problem of financing the overseas subsidiary. Such a mix of funding creates problems should the subsidiary be subject to unforeseen setbacks. While emergency lines of local credit may solve the short-term problem occasioned by a temporary reverse of profit or cash flow, it may be the case that these dry up in adverse circumstances. It then falls upon the group to provide funding.

While the input of parent company equity or borrowing sourced from other than the local territory would solve the problem, the suddenness of the onset of the financing problem may favour another solution, which may be recommended in the short term because it is more prompt and easy to set up. This short-term solution simply lies in a variation of the terms of inter-company credit. This means, in the context of the situation described, that the overseas subsidiary would pay inter-group creditors more slowly than originally prescribed and that inter-group receivables due to the overseas subsidiary would be paid more rapidly. The process is rather like leading and lagging but it is this time triggered by an unforeseen deterioration of local outturns, rather than an imminent movement of exchange rates. Resort to such a tactic must, of course, fall within the latitude on payment terms permitted by exchange control regulations.

28.11 | Taxation effects

International taxation is a complex topic. Clearly, different countries have different tax systems with different rates of tax on profits. The scope for arranging an international group's affairs in order to minimize taxation is therefore extensive and this is true for tax corollaries of financing.

It is worth bearing in mind the almost immutable rule that there is no tax relief against consistent losses in any one country. The best approach is therefore to arrange a group's affairs such that losses are avoided in any one country. To the extent that such losses are caused by artificial practices, such as high transfer pricing, it is far better from a purely tax standpoint to discontinue such dysfunctional tactics.

28.12 | Dividend policy

As part of their exchange control regulations, many developing countries erect barriers that discriminate against dividends being paid to overseas shareholders. While such practices tend to reduce the flow of funds out of the developing country, they also have the effect of discouraging direct investment inwards, which might otherwise hasten the diffusion of technology, help the growth of the developing economy and provide much-needed employment. Governments of developing countries argue that they prefer to keep a greater proportion of their industrial cake in the hands of local investors; multinationals argue that the cake becomes smaller than would otherwise be the case.

The critical question for the international company, though, is not an altruistic one: it concerns cash flows out of and remittable back to the parent. If a project fails to stand up when judged on these criteria the international company should not consider investing.

28.13 | Other methods of profit transfer

Because of their actions in the past, multinationals obtained a reputation for avoiding taxes and transferring cash around the world in spite of exchange controls by such devices as manipulating transfer prices, management fees, service charges, royalty payments and non-commercial interest payments. Over the past twenty years or so, tax authorities have become adept at frustrating such manipulation. It is frequently difficult to make even fair cross-frontier charges between group members without investigation. In short, the pendulum has swung so far in the direction of the taxing authorities that multinationals are basically very concerned about avoiding paying more than their fair burden of tax in many developing countries. Nowadays arm's-length transfer pricing has become the preferred policy of most enlightened multinationals and the use of artificial means of profit transfer as a medium for shifting cash around a group has tended to fall into disrepute. That is not to say that it is non-existent, but it is practised much less frequently than the literature attacking multinationals would have us believe.

28.14 | Parent company guarantees

The use of high levels of debt – especially local debt – to circumvent political risk has been recommended. Where parent company guarantees are given to an overseas subsidiary's creditors, the benefits gained by using high local debt levels tend to evaporate. Many multinationals make it a policy never to give parent company guarantees, although on occasions it is impossible to avoid giving them – for example, if a contract tender is to be seriously considered. However, some treasurers would argue that the multinational company that walks away from its insolvent subsidiary is likely to have problems with lenders in all countries and that relatively little is gained by rigidly avoiding guarantees.

Letters of comfort are, of course, a different matter. These are letters given by the multinational parent to a lender, usually a bank, which acknowledge that the borrower is a subsidiary, that the parent is aware of the indebtedness and that the holding company intends to continue to own the subsidiary. Letters of comfort of this kind have no legal stature, but they do have a moral dimension. They are not guarantees and do not count as such for accounting purposes and for calculating covenant figures. However, letters of comfort that refer to the substitution of a guarantee in prescribed circumstances may be a different kettle of fish again. The key question concerns whether or not such letters constitute guarantees. Legal advice should be sought before signing a letter of this kind. Letters of comfort are sometimes called 'letters of awareness' or 'letters of support'.

The topic is debatable at length. However, it is our belief that as a device to reduce the impact of political risk, particularly confiscation risk, the avoidance of parent company guarantees certainly has substantial advantages for the international company.

28.15 | Partly owned subsidiaries

Deciding about whether an overseas subsidiary should be wholly owned or only partly owned is probably the most critical and far-reaching decision on the financing of overseas operations. The major argument advanced against the presence of outside shareholders is that it makes single-minded management to meet the goals of the majority investor difficult without conflicts of interest with the minorities. The presence of the minority shareholder imposes a need to manage the subsidiary by the most careful application of the arm's-length principle. Any other approach results in constant friction with the outside shareholders, who may become paranoid about the subsidiary's profits and cash flows being syphoned off for the benefit of the majority shareholder. This problem is frequently highlighted when one of the shareholders provides some local facilities for the subsidiary for which it requires financial recompense. At its worst, failure to apply the arm's-length principle results in substantially reduced motivation of local management, especially when such local managers are also minority shareholders. The presence of outside shareholders means that the two sets of investors may have very different objectives on dividend policy. The dividend may be the only tangible reward for the minority, and they may also suffer much less tax on it than the majority shareholder. Furthermore, and most importantly, the minority shareholders may be reluctant to bear their fair share of the burdens of keeping the subsidiary financed or guaranteeing its obligations. At its most acute, this problem may effectively rule out new equity or guaranteed finance. It would, after all, be unfair to the majority shareholders to require them to bear a disproportionate share of such burdens. Such factors have to be carefully weighted against the opposite side of the argument.

The case for having local minority shareholders is that in many countries it is required by law, and in many countries it is an absolute political necessity. It is often argued that, in some countries, influential local shareholders open vital doors to customers, contacts and government authorities and that they can protect the overseas subsidiary against political and commercial discrimination. Moreover, there are frequently very good commercial reasons for local participation in an overseas venture.

Where there are outside shareholders, important consequences ensue. Corporate objectives of the overseas subsidiary may differ from the wholly owned case. We have referred to some obvious examples already. But there are others. For example, in the context of currency risk, local minority shareholders are not interested in group exposure; they are concerned only with that of the overseas subsidiary. Where the local minority shareholders are also the management group, views on perquisites and other managerial trappings are frequently bones of contention.

As a general rule, overseas subsidiaries with minorities are generally very lowly geared and it is often difficult to agree with the minority on profit retentions, extra capital or other finance from shareholders and guarantees from shareholders. Guarantees are altogether impracticable where the minority share is held by the public. Indeed, where the partly owned overseas subsidiary is a company quoted on a local stock exchange, the above problems are reinforced. Public investors cannot give guarantees for such a company, and it is costly and time consuming to raise new capital from such shareholders. And where the law requires that local shareholders must hold a minimum percentage of the capital, the parent company does not even have the option of merely subscribing new capital itself. All these difficulties favour a generous initial capitalization and, probably, a policy of high retention of profits.

There is no single, ultimate answer to the problem of whether an overseas subsidiary company should use outside equity finance or not. In this section we have merely tried to point out the advantages and disadvantages of each policy. Real-world decisions on this topic require careful analysis and commercial judgement, but it must not be forgotten that an investment by a parent company in an overseas subsidiary must stand up in terms of parent cash flow analysis along the lines advocated in the chapter on capital budgeting.

28.16 | Euroequity or crosslisting

Before leaving the topic of multinational financing, some mention must be made of the Euroequity market. Sometimes, so it is claimed, it may be advantageous to issue shares in two or more countries' equity markets. Such share issues are called Euroequity issues and this is also referred to as crosslisting. One of the ideas behind simultaneously floating equity in different countries' markets is the view that any one capital market can absorb only so much of a company's stock at any time. In other words, the rationale for Euroequity issues is that there must be some form of capital market segmentation. If not, it would be possible for a company to issue shares only in London that would simply be bought by Americans, Japanese and European investors without the need to offer the shares on a US, Japanese or European stock exchange. Segmentation might be caused by a factor such as different reporting requirements. It might well be that more shares could be sold to Americans by issuing the shares in the United States and necessarily conforming to US reporting rules – which, in any case, are more stringent than those on stock exchanges in most other countries in the world.

While some non-US firms have listed on US stock exchanges – mostly the New York Stock Exchange and the American Stock Exchange, which list numerous Canadian firms – the shares of many foreign firms trade indirectly as American depository receipts (ADRs). What happens under the ADR system is that a bank holds the underlying foreign shares, receives dividends, reports and accounts and so on, but issues claims against the shares it holds. These claims – the ADRs – then trade in the relatively unregulated over-the-counter market. This has the advantage for foreign firms of reducing listing fees and the information that they must report.

Logically, the highest price a firm might obtain for its shares, net of issuance costs, is in the market with the lowest required rate of return (net of issue costs). The rule for where to issue shares is that they should be sold where the price net of issue costs is the highest. But, again logically, once an issue has been made, arbitrage (sometimes called 'flowback' in this context) should ensure that the two centres quote similar share price equivalents.

Stock exchanges may be measured in a variety of ways – market capitalization, turnover, number of companies listed and so on. But London trades a greater value of foreign equity than any other market and it has a greater number of foreign companies listed. London also has a larger number of companies – domestic and foreign – listed than any other exchange except the electronic over-the-counter market in the United States – popularly known as NASDAQ (the National Association of Securities Dealers Automatic Quotation system).

The simultaneous and international trading of equities in a variety of foreign locations is noticeably increasing. In the United States, foreign equities are traded in the form of ADRs and NASDAQ has been a significant participant.

The reasons why companies seek to list on foreign stock exchanges are numerous. For a variety of reasons, Euroequity provides greater financial flexibility for the multinational and may be said to lower its cost of capital. The mechanism supporting an increase in share price, through lowering the cost of capital, involves overcoming mispricing in an illiquid, segmented, home capital market. Confined to a single market, companies are constrained in a variety of ways. There might be regulatory problems. For example, the authorities may operate queuing procedures on capital issues, or there could be restrictions on the issue of certain kinds of paper. The company might face a shallow, relatively small, domestic capital market with a sharply rising cost of capital function. This would, probably, create clear advantages to issuing debt or equity in deeper capital markets. Furthermore, such equity might be more acceptable in acquisition situations.

Companies with very substantial demands for capital but with shallow domestic capital markets are often obliged to seek funds outside the domestic market. A presence in a variety of financial markets increases the firm's financial flexibility in terms of money-raising techniques available to it. Different capital markets have different preferences for such instruments as convertible issues, warrants and so on.

The issue of equity in foreign markets can help to raise the visibility of a company with, perhaps, some benefit on sales. And having a presence in various capital markets may serve strategic interests. By broadening the shareholder base, the company may be better placed to resist takeover pressure and in turn may itself be able to undertake foreign mergers and acquisitions more easily. Also, having a secondary market for its shares overseas may better enable the firm to issue equity to local managers as part of compensation packages.

But there are disadvantages to overseas listings too. For example, there may be harsher and more expensive disclosure requirements. And there is the problem of flowback. This is the tendency for shares issued into a foreign market to be sold back into the domestic market. This may have the effect of depressing the price of the shares in the domestic market. There are investor relations problems too – the need to maintain a flow of information in several languages adds to the costs of documentation and communication. Compliance with listing and reporting requirements imposed by different foreign stock markets and financial environments may be costly. Differences in the quantity of information, the frequency of disclosure and accounting procedures combine to pose burdens in cost terms. Other problems, such as foreign exchange controls, limitations on domestic ownership of foreign securities, restrictions on issuing activity and different tax regimes, may make international equity financing difficult, although these impediments are slowly being eroded.

A company that has decided to issue shares – or bonds for that matter – abroad must consider whether to issue directly, or indirectly via a subsidiary located abroad. There is frequently a motive to use a specially established financing subsidiary to avoid the need to withhold tax on payments made to foreigners. Until 1984, many US firms established subsidiaries in the Netherlands Antilles and other tax havens to avoid having to withhold 30 per cent of dividend or interest paid to foreigners. The 1984 Deficit Reduction Act repealed, among other things, the requirement for US firms to withhold tax on income paid to foreigners. It also meant that parent companies could sell securities directly. Therefore, at least in the United States, the question of the physical location of the vehicle of share issue is no longer a concern to the firm. This is not the case in every country, and tax havens are still used. Clearly, the need to use subsidiaries in tax havens when raising capital is dependent on the specific tax rules in the parent company's home country.

The arguments in favour of Euroequity issues turn around capital market segmentation. Issuing equity in a variety of capital markets increases financial flexibility and may lower the firm's cost of capital. It may enable the international company to get round domestic regulations such as capital market queuing requirements and restrictions as to types of capital issued. It may be a virtual necessity for some cash-hungry multinationals with shallow capital markets. In any case, it invariably widens the shareholder base, will get the corporate name better known and recognized in international banking circles and may heighten its commercial profile too. But there are costs. It is an expensive process and carries with it burdens in terms of new compliance requirements, documentation and tax difficulties, to say nothing of a new set of foreign regulations. Clearly, Euroequity issues have to be weighed up carefully by financial executives in the multinational. Whether worthwhile gains accrue is an entirely empirical question and, although we have a dearth of real evidence, it is to this that we now turn.

Table 28.1 European gearing ratios of companies

Rank	Country	Gearing ratios*
1	Switzerland	0.55
2	Belgium	0.51
3	Italy	0.45
4	Ireland	0.40
5	Denmark	0.34
6	France	0.34
7	Germany	0.30
8	Sweden	0.27
9	Netherlands	0.26
10	Spain	0.25
11	UK	0.20

* Ratio of debt to debt plus equity.
Source: Tucker (1994).

28.17 | Some more empirical evidence

Let us now consider a small number of interesting empirical studies in the areas of multinational debt/equity ratios, and the effects of Eurodebt and Euroequity issues. As most readers are well aware, there is a big difference between debt ratios in one country and another. This is well borne out by the evidence of Table 28.1. The table shows significantly lower debt levels in the United Kingdom compared with its European counterparts. Why should this be the case?

In Germany, Italy and France, banks are very important owners of equity as well as being providers of debt finance. In these countries, a very substantive percentage of shares in public companies is owned or controlled by banks. In such circumstances, in Germany, France and Italy, banks often nominate directors. They are consequently able to obtain inside information and affect decisions. If banks are in possession of such information, they will, all other things being equal, require a lower margin of safety *vis-à-vis* other countries where the banker's role is much less hands-on. This closeness of banks and corporates is probably the case in countries such as Switzerland, Germany, Italy, France and Japan. And, indeed, debt levels are found to be higher in these countries than for example in the United Kingdom, the United States, Canada and the Netherlands. However, when corrections are made to put accounting practices onto a similar footing, the amount of the difference certainly shades downwards – indeed Rajan and Zingales (1995, 1998) go as far as to call many aspects of debt level difference popular myths which do not stand up to scrutiny. By contrast, Nobes and Parker (2002) argue for the more conventional link between higher debt levels and closer involvement of the lending banks.

There is also an argument that, in countries in which interest payments are tax deductible against corporate taxes, there will, *ceteris paribus*, be a tendency towards higher debt ratios. While this is undoubtedly so, there is perhaps a more cogent reason for some countries to exhibit high relative debt ratios. The risk and expected cost of bankruptcy increases as gearing increases. If expected bankruptcy is less in some countries than in others, the debt/equity ratios should, other things being equat, be higher in the countries with the low expected bankruptcies. In countries where banks are given positions on boards of directors and are both providers of debt and holders of companies' equity, the probability of bankruptcy is relatively low because the banks are given early warnings of trouble and are probably more likely to help in times of adversity. It has been the case that in countries such as Japan and Germany, where bank officials frequently occupy board positions and banks hold considerable amounts of equity, for debt/equity ratios to have been substantially higher than in countries such as the United States and the United Kingdom where banks' positions were the reverse. It may also have been the case that Japanese companies were not perceived to have excessive risk because of potential backing from their government if they experienced financial difficulties. The past tense is used here because recent failures of Japanese banks may reverse their government's past questionable practices.

On the question of capital structure, an interesting study by Collins and Sekely (1983) has found that capital structures of international companies tend to vary by the country in which they are headquartered. The debt ratios of US-based and UK-based multinationals tend to be lower than those headquartered in most other industrialized countries. Madura (2003) suggests that this might be due to the fact that the probability of bankruptcy may be lower for multinationals based in other countries, since their respective governments may rescue them.

The topic of whether there is significant market segmentation in international and domestic debt markets has been investigated by Kidwell, Marr and Thompson (1985) and by Finnerty and Nunn (1985), and their findings are not consistent. Kidwell, Marr and Thompson suggest that US firms issue Eurobonds because they can broaden their financial base, they do not need to disclose so much information since SEC regulations do not apply to Eurobond sales, and they may be able to borrow at a lower interest rate in the Eurobond market since most Eurobonds are bearer bonds and owners may be able to evade taxes. On this last question, the researchers compared the yields of dollar-denominated debt issued by utility companies in the US market versus those in the Eurobond markets and found no significant difference in yields, suggesting that investors in Eurobond markets value bonds in a manner similar to investors in the domestic UK market.

Finnerty and Nunn examined new issues of Eurobonds and matched them with domestic bonds issued in the United States. They ensured comparability on risk rating, industry classification, call features, maturity and issue date, and they were classified according to four credit-rating classes. For the top credit rating, the yields on the matched pairs were not significantly different. But for the other three, the yields of the Eurobonds were significantly less than the corresponding domestic bonds with which they were matched. These results imply that US companies may reduce their financing costs by issuing Eurobonds rather than bonds in the domestic market.

There are also interesting studies on Euroequity issues and their effects on share price. Their results are mixed. Howe and Kelm (1987) estimated abnormal returns from ninety trading days before the actual listing to forty trading days after the listing.

They found that such abnormal returns were consistently negative, and in some cases statistically significant. It may be objected that such negative reactions might be acceptable for a first Euroequity issue because of longer-term awareness and subsequent diversification of equity sources. Some of Howe and Kelm's sample of 161 US firms crosslisting in Basel, Frankfurt or Paris made second and third forays into the Euroequity market. The interesting thing is that when the researchers assessed the abnormal returns for a second and third overseas listing, they again found such abnormal returns to be significantly negative. Clearly, these results suggest that shareholders have reacted unfavourably towards Euroequity listings. The costs involved in such listings may outweigh the potential benefits. While these findings cannot be considered as definitive, they are disturbing.

However, on the other hand, McGoun (1987) found a positive share price reaction to announcements by US firms of intentions to list on the Tokyo, Toronto or London stock exchanges. And Alexander, Eun, and Janakiramanan (1988) found a positive share price effect for thirty-four non-US firms listing on the New York or the America Stock Exchange or NASDAQ, during the period 1969 to 1982; presumably this was a period when markets were more segmented than today. Also, a study by Sundaram and Logue (1996) found that share prices increased for foreign firms that crosslisted their equity in ADR form on the New York and American Stock Exchanges from 1982 to 1992. The researchers argue that crosslisting in the USA enhances equity value by reducing the overall effect of segmentation among difference national securities markets.

A study of 481 multinational firms by Saudagaran (1988) found that the relative size of a firm in its own domestic capital market has a significant influence on the decision to list abroad. The larger the firm relative to its home capital market, the more likely it is to list abroad. He also found that this tendency was more pronounced for firms with a relatively large degree of multinationality.

28.18 ▌ Measuring the cost of international borrowing

Companies may borrow in their own domestic capital markets or they may move further afield and tap international markets to finance their operations. The Eurocurrency market is the largest international source of funds; its mechanism and history were briefly surveyed in Chapter 27. Besides the Eurocurrency markets, the international company may decide to tap the domestic financial markets of overseas countries. In this respect, the international group may choose countries where it already has operations through associated companies or it may finance itself from countries where it does not carry on any operations. Many countries with exchange controls restrict use of domestic capital markets to domestic companies only.

Tapping foreign capital markets may be done directly or indirectly. In the former case this may be achieved by the parent company or a subsidiary borrowing in local markets. In the latter case, this might involve a bilateral arrangement between an entity in the host country and the parent company in the home country. Such an arrangement might involve the exchange of the loan raised in the host country by the local entity in return for a loan in the home country from the parent company. Loan arrangements of this kind are termed 'parallel loans' or 'back-to-back loans' or 'currency exchange agreements' depending upon their exact nature.

Whenever a company decides to borrow uncovered in a foreign currency, it takes on a major complicating factor. This concerns the calculation of the cost of the loan. For a domestic borrowing, the net-of-tax cost would simply be the net-of-tax interest expense. Preferably, this should be expressed in discounted cash flow terms calculated by finding the discount rate which equates the sum raised under the borrowing with the net-of-tax interest costs and capital repayments, allowing for their timing. For a foreign currency borrowing, the framework for the calculation is the same but, because of changes in the exchange rate, the interest payments and capital repayments can be expected to change over time when expressed in home currency terms. Since this difficulty is a distinctive feature of international borrowing, we devote the following sections to developing an approach to the calculation of the true cost of international borrowing.

28.19 | The advantages of borrowing internationally

Many companies carry on their main operations in countries whose domestic capital markets are comparatively small and possibly subject to drying up. Should the parent company be located in such a country and should that company have fairly substantial needs for cash to invest in order to compete in world markets, then its growth and competitive ability may be constrained by the existence of shallow domestic financial markets – unless it taps international financing sources. This was one of the major problems confronting Novo Industri A/S (see Stonehill and Dullum, 1982), the Denmark-based pharmaceutical group, in 1978 when it launched its first dollar convertible Eurobond issue. The economics of the pharmaceutical industry, with its high added value, high research and development levels, high capital intensity and need for constant innovation, make access to deep capital markets a necessary precondition to successful competition on a world scale. Novo was aware that the scale of its corporate strategy turned on the availability of substantial cash resources on an ongoing basis. It saw its domestic capital market as small and subject to periods of illiquidity, which meant that, if it wanted to pursue its strategic plan, it was necessary to look outside domestic capital markets.

These kinds of consideration are much less critical for companies based in the United Kingdom or the United States but they can be very relevant in many other countries. Indeed, the lack of depth and the illiquidity of some countries' capital markets may be one of the historic reasons for most large multinational businesses being based in countries with sophisticated financing sources. This author believes that the lack of ready access to substantial domestic capital markets has constrained the growth of businesses in many smaller European countries and elsewhere in the world.

Besides the benefit of access to deeper financial markets, tapping capital markets outside one's own home country should enable the international company to take

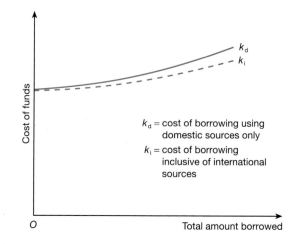

Figure 28.1 The international cost of borrowing.

advantage of market imperfections that prevent the Fisher effect from holding in the short term. It will be recalled that, according to the four-way equivalence model developed in Chapter 4, real interest rates (that is, nominal rates adjusted for anticipated inflation) should tend towards equality. But, given that our model is rarely, if ever, totally in equilibrium, the company which has access to world financial markets, rather than just to its domestic one, should be able to lower its cost of borrowing. Schematically, we would suggest a relationship like that shown in Figure 28.1. It is worth mentioning, however, that when a company taps international financial sources for the first time, it generally finds itself paying slightly more than an established borrower in terms of coupon rates plus underwriting fees.

28.20 | The risks of borrowing internationally

International financing can be broadly categorized into three classes embracing the following situations:

■ Financing in the currency in which cash inflows are expected.

■ Financing in a currency other than that in which cash inflows are expected, but with cover in the forward or swap market or otherwise hedged.

■ Financing in a currency other than that in which cash inflows are expected, but without forward or swap or other cover.

Financing by way of the first two methods avoids foreign exchange risk. But with funds raised via the third method, foreign exchange risk is taken on.

If the international Fisher effect were always to hold as an immutable law and if foreign exchange markets were always in equilibrium, then the benefit accruing to the company through lower nominal interest rates on financing in a hard currency would be exactly offset by the amount by which the harder currency appreciated relative to the other currencies. In other words, if international Fisher holds, then the true cost of funds at the pre-tax level would be equal to the nominal interest rate in the home currency, and this rate would apply irrespective of whence the international company were to draw its funds. As we know from the discussion in Chapter 7, the international Fisher effect does not hold in the short term in the real world, and there is some doubt about whether it holds in the long term. If it is the case that we cannot feel confident about international Fisher asserting itself in the long run, and if it is also the case that exchange rate markets and the interest rate are not always in equilibrium, then the international treasurer may seek either to avoid financing risk by one or more of the techniques discussed earlier or to profit in this area by his or her own insights. Thus the treasurer may seek to raise money denominated in overvalued currencies for relatively long maturities, and by the same token will avoid raising funds in undervalued currencies.

Just as disequilibrium in international Fisher can give rise to financing opportunities for the astute corporation treasurer who is prepared to take on foreign exchange risk, so market imperfections that flow from different tax regimes also create opportunities. Tax legislation on foreign exchange gains and losses varies from one country to another. It is worth mentioning that two or more international financing propositions that appear to have the same pre-tax cost of funds after taking account of interest costs and expected strengthenings and weakenings of currencies may, on a post-tax basis, yield different costs. This phenomenon might result from the fact that corporate tax rates in different centres vary, but it might also flow from the fact that countries have different rules as to whether a capital loss or gain on repayment of an international borrowing is respectively tax deductible or comes into charge for tax.

Most of the discussion to date in this text has focused upon exchange risk problems associated with international financial exposure in the short term – that is, up to one year. In reality, the majority of financing decisions have a time dimension beyond twelve months. But the further we extend this time horizon, the greater become two key problems which impinge upon the international financing decision. First, forward exchange markets become thinner: for many currencies there may not be a forward market beyond twelve months. Secondly, in many developing countries around the world, longer-term local currency financing becomes much more difficult to find.

The non-availability of forward markets for a few currencies for periods beyond twelve months does not mean that the treasurer cannot obtain forward cover for long-term borrowings in foreign currencies. The astute treasurer can use the spot/forward method which was discussed in Chapter 13. Imagine a UK-based international company which has just made a 50m Batavian drac borrowing, requiring repayment of the total sum borrowed in three years' time. If there were no forward market beyond twelve months, the treasurer could manufacture three-year cover by a spot/forward swap. The technique would involve the process shown in Table 28.2.

Remember that the difference between the spot rate and the twelve-month forward rate is underpinned by interest rate differentials. This means that, using the technique summarized in Table 28.2, the treasurer has manufactured three-year

Table 28.2 Spot/forward swap cover for three-year Batavian drac borrowing

End of year		
0	Buy BDc 50 million versus £	12 months forward
1	Sell BDc 50 million versus £	Spot
	Buy BDc 50 million versus £	12 months forward
2	Sell BDc 50 million versus £	Spot
	Buy BDc 50 million versus £	12 months forward
3	Use proceeds of forward purchase at end-of-year 2 to repay borrowing	

cover for the borrowing at an exchange rate equal to the twelve-month forward rate at the end of year 0 plus/minus the twelve-month interest differential at the end of year 1 plus/minus the twelve-month interest differential at the end of year 2. It should be borne in mind that when the treasurer begins this deal at the end of year 0 he or she is exposed in terms of not knowing what the interest rate differential for twelve months will be both at the end of year 1 and at the end of year 2. So this technique minimizes risk, but does not totally eliminate it.

Of course, nowadays the widespread availability of swap markets may provide the ideal alternative route to obtaining cover for the exposure referred to above. Swap markets have far greater liquidity in maturities out to ten years than is available in the long-term forward markets. This usually makes swaps cheaper than long-term forward cover.

What if the treasurer decides not to cover the long-term foreign borrowing? How should the relative merits of competing borrowing propositions be assessed? In short, how should the treasurer assess the cost of international borrowing?

28.21 | Foreign currency financing decisions

In a simple domestic financing situation the true cost of finance may be derived by solving a straightforward discounted cash flow calculation. The amount borrowed, the cash inflow to the company, is set against the interest and principal repayments in each year, the outflows for the company, duly discounted. After a discounting process, the rate that equates the present value of total inflows with the present value of total outflows is the true cost of the borrowing. The general equation may be written as:

$$\text{Amount borrowed} = \frac{[\text{interest paid}_1 + \text{capital repayment}_1]}{(1+r)}$$
$$+ \frac{[\text{interest paid}_2 + \text{capital repayment}_2]}{(1+r)^2} + \cdots$$
$$+ \frac{[\text{interest paid}_n + \text{capital repayment}_n]}{(1+r)^n}$$

where r is the true cost of the loan. The equation would derive from an incremental cash flow analysis in which additional inflows and outflows resulting solely from the financing decision would be specified. The true cost of the borrowing may be calculated on a pre-tax basis or using a post-tax approach. Clearly, if the post-tax cost is required, incremental cash flows must be expressed net of tax.

Where foreign exchange risk is undertaken in an international borrowing, the computation of the cost of the loan is somewhat more complex. But calculations involve the same basic principles. Incremental cash flows arising under a borrowing are specified and the discounted cost is computed. But in this instance we need to recognize that incremental cash flows in home currency terms embrace the initial borrowing, interest to be paid and capital to be repaid, with all of these cash flows duly adjusted to allow for expected or actual (if the analysis is an *ex-post* one) exchange gains and losses. The general equation, in home currency terms, may be expressed as:

$$\text{Amount borrowed} = \frac{\begin{bmatrix} \text{interest paid}_1 + \text{capital repayment}_1 \\ \text{(inclusive of realized exchange gain or loss}_1) \end{bmatrix}}{(1+r)}$$

$$+ \frac{\begin{bmatrix} \text{interest paid}_2 + \text{capital repayment}_2 \\ \text{(inclusive of realized exchange gain or loss}_2) \end{bmatrix}}{(1+r)^2} + \cdots$$

$$+ \frac{\begin{bmatrix} \text{interest paid}_n + \text{capital repayment}_n \\ \text{(inclusive of realized exchange gain or loss}_n) \end{bmatrix}}{(1+r)^n}$$

The solution to the above equation for r gives us the true effective cost of a borrowing. Evidently, if the cost of a foreign borrowing is being made in advance of drawing down a loan, then estimates must be made of future exchange rate movements. For this purpose, the tools in the armoury of the international treasurer were discussed in earlier chapters. Where the currency of borrowing is overvalued or undervalued at the time the loan is drawn down, the treasurer needs to make estimates of the timing and extent of movements towards equilibrium – and this is a major problem.

The true effective cost of a borrowing from international sources may be computed on a pre-tax or on a post-tax basis. The post-tax computation is more complex because we need to consider not only the net-of-tax interest cost but also the foreign exchange gain or loss and whether this is recognized for tax purposes. Analysts also need to be careful in their calculations about whether a borrowing is an amortizing loan or one with a bullet repayment. A bullet repayment involves a single lump sum repayment at maturity. A given currency movement virtually always results in a different true effective cost of funds if the loan is an amortizing one as opposed to one involving a bullet repayment. Also the timing of an appreciation or depreciation of a currency can be extremely material in the calculation of the true cost of borrowing. The sooner the appreciation of a borrowed currency takes place, the greater the increase in the true cost of borrowing. The sooner the devaluation of a borrowed currency occurs, the bigger the decrease to the net effective cost of funds.

Table 28.3 True effective annual cost of borrowing (%)

	Repayment terms		
Year of $ appreciation	Equal amortization	50% by equal amortization 50% by balloon repayment	Bullet repayment
1	14.5	13.7	12.8
2	13.3	13.0	12.6
3	12.3	12.2	12.3
4	11.3	11.7	12.1
5	10.6	11.3	12.0

As an example, consider a UK company financing itself in dollars. The company draws down a five-year $1m borrowing in year 0 and the loan carries a 10 per cent per annum coupon. Assume that the dollar appreciates from $1.30 to the pound at the time of drawdown to $1.17. The true cost of the loan on a pre-tax basis is shown in Table 28.3. The table shows this true cost on the basis that the dollar revaluation takes place in one go either in year 1 or in year 2 or in year 3 and so on. The true effective pre-tax cost in the table is based on a number of assumptions: these are as follows. First, the loan is repayable in equal instalments; second, the loan is assumed to be repaid by annual amortization of $100,000m plus a balloon in year 5 of $500,000m; third, the loan is repaid by a bullet repayment at the end of year 5.

The figures in the table emphasize the need to look beyond the coupon rate of interest. In our example, the devaluation of sterling against the dollar is not a large one by the relative standards of past experience in a floating currency regime. But the impact of that depreciation in the case of the equally amortizing loan is staggering. The impact of a revaluation of the dollar of only around 10 per cent coming early, rather than late, in the borrowing is to raise the coupon cost from around 10 per cent per annum to an effective cost of approaching 15 per cent per annum. The management of a company would have good reason to be critical of the treasurer who talked in terms of this dollar loan as only costing around 10 per cent per annum before tax.

Movements of the Swiss franc and the Deutschmark against sterling through the early 1970s and the strengthening of the dollar in the early 1980s show how naive many corporate treasuries have been in talking their companies into borrowing in cheap interest currencies. Hopefully such financial executives and their companies have learned by bitter, and expensive, experience.

It is also necessary to take account of expected currency movements when calculating the cost of debt as part of a company's exercise of calculating its weighted average cost of capital. This simple procedure is frequently overlooked by financial and planning executives. And in many cases the effect can be very substantial indeed.

There is an increasing tendency for providers of finance in international capital markets to offer floating rate lending with interest tied to LIBOR or some other convenient interest rate base. This creates complexities for the treasurer of an international company. There is a strong temptation to argue that, if international Fisher holds in the long term, the treasurer need not worry whence any borrowing is arranged. Devaluations and revaluations should, according to this theory, cancel out against floating interest rate differentials. This simplistic approach is valid only if the relevant exchange rates move in accordance with the prediction of purchasing power parity and the Fisher effect during the whole course of the loan from drawdown to final repayment. Furthermore, interest and foreign exchange markets must be in equilibrium at the start of a borrowing period for this indifference to financial sourcing to be justified. This is a pretty tall order. Indeed, outside textbook models it will never be found. This has practical implications for the international treasurer even in a world of floating interest rate finance. Imagine that a UK company is considering borrowing via a dollar floating rate loan at a time when the dollar is undervalued by reference to past movements of real effective exchange rates. Even though the loan carries a floating rate, should the dollar/sterling exchange rate move once and for all to correct the previous disequilibrium in PPP but thereafter the rates continue to move in line with international Fisher, then, if this is foreseen, the dollar borrowing will appear relatively expensive. So, even with floating rate notes, the treasurer needs to be very careful. The floating interest rate does not circumvent the problem of potential exchange rate movements.

This whole area of foreign currency financing without forward cover is one that is full of pitfalls. Short cuts are ill-advised. There is no substitute for careful analysis of the interaction between past movements of exchange rates, interest rates and inflation rates. And future estimates are necessary if logical predictions of future exchange rates are to be made over the period of a borrowing. This process is an essential prerequisite to the task of estimating, *ex ante*, the cost of an international borrowing. Hopefully, the framework of analysis laid down in this text should be helpful to potential international borrowers.

28.22 | Summary

- The problems associated with financing an overseas subsidiary differ substantially from those of financing an independent company. The first question to ask is whether the subsidiary is wholly owned or not.

- Where it is only partly owned, it should be capitalized generously and would probably be lowly geared. The reason for this is that it is often difficult to agree with the minority on such things as profit retentions, extra capital needed or guarantees from shareholders. Indeed, guarantees are altogether impracticable where the minority is held by the public. All these difficulties suggest a generous initial capitalization with only a low debt to equity ratio.

- Where the subsidiary is wholly owned, political risk may be reduced by virtue of financing with a high debt level. This was referred to in an earlier chapter.

- Financing, like many aspects of the multinational's activities, should provide an opportunity to minimize global taxes and exploit financial market distortions in order to raise funds at minimum cost. Furthermore, global financing is a means to gain access to a broad range of capital markets and to lessen dependence on any single source. This flexibility can be a great benefit in terms of monitoring and exploiting windows of opportunity to raise relatively cheap money due to capital market imperfections and also in terms of providing reassurances should some markets temporarily dry up.

■ As long as the multinational group has a legal or moral obligation to prevent an overseas affiliate from defaulting, the individual unit really has no independent capital structure. The true debt to equity ratio is equal to that at the consolidated level.

■ International borrowing may enable companies to lower their average cost of finance – see Figure 28.1.

■ International borrowing is important for companies whose headquarters are within countries with shallow capital markets as well as for major multinationals.

■ The true cost of various sources of financing should be calculated by all companies. This involves using the traditional discounted cash flow framework with the amount borrowed showed as an inflow in year 0 and outflows in respect of payment of interest, net of tax, and repayment of principal according to the repayment schedule.

■ Calculating such a true cost is relatively easy in respect of domestic borrowings and those that are fully covered. Using the usual framework referred to above, an IRR in respect of the borrowing can be calculated. Where funding occurs in a currency other than that in which cash inflows are expected, but without forward or swap or other cover, its cost should be estimated with anticipated movements in exchange rate used. However, when presenting data on the costs of relative funding, particular attention needs to be drawn to such uncovered cases.

28.23 | End of chapter questions

Question 1
Why is it necessary to compute the present value when assessing the cost of financing for two alternatives?

Question 2
Is the risk from issuing a floating-rate Eurobond higher or lower than the risk of issuing a fixed-rate Eurobond? Explain.

29 Cash management

Cash management is concerned with planning, monitoring and managing liquid resources. In general terms, the objectives of cash management are as follows:

- To ensure that the organization has the wherewithal to pay its obligations as they fall due.

- To ensure the availability of funds at the right time, in the right place, in the right currency and at an acceptable cost.

- To reduce borrowing requirements and interest cost.

- To minimize idle balances.

- To optimize after-tax earnings on surplus funds.

- To reduce bank charges.

- To increase remittable funds to the parent company from divisions, branches and subsidiaries.

- To reduce tax liabilities.

Cash management has been greatly influenced in recent years by a number of innovations. These include the development of domestic and international cash transmission systems between banks and the rapid growth in electronic banking systems, allowing corporate treasurers to plan and monitor their cash position around the world. Value-dated transfer instructions via a personal computer or terminal are now widespread, as are such techniques as cash pooling, intercompany netting, reinvoicing and factoring.

29.1 Banking relationships

Managing bank accounts has two key aspects: managing the balances and managing the charges. We explore the management of banking relationships in the UK environment; the principles remain the same for other countries, although regulatory environments clearly differ.

In terms of managing bank balances, it is axiomatic that the more bank accounts that are operated, the greater will be the total idle balances, to say nothing of it being more difficult to manage them. One approach is to obtain set-off between accounts. All the major banks in Europe, North America and parts of Australasia offer facilities for domestic currency accounts held at a single bank to be set off against each other for calculation of interest charges and facility utilization. However, many companies have domestic and overseas currency accounts, and set-off should, where possible, be arranged for these too.

Whether the accounts are maintained at one or at several banks, the greatest benefit will accrue only if there is an opportunity to invest surpluses or to fund deficits on a net basis. There are ways of achieving this, of which the following are popular:

- *Automatic investment.* Banks will, for a fee, automatically invest overnight the total of cleared balances on current accounts.

- *Zero balancing, no set-off.* This involves separate automatic transfer of the total cleared balance in each separate account into one central account. The balance on this account is then reported and may be invested for the highest rate available in the market.

- *Full set-off.* This involves keeping the balances on a company's various accounts intact. Having forecast these balances, the net total credit is drawn down on a central account, giving an overall balance equal to zero. The funds drawn down on this central account are automatically invested for the highest overnight return available consistent with risk criteria.

It should be borne in mind when considering investment in interest-bearing accounts that it may, on occasions, be wise to invest even though this means the account going into modest overdraft. The reason for this is simple. Frequently, in many countries, current accounts do not bear interest when in credit. If this is the case, it is usually more profitable to over-invest and incur the risk of a small overdraft overnight than to hold an uninvested current account balance. An example is useful. If an investment is partially funded by a small overdraft, should the investment earn 4 per cent and the overdraft cost 7 per cent then the firm loses, at worst, the difference between the two rates (3 per cent). But, if a balance is left on a non-interest-bearing current account, the firm loses the 4 per cent of the investment rate.

In practice, there may be a good reason for leaving funds on non-interest-bearing current accounts. This is where the balances are accepted by the bank as compensation for bank charges. The value of these balances varies according to the compensation formula agreed with the bank in respect of charges. Usually, though, the compensation rate offered is less than the money would be worth if invested.

There are many methods of charging customers for the operation of bank facilities. It is essential that, when charges are negotiated, each bank's proposal should be converted to a common basis to enable comparisons to be made.

Basically, there are six features of bank charges and these will often be permutated:

- *Interest.* This is related to the bank's own base rate or an external marker rate such as LIBOR.

- *Turnover charge.* This is based on a percentage of the value of entries on the bank statement.

- *Charges for transactions.* These are computed on a per item charge for each type of banking transaction.

- *Compensating balance.* This requires an interest-free deposit to be left with the bank.

- *Minimum balance.* For an expected activity level, the bank requires a minimum level of cash to remain interest free on the account; this compensates the bank for transactions undertaken.

- *Notional interest credit.* This involves a notional interest allowance against transaction charges based on the average cleared credit balance on the current account.

Interest is often calculated on the daily borrowing – this is the case in the United Kingdom and the United States. But there are other methods too. For example, in France banks frequently charge interest on the overnight cleared balance, but they then add an extra percentage of the highest cleared debit balance during the charging period. Thus, if there were a low level for all but one day in a charging period, there could be a very expensive interest surcharge. Clearly, it is essential that corporate treasurers understand banks' interest-charging methods. And to make comparisons easier they should use the true rate (IRR or APR) method. Transaction charges are based on a variety of methods and vary from bank to bank and even within a particular bank. The basis and level of charges are basically a matter for negotiation between the treasurer and the bank. Part of the treasurer's role is to minimize bank operating costs. To do this will involve negotiation.

The compensating balance method is still a feature of charging in banks in some parts of the world. The bank typically requires a non-interest-bearing balance to be maintained equal to, say, 10 per cent of the amount of any loan advanced. The rate quoted for a borrowing – say, 9 per cent – would, when allowing for the compensating balance, come out at 10 per cent. Even US banks used this method until the last couple of decades when they moved towards an all-inclusive interest rate. Whatever method is used, the bank should be paid on a clearly defined and measurable basis.

The corporate treasurer must be aware that there are invisible costs in operating an account; one such is float time. Bank float time may be defined as the interval between a payer losing value from its account and a recipient gaining value in its account. The banking system has the use of funds during this period without cost. To the firm, the cost of bank float time may be considerable. Take a firm with a turnover of £100m per year. One day's float will amount to £280,000 or so. At an interest rate of 12 per cent per annum, this has a cost effect of almost £33,000. With an overdraft averaging £1m throughout the year, this is equal to an increase in the annual interest rate of 3.3 per cent per annum.

Bank float practices and clearing times vary from country to country. In the United Kingdom it may be two days; in Italy it may be ten to twelve days or more. In some countries a payer may be debited one or two days before a transfer and the recipient credited one or more days after. Cheques aside, international payments are usually value dated by the payer. But it is common practice for good value to be given later than the value date of the transfer.

Table 29.1 UK clearing times

	Add
Credits	
In London, for cheques drawn on and paid into a London Town clearing account	0 days
In the UK, for cheques drawn on a non-Town clearing account	+2 days
In the UK, for cheques drawn on a Scottish bank	+3 days
In the UK, for cheques drawn on a Northern Ireland bank	+4 days
In the UK, for computer-generated credits, such as Giro, CHAPS, CHIPS	0 days
In the UK, for cheques drawn in other countries, it is necessary to check with the bank, which will indicate standard transaction clearing time from statement date to value date	varies
Cash	0 days
Debits	
For all debit entries (except where debits are specifically back-valued)	0 days

Of course, the balance on the bank statement is not necessarily the amount upon which interest is charged or credited. Interest is based on the cleared balance; cheques are credited on a bank statement before they are cleared. Banks will provide statements of cleared balances if required.

In order to analyse the impact of bank float time and value dating, it is necessary to obtain bank statements covering an interest calculation period. A value date is applied to each transaction by making adjustments to the details on the statement to reflect the normal period allowed for clearing transactions through the system. This too varies from country to country. As an example, the UK adjustments to be applied are normally as shown in Table 29.1.

Allowing for these adjustments, the daily account balance should be the same as the cleared balance that the bank is using for interest calculations. The interest for the charging period can then be calculated and compared with the actual interest charges. If there is a substantial difference, the bank should be asked to detail its calculations. The difference may arise as a result of the bank's value-dating practices. The knowledge gained by the company may allow it to negotiate revised value dating better.

International electronic payments are specifically value dated. It is worthwhile analysing them to ensure that correct value dates have been applied.

International cheque clearing is a difficult area to review, since the time taken to clear foreign currency cheques will include mail delays, local administration and foreign bank delays. Nonetheless, the treasurer should ask selected overseas customers and suppliers to provide details of the value date applied to transactions in their bank accounts. In theory, the debit and credit should be for the same value date. Resolution of identified problems of excessive bank float is, again, a matter of negotiation.

Generally, banks apply consistent value-dating practices to all of their customers. This rule may alter as customers become aware of the issue and ask for adjustments. In the United Kingdom, banks apply the standard clearing times. But large companies may be able to negotiate better than standard terms and reduce the float time by one day or more.

Float time provides a technique at the treasurer's disposal in cash management efforts. By using cheques to make payments, mail time plus two to three days' clearing time is gained. Making local or foreign currency cheque payments to overseas suppliers may give additional credit that could amount to weeks. The extent to which such extra credit is taken needs to be considered from a commercial viewpoint. It may be possible to negotiate better price terms with the supplier such that the company pays by electronic funds transfer to offset the reduced credit period taken.

In multinational operations, the problem of float involves not just the loss of income on the funds tied up during the longer transfer process but also their exposure to foreign exchange risk during the transfer period. Most aspects of both international and domestic cash management are associated with the concept of float. For purposes of measurement an analysis of float can be considered in five categories:

- Invoicing float refers to funds tied up in the processing and preparing of invoices. Since this float is largely under the control of the company, it may be reduced by more efficient procedures.

- Mail float refers to funds tied up from the time customers mail their remittance cheques until the company receives them.

- Processing float embraces funds tied up in the process of sorting and recording remittance cheques until they are deposited in the bank. Like invoicing float, this float is also under the company's control and may be reduced through more efficient procedures.

- Transit float involves funds tied up from the time remittance cheques are deposited until these funds become usable to the company. This float occurs because it takes a number of days for deposited cheques to clear through the commercial banking system.

- Disbursing float refers to funds available in a company's bank account until they are actually disbursed by the company.

Selecting a commercial bank should be a logical procedure taking cognizance of the plans of the company. Such plans may give rise to requirements that will have to be met by facilities granted by the bank. Facilities that may be sought from a bank include overdraft and short-term working capital funding, medium-term loan finance for capital items, equipment-leasing or hire-purchase facilities, electronic funds facilities, the right to earn interest on surplus funds, facilities for making foreign currency payments and handling receipts, advice on subsidies available from central and local government and easy access to specialist services such as exporting, credit insurance and sales financing. Competition is such that most banks are able to provide for all the above needs.

Bankers assess proposals on the basis of economic and business data available and presented to them. But they still place great store on the quality of the people they are dealing with and their confidence in them. The firm should also feel confident that the bankers with whom it is dealing on a day-to-day basis understand the firm's business operations.

Once a bank has been chosen, the firm should keep it fully apprised of progress. In any long-term relationship, openness is essential – and this applies as much to good news as to bad. In any business, regularly revised financial projections for up to one year, at least, are essential in running the show. Availability of these will ease the negotiation of facilities with the bank. The bank itself will be able to make a judgement based directly upon data presented to it. Regular communication of results will ensure that, when new facilities are required, they can be arranged as quickly as feasible.

As firms grow, it may be appropriate to consider an additional bank to provide specialist facilities. This may arise because the company requires banking facilities outside the home country. These may be arranged through an overseas branch of the firm's home bank, an overseas bank with a relationship with the home banks, or the overseas branch network of one of the major international banks. The firm may require a second bank because it has increasing international trade and requires direct contact with an international bank or the international division of its home bank. Furthermore, where sizeable and regular foreign exchange transactions are undertaken or where money is placed with bankers, the firm may wish to obtain quotes from more than one bank to ensure the best rates.

There are benefits in having relationships established as close to home as possible. Being the big fish in a small pool may be valuable. The quality of day-to-day service obtainable from a local bank may be higher than from a multinational bank. The dedication of staff and management to what is seen by the smaller bank as a major client can be very worthwhile. Some major international companies, while having corporate relationships at the head office of their banks, maintain their routine account business at provincial branches which are geared up to meet their needs and give an outstanding service to the major customer of the branch.

Most large companies have strong relationships with one, two or three banks in the home country. Most small companies have only one relationship bank. Large companies seem, in their home country, to have one or two domestic banks plus one main international bank, which may or may not be one of the domestic banks. In respect of operations in foreign countries, the tendency is to use one domestic bank per country with one principal international bank for all foreign operations. The number of domestic banks chosen will depend upon such factors as geographical convenience – although this is of decreasing importance as technology improves the wish of banks not to be exposed in their lending beyond a particular level and, on the reverse side of the coin, firms' desire not to be exposed to the problems of any one bank. If there is more than one domestic bank involved, it is usual to arrange a lead bank. Many companies look to the banking community for short-term and medium-term funding through the domestic and Eurocurrency markets.

The firm with a good credit rating is faced with a proliferation of banks offering to lend. Unless the treasurer is selective, he or she will gather an array of facilities which might not be used. These facilities are usually uncommitted. This means that they are available for use if it suits the lender. They may be freely withdrawn or suspended; the lower their utilization, the more likely their withdrawal in times of credit squeeze. Many large companies select a panel of banks from which they borrow to meet their needs.

The finance director, or treasurer, should have responsibility for authorizing and controlling new banking facilities. Occasionally one finds, even in large companies, that a subsidiary manager has negotiated credit lines and even gone to the extent of pledging on behalf of the parent board some of the subsidiary's assets, in contravention of loan agreements already arranged.

The bank is often the major source of funds to the company. It follows that the maintenance of good and strong relationships at the highest level cannot be overdone. The day-to-day activity will involve the finance director and treasurer but the availability of the chairman, managing director and other functional directors should ensure that the relationship is strongly welded.

29.2 | Electronic banking

Electronic techniques help to improve cash management. Electronic cash management (ECM) can greatly aid management in terms of reporting data (principally balances and transactions), initiating transactions (mainly funds transfers) and assisting with decision making (mainly cash forecasting). ECM is increasingly providing treasurers with information via personal computers or terminals linked to minicomputers, supplying real-time data and giving consolidated reports for all banks worldwide. ECM can involve the initiation of transactions, such as funds transfers, foreign exchange or money market deals, or opening letters of credit. And ECM is involved in decision-making support. Here the focus is upon, for example, systems for netting cash flows, reporting a company's exposure to interest rate or foreign currency movements, and forecasting and making projections. There are systems that prepare simulations of cash flows under different scenarios.

A frequently asked question on electronic balance reporting is concerned with how to handle data from more than one bank. There are three approaches to this problem:

- Auto-dialling.

- A third-party system into which banks input their data.

- Consolidation of the information by one bank.

The auto-dialling approach involves each bank using the telephone system to record information. Software is purchased to reformat the data and consolidate it on one screen. Clearly, an arrangement has to be made with each bank and this can be expensive.

Currently, the most popular system is the third-party network. The customer enters into an agreement with one bank and an associated bureau involving all banks sending their data to the main bank's bureau for consolidation and onward transmission to the customer. All major bureaux have software available to produce consolidated reports in a standard screen layout. This method has a big advantage in confidentiality – no individual bank knows the information being submitted by another.

The third method involves consolidation at one bank. The firm's banks input balance and transaction reports in an agreed format to a lead bank using SWIFT (the Society for Worldwide Interbank Financial Telecommunications). The lead bank then supplies the consolidated report to the customer. Of course, the lead bank knows what is being reported by the other banks and this lack of confidentiality may create problems.

Some medium sized firms have decided that they need electronic systems. This may also involve receiving information on balances and the current day's transactions. Most UK banks will, on request, supply account statements in real time or as of the previous night, which are available electronically. A major factor is cost. In some countries, companies, especially those that are multibanked, find that the cost of setting up the system plus the fees charged by the bank cannot be justified by the savings made. Clearly, companies need to conduct a cost/benefit review before committing themselves to the costs involved in electronic banking.

29.3 | Cash collection and disbursement

Cash collection starts before the sale of goods or services. The seller should have established a policy on credit terms. This should involve well-administered practices in respect of credit lines for customers and adequate systems for the recording and follow-up of accounts receivable to ensure on-time receipt from sales.

The contract of sale itself is a very important document. It provides the opportunity to negotiate the desired payment mechanism. This helps to ensure that payment is received on the due date and in funds with immediate value to the seller. This is of particular importance with export sales. The time delays in obtaining cleared value for a cheque may be weeks. To avoid this, the contract should provide for payment by confirmed irrevocable letter of credit payable in a business centre convenient to the seller, or by SWIFT transfer to the seller's bank on a specific day. There are many ways to shorten the time-scale of collections nowadays. Cash managers must ensure that they keep abreast of changes taking place in the cash transmission process in international banking.

The signing of the contract is only the beginning. The performance of the contract should be monitored by both parties as this affects the cash settlement by the purchaser. It may be necessary for the cash manager to control the presentation of letters of credit for collection and to ensure that all documents are properly prepared. This will reduce the possibility of rejection by the paying bank. It is vital for the seller to ensure that all documentation to be presented to its customer contains no grounds whatsoever for delay in payment.

The cash manager should seek to reduce the time that it takes to obtain cleared value for cash received in payment. On this front, there are a number of means available, including the following:

■ *Lock boxes for cheque payments*. Effectively, these involve a collection and processing service provided to firms by banks, which collect payments from a dedicated postal box that the firm directs its customers to send payments to. The banks make several collections per day, process the payments immediately and deposit the funds into the firm's bank account. The lock-box account should be opened with a bank able to clear local currency through the domestic system in the shortest possible time. This will allow cleared funds to be handled in bulk and to be transferred or exchanged at the cheapest rate. Should local banks not offer such a facility, it is almost certain that the local branch of an international bank will do so.

■ *Electronic funds transfer and SWIFT.* Wherever possible, international transfers should be effected through these routes.

■ *Automated transfers.* Most advanced countries have domestic banking networks that permit paperless payment, such as CHIPS, CHAPS and Giro. These systems minimize the delay between the customer instructing payment and the seller receiving value for the funds in its account.

■ *Bills of exchange.* In some countries this remains the normal method of payment. This is not the case in northern Europe, the United States or the United Kingdom. But in France and Italy, for example, it remains a common method of payment even for domestic business.

■ *Letter of credit.* This is a letter from the bank of the debtor which undertakes to make payment on the debtor's behalf on presentation by the seller of specified documents. The value of the letter of credit varies according to its terms. A confirmed irrevocable letter of credit (CILC) is a letter of credit issued by the debtor's bank and bearing the confirmation or counter-guarantee of a bank acceptable to the seller. Normally, payment will be made under presentation of documents in the country of the seller. This is the most gilt-edged form of letter of credit. Next in the scale of strength is the irrevocable letter of credit (ILC). This will be issued by a debtor's bank and advised to the seller through a bank in its country, which may also be authorized to make payment on behalf of the issuing bank. The risk of the seller in this instance is the issuing bank. Lower down the scale is a letter of credit that requires documentation to be sent to a foreign bank either directly or through a bank in the seller's country. Letter of credit collections are only as secure as the quality of the documentation presented. Many letter of credit presentations are rejected due to defective documents. This can add months to the collection process in countries of Eastern Europe, Africa and the Middle East. The overall topic of letters of credit is considered in more detail in Chapter 31.

■ It may be worth arranging to collect large cheque payments from suppliers. The break-even point for the cost of using a courier versus the saving in interest is easy to calculate.

29.4 | Cash centres

Company cash management can be centralized, regionalized or decentralized. Decentralization enables subsidiaries to use excess cash in any way they see fit. While this is popular among subsidiary managers, decentralization does not allow a multinational to utilize its most liquid asset on an entirely efficient basis. Effective cash management involves the determination of cash flow centres. For example, a multinational should not choose to hold cash in a country that has violent political upheavals and/or rampant inflation. It should transfer idle cash balances, as quickly as possible, to a stable environment.

Centralized cash management, or cash pooling, calls for local subsidiaries to hold, at the local level, the minimum cash balance for transaction purposes. All funds not needed for transaction purposes are moved to a central cash centre. This cash centre is responsible for placing a central pool of funds in those currencies and money market instruments which will best serve the needs of the group on a worldwide basis.

Centralized cash management has a number of advantages over decentralized cash management, including the following:

- The bank cash centre may collect information more quickly and make better decisions on the strengths and weaknesses of various currencies. Such information and decisions are necessary if the firm plans to invest a central pool of funds most profitably.

- Funds held in a cash centre may rapidly be returned to a subsidiary with cash shortages by the most efficient method. The central pool of funds eliminates the possibility that one subsidiary will borrow at higher rates while another holds idle surplus funds or invests at lower rates.

- By holding all precautionary balances in a central cash centre the multinational firm needs a lower total level of cash to meet unforeseen eventualities.

Before cash is remitted to a central cash centre, local cash needs must be properly assessed. Various factors affect the location of cash centres. From an economic point of view, idle funds should move towards those locations that provide the greatest profitability and safety. These funds are accumulated in cash centres for temporary investment prior to redeployment elsewhere. Thus, the group should choose those locations from which funds can readily be assigned to other places in the world.

The most important factor affecting the location of cash centres is the local government's political stability and attitude towards foreign-based companies. Local laws may required partial ownership of foreign companies by nationals of the host country. Hostility of the courts towards foreign business claims and disclosure requirements may also work against location acting as a cash centre. Tax levels and excessive rates on dividend remittances play an important role in the selection of cash centres.

Cash centres should be located in countries whose currencies are stable in value and readily convertible into other currencies, whose government is stable and accommodating to foreign firms and whose financial structures and banking systems are unlikely to invoke exchange controls and draconian measures against foreign firms.

Cash centres are usually located in the major financial centres of the world such as New York and London. Brussels and Dublin Docks have become popular cash centres with attractive tax concessions. Other popular locations for cash centres are tax havens. Such countries offer most of the prerequisites for a corporate cash centre – political and economic stability, freely convertible currency, access to international communications and definitive legal procedures.

29.5 | Short-term investments

A company may have surplus funds. Frequently, such funds await investments in the business or are earmarked for payment of fixed-date obligations such as taxes or dividends. So, these funds may be specifically required by the company in a short time. In the meantime, the funds are available for short-term investment. Placing money is a subset of liquidity management. The fundamental objectives of liquidity management are concerned with ensuring the following:

- The company meets its liabilities as they fall due – the liquidity objective.

- Investment of surplus cash must not be vulnerable to any unacceptable risk of loss through credit, market or exchange risk. Also, borrowing facilities must not be at risk through the failure of the lender. The criteria applied in assessing these risks will depend on the market in which the risk is being assessed. This is sometimes termed the safety objective.

- After taking into account transaction costs, the aim is to generate an after-tax return commensurate with the risk undertaken – the profitability objective.

- The firm maintains the ability to change its liquidity profile to meet unforeseen circumstances, such as changes in interest rate, changes in economic environment and so on – the flexibility objective.

In ranking these objectives, undoubtedly safety and liquidity take precedence over flexibility and profitability.

In relation to short-term investment, policy should be aimed at ensuring that cash is available for use at the right time, in the right place and in the right currency. Furthermore, it is necessary to maintain the integrity of the principal sum invested by avoiding unnecessary risk. Surplus short-term funds might be invested in the United Kingdom, such as deposits as:

- sterling deposits with clearing banks;

- currency deposits with clearing banks (when funds are required in foreign currency);

- wholesale sterling money market deposits;

- wholesale currency deposits;

- sterling deposits with licensed deposit-taking instructions (LDTI);

- local authority loans;

- bank certificates of deposit;

- local authority yearling bonds;

- British government stocks;

- Treasury bills;

- corporation bills;

- eligible bills;

- ineligible bills;

- floating rate notes.

For a detailed description of the above instruments, see Ross (1990). Similar investment opportunities are available in other countries.

29.6 | Summary

- Cash management is concerned with planning, monitoring and managing liquid resources.

- Cash management is designed to ensure the availability of funds at the right time, in the right place, in the right currency and at an acceptable cost. It is concerned with ensuring that the organization has the wherewithal to meet its obligations as they fall due. Cash management is concerned with borrowing facilities, interest costs, bank charges, idle cash balances and investment of surplus funds. It also has as its objectives the optimization of remittable funds to the parent and the reduction of tax bills.

- Cash management is deeply concerned with banking relationships, electronic banking, cash collection and disbursement and short-term investment.

- This chapter focuses briefly upon each of these topics with a view to giving a flavour of the corporate treasurer's job in cash management terms.

29.7 | End of chapter questions

Question 1
What are the objectives of the cash management function?

Question 2
What is cash management essentially concerned with?

Question 3
How can a centralized cash management system be beneficial to the MNC?

30 Project finance

Project finance is not exactly a newcomer to the international finance scene. Indeed in 1856 financing for the building of the Suez Canal was raised by a variant of this technique. But it was not until some sixty years ago that early project finance techniques were used in the United States to fund the development of oilfields. Small Texan and Oklahoman wildcat explorers lacked sufficient capital to develop their oilfields and could not raise sufficient straight debt on their own credit standings. The bankers developed a form of production payment finance – instead of looking to the company's balance sheet for security, the banks relied on the specific reserves themselves with the direct proceeds of oil sales earmarked for the loan's repayment.

A number of variations on this theme developed, but it was not until the expansion in North Sea oilfields that project finance grew beyond production payment financing and assumed some of the variety that it has today. Subsequently through recession and Third World debt problems, international banks have used project finance concepts first for major mineral developments, then for infrastructural development, and then in the manufacturing sector. Toll roads, tunnelling projects, theme parks, production facilities in the utilities industries, shipping and aircraft finance have also received funding via project finance techniques, although the popularity of particular industries waxes and wanes from time to time.

Project finance is illusive in terms of precise definition because there is no single technique that is immutably used – each facility is tailored specifically to suit the individual project and the needs of the parties sponsoring it. In essence, the expression project finance describes a large-scale, highly leveraged financing facility established for a specific undertaking, the creditworthiness and economic justification of which are based upon that undertaking's expected cash flows and asset collateral. It is the project's own economics rather that its sponsor's (usually the equity owners) financial strength that determines its viability. In this way, the sponsor isolates this activity from its other businesses. Through careful structuring, the sponsor may shift specific risks to project customers, developers and other participants, thus limiting the financial recourse to itself.

This process of sharing risk is not without costs. Project finance borrowing is normally more expensive than conventional company debt and the very large number of contracts that must be specified between the relevant parties entails additional time and expense. But the ultimate result may be more acceptable to the sponsors. Compared with direct funding, it is usually off-balance sheet and this may better reflect the actual legal nature of non-recourse finance. We explain this in more detail later in this chapter.

Lenders are also attracted to project finance. In addition to higher fees, they can be sure that cash generation will be retained within the project rather than diverted to cross-subsidize other activities. The lenders further benefit in terms of their first claim to these funds. They are protected by a range of covenants from the sponsor and other parties. Spreading project risks over several participants lessens their dependence on the sponsor's own credit standing too. The typically large capital requirement necessitates syndication to a group of institutions, so that the credit exposure is shared across many lenders. A properly structured project finance facility does not necessarily entail more risk exposure than a normal corporate advance.

It can be seen that in project lending the focus is entirely upon the project being financed. The lender looks, mainly (often wholly), to the project as a source of repayment. Its cash flows and assets are dedicated to service the project loan. Clearly, the project cannot start to repay a loan until it is operational and continuing to operate soundly, so analysis by lenders is critical. If any major part of the project fails, lenders probably lose money. Projects lack a variety of products and their assets are highly specialized, equipment may be of relatively little value outside the project itself and may, sometimes be geographically remote. A project's assets may provide little in terms of the second exit route that bankers usually like in respect of a loan facility. Because of this, project finance is regarded by bankers as high risk/high reward money – although the risk may be reduced by careful structuring. The other side of the coin is that project cash flows are dedicated to debt repayment.

The owner's risk is often confined to whatever equity or guarantees are needed to make the project viable. Having said this, where the owner plays another role – perhaps contractor or operator – then the owner bears the normal risks associated with these roles. In recompense for the limited risk, the owner will often take nothing out of the project until debt has been repaid – only the strongest of projects can accommodate early withdrawal. Once the project becomes debt-free, then everything that remains is his.

The specific features below distinguish project finance from conventional corporate borrowing. They may not all be present in a particular project financing instance.

- The project is usually established as a distinct, separate entity.

- It relies considerably on debt financing. Borrowings generally provide 70–75 per cent of the total capital with the balance being equity contributions or subordinated loans from the sponsors. Some projects have been structured successfully with over 90 per cent debt.

- The project loans are linked directly to the venture's assets and potential cash flow.

- The sponsors' guarantees to lenders do not, as a rule, cover all the risks and usually apply only until completion (coming on-stream).

- Firm commitments by various third parties, such as suppliers, purchasers of the project's output, government authorities and the project sponsors are obtained and these create significant components of support for the project credit.

- The debt of the project entity is often completely separate (at least for balance sheet purposes) from the sponsor companies' direct obligations.

- The lender's security usually consists only of the project's assets, aside from project cash generation.

- The finance is usually for a longer period than normal bank lending.

Project finance is most frequently used in capital-intensive projects which are expected to generate strong and reasonably certain cash flows and which may consequently support high levels of debt. Many oil companies, which are small relative to the sums involved in the development of major fields, have used project finance to enable them to pursue major new developments using a production payment loan on an existing field already in production to pay for the further development of a new field – rather as a property developer can mortgage existing properties to provide finance for new developments. These kinds of production payment loan tend to be on a limited recourse basis – that is, if the field fails to produce sufficient revenue, the lender has no recourse to the oil company itself except in limited circumstances, such as failure of the oil company to operate the field competently. In this way, the company sheds some of its risk while retaining the long-term benefits of its new discovery.

30.1 | Limited recourse finance

At this point, it is worth distinguishing between limited recourse and non-recourse financing. In project finance terms, non-recourse financing occurs when lenders do not, at any stage during the loan, including the pre-production period, have recourse for repayment from other than project cash flows. In practice, such financing is almost unobtainable. Limited amounts of debt are structured on this basis, and it is becoming more common for major foreign corporate investors buying into energy projects to provide a guarantee to finance the project on a basis that is non-recourse to the original sponsors.

The essential difference between non-recourse and limited recourse finance is highlighted when a project is abandoned prior to becoming operational. In the non-recourse case, the sponsors can, in principle, walk away from the project without liability to repay the debt; this is almost never the case in limited recourse financing. Limited recourse financing is a more accurate description of most project financing involving bank lenders. Such instances include a very wide spectrum of arrangements which restrict the ability of lenders to look to project sponsors for repayment of debt in the event of problems with the loans. Typically, lenders have narrowly defined claims against sponsors for loan repayment prior to completion – that is, until the construction is complete and the project operational. On completion, lenders have recourse only to project cash flows and assets. Completion is thus a vital issue for lender and project borrower alike; this topic is discussed later in this chapter.

30.2 | Ownership structures

Many projects undertaken using project financing techniques are jointly owned or jointly controlled. Reasons for joint ownership or control vary widely between projects but major factors influencing such joint ownership include:

- project development risks may be too large for one participant only and are thus shared by partners;

- benefits from the combination of skills and other resources may be substantial;

- the project development outlays and other considerations (as well as risk tolerance) may be beyond the financial and managerial capacity of a single owner.

The development of a financing plan for a large project involves three key phases – these embrace:

- establishment of an appropriate ownership and operation structure for the project;

- formulation of a suitable financing structure which meets the sponsors' objectives;

- development of appropriate borrowing mechanisms which best meet the capital and cash flow requirements of the project.

The selection of an appropriate ownership structure by sponsors is determined by their objectives and financial, legal, accounting and taxation constraints. Structures vary from project to project. There are four main types of entity used for jointly owned projects. These are set out below.

- *Incorporated entities.* When a corporation is used to own and develop the project, each sponsor holds shares in this company rather than in the project itself. While its corporate structure allows greater flexibility in raising debt capital, tax losses and allowances resulting from the project can usually only be used within the project company itself. Since many projects do not generate profits in the early years, such tax benefits can remain unused for some time. This structure may also result in higher funding costs due to the limited liability and non-recourse features created. Nonetheless it is one of the most popular ownership structures in project finance.

- *Trusts.* Similar to a project company structure, in the trust the sponsors hold units instead of shares in the company. A nominally capitalized company would usually be established to act as trustee and it would handle all of the contracts and hold the legal title to the trust's assets. A trust can be readily dismantled and the project assets transferred back to the sponsors at any time. But there can be some loss of flexibility due to the trustee's strict legal obligations. In project financing, trusts may suffer from the same tax disadvantages as companies.

- *Partnerships.* Here, the project is owned and operated by the partnership and the partners benefit in accordance with the partnership agreement. As the partnership is not usually a taxable entity, partners can gain immediate access to any tax advantages but there is the major disadvantage that the partners have unlimited liability for all of the partnership debts. Sponsors might form separate subsidiaries to shield themselves from this direct liability problem and still retain many tax advantages, but it is not the most popular of ownership structures in project finance.

■ *Joint ventures.* An unincorporated joint venture is a common ownership structure for projects. The joint venture is evidenced by a legal agreement between the sponsors which defines the obligations of the sponsors in the venture. In terms of setting off losses, this structure has tax advantages.

The choice of ownership structure involves a trade-off between the risk exposures of the sponsors and the returns from the project. These include commitments by the sponsors and other third parties to satisfy syndicate lenders' concerns that the project can support, in its own right, a substantial amount of debt. Lenders have a general preference for conventional incorporation of a project venture. In practice, though, the only differences between borrowing through an unincorporated joint venture project and through an incorporated one are the legal costs, tax effects and complexity of the security arrangements.

30.3 | Financing structures

With an appropriate ownership structure agreed, it is necessary to choose a financing structure that meets the sponsors' funding objectives. One of these is usually to arrange finance on a limited recourse basis. The degree of recourse may vary from project to project and, indeed, between different sponsors in the same project. Where limited recourse finance is sought, a separate borrowing vehicle is usually established for the financing and this clearly separates the project liability from the general liabilities of the sponsor. A much less frequently used alternative is for the loan to be extended to the sponsor, with limited recourse being achieved through the terms of the loan agreement.

Another key objective concerns the sharing of project risks between sponsors and other parties. Since sponsors may wish to shed certain project risks, the financing structure might ensure that their impact is shifted to other parties. For example, bank lenders may assume most of the project risks following completion on the condition that marketing risk is covered by pre-arranged sales contracts. Floor pricing arrangements are also a means of risk sharing. In such circumstances, the purchaser takes the commercial risk that it is able to perform given the floor price arrangement, and the bank takes the risk that the loans may not be repaid if the purchaser is unable or unwilling to perform. Also, marketing risks may be reduced by the introduction of minority participants who are buyers of the project's production. In some projects, individual sponsors may have specific objectives which affect the financing structure. The most frequently encountered structures in project financing include:

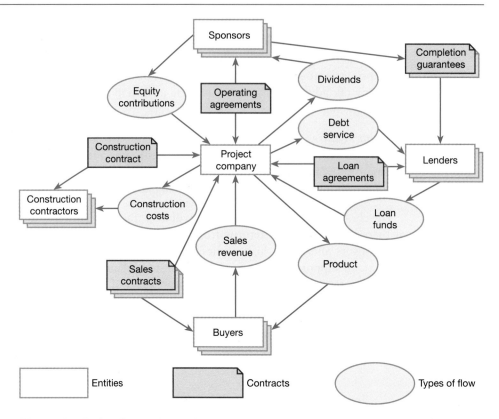

Figure 30.1 Project finance borrowing via a project subsidiary supported by sponsors' undertakings.

■ project sponsors borrowing through a project subsidiary;

■ project sponsors borrowing direct;

■ a structure based upon production payments;

■ use of a joint venture finance/operating/marketing company;

■ use of a finance/tolling company;

■ leveraged leasing as part of a larger project financing facility.

In this text we look briefly at each of these techniques.

Where the project sponsors raise limited recourse money through a project subsidiary, the borrower is a company owned, but not necessarily guaranteed, by the project sponsors. The borrower's assets, which relate solely to the project, and those of the project sponsors pertaining to the project are charged to the lenders. An example of this form of financing is given in Figure 30.1. An essential part of this financing mode is the project sponsors' completion guarantees, so that the lenders' risk is confined to the post-completion period.

This approach to project financing contrasts with that where project sponsors borrow directly. In this latter arrangement, the loan agreement between bank lenders

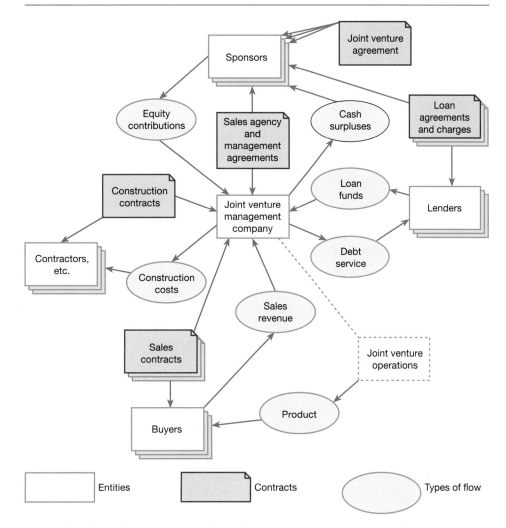

Figure 30.2 Direct borrowing by sponsors for a joint venture project.

and sponsors would, once the project has been completed, specifically prevent lenders seeking recourse against any assets other than those of the project. An example is provided in Figure 30.2. Note that the loan agreement effectively creates an escrow account to control disbursements to the lenders and the project sponsors of cash flows generated by the project. This model of project financing has the disadvantage that the sponsor usually has to borrow and then on-lend the funds. Thus both the asset and the liability may be reflected on the sponsor's balance sheet adversely affecting gearing ratios.

We now turn briefly to production payment financing, a technique common in the United States and elsewhere, especially in the oil and mineral industries.

A production payment involves the sale and purchase of the whole, or a specified proportion, of the rights to future sales proceeds from the producing assets. In this arrangement, lenders, or others, purchase a share of the production from a project and these proceeds become the prime source of project finance. This approach can only be used when the production cash flows can be assessed with a good degree of accuracy and thus represent an acceptable form of collateral. Essentially then, lenders and other production payment purchasers acquire rights to future cash flow from production, secured by a charge over of the mining lease and/or project assets *in situ*. Other factors may include:

■ payment being restricted to sales proceeds of minerals from a specific property and therefore not out of any other production;

■ rights to production being for periods less than the expected life of the project;

■ production payments being derived from proven mineral reserves;

■ sponsor guarantees of minimum production levels; rates and specifications may be required.

A typical production payment financing scheme is illustrated in Figure 30.3. The production payment structure generally requires a borrowing intermediary. This is usually a trust acting on behalf of the sponsors. The project sponsors agree to give the trust the rights to a specified proportion of all sales. This agreement remains in force until a stipulated amount, equal to the initial loan plus accrued interest, has been repaid.

To structure a production payment facility without a trustee, the sale proceeds would then be controlled by way of an escrow account to cover production payment instalments and special conditions. These may embrace regular independent audits of production with an obligation on sponsors that specified levels and rates of production are met.

Variations on this basic production payment financing method abound – they are sometimes termed production loans or production backed loans.

We now turn to the use of a joint venture finance and/or operating company. If an unincorporated joint venture is established to own and operate a project, one has to consider financing possibilities carefully to shed risk. One method, involves management of separate financing by each sponsor, and the separate marketing of production. This preserves the joint venture for tax purposes and provides considerable flexibility in borrowing structures, and differentiation for each sponsor's terms and conditions.

Other means of achieving an acceptable project financing with appropriate risk reduction involve variants of this technique such as the use of a marketing/financing company to conduct the project's operations, marketing and financing – see Figure 30.4 (overleaf).

The sponsors' operating agreement with the financing company makes the latter responsible for project operations, including the borrowing and servicing of loans on behalf of the sponsors, paying expenses and remitting dividends. Depending upon the sponsors' finance and taxation objectives there are many variations on the theme summarized in Figure 30.4. For example, the marketing may be undertaken via a sales agency arrangement or by the use of back-to-back sales contracts with the finance/operating company as an intermediary between project owners and

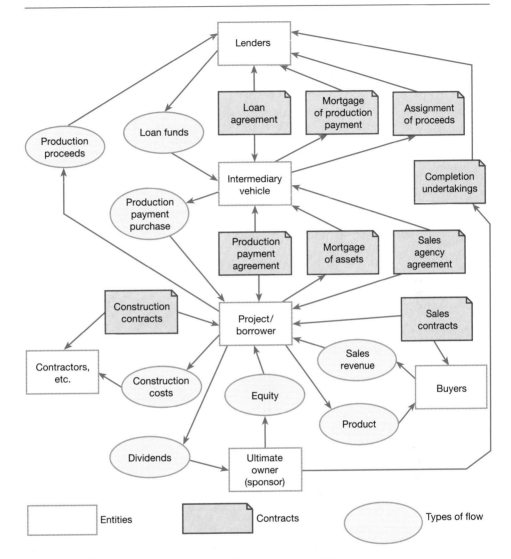

Figure 30.3 Project financing via production payment financing.

purchasers of output. But it should be noted that, as in other structures where the sponsors are not the direct project borrowers, the sponsors would need to guarantee both the completion of the project and the satisfactory management of the finance/operating company.

We now present a summary of the way in which finance/tolling companies may be used as a mechanism in project financing. A tolling arrangement is only applicable where strong throughput contracts or take-or-pay agreements between the provider of a service and end-users of that service are available. Such arrangements are used extensively in financing oil and gas pipelines, mineral transportation facilities, port facilities, rail projects and power stations, among other kinds of project. The take-or-pay agreements require the end-user to make regular payments, over the term of

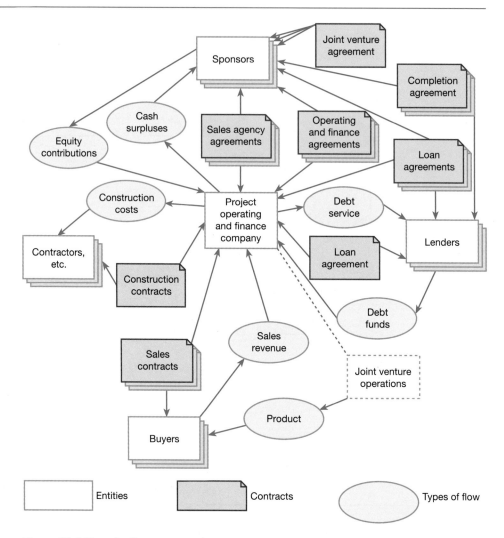

Figure 30.4 Use of a finance-operating company.

the financing, of a specified minimum amount in consideration for the project's output or service, irrespective of whether such benefits are actually fully taken up or not. This unconditional obligation is assigned to the lender as part collateral and usually supported by a completion guarantee by the sponsor. Ideally, such take-or-pay amounts are sufficient to service the project's debt and its operating costs. An example of this type of financing structure appears in Figure 30.5. In the figure shown, note that the sponsors have effectively floated the project as a listed public company. This does not necessarily have to be the case – it is merely set out here to show that a further dimension is possible. Assume that the project floated on the stock exchange is a transportation system. The public company would then construct, own and operate the transportation system and establish take-or-pay contracts with

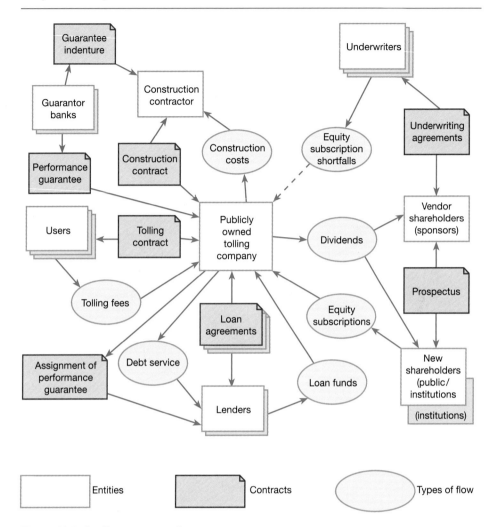

Figure 30.5 A tolling company finance structure.

a number of users. Under the proposed take-or-pay agreements, the user companies would be obliged to make regular payments whether or not the transportation system were used by them. The incentive for the user companies would be substantial savings on transportation costs provided by the new system.

Leveraged leasing is another form of limited recourse financing. Debt and equity parties rely on project cash flows first, and then the project assets financed as the source of repayment of their investment. Leveraged leasing differs from normal leasing because it involves a lender as well as a lessor and lessee. The lessor borrows most of the funds from a third party but still obtains 100 per cent of the tax advantages from owning the leased assets which in turn can be passed on to the lessee through lower lease payments. The lessee benefits too as its payments are also tax deductible.

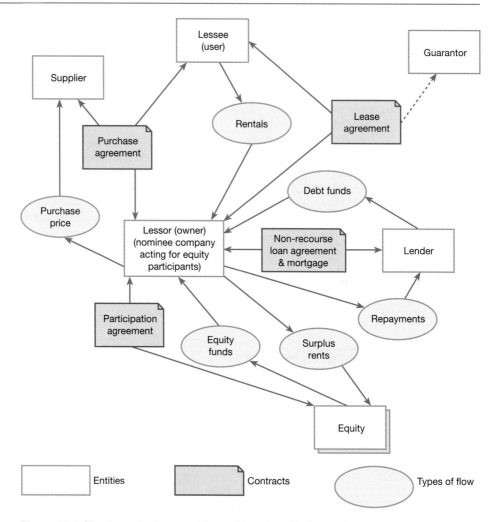

Figure 30.6 Structure of a leveraged lease. Note that this figure shows only the leveraged lease arrangements. Project finance techniques will be superimposed upon them.

This financing structure may be used in natural resource projects, but it is far better suited to financing developments with a substantial component of capital equipment. But there are reasons why leveraged leasing is less attractive than other structures. The prevalence of joint venture structures in limited recourse financings has meant that tax benefits are offset against sponsors' incomes rather than being sold on through a leveraged lease. It is difficult to integrate a leveraged lease into a larger financing. As the asset is leased and not owned, it is not available as security to the project lenders. Figure 30.6 outlines the structure of a typical leveraged lease. Leveraged leasing is a somewhat complex route compared with other project financing methods. This complicates project documentation and adds to the cost of the facility. However, leveraged leasing arrangements may, because of the tax effects, create more competitive financing costs than under other methods.

30.4 | Loan structuring

After establishing a suitable financing structure, project borrowings must be arranged in a form that gives effect to the sponsors' financing objectives. As stated earlier, it is possible to achieve different levels of recourse within the same project loan structure. This may be achieved by several loan structures, of which the following example is typical:

- The project has two sponsors, A and B.

- The project loan is divided into two parts or tranches. Tranche A is supported by a completion guarantee from sponsor A. Sponsor A is also prepared to guarantee repayment of Tranche A. But, while Tranche B is supported by a completion guarantee from sponsor B there is no guarantee of repayment.

- Both tranches are secured on the project's assets.

- The pricing for both tranches is the same until completion, when Tranche B becomes more expensive, reflecting the absence of a guarantee from sponsor B.

Lenders look to project cash flow for repayment of their loan. Hence their need to forecast and analyse cash flows in considerable detail. Their overriding concern is that the cash generated, after all calls on cash, will pay interest and principal payments. A fundamental tool for risk analysis by lenders and borrowers is a cash flow modelling system. It is difficult to contemplate most project financings without this analysis. The basic tools are coverage ratios. These ratios are used to analyse a variety of risk elements but the debt service ratio is the most common. It is concerned with the ability of the project cash flows for a period to meet debt service requirements during that period. By definition, the debt service ratio is given by:

$$\frac{\text{NCFE} + \text{CPD} + (\text{Int} + \text{Lsg})(1 - t)}{\text{CPD} + (\text{Int} + \text{Lsg})(1 - t)}$$

where NCFE is the net generation available to equity participants (but after interest, tax and debt repayments), CPD is the current portion of long-term debt, Int is the interest expense, Lsg is the lease commitment and t is the tax rate for the project. Lenders typically look for debt service ratio of 1.2 or more for relatively predictable projects but ratios of 1.5 or even more are often sought and 2.0 may be required in the case of a project based on a commodity exposed to volatile price movements.

Some lenders use pre-tax debt service ratios for analysing loans to joint ventures. Since tax payments are the responsibility of each sponsor and the lenders have access to pre-tax cash flows, computing pre-tax ratios is then more accepted.

When assessing a financing proposal, lenders set a minimum debt service ratio that reflects the credit support available from sources external to the project. Contracts with take-or-pay provisions and floor price supports are likely to have lower debt service ratios, all other things being equal.

Further analysis undertaken by lenders aims at identifying the level of technical and operating competence of the management (and this must be seen to be undoubted); it also aims at understanding the strategic and competitive position of the project – and, of course, it ultimately aims at identifying repayment ability based solely on project cash generation.

Clearly a critical part of the lenders analysis embraces reaching a view on the risk of the project. In this regard, lenders home in on risk under a number of different headings, including:

■ resource risk;

■ raw materials and supplies risk;

■ completion (or construction) risk;

■ operating risk;

■ marketing risk;

■ financial risks, including foreign exchange risk;

■ political and regulatory risk;

■ *force majeure* risk.

We now consider each of these in turn.

30.5 | Resource risk

Resource risk concerns the ability of the project's recoverable resources to repay the lenders and to provide the sponsors with an adequate return on their investment.

Lenders generally require considerably more reserves than would be necessary to amortize their loan. Such resources are subject to independent evaluations and are audited over the project's life. Reserves are classified as proven or probable with lenders clearly preferring the former and allowing for only a portion of the latter in their calculations.

Lenders measure the degree of resource risk by what is called the reserve coverage ratio. This measures the total of saleable reserves (usually without resorting to probable reserves) to those reserves necessary to meet sales to cover commitments and debt service during the life of the financing. It is calculated as:

$$\text{Reserve coverage ratio} = \frac{\text{total saleable reserve}}{\text{loan life saleable reserve}}$$

where total saleable reserves include all those reserves in the proven category (exceptionally, some probable reserves might be included) extractable with current technology in the existing production plan its extension, and loan life saleable reserves comprise those reserves necessary to meet sales commitments over the life of financing.

The minimum acceptable reserve cover ratio is a matter of judgement, but most lenders would generally expect a reserve coverage ratio of at least 2, although some projects have been financed with lower figures. As the above ratio approaches 1.5, or even falls below it, sponsors may be asked to guarantee a minimum saleable reserve, or to undertake further reserve definition. Another approach involves two-tranche financing where tranche A involves shorter maturities on a limited recourse basis and tranche B is longer term debt with recourse to the sponsors in the event of inadequate reserves. The split between A and B is designed to create adequate reserve coverage for the A tranche.

Oil, gas and mineral financings use a number of ratios to evaluate production payment arrangements and project loans. Both net proceeds (that is, sales less operating costs) and gross sales cash streams are vital for loan structuring, and ratios based on discounted net proceeds or gross sales are used. One such typically used ratio is the net proceeds field life coverage ratio (NPFCR), defined as:

$$NPFCR = \frac{PVNP}{OB}$$

where PVNP is the present value of net proceeds during the oilfield's proven reserve life and OB is the outstanding principal balance. Most lenders seek a ratio, as defined above, of two times or more in each year, with discounting done at the loan interest rate.

30.6 | Raw material and supplies risk

Where raw materials are processed, there is a risk that the plant, though constructed and operationally complete, is unable to fulfil production contracts owing to a shortage of inputs. This risk may become critical because of the prices of inputs or their availability.

Generally, lenders require minimum stockpiles of key raw materials and adequate supply contracts to ensure their cost and availability, both in the short term and in the longer term too. In some cases, the lenders may refuse to carry these risks and seek sponsor or third party guarantees for the raw materials supply.

30.7 | Completion risk

Lenders need to be happy that the project will work and produce an end-product that meets design specifications of quality and quantity, within estimated cost and time limits. This is critical to project lending. Of course, lenders are not necessarily technologists or engineers. So they will look for assurances from the operator on the contractual arrangements under which construction of the various facilities will be undertaken. These contractual arrangements may take different forms. Lenders typically prefer to see one major contracting firm responsible for each section of the project working under a lump-sum fixed contract with a fixed completion date, penalties for delay and turnkey responsibility for the commissioning of that section. A precise definition of tasks and responsibilities is of paramount importance for projects especially where several companies, perhaps from different countries, are involved.

Lenders will expect to receive an independent consultant's report on the feasibility of the project. This will evaluate the technology and confirm that the project can be completed to meet the technical specification within the estimated cost. Based on track records of similar plants and the companies involved in construction and operation, lenders will need to be satisfied that the plant is likely to be successfully completed and operated to produce the products in the quantities and the qualities and at the cost levels required.

Lenders look for an economic projection with forecasts of production and sales levels, operating costs and earnings anticipated over the life of the project. They look at the ability of a project to cover the required debt service payments in each year and at the average of the debt service over the repayment period. Lenders also look for an assessment of future net cash flows before loan repayment and also after the loan is due to be finally repaid – this latter estimate gives an indication of the extent to which the project has something in reserve.

Typically, lenders also seek a guarantee from a party other than the sponsors that the project facilities will be completed on time. The financial strength of the party giving this completion guarantee is clearly of essence. The arrangement of further financing, on a standby facility basis, with a much lower debt ratio than in the main project finance package may, in some cases, overcome the need for a completion guarantee.

Lenders need to be satisfied that the party giving any completion guarantee will meet cost overruns incurred up to completion and that it will have the ability to do so. The guarantor is obliged to arrange for completion by a certain date and to subscribe equity to meet any cost overruns.

Successful completion of the project is the essence of cash flow based project financing. It receives the most attention in loan negotiation and documentation. Where a separate borrowing vehicle is used, the loan will be between the borrowing vehicle and the lenders. Lenders will require either a direct completion guarantee, or a guarantee by the sponsors to the borrowing vehicle in the case of default in terms of failing to complete construction and functioning of the project according to a set of independently certified completions tests.

Completion agreements define covenants between lenders and sponsors and embrace such areas as the following:

■ Unconditional agreements to provide funds and management expertise to ensure completion in accordance with specified completion tests.

■ Financial guarantees requiring sponsors to repurchase project debt or convert it to a corporate obligation of the sponsors should completion conditions not be met.

■ Cash or working capital deficiency agreements where the sponsors agree to provide sufficient cash to meet minimum specified levels of working funds during part or all of the loan's term. These arrangements use junior obligations to support the position of senior lenders and may not always be used. However, export credit agencies often favour these covenants.

- Completion and performance agreements whereby the sponsors agree to meet the completion tests, but not responsibility for the debt if they fail to do so. This puts the onus on lenders to sue for and prove damages if completion problems occur.

- Best efforts undertakings which may take a variety of forms from 'full faith and credit' best efforts undertakings to agreements to use prudent commercial practice to secure completion.

- Completion pool of funds agreements, specifying so much debt and so much equity subscription, which commits owners to spend no more than a fixed sum in attempting completion.

The strength of the completion agreements is a function of how completion is defined. Completion tests may include the following:

- Completion and performance tests that require physical completion of the facilities and their operation for a period – typically between 3 and 12 months – at design performance levels. A key test is to maintain actual production costs within a specified percentage of budgeted costs.

- Physical completion tests are weaker because they do not include a performance measure. This means that lenders may share some of the design risks inherent in completion.

- Cash flow completion tests requiring a defined level of cash, working capital and rate of cash generation by the project.

- Other tests, for example minimum levels of sales committed under satisfactory long-term contracts, have been required where loan drawdowns occur beforehand.

Completion and performance certification requires the sponsors and an independent engineer to make several warranties. These may include the following:

- Technical and physical completion in accordance with agreed completion tests warranted by independent engineers.

- Sponsors' warranties that an agreed level of minimum working capital exists in the project.

- Sponsors' warranties that no situation exists which would result in the project being unable to service debt.

- Other special tests and warranties may be written into individual certification requirements as necessary.

30.8 | Operating risk

Operating risk is concerned with whether the project produces in a cost-effective manner. The technology used and the sponsors' past experience of it and track record of operating it are key aspects when assessing the level of operating risk and its potentially adverse impact. Project finance lenders seldom advance funds for a project on a new or unproven technology. Labour availability and industrial relations and safety regulations may also be important. Sponsor covenants are used to ensure that the project follows the accepted procedures.

In essence, then, lenders need to be satisfied that the project facilities will operate satisfactorily during the project's life so that the end-product may be produced in the quantities and qualities required. In this respect, they will analyse factors including the following:

- The track record of the operator of the project over a number of years in the operation of plants of the type involved.

- The availability of able and proven management and a trained workforce.

- The quality of financial plans and projections, with indications of abilities to monitor expenditure during the construction phase and to control operating costs thereafter.

- The availability of all necessary governmental consents.

- The location of the project, including the infrastructure and transport facilities available or planned, plus an indication of the potential environmental impact.

- The certainty and availability and cost of key inputs such as feedstocks and power required by the project. It may be necessary that feedstock and power supply be covered by long-term fixed price contracts.

The above factors are critical in assessing the risks associated with the functioning of the project. An appropriate insurance policy with a loss-payable clause in favour of the lenders may also cover, on an all-risks basis, the construction and operation period and may cover loss of profits due to delay resulting from *force majeure* risks – see below. Loss of profit as a result of breakdown may not be recoverable and this may jeopardize the ability of a project to meet its debt service. It is necessary, in these circumstances, to establish which party will bear such losses and to assess the ability of such a party to meet them.

30.9 | Marketing risk

Once the project commences production, there remains the risk that output cannot be sold for the price or in the volume originally planned. The extent of these two risk factors varies significantly among projects. These risks can be overcome through a variety of means, such as long-term sales contracts, supply and demand estimates or take-or-pay clauses. The sponsor may be forced to give a loan covenant or separate support agreement covering this area.

A few projects may attract strong and effective long-term fixed price sales arrangements with an escalator. Where these are the basis for financing, lenders carefully analyse escalator mechanisms. Lenders tend to have greater confidence in projects where a high volume on contracted sales is to companies with some ownership of the project.

Essentially then, the focus of lenders in a project finance situation is upon the ability of the operator to sell sufficient volumes of end-product to generate the required revenues to meet debt service. Lenders are generally reluctant to accept the risk that an undefined quantity of product will be sold to undefined buyers at some date in the future. Consequently, a lot of attention is paid to agreements which the operating company seeks with potential purchasers of the plant's output following completion. Offtake contracts, which the operating company enters, for the sale of output will have to provide lenders with enforceable claims against the purchasing entities in the event of production being delayed or the purchaser failing to meet its commitment to buy the product at a specific date and price. The identity of the purchaser and the enforceability of the claims against such a purchaser are of vital importance in satisfying lenders. Lenders will need to be certain that any new projects linked to the supply of the end-product will be completed in step with the project which they are financing.

Lenders expect the project sponsor to enter into offtake commitments for the sale of the product with a party or parties which can be expected to meet such commitments and which are sufficiently financially strong to meet any judgement for damages that might be awarded against them. Lenders seek to be protected by the allocation of a substantial proportion of the output of the plant under sales contracts, running well after final repayment of the financing, with acceptable parties at a minimum price.

In assessing offtake commitments, lenders generally look at such factors as the strength and creditworthiness of the buyer, the period of commitment, the proportion of the designed capacity covered by the commitment, requirements for the quality of the product in the offtake agreement, *force majeure* provisions, the conditions under which the buyer can refuse to accept the product, the sale price (with any provision for price escalation to cover cost increases) and the currency of payments. The assurance provided to lenders by offtake arrangements is strengthened if the purchasers have a financial commitment to the project – perhaps in the form of direct loans or a significant equity stake.

30.10 | Financial risk

Various means are available to offset foreign exchange and interest rate risk in a project financing situation. For example, as we have seen earlier in this text, a certain amount of foreign exchange risk may be eliminated by borrowing in the same currency as that generated by commodity sales and managing the residual risk by a combination of short- and long-dated foreign exchange contracts, swaps and other instruments. Interest rate risk may be managed by using similar means designed for the interest rate markets, such as forward rate agreements (FRAs) and options for short-term management and swaps, caps and collars for longer term management.

The price risk of commodities consumed by the project may be managed, to an extent, by the use of commodity futures or swaps markets. The use of swaps exposes the producer to counterparty risk, of course.

30.11 | Political and regulatory risk

Investment in foreign countries is subject to a variety of risks such as expropriation or nationalization. There may be changes in local tax regimes, currency and foreign exchange problems. Sponsors and lenders may arrange insurance against some of these risks. Certainly agreements usually require sponsors to indemnify lenders against these risks.

Although utter avoidance of all political risk is impossible, lenders will certainly want to be satisfied that all necessary consents and authorizations have been granted and that there is every possible assurance that they will continue to be in force so that the project can be consistently operated according to plan. Lenders will be reassured if undertakings covering such matters as supply of essential services like power, feedstock, overheads, water and so on, and the maintenance of all relevant consents, have been obtained. Strong lenders have insisted that, if the host government alters the basic political and regulatory foundations under which the project was originally conceived, then it should immediately become a full guarantor of all project debt. This kind of clause has frequently been upheld in law.

30.12 | *Force majeure* risk

Force majeure risk refers to those intrusions of circumstances beyond the control of either sponsors or lenders. These include such acts of nature as earthquakes, floods, tidal waves, typhoons, fire and explosion as well as some man-made disasters such as war or terrorism. Some may be covered by insurance but premiums are often high or even prohibitive. The actual exposure may be borne jointly by sponsors and lenders or this may be varied by the lending agreement.

30.13 | How does project finance create value?

It has been suggested that raising money through project finance rather than direct borrowing by the parent company adds shareholder value. The worth of a project to the parent, so the argument goes, is enhanced if it can be made to stand alone as a self-financing entity so that the parent benefits from its success and is isolated against its failure. Also, project finance debt ratios are higher than for the sponsoring companies. The argument that this adds shareholder value is frail. If risk is transferred, one would expect the taker of the risk to have asked for some compensation – perhaps in terms of a better contract price, or a higher interest rate. On the debt question, the proposition that the project can bear a higher debt ratio than the company seems naive. If lenders were able to ask for the sort of undertakings referred to earlier in this chapter, including perhaps escrow accounts (under which project cash flows are held in a separate bank account against debt service payment being met), for normal company lending, it is not apparent why debt ratios should be any different from project finance levels. Banks look for a higher gross margin in respect of project finance lending than is typical with wholesale corporate lending. While the former may attract a 1 per cent gross margin over the cost of inter-bank funds, the latter typically earns only $^1/_2$ per cent gross. Having said this, project finance does allow the sponsoring parties to transfer particular risks to others. Indeed, the interest rate charged by project-financing lenders usually reflects the degree of support provided by the sponsors.

Turning to the question of political risk, some companies believe that expropriation by a foreign government is less likely when they raise money by project financing. The argument goes that few host governments would want to take an action that would anger a group of leading international banks – and this may be true. Often, of course, the host government is a shareholder in the project equity. This is a two-edged sword inasmuch as it may or may not motivate expropriation. Would the host government wish to alienate its partners and the international banking community? Or does the host government gain know-how during the partnership which may hasten nationalization?

Another motive for project financing which has been suggested is that it may not be shown as debt on the company's balance sheet. Whether this argument has any validity turns on whether lenders or shareholders recognize the existence and potential effect of these hidden liabilities. It would be naive to suggest that the financial world would be hoodwinked or deceived by such off-balance sheet devices.

Certainly, project financing is expensive and time consuming to arrange. But it may be the appropriate kind of finance for a particular circumstance. For example, a lender's security for a pipeline project loan depends on the existence of throughput arrangements. The lender's security for a tanker loan depends on the charter agreements. In these circumstances, it may be simplest to tie the loan directly to the underlying contracts, and it is certainly appropriate.

So, should we conclude that structuring investments on a project finance basis does not add shareholder value? This would be wrong – project finance may increase shareholder value or it may destroy it. It all depends on how it is done.

In structuring a deal involving for example, mineral extraction, the firm owning the reserves of ore trades potential cash generation when it takes on co-sponsors in return for sharing some of the risks. A perfectly offsetting trade of return for risk should neither add nor destroy value.

However, we believe that the potential for creating shareholder value lies in the domain of taxation and systematic/unsystematic risk. Let us look further at these points.

Certainly whether one approaches valuation via an NPV or an APV route, two relevant conclusions are apparent. First of all, using higher levels of debt will have a tendency towards the lowering of the weighted average cost of capital (relevant for the NPV approach) or an increase in the tax shield due to debt financing (relevant in the APV approach). The former effect will be offset, to some extent, in the NPV case by the increase in the geared cost of equity capital. But, on the other side of the equation, risk shedding in structuring the project financing along the lines suggested in this chapter should tend to reduce the volatility of project earnings – for example, take or pay agreements may be in place, and similar stabilizing features too. The reduction in volatility of the project profit and loss account bottom line should result in the project having lower systematic risk than would otherwise be the case. This will reduce the discount rate to be used in project evaluation. But this, of itself, may not create value. Remember that cash flows for the project will be lower by virtue of giving up return for sharing of risk. And if the trade of return for risk is fair, these minus and plus effects should cancel out. The potential for value creation derives from another area.

In Chapter 28 of this book, we pointed out that, in opposition to the capital asset pricing model, Adler and Dumas (1977a, b) and Lessard and Shapiro (1983) have proposed the valuation model:

$$V_F = \Sigma V_i - P(\sigma)$$

where V_F is the value of the firm, V_i is the present value of each of the firm's projects and $P(\sigma)$ is a penalty factor that reflects the impact on expected after-tax cash flows of the total risk of the firm. It is possible to argue that with respect for example, to a large mineral project, its size and potentially adverse effects if it were to go wrong could make $P(\sigma)$ very significant indeed. If the firm were to shed some of this risk it should reduce the impact of the penalty factor. Assuming that, in structuring the project finance, the risk/return trade-off was entirely fair, then ΣV_i in the above equation would not alter. As total risk should fall as a result of use of project finance in the mineral investment, shareholder value would be created.

According to this analysis, the potential for shareholder value creation through project financing derives from two sources, namely a higher value of the tax shield on debt and a reduction in the penalty factor owing to the impact of total risk on the value of the firm.

In addition, we believe that there is potential for corporate value creation in two other areas. First of all, in undertaking for example, an infrastructure project for a foreign country, the host government, in pursuit of political rather than economic motives, may allow a deal to be structured that involves a less than exact risk/return trade-off. So, in its pursuit of political ends it may enter into a contract that gives a beneficial risk/return trade-off favouring the corporations undertaking the project. The second source of value creation for the corporate entity is through the creation of valuable real operating options in a foreign territory – although this cannot be quantified as precisely as other value-creating devices.

30.14 | The financial analysis of investments with project financing

At least three critical present values should be highlighted during the course of appraisal of investments with project financing. Assume that we are looking at the profitability of a project from the standpoint of a company with large mineral reserves. The decision makers in the company might go ahead and extract ore entirely for the company's account – in other words with no project finance. The company might sell the reserves. Or it might decide to shed risk on the ore extraction by resorting to project finance techniques. The company should choose that course of action which promises greatest shareholder value. To justify using project financing techniques, the firm's appraisal should result in this mode of expansion giving the largest payoff in present value terms when compared with the two other routes mentioned above. In reality, there may be more than three ways of exploiting the mineral reserves, perhaps through joint venture and so on.

In any case, if we are looking at the three possibilities referred to above, the firm putting some of its mineral-bearing reserves into the project should undertake cash flow appraisals in the following terms:

- Calculating the present value for the project as a whole in the usual way and assuming no project finance input. After deducting the value of debt assumed, a figure for potential shareholder value created by the project – without project financing – may be identified. For convenience, let us call this present value PV_1.

- Calculating the present value of incremental flows to the mineral reserve providing sponsor assuming a project finance structure. Such returns will probably be by way of dividend flows. We term this present value PV_2.

- Estimating the proceeds from merely selling off the reserves. We term this present value PV_3.

To justify project financing, on rational profit-maximizing grounds, we should find that:

$$PV_2 > PV_1$$

and:

$$PV_2 > PV_3$$

As we have stated before, project financing does not automatically create shareholder value – indeed badly structured project financing actually destroys it.

In calculating the above present values, a number of points ought to be made. In the calculation of PV_1, the route used may involve a weighted average approach or an adjusted present value methodology. Remember that if the project – without project financing – is so large as to endanger the future of the company as a whole, a case can be made for using a discount rate which would reflect total risk rather than merely systematic risk. This idea would apply whether the weighted average cost of capital or an adjusted present value methodology were applied.

When it comes to the calculation of PV_2, the discount rate to be used is critical. Although we would usually be looking at dividend cash inflows and the temptation is therefore to discount at an equity cost of capital, we must bear in mind that the flows might, by virtue of the structuring of the project finance, be of a much lower risk order than normal dividend inflows. For example, if the project had a take-or-pay agreement with a sovereign state and completion guarantees from a government-owned construction company and indeed (just for the purpose of explanation) all possible of the project financing risk-shedding agreements were with governmental agencies and set up in a watertight legal way, the logical discount rate might be the risk-free rate. Of course, such a situation is rarely encountered. To relax this basic assumption somewhat, assume that all possible risk-shedding arrangements were in place and that these arrangements were with financially strong private sector corporations, then the discount rate might be the corporate bond rate, perhaps R_F plus 1–2 per cent depending upon the strength of the corporations concerned. However, it has to be said that this argument is not a strong one. The prudent company may feel more relaxed using a normal equity cost of capital. Note that it is a cost of equity capital that is called for since the effect of the project financing is to create a common stock investment. But, remember the use of a geared beta is called for, and the debt ratio will alter year by year. Of course, the inflows to the mineral-providing sponsor may be in terms of dividend, interest and loan repayment. Where the sponsor's loan is made to the project and where such a loan is not a subordinated loan, there is a case for treating such flows in terms of using a debt interest discount rate. The strength of this argument is less with subordinated finance from the sponsor.

By contrast to the calculation of PV_2, estimating PV_3 is less complicated and would normally be derived from valuation ideas about the market price of mineral reserves per tonne.

Of course, we should bear in mind the worth of real options (see Chapter 23) in each valuation case. Clearly in the estimation of PV_1, the firm would retain all such options itself. By contrast, note that one of the effects of a take or pay clause, which may exist in a particular project financing situation, is that the sponsors give up some of the option value associated with mineral price rises and this should be allowed for in assessing PV_2. If mineral rights are sold off (that is what PV_3 focuses upon), the vendor would presumably wish to be remunerated for giving up the base case present value plus any real option estimates. We could imagine scenarios in which the purchaser might appear to overpay to obtain synergy benefits perhaps through internalizing strategically located raw material supplies in a vertically integrated business. Also, it is worth mentioning that whenever divestment is being considered, the vendor should ensure that adequate compensation is received not just for the base case present value but also in respect of the estimated worth of real operating options for the business to be sold off.

In project financing, there may be a number of sponsors. Those whose input is via other means than mineral reserves, oilfields or similar assets should, of course, also go through a process not dissimilar to the calculations above, although their cash outflows might be in terms of construction costs, management time or whatever and their inflows in terms of dividends. Their equation is somewhat less complicated given that they will not have possibilities similar to those described in PV_3.

Logical, well-honed cash flow analysis, on top of careful legal structuring and project financing, is critical to the creation of shareholder value in this complex and fascinating field of financial management. It deserves attention. Skimping on it is one of the easiest ways of destroying shareholder value.

30.15 | Summary

- The term 'project finance' covers a variety of financing structures.

- Generally and legally, project finance refers to funds provided to finance a project that will, in varying degrees, be serviced out of the revenues derived from that project.

- The level of recourse and the type of support given may vary from one project to another.

- In project finance, lenders usually take some degree of credit risk on the project itself.

- In deciding whether to finance a project, lenders must consider its technical feasibility and its economic projections. This means that the commercial, legal, political and technical risks of a project must all be evaluated.

- Having analysed the risks associated with a project, lenders try to establish a method of financing that covers those risks in the most effective way. It is necessary that the financial structure in project finance should be creative enough to allow the project to succeed.

- From the lender's point of view, effective security must be structured. Lenders are usually deeply concerned about the cost of over-runs and they frequently seek completion guarantees and performance bonds.

- Project financiers are very concerned about the availability of all raw materials and customers, and try to ensure ability to service and repay debt.

- Lenders frequently require assurances regarding the revenues which the project will generate. Evidence of sales contracts may be asked for with respect to the short to medium term or even the longer term. Provisions relating to price adjustments may be critical.

30.16 | End of chapter questions

Question 1
Project finance is difficult to define. What are its essential features?

Question 2
When deciding whether or not to back a project finance proposition, what essential features do potential lenders home in on?

31 Financing international trade and minimizing credit risk

Two problem areas dominate the financing of international trade: these concern foreign exchange risk and credit risk. The former topic is wide ranging and is considered in detail in various sections of this book. This chapter focuses upon credit risk. This may be defined as the risk that one may not be paid for goods or services supplied. Its complexities in an international arena arise because of the difficulties of taking repossession of goods following non-payment when they are outside the country of the supplier.

Before goods are shipped, the importer and exporter agree the terms of a transaction, including price, insurance, freight, dates of shipment and so on. The banking system provides several methods of making or receiving payment in international trade. Payment method usually lies among a number of choices including cash with order, open account, bills of exchange, documentary letters of credit and government assistance schemes. These choices are not mutually exclusive. For example, bills of exchange and letters of credit are often used as part of a package with government assistance as well. In this chapter we consider each of the above methods of financing international trade. It must be borne in mind that this whole topic is a broad one and the coverage here can only be superficial. In summary, the main trade finance possibilities are shown in Table 31.1. The trade finance solutions listed in the table are arranged in order of risk – from the highest risk to the exporter (which is the lowest risk to the importer) to the lowest risk to the exporter (which is the highest risk to the importer). An appendix explaining trade finance terms can be found at the end of this chapter. Readers dealing with the topics of financing international trade and minimizing credit risk in the real world would be well advised to obtain advice from a banker or other specialist.

31.1 | Cash with order

From the standpoint of the exporter, this is the most desirable payment method, but in international trade it is the least used, since some credit period is generally given to the importer. If the seller receives cash with order (CWO), it has possession of both the money and the goods for a limited period. Cash with order is unattractive to the purchaser, since the purchaser bears the whole burden of financing the shipment. The buyer loses the use of funds for a significant time period, being forced to finance working capital and to lose interest on funds.

Table 31.1 Trade finance possibilities from highest risk to exporter
(lowest risk to importer) to lowest risk to exporter (highest risk to importer)

Term	Description
Extended terms	Importer pays for goods over period of time during which they are used by importer, often three to ten years. A set of promissory notes is normally issued upon shipment, payable at six-month or one-year intervals.
Open account, clean draft	Exporter makes shipment and awaits payment direct from importer. Any documents needed by importer sent directly by exporter when sale is invoiced though a draft may also be presented separately through banking channels.
Time or date draft, documents against acceptance	Exporter makes shipment and presents draft and documents to bank with instructions that documents are to be released to importer upon importer's acceptance of the draft (importer's acknowledgement of his/her debt and promise to pay at a future date).
Consignment, retention of title	Exporter makes shipment and receives payment as goods are sold by importer. Sales contract and/or other legal documentation gives exporter right to repossess any unsold goods.
Sight draft, cash against documents/delivery against payment	Exporter makes shipment and entrusts documents to a bank with instructions that documents be released to importer only upon payment of draft.
Cash against goods, shipment into bonded warehouse	As opposed to traditional cash on delivery, usually involves shipping goods to a warehouse operated by exporter in importer's country. Goods are released in relatively small amounts from warehouse by exporter's local agent.
Irrevocable letter of credit	Instrument issued by importer's bank in favour of exporter, payable against presentation to the issuing bank of specified documents. May be payable at sight or may incorporate bank-guaranteed financing.
Confirmed irrevocable letter of credit	Same as above, except importer's bank asks advising bank to add its confirmation. Payable upon presentation of compliant documents to the confirming bank. May be payable at sight or may incorporate bank-guaranteed financing.
Cash in advance	Importer sends good funds before exporter ships.

Cash with order often has a stigma associated with it – namely, that the purchaser is less than creditworthy. When it is used, the buyer loses control of the situation. The buyer is at the mercy of the supplier in terms of the latter's honesty, solvency and ability to deliver goods promptly. The purchaser also has to be certain that the seller's country will not prohibit, for various reasons, the export of the goods concerned. Cash with order clearly creates risks for the buyer.

In international trade, cash with order is found where the importer is of doubtful credit standing and where the exporter is competitively very strong. This form of payment is extremely rare in exporting. It clearly involves an overseas buyer in extending credit to an exporter – the opposite procedure is the normal method of trade. A variation of this form of payment is cash on delivery (COD). This is used for small-value goods which are sent via Post Office parcel post and are released only after payment of the invoice plus COD charges.

31.2 | Open account

Under this method of financing, exporter and importer agree that the account will be settled at a predetermined date. In the meantime, goods and shipping documents are sent to the buyer so that it may receive the goods and use them as it wishes. Open account has risks for the exporter, since no documentary evidence of ownership or obligation is usually available. Differences of law and custom in various countries make it difficult to safeguard the interests of the exporter, which loses control of the goods. If payment is not forthcoming, the exporter is in a weak position.

Using open account also means that financing falls upon the exporter. The exporter needs enhanced working capital levels and loses interest on funds. Open account trading is used in international trade where there is a trusted business relationship between the parties and the importer is of undoubted creditworthiness.

Payment of indebtedness under open account may be made by electronic funds transfer, telegraphic transfer, mail transfer, cheque or banker's draft. Electronic funds transfer involves instructions to bankers to move funds electronically from one bank account to another. They are faster and more efficient than cheques and involve relatively low cost. Telegraphic transfer involves an instruction from the importer's bank to the exporter's bank to transfer some funds on the importer's account to the exporter's credit. The importer has to pay its own bank the local currency equivalent to meet the amount of the invoice. The invoice may be expressed in the currency of either the exporter or the importer, or in any other currency. Mail transfer payment involves the same process except that the payment from the importer is mailed by the importer's bank to the exporter's bank and is therefore a slower means of payment. Payment by cheque simply involves the importer mailing a cheque to the exporter. Finally, payment under banker's draft involves the importer obtaining a banker's draft from its bank and sending it to the exporter's bank. It should be noted that, under telegraphic and mail transfer, cleared funds are released to the exporter. Cheque and banker's draft require collection and clearing, and this can take time.

Thus, while an exporter receives the greatest security from cash with order or cash on delivery, open account is at the other extreme and offers the least security to the exporter. The open account method of payment is increasingly popular within the EU because it is simple and straightforward. The vast majority of UK exports within the EU are paid for under open account terms. It saves money and procedural difficulties but its risk to the exporter is obviously greater. It is used only when an exporter trusts the business integrity and ability of an overseas buyer, a trust that has probably been established through a sustained period of trading between many businesses within the EU.

A variation of open account payment is the consignment account, where an exporter supplies an overseas buyer in order that stocks are built up in quantities sufficient to cover continued demand. The exporter retains ownership of the goods until they are sold, or for an agreed period, after which the buyer remits the agreed price to the exporter.

However, a large proportion of export contracts cannot be settled by payment in advance or by open account: this is particularly so for sales outside the EU. So the trading community throughout the world has developed methods of payment which involve the transfer of documents for exported goods using the international banking system – with the aim of speedily settling export transactions at minimum risk to exporters and to overseas buyers.

31.3 | Documentation in foreign trade

There are three important key documents involved in foreign trade. The first is bill of exchange or draft, which is an order to pay; the second is the bill of lading, which is a document involved in the physical movement of the merchandise by a common carrier; the third is the letter of credit, which is a third-party guarantee of an importer's creditworthiness.

Documentation in foreign trade is designed to ensure that the exporter will receive payment and the importer will receive the merchandise. Also, documents in foreign trade are used to eliminate non-completion risk, to reduce foreign exchange risk and to finance trade transactions.

The risk of non-completion is greater in foreign trade than in domestic transactions. Thus, exporters wish to keep title to the goods until they are paid for and importers are reluctant to pay until they receive the goods. Most domestic sales are on open account credit. Under open account, the buyer does not sign a formal debt instrument because credit sales are made on the basis of a seller's credit evaluation of the buyer. Buyers and sellers are also, usually, further apart, physically and culturally, in foreign trade than in domestic trade. Consequently, sellers are less able to ascertain the credit standing of their overseas customers. Buyers may also find it difficult to determine the reputation and integrity of their foreign suppliers. Much of the non-completion risk is reduced through the use of the bill of exchange, the bill of lading and the letter of credit.

Of course, foreign exchange transaction risk arises when export sales are denominated in a foreign currency and are paid at a later date. Forward contracts, swaps, currency options and currency denominating practices, referred to elsewhere in this text, may be used to reduce foreign exchange risk in foreign trade.

Because all foreign trade involves a time lag, funds become tied up in the shipment of goods for some period of time. Trade transactions become free of non-completion and foreign exchange risk due to well-drawn trade documents and forward contracts.

Thus, banks are prepared to finance goods in transit and even prior to shipment. Financial institutions at either end of the trade offer a variety of financing alternatives that reduce or eliminate risk for both exporter and importer.

Drafts

A bill of exchange (or draft) is an order written by an exporter that requires an importer to pay a specified amount of money at a specified future date. Through the use of drafts, the exporter may use its bank as a collection agent on accounts that the exporter finances. The bank forwards the exporter's drafts to the importer, either directly or indirectly (through a branch or a correspondent bank), and then remits the proceeds back to the exporter.

A draft involves three parties – these are the drawer or maker, the drawee and the payee. The drawer is the person or the business issuing a draft. This person is usually the exporter who sells and ships the merchandise. The drawee is the person or the business against whom the draft is drawn. This person or business is usually the importer who must pay the draft at maturity. The payee is the person or the business to whom the drawee must eventually pay the funds. If the draft is not a negotiable instrument, it designates the person or bank to whom payment is to be made. Such a person, know as the payee, may be the drawer or a third party such as the drawer's bank. However, most drafts are negotiable instruments. Drafts are negotiable if they meet a number of conditions. The draft must:

- be in writing and signed by the drawer (the exporter);

- contain an unconditional promise or order to pay an exact amount of money;

- be payable on sight or at a specified time;

- be made out to order or to bearer.

If the draft is made to order, the funds involved would be paid to a person specified. If it is made to bearer, the funds should be paid to the person who presents the draft for payment.

When a draft is presented to a drawee, either the drawee or his bank accepts it. This acceptance acknowledges in writing the drawee's obligation to pay the sum indicated on the face of the draft. When drafts are accepted by banks, they are termed banker's acceptances. Some bankers' acceptances are highly marketable. This means that the exporter can sell them in the bill marker or discount them at his bank. Whenever they are sold or discounted, the seller writes his endorsement on the back of the draft. In the event that an importer fails to pay at maturity, the holder of the draft will have recourse for the full amount of the draft from the immediately previous endorser and then the endorser before that – and so on.

Drafts are used in foreign trade for a number of reasons. First of all, they provide written evidence of obligations in a comprehensive and fairly standard form. Second, they allow both the exporter and the importer to reduce the cost of financing and to divide costs equitably. Third, they are negotiable and unconditional. This means that drafts themselves are not subject to disputes that may occur between the parties involved.

Drafts may be either sight drafts or time drafts. A sight draft is payable upon demand. Here, the drawee must pay the draft immediately or dishonour it. A time draft is payable a specified number of days after presentation to the drawee. When a time draft is presented to the drawee, he may have his bank accept it in writing or by stamping a notice of acceptance on its face. When a draft, or bill of exchange, is drawn on and accepted by a bank, it becomes a bankers' acceptance.

Drafts may be documentary drafts or clean drafts. Documentary drafts require shipping documents such as bills of lading, insurance certificates and commercial invoices. Most drafts are documentary since all of these shipping documents are necessary to obtain the goods shipped. The documents attached to a documentary draft are passed on to an importer either upon payment, for sight drafts, or upon acceptance, for time drafts. If documents are to be delivered to an importer upon payment of the draft, the draft is referred to as a D/P (documents against payment) draft. If the documents are passed on to an importer upon acceptance, the draft is called a D/A (documents against acceptance) draft.

When a time draft is accepted by an importer, it is termed a trade acceptance or a clean draft. When clean drafts are used in international trade, the exporter usually sends all shipping documents directly to the importer and only the draft to the collecting bank. The clean draft involves a fair amount of risk. Thus, clean drafts are generally used in cases in which there is considerable faith between exporter and importer or in cases in which firms send goods to their foreign subsidiaries.

Bills of lading

We now turn to bills of lading. A bill of lading is a shipping document issued to an exporter firm or its bank by the carrier which transports the goods. It acts as receipt, a contract and a document of title. As a receipt, the bill of lading indicates that the goods specified have been received by the carrier. As a contract, it is evidence that the carrier is required to deliver the goods to the importer in exchange for certain charges. As a document of title, it is evidence of ownership of the goods. So, the bill of lading is used to ensure payment before the goods are delivered. The importer cannot obtain title to the goods until he obtains the bill of lading from the carrier.

Bills of lading may be straight bills of lading or order bills of lading. A straight bill of lading requires that the carrier deliver the goods to a specified party, usually the importer. This technique is used where the goods have been paid for in advance. An order bill of lading requires the carrier to deliver the goods to the order of a specified party, usually the exporter. In this case, the exporting firm retains title to the goods until it receives payment. Once payment is forthcoming, the exporting firm endorses the order bill of lading in blank or to its bank. The endorsed document can be used as security for financing.

Bills of lading may be on-board bills of lading or received-for-shipment bills of lading. On-board bills of lading indicate that the goods have been placed on board the vessel. A received-for-shipment bill of lading merely acknowledges that the carrier has received the goods for shipment but does not guarantee that the goods have been loaded on the vessel. A received-for-shipment bill of lading may readily be converted into an on-board bill of lading by the appropriate stamp which shows the name of the vessel, the date and the signature of an official of the vessel.

In addition, bills of lading may be classified as clean bills of lading or foul bills of lading. A clean bill of lading indicates that the carrier has received the goods in apparently good condition. By contrast, a foul bill of lading bears an indication from the carrier that the goods appeared to have suffered some damage before the carrier received them for shipment. Foul bills of lading are, generally, not acceptable under a letter of credit. With a letter of credit it is important that the exporter obtain a clean bill of lading.

Letters of credit

We now turn to letters of credit. A letter of credit is a document issued by a bank at the request of an importer. In the letter of credit, the bank agrees to honour a draft drawn on the importer if the draft accompanies specified documents such as the bill of lading. Typically, the importer requests his or her local bank to write a letter of credit. In exchange for the bank's agreement to honour the demand for payment that results from the transaction, the importer promises to pay the bank the amount of the transaction plus a specified fee.

Letters of credit facilitate foreign trade and are advantageous to both exporter and importer. They give a number of benefits to the exporter. First, they mean that the exporter sells his goods abroad against the promise of a bank rather than a commercial firm. Because banks are usually better credit risks than most business firms, exporters are almost assured of payment if specific conditions are met. Second, exporters may obtain funds as soon as they have the necessary documents such as the letter of credit and the bill of lading. When shipment is made, the exporter prepares a draft in accordance with the letter of credit and presents it to his local bank. If the bank finds that all papers are in order, it advances the face value of the draft less fees and interest.

The letter of credit also gives a number of benefits to importers. It assures them that the exporter will only be paid if he or she provides certain documents, all of which are carefully examined by the bank. If the exporter is unable or unwilling to make proper shipment, recovery of the deposit is more easily achieved from the bank than from the overseas exporter. Also, the letter of credit enables the importer to remove commercial risk to the exporter in exchange for certain considerations. Moreover, it is less expensive to finance goods under a letter of credit than by borrowing.

Letters of credit may be irrevocable or revocable. Most letters of credit between unrelated parties are irrevocable. An irrevocable letter of credit cannot be cancelled or modified by the importer's bank without the consent of all parties. A revocable letter of credit can be revoked or modified by the importer's bank at any time prior to payment. Banks do not favour revocable letters of credit. Indeed, some banks refuse to issue them because of their potential for subsequent litigation.

Letters of credit may be confirmed or unconfirmed. A confirmed letter of credit is a letter of credit confirmed by a bank other than the issuing bank. Why might this be necessary? An exporter may want a foreign bank's letter of credit confirmed by a domestic bank when the exporter has some doubt about the foreign bank's ability to pay. In this case, these banks are obligated to honour drafts drawn in accordance with the letter of credit. Unconfirmed letters of credit are guarantees only of the opening bank. The strongest letter of credit is clearly a confirmed, irrevocable letter of credit. Such a letter of credit cannot be cancelled by the opening bank and, moreover, it requires both the opening and confirming banks to guarantee payment on drafts issued in connection with an export transaction.

Also, letters of credit may be either revolving or non-revolving. A revolving letter of credit is a letter of credit whose duration revolves, for example, weekly or monthly. Thus, a £50,000 revolving credit might authorize an exporter to draw drafts up to £50,000 each week until the expiry of the credit. A revolving letter of credit might be used when an importer has to make frequent and known purchases and payments. Most letters of credit are non-revolving. Thus, typically, letters of credit are issued and valid for a single transaction.

Other documentation

There is other documentation required too. In addition to the draft, the bill of lading and the letter of credit, some additional documents frequently required in international trade are commercial invoices, insurance documents and consular invoices. These, and some other documents, are required to obtain the goods shipped. Furthermore, they may be essential to clear the merchandise through customs at ports of entry and departure.

A commercial invoice is issued by the exporter. It contains a precise description of the merchandise, indicating unit prices, quality, total value, financial terms of sale and various shipping features. The commercial invoice may include other information such as the names and addresses of both exporter and importer, the number of packages, transportation and insurance charges, the name of the vessel, the ports of departure and destination, export or import permit numbers and so on.

Shipments in international trade are all insured. Most insurance contracts nowadays automatically cover all shipments made by the exporter. The risks of transportation range from damage to total loss of merchandise. Most ocean carriers do not have any responsibility for losses during the actual transportation except those directly attributed to their negligence. Therefore, some form of marine insurance is arranged to protect both the exporter and the importer. This additional insurance coverage ranges from limited cover for losses through collision, fire and sinking to the broad coverage of all risks.

Exports to some countries require a consular invoice issued by the consulate of the importing country. Specifically, a consular invoice is necessary to obtain customs clearance. It also provides officials with information necessary to assess import duties. The consular invoice does not carry title to the goods and is negotiable.

Various other documents may be required by the importer or may be necessary in clearing the goods through ports of entry or exit. These include certificates of origin, weight lists, packing lists and inspection certificates. A certificate of origin certifies the country in which the goods were manufactured or grown. A weight list specifies the weight of each item. A packing list identifies the contents of each individual package. An inspection certificate is a document issued by an independent inspection company to verify the contents and quality of the shipment.

No. 45/1 Date 30th October 2003 For £20,000

At sight pay this first of Exchange

to the order of ourselves

twenty thousand pounds only

Value in merchandise shipped to South Africa as per invoice

number 91/69/2 which place to account

To: Delany Capetown (Pty) Ltd.
Paarl Street
Rondebosch
Capetown
South Africa

For and on behalf of
Jacksons Export (UK) Ltd.

Figure 31.1 Example of a bill of exchange.

31.4 Bills of exchange

In our analysis at the beginning of this chapter, one of the methods of making payment in international trade was identified as the bill of exchange (or draft). A bill of exchange is defined in UK law as an unconditional order in writing addressed by one person to another, signed by the person giving it, requiring the person to whom it is addressed to pay, on demand or at a fixed or determinable future time, a certain sum in money to, or to the order of, a specified person, or to bearer.

An exporter can send a bill of exchange for the value of goods through the banking system for payment by an overseas buyer on presentation. Typically, an exporter prepares a bill of exchange which is drawn on an overseas importer, or on a third party designated in the export contract, for the sum agreed as settlement. The bill of exchange, or draft, resembles a cheque; indeed a cheque is defined by the Bills of Exchange Act 1882 as a bill of exchange drawn on a banker, payable on demand. An example of a bill of exchange is given in Figure 31.1.

The bill of exchange is called a sight draft if it is made out payable at sight – that is, on demand. If it is payable at a fixed or determinable future time, it is called a term draft, since the buyer is receiving a period of credit, known as the tenor of the bill. The buyer signifies an agreement to pay on the due date by writing an acceptance across the face of the bill.

By using a bill of exchange with other shipping documents through the banking system, an exporter can ensure greater control of the goods because, until the bill is paid or accepted by the overseas buyer, the goods cannot be released. Also, the buyer does not have to pay or agree to pay until delivery of the goods from the exporter.

A UK exporter might pass a bill of exchange to a bank in the United Kingdom. The UK bank forwards the bill to its overseas branch or to a correspondent bank in an overseas buyer's country. This bank, known as the collecting bank, presents the bill to whoever it is drawn upon for immediate payment if it is a sight draft, or for acceptance if it is a term draft. This procedure is known as a 'clean bill collection' because no shipping documents are required. Clean bill collections have recently become more popular. Such collections provide more security than open account terms if there is some doubt about a buyer's financial status.

However, it is more likely that bills are used in a documentary bill collection method of payment. In this case, an exporter sends the bill to the buyer by way of the banking system with the shipping documents, including the document of title to the goods, usually an original bill of lading. The bank releases the documents only on payment or acceptance of the bill by the overseas buyer. This was detailed in the previous section of this chapter.

An exporter may even use the banking system for a cash against documents (CAD) collection. In this case only the shipping documents are sent and the exporter instructs the bank to release them only after payment by the overseas buyer. This method is used in some European countries whose buyers prefer CAD to a sight draft if the exporter insists on a documentary collection for settlement of the export contract.

In all the methods of payment using a bill of exchange, or draft, a promissory note can be used as an alternative. This is issued by a buyer which promises to pay an exporter a certain amount of money within a specified time. For a UK exporter, it is also possible to send the documents and bill of exchange directly to an overseas buyer's bank, thus bypassing the UK bank. This system of direct collection is widely supported by US banks.

In order to make clear what procedures an exporter wants from a particular collection and what action should be taken if an overseas buyer does not meet the payment terms of the contract, most UK banks ask exporters to fill out a bank lodgement form. This is a checklist which ensures that all the instructions are remembered in order to make a successful collection.

As an illustration of how bills of exchange work, consider the following example of a US exporter and a UK importer using a 60-day sight draft.

1. The US exporter makes a shipment to a UK importer with the billing made out to the name of the exporter.

2. The exporter delivers the draft and shipping documents to the US bank, which sends the draft and shipping documents to the UK bank.

3. The UK bank notifies the importer that the documents have arrived and presents the draft to the importer for acceptance, payment in 60 days.

4. Upon accepting the bill of exchange, the shipping documents are surrendered to the importer and the shipment can now be claimed.

5. The accepted bill of exchange is returned to the US bank by the UK bank.

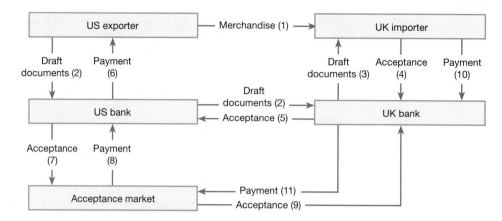

Figure 31.2 Example of international trade financing under a 60-day sight draft.

6. The exporter discounts the draft and receives advance payment.

7. The US bank, in turn, disposes of the bill of exchange in the acceptance market.

8. Upon receiving such funds, the US bank is now in a liquid position again.

9. When the 60-day maturity approaches, the bill of exchange is sent to the UK bank by the financial institution that had purchased it from the US bank.

10. The UK bank receives payment from the UK importer in pounds sterling and the conversion of sterling to dollars is made by the UK bank.

11. The funds are transmitted to the present holder of the trade acceptance.

The above example can be summarized in schematic form, as shown in Figure 31.2.

Given that title documents may be released only upon payment, the exporter's position is superior to that achieved with open account exporting. Bills of exchange also have the advantages of being cheaper than documentary credits and of opening further arenas for financing. Bills of exchange may be discounted by negotiation. This means that a bank buys its customer's outward collection (that is, the foreign currency proceeds of an export) at the time that the collection is remitted abroad. This provides the exporter with short-term funds. Banks may also give an advance against an outward collection of bills of exchange.

Exporters of substantial creditworthiness may also use a merchant bank acceptance facility. Under this financing mechanism, documentary drafts drawn by the exporter on the overseas buyer become security and are handled as documentary collections by the merchant bank. These documents are pledged to the merchant bank. The exporter draws a draft on the bank and, after acceptance by the bank, the draft, now known as an accommodation bill, is discounted, usually with a discount house, and the proceeds are paid to the exporter.

Using bills of exchange offers less security to the exporter than obtaining cash with order or using letters of credit. Bills of exchange provide the importer with a period of credit and the chance to ensure that the goods are what was ordered before payment is authorized. Transacting international trade via bills of exchange reduces the risk of non-payment. Although more expensive than cash with order and open account, bills of exchange are cheaper than trading via letters of credit.

31.5 | Documentary letters of credit trading

As discussed earlier in this chapter, a documentary letter of credit is a credit under which drawings are honoured, provided the beneficiary delivers the documents evidencing shipment of the goods ordered. With a documentary letter of credit, exporters are able to receive payment for goods in their own country, once shipment has taken place. At the same time, the buyer is secure in the knowledge that payment will not have been made unless the terms and conditions of the credit have been met. With the security of the documentary credit, the exporter is able to produce goods knowing that it will receive payment promptly. At the same time the importer is as sure as it can be that the goods will be received when they are required.

The first contractual step in an export transaction is the sale contract. If it is agreed as part of the contract that a documentary credit is to be used for payment of the goods, then the buyer will make arrangements with its bank for the issue of the credit. The onus of drawing up the letter of credit lies with the importer, which gives its bank detailed instructions about the nature of the goods, their quality and price, the total value of the credit, the documents required, the dates between which documents may be presented for payment and any special provisions which may have been agreed between purchaser and seller. These terms and conditions will be contained in the advice of issue of the documentary credit sent to the seller, which is technically referred to as the beneficiary. The documentary credit is separate from the sales contract. As such the beneficiary checks that the terms comply with those agreed in the sale contract. If they differ, the beneficiary contacts the seller – technically known as the taker – and requests that the seller instructs its bank to issue an amendment to the credit.

Banks advise the beneficiary in one of three ways that a credit has been opened in its favour. They may advise the beneficiary direct, indicating a bank in the beneficiary's country where payment may be obtained against the documents. Secondly, they may address the advice of opening to the beneficiary and send it to their branch or correspondent for onward transmission. Thirdly, they may address it to their branch or correspondent in the beneficiary's country and request that the beneficiary should be notified.

Letters of credit are of various types. The most frequently encountered are revocable, irrevocable and confirmed irrevocable credits. The differences between revocable and irrevocable credits are important and have been referred to earlier in this chapter.

To reiterate, a revocable credit may be amended or cancelled at any time without prior notice to the beneficiary. However, the issuing bank is bound to reimburse a branch or other bank to which such a credit has been transmitted and made available for payment, acceptance or negotiation, for any payment, acceptance or negotiation complying with the terms and conditions of the credit, and for any amendments received up to the time of the payment, acceptance or negotiation made by such branch or other bank prior to receipt by it of notice of amendment or cancellation.

An irrevocable credit constitutes a definite undertaking of the issuing bank, provided that the terms and conditions of the credit are complied with:

- To pay, or that payment will be made, if the credit provides for payment, whether against a draft or not.

- To accept drafts if the credit provides for acceptance by the payment at maturity, if the credit so provides, for the acceptance of drafts drawn on the applicant for the credit or any other drawee specified in the credit.

- To purchase/negotiate, without recourse to drawers and/or bona fide holders, drafts drawn by the beneficiary at sight or at a tenor, on the applicant for the credit or on any other drawee specified in the credit, or to provide for purchase/negotiation by another bank, if the credit provides for purchase/negotiation.

A revocable credit is not a legally binding undertaking between the bank or banks concerned and the beneficiary, since it may be modified or cancelled at any time without the beneficiary being notified, though payment made before receipt of a modification or cancellation remains valid. Thus it is never a confirmed credit. An irrevocable credit may not be modified or cancelled without the consent of all the parties concerned.

The beneficiary of a credit may not know the standing of the opening bank. If the opening bank becomes bankrupt after the beneficiary's bank has negotiated the credit, but before it has been reimbursed, then the beneficiary's bank has recourse to the beneficiary. As a precaution, the beneficiary can ask its bank to confirm the credit for a fee, provided the bank is satisfied about the standing of the opening bank. Once confirmed, the confirming bank has no recourse to the beneficiary after negotiation of the credit. This constitutes a confirmed irrevocable documentary letter of credit.

After the beneficiary has received the documentary credit in the form required, and the goods are available for shipment, arrangements are made via an agent to draw up the documents. The agent receives a copy of the credit to ensure that the documents are prepared according to it. After the goods have been shipped, the beneficiary delivers all the documents to its bank, with the credit. The bank compares the documents with the credit. If it is satisfied that they are in order, the bank pays the beneficiary.

When an exporter has negotiated in the contract with a buyer for a confirmed irrevocable letter of credit, then security of payment, as far as is humanly possible, is achieved.

Whether or not the credit is confirmed, it is essential that the exporter checks the credit terms immediately to make sure that they are compatible with the sales contract made with the buyer. When dealing with documentary credits, the bank is concerned only with the documents to be presented and not with the goods or services involved. Documentary credits may provide for payment at sight or for acceptance of a term bill of exchange by either the issuing bank in a buyer's country or the correspondent bank in the United Kingdom. A schematic representation of the

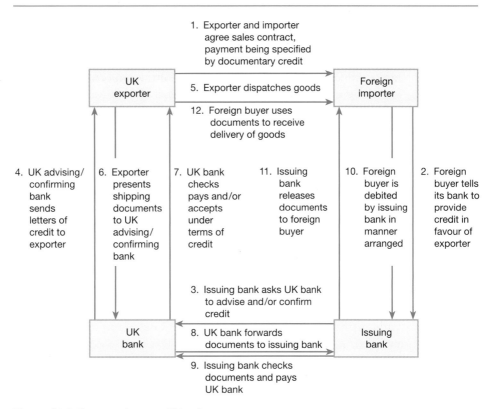

Figure 31.3 Documentary credit trading.

typical series of steps involved in trading under a documentary credit is set out in Figure 31.3.

Under a letter of credit transaction, the onus of financing falls squarely upon the buyer. The main benefit derived by the importer is the protection of a definite date by which the seller is required to ship goods. The buyer therefore expects prompt delivery. Also the buyer may expect to receive lower prices when a letter of credit is submitted, since difficulties are so fully safeguarded that the exporter finds it unnecessary to cover them in the price. Advance orders, or orders running throughout a period of time, are well protected by the expiration date of the letter of credit, as well as by the limit of the sum of money for which it is drawn. Attractive discounts are frequently offered to importers for providing letter of credit payment.

Letters of credit are of great benefit when the parties involved are relatively unknown to each other, or where one of the parties is in a country where political risk of non-payment is high. Over recent years, an increasing portion of world trade has been conducted between multinationals and their subsidiaries and associates, or between well-established trading partners. In these cases the risk of default is greatly reduced and trading on open account has reasserted itself.

Letters of credit do have drawbacks and there are popular alternatives. For example, a small importer wishing to open a letter of credit may be called upon by its bank to provide partial – or even full – cash cover. The cash flow impact of this may be so acute as to force the importer to find other ways of arranging payment. This may be via a confirming house or an international credit union which arranges extended payment terms. Exporters are usually happy to deal with the confirming house, which makes payment on behalf of the importer, without the security of a letter of credit. Exporters can also improve cash flows by selling their debt books to a factoring house. Factoring houses give the seller credit insurance by taking over its invoices as the goods are supplied, and they provide cash – either immediately or at some agreed future date – for up to three-quarters of the invoice value less various incidental charges.

Before entering the arena of trading via documentary credit, the reader should note that well over 50 per cent of the sets of documents lodged under letters of credit are rejected by banks upon first presentation because they are either incomplete or incorrect. Delays or refusals to pay inevitably ensue. The main reasons for this are as follows:

■ The letter of credit has expired.

■ The documents are presented after the period stipulated in the letter of credit.

■ The shipment is late.

31.6 | Government assistance schemes

Most countries operate a system of credit insurance through agencies such as the Export Credit Guarantee Department (ECGD) in the United Kingdom (this department has now been partially privatized). The overall services of these agencies vary from one country to another and for precise details it is necessary to refer to their booklets of services rendered. In the remainder of this chapter we concentrate upon ECGD's services in the export credit field.

ECGD insures exporters against the risk of not being paid, whether this results from the default of the purchaser or from other causes. It also offers unconditional guarantees of 100 per cent repayment to banks, thus creating security for banks to provide finance to exporters at favourable interest rates. ECGD insures new investment overseas against the risks of war, expropriation and the imposition of restrictions on remittance. It also provides protection against part of the increases in UK costs for large contracts with long manufacturing periods. For major contracts it supports the issue of performance bonds, and for members of a UK consortium it provides protection against losses arising through the insolvency of a member of the consortium.

ECGD classifies export trade into two categories. First, there is trade of a repetitive type, involving standard, or near standard, goods. Credit risk cover on these is provided on a comprehensive basis. The exporter must offer for cover all or most of its export business for at least a year in both good and bad markets. Secondly, there are projects and large capital goods deals of a non-repetitive nature, usually of high value and involving lengthy credit periods. This business is not suited to comprehensive treatment and specific policies are negotiated for each contract. Cover for this specific insurance is given in one of two ways. With a supplier credit, the manufacturer sells on deferred payment terms, borrowing from a UK bank to finance the period from shipment until payment is received. ECGD insures the exporter and often gives a guarantee direct to the bank. With a buyer credit, the exporter receives prompt payment from its buyer, which draws on a loan from a UK bank to provide this payment. The loan is repaid in instalments and ECGD guarantees the bank repayment by the overseas customer.

In the area of supplier credit, ECGD's comprehensive short-term guarantee provides an insurance on sales with credit periods of up to six months. The risks covered embrace the following:

- Insolvency of the buyer.

- The buyer's failure to pay within six months of the due date for goods which it has accepted.

- The buyer's failure to take up goods that have been despatched (where not caused or excused by the policy holder's actions, and where ECGD decides that the institution or constitution of legal proceedings against the buyer would serve no useful purpose).

- A general moratorium on external debt decreed by the government of the buyer's country or of a third country through which payment must be made.

- Any other action by the government of the buyer's country which prevents performance of the contract in whole or in part.

- Political events, economic difficulties, and legislative or administrative measures arising outside the United Kingdom which prevent or delay the transfer of payments or deposits made in respect of the contract.

- Legal discharge of a debt (not being legal discharge under the proper law of the contract) in a foreign currency, which results in a shortfall at the date of transfer.

- War and certain other events preventing performance of the contract, provided that the event is not one normally insured with commercial insurers.

- Cancellation or non-renewal of a UK export licence or the prohibition or restriction on export of goods from the United Kingdom by law.

ECGD covers 90 per cent of the loss where it arises through the first two categories of risk. With the third, the exporter bears the first 20 per cent of the original price, and ECGD bears 90 per cent of the remainder. For the other risks, ECGD covers 95 per cent of the loss, except where the loss arises before the goods are despatched overseas. Here the loss is limited to 90 per cent.

Under comprehensive policies, the exporter offers for insurance a broad spread of business to be transacted over a future period. But transactions involving large projects or contracts are negotiated individually between the exporter and ECGD. This gives rise to a specific guarantee where cover runs from either the date of contract or the date of shipment. Risks covered are similar to those covered under the comprehensive policies, except that the top percentage of cover remains at 90 per cent.

ECGD also offers guarantees for supplier credit financing. Here the credit period must be less than two years from the date of export of goods or completion of services, and the buyer gives a promissory note or accepts a bill of exchange. ECGD may give an unconditional guarantee to the exporter's bank that it will pay 100 per cent of any sum three months overdue. ECGD agrees a limit for the finance it will guarantee based on experience and the exporter's financial standing. Operationally, the exporter presents the notes or bills to its bank after shipment of the goods with the appropriate documentary evidence and a standard form of warranty that its ECGD cover for the transaction is in order.

British banks have agreed to finance 100 per cent of the value of such transactions and to charge interest at a very small spread over base rate. The exporter signs a recourse undertaking to give ECGD the right to recover from the exporter should the bank claim sums due in advance of, or in excess of, claims payable under the standard policy. All classes of UK exports qualify for this facility.

With exports ranging from cash against documents to six-month credit, ECGD guarantees a straight loan from the bank to the exporter in respect of the export transaction and it guarantees 100 per cent of the bank loan.

A further area through which ECGD picks up credit risk is effectively via buyer credit financing. In many large contracts where specific supplier credit insurance is available, exporters may prefer to negotiate on cash terms and to arrange a loan to the buyer with repayment terms similar to the credit it might expect from the supplier. ECGD buyer credit guarantees are available to banks making such loans in respect of contracts of £1m or more.

A buyer credit guarantee normally involves the overseas purchaser in paying, direct from its own resources to the supplier, 15–20 per cent of the contract price, including a sufficient downpayment on signature of the contract. The remainder is paid to the supplier direct from a loan made to the buyer or a bank in the buyer's country by a UK bank and guaranteed by ECGD, as to 100 per cent of capital and interest, against non-payment for any reason. The contract may include some foreign goods and services, but the amount of the loan will then be less than the British goods and services to be supplied.

31.7 | Sources of export finance

Buying credit risk can be expensive. So it pays not to duplicate cover – for example, by taking out ECGD cover together with an irrevocable letter of credit. On occasions this duplication may be unavoidable, such as where ECGD makes a confirmed irrevocable letter of credit a condition of its cover on a particular buyer. This happens when the buyer is especially risky and would not otherwise qualify for cover.

In Table 31.2 the various sources of short-term export finance are summarized. One of the headings in the table is important and its implications deserve further comment. This is the term 'recourse'. Non-recourse finance means that the lender has no right of action against the exporter due to the overseas buyer failing to meet its obligations. However, it is worth mentioning that ECGD retains a right of recourse

Table 31.2 Sources of export credit

Source	Nature	Is buyer aware?	Is 100% advanced?	Is the exporter relieved of:		
				Sales ledger work?	Credit risk?	Recourse?
Overdraft	Borrowing	No	Yes	No	No	No
Acceptance credit	Borrowing	No	Yes	No	No	No
Advance against bills	Borrowing	No	Less	No	No	No
Negotiating bills	Sale of bills	No	Less	No	No	No
Factoring	Sale of book debt	Yes	Less	Yes	Yes	Yes
Invoice discounting	Sale of invoices	No	Less	No	No	No
Export merchant	Sale of goods	Yes	Yes	Yes	Yes	Yes
Confirming house						
Traditional	Sale of goods	Yes	Yes	Yes	Yes	Yes
Modern	Sale of book debt	Yes	Yes	Yes	Yes	Yes
ECGD comprehensive bank guarantee						
Bills	Sale of bills	No	Yes	No	90/95%	Yes
Open account	Borrowing	No	Yes	No	90/95%	No
Forfaiting	Sale of bills	Yes	Yes	Yes	Yes	Yes

against the exporter on two grounds. The first relates to the extra percentage cover given to the bank. The bank advancing funds is indemnified 100 per cent by ECGD should the buyer fail to pay, but the exporter's cover is for only 90 or 95 per cent. Thus ECGD may claim back the difference of 5 or 10 per cent from the exporter. Also the right of recourse may be retained in respect of the whole 100 per cent paid out by ECGD to the bank should ECGD consider that default has arisen due to a factor not covered in the comprehensive guarantee. In effect, this is where there is a dispute about the exporter's performance of its contract. The exporter does, of course, continue to enjoy 90/95 per cent immunity to pure default risk, irrespective of whether the default is commercial, arising from the buyer's financial weakness, or political.

The accounting impact of non-recourse finance is interesting. If the finance is with recourse, it appears on the exporter's balance sheet as a liability financing the receivable on the assets side. But if the finance is without recourse, it is treated as an outright sale of the receivable to the bank. There is then no liability on the balance sheet. For the six categories of export finance in which the response of 'no' appears in the last column of Table 31.2 – that is, where the finance is with recourse to the exporter – receivables and liabilities would be greater on the balance sheet than would be the case with non-recourse finance.

Referring to data in Table 31.2, various caveats should be noted. Regarding the column 'Is 100% advanced?', where less than 100 per cent is given under an export-financing source it will usually be above 80 per cent of invoice value. Factoring without invoice discounting essentially amounts to credit insurance and is expensive.

Nowadays factors increasingly hold their own ECGD cover. Many have overseas associates and they often restrict their factoring to customers approved by such associates. Export merchants and confirming houses operating in the traditional mode buy goods as a legal principal, although the modern confirmer does not acquire title to the goods. Confirmers usually accept risks that exporters cannot deal with through their normal channels. Confirming is effectively a way of obtaining ECGD cover without incurring the substantial administrative cost of operating that cover. It should be noted that forfaiting normally differs from factoring in that it applies mainly to medium-term credit and requires that a guarantee, called an aval, of a local bank be obtained; this makes the credit costly. In some cases, buyers are asked to obtain this aval without being informed of the forfaiting operation. Forfaiting and factoring are both relatively expensive media of export finance.

The forms of finance set out in Table 31.2 are all fairly complex and readers desirous of obtaining a detailed insight of their real-world operation are referred to the fairly substantial literature on their practical use. In-depth descriptions are outside the scope of a book of this nature. However, since both forfaiting and countertrade are growing methods of international trade, brief sections are now devoted to each in turn.

31.8 | Forfaiting

Forfaiting is a form of medium-term financing of international trade. It involves the purchase by a bank (the forfaiter) of a series of promissory notes, usually due at six-month intervals for three to five years, signed by an importer in favour of an exporter. These notes are frequently avalled (guaranteed) by the importer's bank. The promissory notes are sold by the exporter to the forfaiting bank at a discount. The bank pays the exporter straight away, allowing the exporter to finance the production of the goods for export and for the importer to pay later. The notes are held by the forfaiter for collection as they become due, without recourse to the exporter in whose favour the notes were originally drawn before assignment. The absence of recourse distinguishes the forfaiting of promissory notes from the discounting of trade drafts, for which the exporter is open to recourse in the case of non-payment. Forfaiting may be summarized as a medium-term, non-recourse, exporter-arranged financing of importers' credits.

A forfaiting transaction is summarized in Figure 31.4. It shows what happens when a UK machine manufacturer sells its machines to a Russian firm. The unshaded arrows show the exchanges occurring at the time the export deal is done; the shaded arrows show subsequent settlements.

The discount rates that apply to forfaiting depend on the terms of the notes, the currencies in which they are denominated, the credit ratings of the importers and the banks avalling the notes, and the country risks of the importing entities. The spreads between forfaiting rates and Eurocurrency deposit rates, with which forfaiting rates move, are generally around one and a half times the spreads between straight Eurocurrency loans and deposits. The higher spreads reflect the lack of recourse and

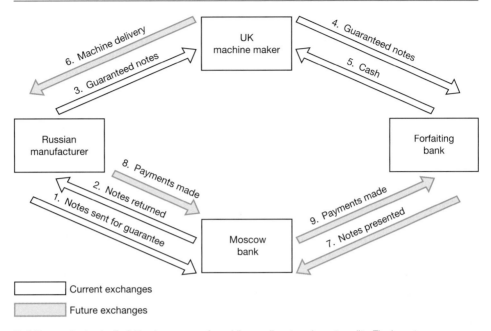

Forfaiting made simple: Forfaiting is a means of providing medium-term import credits. The importer prepares promissory notes which are guaranteed by a bank. These are sent to the exporter, who sells them for cash to a forfaiting bank. The bank may sell the notes. The holder of the notes has no recourse to the exporter. The credit risk is borne entirely by the noteholder.

Figure 31.4 The steps in forfaiting.

interest rate risk. The typical five-year term of forfaiting deals means that forfaiters have difficulty matching credit maturities with the generally much shorter-maturity Eurocurrency deposits and futures contracts. There have been some floating-rate notes but fixed rate deals predominate.

Leading forfaiting banks are flexible and often quote rates over the telephone once they know the name of the importer or the avalling bank. The forfaiter may charge a fee for this service. This allows exporters to quote their selling prices after working out what they will net from their sales after forfaiting costs. Because there is no recourse, the promissory notes are not carried on the exporter's books as a contingent liability. Another advantage of forfaiting is that there is no need to arrange credit insurance. The advantage of forfaiting to importers is that they receive credit when it might not otherwise be offered, or might not be offered on the same terms.

Like the birth of the Eurodollar market, the development of forfaiting owes its origins, but not its subsequent development, to the difficulties faced in East–West trade. The practice of forfaiting goes back to the 1960s and the placing of orders by the Eastern-bloc Comecon countries for capital equipment and grain. Many of these orders were placed with West German firms that were not in a position to supply credit themselves, or to arrange financing with banks or official lending agencies. The exporters were unable to offer supplier credits, and they were unable to arrange buyer credits through lending institutions. Instead, they found banks that were willing to purchase the importers' promissory notes at a good-sized discount. The original deals involved the sale of US grain to Germany, which resold the grain to Eastern European countries. Forfaiting allowed the US exporters to be paid immediately and gave the Eastern European buyers a medium-term credit.

Forfaiting has grown in popularity, spreading from Switzerland and Germany, where it began, to London, thence to the rest of Europe, and to the United States. Forfaiting is still not as important as payment by bills of exchange or credit from official export finance agencies, but it is now an important source of financing, especially for the medium-term maturities.

31.9 | Countertrade

Countertrade involves a reciprocal agreement for the exchange of goods or services. The parties involved may be firms or governments, and the reciprocal agreements can take a number of forms – for example, barter, counterpurchase, industrial offset, buy-back and switch trading. Details were discussed in Chapter 21.

31.10 | Summary

- The usual methods of payment in international trade involve either cash with order, open account, bills of exchange, documentary letters of credit or government assistance schemes. Ensure that you understand the generalities of each. Note that government agencies, such as ECGD in the United Kingdom, will take up to 90 per cent of the credit risk on exports subject to the exporter paying a fee.

- Government agencies also provide supplier credits and buyer credits which are sources of finance to ease smooth export trading. Note how these work.

- Try to obtain, from your reading of this chapter, a reasonable idea of the hierarchy of letters of credit.

31.11 | End of chapter questions

Question 1
What is forfaiting? Specify the type of traded goods for which forfaiting is applied.

Question 2
What is countertrade?

Question 3
What motivates governments to establish so many guarantee and insurance schemes to aid international trade?

31.12 ┃ Appendix

Some terms encountered in trade finance

Acceptance – time draft 'accepted' by the party upon whom it is drawn by endorsing the front of the draft to this effect. Acceptance constitutes an unconditional obligation on the part of the accepting party to pay the draft at maturity. A draft accepted by a bank is called a 'banker's acceptance' whereas one accepted by a company is called a 'trade acceptance'.

Advising bank – bank that receives a letter of credit from the issuing bank for authentication and delivery to the beneficiary. The advising bank is usually a correspondent of the issuing bank located in the vicinity of the beneficiary.

Aval – guarantee added by a bank to an accepted time draft by endorsing the front of the draft 'per aval'. The avalizing bank becomes obligated to pay the draft at maturity if the drawee/acceptor fails to do so.

Bill of exchange – synonym for draft.

Bill of lading – document signed by a transportation company ('carrier') to show receipt of goods for transportation from and to the points indicated. A 'clean' bill of lading bears no clause or notation which expressly declares a defective condition of the goods and/or the packaging.

Cash against documents/documents against payment – terms for documentary collection instructions requesting the presenting bank to deliver documents only upon receipt of payment from the drawee/importer.

Clean draft – draft (bill of exchange) which is not accompanied by documents.

Clean letter of credit – letter of credit that calls for presentation of nothing more than a draft to trigger payment. The term is sometimes used (incorrectly) to mean 'standby letter of credit'.

Collecting bank – any bank other than the remitting bank involved in the collection of a draft and/or documents.

Confirmed letter of credit – letter of credit to which the advising bank has added its own, independent undertaking to honour presentation of the required documents, i.e. pay the beneficiary at sight or at maturity, as specified by the letter of credit.

Confirming bank – bank that has added its confirmation to a letter of credit. Sometimes this term is also used loosely to refer to a bank that has issued a commitment to purchase letter of credit documents without recourse, a practice called 'silent confirmation'.

Direct collection – service for handling export draft collections in which the exporter's bank provides the exporter with forms that bear the bank's own letterhead for mailing documents to the buyer's bank for collection. To the buyer's bank, it will appear that the documents were sent from the exporter's bank, but time and expense are saved by by-passing unnecessary processing at the exporter's bank.

Documentary credit – synonymous with 'letter of credit'.

Documentary draft collection – process for collecting payment in a sale of goods wherein a legal demand for payment from the buyer is made by a bank acting as collecting agent for the seller. The demand is made by presenting a draft. The collecting bank is also entrusted with documents to deliver in accordance with accompanying instructions, usually once the draft is either paid or accepted. These documents are generally needed by the buyer to show title to the goods and/or to clear customs.

Documents against acceptance – term for documentary collection instructions requesting the presenting bank to deliver documents only upon acceptance of the draft (bill of exchange) by the drawee/buyer.

Draft – written demand for payment of a specified amount addressed to a named party, called the 'drawee', and signed by the 'drawer'. A draft may demand payment immediately upon presentation ('at sight') or on a specified maturity date and must also specify a party to be paid (the 'payee'). Most drafts are 'negotiable', meaning the payee's right to payment can be transferred by the payee to another party by endorsement and delivery of the draft. Also called a bill of exchange.

eUCP – a 12-article supplement to the UCP containing rules for electronic presentation of documents under a letter of credit.

Evergreen letter of credit – standby letter of credit with an initial expiration date but containing a clause that states that it will be automatically extended for additional periods unless the issuing bank provides notice to the beneficiary stating otherwise.

Freely negotiable letter of credit – letter of credit that indicates it is 'available with any bank by negotiation'. By including this wording, the issuing bank authorizes the beneficiary to present documents to the bank of his/her choice for examination and collection of payment.

Instalment letter of credit – letter of credit calling for multiple shipments within specified date ranges.

International standby practices (ISP) – international standards of practice for demand guarantees and standby letters of credit established for bankers by the International Chamber of Commerce. The term 'standby' is used to include both letters of credit and guarantees, but it must be kept in mind that the ISP, like all ICC publications, only applies to standbys that say they are subject to it.

Irrevocable letter of credit – letter of credit that cannot be amended or cancelled without agreement of both the beneficiary and the issuing bank. Any letter of credit subject to the UCP500, the ISP, or to US law, is irrevocable unless it specifies otherwise.

Issuing bank – bank that has issued a letter of credit. The issuing bank is obligated to pay if documents arc presented that comply with the letter's requirements.

Letter of credit – undertaking, usually on the part of a bank and at the request of one of the bank's customers, to pay a named beneficiary a specified amount of money (or to deliver an item of value) if the beneficiary presents documents in accordance with the terms and conditions specified in the letter of credit.

Negotiable – quality belonging to a document of being able to transfer ownership of money, goods, or other items of value specified in the document by endorsement and/or delivery of the document. Cheques, drafts, promissory notes, bonds, stock certificates, bills of lading, and warehouse receipts are examples of documents often issued in negotiable form.

Negotiating bank – bank, usually in the seller's country, nominated by the bank issuing a letter of credit to purchase (negotiable) documents presented by the seller. The term is also used, imprecisely, to refer to banks nominated to pay or to accept drafts.

Presenting bank – in a draft collection transaction, the bank that contacts the drawee, generally the buyer of goods, for acceptance and/or payment.

Reimbursing bank – in a letter of credit transaction, the bank with which the issuing bank maintains an account and which is authorized by the issuing bank to charge that account to pay claims received from the negotiating bank for documents that have been presented.

Remitting bank – in a draft collection transaction, the first bank in the chain of collection, i.e. the principal's or seller's bank.

Retention of title – legal arrangement under which a seller delivers these goods 'on consignment' into someone's custody but ownership remains with the seller until he/she is paid. In many countries, retention of title allows the seller to repossess the goods whenever desired and to establish a claim against the custodian if the goods are sold or used without being paid for.

Revocable letter of credit – letter of credit that can be amended or cancelled at any time without notice to, or consent of, the beneficiary. A letter of credit that is subject to the UCP500, the ISP, or to US law, is revocable only if it clearly specifies so.

Sight draft – draft that demands payment 'at sight', or immediately, as opposed to a time draft, which may be payable, e.g. '90 days after sight' or '30 days after bill of lading date'.

Silent confirmation – term used for a bank's commitment to negotiate (i.e. purchase) documents under a letter of credit without recourse at a future date. A silent confirmation is not a confirmation in the true sense, and will not use the word 'confirm', but is rather an equivalent form of protection for the beneficiary. The bank will require that the letter of credit be negotiable by itself to be able to establish holder-in-due-course rights equivalent to those of a confirming bank.

Standby letter of credit – as opposed to a commercial letter of credit, a letter of credit that does not cover the direct purchase of merchandise, so called because it is often intended to be drawn on only when the applicant for whom it is issued fails to perform an obligation. There is, nonetheless, a type of standby letter of credit that is intended to be drawn on, referred to as a 'direct pay letter of credit'. Standby letters of credit are based on the underlying principle of letters of credit that payment is made against presentation of documents – whatever documents the applicant, beneficiary, and issuing bank may agree to, not necessarily documents showing shipment of goods.

Time draft – draft that demands payment at a specified future date rather than immediately upon presentation.

Transferable letter of credit – type of letter of credit that names a 'middleman' as beneficiary and allows him/her to give another party, the actual supplier, certain rights to present documents and receive payment under the letter of credit.

Uniform customs and practice for documentary credits (UCP) – international standards of letter of credit practice established for bankers by the International Chamber of Commerce. Historically, the UCP has been revised about every 10 years to keep up with changing practice, the most recent revision, UCP500, having been completed in 1993. Although the UCP defines rights and obligations of the various parties in a letter of credit transaction, it is not law and any given letter of credit is subject to the UCP only to the extent indicated in the letter of credit itself.

Uniform rules for collection – international standards of draft collection practice established for bankers by the International Chamber of Commerce. The uniform rules are not law but are more properly viewed as a handbook for banks used to establish common understanding of terminology and expectations.

Part G

Miscellaneous

32 Miscellaneous issues in multinational finance

In this chapter we focus on a number of topics which are much too important not to be covered in a book of this sort and are relevant to the study of multinational finance, but that do not warrant a separate chapter. In particular, parts of this chapter are devoted respectively to the questions of performance measurement, treasury centralization versus decentralization, the treasury of a profit centre or cost centre, authority and limits in foreign exchange management, dealing with banks, security in the dealing room, commercial paper, credit rating, transfer pricing, capital flight and actual corporate ledging policies.

32.1 | Overseas subsidiary performance measurement

The development of a system for evaluating the performance of an overseas affiliate logically involves four distinct phases:

- Specification of the purpose of the system.

- Determining information requirements.

- Designing an information collection system.

- Assessing the system in cost/benefit terms.

The first step, then, is to specify the system's purpose. Immediately a key question arises: is head office management concerned with managerial performance or flows back to headquarters? In any case, how do we ensure that subsidiary management is insulated, in terms of evaluation, from factors beyond its control, such as exchange rate charges, local inflation rates and so on? We return to these questions later in this chapter.

First of all, we take a couple of steps back and ask what the main objectives of a system of performance evaluation are. They embrace the following:

- To provide a basis to aid global resource allocation.

- To provide an early warning system to highlight things going wrong.

- To ensure that adequate profit and/or cash are generated and to measure them.

- To provide a set of standards to motivate individual managers.

- To provide a basis for evaluating the performance of individual managers.

That seems fairly straightforward. So what are the problems?

32.2 | Problems in overseas performance evaluation

Exchange rate movements create difficulties in terms of evaluating the performance of an overseas affiliate. The first difficulty is whether one should measure using home or host currency. If evaluation is in home currency terms, then, in drafting a budget, assumptions have to be made about exchange rates. But actual performance will be realized, in all probability, at some other exchange rate. An unbudgeted change in exchange rates automatically makes for a variance between budget and actual. If the firm in the overseas territory is involved in competing with imports or in exporting, this variance will impact upon local currency outturns. Furthermore, if performance is looked at in home currency terms, then there will not only be a variance due to the above economic exposure but there will also be one associated with translation.

Focusing just upon the impact of translation problems, Lessard and Lorange (1977) point out that there are three exchange rates that can be used in setting a budget and these three can also be used to monitor (or track, as they refer to it) performance. The three exchange rates are the initial rate, the projected rate and the end rate, and their permutation in a 3×3 matrix produces nine possible combinations of budgeted and actual exchange rates. Lessard and Lorange summarize the situation as shown in Figure 32.1. Given that only three of these monitor on the same basis as budgeting, the logical contenders would appear to be:

- budget at initial rate, monitor at initial rate;

- budget at projected rate, monitor at projected rate;

- budget at ending rate, monitor at ending rate.

Exchange rate used to track performance versus budget

		Initial	Projected	Ending
Exchange rate used in budget	Initial	Budget – Initial Track – initial	Budget – initial Track – projected	Budget – initial Track – ending
	Projected	Budget – projected Track – initial	Budget – projected Track – projected	Budget – projected Track – ending
	Ending	Budget – ending Track – initial	Budget – ending Track – projected	Budget – ending Track – ending

Figure 32.1 Exchange rates and control.
Source: Lessard and Lorange (1977).

Lessard and Lorange prefer the second method. They show that two of the major criteria for good management control systems are satisfied. They claim that 'goal congruence exists because a corporate-wide point of view will prevail in making decisions in which exchange rate changes might have an impact'. Furthermore, they claim that operating managers are treated fairly, since they receive neither blame nor credit for variations in performance caused by exchange rate changes that are unanticipated.

Stewart (1983) proposes measuring performance by use of a normalized exchange rate, based on what the exchange rate would be if the market adjusted fully to purchasing power parity (PPP) over the short run. The argument advanced is that actual exchange rates fluctuate around an intrinsic value; sometimes the market rate is overvalued, sometimes it is undervalued. In the long run, exchange rates and local profitability return to PPP conditions. It follows that, should performance be measured by intrinsic value or normalized exchange rates, firms may avoid the ups and downs created by excessive exchange rate movements. Stewart asserts that, if asset values and operating profit are measured in the home currency using a PPP-normalized exchange rate, then rates of return on investment will tend to measure performance effectively. This approach assumes that exchange rates are in equilibrium in some base period. The disadvantage of Stewart's approach is that it fails to take account of economic exposure effects and homes in solely upon translation aspects of the problem. It does not, in other words, take account of competitive aspects of changing exchange rates. And it seems to focus upon a hypothetical state of the world rather than looking at the way it really is.

Lessard and Sharp (1984), taking up the challenge of this objection, propose a measure of performance that addresses the need both to translate foreign currency profits into home currency and to take cognizance of the impact of exchange rates on underlying profitability. They suggest the use of a technique that might be termed 'contingent budgeting'. Their recommended procedure involves three steps which they describe as follows:

1. Prepare a budget based on a 'most-likely' scenario. This is the traditional budget preparation process. It seems to be natural to prepare the budget in terms of local currency units.
2. Prepare an audit of the likely effect of a range of surprise deviations from existing exchange rate parities, in terms of impact on prices, costs and hence operating cash flows. The objective of this procedure is to develop, in advance, an expectation of the relationship between exchange rates, operating management's best efforts, and operating cash flows.
3. At the end of the year, when the exchange rates are known, use the results of the audit to compute a set of standards or benchmarks of performance, given the exchange rates that actually materialized. Actual results should then be compared with the contingent standards as the point of departure in discussing management performance.

Lessard and Sharp's approach is theoretically acceptable but whether it is cost effective and practical is another question. Admittedly, the whole budget process is bathed in subjectivity – Lessard and Sharp's recommended method seems to have more than its fair share.

In proposing an eminently practical approach, Carsberg (1983) suggests that an affiliate's actual performance should be compared with budget using local currency.

He argues that, rather in the manner used to assess performance of managers in home country subsidiaries, 'the performance of an overseas manager may best be judged in terms of the results measured in overseas currency, and set against standards of performance in the country concerned'. Carsberg admits that:

> for the purpose of capital allocation, however, the home country financial management must attempt to estimate the effects of currency changes on the long-run profitability of proposed international investments; and control procedures will need to focus on a comparison of actual and estimated returns in the home currency.

Carsberg's pragmatic solution is summed up in his observation that:

> the best way to assess whether an overseas investment has been satisfactory is to measure the net cash flows generated by the investment, translate them into terms of the home currency, and discount them at the appropriate cost of capital to obtain a net present value.

But any system of overseas performance evaluation needs to exclude the effects of certain multinational practices which may be deemed valuable at the level of the group but which are imposed upon subsidiaries – such practices include transfer pricing, funds flow adjustments (for example, leading and lagging) and group hedging requirements.

Transfer pricing can have a significant impact on an overseas subsidiary's performance. A manager who is deemed accountable for the influence of transfer prices on reported profits is likely to react in ways that are counterproductive to the group as a whole. Transfer pricing is virtually always a centralized decision emanating from the multinational headquarters. Its purpose may be tax minimization or to inflate costs where prices are based on cost plus or something similar. In performing an appraisal of an overseas subsidiary, the distorting effect of less than arm's-length pricing should be eliminated. Certainly, managerial evaluations should be decoupled from the transfer prices being used. This decoupling may be done by charging purchasers market prices, if available, or by using the marginal cost of production and shipping plus a reasonable profit on sales. Managers of subsidiaries that produce solely for sale to other subsidiaries ought to be evaluated on the basis of their production costs, rather than their profits. After all, they are essentially cost centres with no control over the revenues, which are set at headquarters level to achieve maximum net-of-tax profits.

Decoupling in the way suggested above may present problems at times. Transfer prices of multinational drug companies are monitored closely throughout the world. To disclose, even with the group, the effect and level of transfer prices and true costs may not be expedient from the standpoint of the drug company concerned.

The next area that needs to be disaggregated for performance evaluation purposes is the effect of funds flow adjustment – in particular, the effects of leading and lagging and suchlike. Leading and lagging may be directed from the central treasury at headquarters with a view to maximizing group profits. The results obtained at operating overseas subsidiary level would be unlikely to reflect that operating performance of managers in the host country – certainly, it is not them who usually instigate the action. Leading and lagging is likely to distort working-capital levels and ratios of affiliates. A subsidiary ordered to extend longer credit terms to another group company will require more working capital to finance its business and will show an increase in its debtors to sales ratio. Also, its interest expenses will increase. Since leading and lagging is a group policy, its effects should not be included when evaluating subsidiary management. These effects should be reversed by eliminating the cost of carrying intra-corporate debtors and adding these costs to those subsidiaries invoiced with intra-corporate creditors. Also, each affiliate's investment base should reflect only those corporate assets required for its operating business.

There is also the question of covering. Foreign operational management may wish to take cover from transaction exposure. If this is the case, performance evaluation should allow for covering even though all covering is only carried out at group level. It is usual to require that divisions do not use outside bankers to cover foreign exchange exposure but that all hedging be dealt with according to one of three approaches:

■ Subsidiaries hedge all foreign exchange transaction exposures with the group treasury.

■ Subsidiaries hedge only those foreign exchange transaction exposures that they consider wise with the group treasury.

■ Subsidiaries hedge no foreign exchange transaction exposure at all but leave this function to the group treasury, to which all exposures are routinely reported.

Whichever system is used, all transaction exposure should be reported to the group treasury. And where the central treasury is used for covering, it is required to quote to divisions rates for forward cover which the divisions could get in the foreign exchange market.

For reporting purposes, we believe that the middle course is the preferred one. It ensures that subsidiaries are responsible for their selective hedging actions. Using this system, divisional management accounts will reflect operational outturns plus the results of covering which has been duly instigated by the subsidiaries concerned. It should be recalled that, even though this system is used, all hedging is done with the centre and the group treasury obtains information on all transaction exposures, whether hedged or not. So it can take action in response to the total group exposure.

Neither the first system nor the last gives operating management any discretion on hedging and the withdrawal of this discretion may be a demotivating factor. Given that we wish our control system to be functional as well as being a motivator, it is preferable for divisions to report all transaction exposures, but to hedge whatever they wish of this exposure with the head office treasury. This system is also preferable where there are minority interests in a subsidiary. Clearly, selective hedging at the level of the partly owned subsidiary may be beneficial to minority shareholders. If a system is to be designed that does not act against the interest of minority shareholders, which the 'hedge everything' or 'hedge nothing' system may do, then care must be taken to ensure that subsidiary results are not distorted by requirements which may be optimal at the group level but not at the subsidiary level.

The whole area of empirical work on overseas performance evaluation is somewhat under-researched. Choi and Czechowicz (1983) found that budget compared with actual is the single most important performance criterion for sixty-four US multinational firms and for twenty-four non-US multinational firms; return on investment comes second. Interestingly, in their survey they found that US multinationals rate cash flow to the parent as more important than cash flow to the affiliate, whereas non-US multinationals reverse the ranking order. Persen and Lesig (1980) also found that actual performance versus budget topped the list of evaluation criteria.

In connection with monitoring budgeted performance, a Business International (1977) survey of 200 multinationals found that only three of Lessard and Lorange's nine combinations were used. Half of the firms polled used a projected rate for budgeting but measured performance with the end-of-period rate; 30 per cent used a projected rate both for budgeting and for performance evaluation; and the remaining 20 per cent used the spot rate for budgeting and the end-of-period rate for monitoring performance.

On the question of centralization versus decentralization of treasury control, Meister (1970) indicates that, of a sample of multinationals, 85 per cent indicated that decisions involving repatriation of funds were made at the corporate level. Furthermore, where companies were minority partners in joint ventures, they appeared to have little control over the repatriation decision. On the issue of inter-subsidiary financing, in most companies either the chief financial executive of the parent company or the treasurer, with the aid of tax advice, appeared to decide on intra-corporate flows of money. And on the question of negotiation of funds, 85 per cent of firms indicated that all medium-term and long-term financing was approved at corporate headquarters, although many firms allowed their subsidiaries more leeway with regard to raising short-term finance.

An interesting study by Stobaugh (1979) indicated different attitudes towards centralization among small (average annual foreign sales of $50m), medium (average annual foreign sales of $200m) and large (average annual foreign sales of $1bn) multinationals. The small-firm group generally allowed subsidiaries a lot of leeway in financial management, perhaps owing to lack of sophistication in international financial management at headquarters or to cost/benefit factors. Medium-sized firms tended to have very sophisticated control and reporting systems designed to optimize world results and cash flows. But the largest-firm group tended to reverse the centralization trend to some extent by providing subsidiaries with formal guidelines but allowing them considerable leeway within these boundaries. This latitude seemed to be due to a recognized inability to optimize in such a complex area as global financial flows.

32.3 | Treasury management performance

There is also the problem of treasury performance measurement. Treasury management is concerned with borrowing, investing liquid resources and managing foreign exchange and interest rate exposures. The objectives of the treasury function embrace the raising of funds as cheaply as possible, the investment of liquid funds to earn an adequate return, the control of currency and interest rate exposures and ensuring that the firm can meet its liabilities as they fall due. Corporate treasurers are frequently judged, in terms of performance achieved, by the effect of their decisions on bottom-line reported profits. But the literature on treasury management is virtually devoid of serious articles on performance measurement. One notable exception is a pioneering article by Cooper and Franks (1987), which attempts to set benchmarks for measuring treasury performance. Interested readers are referred to the article. The topic is an important one which is currently at the cutting edge of treasury research. Logically, the benchmarking and performance-measurement techniques would parallel those applied in fund management.

32.4 | Centralization of exposure management

The argument against centralized control is simple. Central bureaucracies can be expensive, slow to respond to problems and inflexible – particularly from the viewpoint of the manager in the front line. But there are some decisions that cannot sensibly be delegated. Many financial decisions fall into this category. The case for centralizing foreign exchange management rests on the following arguments:

- It ensures that the company as a whole follows a consistent policy.

- It facilitates the matching of exposures. Without a centralized approach, there is a big danger that one subsidiary might be buying a currency at the same moment as another is selling it.

- It helps to get the best rates in the market. Banks charge far wider spreads on their buying and selling rates when dealing for small amounts via branches. The finest rates may be obtained by dealing large amounts directly with the bank's own dealing room. Dealing through the local branch of the bank always results in a poorer rate of exchange and some loss of control of the transaction.

- It ensures the concentration of limited expertise. If centralized, exposure management will be handled by a team for whom it is a primary function rather than a secondary aspect of a divisional finance or accounting role. Concentration of skills in this way should ensure a better understanding of the problem and an enhanced execution.

- Centralization will pool both skills and systems investment. It usually justifies proper dealing facilities, direct lines and computer systems for data management and communication.

- It helps integration with cash management.

By contrast, there are a number of arguments advanced to support decentralization of exposure management. These include the following:

- There are substantial up-front costs in recruitment, office space and equipment in establishing a central foreign exchange expertise.

- Foreign exchange risk management is interesting and stimulating. Line managers may resist attempts to take this authority away.

A further, somewhat spurious, argument against centralization is that it may demotivate divisional management by transferring authority and control from individual units and profit centres. Centralization need not involve this. The approach recommended in this book is that individual units should regard the central treasury as their banker and run an account with head office. Divisions may or may not hedge exposure with the treasury; this should maintain their autonomy. They will, of course, report all exposures to the centre. A more valid argument against the centralization of foreign exchange exposure activities is that divisional staff may become blind to the risks involved and the expertise necessary to handle foreign exchange problems as they inevitably arise in the course of their work. Clearly, good training of line managers who may come up against foreign exchange problems is essential.

Factors influencing the centralization/decentralization discussion are many. For example, the corporate philosophy on autonomy is pertinent, as is ownership. With a larger number of partly owned subsidiaries or associates with substantial minority holdings, it may be appropriate to adopt a decentralized approach. After all, minority shareholders will want optimization at the level of their own investment – and this is not the group level.

The proportion of value or turnover exposed is obviously a relevant factor in deciding whether to centralize or not. Where performance will not be materially affected by changes in exchange rates, foreign exchange risk is unlikely to be an issue. But clearly, where group profit and balance sheet are substantially exposed to currency volatility, the reverse is true.

Large multinational groups, with a number of subsidiaries trading in different countries and with each other, will create complex exposures. There will be correspondingly greater opportunity for inconsistency in exposure management, unless centralized.

In a purely decentralized system, the unit looks after its own exposures only, having no regard for exposures occurring elsewhere in the group. It will decide on the timing of cover and implement that decision using external methods if necessary. Reports to the parent may not even identify the currency flows.

At the opposite end of the spectrum is the completely centralized system. Here the treasury receives and co-ordinates data and forecasts of currency flows from all group members to determine the total net position, and undertakes appropriate hedging action determined by group exposure positions and strategy. The subsidiary will not be consulted on group hedging strategy.

There are many intermediate variations possible too. The treasury may exist merely as an advisory function, directing when and how the subsidiary should hedge its exposures; this may be appropriate where a company has many relatively independent overseas subsidiaries. A centralized treasury may provide a dealing service to carry out the cover decisions of the subsidiaries. It may deal only with exceptional or very large currency exposures. Many companies operate a system under which the subsidiaries are obliged to report all exposures to the centre, and must undertake any cover they wish to put in place with the centre, but can choose if or when to hedge; the centre covers the group position according to overall exposure and policy, while the subsidiary remains in control of its own performance. If justified by cost/benefit considerations, this latter kind of approach is most effective.

Empirically, Evans, Folks and Jilling (1978) have observed an increasing tendency towards centralization in the US-based multinationals. Oxelheim (1984) has found a similar trend with Swedish-based international groups, stimulated by improved global tax planning, knowledge concentration and other financial economies of scale.

To round off this summary of the centralization/decentralization debate, it must be stressed that, whatever system is adopted, it needs to be justified on cost/benefit grounds and it needs to be regularly checked to ensure that the system chosen continues to deliver the goods in cash terms. The need for *ad hoc* post-audits should be clear.

32.5 | The treasury as a profit centre

The centralization of foreign exchange exposure management creates the opportunity to run it as a profit centre. In this context, profit may accrue first from improved exchange rates on deals, secondly by taking selective hedging decisions and thirdly by generating profits from speculation in currencies.

The extent to which the treasury is allowed to play currency markets – to punt – is a matter for board decision, taking into account shareholders' best interests. Given the caveat about equity investors' interests, any position taking can be justified only by some superior knowledge possessed by a treasury executive or adviser. This would probably imply only minimal speculation. Whatever approach is used in terms of profit or cost centre, treasury performance needs to be measured. If the track record fails to indicate superior outturns given the level of risk incurred, then any position taking at all should be ruled out. Failure to match appropriate return levels for the amount of risk incurred presumably raises questions about whether the treasurer is up to the job.

The author is aware that some companies, such as BP, have set up their treasury with a remit to make money by taking positions in foreign exchange markets (with performance measured and controlled), rather as banks do. It is worth mentioning that, according to Dallas (1990), interest rate mismatching and running the treasury as a profit centre are scored negatively by credit-rating agencies.

32.6 | Authority and limits

It is critically important that individuals working in the area of foreign exchange exposure know clearly the limits of their authority to act and the circumstances in which they are expected to do so. It is probably easier for a bank to set limits for its dealers than it is for a corporation to do so. The limit on a bank dealer only constrains the size of position he or she may take. Within that limit the dealer is left free to buy and sell currencies as profitable opportunities arise. The activities of dealers in non-financial institutions must be constrained – but in a different way. Their job is not normally to speculate in currency. It is rather to buy and sell the currency arising specifically from their company's trading activities. But timing is of the essence. And corporate dealers may deliberately leave a trading position exposed for a short time, hoping to deal later at a more favourable rate. Many companies are unwilling to leave decisions of this importance to a single dealer, however expert he or she is.

Often, the responsibility for the setting of the company's policy on exposures is shared by a small committee. The committee should give clear instructions, authority and limits to the dealing staff, whose activities should be monitored as a matter of routine. The idea of limits goes beyond dealer authority. Effectively, it sets the maximum figure for exposure to any single type of risk. The figure may be the maximum loss that the management is prepared to suffer for that risk. Limits might be set for a range of exposures and include counterparty credit limits, capacity limits, sovereign limits, currency limits, liquidity limits, delivery limits and interest rate limits. There might be an overall level for limits during dealing hours (daylight limits) and another for overnight exposures. Overnight limits are essential. They relate to a period of currency movement that is probably not being monitored by the business as the dealing room is closed at night. Excessive overnight positions could clearly accumulate large losses. We now look briefly at each of the seven limits listed above.

Counterparty credit limits are required to protect the company from excess loss in the event of default by the counterparty to a transaction. But remember that, in foreign exchange dealing, the credit risk is normally a margin risk, not the full capital risk as with a loan. The possible loss on a forward deal if the counterparty defaults is that the deal has to be closed out at the current forward market for the original maturity date. The possible loss is the difference between the original forward price and that obtained to close out the deal. The result might be a profit, although it is unlikely that a counterparty would default on a valuable forward. The full capital sum is at risk at the time of delivery – see delivery limits below.

Capacity limits relate to the total risk that an undertaking may assume. The Articles or Memorandum of Association will stipulate company borrowing limits. This may be as a proportion of capital or assets or it may be an absolute figure.

The next limit relates to country risk. Sovereign limits concern the accepted level of risk exposure to a foreign country imposing restrictions on the business. The restrictions may not be just about payment of a debt, but this is normally the main concern. Sovereign exposure includes a number of risks – for example, an embargo on payment or a regulation that reduces the value of the payment, or remittances simply becoming blocked.

Currency limits are considered the most important of limits for dealers. Currency limits may be set by reference to measuring the volatility of each currency and the maximum loss sustainable. Bankers take the following views in arriving at currency limits for dealers. More volatile currencies do not necessarily require lower limits. To limit dealers to very stable currencies is to limit severely the opportunities to make profits. Bank currency limit systems generally have three parts: a gross long position limit (total currency assets), a gross short position limit (total currency liabilities) and a net position limit (the net of assets and liabilities).

Next we turn to liquidity limits. These seek to ensure that a business is not short of liquid funds when they are needed. Liquidity or maturity risk is most easily shown as a gap report or ladder. This is a report that shows maturities in chronological order. Liquidity limits set ceilings on the extent of any maturity mismatch.

Delivery limits are now looked at. All currency transactions require delivery of some form of value at some point. Any movement of funds contains an element of risk. The banking system is geared to make a vast quantity of receipts and payments. It is easy to forget that there is a risk and that this risk can be for the full capital value of the foreign exchange deal. The full capital value of a currency deal is at risk when the different currencies of the deal are delivered in different time zones. The party that has to deliver in the first time zone is at full value risk until the matching payment is made in the later time zone. Delivery risk is still sometimes called 'Herstatt risk' after the German bank that defaulted in 1974. Herstatt defaulted after collecting funds in the European time zone but before making payments due in US dollars in the later US time zone. The only way to cover against the risk, in cases of doubt, is to delay payment against proof of receipt of the other currency. This will lead to a penalty interest payment, but may be worth it for the added security.

Finally, there should be a limit on interest rate risks incurred. Admittedly, this has little to do with foreign exchange except inasmuch as the forward currency rate is a function of differential interest rates, so that forward rate exposure can be said to consist, in part, of interest rate risk. In a similar way to liquidity limits, a gap report may readily be produced showing mismatch.

32.7 | Foreign exchange dealing with banks

Foreign exchange deals should be done by corporations on a competitive basis. Rates quoted by various banks may differ to a greater extent than might at first be thought. After all, the banks' quotations are a function of their own currency positions that they happen to have at the time. A bank that was able to quote a very competitive rate on one occasion will not necessarily be able to do so next time around. The more banks that are approached for quotations, the better the chance of an advantageous rate. Differences of a few points in the fourth decimal place can be worth a lot of money on a really big deal.

The size of a deal is important when competitive quotes are being sought. Banks will not be grateful if kept waiting for a decision while rates are checked elsewhere for a deal of $10,000 or so. More important, there is the possibility of driving the market against oneself by seeking a large number of quotations for an amount that is relatively large in that particular market at that time. Calls to a dozen banks could easily move the price. On a large deal, three quotations or so is generally a maximum and it is essential that they be obtained simultaneously, not one after the other.

Spot currency transactions are normally carried out for value two working days after the date on which the deal is done to allow adequate time for the settlement arrangements to be made. Special arrangements may be made for settlement on a one-day or even a same-day basis, but there is liable to be some cost involved in this.

In theory, currency is bought and sold on the foreign exchange market with a cash settlement. For most larger corporates, no cash actually changes hands on the settlement day. What the purchaser buys is the right to a credit balance of a given amount in a bank account of its choosing, but almost always with a bank in the territory of which the currency purchased is the domestic currency. In other words, US dollars may not leave the United States and sterling tends not to leave London. A purchaser of dollars for sterling will, after two working days, obtain a dollar credit in a nominated bank account in New York in exchange for a debit to its sterling account in London. Even if the purchaser has a dollar account with a London bank, the balance on that account is reflected in the balance of the London bank with its New York correspondent bank. The position is the same when borrowing or depositing. Two-day value applies and settlement is by credit to a bank account in the appropriate territory. There is, of course, an obligation to return the funds at maturity.

Donaldson (1987) has a wealth of good advice for relatively small corporate players in the foreign exchange market in terms of obtaining quotations from banks for deals.

Nowadays, computer systems are available to enable the finance director or corporate treasurer to identify and deal at the best rates on offer.

32.8 | Dealing room security

Foreign exchange deals are made on the telephone or electronically and subsequently confirmed in writing, normally within twenty-four hours. Telephone calls can be made from anywhere and by anyone. In theory, a company could be fraudulently committed without being aware of what had happened until the following day. Steps are taken to provide a substantial degree of protection. First of all, bank dealers usually know the people authorized to do deals within the corporation. Furthermore, every telephone deal is usually recorded by the bank. One of the most effective internal checks concerns the handling of the confirmation documentation. Banks always send out formal documentation confirming the terms of each deal; these are normally received by the customer on the following day. It is normal practice for companies to raise confirmation documents themselves and also to send these to the banks with which they have dealt. The absence of such a confirmation would alert the bank if an unofficial deal had been made in the company's name. For this control to be effective, tight security must be maintained over the confirmation forms, which should be serially numbered, and a record kept of the use to which each is put.

Under no circumstances should banks' dealing confirmations be sent to the dealing room. And under no circumstances should front office dealers be involved in creating and checking back office documentation. The flow should be structured in such a way that some responsible member of the staff, the internal auditor, perhaps, has the task of matching dealing record slips prepared in the corporate dealing room with the relevant bank confirmations. All banks that the company deals with on foreign exchange should be given the name of the person to whom all documentation should be sent – and clearly this should not be someone in the dealing room itself. Frauds perpetuated by a company's dealers fall into the following categories:

- Dealers being involved in back office documentation – either directly or in collusion.

- Overstating the cost or understating the realization on a deal and then by some means syphoning off the excess proceeds into a personal account. This may involve collusion with one of the bank's dealers.

- Directing the proceeds of a deal to a personal account, then somehow teeming and lading before ultimately absconding.

- Speculating in currencies by opening up unauthorized long or short positions. The intention is that profits are kept personally, but if the currency moves the wrong way then losses are for the company.

Checking of bank confirmations is the first line of defence. Regular audit checks in the dealing room are a further safeguard. Individuals involved in such audits need to be experienced in foreign exchange practices. And, to reiterate, the doing of front-office deals and the raising and/or checking of back-office documentation must be entirely separate – 100 per cent so. The losses revealed in 1995 at Barings in Singapore and by Daiwa Bank in New York both involved such a situation. In the author's opinion, for every bank fraud which hits the front pages there are in excess of a hundred, on a smaller scale, that do not. Dealing losses or incompetences followed by fraud involving a dealer in the back office are not new and will only go away if banks are diligent all of the time in both their head offices and throughout their empires – a set of circumstances that is very likely. So do not be surprised when the financial newspapers carry reports of further dealer incompetence and fraud resulting in big losses at ABCD Bank or BCDE Company.

32.9 | Commercial paper

Commercial paper (CP) – basically a corporate or other institutional IOU – is an instrument for raising short-term funds used by companies and financial and sovereign issuers. It is issued in the form of unsecured promissory notes in bearer form with maturities of under one year. CP is a cheap and easy method of raising short-term funds for top-rated issuers. It provides a further source of funding besides bank borrowing. In the sterling CP market, a top-rated issuer might raise funds at five basis points below LIBID, the London inter-bank bid rate. An unrated medium-quality name might raise funds at five basis points over LIBOR, the London inter-bank offered rate.

CP is purchased by a wide range of companies and institutional investors wishing to invest short-term cash surpluses at rates competitive with bank deposits. The credit quality of most CP issues is high. Ninety per cent of commercial paper sold in the United States is rated A1/P1, the highest rating for short-term money.

CP programmes are uncommitted facilities or arrangements between an issuer and dealers who agree to distribute the paper to investors whenever the issuer wishes to raise funds by this means. The issuer is not obliged to raise the entire amount of the programme. The issuer may drawdown only 50 per cent of the programme, leaving the balance unused, or the company might repay the entire amount on the maturity of the notes and then draw up to the entire amount of the programme at a later date. The major CP markets are in US commercial paper (USCP), Euronotes or Euro-commercial paper (ECP) and sterling commercial paper (SCP), although there are CP markets in a wide range of other countries and currencies.

The USCP market originated in the nineteenth century: corporate treasurers lent their surplus funds to other corporations via commercial paper. Nowadays, there are around 2,500 CP programmes with some US$700bn of paper outstretching. The market is largely domestic and is weighted to short maturities: the average maturity is 22 days. About 55 per cent of USCP is sold through dealers and the remainder is placed directly by the issuing company with the investor. The USCP market is highly liquid, but there is little secondary trading in the paper due to the very short maturities of most USCP. Yields are consistently lower than LIBOR; the low cost is, of course, the main attraction.

We now turn to ECP. But before we do, a brief word about ECP's big brother, Euronotes. The Euronote market developed in the last decade. A Euronote is a short-term bearer promissory note issued under a medium-term Euronote facility, such as a revolving underwriting facility or a note issuance facility. The borrower under such a facility has a commitment from the underwriting banks that it will be able to issue the Euronotes under the medium-term facility.

ECP refers to short-term bearer promissory notes issued without the benefit of the associated medium-term underwriting commitment. The issuer cannot be certain that it will be able to issue paper whenever it wishes – for example, if investors lose confidence in the issuer's credit standing or if the market collapses. The ECP market has around $90bn of paper in issue. Major investors are based in London and Switzerland. Typical ECP maturities are one, three and six months; the average maturity is three months. The US dollar is the most popular currency for issues, although programmes have been established in various other currencies. The market in euros is a growing one.

Until 1986, UK legislation imposed restrictions on the issue of sterling CP, but since then the SCP market has grown and it now has over £6bn in issue from around 180 programmes placed mainly with domestic UK investors.

The main issuers are corporations with an estimated 45 per cent of the market; government agencies account for 20 per cent of issues, sovereign issues total 15 per cent and banks and financial institutions each account for 10 per cent of issues. On the other side of the equation, the largest investor group comprises companies with some 30 per cent; commercial banks account for 25 per cent of investment, while central banks, sovereign and quasi-sovereign entities have 20 per cent of the market and commercial companies and other financial institutions account for 25 per cent of investment. The attractions to both investors and borrowers are that bank returns and costs are bettered. The normal denomination of notes, which are in bearer form, are as follows:

USCP	$100,000 to $1m
ECP	$100,000 to $500,000 (some issues have had denominations as small as $10,000)
SCP	£100,000 to £1m

Commercial paper is normally issued at a discount of its face value, but it may be interest bearing at the rear end.

32.10 | Credit rating

Banks undertake their own assessments of credit risk for the loans that they make to customers. Banks are equipped to analyse a range of specialized credit situations via their large and diverse credit departments. Financial institutions that are involved in investing savings do not lend as banks do. But they do invest funds in government and corporate securities. These securities may be in the form of bonds and other debt obligations that carry redemption risk. In the absence of a credit department, such financial institutions rely on third-party evaluations of credit risk. Assessments are in the form of credit ratings and are provided by the rating agencies.

The major rating agencies are US-based firms, most notably Standard and Poor's (owned by US publisher McGraw-Hill) and Moody's (owned by Dun & Bradstreet). The two major agencies attach credit ratings to debt issues of corporations, sovereigns, utilities, supranationals and so on. The rating is a current assessment of the creditworthiness of a borrower with respect to a specific obligation. Credit ratings are based on the following considerations:

■ Likelihood of default – the capacity of the borrower to meet obligations in respect of interest and repayment of principal in accordance with the terms of the borrowing.

■ The nature of and provisions of the obligation – that is, short- or long-term debt, events of default, covenants and so on.

■ The protection afforded by, and the relative position of, the obligation in the event of bankruptcy, reorganization or other arrangement under bankruptcy law.

A credit rating may be defined as an indication of the relative probability of timely payment of principal and interest. Standard and Poor's (S & P's) and Moody's each have two rating systems – one for long-term obligations and one for short-term obligations.

We first of all look at the S & P rating method. Its long-term rating system is divided into two parts: investment grade and speculative grade. Investment grade ratings are defined as those issues that should pay principal and interest on time. These are the four highest-rating categories, namely AAA, AA, A and BBB. The higher the rating, the greater the likelihood of timely payment. A bond rated AA has a greater probability of paying principal and interest on time than one rated BBB, although both bonds should pay principal and interest on time. Bonds rated AA to B are further qualified by the addition of a plus or minus sign to indicate their standing within the category. The other half of S & P's long-term rating system relates to those bonds where there is some uncertainty as to whether they will pay principal and interest on time. These are classed as speculative grade and are assigned ratings of BB, B, CCC, CC and C. Bonds in default are rated D. Obviously, the system implies that the lower the rating of a bond, the greater the probability of default. To summarize S & P's bond rating, investment grade status is given as follows:

AAA   The highest rating assigned by S & P. Capacity to pay interest and to repay principal is extremely strong.

AA   Debt rated AA has a very strong capacity to pay interest and to repay principal and differs from the highest-rated issues only to a small degree.

A   Debt rated A has a strong capacity to pay interest and to repay principal, but it is somewhat more susceptible to the adverse effects of change in circumstance and economic conditions than obtain higher-rated categories.

BBB   Debt rated BBB is regarded as having an adequate capacity to pay interest and to repay principal. While it normally exhibits adequate protection, adverse economic conditions or changing circumstances are more likely to lead to a weakened capacity to pay interest and to repay principal for debt in this category than in higher-rated categories.

Debt rated BB, B, CCC, CC and C is regarded as having predominantly speculative characteristics, with respect to capacity to pay interest and repay principal. BB indicates the least degree of speculation and C the highest. Although such debt will probably have some quality and protective characteristics, these are outweighed by large uncertainties or major exposure to adverse conditions. Debt rated D is in default.

Moody's bond-rating gradations follow a similar format but their coding is different. Moody's uses the following definitions:

Aaa   Bonds rated Aaa are judged to be of the best quality. They carry the smallest degree of investment risk. Interest payments are well protected by a substantial and stable margin and principal is secure. Foreseeable changes are most unlikely to impair the fundamentally strong position of the bond-holder.

Aa   Bonds rated Aa are of high quality by all standards. With the Aaa group, they constitute what are generally known as 'high-grade bonds'. They are rated lower than the best bonds because margins of protection may not be as large as in the Aaa case, or fluctuation of cover factors may be of greater amplitude, or there may be other elements present which make the long-term risks somewhat larger than in Aaa securities.

A   Bonds rated A have many favourable investment attributes and are considered as upper-medium-grade obligations. Factors giving security to principal and interest are considered adequate, but there may be suggestions of a susceptibility to impairment sometime in the future.

Baa   Bonds rated Baa are considered as medium-grade obligations. In other words, they are neither highly protected nor poorly secured. Interest payments and principal security appear adequate at present, but longer-term protection may be lacking or may be unreliable over any great length of

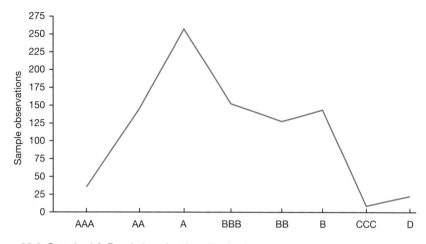

Figure 32.2 Standard & Poor's bond-rating distribution.
Source: Standard & Poor.

time. Such bonds lack outstanding investment characteristics and have speculative elements.

Ba   Bonds rated Ba are considered to have speculative elements and their future cannot be classified as well assured. The protection of interest and principal payments may be very moderate; they are not well safeguarded during both good and bad times in the future. Uncertainty of position characterizes these bonds.

B   Bonds rated B lack the general characteristics of desirable investment. Assurance of interest and principal payments over the long term may be small.

Caa   Bonds rated Caa are of poor standing. Such issues may be in default or there may be elements of danger with respect to principal or interest currently present.

Ca   Bonds rated Ca are speculative to a high degree. Such issues are often in default or have other shortcomings.

C   Bonds rated C are the lowest class of bonds, and such issues are regarded as having extremely poor prospects of ever attaining any real investment standing.

According to Emmer (1984), S & P rated fewer than 9 per cent of all industrial companies AAA. Figure 32.2 indicates how many bonds are typically rated by them – the chart draws from Emmer's work.

The other system produced by S & P is their commercial paper rating. Such ratings are assigned to short-term obligations with a maturity of less than one year. This system is also divided into investment grade and speculative grade. The investment grade category is the A category and it is subdivided into A1+, A1, A2 and A3. The speculative grade categories are rated B and C, and D refers to those issues that are in default.

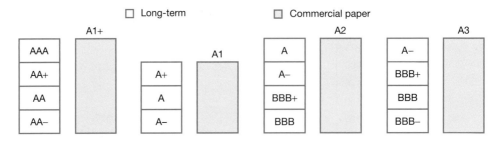

Figure 32.3 Standard & Poor's long-term and commercial paper ratings.
Source: Standard & Poor.

S & P's longer-term rating looks further into the future and places more emphasis on the fundamental characteristics of the issuer, while the short-term rating does not look out as far and places more emphasis on liquidity. Emmer draws a parallel between S & P's short- and long-term rating categories as set out in Figure 32.3. In this, there is some overlap of categories.

Moody's has the following rating categories for commercial paper: P1, P2, P3 and 'not prime'. Their top rating of P1 is the equivalent of S & P's A1 and A1+ ratings. Commercial paper given an A1 rating by Standard & Poor's and P1 by Moody's is commonly known as A1/P1 paper.

In the US commercial paper market, the practice is that two ratings should be obtained. Over 90 per cent of all paper issued in the New York market is rated A1/P1 or better. US commercial paper issuers are normally prime-quality credits. If the issuer is a lower-quality credit or a private company which does not wish to disclose its financial statements to the rating agencies, its paper can be issued if backed by a bank letter of credit from a bank of acceptable credit standing – that is, A1/P1 rated. The paper will then trade at a price reflecting the quality of the bank's credit and not that of the issuer. In the Euro-commercial paper market a rating is not mandatory but advisable. And in the sterling commercial paper market, ratings are the exception rather than the rule.

In the bond markets in particular, the rating is the single most important determinant of the interest rate which a company is likely to pay on raising funds. Emmer (1984), referring to yields current then, points out that the average yield on AAA industrial bonds was 12.08 per cent, while for AA bonds the yield was 12.37 per cent, for A bonds it was 12.62 per cent and for BBB bonds it was 13.28 per cent. The spread between A and BBB is quite marked. Corporate boards of directors often seek to maintain at least an A rating. Companies rated below A find it difficult to tap the Eurobond markets. Of course, the differences in interest costs between different rating classes varies from time to time. The above spreads are merely related as indicative.

For non-US companies selling securities in the US market, rating has become a very significant factor. Many US investors, not being familiar with foreign companies, their financial policies or local business practices, rely heavily on credit ratings. No single investor can afford to devote the resources that are necessary to evaluate and understand all the different corporate credits in the market place.

Obtaining a rating can be broken down into four parts – preparation, meeting the agency, the rating committee and informing the company. The first is preparation. Prior to meeting with a company, the rating agency needs basic background information about the company's business, history, organization and management structure. This would generally be obtained from published sources, such as annual reports, supplemented by the submission of additional information not disclosed in annual reports. All of the information presented to the rater is strictly confidential. The second part of the rating process is a meeting between the management of the company and the agency. Such meetings usually take place at the company's headquarters. The analysis team assigned by the rating agency to meet with a company generally consists of two or three individuals. The company generally fields a cross-section of management. Discussion concerns current operations and long-term strategies. Meetings generally last a couple of days. Rating agency executives then prepare a report to be presented to a rating committee. The rating committee is composed of officers with an in-depth knowledge of the industry and the economic and business environment. At this meeting the analyst reviews the company's profile and recommends a rating. The committee votes on this recommendation and then informs the company of the decision.

Should the company agree with this decision, rating goes ahead (see below). If the company does not agree, the rating agency will schedule another meeting with the company to review the reasons behind the decision. At that time, if it chooses, the company may present further information. After this meeting, the rating committee reconvenes and reviews the new information presented by the company. A further vote on rating ensues. At this point, the company may choose to accept the rating, in which case it becomes official, or it may reject it.

If the rating is rejected, it will not be made public in the following circumstances: if it is a commercial paper rating, or if the proposed financing is done outside the United States. However, if the bonds are publicly offered in the United States, the agency releases the rating as soon as the issue is filed with the SEC. Ratings are under continuous surveillance with an annual formal review. Ratings may be changed upon a permanent or fundamental change in either the issuer's financial condition or the industry in which it operates.

32.11 | Transfer pricing

The repatriation of profit by a multinational firm from its overseas operations can be a politically sensitive problem. In order to get monies out of an overseas subsidiary that restricts flows outwards, it may use transfer pricing. It may set high transfer prices on goods and services supplied to a foreign subsidiary by the head office or by divisions in environments that are less restrictive. Or the multinational may lower the transfer prices of products which the foreign division sells to the head office or to other divisions.

Transfer pricing is also used to reduce overall corporate taxes. The multinational may shuffle income to keep profits low in high-tax countries and relatively high in low-tax countries. The gains from profit shuffling via transfer prices are limited by the authorities in some countries; they may reallocate income if it is deemed that transfer prices have distorted profits.

Transfer prices may also be used to reduce import tariffs and to avoid quotas. When tariffs on imports are based on values of transactions, the value of goods moving between divisions may be artificially reduced by keeping down the transfer prices. This could put the multinational at an advantage over domestic firms. Also, where quotas are based on values of trade, the multinational can keep down prices to maintain the volume. Again, the multinational may turn this to advantage over purely domestic competitors. However, import authorities frequently adopt their own 'value for duty' on goods entering to help prevent revenues from being lost through transfer pricing manipulation.

For resource allocation in the multinational, it is important that divisional profitability be measured accurately. The record of profitability of different divisions is often relevant in allocating resources to capital projects and in sharing corporate resources. To discover the true profitability, the group should be sure that interdivisional transfer prices are the prices that would have been paid had the transactions been with independent companies – arm's-length prices. But there may be problems inasmuch as multinational group management may not want true profits to be known outside of a tight central coalition of executives.

32.12 | Capital flight

Capital flight refers to large capital outflows resulting from unfavourable investment conditions in a country. When the risk of maintaining funds in a country rises sharply and/or the expected returns fall, one frequently observes large outflows of funds so that the country experiences, in total, massive capital account deficits. The change in the risk–return relationship that gives rise to capital flight may be due to political or financial crises, tightening capital controls, tax increases or fear of a domestic currency devaluation owing to the government maintaining a previous unrealistic level.

During the 1980s, in the wake of the developing country debt crisis, funds were allegedly misappropriated from national borrowings to individual bank accounts overseas by people in powerful positions, to say nothing of wealthy individuals and business firms shipping capital out of the debtor nations to more financially secure shores. It has been suggested that, during the decade to 1986, $26bn of capital left Argentina. This $26bn is more than half the total debt of $46bn incurred throughout 1984. During this period, Mexico lost $53bn in capital flight versus $97bn of gross external debt in 1984. Venezuelan capital flight totalled $30bn against gross external debt of $34bn. The saga has continued ever since with increasing sums leaving South America in the expectation of a devaluation of the local currency with flows moving to Switzerland, the USA and various offshore tax havens.

The important aspect of capital outflow is that fewer resources are available at home to service debt and more borrowing is consequently required. In addition, capital flight may be associated with a loss of international reserves and greater pressure for devaluation of the domestic currency.

32.13 | Corporate hedging policies

Finally, we present an overview of what we know about companies' actual hedging policies. It draws on a few empirical studies of corporate practices. The studies reported here are by no means all-encompassing and constitute nothing more than an indication of treasury management practices.

One of the first studies of corporate exposure management in the United States dealt with the choice among foreign exchange hedging tools available to corporations. The survey undertaken by Evans, Folks and Jilling (1978) was undertaken in the mid-1970s. At the time of the study, options and swaps were not available and the futures market was very much in its infancy. Financial executives within multinational companies, responding to a questionnaire survey conducted on behalf of the FASB, were asked to rate foreign exchange risk management techniques according to usage in their company and according to perceived usefulness. Table 32.1 summarizes the findings. It should be noted that, in respect of the usefulness rating, scores were in a range from 1 to 3. A rating of 1 implied low usefulness; a rating of 3 implied high usefulness. It can be seen from the table that the most useful tools in the mid-1970s were the borrowing hedge and the forward contract, in that order.

Another pioneering study, published in the early 1980s, was undertaken by Rodriguez (1980, 1981). Drawing data from a sample of interviews with financial executives in seventy of the largest US-based multinationals, Rodriguez compared views in 1974 with those of 1977. She observed an interesting refocus, stating that:

> during 1974 interviews, translation exposure for the current reporting period was used almost exclusively as the measure of exposure to exchange risk and as the basis for hedging this risk in these companies. By 1977, transaction exposure was followed simultaneously in most of the companies. And, when the decision was whether to hedge an exposure, only 20% of the companies interviewed in 1977 based their hedging decision solely on translation exposure.

The same survey found that economic exposure was largely ignored by financial executives; their efforts were concentrated largely upon transaction and translation exposure.

As a follow-up to the Rodriguez studies, Doukas (1983) found that FAS 52 caused a shift in the focus of finance executives in US firms. His findings are that, once translation gains and losses were removed from the consolidated income statement – which it will be recalled was the key effect of FAS 52 – only a very small percentage of US firms continued to hedge translation exposure. This finding is borne out by Collier, Davis, Coates and Longden (1990a, b). But they further found, as had Collier and Davis (1985), that a fair number of UK companies seemed to spend time and effort on hedging pure translation exposures. In Scandinavia, Oxelheim (1984) reports that, based on a study of Swedish firms, almost all companies gave priority

Table 32.1 How financial executives rate foreign exchange rate techniques

Technique	Usage rate (%)	Usefulness rating*
(1) Increase borrowing levels in currency	83.3	2.462
(2) Use forward exchange contracts	82.1	2.297
(3) Decrease borrowing levels in currency	71.8	2.286
(4) Lead/lag intra-company receivables/payables	71.2	2.243
(5) Adjust product price in local markets	67.9	2.075
(6) Lead/lag local currency external receivables/payables	51.3	2.050
(7) Reschedule intra-company debt payments	55.8	2.000
(8) Accelerate/decelerate subsidiary dividend payments	82.7	1.979
(9) Adjust transfer prices	28.8	1.867
(10) Adjust product price levels in export markets	48.7	1.855
(11) Finance fund requirements or invest excess cash of third-country subsidiaries in currency	36.5	1.789
(12) Net exposure with exposure in other currencies	41.7	1.753
(13) Adjust inventory levels	41.7	1.723
(14) Use contractual clauses calling for assumption of exchange risk by supplier's customers	40.4	1.716
(15) Vary currency of billing to external parties	39.1	1.705
(16) Seek different credit terms from suppliers	32.1	1.540
(17) Formally alter credit terms to customers	25.0	1.513
(18) Lease rather than buy from suppliers	10.3	1.438
(19) Utilize government exchange risk guarantee programmes	24.4	1.395
(20) Lease rather than sell to customers	7.1	1.272
(21) Factor receivables	28.8	1.244

* Figures in this column range from 3 for high usefulness to 1 for low usefulness.
Source: Evans, Folks and Jilling (1978).

to transaction exposure in preference to translation exposure. In a survey undertaken by Khoury and Chan (1988) and based upon replies received from seventy-three companies drawn from the 1985 *Fortune Directories* in the United States, a surprisingly large number – almost two-thirds – said they did little or no hedging. Companies that did hedge used forwards, matching, futures contracts and over-the-counter options, in that order. Of the companies that responded in detail to Khoury and Chan's questionnaire, none saw itself as risk seeking. Respondents classified themselves virtually half and half in the risk-neutral and risk-averse category. Respondents viewed liquidity, flexibility and certainty about cost as the three critical considerations in choosing a hedging vehicle.

This finding of general risk aversion is borne out in a study by Booth, Smith and Stolz (1984) of 238 financial institutions. The goals of risk management that they found in their survey are summarized in Table 32.2, in which it can be seen that only a minimum of financial institutions report that they actively sought profit from their hedging activities.

A study by Millar (1990) of 173 subscribers to Business International publications makes interesting reading. Millar found that the main objective of risk management

Table 32.2 Goals of risk management according to Booth, Smith and Stolz's (1984) survey

Eliminate all risks or eliminate risk selectively	67%
Seek competitive advantage	32%
Actively seek profits	1%

Table 32.3 Goals of risk management according to Millar's (1990) survey

	Interest rate (%)	*Foreign exchange (%)*
Eliminate all risk	58	59
Eliminate risk selectively	52	52
Allow profits	8	16
Actively seek profits	5	7
Seek competitive advantage	29	25
Tax arbitrage, etc.	0	4
Do not manage risk	16	1

was to minimize borrowing costs. This was reported as the key objective by almost 60 per cent of respondents. Approximately 30 per cent were primarily concerned with managing financial risk as the primary objective of exposure management, and around 10 per cent had broadening funding sources as their major objective. In the Millar survey, 16 per cent of firms reported that their treasury function was managed as a profit centre in respect of foreign exchange operations, while only 3 per cent reported similarly in respect of interest rate management. In terms of goals for risk management, Millar's findings are summarized in Table 32.3. It is interesting to note that a substantial number of companies report that they are seeking profit through risk management; it is also interesting to note that, while only a very small number do not manage foreign exchange risk, the proportion which does not pursue an active policy for interest rate management is substantial.

In terms of managing interest rate risk, Millar found that the majority of the firms used simulation techniques (52 per cent of his sample). Gap analysis was used by 26 per cent of respondents and duration analysis by 14 per cent. Turning now to the nature of foreign exchange exposures with which Millar's respondents were concerned, his findings are summarized in Table 32.4 (overleaf). It is interesting to note that transaction exposure seems to be the major concern of corporations – as it should be – but it is a little sobering, although rather what one would expect, that economic exposure receives such small concern. In terms of risk management instruments which firms have used, Millar reports for foreign exchange, again as one would expect, that the forward is by far the most frequently used vehicle. But the use of swaps, for both foreign exchange and interest rate management, can be seen to be very substantial indeed. Millar's findings are summarized in Table 32.5 (overleaf).

A survey undertaken by Davis (1989) of 255 members of the Financial Executives Institute (FEI) is also worth mentioning. In comparing the findings of Davis and

Table 32.4 Focus of foreign exchange management according to Millar's (1990) survey

	(%)
Translation	39
Transaction (firm commitment)	79
Transaction (within one year)	62
Transaction (beyond one year)	16
Contingent exposure	15
Competitive exposure	15

Table 32.5 Instruments used to hedge exposures according to Millar's (1990) survey

	Interest rate (%)	Foreign exchange (%)
Forwards	35	99
Futures	25	20
Swaps	68	64
Options	43	48

Millar it must be mentioned that there is a far greater chance of respondents to the Business International subscribers' survey being large corporations as opposed to members of the FEI; its membership embraces a large proportion of small firms. In terms of the major objective of risk management, Davis found that approximately 40 per cent of his firms rated the minimization of borrowing costs as the major financial objective of exposure policy. Fifteen per cent of respondents were concerned as a major objective with broadening funding sources. On the question of the organization of the treasury as a profit centre, 7 per cent of the Davis survey reported that foreign exchange management was run as a profit centre. It is interesting to note that none in the Davis survey reported that interest rate management was run in this way. On the question of the goals of risk management, the Davis survey reported that 22 per cent of firms surveyed did not manage foreign exchange risk, 34 per cent were concerned with eliminating risk selectively and 7 per cent were concerned with eliminating all foreign exchange risk. On the question of interest rate management, 46 per cent of Davis's respondents said that they did not manage this risk, 31 per cent said that they were concerned with eliminating interest rate risk selectively and 2 per cent said that they were concerned with eliminating all interest rate risk. The relative unsophistication of the respondents to the FEI survey is borne out by the fact that, when asked what foreign exchange risk management instruments they had used, only 45 per cent reported that they had used forwards, 14 per cent said that they had used futures, 9 per cent reported that they had used swaps and 9 per cent said that they had used options. On the interest rate management front, 24 per cent of Davis's respondents had used swaps, 24 per cent had used options, only 8 per cent had used futures and none had used forwards.

Table 32.6 Findings of survey by Soenen and Aggarwal (1989)

	UK	Netherlands	Belgium
Questionnaires mailed	200	250	300
Questionnaires completed	56	103	58
	%	%	%
Lack of of formal policy on			
Cash management	20	33	49
Foreign exchange management	10	46	80
Extent of centralization			
Cash management	69	70	40
Foreign exchange management	68	73	73
Focus of exposure management			
Transaction	39	47	57
Translation	9	11	12
Both	52	42	31
Transaction headging strategy			
Full cover	19	26	0
Selective covering	67	67	63
No covering	14	9	37
Foreign exchange hedging methods			
Forwards	83	71	62
Money market hedging	47	17	14
Currency of import/export	42	28	36
Credit term adjustments	37	15	21
Leading and lagging	35	27	48
Inventory adjustments	23	9	16
Commodity futures markets	5	7	4
Adjustment of inter-company payment terms	–	29	30
No answer	8	22	18

The next study summarized here was undertaken by Soenen and Aggarwal (1989). They mailed a questionnaire to 200 companies in the United Kingdom, 250 companies in the Netherlands and 300 companies in Belgium. The questionnaire was concerned with cash and foreign exchange management practices. The overall response rate was almost 30 per cent. The breakdown in terms of response rate and findings is summarized in Table 32.6. There is an interesting contrast in the specification of a formal policy on foreign exchange management. This is particularly borne out in the contrast between UK and Belgian companies. Out of a total of fifty-six companies from the United Kingdom, only 10 per cent lacked a formal policy on foreign exchange management; for the fifty-eight Belgian companies that replied, 80 per cent lacked a formal policy. Most companies in all three countries had a fairly centralized policy for cash management and foreign exchange management, with a focus biased towards managing transaction exposure. It is interesting to note that most of the companies in the Soenen and Aggarwal study reported that they pursued a policy of selective covering. UK companies reported a broader use of hedging instruments. Since this survey is drawn from major corporations, it represents a unique addition to our knowledge of multinationals' hedging policies.

The next study which we focus upon is concerned with the management of foreign exchange risk in UK-based multinationals. The study by Belk and Glaum (1990) does not claim to be representative and is based upon interviews with treasurers in seventeen major UK industrial companies during 1988. It is interesting to note that, out of their sample, only three companies considered accounting exposures to be without relevance. Of those that did consider accounting exposure to be relevant, two adjusted their exposure through the gearing of their overseas subsidiaries but would not attempt to hedge the remaining net asset exposure. Eleven companies were prepared to manage their net accounting exposures mainly via parent company borrowing in the currencies of the net asset exposures of the subsidiaries. One company claimed to hedge its accounting exposures completely. Of the companies surveyed, six reported that they did not continuously manage their accounting exposure but that they closely monitored it and would be prepared to take appropriate action in certain circumstances – the appropriate action was generally to borrow in the relevant foreign currency.

On the question of transaction exposure, fourteen out of the seventeen companies interviewed regarded this as the focus of their foreign exchange risk management policy. Two companies declared that their transaction exposure management was of minor importance and that the centre of attention was on-balance sheet exposure. One company was of the opinion that there was no point in attempting to manage transaction exposure; it had developed an approach to manage its economic exposure with financial instruments. The management at this company added that it perceived foreign exchange markets to be efficient enough that they render it futile to attempt to gain by managing transaction exposure. The approaches of companies that did manage their transaction exposure were found to be diverse, spanning the whole spectrum of methods available.

Of the sample of seventeen companies, six appeared to pursue a policy of selective hedging. Two other companies had a rule of always covering a minimum of their transaction exposures amounting to 60 per cent and 75 per cent respectively. As regards the remaining proportion, covering was at the discretion of treasury management. Four of the seventeen multinationals surveyed were actively engaged in foreign exchange dealing. Two of these stated that their positions were limited according to the exposures incurred in the ordinary course of business, while the other two companies appeared to be dealing in foreign exchange for profit rather as if they were a small to medium-sized bank. The four multinationals involved in foreign exchange dealing belonged to the largest companies in the sample.

On the question of economic exposure, company policies varied. Six made no attempt at managing economic exposure. At the other extreme, three companies within the sample used a highly sophisticated form of regression analysis which determined their real as opposed to their nominal exposures. What they were concerned with identifying was the extent to which they carried exposure in terms of their underlying cash flows and profits against foreign currencies. They would then adopt a policy of financing in a basket of currencies against which there was an economic exposure. In between these two extremes, most companies surveyed attempted to identify future cash flows and, to a greater or lesser extent, hedge these. More than one company reported that an attempt was made to identify the hedging strategy of key competitors and, based upon this, an informed policy was developed for the company.

On the question of centralization, one of the seventeen companies was completely decentralized in its foreign exchange risk management, seven companies showed a low degree of centralization and nine exhibited a high degree of centralization. The treasuries of two of the seventeen companies surveyed were run as profit centres; six treasurers reported that, while their treasuries were not profit centres, they were nonetheless expected to contribute profits; the remaining treasuries were effectively service centres. Nine of the treasurers of the companies reporting described their companies as totally risk averse; four treasurers in addition regarded themselves as risk averse, although they did not hedge all of their exposures; three of the interviewed treasurers regarded themselves as risk-seeking in relation to additional returns.

On the question of use of specific instruments it is interesting to note that in the Belk and Glaum survey, none of the seventeen multinationals surveyed used currency futures as a tool for foreign exchange management. All of the seventeen had used currency options and fifteen of the seventeen were users of swaps. Two of the sample had even gone as far as to utilize the debt equity swap market in respect of South American debt.

The increasing tendency towards centralization of foreign exchange management was also found in the Evans, Folks and Jilling (1978) survey referred to earlier and also in the Oxelheim (1984) survey.

In addition to formal surveys of company practices on foreign exchange management, the literature contains interesting references to various practices within individual companies. For example, there are fascinating details on corporate use of regression analysis to identify those currencies and commodity prices against which corporate income streams are exposed. Garner and Shapiro (1984) report such practices at Vulcan Materials Co., Lighterness (1987) relates practices at RTZ, and Maloney (1990) indicates policies at Western Mining. Having identified exposures, all of the companies concerned specified a debt policy designed to minimize adverse cash flow and profit impact. On the more basic question of transaction exposure, there is a wealth of articles relating the policy of individual companies: Clifford (1989) and Lewent and Kearney (1990) provide particularly good examples. Experiential indications of treasury practices can be found in Kendall and Sheridan (1991).

A further study worthy of attention was undertaken by Davis, Coates, Collier and Longden (1991), who used case studies to examine foreign exchange risk management in twenty-three large UK and US multinational companies. They focused on four aspects of exposure management – namely, foreign exchange risk characteristics of companies, control over subsidiaries, the use of information technology in foreign exchange management and development of corporate policies over time given changing risks – and came to the following conclusions:

■ Firms were found to be highly risk averse with respect to transaction risk, with translation risk lower in their risk-aversion priorities. Economic exposure was managed by several companies through a portfolio approach to international marketing and production.

■ In foreign exchange risk management, there was a clear tendency towards centralization.

■ There was also a clear trend towards increased use of more sophisticated information systems in the management of foreign exchange risk.

■ Generally, firms had not changed their policies towards risk over time. This was partially due to the fact that formalized foreign exchange risk management systems were relatively new – under ten years old in several firms – but it also reflected the lack of substantial change in the foreign exchange risk profiles of most of the companies.

In a study by Steil (1993), who examined the foreign exchange risk management practices of twenty-six US multinationals, the investigator reports a widespread and growing support for option-based hedging. The research was carried out in two phases with companies surveyed both in 1987 and 1990 with emphasis put on the use of options and forwards as hedging instruments.

Another recent investigation was carried out by Nance, Smith and Smithson (1993) who examined the use of forwards, futures, swaps and options by large US companies in the fiscal year 1986. Of the 169 firms sampled, 104 used hedging instruments. The researchers hypothesized that hedging is beneficial because it may lower taxes, the expectation of financial distress and agency costs. Their findings indicate that hedging firms have more convex tax schedules – that is, more of their income in the progressive region of the tax schedule – and they perceive hedging as valuable in terms of lowering the risk of financial distress.

Hakkarainen, Kasanen and Puttonen (1994) studied the foreign exchange and interest rate risk management practices of 84 respondents out of a possible 100 major companies with their headquarters in Finland. Most of the participants in the survey assessed their exchange rate exposure as large. Almost all of the firms forecast exchange rate movements. In addition to exchange rate forecasts by outsiders, many firms carry out exchange rate analysis of their own. Half of the respondents felt that exchange rate changes are predictable in a range from a month to a year. Their self-rated ability to predict diminishes when the horizon is lengthened. Almost all of the firms hedge the exchange rate risk of their foreign-currency-denominated loans. The home currency value of the equity of a foreign subsidiary and the exchange rate risk of financial assets are hedged by about half of the firms. The survey reveals that the popularity of leading and lagging as an internal exchange rate management technique has diminished over the years. It was used often or continuously by only 10 per cent of the respondents to the survey. Two-thirds of the firms match their currency inflows and outflows, and take loans in various currencies (for hedging purposes) often or continuously. Foreign exchange forward contracts, currency accounts and foreign currency swaps are the most popular external exchange rate risk-hedging methods. Forwards were especially used by firms which invoice or buy in foreign currencies. Currency swaps were most heavily used by firms that carry much foreign-exchange-denominated long-term debt. Evidence was found that many respondents increased the use of foreign exchange options relative to forwards as exchange rate volatility and uncertainty about exchange rate development has increased. The responsibility for exchange rate risk management was centralized in most firms. Subsidiaries tended to acquire their external exchange rate risk-hedging instruments mainly from the parent company.

Turning to interest rate hedging, the Finnish survey found this to be a lower priority than foreign exchange management. The main goal was the minimization of risk. The choice between fixed and floating rate loans was, for many firms, based upon the view of future interest rate movements; target fixed-to-floating ratios were found in only a few firms. Most respondents felt that they could forecast interest rate movements. The success of the firms' foreign exchange and interest rate forecasting was not empirically investigated in this study. The most commonly used interest rate-hedging instruments were found to be swaps and forward rate agreements. Firm size was positively related to the usage of interest rate swaps and forward rate agreements. No clear association was detected between the degree of leverage and the use of hedging instruments.

Next, we turn to the findings of a recent survey of 189 large UK-based companies (out of 600 to whom questionnaires were sent) as to their currency management practices. The investigation, by Edelshain (1995), throws a number of interesting shafts of light on currency risk management, for example:

- 34 per cent of firms use currency forecasting services;

- 64 per cent believe that foreign exchange movements cannot be accurately predicted;

- 43 per cent of firms required all currency exposure to be reported to the parent which decided whether or not to hedge;

- 26 per cent of firms gave to each operation or subsidiary the responsibility to hedge independently;

- 25 per cent of firms gave each operation or subsidiary the responsibility to hedge but only via the parent;

- 9 per cent of firms ran their treasury as a profit centre;

- 26 per cent of firms responded positively that their philosophy was to make money from foreign exchange opportunities, including currency movements;

- 29 per cent of firms reckoned that their policy on currency exposure was one of complete risk aversion;

- 53 per cent reckoned that they hedged all quantifiable currency risk arising in trading;

- 39 per cent hedged all long-term foreign currency asset exposures;

- 55 per cent attempted to minimize balance sheet exposures in each foreign currency.

Table 32.7 British firms' use of currency risk management instruments/techniques

Used by	% of respondents
Spot contracts	74
Forward contracts	78
Futures contracts	15
Option contracts	51
Swaps	40
Collars	14
Parallel loans	17
Selective hedging	46
Insurance (inconvertibility/export)	17
Government schemes	10
Switching to using a different currency of invoicing	34
Reinvoicing centres	5
Indexation of contracts	21
Using a stable currency	16
Using a basket of currencies	12
Price alteration to reflect exposure	23
Transfer pricing	10
Leading and lagging	20
Delaying and/or bringing forward sales/purchases	14
Timing of dividend remittances	26
Royalty schemes	10
Centralized treasury	53
Netting	31
Matching asset/liability and/or income/outgoing in same currencies	61
Matching asset/liability and/or income/outgoing in proxy currencies	8
Using local-denominated debt	60
Selective plant location	12
Matching competitor sourcing	8
Applying sensitivity analysis to currency in planning	22
Using others in the supply chain to take exposure	9

Source: Edelshain (1995).

He also summarized techniques currently being used by respondent companies in terms of managing currency issues. These are interesting and are tabulated in Table 32.7.

The findings, for which the tabulation is fairly self-explanatory, of a recent US survey of corporate foreign exchange risk management practices (see Table 32.8). It was conducted by Bank of America in 1996. Among other things, the survey uses the term anticipated exposures. These are transactions for which there are – at the time – no contracts or agreements between parties, but they are anticipated on the basis of trends and continuing relationships.

A relatively recent move has been in the area of explaining corporate hedging rationale using statistically-based research methods. In Table 32.9 (overleaf), we summarize the findings of seven such investigations. Looking at the table, under the heading of taxes, we have already suggested in Chapter 11 that if a firm's tax

Table 32.8 US corporate foreign exchange policies, 1996

- **Translation exposure**
  80% identify this exposure; 15% fully hedge, 15% partially or selectively hedge, 70% do not hedge; forwards used 73% of the time, options used 27% of the time

- **Transaction exposure**
  60% identify this exposure; 30% fully hedge, 55% partially or selectively hedge, 20% do not hedge; forwards used 83% of the time, options used 17% of the time

- **Anticipated exposure**
  70% identify this exposure; 2% fully hedge, 55% partially or selectively hedge, 43% do not hedge; forwards used 71% of the time, options used 29% of the time

- **Contingent exposure**
  52% identify this exposure; 4% fully hedge, 11% partially or selectively hedge, 85% do not hedge; forwards used 63% of the time, options used 37% of the time

- **Economic exposure**
  54% identify this exposure; 5% fully hedge, 95% do not hedge; forwards used 54% of the time, options used 46% of the time

- **Balance sheet exposure**
  30% identify this exposure; 6% fully hedge, 15% partially or selectively hedge, 78% do not hedge; forwards used 74% of the time, options used 26% of the time

- **Income statement exposure**
  44% identify this exposure; 6% fully hedge, 33% partially or selectively hedge, 61% do not hedge; forwards used 66% of the time, options used 34% of the time

- **Firm hedging maturities**
  21% of hedges are for maturities of less than six months, 62% are for maturities of six months to one year, 17% are for maturities over one year

- **Functional currency of foreign affiliates**
  33% US dollar, 66% local currency

Source: Global Capital Markets Group, Bank of America (1996–1997).

schedule is convex, hedging can reduce expected taxes. The tax schedule may be convex by statutory progressivity and through such items as tax carry forwards and investment tax credits. In Table 32.9, the three tax items with an expected positive sign associated with them suggest that the more convex the tax schedule the greater the hypothesized tendency to hedge. Next in the table, the greater the possibility of financial distress the greater the hypothesized tendency to hedge. The reader can continue down the table and see how the research studies' results have delivered relative to the expected sign. Readers who are really interested are referred to the original studies in terms of looking at the detailed sampling frame and other similar factors.

Finally, two recent studies indicated an inclination to hedge as a function of the business culture in a country. Judge (2001) found that various proxies of financial distress provide the strongest indicator of a tendency to hedge foreign currency risk. He also observed, like all of the studies summarized in Table 32.9, that larger firms were more likely to hedge than their smaller counterparts. Judge also pointed out that the driving force to hedge to minimize financial distress was greater in Britain

Table 32.9 Empirical results on drivers of the use of risk management techniques by companies

Researchers	Predicted sign	Nance, Smith and Smithson	Berkman and Bradbury	Tufano	Geczy, Minton and Schrand	Graham and Smith	Haushalter	Allayannis and Ofek
Year of publication		1993	1996	1996	1997	1999a 1999b	2000	2001
Variable								
Taxes								
Tax loss carry forwards	+	−	+**	+	+	FX +* IR −**		+
Investment tax credits	+	+*						
Convex tax schedule	+	+				−	+**	+
Financial distress								
Interest cover ratio	−	−	−***					
Debt to equity ratio	+	−	+***	+*	−	+**	+***	+
Agency costs: underinvestment								
R&D to firm value	+	+*				+*		
R&D to sales	+				+***			+**
P/E ratios	+		+*					
Market/book ratio	+	+			−*			
Exploration to investment expenditure	+			−*				
Acquisition activities	+			+			+	
Managerial utility maximization								
Managerial share ownership	+		+	+*	+	FX − IR +**		
Managerial option ownership	−			−**	+	FX − IR +	−**	
Large block shareholdings	−			−**			−	
Firm size								
Firm value	+	+**	+***	+				
Total assets	+				+***	+***	+	+***
Miscellaneous								
Liquidity	−	−	−**					
Dividend payout	+	+***	+*		−*			−*
Convertible debt/equity	−	+					+	
Preferred stock/equity	−	−						
Cash balances	+			−*			+	
Diversification	−			+			+	

* indicates significance level of 10%
** indicates significance level of 5%
*** indicates significance level of 1%

than in the United States. One possible explanation for this is that the costs of financial distress are higher in the United Kingdom than in the United States. The main objective of Chapter 11 of the US Bankruptcy Code is to maintain the business as a going concern, even if it reduces the proceeds to creditors. The main objective of the UK code is to increase the likelihood of payment of creditor's claims. If the UK rules encourage premature liquidation, then it could be argued that UK firms face higher expected costs of financial distress and this provides a greater incentive to hedge to avoid these costs.

In a study by Macrae (2003), the researcher found that Dutch firms hedge more financial risk than their US counterparts. The author claims that this reflects the more openness of the Dutch economy and, possibly, the greater orientation towards stakeholder interests rather than towards shareholder interests, a feature more apparent in The Netherlands than in the United States.

32.14 | Summary

This chapter covers a number of topics and each of these is summarized under separate bullet points below.

■ On the topic of subsidiaries' performance measurement, on practical grounds, comparison of actual outturns with budgeted performance in foreign currency terms may be the most sensible, cost-effective approach. This is especially so if it is coupled with an emphasis upon cash generation in home currency terms which may then be discounted to provide a focus upon performance in present value terms. Performance evaluation based upon accounting outturns needs to be adjusted to allow for the effects of transfer pricing, funds flow adjustments (such as leading and lagging) and hedging policy.

■ Exposure management may be centralized or decentralized. The case for centralization involves the following arguments: it ensures that the company follows a consistent policy; it facilitates the matching of exposures; it helps ensure that the best rates in the market are obtainable; it ensures the concentration of limited expertise, skills and systems investment; it helps integrate with cash management. The case against centralization involves the following points: there are substantial up-front costs in recruitment, office space and equipment in establishing a centralized foreign exchange expertise; foreign exchange risk management may be an interesting and stimulating aspect of the subsidiary company's life; taking this away from the subsidiary may, at the margin, be a demotivating factor. Centralization need not involve this. The approach recommended in this book is that individual units should regard the central treasury as their banker and run an account with head office as if it were their banker. Divisions may hedge some exposures with the treasury – this means that autonomy will be maintained. They will, of course, report all exposures to the centre. Another argument against the centralization of foreign exchange exposures is that divisional staff may become blind to the risks and expertise needed to handle foreign exchange problems.

- With a large number of partly owned subsidiaries, it may be appropriate to adopt a decentralized approach. Minority shareholders will want optimization at the level of their own investment – not at group level.

- The proportion of value or turnover exposed is obviously a relevant factor in deciding whether to centralize or not. Where performance will not be materially affected by changes in exchange rates, foreign exchange risk is unlikely to be an issue. In a purely decentralized system, the unit looks after its own exposures only, having no regard for exposures occurring elsewhere in the group. At the opposite end of the continuum is the completely centralized system in which the treasurer receives and co-ordinates data from all group members determining a net position and undertaking appropriate hedging action. The subsidiary will not be consulted on group hedging strategy. Many intermediate variations are possible too. It must be stressed that whatever system is adopted, it needs to be justified on cost–benefit grounds and must be regularly checked to ensure that the system chosen continues to deliver the goods in cash terms. The need for *ad hoc* post-audits is clear.

- Whether the treasury should be a profit centre or a cost centre is a question frequently discussed. If foreign exchange exposure management is centralized, it creates the opportunity to run as a profit centre. In this context profit may accrue from improved exchange rates on deals, by selective hedging actions and, thirdly, by speculating in currencies. Of course, any position-taking can only be justified by some superior knowledge possessed by a treasury executive or adviser. The result of this is that only minimal speculation – if any – could be justified. It is worth noting that non-bank organizations which involve themselves in interest rate mismatching and running the treasury as a profit centre are scored negatively by credit-rating agencies. One of the dangers of running the treasury as a profit centre is that it may go for profit by ripping off divisions.

- It is very important that companies establish authorities and limits for currency and interest rate deals. It is equally important that individuals working in these areas know clearly their limits of authority to act and the circumstances in which they are expected to do so. Corporate limits might be set for a range of exposures such as counterparty credit limits, capacity limits, sovereign limits, currency limits, liquidity limits, delivery limits, and interest rate limits. A general understanding of what each of these entails should be sought from the text.

- The major credit-rating agencies are US-based firms, most notably Standard and Poor's and Moody's. A credit rating is an assessment of the credit worthiness of a borrower with respect to a specific obligation. Credit ratings are based upon a number of considerations including the likelihood of default, the nature of and provisions of the borrowing obligation and the protection afforded in the event of bankruptcy or reorganization. A credit rating may be defined as an indication of the relative probability of timely payment of interest and principal in respect of a particular borrowing.

- Transfer pricing may be used to get monies out of an overseas subsidiary that restricts flows upwards. The multinational may set high transfer prices on goods and services supplied to a foreign subsidiary by the head office or by divisions in environments that are less restrictive. The multinational may lower the transfer prices of products which the foreign division sells to the head office or to other divisions. Transfer pricing may be used to reduce overall corporate taxes. The multinational may shuffle income to keep profits low in high-tax countries and relatively high in low-tax countries. Transfer prices may also be used to reduce import tariffs and to avoid quotas. For purposes of resource allocation in the multinational, it is important that divisional profitability be accurately measured. To discover true profitability, the group should be sure that inter-divisional transfer prices are the prices that would have been paid had the transactions been with independent companies – that is at arm's length. But there may be problems inasmuch as multinational group management may not want true profits to be known outside a tight central coalition of executives.

32.15 | End of chapter questions

Question 1
Explain how transfer pricing can be used to reduce a MNC's overall tax liability.

Question 2
Briefly describe the role of tax planning by the MNC. What are its key functions?

Question 3
Describe the possible conflict of interests between a subsidiary and centralized management.

Test bank 5

Exercises

1. Global Enterprises plc (see balance sheet below) believes broadly in currency neutrality. The board prefers not to risk a loss to the sterling amount of shareholders' funds from exchange rate movements rather than to have the chance of making gains from such movements. The group had long had a surplus of some US $60m assets over US liabilities. It had been decided in principle to take corrective action. However, this was in 1980 when the spot rate was $2.30 = £1. You advised that the timing was not felicitous. In 1984 when the rate reached $1.20 = £1 you felt that the time had come to take immediate action, but you also judged that a desirable restructuring of the balance sheet for the longer term needed more time. For example, you had little short-term sterling debt that could be immediately repaid and you did not wish to increase the gearing in the meantime.

    What immediate steps could you take to neutralize the $60 million exposure, and what options should you then investigate for a longer-term solution?

	£m		£m
Fixed assets	460	Capital reserves	590
Stocks and debtors	850	Minorities	50
Trade creditors	(380)	Loan capital	300
Tax & dividends	(50)	Cash and deposits	(270)
Other current liabilities,			
provisions & accruals	(210)		
	670		670

    (Association of Corporate Treasurers: Part II, Specimen Paper in Treasury Management)

2. You are the treasurer of a major chemical producer, one of whose divisions has postponed a major plant on a greenfield site in the UK because of restrictions on resources in a period of high capital expenditure. An investment bank acting on behalf of the plant supplier proposes that you set up a special-purpose company to revive the project, financing it on a limited recourse basis. The £100m cost would be provided:

	£ million	
Equity		
Your company	18	(of which £6m is to be preference shares)
Plant supplier	8	
Plant contractor	4	
	30	

Debt

Bank loans	70
	100

The concept would be that the banks would rely on the cash flow from the project to service the debt. Your company would be expected to manage the construction process as it would with any plant and purchase the end product but there would be no recourse to your company's general credit. At the point when the banks have been repaid, you would have the option to buy out the other shareholders at cost plus a rate of return equal to current interest rates. Your finance director asks you:

(a) What undertakings your company is likely to have to give in order to make the project bankable.
(b) How you would propose that the risks arising from the undertakings be managed.
(c) Whether to apply to the revived project your normal hurdle rate for greenfield projects. This is a 23 per cent after-tax discount rate and is based on a target corporate gearing of 65 per cent equity : 35 per cent debt.

Draft a response.

(Association of Corporate Treasurers: Part II, September 1988, Paper in Corporate Finance)

3. You are the international treasurer of a major multinational processing and selling food products. The fruit products division is planning a greenfield plant to produce canned orange juice from locally grown fruit in a high-inflation (currently 60 per cent p.a.) South American country. The equipment is available from the United States or from Europe. The production will be 25 per cent for the local market with the balance exported to meet existing demand in European countries. You will have to advise on the financing structure of the company being formed to own the plant (local regulations require a separate legal entity) and the impact on the group's situation.
    What factors will you consider in formulating your advice?

(Association of Corporate Treasurers: Part II, September 1990, Paper in Corporate Finance)

▌Multiple choice questions

1. A multinational has one subsidiary in a 45 per cent tax rate country, and another in a 30 per cent tax rate country. To increase its overall after-tax earnings, the headquarters should arrange to:

    (a) lower the price of supplies from the low-tax-rate subsidiary to the high-tax-rate subsidiary;
    (b) move expenses from the high-tax rate subsidiary to the low-tax-rate subsidiary;
    (c) have the low-tax-rate subsidiary lower its prices charged for materials transferred to the high-tax rate subsidiary;
    (d) none of the above.

2. A firm produces goods for which substitutes are universally available. Depreciation of the firm's home currency should:

(a) reduce local sales because foreign competition in the home market is reduced;
(b) reduce the firm's exports denominated in the firm's home currency;
(c) reduce returns earned on the firm's foreign bank deposits;
(d) reduce payments required to pay for imports denominated in foreign currency;
(e) none of the above.

3. Which of the following creates an effective hedge of net payables in US dollars for a UK firm?

(a) Purchase of a sterling put option.
(b) Sale of pounds forward for dollars.
(c) Sale of sterling futures.
(d) All of the above.
(e) None of the above.

4. A US-based multinational is due to receive Sfr8m in 90 days. The current spot rate of the Swiss franc is $0.62 and the 90-day forward rate is $0.635. Managers at the multinational have come up with the following estimate for the spot rate of the US dollar against the Sfr in 90 days:

	Probability
$0.61	10 per cent
$0.63	20 per cent
$0.64	40 per cent
$0.65	30 per cent

The probability that the forward hedge will result in more US dollars being received compared to the outturn assuming no hedging is:

(a) 10 per cent;
(b) 20 per cent;
(c) 30 per cent;
(d) 50 per cent;
(e) 70 per cent.

5. A multinational based in the United States is due to receive CHF10m in 180 days. The current Swiss franc/dollar spot rate is $0.50; the 180-day forward rate is $0.51. A Swiss franc call option with a strike price of $0.52 and a 180 day expiration date attracts a premium of 2 cents. A Swiss franc put option with a 180-day expiration date and an exercise price of $0.51 has a premium of 2 cents The management of the firm reckons that the spot rate in 180 days might be:

	Probability
$0.48	10 per cent
$0.49	60 per cent
$0.55	30 per cent

Including the cost of the premium in your calculation, what is the probability that the forward hedge will result in more dollars received than the options hedge?

(a) 10 per cent
(b) 30 per cent
(c) 40 per cent
(d) 70 per cent
(e) None of the above

6. *Ceteris paribus*, a firm will benefit from geographical diversifying if:

(a) the correlation between country economies is high;
(b) the correlation between country economies is low;
(c) the correlation between country economies is positive;
(d) two of the above are correct.

7. Financial theory suggests that achieving which of the following, all other things being equal, is likely to increase shareholder wealth?

(a) Seeking to profit from capital market distortions.
(b) Reducing the riskiness of operating cash flows.
(c) Maintaining the debt to capital employed ratio.
(d) All of the above.
(e) None of the above.

8. A bank raises finance with a preponderance of fixed interest short-term borrowings and lends with a preponderance of longer-term lendings at fixed interest rates. It justifies its policy on the grounds that the term structure of interest rates is upwards sloping. If interest rates increase by 150 basis points ($1\frac{1}{2}$ per cent) all along the term structure, what effect does this have on the bank?

(a) It will make more money than that previously planned.
(b) It will make less money than that previously planned.
(c) It will be indifferent because the effect will be felt equally on its short-term borrowings and its longer-term lendings.
(d) It should increasingly resort to financial disintermediation by off-balance-sheet operations.
(e) None of the above is correct.

9. Transfer pricing:

(a) includes the pricing of goods, services and technology exchanged among associated companies in different countries;
(b) is used by multinationals to achieve a number of objectives;
(c) is subject to limitations imposed by tax authorities;
(d) may influence managerial incentives and performance;
(e) all of the above are correct.

10. A sterling call option exists with a strike price of $1.60 and a 90-day expiration date and it attracts a premium of 3 cents per unit. A sterling put option with an exercise

price of $1.60 and a 90-day expiration date has a premium of 2 cents per unit.
A US multinational plans to deal options to cover its receivable of £7m in 90 days.
The options concerned are European options. The sterling/dollar spot rate is expected
to be $1.57 in 90 days. On this basis, what would be the dollar proceeds after allowing
for the option premium?

(a) $11.69m
(b) $10.99m
(c) $11.06m
(d) $11.43m
(e) $11.34m.

Suggested answers to end of chapter questions

Chapter 2

Answer 1

Under the fixed exchange rate system, governments attempted to maintain exchange rates within 1 per cent of a predetermined value. This would be achieved by government intervention. Devaluations and revaluations were necessary ever so often. Under a freely floating system, government intervention is non-existent. The market arrives at a rate. Under a managed-float system, governments allow exchange rates to move according to market forces, but they intervene when they believe it is necessary.

Answer 2

Central banks may use their currency reserves to buy a specific currency in the foreign exchange market to place upward pressure on that currency. Central banks can also attempt to force currency depreciation by selling that currency in the foreign exchange market in exchange for other currencies, thus flooding the market.

Answer 3

Briefly, a freely floating system may help to correct balance of trade imbalances as the currency should adjust according to market forces. A strong current account balance should create a strengthening currency which, in turn, should dampen demand for the country's exports and, at the same time, increase imports into the country. The result of this should be a movement towards current account balance. A disadvantage of freely floating exchange rates is that firms have to manage their international exposures.

Chapter 3

Answer 1

Probably has a lot to do with the magnitude of bond markets (United Kingdom relatively low on bonds but high on equities) and the nature of the banking system. Where bankers are close to business in terms of seeking board representation, the result may be reflected in a lesser need for resorting to equity markets to raise finance and hence a lesser equity culture (France and Germany).

Answer 2

In the short run it has reduced it. Nowadays, trade between France and the Netherlands, previously denominated in either of the home currencies, does not need to resort to the foreign currency market.

Answer 3

Probably the bond-oriented countries would have experienced low inflation with few surprises in the actual level of inflation. A history of inflation overshooting expectations would be detrimental to bond markets because it would depress bond prices. Even if held to maturity, the bond's real return would become depressed – and possibly move into negative territory.

Chapter 4

Answer 1

Demand for pounds should increase, supply of pounds for sale should decrease, and the pound's value should increase.

Answer 2

The higher the real interest rate of a country relative to another country, the stronger will be its home currency, other things equal.

Answer 3

The Latin American countries concerned have very high inflation, which places downward pressure on their currencies. Effective anti-inflationary policies are needed to prevent further depreciation. They could begin by cutting inflation and controlling it via the money supply.

Chapter 5

Answer 1

Yes! One could purchase Swiss francs at Bank Y for $0.40 and sell them to Bank X for $.401. With $1 million available, CHF2.5 million would be purchased at Bank Y. These Swiss francs would then be sold to Bank X for $1,002,500, thereby generating a profit of $2,500.

Answer 2

The large demand for CHF at Bank Y will force this bank's ask price for CHF to increase. The large sales of CHF to Bank X will force its bid price down. Once the ask price of Bank Y is no longer less than the bid price of Bank X, locational arbitrage will no longer be profitable.

Answer 3

Yes. The appropriate cross exchange rate should be 1 Batavian drac = 3 Ulerican crowns. The actual value of the BTD in terms of ULC is more than it should be. One could obtain BTD with USD, sell the BTD for ULC and then exchange ULC for US$. With $1,000,000, this strategy would generate $1,006,667 – creating a profit of $6,667.

$$(\$1,000,000/\$.90 = BTD1,111,111 \times 3.02 = ULC3,355,556 \times \$0.30 = \$1,006,667)$$

Chapter 6

Answer 1

All other things being equal, a high inflation rate tends to increase imports and decrease exports, thereby increasing the currency account deficit.

Answer 2

A weakening home currency increases the price of imports purchased by the home country and reduces the prices paid by foreign businesses for the home country's exports. This should cause a decrease in the home country's demand for imports and an increase in the foreign demand for the home country's exports, and improve the current account balance.

Answer 3

A current account deficit is reflected in a net sale of the home currency in exchange for other currencies. This places downward pressure on the home currency's value. If the home currency weakens, it will reduce the home demand for foreign goods (since goods will now be more expensive), and will increase the home export volume (since exports will appear cheaper to foreign countries). In some cases, the home currency will remain strong even though a current account deficit exists, since other factors (such as international capital flows), other than the current account, can affect the forces on the currency by the currency account.

Chapter 7

Answer 1

PPP suggests that the purchasing power of a consumer will be similar when purchasing goods in a foreign country or in the home country. If inflation in a foreign country differs from inflation in the home country, the exchange rate will adjust to maintain equal purchasing power. So, higher inflation depresses the exchange rate of the high inflation country, all other things being equal.

Currencies of high inflation countries will be weak according to PPP, causing the purchasing power of goods in the home country versus these countries to be similar.

Answer 2

One method would be to track the currencies of two countries over time and compare their inflation levels over these periods. Then, you could determine whether the exchange rate changes were similar to what would have been expected under PPP theory.

A second method would be to choose a variety of countries and compare the inflation differential of each foreign country relative to the home country for a given period. Then, you might determine if the exchange rate changes of each foreign currency were what would have been expected based on the inflation differentials under PPP theory.

Answer 3

(a) The value of the dollar should rise as more rapidly rising GNP in the United States should lead to a relative increase in demand for dollars.

(b) The value of the dollar should fall in line with PPP.

(c) According to PPP, the exchange rate should remain the same.

(d) The value of the dollar should rise as the higher real rates attract capital from Japan that must first be converted into dollars.

(e) The value of the dollar should fall as foreigners find it less attractive to own US assets and the demand for dollars falls.

(f) Higher US wages and declining relative productivity weaken the American economy and make it less attractive for investment purposes. Assuming that a weak economy leads to a weak currency, the dollar will fall. From a somewhat different perspective, when a nation's productivity growth lags behind that of its major trading partners, the other countries will become more competitive. The depreciating currency is the market's way of restoring balance. The lagging country regains its balance, but only by accepting a lower real price for its goods. In effect, the cheaper currency is the market's way of cutting wages in the lagging country. From another perspective, US inflation rises relative to Japanese inflation and, through PPP, the dollar should fall.

Chapter 8

Answer 1

Transaction exposure is due to international transactions by a firm and affects cash flows. Economic exposure impacts the present value of future cash flows. The two are alike because they are cash flow exposures. They are different because economic exposure affects all future cash flows but transaction exposure involves a limited future time window for cash flows. Transaction exposure is easy to hedge. Economic exposure is very difficult to hedge perfectly.

Answer 2

If the firm competes with foreign firms that also sell in the same market, then the consumers may switch to foreign products if the local currency strengthens – or vice versa.

Answer 3

Most companies use strategic methods such as diversified production, marketing and financing. The biggest problem with the diversification strategy is the loss of economies of scale. The biggest advantage is that it can yield lower costs – subject to quality maintenance.

Chapter 9

Answer 1

The consolidated earnings will be increased due to the strength of the subsidiaries' local currencies.

Answer 2

Exactly the opposite of Answer 1 above. The consolidated earnings will be reduced due to the weakness of the subsidiaries' local currencies.

Answer 3

MNCs might emphasize in their annual reports how consolidated earnings were adversely influenced by the translation effect. They could indicate the effect that constant currencies would have had on their reported earnings. So, the effect of converting income statements at the same rate this year as last year, could be shown. In truth, this only creates a partial comparison because there could also be economic exposure effects too.

Chapter 10

Answer 1

(a) It affects consolidated financial statements, which are often used by shareholders to assess the performance of the MNC.

(b) Pure translation exposure does not affect cash flow. It simply reflects the impact of exchange rate fluctuations on consolidated financial statements rather than cash flow.

Answer 2

The typical first reaction to this question is to say that Walt Disney's world exposure must increase, as EuroDisney would generate revenues in French francs (latterly euros), which may be converted to dollars in the future. If the French franc (euro) were to weaken against the dollar, the revenues would be converted to fewer dollars – and vice versa – thereby increasing economic exposure.

But, Walt Disney Inc was already affected by movements in the French franc and other major currencies before EuroDisney was built. When major currencies weaken against the dollar, foreign tourism to the United States is likely to decrease and Walt Disney's revenue in the United States would fall. By having a European amusement park, Disney may offset the declining US business during strong dollar cycles, as more European tourists may go to the EuroDisney in France. So, Disney may become less exposed to exchange rate movements because of the existence of EuroDisney.

Chapter 11

Answer 1

Consideration of all cash flows in a particular currency is not necessary when some inflows and outflows offset each other. Only net cash flows between currencies are truly relevant when looking at transaction exposure.

Answer 2

The net exposure in each currency in US dollars is derived below:

Foreign currency	Net inflows in foreign currency	Current exchange rate	Value of exposure
Ruritania doppels (RUD)	+RUD 2 million	$ .15	$ .3 million
British pounds (GBP)	+GBP 1 million	$1.50	$1.5 million
Batavian dracs (BTD)	−BTD 1 million	$ .30	$−.3 million

Since the RUD and BTD move in tandem against the dollar, their dollar value of net exposures cancels out. Their exposures should be offset if their exchange rates against the US dollar continue to be highly correlated. The firm's main concern about exposure should be the GBP net inflows.

Answer 3

No! Thus, past correlations will not serve as perfect forecasts of future correlations. However, historic data may still be useful if the correlations are reasonably expected to be pretty stable.

Chapter 12

Answer 1

Netting uses a centralized compilation of inter-subsidiary potential cross-border cash flow. It is designed to reduce currency conversion costs and processing costs associated with payments between subsidiaries. By specifying a single net payment to be made instead of all individual payments owed between subsidiaries, transaction costs may be reduced.

Answer 2

A subsidiary in need of funds would receive cash inflows from another subsidiary sooner than is required. This early payment provides the necessary funds. If the subsidiary in need of funds is making payment, it may be allowed by the MNC parent or recipient subsidiary to delay on its payment. The technique is particularly pertinent when devaluations are expected. In these circumstances you would wish to increase monetary liabilities in the devaluing currency and decrease monetary assets in the devaluing currency.

Chapter 13

Answer 1

The firm could borrow an amount of Swiss francs such that CHF100,000 to be received in 90 days could be used to pay off the loan. This amounts to (100,000/1.02), around CHF98,039, which could be borrowed now and converted to about $49,020 and invested in a US$ deposit for 90 days. The borrowing of CHF has offset the transaction exposure due to the future receipt of CHF.

Answer 2

If US Co Inc deposits BLW186,916 (computed as BLW200,000/1.07) into a bank account denominated in BLW earning 7 per cent over six months, the deposit would be worth BLW200,000 at the end of the six-month period. This amount would then be used to make the net BLW payments. To make the initial deposit of BLW186,916, USA Co Inc would need about $18,692 (computed as 186,916 × $.10). If necessary, it could borrow these funds. The money market hedge eliminates transaction exposure.

Answer 3

It should be equal in terms of favourability. If IRP exists, the forward premium on the forward rate would reflect the interest rate differential. The hedging of future payables with a forward purchase provides the same results as borrowing at the home interest rate and investing at the foreign interest rate to hedge the payables.

Chapter 14

Answer 1

An interest rate swap usually involves an exchange of fixed (floating) rate interest payments for floating (fixed) rate interest payments in the same currency. A currency swap typically involves an exchange of principal plus interest payments in one currency for equivalent payments in another currency.

The credit risk on a currency swap is greater than that on interest rate swap. First, the credit risk on the interest rate swap is confined only to interest payments, while the credit risk on the currency swap involves both principal and interest payments. Second, because the exchange rate changes that occur during the lifetime of a currency swap may be large, the credit risk of the currency swap can be correspondingly larger.

Answer 2

In some instances, a domestic company may borrow money at a lower rate of interest in the domestic capital market than a foreign firm. Note that, we stress 'in some instances'. For example, a US company may borrow money at a better rate (versus foreign companies) in the United States, but it might have less favourable access to capital markets in Europe. At the same time, a European company may have good borrowing opportunities domestically (borowing in euros versus market rates in euros) but less good opportunities in US$ (versus US$ market rates) in the United States. These rate differentials raise the possibility that each firm can exploit its comparative advantage in the domestic market and share the gains by reducing net borrowing costs. In fact, if the firm can access funds at below market rate in any currency, it may, via a swap, convert the borrowing to a currency in which it wants to raise funds. For example, a US firm building a new plant using Japanese equipment may, through the Japanese Exim bank, have access to JPY at below market rates. It might take the JPY although it has no other exposure to JPY and, through a swap, convert the borrowing to US$, the currency in which most of its operating cash flows arise. And this may yield a rate below the market rate for US$.

Answer 3

You prefer to pay a fixed long-term rate and receive a floating short-term rate. The initial short-term rate that you receive will merely be the spot rate that prevails today. However, if your expectation is correct, the short-term rate will rise more than the market expects and you will then receive that higher rate. Because your payments are fixed, you will gain from your insight.

Chapter 15

Answer 1

The US corporation could agree to a futures contract to sell GBP at a specified date in the future and at a specified price. This locks in the exchange rate at which the GBP could be sold.

Answer 2

The basis is the difference between the cash price (often the source of risk being hedged by a futures position) and the futures price. The performance of a futures hedge depends on whether or not the basis changes over the time of the hedge, or whether such changes are predicted and accounted for when the hedge is established. Unless anticipated *ex ante*, a change in the basis over the time of a hedge implies that the value of the cash position will change by a different amount than the value of the futures position, resulting in an unanticipated gain or loss. Basis risk is the risk associated with changes in the basis which will have a direct bearing on how well a hedge performs.

Changes in the basis are more likely when the characteristics of the cash position being hedged are more different from the characteristics of the future being used as a hedge. Ideally, one would choose the futures contract based on the same position being hedged in the cash market. This results in a minimal change in the basis over time and provides the most effective hedge. However, when futures contracts are not traded on exactly the same thing being hedged in the cash market, a greater degree of basis risk is inherent. Under these circumstances, the hedge is referred to as a cross-hedge since the hedge is being applied across markets. The more similar the futures instrument is to the cash instrument being hedged, the more likely their price movements will be equal over time and the less basis risk will be involved. A futures instrument which is very dissimilar to the cash instrument will involve greater basis risk than instruments (cash and futures) which have similar characteristics.

A mismatch in maturities between the futures instrument and the cash instrument being hedged can contribute to basis risk. Assume that 180-day Treasury Bills are being hedged with (90-day) Treasury Bill futures contracts. Even though Treasury Bills are involved in both the cash and futures positions, they are in different commodities. The value of the futures contract will be influenced by changes in expected 90-day interest rates whereas the value of the cash instrument will be influenced by 180-day interest rates. It is unlikely that changes in these rates will be exactly the same. At the same time the value of a 90-day Treasury Bill will respond differently to a unit change in interest rates than will a 180-day Treasury Bill. Even when rate changes are equal, price changes may not be equal and basis changes will occur.

Answer 3

(a) The December futures price would have decreased, because it reflects expectations of the future spot rate as of the settlement date. If the existing spot rate were $1.51, the spot rate expected on the December futures settlement date is also likely to be near to $1.51.

(b) You would have sold futures at the existing futures price of $1.59. That is equal to 'sell GBP at $1.59'. Then, as the spot rate of the pound declined, the futures price would decline and you could close out the futures position by purchasing a futures contract at a lower price. Alternatively, you could wait until the settlement date, purchase the pounds in the spot market, and fulfil the futures obligation by delivering pounds.

Chapter 16

Answer 1

An options premium is the sum of intrinsic value and time value. Both intrinsic value and time value are influenced by volatility of the underlying. With a currency contract, intrinsic value is the difference between the exchange rate of the underlying currency and the strike price of the currency option. Time value is the amount of money that options buyers are willing to pay for an option in the anticipation that the price of the option may increase over time.

Answer 2

Options have positive values even if they are out-of-the-money because investors will usually pay something today for out-of-the-money options on the chance of profit before maturity.

They are also likely to pay some additional premium today for in-the-money options on the chance of an increase in intrinsic value before maturity.

Answer 3

An option is in-the-money if it can be exercised for a gross profit immediately. Gross profit here means that the profit excludes the initial price paid for the option. This means that a call is in-the-money when the value of the underlying security exceeds the exercise price. A put is in-the-money when the value of the underlying security is less than the exercise price.

Chapter 17

Answer 1

A call option can hedge a firm's future payables denominated in a foreign currency. It effectively locks in the maximum price to be paid for a currency.

Answer 2

A put option can hedge a firm's future receivables denominated in a foreign currency. If effectively locks in the minimum price at which a currency may be sold.

Answer 3

Currency options not only provide a hedge, but they provide flexibility since they do not require an actual commitment to buy or sell a currency (whereas the forward contract does).

A disadvantage of currency options is that a price (the up-front premium) is paid for the option itself. The only payment by a firm using a forward contract is the exchange of a currency as specified in the contract.

Chapter 18

Answer 1

(a) By having a mismatch in terms of inflows of cash falling as a consequence of an interest rate rise but the firm is financed by floating rate interest. Clearly, this kind of mismatch could also involve stable inflows financed by floating rate finance.

(b) By granting more floating rate loans for a particular maturity than it has deposits at floating rate for that maturity.

Answer 2

Using the interest rate swap market, or if it is exposed as in 1(a), it might finance at a fixed rate.

Answer 3

By ensuring that, within maturities, fixed rate deposits and fixed rate loans are equal and ensuring that, within maturities, the same is achieved for floating rates. Adjustments to imbalances may be achieved via swaps and futures.

Chapter 19

Answer 1

It really consists of bolting together financial instruments, LEGO-like. So options, and forwards or puts and calls of different maturities are bolted together to form a new financial instrument that can be priced according to its underlying LEGO pieces and in accordance with their logical prices.

Answer 2

Because their financial staff have failed to analyse instruments via their underlying components – their LEGO pieces and their LEGO prices.

Answer 3

The players need the ability to recognize the needs for financial instruments in corporate treasury (at least, this is true for the salesmen) and then they need the logic and mathematical ability to bolt together the underlying financial LEGOs to create a instrument that is profitable to the bank and meets the customer's needs.

Chapter 20

Answer 1

King Company is likely to benefit because it is maintaining all of its manufacturing in one area. All other things being equal, if President Inc. spreads its production facilities, it will incur higher fixed costs per unit of output. But, presumably, President Inc is seeking lower costs in countries into which it is directing its FDI. This could result in lower costs per unit (subject to maintenance of quality). But this is not an economy of scale.

Answer 2

Foreign governments sometimes expect that FDI will provide needed employment or technology for a country, or exports from the country, or reduced imports. For these reasons, they may provide incentives to encourage FDI.

Answer 3

The theory of comparative advantage implies that countries specialize in the production of goods which they can produce most efficiently and that they rely on other countries for other goods. Many countries can produce certain goods more efficiently than other countries because countries are endowed differently in their economic resources. You specialize where you can best apply your limited resources. And buy in the rest.

Chapter 21

Answer 1

Before and after a devaluation, they may wish to control companies' and individuals' abilities to move their money around as they wish. In other words, they wish to fetter free markets in financial assets to meet balance of payments objectives and other goals.

Answer 2

Probably, overall, discourage because they invariably involve restrictions on remittances. However, multinationals may still invest because they hope for changes in the regime later on, by which time they will have developed a strongly cash-generating business.

Chapter 22

Answer 1

When a parent allocates funds for a project, it should view the project's feasibility from its own perspective. It is possible that a project might be feasible from a subsidiary's perspective, but be infeasible when viewed from a parent's cash flow perspective (due to remittance restrictions, foreign withholding taxes or exchange rate changes affecting funds remitted to the parent).

Answer 2

Some of the more obvious factors are:

(a)   exchange rates;

(b)   whether remittance restrictions exist;

(c)   the probability of a host government takeover;

(d)   foreign demand for product;

(e)   foreign attitude toward the firm; and

(f)   tax effects.

Chapter 23

Answer 1

Debt-equity swaps allow the lender (or whoever has a claim on the debt) to exchange the claim for an equity investment in the borrower's assets. MNCs may consider purchasing claims on LDC debt in the secondary market to swap these claims for an equity investment in the LDC's assets. In this way, debt-equity swaps can increase activity in the secondary loan market. In fact, this has been a feature of the attempts at solving the debt crisis affecting developing countries.

Answer 2

Additional factors that merit consideration in a foreign project analysis include: the host government attitude toward foreign companies, exchange rates, currency controls, foreign demand for product, possible expropriation – and others too.

Chapter 24

Answer 1

The following characteristics of MNCs can influence the cost of capital:

- Size. MNCs may be stable firms which are better known and therefore receive preferential treatment by creditors.

- Access to international capital markets. MNCs have access to more sources of funds than domestic firms. To the extent that financial markets are segmented, MNCs may be able to obtain financing from accessing various sources at a lower cost.

- International diversification. If an MNC can achieve favourable tax breaks on foreign operations, it might enhance after-tax cash flows.

- Country risk. MNCs with subsidiaries in politically unstable countries may experience volatile cash flows over time and be more susceptible to financial problems. This may increase the cost of capital.

- Host country interest rates. MNCs may be offered subsidized loans to locate in some territories. This reduces their overall cost of capital.

Answer 2

Yes. But beware – their standard deviation of returns has been greater too. So, they have earned higher returns but they have exhibited higher risk.

Chapter 25

Answer 1

If the MNC can set up foreign projects in countries whose country risk levels are not highly correlated over time, then it reduces the exposure to the possibility of high country risk in all of these areas simultaneously.

Answer 2

Disagree! Even if the MNC is already in country X, it should always be asking should we continue here? Country risk needs to be monitored continually. If country risk is so high that there is great danger to employees, it may be argued that no expected return is high enough to warrant the project.

Answer 3

No. Country risk analysis is not intended to estimate all project cash flows and determine the present value of these cash flows. It is intended to identify forms of country risk and their potential impact. This is important for capital budgeting but it is not a substitute for an international project appraisal aimed at homing in on a parent net present value.

Chapter 26

Answer 1

Point estimates of exchange rates lead to a point estimate of a project's NPV. It is more desirable to have a feel for a variety of outcomes (NPVs) that might occur.

This might mean sensitivity or scenario analysis.

Answer 2

Develop a range of possible values that each input variable (such as price, quantity sold, exchange rates) may take on. Then apply a simulation model to these ranges. The result is a distribution of NPVs that may occur.

Chapter 27

Answer 1

It may offset some exchange rate risk if it has cash inflows in euros. These euros could be used to make coupon payments.

Answer 2

Syndicated lending reflects a group of banks (called a syndicate) providing a large loan to a customer. This is sometimes desirable as a single loan may be highly damaging to a single bank if the borrower defaulted on the loan. With a syndicate, the potential loss to any bank is limited.

Answer 3

Eurobonds are bonds that are underwritten by a multinational syndicate of banks and sold simultaneously in many countries other than the country of the currency in which they are denominated. Foreign bonds are bonds which are sold in a particular country by a foreign borrower, and underwritten by a syndicate of members from that country; foreign bonds are denominated in the currency of that country.

Chapter 28

Answer 1

Two alternatives could show similar cash inflows when summing all periods. Yet, the alternative with most of its outflows occurring later would be preferable because of the time value of money. It would have a lower present value.

Answer 2

The risk from issuing a floating-rate Eurobond is that the interest rate may rise over time. The risk from issuing a fixed-rate Eurobond is that the firm is obligated to pay that coupon rate even if interest rates decline. Most would argue that a fixed-rate Eurobond is less risky. At least they know with certainty the coupon rate they must pay in the future.

Chapter 29

Answer 1

Cash management is concerned with planning, monitoring and managing liquid resources.

Answer 2

Cash management is designed to ensure the availability of funds at the right time, in the right place, in the right currency and at an acceptable cost. It is concerned with ensuring that the organization has the wherewithal to meet its obligations as they fall due. Cash management is concerned with borrowing facilities, interest costs, bank charges, idle cash balances and investment of surplus funds. It also has as its objectives the optimization of remittable funds to the parent and the reduction of tax bills. Cash management is also concerned with banking relationships, electronic banking, cash collection and disbursement and short-term investment.

Answer 3

A centralized cash management system is beneficial in that it allows for netting, which can reduce transactions costs and improve cash budgeting. In addition, it can increase yields on short-term investments by pooling the excess cash of various subsidiaries.

Chapter 30

Answer 1

The term project finance covers a variety of financing structures. Generally and legally, project finance refers to funds provided to finance a project that will, in varying degrees, be serviced out of the revenues derived from that project. The level of recourse and the type of support given may vary from one project to another. In project finance, lenders usually take some degree of credit risk on the project itself.

Answer 2

In deciding whether to finance a project, lenders must consider its technical feasibility and its economic projections. This means that the commercial, legal, political and technical risks of a project must all be evaluated. Having analysed the risks associated with a project, lenders try to establish a method of financing that covers those risks in the most effective way. It is necessary that the financial structure in project finance should be creative enough to allow the project to succeed. From the lender's point of view, effective security must be structured. Lenders are usually deeply concerned about the cost of over-runs and they frequently seek completion guarantees and performance bonds. Project financiers are very concerned about the availability of all raw materials and customers, and try to ensure ability to service and repay debt. Lenders frequently require assurances regarding the revenues which the project will generate. Evidence of sales contracts may be asked for with respect to the short- to medium-term or even the longer term. Provisions relating to price adjustments may be critical.

Chapter 31

Answer 1

A forfaiting transaction involves an importer that issues a promissory note to pay for the imported goods over a period of three to seven years. Notes are offered to the exporter who sells them at a discount to a forfaiting bank. Forfaiting is mostly used for capital goods.

Answer 2

Countertrade involves the sale of goods to one country in exchange for goods from that country.

Answer 3

Governments may be able to boost exports by establishing policies that either protect the exporters from various types of risk, or encourage lenders to provide financing to exporters.

Chapter 32

Answer 1

The MNC could set a pricing policy (within provisions set out by the governments concerned) to impose high prices or interest costs on goods or funds transferred to those subsidiaries that are in high-tax countries and are profitable at a pre-tax level.

Answer 2

Tax planning involves (1) knowing the tax laws of each country (2) using the tax laws to analyse the feasibility of alternative policies and (3) minimizing the MNC's overall tax liability.

Answer 3

If centralized management makes decisions to benefit the MNC overall, this may hamper one subsidiary at the expense of another (transfer pricing is an example). The subsidiary adversely affected by the policy may disapprove the MNC's tactics, thereby creating a conflict of interests.

Suggested answers to selected exercises

Test bank 1

1. (a) New York   USD0.55   = CHF1
    Zurich should be the same
    Zurich   USD0.55   = CHF1
    Zurich (Direct)   CHF1.8181 = USD1

  (b) New York   USD0.55   = CHF1
    i.e.   CHF1.8181 = USD1
    Zurich should be   CHF1.8181 = USD1
    Zurich is   CHF1.8500 = USD1

    Arbitrage is:
    Buy CHF   Sell USD in Zurich, and
    Sell CHF   Buy USD in New York

2. (a) New York   USD0.55 = CHF1
                       USD1.60 = GBP1

    We want CHF for GBP1
$$GBP1 = USD1.60$$
$$= CHF\ 1.60 \times \frac{1}{0.55}$$
$$= CHF2.9091$$

  (b) New York   CHF2.9091 = GBP1
    Zurich quote   CHF2.80 = GBP1

    Arbitrage involves:
    Buy CHF   Sell GBP in New York
    Sell CHF   Buy GBP in Zurich

3. (a) US$ investment
    Proceeds in three months' time
    $1,000,000 \times 1.02 = \$1,020,000$

    £ investment
    Buy £ spot $1m ÷ 1.8 = £555,556$
    Invest 90 days
    $£555,556 \times 1.025 = £569,445$
    Sell proceeds forward at day 0 for 90 days
    $£569,445 \times 1.78 = \$1,013,612$

£ investment in $ yields a riskless profit of $6,388 after interest costs.
(Using formula)

Forward discount

$$\frac{f_0 - s_0}{s_0} = \frac{1.78 - 1.80}{1.80}$$

$$= -1.111\%$$

Interest differential

$$\frac{i_\$ - i_£}{1 + i_£} = \frac{0.02 - 0.025}{1.025}$$

$$= -0.488\%$$

Interest rate parity not holding. Scope for covered interest arbitrage.
Keep forward discount constant. Interest differential needs 'more minus'.

$$i_£ \uparrow \quad i_\$ \downarrow$$

(b) US$ investment proceeds – see question 3(a): $1,020,000.

Investment proceeds – see question 3(a): £569,445.

Equilibrium forward rate:

$$\frac{1,020,000}{569,445} = 1.7912$$

(Using formula)
Interest differential (3 months):

$$\frac{0.02 - 0.025}{1.025} = -0.004878$$

Forward discount (3 months):

$$\frac{f - 1.80}{1.80}$$

In equilibrium, interest differential equals forward discount:

$$\frac{f - 1.80}{1.80} = -0.004878$$

Solving: $f = 1.7912$

(c) Forward discount:

$$\frac{1.78 - 1.80}{1.80} = -1.111\%$$

Interest differential:

$$\frac{0.02 - 0.035}{1.035} = -1.449\%$$

Interest rate parity not holding. Scope for covered interest arbitrage.
Keep forward discount constant. Interest differential needs 'less minus'.

$$i_£ \downarrow \quad i_\$ \uparrow$$

$i_£$ too high; $i_\$$ is too low. Borrow $; invest £.

(d) Three-month forward discount

$$\frac{1.78 - 1.80}{1.80} = -1.111\%$$

Interest differential – 3 months

$$\frac{0.02 - x}{1 + x}$$

In equilibrium:

$$\frac{0.02 - x}{1 + x} = 0.0111$$

Solving, $x = 0.0314$.

Three-month £ interest rate is 3.14%, that is, 12.56% p.a.

6. (a) We want to sell CHF, buy AUD and to buy CHF, sell AUD.
   To get the rate for selling CHF, buying AUD, we go via

Sell CHF	Buy USD	CHF1.5495
Sell USD	Buy AUD	AUD1.7935

   So   Sell CHF1.5495 = USD1
         Sell USD1   = AUD1.7935

   CHF1 = AUD1.157470

   Picking up opposite quotes will give us the offer quote of 1.158863. The answer is

   CHF1 = AUD1.157470 – 1.158863

   or   AUD1 = CHF0.8629 – 0.8640

   (b) We want the rate to sell GBP buy AUD and to buy GBP sell AUD. We go via

Sell GBP buy USD	1.6325
Sell USD buy AUD	1.7935

   Sell GBP1   = USD1.6325
   Sell USD1.6325 = AUD2.927889

   Using the opposite quotes will give us the offer quote of AUD2.931316. The answer is:

   GBP1 = AUD2.9279 – 2.9313
   AUD1 = GBP0.3411 – 0.3415

Foreign exchange rates

FX rates matrix

GBP against	US$	AU$	JPY
Spot	1.6325–1.6335	2.30–2.30³/₄	263.15–263.25
1 month	1.6250–1.6262	2.29³/₈–2.30¹/₄	263.00–263.35
2 month	1.6190–1.6203	2.28⁷/₈–2.29³/₄	262.98–263.33
3 month	1.6122–1.6135	2.28³/₈–2.29¹/₄	262.96–263.31

FX rates

1. 1.6335
2. 262.96
3. 1.6262
4. 263.15
5. 2.30
6. 263.33
7. 1.6190
8. $2.28^7/_8$
9. $2.29^1/_4$
10. 263.35
11. 1.6135
12. 263.31
13. 1.6135
14. 263.00
15. $2.30^1/_4$
16. $2.28^3/_8$

17. $\dfrac{1.6250 - 1.6325}{1.6325} \times \dfrac{12}{1} \times 100\% = 5.51\%$ p.a.

   US\$ at premium: $i_£ > i_{US\$}$

18. $\dfrac{1.6135 - 1.6335}{1.6335} \times \dfrac{12}{3} \times 100\% = 4.90\%$ p.a.

   US\$ at premium: $i_£ > i_{US\$}$

19. Same as 18.

20. $\dfrac{263.135 - 263.20}{263.20} \times \dfrac{12}{3} \times 100\% = 0.10\%$ p.a.

   Yen at premium: $i_£ > i_{Yen}$

21. $\dfrac{262.96 - 263.15}{263.15} \times \dfrac{12}{3} \times 100\% = 0.29\%$ p.a.

   Yen at premium: $i_£ > i_{Yen}$

22. $\dfrac{2.2975 - 2.3075}{2.3075} \times \dfrac{12}{2} \times 100\% = 2.60\%$ p.a.

   AU\$ at premium: $i_£ > i_{AUD}$

Test bank 2

2. (a) Transaction exposure in respect of export receipts from sales invoiced in foreign currency. Economic exposure in all markets against Japanese yen and the euro. This arises because the UK company concerned has its cost base in sterling (presumably) whereas competitors have theirs in yen and euros. (Note that this is a presumption since it is possible that all competitors could have their main cost inputs in dollars, for example.) If the presumption about cost bases being in the respective home currencies of the key competitors, then, should sterling's real effective exchange rate strengthen against the yen and the euro, the UK competition would lose out. Were sterling's real exchange rate to weaken, then the UK competition should gain.

(b) The economic exposure should be measured in terms of how the present value of the business alters as real exchange rates alter. This is not as easy as it sounds and would involve a lot of work (perhaps involving regression analysis, perhaps involving deductive reasoning) on cash generation, profit outturns and so on and how they change in response to exchange rate movements. This work would draw from analysis of various elasticities – but the essential point is that it is concerned with present value changes.

(c) Economic exposure may be reduced by establishing the same cost base as competitors. So relocation of manufacturing facilities to acquire cost inputs in yen and euros, of a relatively similar magnitude to competitors, should achieve a reduction in economic exposure.

3. Full quotations are:

	US$	NKr
Spot	1.2775–1.2785	11.2500–11.2600
1m	1.2719–1.2732	11.2475–11.26375
2m	1.2672–1.2686	11.2550–11.2725
3m	1.2625–1.2640	11.25875–11.2775

Answers:
(a) 11.2775
(b) If interpreted as option from day 30 to day 90 = 11.2475
    If interpreted as day 60 to day 90 = 11.2550
(c) 1.2625
(d) 1.2686
(e) 11.26375
(f) 11.2475

4. (a) 13.8735
   (b) 1.3900
   (c) 1.3870
   (d) 1.3915
   (e) 13.8735
   (f) 13.8575

5. The solution to this question involves us in preparing a multinational netting matrix similar to that set out below (figures in ax000):

	Receiving subsidiary				Total payments	Net	Eliminated
	Alpha	Beta	Gamma	Delta			
Alphaland	–	125		200	325	–	325
Betaland	250	–	100	300	650	275	375
Gammaland	–	150	–	250	400	175	225
Deltaland	200	100	125	–	425	–	425
Total receipts	450	375	225	750			
Net	125	–	–	325			
Eliminated	325	375	225	425			

The net result is that the Betaland and the Gammaland subsidiaries pay the equivalent of ax275,000 and ax175,000 respectively and this is received by the Alphaland and Deltaland subsidiaries as to the equivalent of ax125,000 and ax325,000. Transaction costs are saved on the eliminated transfers totalling the equivalent of ax1.35m.

Test bank 3

1. Justification for foreign currency borrowings might include:

	Ex ante	*Ex post*
■ Matching against exposures	■ versus projected foreign currency cash flows	■ versus actual foreign currency cash flows
■ Matching against translation exposures	■ versus projected foreign currency net assets	■ versus actual foreign currency net assets
■ Matching against competitive exposure	■ to neutralize, partially, expected foreign competition	■ to neutralize, partially, actual foreign competition
■ Accessing below market funds in foreign currency and covering to move liability to desired currency	■ financial attractiveness of proposition	■ financial attractiveness of proposition
■ PPP disequilibria	■ fundamental overvaluation of currency borrowed	■ actual financial outturns

3. (a) Possible sources of cover

	Amount/maturity	*Comment*
Option:	$12m, 11 months	Excess cost, but opportunity for profit
	$10m, 11 months	May leave $2m exposed
	$12m, 8 months + swap	Excess cost, plus interest rate risk for months 8–11.
Forward:	$10m, 8 months + swap	May leave $2m exposed plus interest rate risk for months 8–11
	$12m, 11 months	Could be creating a $2m exposure
	$10m, 11 months	Could be leaving a $2m exposure
Combination:	$10m, 11 month forward plus $2m, 11 months option	The exposure is covered but the cost of the option may be unnecessary
	$10m, 11 months forward plus $2m, 8 months option + swap if necessary.	Exposure is covered and option premium reduced. Risk to interest rates on swap remain.

(b) Factors that could influence choice:
- *Cost.*   Option premium cost increases as maturity is further away.
- *Forecasts.* If there is a firm view on rates (interest or currency) then the $12m option for 8 months plus swap may be justified. The combination shown above might be appropriate if there is no firm view.
- *Year-end.* The hedge will, most likely, be in place over a year end. What are the implications of valuation of hedges in accounting and tax treatment terms?
- *Tax.*   Will receipt and hedge be tax symmetrical?

4. (a) Sun and Sand has revenues in sterling and costs in US$ as well as euros, Moroccan dinars and other currencies. Relatively little of the cost may be assumed to be in sterling. This cost/revenue mismatch, coupled with the narrow net margin, at a mere 5 per cent, means that small currency fluctuations may dramatically improve profitability or eliminate it altogether.

Should the largest competitor decide not to cover any of its exposures, this may lead to very high profitability relative to Sun and Sand or very low or negative outturns leading to either a stronger or weaker competitor. Depending on the concentration of the market this may be a very significant factor. For example, if there are only two participants, Sun and Sand and the competitor, then this would have a very significant impact on the competitive positions.

The competitor could, if rates moved favourably, offer discounts on holidays or reissue its brochure to gain market share. If the competitor gained significant market share this could impact on Sun and Sand's ability to fill the chartered and/or contracted aircraft seats and hotel accommodation. Clearly this would have an even greater impact on profitability.

While favourable exchange rate movements may lead to discounts, unfavourable movements may be more difficult to offset by surcharges, reversing the competitive situation.

There are therefore major risks to current year profitability, and to the relative strength of Sun and Sand and its major competitor for the future.

(b) The question of management of the risk resolves into two issues, volume and price. Forecasts are required showing the level of demand that is reasonably certain as well as an expected level. It may be possible then to cover some of the volume risk by taking options on holiday accommodation and aircraft seats rather than straightforward contracts.

Regarding the price risk, forward contracts may be appropriate for the minimum expected sales, bearing in mind the payment profile; that is, when cash is expected to be received and when currency payments have to be made. The use of options is probably not appropriate for the majority of costs because of the premium involved relative to the narrow profit margin.

Other than these methods, it may be possible to include a surcharge option in the terms and conditions of sale. This, however, is likely to meet with customer resistance and impact further on the volume risk.

It may be possible in the future to sell holidays in the United States to provide a US$ revenue stream, or to sell in Spain and provide a euro revenue stream. It may also be possible to pay for hotel accommodation in either sterling or euro, although this may create further problems of hotels providing an unsatisfactory service if the exchange rate is unfavourable to them and no cover has been taken. Alternatively, the hotels may price less competitively if they are being asked to carry the risk. There are also such things as trade associations through which data on exposure and its management may be talked through and, possibly, standardized.

Test bank 4

1. (a) Relevant factors are:
   - assumptions underpinning the forecast;
   - Swiss inflation;
   - Swiss required rate of return;
   - future exchange rate changes $/CHF;
   - US inflation;
   - US required rate of return.

   In essence the firm is concerned in the comparison of:

   $$\$2\text{m now versus } \$\frac{6.5e}{(1+r)^6} \text{ million}$$

   where e is the exchange rate six years out and r is the required dollar return on the investment or in purely domestic terms:

   $$\text{Sfr4m now versus Sfr6.5m ten years out}$$

   (b) It is fluctuations in the real value of the Sfr that matter; fluctuations in the nominal value of the Sfr that are wholly offset by higher inflation in the US should not affect the investment. If the real value of the Sfr rises, the real dollar price of hotel service being sold by Inter-Continental should also rise. If demand for their services is elastic, which it may be given the heavy dependence of the Swiss hotel industry on foreign tourists, real dollar revenues will decline. Inelastic demand will lead to an increase in real dollar revenues. The hotel's real dollar cost of Swiss labour and services will rise. The overall impact is that if PPP holds, nominal currency changes should not affect Inter-Continental's Verbier investment. If PPP does not hold, an increase in the real exchange rate is likely to cause a decrease in the real value of the Verbier investment.

   (c) - Projection on the international Fisher effect, using nominal interest differentials between US and Swiss bonds with maturities of ten years.
   - Forecast relative US and Swiss prices and then use PPP to forecast the rate change.
   - Use the forward rate if a ten-year swap can be found.

   Over the long run PPP tends to hold leaving a relatively constant real exchange rate. But whether or not the exchange rates are in equilibrium at the date of Inter-Continental's initial investment is a material factor in estimating future exchange rate movements.

4. The cash flow profile of the project under consideration is set out, month by month, below:

Month (end of month)	0	1	2	3	4	5	6
Cash flow (£m)	−4	+2	–	−5	–	–	(+7+π)

(where π is the project profit)

   (a) Students usually begin this question by trying to establish whether it is better to rely on LIBOR borrowing or to lock in an FRA rate, all other things being equal. From the interest rates quoted for LIBOR, the implied rates for 1 v 3 and 3 v 6 can be calculated as below:

Borrow	*Lend*

1 v 3 implied rate:

$$= \frac{1 + (0.13875 \times 3/12)}{1 + (0.14 \times 1/12)}$$

$$= \frac{1.346875}{1.0116667}$$

$$= 1.0227553$$

1 v 3 rate $= 2.27553\% \times 6$ p.a.

$\qquad = 13.65318\%$ p.a.

$$= \frac{1 + (0.13625 \times 3/12)}{1 + (0.13875 \times 1/12)}$$

$$= \frac{1.0340625}{1.0115625}$$

$$= 1.0222428$$

1 v 3 rate $= 2.22428 \times 6$ p.a.

$\qquad = 13.34568\%$ p.a.

3 v 6 implied rate:

$$= \frac{1 + (0.135 \times 1/2)}{1 + (0.13875 \times 1/4)}$$

$$= \frac{1.0675000}{1.0346875}$$

$$= 1.0317125$$

3 v 6 rate $= 3.17125\% \times 4$ p.a.

$\qquad = 12.685\%$ p.a.

$$= \frac{1 + (0.1325 \times 1/2)}{1 + (0.13625 \times 1/4)}$$

$$= \frac{1.06625}{1.0340625}$$

$$= 1.0311272$$

3 v 6 rate $= 3.11272\% \times 4$ p.a.

$\qquad = 12.45088\%$ p.a.

From the above calculation, the implied rates are:

$$
\begin{array}{lc}
1 \text{ v } 3 & 13.65\text{--}13.35 \\
3 \text{ v } 6 & 12.68\text{--}12.45
\end{array}
$$

It can be seen that these rates are lower than the FRA rates for comparable periods. *Ceteris paribus*, borrowing is preferred to FRA usage.

Given the cash flow profile in the question, the cheaper route is probably:

$$
\begin{array}{lll}
0\text{--}6 & \text{Borrow} & £2\text{m} \\
0\text{--}1 & \text{Borrow} & £2\text{m} \\
3 \text{ v } 6 & \text{Buy FRA} & £5\text{m}
\end{array}
$$

Interest costs on this basis are calculated below. Remember that borrowing will be at a $\frac{1}{2}\%$ p.a. premium on LIBOR.

	£
0–6 $(13\frac{1}{2} + \frac{1}{2})\%$ p.a. on £2m	140,000
0–1 $(14 + \frac{1}{2})\%$ p.a. on £2m	24,167
Interest thereon month 1–6 to put interest costs in terms of terminal value	1,359
3 v 6 FRA $(12.70 + \frac{1}{2})\%$ p.a. on £5m	165,000
	330,526

There are other borrowing routes. Interest costs of some are shown below. The figures are calculated in terminal value terms. The first involves:

0–1	Borrow	£4m
0–3	Buy FRA	£2m
3–6	Buy FRA	£7m

Interest costs on this choice amount to:

	£
0–1 $(14 + \frac{1}{2})$% p.a. on £4m	48,333
Interest thereon $1 \rightarrow 6$ to put interest costs in terminal value	2,719
1 v 3 FRA $(13.70 + \frac{1}{2})$% p.a. on £2m	47,333
Interest thereon $3 \rightarrow 6$ to put interest costs in terms of terminal value	1,597
3 v 6 FRA $(12.70 + \frac{1}{2})$% p.a. on £7m	231,000
	330,982

Another borrowing route might be:

0–6	Borrow	£4m
1–3	Sell FRA	£2m
3 v 6	Buy FRA	£3m

Interest costs on this choice amount to:

	£
0–6 $(13\frac{1}{2} + \frac{1}{2})$% p.a. on £4m	280,000
1 v 3 Sell FRA (13.5)% p.a. on £2m	(45,000)
Interest thereon $3 \rightarrow 6$ to put interest costs in terms of terminal value	(1,491)
3 v 6 Buy FRA $(12.70 + \frac{1}{2})$% p.a. on £3m	99,000
	332,509

All of the above calculations reinforce the choice of action proposed originally.

(b) If interest rates were expected to fall within the first month we might adopt the original policy by borrowing £4m for one month and not doing any FRAs. This is clearly risky and the critical factor would be the strength of our opinion about the interest rate fall. Interest rate options could be built into the equation based on the original borrowing policy.

(c) If interest rates were expected to rise over the next few weeks we could finance the original borrowing suggested but add in caps or other interest rate option devices.

Test bank 5

1. Possible solutions would include:

(a) Do not worry about it if it were a pure translation exposure. However, note that gross gearing on a debt-to-equity ratio basis is 51 per cent although, on a net basis, it is only 5 per cent. Perhaps there is a covenant on gross debt-to-equity ratio level of around 50 per cent (which is not unusual) – in which case we may have to be more than concerned with the exposure.

(b) Drawdown $ debt to replace £ debt. Justified on grounds of matching against $ economic exposure. Need to generate sufficient $ inflows to service debt.

(c) Drawdown $ debt, convert to £. Pay dividend for US company to holding company?

(d) Drawdown $ debt. Lend $60m to holding company denominated in £. Repay £ debt.

2. (a) and (b) It is essential to identify and understand all the types of risks involved for the company and for the bank. The question should be raised of whether the company is so tied into this project as effective owner that it would not in practice be able to take advantage of the limited recourse package and walk away. Is the whole thing an expensive charade? If not, the following undertakings and risk management factors are relevant:

- *Completion risk.* The bank will want guarantees that
  (i) the plant can be built for the price stated (demand fixed prices from supplier and contractor);
  (ii) the debt will be serviced if the plant is late on stream or does not perform to specifications (take liquidated damages equal to debt services from supplier/contractor; query; insure their credit; take bonds);
  (iii) they get paid if the plant is damaged (insurance).

If there is residual risk left with the majority shareholder, recourse should be limited to a stated cash amount.

- *Sales risk.* The chemical company will have to commit to buying the product but it should avoid committing to purchase at a preset price. Risk of being tied into uncommercial sources when competitors get the benefit of failing costs, therefore commitment to be at market price.

- *Operational risk.* If the process is proven, banks may be prepared to take the risk of unexpected operating costs, but they will expect a commitment to provide management expertise.

- *Interest risk:*
  (i) During the construction period. It is probably sensible to arrange to fix (through FRAs, swaps) or cap interest rates to ensure that overall cost stays within finance available.
  (ii) During operational period. Fixing interest rates may make banks feel more secure about allowing a sales price tied to market rates.

(c) Hurdle rates for the non-recourse project. Obviously the fact that risk is reduced in the project should mean that the firm uses a lower hurdle rate than usual. It is clearly inappropriate for the normal hurdle rate to be applied to the overall pre-interest cash flows. It would probably be appropriate to look at the firm's cash out for equity versus cash back as dividends and terminal value (if any). Furthermore, the project finance alternative should be justified in terms of its NPV versus the NPV with the firm doing the project on its own with no limited resource finance.

3. There is no single answer to this question. The good answer needs to be structured to deal with:
- sources of funding;
- factors relevant to gearing;
- currency-related issues and exposure generally;
- wider issues.

Sources of funding:
- Local currency equity.
- Equity form debt/equity swaps.
- Local currency debt.
- International debt market.
- Local expatriate credit agencies.
- Parent funds.

Gearing-related issues:
- Arguments for debt:
    - (i)   High local taxes? Is this the case?
    - (ii) Local withholding tax.
    - (iii) Minimize translation losses.
    - (Iv) Minimize political risk if local debt.
- Arguments for equity:
    - (i)   Risk of low and fluctuating profit on project.
    - (ii) Group policy re guarantees of subsidiary debt.
    - (iii) Thin capitalization rules.

Currency-related issues:
- Combined effects of inflation, interest rates, currency movements.
- Real costs of local debt – may be cheap.
- Mechanism for adjustments in exchange rate – automatic or big lag?
- Can hard currency income be obtained for debt servicing?
- Exposure effects – transaction, translation and economic on P & L, B/S, cash flow.
- Key question is how to protect economic value of project.
- Consider exposure issues re sales pattern, raw material costs, labour costs, plant depreciation, interest costs and overheads.

Wider issues:
Discussion usually involves mention of the following:
- Debt service implications of 25/75 local/export sales split.
- Servicing hard currency purchase of equipment.
- High local tax rates suggest debt.
- Withholding taxes suggest debt.
- Export credits?
- Local versus international debt.
- Currency exposure.
- Interaction of inflation/devaluation/local interest rates.
- Currency controls.
- Thin capitalization rules.

Solutions to multiple choice questions

Summary of answers

Question	1	2	Test bank 3	4	5
1	b	e*	b	d	d
2	c	c	a	d	e
3	d	e	e*	c	d
4	c	c	d	d*	c
5	a	e*	a	f	d
6	c	c	d	d*	b
7	a	b	b	d	a
8	d	a	e	d	b
9	c	b	a	c	e
10	c	a	c	c*	c

* Indicates complicated answers – see below.

Test bank 2

1. $500,000 \times 1.70 = CHF850,000$
Invest at 10% gives CHF935,000
Convert to \$ twelve months forward $935,000 \div 1.76 = \$531,250$
% return $= 31,250 \div 500,000 \times 100 = 6.25\%$

5. $\dfrac{(1 + 0.05)^5}{(1 + 0.08)^5} - 1 = -13\%$

$\$0.20\,[1 + (-0.130)] = \$0.174$

Or, using $\dfrac{i_\$ - i_{kr}}{1 + i_{kr}} = \dfrac{s_t - s_0}{s_0}$

We can come up with a year 1 rate of DKK/US\$ 0.194175
Repeating this constantly to year 5 gives DKK/US\$ 0.174 (approx.)

Test bank 3

3. Profit per unit = $0.61 - $0.58 - $0.02

$\qquad\qquad$ = $0.01

Test bank 4

4. Cash flows (no expropriation)

	Year					
	0	1	2	3	4	5
Cash flow	−79	+10	+12	+16	+20	+20 → inf
PV at 17%	−79	+8.6	+8.8	+10.0	+10.7	+(117.6 × 0.5336) = 62.8

NPV (no expropriation) = −40.9 + 62.8 (1 − p)
p = probability of expropriation

Cash flows (with expropriation)

	Year					
	0	1	2	3	4	5
Cash flow	−79	+10	+12	+16	+20	+36
PV at 17%	−79	+8.6	+8.8	+10.0	+10.7	+16.4

NPV (with expropriation) = −40.9 + 16.4p

Putting these two scenarios together, the expected NPV will be
$$-40.9 + 62.8 (1 - p) + 16.4p$$

For break-even, we put this expression equal to zero and solve for p
$$-40.9 + 62.8 - 62.8p + 16.4p = 0$$
$$p = 47.2 \text{ per cent}$$

6. Cash flows

	Year		
	0	1	2
Cash inflows – M$ million		12	30 + x
FX rates		1.35	1.35
12% discount		0.8929	0.7973
Net present value in CHF million	−30	+7.94	17.72 + 0.5906x

Break even

$$-30 + 7.94 + 17.72 + 0.5906x = 0$$
$$4.34 = 0.5906x$$
$$x = 7.35$$

10. Gain $ = \$3m per annum

   Net of tax = \$2m per annum

   PV   = \$2m (annuity factor 6 year 12%)

              = \$2m $\times$ 4.1114

              = \$8.2m

Appendix 1
Present value of $1

Years hence	1%	2%	4%	6%	8%	10%	12%	14%	15%	16%	18%
1	0.990	0.980	0.962	0.943	0.926	0.909	0.893	0.877	0.870	0.862	0.847
2	0.980	0.961	0.925	0.890	0.857	0.826	0.797	0.769	0.756	0.743	0.718
3	0.971	0.942	0.889	0.840	0.794	0.751	0.712	0.675	0.658	0.641	0.609
4	0.961	0.924	0.855	0.792	0.735	0.683	0.636	0.592	0.572	0.552	0.516
5	0.951	0.906	0.822	0.747	0.681	0.621	0.567	0.519	0.497	0.476	0.437
6	0.942	0.888	0.790	0.705	0.630	0.564	0.507	0.456	0.432	0.410	0.370
7	0.933	0.871	0.760	0.665	0.583	0.513	0.452	0.400	0.376	0.354	0.314
8	0.923	0.853	0.731	0.627	0.540	0.467	0.404	0.351	0.327	0.305	0.266
9	0.914	0.837	0.703	0.592	0.500	0.424	0.361	0.308	0.284	0.263	0.225
10	0.905	0.820	0.676	0.558	0.463	0.386	0.322	0.270	0.247	0.227	0.191
11	0.896	0.804	0.650	0.527	0.429	0.350	0.287	0.237	0.215	0.195	0.162
12	0.887	0.788	0.625	0.497	0.397	0.319	0.257	0.208	0.187	0.168	0.137
13	0.879	0.773	0.601	0.469	0.368	0.290	0.229	0.182	0.163	0.145	0.116
14	0.870	0.758	0.577	0.442	0.340	0.263	0.205	0.160	0.141	0.125	0.099
15	0.861	0.743	0.555	0.417	0.315	0.239	0.183	0.140	0.123	0.108	0.084
16	0.853	0.728	0.534	0.394	0.292	0.218	0.163	0.123	0.107	0.093	0.071
17	0.844	0.714	0.513	0.371	0.270	0.198	0.146	0.108	0.093	0.080	0.060
18	0.836	0.700	0.494	0.350	0.250	0.180	0.130	0.095	0.081	0.069	0.051
19	0.828	0.686	0.475	0.331	0.232	0.164	0.116	0.083	0.070	0.060	0.043
20	0.820	0.673	0.456	0.312	0.215	0.149	0.104	0.073	0.061	0.051	0.037
21	0.811	0.660	0.439	0.294	0.199	0.135	0.093	0.064	0.053	0.044	0.031
22	0.803	0.647	0.422	0.278	0.184	0.123	0.083	0.056	0.046	0.038	0.026
23	0.795	0.634	0.406	0.262	0.170	0.112	0.074	0.049	0.040	0.033	0.022
24	0.788	0.622	0.390	0.247	0.158	0.102	0.066	0.043	0.035	0.028	0.019
25	0.780	0.610	0.375	0.233	0.146	0.092	0.059	0.038	0.030	0.024	0.016
26	0.772	0.598	0.361	0.220	0.135	0.084	0.053	0.033	0.026	0.021	0.014
27	0.764	0.586	0.347	0.207	0.125	0.076	0.047	0.029	0.023	0.018	0.011
28	0.757	0.574	0.333	0.196	0.116	0.069	0.042	0.026	0.020	0.016	0.010
29	0.749	0.563	0.321	0.185	0.107	0.063	0.037	0.022	0.017	0.014	0.008
30	0.742	0.552	0.308	0.174	0.099	0.057	0.033	0.020	0.015	0.012	0.007
40	0.672	0.453	0.208	0.097	0.046	0.022	0.011	0.005	0.004	0.003	0.001
50	0.608	0.372	0.141	0.054	0.021	0.009	0.003	0.001	0.001	0.001	

Appendix 1 – (cont'd)

Years hence	20%	22%	24%	25%	26%	28%	30%	35%	40%	45%	50%
1	0.833	0.820	0.806	0.800	0.794	0.781	0.769	0.741	0.714	0.690	0.667
2	0.694	0.672	0.650	0.640	0.630	0.610	0.592	0.549	0.510	0.476	0.444
3	0.579	0.551	0.524	0.512	0.500	0.477	0.455	0.406	0.364	0.328	0.296
4	0.482	0.451	0.423	0.410	0.397	0.373	0.350	0.301	0.260	0.226	0.198
5	0.402	0.370	0.341	0.328	0.315	0.291	0.269	0.223	0.186	0.156	0.132
6	0.335	0.303	0.275	0.262	0.250	0.227	0.207	0.165	0.133	0.108	0.088
7	0.279	0.249	0.222	0.210	0.198	0.178	0.159	0.122	0.095	0.074	0.059
8	0.233	0.204	0.179	0.168	0.157	0.139	0.123	0.091	0.068	0.051	0.039
9	0.194	0.167	0.144	0.134	0.125	0.108	0.094	0.067	0.048	0.035	0.026
10	0.162	0.137	0.116	0.107	0.099	0.085	0.073	0.050	0.035	0.024	0.017
11	0.135	0.112	0.094	0.086	0.079	0.066	0.056	0.037	0.025	0.017	0.012
12	0.112	0.092	0.076	0.069	0.062	0.052	0.043	0.027	0.018	0.012	0.008
13	0.093	0.075	0.061	0.055	0.050	0.040	0.033	0.020	0.013	0.008	0.005
14	0.078	0.062	0.049	0.044	0.039	0.032	0.025	0.015	0.009	0.006	0.003
15	0.065	0.051	0.040	0.035	0.031	0.025	0.020	0.011	0.006	0.004	0.002
16	0.054	0.042	0.032	0.028	0.025	0.019	0.015	0.008	0.005	0.003	0.002
17	0.045	0.034	0.026	0.023	0.020	0.015	0.012	0.006	0.003	0.002	0.001
18	0.038	0.028	0.021	0.018	0.016	0.012	0.009	0.005	0.002	0.001	0.001
19	0.031	0.023	0.017	0.014	0.012	0.009	0.007	0.003	0.002	0.001	
20	0.026	0.019	0.014	0.012	0.010	0.009	0.005	0.002	0.001	0.001	
21	0.022	0.015	0.011	0.009	0.008	0.006	0.004	0.002	0.001		
22	0.018	0.013	0.009	0.007	0.006	0.004	0.003	0.001	0.001		
23	0.015	0.010	0.007	0.006	0.005	0.003	0.002	0.001			
24	0.013	0.008	0.006	0.005	0.004	0.003	0.002	0.001			
25	0.010	0.007	0.005	0.004	0.003	0.002	0.001	0.001			
26	0.009	0.006	0.004	0.003	0.002	0.002	0.001				
27	0.007	0.005	0.003	0.002	0.002	0.001	0.001				
28	0.006	0.004	0.002	0.002	0.002	0.001	0.001				
29	0.005	0.003	0.002	0.002	0.001	0.001	0.001				
30	0.004	0.003	0.002	0.001	0.001	0.001					
40	0.001										
50											

Appendix 2
Present value of $1 received annually for *n* years

Years (n)	1%	2%	4%	6%	8%	10%	12%	14%	15%	16%	18%
1	0.990	0.980	0.962	0.943	0.926	0.909	0.893	0.877	0.870	0.862	0.847
2	1.970	1.942	1.886	1.833	1.783	1.736	1.690	1.647	1.626	1.605	1.566
3	2.941	2.884	2.775	2.673	2.577	2.487	2.402	2.322	2.283	2.246	2.174
4	3.902	3.808	3.630	3.465	3.312	3.170	3.037	2.914	2.855	2.798	2.690
5	4.853	4.713	4.452	4.212	3.993	3.791	3.605	3.433	3.352	3.274	3.127
6	5.795	5.601	5.242	4.917	4.623	4.355	4.111	3.889	3.784	3.685	3.498
7	6.728	6.472	6.002	5.582	5.206	4.868	4.564	4.288	4.160	4.039	3.812
8	7.652	7.325	6.733	6.210	5.747	5.335	4.968	4.639	4.487	4.344	4.078
9	8.566	8.162	7.435	6.082	6.247	5.759	5.328	4.946	4.772	4.607	4.303
10	9.471	8.983	8.111	7.360	6.710	6.145	5.650	5.216	5.019	4.833	4.494
11	10.368	9.787	8.760	7.887	7.139	6.495	5.937	5.453	5.234	5.029	4.656
12	11.255	10.575	9.385	8.384	7.536	6.814	6.194	5.660	5.421	5.197	4.793
13	12.134	11.343	9.986	8.853	7.904	7.103	6.424	5.842	5.583	5.342	4.910
14	13.004	12.106	10.563	9.295	8.244	7.367	6.628	6.002	5.724	5.468	5.008
15	13.865	12.849	11.118	9.712	8.559	7.606	6.811	6.142	5.847	5.575	5.092
16	14.718	13.578	11.652	10.106	8.851	7.824	6.974	6.265	5.954	5.669	5.162
17	15.562	14.292	12.166	10.477	9.122	8.022	7.120	6.373	6.047	5.749	5.222
18	16.398	14.992	12.659	10.828	9.372	8.201	7.250	6.467	6.128	5.818	5.273
19	17.226	15.678	13.134	11.158	9.604	8.365	7.366	6.550	6.198	5.877	5.316
20	18.046	16.351	13.590	11.470	9.818	8.514	7.469	6.623	6.259	5.929	5.353
21	18.857	17.011	14.029	11.764	10.017	8.649	7.562	6.687	6.312	5.973	5.384
22	19.660	17.658	14.451	12.042	10.201	8.772	7.645	6.743	6.359	6.011	5.410
23	20.456	18.292	14.857	12.303	10.371	8.883	7.718	6.792	6.399	6.044	5.432
24	21.243	18.914	15.247	12.550	10.529	8.985	7.784	6.835	6.434	6.073	5.451
25	22.023	19.523	15.622	12.783	10.675	9.077	7.843	6.873	6.464	6.097	5.467
26	22.795	20.121	15.983	13.003	10.810	9.161	7.896	6.906	6.791	6.118	5.480
27	23.560	20.707	16.330	13.211	10.935	9.237	7.943	6.935	6.514	6.136	5.492
28	24.316	21.281	16.663	13.406	11.051	9.037	7.984	6.961	6.534	6.152	5.502
29	25.066	21.844	16.984	13.591	11.158	9.370	8.022	6.983	6.551	6.166	5.510
30	25.808	22.396	17.292	13.765	11.258	9.427	8.055	7.003	6.566	6.177	5.517
40	32.835	27.355	19.793	15.046	11.925	9.779	8.244	7.105	6.642	6.234	5.548
50	39.196	31.424	21.482	15.762	12.234	9.915	8.304	7.133	6.661	6.246	5.554

Appendix 2 – (cont'd)

Years (n)	20%	22%	24%	25%	26%	28%	30%	35%	40%	45%	50%
1	0.833	0.820	0.806	0.800	0.794	0.781	0.769	0.741	0.714	0.690	0.667
2	1.528	1.492	1.457	1.440	1.424	1.392	1.361	1.289	1.224	1.165	1.111
3	2.106	2.042	1.981	1.952	1.923	1.868	1.816	1.696	1.598	1.493	1.407
4	2.589	2.494	2.404	2.362	2.320	2.241	2.166	1.997	1.849	1.720	1.605
5	2.991	2.864	2.745	2.689	2.635	2.535	2.436	2.220	2.035	1.876	1.737
6	3.326	3.167	3.020	2.951	2.885	2.759	2.643	2.385	2.168	1.983	1.824
7	3.605	3.416	3.242	3.161	3.083	2.937	2.802	2.508	2.263	2.057	1.883
8	3.837	3.619	3.421	3.329	3.241	3.076	2.925	2.598	2.331	2.108	1.922
9	4.031	3.786	3.566	3.463	3.366	3.184	3.019	2.665	2.379	2.144	1.948
10	4.192	3.923	3.682	3.571	3.465	3.269	3.092	2.715	2.414	2.168	1.965
11	4.327	4.035	3.776	3.656	3.544	3.335	3.147	2.752	2.438	2.185	1.977
12	4.439	4.127	3.851	3.725	3.606	3.387	3.190	2.779	2.456	2.196	1.985
13	4.533	4.203	3.912	3.780	3.656	3.427	3.223	2.799	2.468	2.204	1.990
14	4.611	4.265	3.962	3.824	3.695	3.459	3.249	2.814	2.477	2.210	1.993
15	4.675	4.315	4.001	3.859	3.726	3.483	3.268	2.825	2.484	2.214	1.995
16	4.730	4.357	4.033	3.887	3.751	3.503	3.283	2.834	2.489	2.216	1.997
17	4.775	4.391	4.059	3.910	3.771	3.518	3.295	2.840	2.492	2.218	1.998
18	4.812	4.419	4.080	3.928	3.786	3.529	3.304	2.844	2.494	2.219	1.999
19	4.844	4.442	4.097	3.942	3.799	3.539	3.311	2.848	2.496	2.220	1.999
20	4.870	4.460	4.110	3.954	3.808	3.546	3.316	2.850	2.497	2.221	1.999
21	4.891	4.476	4.121	3.963	3.816	3.551	3.320	2.852	2.498	2.221	2.000
22	4.909	4.488	4.130	3.970	3.822	3.556	3.323	2.853	2.498	2.222	2.000
23	4.925	4.499	4.137	3.976	3.827	3.559	3.325	2.854	2.499	2.222	2.000
24	4.937	4.507	4.143	3.981	3.831	3.562	3.327	2.855	2.499	2.222	2.000
25	4.948	4.514	4.147	3.985	3.834	3.564	3.329	2.856	2.499	2.222	2.000
26	4.956	4.520	4.151	3.988	3.837	3.566	3.330	2.856	2.500	2.222	2.000
27	4.964	4.524	4.154	3.990	3.839	3.567	3.331	2.856	2.500	2.222	2.000
28	4.970	4.528	4.157	3.992	3.840	3.568	3.331	2.857	2.500	2.222	2.000
29	4.975	4.531	4.159	3.994	3.841	3.569	3.332	2.857	2.500	2.222	2.000
30	4.979	4.534	4.160	3.995	3.842	3.569	3.332	2.857	2.500	2.222	2.000
40	4.997	4.544	4.166	3.999	3.846	3.571	3.333	2.857	2.500	2.222	2.000
50	4.999	4.545	4.167	4.000	3.846	3.571	3.333	2.857	2.500	2.222	2.000

Appendix 3
Table of areas under the normal curve

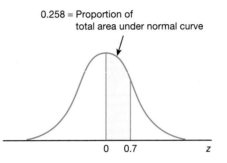

0.258 = Proportion of total area under normal curve

0   0.7   z

Graph of an Appendix 3 table value

z	0.00	0.01	0.02	0.03	0.04	0.05	0.06	0.07	0.08	0.09
0.0	0.0000	0.0040	0.0080	0.0120	0.0160	0.0199	0.0239	0.0279	0.0319	0.0359
0.1	0.0398	0.0438	0.0478	0.0517	0.0557	0.0596	0.0636	0.0675	0.0714	0.0753
0.2	0.0793	0.0832	0.0871	0.0910	0.0948	0.0987	0.1026	0.1064	0.1103	0.1141
0.3	0.1179	0.1217	0.1255	0.1293	0.1331	0.1368	0.1406	0.1443	0.1480	0.1517
0.4	0.1554	0.1591	0.1628	0.1664	0.1700	0.1736	0.1772	0.1808	0.1844	0.1879
0.5	0.1915	0.1950	0.1985	0.2019	0.2054	0.2088	0.2123	0.2157	0.2190	0.2224
0.6	0.2257	0.2291	0.2324	0.2357	0.2389	0.2422	0.2454	0.2486	0.2517	0.2549
0.7	0.2580	0.2611	0.2642	0.2673	0.2704	0.2734	0.2764	0.2794	0.2823	0.2852
0.8	0.2881	0.2910	0.2939	0.2967	0.2995	0.3023	0.3051	0.3078	0.3106	0.3133
0.9	0.3159	0.3186	0.3212	0.3238	0.3264	0.3289	0.3315	0.3340	0.3365	0.3389
1.0	0.3413	0.3438	0.3461	0.3485	0.3508	0.3531	0.3554	0.3577	0.3599	0.3621
1.1	0.3643	0.3665	0.3686	0.3708	0.3729	0.3749	0.3770	0.3790	0.3810	0.3830
1.2	0.3849	0.3869	0.3888	0.3907	0.3925	0.3944	0.3962	0.3980	0.3997	0.4015
1.3	0.4032	0.4049	0.4066	0.4082	0.4099	0.4115	0.4131	0.4147	0.4162	0.4177
1.4	0.4192	0.4207	0.4222	0.4236	0.4251	0.4265	0.4279	0.4292	0.4306	0.4319
1.5	0.4332	0.4345	0.4357	0.4370	0.4382	0.4394	0.4406	0.4418	0.4429	0.4441
1.6	0.4452	0.4463	0.4474	0.4484	0.4495	0.4505	0.4515	0.4525	0.4535	0.4545
1.7	0.4554	0.4564	0.4573	0.4582	0.4591	0.4599	0.4608	0.4616	0.4625	0.4633
1.8	0.4641	0.4649	0.4656	0.4664	0.4671	0.4678	0.4686	0.4693	0.4699	0.4706
1.9	0.4713	0.4719	0.4726	0.4732	0.4738	0.4744	0.4750	0.4756	0.4761	0.4767
2.0	0.4772	0.4778	0.4783	0.4788	0.4793	0.4798	0.4803	0.4808	0.4812	0.4817
2.1	0.4821	0.4826	0.4830	0.4834	0.4838	0.4842	0.4846	0.4850	0.4854	0.4857
2.2	0.4861	0.4864	0.4868	0.4871	0.4875	0.4878	0.4881	0.4884	0.4887	0.4890
2.3	0.4893	0.4896	0.4898	0.4901	0.4904	0.4906	0.4909	0.4911	0.4913	0.4916
2.4	0.4918	0.4920	0.4922	0.4925	0.4927	0.4929	0.4931	0.4932	0.4934	0.4936
2.5	0.4938	0.4940	0.4941	0.4943	0.4945	0.4946	0.4948	0.4949	0.4951	0.4952
2.6	0.4953	0.4955	0.4956	0.4957	0.4959	0.4960	0.4961	0.4962	0.4963	0.4964
2.7	0.4965	0.4966	0.4967	0.4968	0.4969	0.4970	0.4971	0.4972	0.4973	0.4974
2.8	0.4974	0.4975	0.4976	0.4977	0.4977	0.4978	0.4979	0.4979	0.4980	0.4981
2.9	0.4981	0.4982	0.4982	0.4983	0.4984	0.4984	0.4985	0.4985	0.4986	0.4986
3.0	0.4987	0.4987	0.4987	0.4988	0.4988	0.4989	0.4989	0.4989	0.4990	0.4990

Appendix 4
Black and Scholes value of call option expressed as a percentage of the share price

σ√t	Share price divided by present value of exercise price, that is S/PV(E)														
	0.30	0.35	0.40	0.45	0.50	0.55	0.60	0.65	0.70	0.75	0.80	0.82	0.84	0.86	0.88
0.05	0.0	0.0	0.0	0.0	0.0	0.0	0.0	0.0	0.0	0.0	0.0	0.0	0.0	0.0	0.0
0.10	0.0	0.0	0.0	0.0	0.0	0.0	0.0	0.0	0.0	0.0	0.0	0.1	0.2	0.3	0.5
0.15	0.0	0.0	0.0	0.0	0.0	0.0	0.0	0.0	0.1	0.2	0.5	0.7	1.0	1.3	1.7
0.20	0.0	0.0	0.0	0.0	0.0	0.0	0.0	0.1	0.4	0.8	1.5	1.9	2.3	2.8	3.4
0.25	0.0	0.0	0.0	0.0	0.0	0.1	0.2	0.5	1.0	1.8	2.8	3.3	3.9	4.5	5.2
0.30	0.0	0.0	0.0	0.1	0.1	0.3	0.7	1.2	2.0	3.1	4.4	5.0	5.7	6.3	7.0
0.35	0.0	0.0	0.1	0.2	0.4	0.8	1.4	2.3	3.3	4.6	6.2	6.8	7.5	8.2	9.0
0.40	0.0	0.1	0.2	0.5	0.9	1.6	2.4	3.5	4.8	6.3	8.0	8.7	9.4	10.2	11.0
0.45	0.1	0.2	0.5	1.0	1.7	2.6	3.7	5.0	6.5	8.1	9.9	10.6	11.4	12.2	12.9
0.50	0.2	0.5	1.0	1.7	2.6	3.7	5.1	6.6	8.2	10.0	11.8	12.6	13.4	14.2	14.9
0.55	0.5	1.0	1.7	2.6	3.8	5.1	6.6	8.3	10.0	11.9	13.8	14.6	15.4	16.1	16.9
0.60	0.9	1.6	2.5	3.7	5.1	6.6	8.3	10.1	11.9	13.8	15.8	16.6	17.4	18.1	18.9
0.65	1.4	2.4	3.6	4.9	6.5	8.2	10.0	11.9	13.8	15.8	17.8	18.6	19.3	20.1	20.9
0.70	2.1	3.3	4.7	6.3	8.1	9.9	11.9	13.8	15.8	17.8	19.8	20.6	21.3	22.1	22.9
0.75	3.0	4.4	6.1	7.9	9.8	11.7	13.7	15.8	17.8	19.8	21.8	22.5	23.3	24.1	24.8
0.80	4.0	5.7	7.5	9.5	11.5	13.6	15.7	17.7	19.8	21.8	23.7	24.5	25.3	26.0	26.8
0.85	5.1	7.1	9.1	11.2	13.3	15.5	17.6	19.7	21.8	23.8	25.7	26.5	27.2	28.0	28.7
0.90	6.4	8.5	10.7	13.0	15.2	17.4	19.6	21.7	23.8	25.8	27.2	28.4	29.2	29.9	30.6
0.95	7.8	10.1	12.5	14.8	17.1	19.4	21.6	23.7	25.7	27.7	29.6	30.4	31.1	31.8	32.5
1.00	9.3	11.8	14.3	16.7	19.1	21.4	23.6	25.7	27.7	29.7	31.6	32.3	33.0	33.7	34.4
1.05	10.9	13.6	16.1	18.6	21.0	23.3	25.6	27.7	29.7	31.6	33.5	34.2	34.9	35.6	36.2
1.10	12.6	15.4	18.0	20.6	23.0	25.3	27.5	29.6	31.6	33.5	35.4	36.1	36.7	37.4	38.1
1.15	14.4	17.2	20.0	22.5	25.0	27.3	29.5	31.6	33.6	35.4	37.2	37.9	38.6	39.2	39.9
1.20	16.2	19.1	21.9	24.5	27.0	29.3	31.5	33.6	35.5	37.3	39.1	39.7	40.4	41.0	41.7
1.25	18.1	21.1	23.9	26.5	29.0	31.3	33.5	35.5	37.4	39.2	40.9	41.5	42.2	42.8	43.4
1.30	20.0	23.0	25.9	28.5	31.0	33.3	35.4	37.4	39.3	41.0	42.7	43.3	43.9	44.5	45.1
1.35	21.9	25.0	27.9	30.5	33.0	35.2	37.3	39.3	41.1	42.8	44.4	45.1	45.7	46.3	46.8
1.40	23.9	27.0	29.9	32.5	34.9	37.1	39.2	41.1	42.9	44.6	46.2	46.8	47.4	47.9	48.5
1.45	25.8	29.0	31.9	34.5	36.9	39.1	41.1	43.0	44.7	46.4	47.9	48.5	49.0	49.6	50.1
1.50	27.8	31.0	33.8	36.4	38.8	40.9	42.9	44.8	46.5	48.1	49.6	50.1	50.7	51.2	51.8
1.55	29.8	33.0	35.8	38.4	40.7	42.8	44.8	46.6	48.2	49.8	51.2	51.8	52.3	52.8	53.3
1.60	31.8	35.0	37.8	40.3	42.6	44.6	46.5	48.3	49.9	51.4	52.8	53.4	53.9	54.4	54.9
1.65	33.8	36.9	39.7	42.2	44.4	46.4	48.3	50.0	51.6	53.1	54.4	54.9	55.4	55.9	56.4
1.70	35.8	38.9	41.6	44.0	46.2	48.2	50.0	51.7	53.2	54.7	56.0	56.5	57.0	57.5	57.9
1.75	37.7	40.8	43.5	45.9	48.0	50.0	51.7	53.4	54.8	56.2	57.5	58.0	58.5	58.9	59.4
2.00	47.3	50.1	52.5	54.6	56.5	58.2	59.7	61.1	62.4	63.6	64.6	65.0	65.4	65.8	66.2
2.25	56.1	58.6	60.7	62.5	64.1	65.6	66.8	68.0	69.1	70.0	70.9	71.5	71.6	71.9	72.2
2.50	64.0	66.1	67.9	69.4	70.8	72.0	73.1	74.0	74.9	75.7	76.4	76.7	77.0	77.2	77.5
2.75	70.9	72.7	74.2	75.4	76.6	77.5	78.4	79.2	79.9	80.5	81.1	81.4	81.6	81.8	82.0
3.00	76.9	78.3	79.5	80.5	81.4	82.2	82.9	83.5	84.1	84.6	85.1	85.3	85.4	85.6	85.8
3.50	86.0	86.9	87.6	88.3	88.8	89.3	89.7	90.1	90.5	90.8	91.1	91.2	91.3	91.4	91.5
4.00	92.0	92.5	92.9	93.3	93.6	93.9	94.2	94.4	94.6	94.8	94.9	95.0	95.0	05.1	95.2
4.50	95.7	96.0	96.2	96.4	96.6	96.7	96.9	97.0	97.1	97.2	97.3	97.3	97.3	97.4	97.4
5.00	97.8	97.9	98.1	98.2	98.3	98.3	98.4	98.5	98.5	98.6	98.6	98.6	98.6	98.7	98.7
6.00	99.5	99.5	99.6	99.6	99.6	99.6	99.7	99.7	99.7	99.7	99.7	99.7	99.7	99.7	99.7

Row label (left axis): Square root of cumulative variance, that is $\sigma\sqrt{t}$

	Share price divided by present value of exercise price, that is $S/PV(E)$														
	0.90	0.92	0.94	0.96	0.98	1.00	1.02	1.04	1.06	1.08	1.10	1.12	1.14	1.16	1.18
0.05	0.0	0.1	0.3	0.6	1.2	2.0	3.1	4.5	6.0	7.5	9.1	10.7	12.3	13.8	15.3
0.10	0.8	1.2	1.7	2.3	3.1	4.0	5.0	6.1	7.3	8.6	10.0	11.3	12.7	14.1	15.4
0.15	2.2	2.8	3.5	4.2	5.1	6.0	7.0	8.0	9.1	10.2	11.4	12.6	13.8	15.0	16.2
0.20	4.0	0.7	5.4	6.2	7.1	8.0	8.9	9.9	10.9	11.9	13.0	14.1	15.2	16.3	17.4
0.25	5.9	6.6	7.4	8.2	9.1	9.9	10.9	11.8	12.8	13.7	14.7	15.7	16.7	17.7	18.7
0.30	7.8	8.6	9.4	10.2	11.1	11.9	12.8	13.7	14.6	15.6	16.5	17.4	18.4	19.3	20.3
0.35	9.8	10.6	11.4	12.2	13.0	13.9	14.8	15.6	16.5	17.4	18.3	19.2	20.1	21.0	21.9
0.40	11.7	12.5	13.4	14.2	15.0	15.9	16.7	17.5	18.4	19.2	20.1	20.9	21.8	22.6	23.5
0.45	13.7	14.5	15.3	16.2	17.0	17.8	18.6	19.4	20.3	21.1	21.9	22.7	23.5	24.3	25.1
0.50	15.7	16.5	17.3	18.1	18.9	19.7	20.5	21.3	22.1	22.9	23.7	24.5	25.3	26.1	26.8
0.55	17.7	18.5	19.3	20.1	20.9	21.7	22.4	23.2	24.0	24.8	25.5	26.3	27.0	27.8	28.5
0.60	19.7	20.5	21.3	22.0	22.8	23.6	24.3	25.1	25.8	26.6	27.3	28.1	28.8	29.5	30.2
0.65	21.7	22.5	23.2	24.0	24.7	25.5	26.2	27.0	27.7	28.4	29.1	27.8	30.5	31.2	31.9
0.70	23.6	24.4	25.2	25.9	26.6	27.4	28.1	28.8	29.5	30.2	30.9	31.6	32.6	32.9	33.6
0.75	25.6	26.3	27.1	27.8	28.5	29.2	29.9	30.6	31.3	32.0	32.7	33.3	34.0	34.6	35.3
0.80	27.5	28.3	29.0	29.7	30.4	31.1	31.8	32.4	33.1	33.8	34.4	35.1	35.7	36.3	36.9
0.85	29.4	30.2	30.9	31.6	32.2	32.9	33.6	34.2	34.9	35.5	36.2	36.8	37.4	38.0	38.6
0.90	31.3	32.0	32.7	33.4	34.1	34.7	35.4	36.0	36.6	37.3	37.9	38.5	39.1	39.6	40.2
0.95	33.2	33.9	34.6	35.2	35.9	36.5	37.2	37.8	38.4	39.0	39.6	40.1	40.7	41.3	41.8
1.00	35.1	35.7	36.4	37.0	37.7	38.3	38.9	39.5	40.1	40.7	41.2	41.8	42.4	42.9	43.4
1.05	36.9	37.6	38.2	38.8	39.4	40.0	40.6	41.2	41.8	42.4	42.9	43.5	44.0	44.5	45.0
1.10	38.7	39.3	40.0	40.6	41.2	41.8	42.3	42.9	43.5	44.0	44.5	45.1	45.6	46.1	46.6
1.15	40.5	41.1	41.7	42.3	42.9	43.5	44.0	44.6	45.1	45.6	46.2	46.7	47.2	47.7	48.2
1.20	42.3	42.9	43.5	44.0	44.6	45.1	45.7	46.2	46.7	47.3	47.8	48.3	48.7	49.2	49.7
1.25	44.0	44.6	45.2	45.7	46.3	46.8	47.3	47.8	48.4	48.8	49.3	49.8	50.3	50.7	51.2
1.30	45.7	46.3	46.8	47.4	47.9	48.4	48.9	49.4	49.9	50.4	50.9	51.3	51.8	52.2	52.7
1.35	47.4	47.9	48.5	49.0	49.5	50.0	50.5	51.0	51.5	52.0	52.4	52.9	53.3	53.7	54.1
1.40	49.0	49.6	50.1	50.6	51.1	51.6	52.1	52.6	53.0	53.5	53.9	54.3	54.8	55.2	55.6
1.45	50.7	51.2	51.7	52.2	52.7	53.2	53.6	54.1	54.5	55.0	55.4	55.8	56.2	56.6	57.0
1.50	52.3	52.8	53.5	53.7	54.2	54.7	55.1	55.6	56.0	56.4	56.8	57.2	57.6	58.0	58.4
1.55	53.8	54.3	54.8	55.3	55.7	56.2	56.6	57.0	57.4	57.8	58.2	58.6	59.0	59.4	59.7
1.60	55.4	55.9	56.3	56.8	57.2	57.6	58.0	58.5	58.9	59.2	59.6	60.0	60.4	60.7	61.1
1.65	56.9	57.3	57.8	58.2	58.6	59.1	59.5	59.9	60.2	60.6	61.0	61.4	61.7	62.1	62.4
1.70	58.4	58.8	59.2	59.7	60.1	60.5	60.9	61.2	61.6	62.0	62.3	62.7	63.0	63.4	63.7
1.75	59.8	60.7	60.7	61.1	61.5	61.8	62.2	62.6	62.9	63.3	63.6	64.0	64.3	64.6	64.9
2.00	66.6	66.9	67.3	67.6	67.9	68.3	68.6	68.9	69.2	69.5	69.8	70.0	70.3	70.6	70.8
2.25	72.5	72.8	73.1	73.4	73.7	73.9	74.2	74.4	74.7	74.9	75.2	75.4	75.6	75.8	76.0
2.50	77.7	78.0	78.2	78.4	78.7	78.9	79.1	79.3	79.5	79.7	79.9	80.0	80.2	80.4	80.6
2.75	82.2	82.4	82.6	82.7	82.9	83.1	83.3	83.4	83.6	83.7	83.9	84.0	84.2	84.3	84.4
3.00	85.9	86.1	86.2	86.4	86.5	86.6	86.8	86.9	87.0	87.1	87.3	87.4	87.5	87.6	87.7
3.50	91.6	91.6	91.7	91.8	9.19	92.0	92.1	92.1	92.2	92.3	92.4	92.4	92.5	92.6	92.6
4.00	95.2	95.3	95.3	95.4	95.4	95.4	95.5	95.5	95.6	95.6	95.7	95.7	95.7	95.8	95.8
4.50	97.4	97.5	97.5	97.5	97.5	97.6	97.6	97.6	97.6	97.6	97.7	97.7	97.7	97.7	97.8
5.00	98.7	98.7	09.7	98.7	98.7	98.8	98.8	98.8	98.8	98.8	98.8	98.8	98.8	98.8	98.8
6.00	99.7	99.7	99.7	99.7	99.7	99.7	99.7	99.7	99.7	99.7	99.7	99.7	99.7	99.7	99.8

Left axis label: Square root of cumulative variance, that is $\sigma\sqrt{t}$

Appendix 4 – (cont'd)

| | Share price divided by present value of exercise price, that is $S/PV(E)$ | | | | | | | | | |
	1.20	1.25	1.30	1.35	1.40	1.45	1.50	1.75	2.00	2.50
0.05	16.7	20.0	23.1	25.9	28.6	31.0	33.3	42.9	50.0	60.0
0.10	16.8	20.0	23.1	25.9	28.6	31.0	33.3	42.9	50.0	60.0
0.15	17.4	20.4	23.3	26.0	28.6	31.0	33.3	42.9	50.0	60.0
0.20	18.5	21.2	23.9	26.4	28.9	31.2	33.5	42.9	50.0	60.0
0.25	19.8	22.3	24.7	27.1	29.4	31.7	33.8	42.9	50.0	60.0
0.30	21.2	23.5	25.8	28.1	30.2	32.3	34.3	43.1	50.1	60.0
0.35	22.7	24.9	27.1	29.2	31.2	33.2	35.1	43.5	50.2	60.0
0.40	24.3	26.4	28.4	30.4	32.3	34.2	36.0	44.0	50.5	60.1
0.45	25.9	27.9	29.8	31.7	33.5	35.3	37.0	44.6	50.8	60.2
0.50	27.6	29.5	31.3	33.1	34.8	36.4	38.1	45.3	51.3	50.4
0.55	29.2	31.0	32.8	34.5	36.1	37.7	39.2	46.1	51.9	60.7
0.60	30.9	32.6	34.3	35.9	37.5	39.0	40.4	47.0	52.5	61.0
0.65	32.6	34.2	35.8	37.4	38.9	40.3	41.7	48.0	53.3	61.4
0.70	34.2	35.8	37.3	38.8	40.3	41.6	43.0	49.0	54.0	61.9
0.75	35.9	37.4	38.9	40.3	41.7	43.0	44.3	50.0	54.9	62.4
0.80	37.5	39.0	40.4	41.8	43.1	44.4	45.6	51.1	55.8	63.0
0.85	39.2	40.6	41.9	43.3	44.5	45.8	46.9	52.2	56.7	63.6
0.90	40.8	42.1	43.5	44.7	46.0	47.1	48.3	53.3	57.6	64.3
0.95	42.4	43.7	43.5	44.7	46.0	48.5	49.6	54.5	58.6	65.0
1.00	44.0	45.2	46.5	47.6	48.8	49.9	50.9	55.6	59.5	65.7
1.05	45.5	46.8	48.0	49.1	50.2	51.2	52.2	56.7	60.5	66.5
1.10	47.1	48.3	49.4	50.5	51.6	52.6	53.5	57.9	61.5	67.2
1.15	48.6	49.8	50.9	51.9	52.9	53.9	54.9	59.0	62.5	68.0
1.20	50.1	51.3	52.3	53.4	54.3	55.2	56.1	60.2	63.5	68.8
1.25	51.6	52.7	53.7	54.7	55.7	56.6	57.4	61.3	64.5	69.6
1.30	53.1	54.1	55.1	56.1	57.0	57.9	58.7	62.4	65.5	70.4
1.35	54.6	55.6	56.5	57.4	58.3	59.1	59.9	63.5	66.5	71.1
1.40	56.0	56.9	57.9	58.7	59.6	60.4	61.2	64.6	67.5	71.9
1.45	57.4	58.3	59.2	6.00	60.9	61.6	62.4	65.7	68.4	72.7
1.50	58.8	59.7	60.5	61.3	62.1	62.9	63.6	66.8	69.4	73.5
1.55	60.1	61.0	61.8	62.6	63.3	64.1	64.7	67.8	70.3	74.3
1.60	61.4	62.3	63.1	63.8	64.5	65.2	65.9	68.8	71.3	75.1
1.65	62.7	63.5	64.3	65.0	65.7	66.4	67.0	69.9	72.2	72.9
1.70	64.0	64.8	65.5	66.2	66.9	67.5	68.2	70.9	73.1	76.6
1.75	65.3	66.0	66.7	67.4	68.0	68.7	69.2	71.9	74.0	77.4
2.00	71.1	71.7	72.3	72.9	73.4	73.9	74.4	76.5	78.3	81.0
2.25	76.3	76.8	77.2	77.7	78.1	78.5	78.9	80.6	82.1	84.3
2.50	80.7	81.1	81.5	81.9	82.2	82.6	82.9	84.3	85.4	87.2
2.75	84.6	84.9	85.2	85.5	85.8	86.0	86.3	87.4	88.3	89.7
3.00	87.8	88.1	88.3	88.5	88.8	89.0	89.2	90.0	90.7	91.8
3.50	92.7	92.8	93.0	93.1	93.3	93.4	93.5	94.0	94.4	95.1
4.00	95.8	95.9	96.0	96.1	96.2	96.2	96.3	96.6	96.8	97.2
4.50	97.8	97.8	97.9	97.9	97.9	98.0	98.0	98.2	98.3	98.5
5.00	98.9	98.9	98.9	98.9	98.0	99.0	99.0	99.1	99.1	99.2
6.00	99.8	99.8	99.8	99.8	99.8	99.8	99.8	99.8	99.8	99.8

Square root of cumulative variance, that is $\sigma\sqrt{t}$

Appendix 5
Present value of $1 with a continuous discount rate, r, for T periods. Values of e^{-rt}

Period (T)	Continuous discount rate (r)							
	1%	2%	3%	4%	5%	6%	7%	8%
1	0.9900	0.9802	0.9704	0.9608	0.9512	0.9418	0.9324	0.9231
2	0.9802	0.9608	0.9418	0.9231	0.9048	0.8869	0.8694	0.8521
3	0.9704	0.9418	0.9139	0.8869	0.8607	0.8353	0.8106	0.7866
4	0.9608	0.9231	0.8869	0.8521	0.8187	0.7866	0.7558	0.7261
5	0.9512	0.9048	0.8607	0.8187	0.7788	0.7408	0.7047	0.6703
6	0.9418	0.8869	0.8353	0.7866	0.7408	0.6977	0.6570	0.6188
7	0.9324	0.8694	0.8106	0.7558	0.7047	0.6570	0.6126	0.5712
8	0.9231	0.8521	0.7866	0.7261	0.6703	0.6188	0.5712	0.5273
9	0.9139	0.8353	0.7634	0.6977	0.6376	0.5827	0.5326	0.4868
10	0.9048	0.8187	0.7408	0.6703	0.6065	0.5488	0.4966	0.4493
11	0.8958	0.8025	0.7189	0.6440	0.5769	0.5169	0.4630	0.4148
12	0.8869	0.7866	0.6977	0.6188	0.5488	0.4868	0.4317	0.3829
13	0.8781	0.7711	0.6771	0.5945	0.5220	0.4584	0.4025	0.3535
14	0.8694	0.7558	0.6570	0.5712	0.4966	0.4317	0.3753	0.3263
15	0.8607	0.7408	0.6376	0.5488	0.4724	0.4066	0.3499	0.3012
16	0.8521	0.7261	0.6188	0.5273	0.4493	0.3829	0.3263	0.2780
17	0.8437	0.7118	0.6005	0.5066	0.4274	0.3606	0.3042	0.2567
18	0.8353	0.6977	0.5827	0.4868	0.4066	0.3396	0.2837	0.2369
19	0.8270	0.6839	0.5655	0.4677	0.3867	0.3198	0.2645	0.2187
20	0.8187	0.6703	0.5488	0.4493	0.3679	0.3012	0.2466	0.2019
21	0.8106	0.6570	0.5326	0.4317	0.3499	0.2837	0.2299	0.1864
22	0.8025	0.6440	0.5169	0.4148	0.3329	0.2671	0.2144	0.1720
23	0.7945	0.6313	0.5016	0.3985	0.3166	0.2516	0.1999	0.1588
24	0.7866	0.6188	0.4868	0.3829	0.3012	0.2369	0.1864	0.1466
25	0.7788	0.6065	0.4724	0.3679	0.2865	0.2231	0.1738	0.1353
30	0.7408	0.5488	0.4066	0.3012	0.2231	0.1653	0.1225	0.0907
35	0.7047	0.4966	0.3499	0.2466	0.1738	0.1225	0.0863	0.0608
40	0.6703	0.4493	0.3012	0.2019	0.1353	0.0907	0.0608	0.0408
45	0.6376	0.4066	0.2592	0.1653	0.1054	0.0672	0.0429	0.0273
50	0.6065	0.3679	0.2231	0.1353	0.0821	0.0498	0.0302	0.0183
55	0.5769	0.3329	0.1920	0.1108	0.0639	0.0369	0.0213	0.0123
60	0.5488	0.3012	0.1653	0.0907	0.0498	0.0273	0.0150	0.0082

Appendix 5 – (cont'd)

Period	Continuous discount rate (r)								
(T)	9%	10%	11%	12%	13%	14%	15%	16%	17%
1	0.9139	0.9048	0.8958	0.8869	0.8781	0.8694	0.8607	0.8521	0.8437
2	0.8353	0.8187	0.8025	0.7866	0.7711	0.7558	0.7408	0.7261	0.7118
3	0.7634	0.7408	0.7189	0.6977	0.6771	0.6570	0.6376	0.6188	0.6005
4	0.6977	0.6703	0.6440	0.6188	0.5945	0.5712	0.5488	0.5273	0.5066
5	0.6376	0.6065	0.5769	0.5488	0.5220	0.4966	0.4724	0.4493	0.4274
6	0.5827	0.5488	0.5169	0.4868	0.4584	0.4317	0.4066	0.3829	0.3606
7	0.5326	0.4966	0.4630	0.4317	0.4025	0.3753	0.3499	0.3263	0.3042
8	0.4868	0.4493	0.4148	0.3829	0.3535	0.3263	0.3012	0.2780	0.2576
9	0.4449	0.4066	0.3716	0.3396	0.3104	0.2837	0.2592	0.2369	0.2165
10	0.4066	0.3679	0.3329	0.3012	0.2725	0.2466	0.2231	0.2019	0.1827
11	0.3716	0.3329	0.2982	0.2671	0.2393	0.2144	0.1920	0.1720	0.1541
12	0.3396	0.3012	0.2671	0.2369	0.2101	0.1864	0.1653	0.1466	0.1300
13	0.3104	0.2725	0.2393	0.2101	0.1845	0.1620	0.1423	0.1249	0.1097
14	0.2837	0.2466	0.2144	0.1864	0.1620	0.1409	0.1225	0.1065	0.0926
15	0.2592	0.2231	0.1920	0.1653	0.1423	0.1225	0.1054	0.0907	0.0781
16	0.2369	0.2019	0.1720	0.1466	0.1249	0.1065	0.0907	0.0773	0.0659
17	0.2165	0.1827	0.1541	0.1300	0.1097	0.0926	0.0781	0.0659	0.0556
18	0.1979	0.1653	0.1381	0.1153	0.0963	0.0805	0.0672	0.0561	0.0469
19	0.1809	0.1496	0.1237	0.1023	0.0846	0.0699	0.0578	0.0478	0.0396
20	0.1653	0.1353	0.1108	0.0907	0.0743	0.0608	0.0498	0.0408	0.0334
21	0.1511	0.1225	0.0993	0.0805	0.0652	0.0529	0.0429	0.0347	0.0282
22	0.1381	0.1108	0.0889	0.0714	0.0573	0.0460	0.0369	0.0296	0.0238
23	0.1262	0.1003	0.0797	0.0633	0.0503	0.0400	0.0317	0.0252	0.0200
24	0.1153	0.0907	0.0714	0.0561	0.0442	0.0347	0.0273	0.0215	0.0169
25	0.1054	0.0821	0.0639	0.0498	0.0388	0.0302	0.0235	0.0183	0.0143
30	0.0672	0.0498	0.0369	0.0273	0.0202	0.0150	0.0111	0.0082	0.0061
35	0.0429	0.0302	0.0213	0.0150	0.0106	0.0074	0.0052	0.0037	0.0026
40	0.0273	0.0183	0.0123	0.0082	0.0055	0.0037	0.0025	0.0017	0.0011
45	0.0174	0.0111	0.0071	0.0045	0.0029	0.0018	0.0012	0.0007	0.0005
50	0.0111	0.0067	0.0041	0.0025	0.0015	0.0009	0.0006	0.0003	0.0002
55	0.0071	0.0041	0.0024	0.0014	0.0008	0.0005	0.0003	0.0002	0.0001
60	0.0045	0.0025	0.0014	0.0007	0.0004	0.0002	0.0001	0.0001	0.0000

Period	Continuous discount rate (r)								
(T)	18%	19%	20%	21%	22%	23%	24%	25%	26%
1	0.8353	0.8270	0.8187	0.8106	0.8025	0.7945	0.7866	0.7788	0.7711
2	0.6977	0.6839	0.6703	0.6570	0.6440	0.6313	0.6188	0.6065	0.5945
3	0.5827	0.5655	0.5488	0.5326	0.5169	0.5016	0.4868	0.4724	0.4584
4	0.4868	0.4677	0.4493	0.4317	0.4148	0.3985	0.3829	0.3679	0.3535
5	0.4066	0.3867	0.3679	0.3499	0.3329	0.3166	0.3012	0.2865	0.2725
6	0.3396	0.3198	0.3012	0.2837	0.2971	0.2516	0.2369	0.2231	0.2101
7	0.2837	0.2645	0.2466	0.2299	0.2144	0.1999	0.1864	0.1738	0.1620
8	0.2369	0.2187	0.2019	0.1864	0.1720	0.1588	0.1466	0.1353	0.1249
9	0.1979	0.1809	0.1653	0.1511	0.1381	0.1262	0.1153	0.1054	0.0963
10	0.1653	0.1496	0.1353	0.1225	0.1108	0.1003	0.0907	0.0821	0.0743
11	0.1381	0.1237	0.1108	0.0993	0.0889	0.0797	0.0714	0.0639	0.0573
12	0.1154	0.1023	0.0907	0.0805	0.0714	0.0633	0.0561	0.0498	0.0442
13	0.0963	0.0846	0.0743	0.0653	0.0573	0.0503	0.0442	0.0388	0.0340
14	0.0805	0.0699	0.0608	0.0529	0.0460	0.0400	0.0347	0.0302	0.0263
15	0.0672	0.0578	0.0498	0.0429	0.0369	0.0317	0.0273	0.0235	0.0202
16	0.0561	0.0478	0.0408	0.0347	0.0296	0.0252	0.0215	0.0183	0.0156
17	0.0469	0.0396	0.0334	0.0282	0.0238	0.0200	0.0169	0.0143	0.0120
18	0.0392	0.0327	0.0273	0.0228	0.0191	0.0159	0.0133	0.0111	0.0093
19	0.0327	0.0271	0.0224	0.0185	0.0153	0.0127	0.0105	0.0087	0.0072
20	0.0273	0.0224	0.0183	0.0150	0.0123	0.0101	0.0082	0.0067	0.0055
21	0.0228	0.0185	0.0150	0.0122	0.0099	0.0080	0.0065	0.0052	0.0043
22	0.0191	0.0153	0.0123	0.0099	0.0079	0.0063	0.0051	0.0041	0.0033
23	0.0159	0.0127	0.0101	0.0080	0.0063	0.0050	0.0040	0.0032	0.0025
24	0.0133	0.0105	0.0082	0.0065	0.0051	0.0040	0.0032	0.0025	0.0019
25	0.0111	0.0087	0.0067	0.0052	0.0041	0.0032	0.0025	0.0019	0.0015
30	0.0045	0.0033	0.0025	0.0018	0.0014	0.0010	0.0007	0.0006	0.0004
35	0.0018	0.0013	0.0009	0.0006	0.0005	0.0003	0.0002	0.0002	0.0001
40	0.0007	0.0005	0.0003	0.0002	0.0002	0.0001	0.0001	0.0000	0.0000
45	0.0003	0.0002	0.0001	0.0001	0.0001	0.0000	0.0000	0.0000	0.0000
50	0.0001	0.0001	0.0000	0.0000	0.0000	0.0000	0.0000	0.0000	0.0000
55	0.0001	0.0000	0.0000	0.0000	0.0000	0.0000	0.0000	0.0000	0.0000
60	0.0000	0.0000	0.0000	0.0000	0.0000	0.0000	0.0000	0.0000	0.0000

Appendix 5 – (cont'd)

Period	Continuous discount rate (r)								
(T)	27%	28%	29%	30%	31%	32%	33%	34%	35%
1	0.7634	0.7558	0.7483	0.7408	0.7334	0.7261	0.7189	0.7188	0.7047
2	0.5827	0.5712	0.5599	0.5488	0.5379	0.5273	0.5169	0.5066	0.4966
3	0.4449	0.4317	0.4190	0.4066	0.3946	0.3829	0.3716	0.3606	0.3499
4	0.3396	0.3263	0.3135	0.3012	0.2894	0.2780	0.2671	0.2567	0.2466
5	0.2592	0.2466	0.2346	0.2231	0.2122	0.2019	0.1920	0.1827	0.1738
6	0.1979	0.1864	0.1755	0.1653	0.1557	0.1466	0.1381	0.1300	0.1225
7	0.1511	0.1409	0.1313	0.1225	0.1142	0.1065	0.0993	0.0926	0.0863
8	0.1153	0.1065	0.0983	0.0907	0.0837	0.0773	0.0714	0.0659	0.0608
9	0.0880	0.0805	0.0735	0.0672	0.0614	0.0561	0.0513	0.0469	0.0429
10	0.0672	0.0608	0.0550	0.0498	0.0450	0.0408	0.0369	0.0334	0.0302
11	0.0513	0.0460	0.0412	0.0369	0.0330	0.0296	0.0265	0.0238	0.0213
12	0.0392	0.0347	0.0308	0.0273	0.0242	0.0215	0.0191	0.0169	0.0150
13	0.0299	0.0263	0.0231	0.0202	0.0178	0.0156	0.0137	0.0120	0.0106
14	0.0228	0.0198	0.0172	0.0150	0.0130	0.0113	0.0099	0.0086	0.0074
15	0.0174	0.0150	0.0129	0.0111	0.0096	0.0082	0.0071	0.0061	0.0052
16	0.0133	0.0113	0.0097	0.0082	0.0070	0.0060	0.0051	0.0043	0.0037
17	0.0102	0.0086	0.0072	0.0061	0.0051	0.0043	0.0037	0.0031	0.0026
18	0.0078	0.0065	0.0054	0.0045	0.0038	0.0032	0.0026	0.0022	0.0018
19	0.0059	0.0049	0.0040	0.0033	0.0028	0.0023	0.0019	0.0016	0.0013
20	0.0045	0.0037	0.0030	0.0025	0.0020	0.0017	0.0014	0.0011	0.0009
21	0.0034	0.0028	0.0023	0.0018	0.0015	0.0012	0.0010	0.0008	0.0006
22	0.0026	0.0021	0.0017	0.0014	0.0011	0.0009	0.0007	0.0006	0.0005
23	0.0020	0.0016	0.0013	0.0010	0.0008	0.0006	0.0005	0.0004	0.0003
24	0.0015	0.0012	0.0009	0.0007	0.0006	0.0005	0.0004	0.0003	0.0002
25	0.0012	0.0009	0.0007	0.0006	0.0004	0.0003	0.0003	0.0002	0.0002
30	0.0003	0.0002	0.0002	0.0001	0.0001	0.0001	0.0001	0.0000	0.0000
35	0.0001	0.0001	0.0000	0.0000	0.0000	0.0000	0.0000	0.0000	0.0000
40	0.0000	0.0000	0.0000	0.0000	0.0000	0.0000	0.0000	0.0000	0.0000
45	0.0000	0.0000	0.0000	0.0000	0.0000	0.0000	0.0000	0.0000	0.0000
50	0.0000	0.0000	0.0000	0.0000	0.0000	0.0000	0.0000	0.0000	0.0000
55	0.0000	0.0000	0.0000	0.0000	0.0000	0.0000	0.0000	0.0000	0.0000
60	0.0000	0.0000	0.0000	0.0000	0.0000	0.0000	0.0000	0.0000	0.0000

Appendix 6
Swift codes

Country	Code	Currency	Code
Afghanistan	AF	Afghani	AFA
Albania	AL	Lek	ALL
Algeria	DZ	Algerian Dinar	DZD
American Samoa	AS	US Dollar	USD
Andorra	AD	Andorra Peseta	ADP
		& Euro	EUR
Angola	AO	Kwanza	AOA
Anguilla	AI	East Caribbean Dollar	XCD
Antigua & Barbuda	AG	East Caribbean Dollar	XCD
Argentina	AR	Argentine Peso	ARS
Armenia	AM	Armenian Dram	AMD
Aruba	AW	Aruban Guilder	AWG
Australia	AU	Australian Dollar	AUD
Austria	AT	Euro	EUR
Azerbaijan	AZ	Azebaijan Manat	AZM
Bahamas	BS	Bahamian Dollar	BSD
Bahrain	BH	Bahraini Dinar	BHD
Bangladesh	BD	Taka	BDT
Barbados	BB	Barbados Dollar	BBD
Belarus	BY	Belarussian Ruble (New)	BYR
Belgium	BE	Euro	EUR
Belize	BZ	Belize Dollar	BZD
Benin	BJ	CFA Franc BCEAO	XOF
Bermuda	BM	Bermudian Dollar	BMD
Bhutan	BT	Ngultrum	BTN
		& Indian Rupee	INR
Bolivia	BO	Boliviano	BOB
		& Mvdol	BOV
Bosnia & Herzegovina	BA	Convertible Marks	BAM
Botswana	BW	Pula	BWP
Bouvet Island	BV	Norwegian Krone	NOK
Brazil	BR	Brazilian Real	BRL
British Indian Ocean Territory	IO	US Dollar	USD
Brunei Darassalam	BN	Brunei Dollar	BND
Bulgaria	BG	Lev	BGL

Country	Code	Currency	Code
Burkina Faso	BF	CFA Franc BCEAO	XOF
Burundi	BI	Burundi	BIF
Cambodia	KH	Riel	KHR
Cameroon	CM	CFA Franc BEAC	XAF
Canada	CA	Canadian Dollar	CAD
Cape Verde	CV	Cape Verde Escudo	CVE
Cayman Islands	KY	Cayman Islands Dollar	KYD
Central African Republic	CF	CFA Franc BEAC	XAF
Chad	TD	CFA Franc BEAC	XAF
Chile	CL	Chilean Peso	CLP
		& Unitades de Formento	CLF
China	CN	Yuan Renminibi	CNY
Christmas Island	CX	Australian Dollar	AUD
Cocos (Keeling) Islands	CC	Australian Dollar	AUD
Colombia	CO	Colombian Peso	COP
Comoros	KM	Comoro Franc	KMF
Congo	CG	CFA Franc BEAC	XAF
Congo Democ. Republic	CD	Franc Congolais	CDF
Cook Islands	CK	New Zealand Dollar	NZD
Costa Rica	CR	Costa Rican Colon	CRC
Cote d'Ivoire	CI	CFA Franc BCEAO	XOF
Croatia	HR	Kuna	HRK
Cuba	CU	Cuban Peso	CUP
Cyprus	CY	Cyprus Pound	CYP
Czech Republic	CZ	Czech Koruna	CZK
Denmark	DK	Danish Krone	DKK
Djibouti	DJ	Djbouti Franc	DJF
Dominica	DM	East Caribbean Dollar	XCD
Dominican Republic	DO	Dominican Peso	DOP
East Timor	TP	Rupiah	IDR
		& Timor Escudo	TPE
Ecuador	EC	US Dollar	USD
Egypt	EG	Egyptian Pound	EGP
El Salvador	SV	Colon	SVC
		& US Dollar	USD
Equatorial Guinea	GQ	CFA Franc BEAC	XAF
Eritrea	ER	Nakfa	ERN
Estonia	EE	Kroon	EEK
Ethiopia	ET	Ethiopian Birr	ETB
Faeroe Islands	FO	Danish Krone	DKK
Falkland Islands (Malvinas)	FK	Falkland Islands Pound	FKP
Fiji	FJ	Fiji Dollar	FJD
Finland	FI	Euro	EUR
France	FR	Euro	EUR
French Guiana	GF	Euro	EUR

Country	Code	Currency	Code
French Polynesia	PF	CFP Franc	XPF
French Southern Territories	TF	French Franc	FRF
Gabon	GA	CFA Franc BEAC	XAF
Gambia	GM	Dalasi	GMD
Georgia	GE	Lari	GEL
Germany	DE	Euro	EUR
Ghana	GH	Cedi	GHC
Gibraltar	GI	Gibraltar Pound	GIP
Greece	GR	Euro	EUR
Greenland	GL	Danish Krone	DKK
Grenada	GD	East Caribbean Dollar	XCD
Guadeloupe	GP	Euro	EUR
Guam	GU	US Dollar	USD
Guatemala	GT	Quetzal	GTQ
Guernsey, C.I.	GG	Pound Sterling	GBP
Guinea	GN	Guinea Franc	GNF
Guinea-Bissau	GW	Guinea-Bissau Piso	GWP
		& CFA Franc BCEAO	XOF
Guyana	GY	Guyana Dollar	GYD
Haiti	HT	Gourde	HTG
		& US Dollar	USD
Heard & McDonald Islands	HM	Australian Dollar	AUD
Holy See (Vatican City State)	VA	Euro	EUR
Honduras	HN	Lempira	HNL
Hong Kong	HK	Hong Kong Dollar	HKD
Hungary	HU	Forint	HUF
Iceland	IS	Iceland Krona	ISK
India	IN	Indian Rupee	INR
Indonesia	ID	Rupiah	IDR
Iran, Islamic Republic of	IR	Iranian Rial	IRR
Iraq	IQ	Iraqi Dinar	IQD
Ireland	IE	Euro	EUR
Isle of Man	IM	Pound Sterling	GBP
Israel	IL	New Israeli Shekel	ILS
Italy	IT	Euro	EUR
Jamaica	JM	Jamaican Dollar	JMD
Japan	JP	Yen	JPY
Jersey, C.I.	JE	Pound Sterling	GBP
Jordan	JO	Jordanian Dinar	JOD
Kazakhstan	KZ	Tenge	KZT
Kenya	KE	Kenyan Shilling	KES
Kiribati	KI	Australian Dollar	AUD
Korea, Democratic People's Republic of	KP	North Korean Won	KPW

Country	Code	Currency	Code
Korean, Republic of	KR	Won	KRW
Kuwait	KW	Kuwait Dinar	KWD
Kyrgyzstan	KG	Som	KGS
Lao, People's Democratic Republic	LA	Kip	LAK
Latvia	LV	Latvian Lats	LVL
Lebanon	LB	Lebanese Pound	LBP
Lesotho	LS	Loti &	LSL
		Rand	ZAR
Liberia	LR	Liberian Dollar	LRD
Libian Arab Jamahiriya	LY	Libyan Dinar	LYD
Liechtenstein	LI	Swiss Franc	CHF
Lithuania	LT	Lithuanian Litas	LTT
Luxembourg	LU	Euro	EUR
Macau	MO	Pataca	MOP
Macedonia, The Former Yugoslav Republic of	MK	Denar	MKD
Madagascar	MG	Malagasy Franc	MFG
Malawi	MW	Kwacha	MWK
Malaysia	MY	Malaysian Ringgit	MYR
Maldives	MV	Rufyaa	MVR
Mali	ML	CFA Franc BCEAO	XOF
Malta	MT	Maltese Lira	MTL
Marshall Islands	MH	US Dollar	USD
Martinique	MQ	Euro	EUR
Mautitania	MR	Ouguiya	MRO
Mauritius	MU	Mauritius Rupee	MUR
Mayotte	YT	Euro	EUR
Mexico	MX	Mexican Peso	MXN
		& Mexican Unidad de Inversion (UDI)	MXV
Micronesia, Fed. States of	FM	US Dollar	USD
Moldova, Republic of	MD	Moldovian Leu	MDL
Monaco	MC	Euro	EUR
Mongolia	MN	Tugrik	MNT
Montserrat	MS	East Caribbean Dollar	XCD
Morocco	MA	Moroccan Dirham	MAD
Mozambique	MZ	Metical	MZM
Myanmar	MM	Kyat	MMK
Namibia	NA	Namibian Dollar &	NAD
		Rand	ZAR
Nauru	NR	Australian Dollar	AUD
Nepal	NP	Nepalese Rupee	NPR
Netherlands	NL	Euro	EUR
Netherlands Antilles	AN	NA Guilders	ANG
New Caledonia	NC	CFP Franc	XPF
New Zealand	NZ	New Zealand Dollar	NZD

Country	Code	Currency	Code
Nicaragua	NI	Cordoba Oro	NIO
Niger	NE	CFA Franc BCEAO	XOF
Nigeria	NG	Naira	NGN
Niue	NU	New Zealand Dollar	NZD
Norfolk Island	NF	Australian Dollar	AUD
Northern Mariana Islands	MP	US Dollar	USD
Norway	NO	Norwegian Krone	NOK
Oman	OM	Rial Omani	OMR
Pakistan	PK	Pakistan Rupee	PKR
Palau	PW	US Dollar	USD
Palestinian Territory, Occ	PS	New Israeli Shekel	ILS
Panama	PA	Balboa &	PAB
		US Dollar	USD
Papua New Guinea	PG	Kina	PGK
Paraguay	PY	Guarani	PYG
Peru	PE	Nuevo Sol	PEN
Philippines	PH	Philippine Peso	PHP
Pitcairn	PN	New Zealand Dollar	NZD
Poland	PL	Zloty	PLN
Portugal	PT	Euro	EUR
Puerto Rico	PR	US Dollar	USD
Qatar	QA	Qatari Riyal	QAR
Reunion	RE	Euro	EUR
Romania	RO	Leu	ROL
Russian Federation	RU	Russian Ruble (New)	RUB
Rwanda	RW	Rwanda Franc	RWF
Samoa	WS	Tala	WST
San Marino	SM	Euro	EUR
Sao Tome & Principe	ST	Dobra	STD
Saudi Arabia	SA	Saudi Riyal	SAR
Senegal	SN	CFA Franc BCEAO	XOF
Seychelles	SC	Seychelles Rupee	SCR
Sierra Leone	SL	Leone	SLL
Singapore	SG	Singapore Dollar	SGD
Slovakia	SK	Slovak Koruna	SKK
Slovenia	SI	Tolar	SIT
Solomon Islands	SB	S.I. Dollar	SBD
Somalia	SO	Somali Shilling	SOS
South Africa	ZA	Rand	ZAR
Spain	ES	Euro	EUR
Sri Lanka	LK	Sri Lanka Rupee	LKR
St Helena	SH	St Helena Pound	SHP
St Kitts & St Nevis	KN	East Caribbean Dollar	XCD
St Lucia	LC	East Caribbean Dollar	XCD

Country	Code	Currency	Code
St Pierre & Miquelon	PM	Euro	EUR
St Vincent & The Grenadines	VC	East Caribbean Dollar	XCD
Sudan	SD	Sudane Dollar	SDD
Suriname	SR	Surinam Guilder	SRG
Svalbard & Jan Mayen Islands	SJ	Norwegian Krone	NOK
Swaziland	SZ	Lilangeri	SZL
Sweden	SE	Swedish Krone	SEK
Switzerland	CH	Swiss Franc	CHF
Syrian Arab Republic	SY	Syrian Pound	SYP
Taiwan	TW	New Taiwan Dollar	TWD
Tajikstan	TJ	Somoni	TJS
Tanzania, United Republic of	TZ	Tanzanian Shilling	TZS
Thailand	TH	Baht	THB
Togo	TG	CFA Franc BCEAO	XOF
Tokelau	TK	New Zealand Dollar	NZD
Tonga	TO	Pa'Anga	TOP
Trinidad & Tobago	TT	T & T Dollar	TTD
Tunisia	TN	Tunisian Dinar	TND
Turkey	TR	Turkish Lira	TRL
Turkmenistan	TM	Manat	TMM
Turks & Caicos Islands	TC	US Dollar	USD
Tuvalu	TV	Australian Dollar	AUD
Uganda	UG	Uganda Shilling	UGX
Ukraine	UA	Hryvnia	UAH
United Arab Emirates	AE	UAE Dirham	AED
United Kingdom	GB	Pound Sterling	GBP
United States	US	US Dollar	USD
United States Minor Outlaying Islands	UM	US Dollar	USD
Uruguay	UY	Peso Uruguayo	UYU
Uzbekistan	UZ	Uzbekistan Sum	UZS
Vanatu	VU	Vatu	VUV
Venezuela	VE	Bolivar	VEB
Viet Nam	VN	Dong	VND
Virgin Islands, British	VG	US Dollar	USD
Virgin Islands, US	VI	US Dollar	USD
Wallis & Fatuna Islands	WF	CFP Franc	XPF
Western Sahara	EH	Moroccan Dirham	MAD
Yemen	YE	Yemen Rial	YER
Yugoslavia	YU	New Dinar	YUM
Zambia	ZM	Kwacha	ZMK
Zimbabwe	ZW	Zimbabwe Dollar	ZWD

Glossary

Absolute purchasing power parity A form of purchasing power parity which claims that under a fully floating exchange rate regime the ratio between domestic and foreign price levels equals the equilibrium rate of exchange between the domestic and foreign currencies.

Acceleration In relation to a loan, the action of a lender in demanding early repayment of principal in the event of default.

Acceptance The signing of a bill of exchange in formal acknowledgement of the obligation to honour the bill.

Acceptance credit A UK money-market term for a bill of exchange drawn by a customer on its bank, which is accepted and then discounted by the bank, the proceeds being paid to the customer.

Accounting exposure Exposure which arises from the process of consolidating items denominated in foreign currency into the group financial accounts denominated in the parent's currency. Sometimes called translation exposure.

Alienation of assets The risk that a borrower may realize some or all of the assets that form the lender's security.

All-current rate method A foreign currency translation method. All items denominated in foreign currency are translated at current exchange rates. Sometimes called the closing rate method or current rate method – but not to be confused with the current/non-current rate method.

American depository receipt (ADR) Certificate of ownership issued by a US bank to investors in place of the underlying corporate shares, which are held in custody.

American option An option which may be exercised on any business day within the option period.

Amortization The repayment of, or obligation to repay, the principal of a loan in more than one instalment.

Appreciation An increase in the value of a currency.

Arbitrage A purchase of foreign exchange, securities or commodities in one market coupled with immediate resale in another market in order to profit risklessly from price discrepancies. The effect of arbitrageurs' actions is to equate prices in all markets for the same commodity.

Arm's-length price The price at which a willing seller and an unrelated willing buyer will freely agree a transaction.

Ask price The larger price in a foreign exchange quotation. Sometimes called the offer price.

Asset-based swap An interest rate or cross-currency interest rate swap entered into by a party to convert the coupon on an asset to another rate or another currency rate basis.

At the money An option when the value of its underlying security is equal to the option strike price.

Average life   The effective life of a bond issue calculated as the average of the time-periods for which funds are made available to the borrower, weighted by the amount available in each such period.

Back-to-back loan   One of two loans of the same initial amount made by one party to another in different countries, the loans being denominated in different currencies and each maturing on the same date. Used as a method of borrowing foreign currency and unblocking funds.

Balance of payments   A financial statement prepared for a country summarizing the flow of goods, services and funds between the residents of that country and the residents of the rest of the world during a particular period.

Balance of trade   The net of imports and exports of goods reported in the balance of payments.

Balance sheet exposure   Exposure which arises from the process of translating balance sheet items denominated in foreign currency into the group accounts denominated in the parent's currency.

Balloon   The principal amount repaid on maturity of a loan that is significantly larger than the annual repayments. For example an issue could have six payments of 10 per cent, followed by a balloon of 40 per cent at maturity.

Basis   The difference between cash and futures prices. Also the difference between yields on similar but different financial instruments.

Basis point   A hundredth of 1 per cent. Used in relation to interest rates.

Basis risk   With respect to futures contracts, the basis represents the difference between the price of the cash commodity and a related futures contract, a difference that widens or narrows as the cash and futures prices fluctuate. Basis risk refers to the possibility that this difference will change during the life of the contract, resulting in an unexpected loss or gain. The basis is the key to hedging: if it remains constant over the life of a position, a perfect hedge (losses exactly equal to gains) results. Basis risk results when a particular futures contract is used to hedge a portfolio that differs from the underlying futures instrument.

Basis swap   An interest rate or cross-currency swap in which the payment obligations of each of the parties are determined on the basis of a floating rate index. A US dollar LIBOR/sterling LIBOR swap would be a basis swap, as would a LIBOR/CD swap in which both parties' payment obligations were in US dollars.

Basket   An artificial currency based on a mixture of actual currencies. For example, the ECU is an artificial currency based upon a basket of EU currencies.

Bearer bond or bearer security   A negotiable security that is presumed in law to be owned by the holder. Title to bearer securities is effected by delivery.

Bearer instrument   A negotiable instrument on which title passes by mere delivery without endorsement or registration.

Bells and whistles   The additional features of a security intended to attract investors or reduce issue costs or both.

Benchmark security   The choice of a security as a standard for the return on a particular class of securities that serves as a guide for other comparable issues.

Beta   A measure of the sensitivity of an asset to changes in the market. A beta of 0.5 means that on average a 1 per cent change in the market in the short run implies a 0.5 per cent change in the value of the asset. *See also* systematic risk.

Bid–ask spread or bid–offer spread   The difference between the prices quoted by a dealer for buying and selling a security.

Bid price   The smaller price in a foreign exchange quotation.

Bill of exchange   A negotiable instrument, used mainly in international trade, instructing one person, the drawee, to pay a certain sum of money to another named person, the drawer, on demand or at a certain future time. If the drawee, or acceptor, of the bill is a bank, the bill is a bank bill (known as a banker's acceptance); if it is a trader, the bill is a trade bill; if it is the UK or US government, it is a treasury bill. Such bills are normally issued with 90-day lives, and their marketability depends on the standing of the drawee or acceptor, the nature of the underlying transaction and whether the bill is eligible for rediscounting with the central bank.

Black and Scholes model   A model that provides a means by which to value option contracts. It involves using information on the underlying asset, the strike price, volatility, time to expiry and risk-free interest rates. First formulated by Fischer Black and Myron Scholes in 1973.

Blocked currency   A currency that is not freely convertible to other currencies due to exchange controls.

Blue chip   An equity share that is considered to be of the highest quality.

Bond   A promise under seal to pay money. The term is generally used to designate the promise made by a corporation, either public or private, or a government to pay money, and it generally applies to instruments with an initial maturity of one year or more.

Bond basis   The method used to compute accrued interest on some bonds and on some short-term money-market instruments. In the Eurobond market the accrued interest calculated on the bond basis is equal to the coupon rate multiplied by the number of lapsed bond days divided by 360 (known as the 360-day year convention). *See also* money-market basis.

Bonus issue   An issue of shares to existing holders, usually in some set proportion to the holding, but requiring no payment. This has the effect of increasing the company's issued capital and is normally made possible by the capitalization of reserves. Sometimes known as a scrip or capitalization issue.

Bretton Woods Conference   A meeting of representatives of non-communist countries in Bretton Woods, New Hampshire, USA, in 1944. Representatives agreed on the characteristics of the international monetary system, effectively the fixed exchange rate system, which prevailed until 1971.

Bridge financing   A type of loan, usually at fluctuating interest rates, that takes the form of renewable overdrafts or discounting facilities. It is used as a continuing source of funds until the borrower obtains medium- or long-term financing to replace it.

Bulldog bond   A sterling-denominated bond issue made in the UK market by a foreign (non-UK) borrower.

Bullet   A straight debt issue with repayment in one go at maturity.

Buyer credit   One of the two main techniques by which the United Kingdom supports UK companies in winning and financing engineering and construction projects overseas. Under a buyer credit, the customer settles with the supplier on a cash basis, funds for this purpose being provided to the customer directly by a bank under ECGD guarantee.

Callable bond   A bond with a call provision giving the issuer the right to redeem the bonds under specified terms prior to the normal maturity date.

Call option   The right, but not the obligation, to buy an amount of foreign exchange at a specified price within a specified period.

Cap   A limit on the upward movement of a coupon or interest rate.

Capital account   A balance of payments term meaning the part of the balance of payments which records the changes in financial assets and liabilities. The capital account is divided into long-term flows and short-term flows.

Capital adequacy   The minimum amount of capital that bank, non-bank financial intermediaries and other financial market operators must maintain in proportion to the risks that they assume.

Capital asset pricing model (CAPM)   A model that promotes a basis for pricing risk associated with holding securities. Its essence is that rates of return are directly related to a single common factor: namely, the return on the market portfolio adjusted for non-diversifiable risk.

Capital mobility   The extent to which private capital is free to be invested abroad. Capital mobility is predicated upon well-developed foreign exchange and financial markets, freedom from official restrictions on foreign investment and confidence that future government policies will not obstruct the repatriation of invested funds.

Capital structure   The distribution of a company's issued capital as between bonds, debentures, preferred and ordinary shares, earned surplus and retained income.

Capped FRN   An issue with an upper limit on the coupon rate. Under this type of issue, the lender forgoes the possibility of receiving a return above the cap rate should the market interest rate exceed the cap rate.

Cash flow exposure   This is concerned with the effect of currency changes on the present value of future cash flows generated by a company's domestic and foreign operations. Sometimes called economic exposure.

Cash market   Where delivery and settlement of the deal is immediate, or within a few days, as compared with the future and options markets where delivery and settlement are delayed.

Central bank   The institution with the primary responsibility to control the growth of a country's money stock. It also has regulatory powers over commercial banks and over other financial institutions. It usually serves as the monetary agent for the government.

Certificate of deposit (CD)   A placement of money for a specified period of time with a bank. The depositor receives a confirmation, the deposit receipt, which is a negotiable instrument. Bankers dealing in CDs make a secondary market where they may be sold and purchased prior to maturity. Investors usually accept a smaller interest rate on CDs than on regular time deposits because the investment has greater liquidity via the secondary market.

CHAPS   *See* clearing house automated payments system.

Chartism   Interpreting foreign exchange (and other) market activity and predicting future movements over the near term from graphic depictions of past prices and volumes. Sometimes called technical analysis or momentum analysis.

CHIPS   *See* clearing house inter-bank payments system.

Clean float   An exchange rate system characterized by the absence of government intervention. Sometimes called a free float.

Cleared balance   The true balance of a customer's account with its banker on which its funds' availability depends.

Clearing house   An institution through which Eurobond contracts, futures contracts and other financial instruments, including cheques, are cleared.

Clearing house automated payments system (CHAPS)   A network of linked computers operated by UK clearing banks which provides for the rapid transfer of large balances.

Clearing house inter-bank payments system (CHIPS)   An automated clearing facility set up in 1970 and operated by the New York Clearing House Association. It processes international money transfers for its membership which includes over a hundred US financial institutions – mostly major US banks and branches of foreign banks.

Clearing system   A transaction or depository system set up for efficient physical delivery.

Close out   For a futures contract this means taking a second offsetting position in order to remove the delivery obligation.

Closing exchange rate   The exchange rate prevailing at a financial reporting date.

Closing price   The price, or spread of prices, at which deals are made just before the close of official business in a particular market.

Closing rate method   *See* all-current rate method.

Collar   A transaction that combines a cap and a floor so as to provide cap or floor protection at a lower cost. For example, the buyer of a cap might give up some of the benefits of a decline in interest rates by selling a floor to the writer of the cap, thereby reducing the cost of the cap by the value of the floor. Or, the purchaser of the floor might be willing to give up some benefits of a rise in interest rates by selling a cap to reduce the floor purchase price. The cap and floor portions of a collar operate as described in the definitions of those terms if actual interest rates rise above the agreed cap rate or decline below the agreed floor rate, respectively, for any period. Sometimes called a floor/ceiling arrangement.

Collateral Security placed with a lender to assure the performance of the obligation. Assuming that the obligation is satisfied, the collateral is returned by the lender.

Comfort letter A formal letter written to a lender, normally by a parent company, indicating its willingness to accept some responsibility to honour the borrowing obligations of a subsidiary or associate company, but without constituting a legal obligation to do so. Such letters may be written in varying degrees of strength. At one extreme, there is the letter of awareness, which does no more than acknowledge the existence of the relevant borrowing, while at the other comes the unenforceable guarantee. In this latter form, the writer would indicate that it undertook to meet the borrower's obligations in the event of its failing to do so, but that the recipient could not use the letter as a means of forcing it to do so. The essential point is that, while such letters constitute a significant moral obligation, they do not constitute a legally binding obligation. For this reason, they have come to be known in the United States as LOMIs, letters of moral intent. They do not have to be treated as contingent liabilities and have no impact on the parent company's balance sheet.

Commercial paper An unsecured promissory note issued usually for maturities of 60 days or less.

Commitment fee A percentage per annum rate charged by a lender on the daily undrawn balance of a borrowing facility.

Compensating balance A minimum sum of money which, as a condition of a term loan, the borrower undertakes to maintain on current account with the lender, in theory to increase the bank's security by reducing the risk that the account will be overdrawn. The effect of maintaining a non-interest-bearing deposit is to reduce the true sum borrowed: since interest is payable on the gross sum, the effective rate on the net amount is higher than that quoted. This mechanism was common in the United States until the end of the 1970s but has now gone out of general use, maybe because of the growth in professionalism among treasury staff.

Confirmation The written document confirming the oral foreign exchange contract agreed by telephone between either dealer and dealer or dealer and client.

Confirmed irrevocable letter of credit A type of credit issued by the importer's bank and confirmed by a bank in the exporter's country. The importer's bank commits itself irrevocably to pay the exporter's draft, and the confirming bank (the exporter's bank) adds to this commitment by assuming the responsibility to pay the exporter's draft, provided that all conditions contained in the letter of credit are satisfied.

Convertibility The ability to convert one currency into another without special permission from exchange control authorities.

Convertible bond A fixed interest security that is exchangeable into equity shares under stipulated conditions.

Convertible Eurobond A Eurobond that can be converted into equity under stipulated conditions.

Convertible FRN A floating rate note that can be converted into a fixed rate bond or into another FRN with a different maturity or a different currency denomination.

Correlation A standardized statistical measure of the dependence of two random variables. It is defined as the covariance divided by the standard deviations of two variables.

Correspondent bank A bank that handles the business of a foreign bank.

Cost of capital   The rate of return expected by a party financing the firm.

Cost-plus loan pricing   The interest rate on a loan expressed as a function of some publicly available cost-of-funds measure, such as LIBOR.

Countertrade   A generic term for a range of commercial mechanisms for reciprocal trade that include barter, counterpurchase, offsets buy-back and switch trading. The common characteristic of these arrangements is that export sales to a particular market are made conditional upon undertakings to accept imports from that market. Latterly, they are used as a way of promoting trade between developed and less-developed nations, and are intended to avoid, or mitigate, the problems associated with sovereign debt by allowing settlement in the produce of the buying country. A number of specialist intermediaries have grown up prepared to exchange the output/produce received by the seller for money/currency, and then to place the output/commodities with the ultimate user for a fee, known as disagio, or by discounting the value of the output.

Country risk   A wide range of risk, including political as well as economic risk. Corporate goals of multinationals and the national aspirations of host countries may not be congruent; the essential element in country risk is the possibility of some form of government action preventing the fulfilment of a contract.

Coupon or coupon rate   The fixed interest rate attached to a loan.

Covariance   A statistical measure of the degree to which random variables move together.

Covenant   An obligation in writing. There are covenants in term loan agreements, deeds, mortgages and other similar instruments.

Covered interest arbitrage   The process of borrowing a currency, converting it to a second currency where it is invested, and selling this second currency forward against the initial currency. Riskless profits are derived from discrepancies between interest differentials and the percentage discount or premium between the currencies involved in the forward transaction. Covered interest arbitrage is based on disequilibrium in interest rate parity.

Covered position   A position in a security that is matched by a counter position in another security, thereby neutralizing the initial position.

Covering   Protecting the cash value of future proceeds usually from an international trade transaction, by buying or selling the proceeds in the forward market. Although used interchangeably with the term 'hedging', covering is, strictly speaking, protecting a future cash flow amount whereas hedging refers to the protection of foreign-denominated accounting assets or liabilities against pure translation losses.

Crawling peg system   An exchange rate system in which the exchange rate is adjusted frequently and deliberately, perhaps many times a year, usually to reflect prevailing rates of inflation.

Credit risk   The likelihood, in lending operations, that a borrower will not be able to repay the principal or pay the interest.

Cross default provision   A clause in a loan agreement that allows the lender to declare the loan immediately repayable and to terminate any further extension of credit if the borrower defaults on any other debt.

Cross-rate   The exchange rate between currencies A and B based upon the rates between currencies A and C and currencies B and C.

Currency basket   A means of expressing the value of a financial asset or currency as a weighted average of more than one foreign exchange rate. The weights in this average are usually defined as specific quantities of currencies, hence the term 'currency basket'.

Currency option   A contract conferring the right, but not the obligation, to buy or sell a specified currency against another currency at a specific price on or prior to a specified date.

Currency swap   The simultaneous borrowing and lending operation in which parties transfer currencies from one to the other at the spot rate and agree to reverse the exchange at a future date and at an agreed exchange rate.

Current account   As used in the balance of payments, it is that section that records the trade in goods and services and the exchange of gifts among countries.

Current/non-current method   A foreign currency translation method in which current items in balance sheets denominated in foreign currencies are translated at current exchange rates and long-term items are translated at historical rates.

Current rate method   *See* all-current rate method.

Dealer   A specialist in a bank or company who is authorized to undertake foreign exchange transactions.

Debenture   In the United Kingdom, a fixed interest secured loan which can be for a fixed maturity or irredeemable. There are two main types: mortgage debentures, which are secured against a specific asset of the issuer; and floating debentures, which are secured against the entire asset base of the issuer.

Debt capacity   The total amount which a company is capable of borrowing.

Debt–equity swaps   A secondary debt market involving the trading of sovereign debt as between the major lending banks. Recognizing that large parts of Third World debts will not be readily cleared from their books, banks have sought new ways of trading their positions by swapping and selling debts between one another and to corporations desiring to undertake projects in the Third World countries concerned. The corporation offers the acquired debt to the less-developed country (LDC) in return for local currency: the LDC thereby redeems the debt.

Debt factoring   The purchasing, normally with recourse to the seller, of accounts receivable as a mechanism for providing short-term finance on a continuing basis. The practice is common among small companies in the United Kingdom.

Debt service ratio   A ratio used to assess a country's creditworthiness. It is the ratio of a country's debt service payments to exports.

Deep discount bond   A low- or zero-coupon bond issued at a discount.

Deep market   The situation in which it is possible to trade large amounts of securities without significantly affecting the price.

Default   The act of breaching a covenant or warranty in a loan agreement.

Delivery risk   The risk, on a payment date when each party has an obligation to make a payment, that one party will make its required payment but the other party will fail to do so. In swaps, this risk is often avoided by providing for net payments. In a currency swap, delivery risk is increased because net payments are often not acceptable, since the parties want to receive actual payments in different currencies. Additional risk results from the fact that the payments may be due in different time zones so they cannot, even in theory be made simultaneously. On the maturity date of a currency swap the notional amounts are usually exchanged, thus further increasing the magnitude of the risk.

Delta   The change in the value of an option given a change in the value of the underlying security. The inverse of the delta gives the hedge ratio.

Delta hedge   A method of hedging risk exposure for option writers, involving buying or selling the underlying security in proportion to the delta. For example, when a call option writer is committed on an option with a delta of 0.5, it may effect a delta hedge by buying an amount of the underlying security equal to one-half of the amount of the underlying currency that must be delivered on exercise.

Demand deposit   Funds in a current account that may be withdrawn at any time without notice. Demand deposits may or may not be interest-bearing deposits.

Depreciation   *See* devaluation.

Deregulation   The removal or relaxation of the barriers or rules that have previously restricted the scope of securities trading and the nature of the operations undertaken by financial institutions.

Derivative products   A generic term for the range of traded instruments that have grown up around securities and currency and commodity trading.

Devaluation   A substantial decline in an exchange rate, usually effected in one go by government decree.

Direct investment   Purchase of a foreign financial asset in which substantial involvement in the management of the foreign asset is presumed. In practice, it is any holding that represents more than 10 per cent ownership of the foreign asset. Also termed foreign direct investment.

Direct quote   A rate of exchange quoted in terms of x units of home currency to 1 unit of foreign currency.

Dirty float   *See* managed float.

Discount house   A UK institution that acts as an intermediary between the Bank of England and the banking system. Discount houses participate in auctions of gilt-edged stock, enjoy lender-of-last-resort facilities with the Bank of England and discount bills.

Discounting   Where a sale is to be settled by a bill of exchange, the seller may surrender it to a financial institution in exchange for immediate payment of an amount less than the face value to reflect interest.

Discount market   UK institutions and dealers that trade bills of exchange.

Disintermediation   The process of bypassing normal financial intermediaries.

Double taxation   Taxes paid twice, once abroad where income is earned and a second time in the United Kingdom, if the company is UK owned. A principle of tax law is that double taxation should be avoided. If the UK company has already paid taxes abroad, it should only pay enough taxes in the United Kingdom to bring the overall rate up to the UK rate.

Drawdown   When a part of a borrowing facility is used.

Drop-lock bond   A bond or similar instrument which initially bears interest at a variable rate as if it were a floating rate obligation, but which will change to bear interest at a predetermined fixed rate in the event that a defined market rate falls to a stated level.

Dual currency bond   A security denominated in one currency with interest or principal or both paid in another at a pre-agreed rate.

Duration   A measure of a security's 'length' that considers the periodic coupon payments. It is the weighted average maturity of all payments of a security, coupons plus principal, where the weights are the discounted present values of the payments. Therefore, the duration is shorter than the stated term to maturity on all securities except for zero-coupon bonds, for which they are equal.

ECB   *See* European Central Bank

ECGD   *See* Export Credit Guarantee Department.

Economic and Monetary Union   A plan to create a single European market with a single currency, to be called the 'euro'. The detailed plan for the single currency was first formulated in the 1989 Delors report. It was refined in the Maastricht Treaty which came into effect on 1 November 1993.

Economic exposure   The extent to which the value of the firm will change due to an exchange rate change. This arises due to the effect of currency changes upon the parent currency present value of expected future cash flows to be generated by a company's operations.

ECU   *See* European currency unit.

Effective exchange rate   A rate measuring the overall nominal value of a currency over time in the foreign exchange market. It is calculated via a weighted average of bilateral exchange rates, using a weighting scheme that reflects the importance of each country's trade with the home country.

Efficient market   A market in which there is a sufficiently large number of buyers and sellers to eliminate an incentive for arbitrage transactions, and in which the trade-off between return and risk is fully reflected in prices.

Electronic funds transfer at point of sale (EFTPOS)   A system that allows funds to be moved automatically from a buyer's account to a seller's, the transfer taking place at the time of the transaction.

EMS   *See* European Monetary System.

EMU   *See* Economic and Monetary Union.

ERM   *See* exchange rate mechanism.

EURIBOR   European interbank-offered rate sponsored by the European Banking federation, the Association Cambiste Internationale, and the European Savings and Cooperative Organization as a reference rate for the euro zone. EURIBOR is to be set using quotations from a panel of banks from across the euro zone.

Euro   The currency unit that will replace the currencies of the (so far) eleven subscribing EU countries to EMU. The euro replaced the ECU on a one for one basis. So one euro equals one ECU.

Eurobanks   Financial intermediaries that bid for time deposits and make loans in currencies other than that of the country in which they are located.

Eurobond   A bond underwritten by an international syndicate of banks and marketed internationally in countries other than the country of the currency in which it is denominated. This issue is thus not subject to national restrictions.

Euroclear   One of the Eurobond market's two clearing systems. It is provided by Morgan Guaranty for over 100 banks and is based in Brussels.

Eurocommercial paper   A generic term used to describe Euronotes that are issued without being underwritten.

Eurocredit   The Eurocredit market is where highly rated borrowers can gain access to medium-term (one to fifteen years) bank lending. The loan can be denominated in one or several Eurocurrencies as can the interest and the principal. The interest rate is normally fixed as a margin over LIBOR.

Eurocurrency   A time deposit in a bank account located outside the banking regulations of the country which issues the currency.

Eurodollars   Dollars held in time deposits in banks outside the United States. These banks may be foreign owned or overseas branches of US banks. But see international banking facilities.

Euroland   The name for the eleven countries as a whole adopting EMU in full.

Euro LIBOR   London interbank-offered rate for euro.

Euromarkets   A collective term used to describe a series of offshore money and capital markets operated by international banks. They comprise Eurocurrency, Eurocredit and Eurobond markets. The centre of these markets is London, except for the Eurosterling market which is centred in Paris.

Euronote   The Euronote market is one in which borrowers raise money by the issue of short-term notes, generally with maturities of three and six months, that are negotiable like certificates of deposit. As one issue of notes matures, the borrower issues some more so that, while the holders of the debt change over time, the total amount outstanding can be maintained in the medium term. A group of commercial banks may ensure that the borrower in a particular issue will be able to place such notes by standing by ready to purchase the paper should the appetite of short-term investors wane.

Euronote facility   This allows borrowers to issue short-term notes through a variety of note distribution mechanisms, under the umbrella of a medium-term commitment from banks.

European Central Bank (ECB)   The European Central Bank, which determines monetary policy for the participating member states in EMU from 1 January 1999.

European currency unit (ECU)   A currency basket composed of specific quantities of the currencies of European Monetary System members. Following EMU, the euro replaced the ECU one for one.

European Monetary System (EMS)   A structure of agreements governing the exchange market activities of participating members of the European Union. Agreements require members closely to manage the exchange values of their currencies relative to those of other members.

European option   An option that can be exercised on the fixed expiration date only.

Euro zone   The name for the eleven countries as a whole adopting EMU in full.

Exchange controls   Restrictions imposed by the central bank or other government authorities on the convertibility of a currency, or on the movement of funds in that currency.

Exchange rate   The number of units of one currency expressed in terms of a unit of another currency.

Exchange rate mechanism (ERM)   A system of intervention in the foreign exchange markets designed to keep participating EU currencies within a narrow range versus the old ECU.

Exercise   To carry out a transaction, usually applied to the options market.

Exercise price   The exchange rate at which a foreign exchange option may be exercised.

Expiry or expiration date   The date upon which an option or warrant contract terminates.

Export–Import Bank (Eximbank)   US government agency established in 1934 to stimulate US foreign trade. The Eximbank supports commercial banks that are financing exports and provides direct financing, loan guarantees and insurance to exporters and foreign buyers of US goods. Similar to the ECGD in the United Kingdom.

Export Credit Guarantee Department (ECGD)   A UK agency dedicated to facilitating UK exports primarily through subsidized export financing and offering export credit insurance to UK exporters.

Factoring   A financing method in which the borrower assigns or sells its receivables as collateral to a firm, called a factor, which normally assumes responsibility for collection.

FASB 8   A US accounting standard in force from 1976 to 1981 that required companies to translate their foreign-affiliate financial statements using the temporal method. Foreign currency translation gains and losses were reported in the income statement as ordinary income.

FASB 52   *See* SFAS 52.

Federal funds   Money deposited with the Federal Reserve Bank, the central bank of the United States. This money is available on demand. Purchases of US treasury bills and most other money-market instruments in the domestic US money market may only be made with Federal funds.

Federal Reserve System (Fed)   The central banking system of the United States.

Filter rule   A rule for buying and selling securities based on the premise that, once a movement in a currency's exchange rate has exceeded a given percentage, it will continue to move in the same direction.

Finance vehicle   An operation involving the setting up of an offshore subsidiary for the purpose of issuing debt and lending the borrowings on to the parent or another subsidiary. The parent normally guarantees the debt issues.

Fisher effect   The hypothesis that the nominal interest rate differential between two countries should equal the expected inflation differential between those countries. Also called Fisher's closed hypothesis.

Fisher's closed hypothesis   *See* Fisher effect.

Fisher's open hypothesis   *See* international Fisher effect.

Fixed exchange rate system   A system in which the value of a country's currency is tied to a major currency, such as the US dollar, gold or the SDR. The term usually allows for fluctuations within a range of 1 or 2 per cent on either side of the fixed rate.

Fixed rate interest   When the interest on a security is calculated as a constant specified percentage of the principal and is paid at the end of stated periods until maturity.

Fixed rate payer   A party that makes swap payments calculated on the basis of a fixed rate.

Floating exchange rate system   A system in which the value of a currency relative to others is established by the forces of supply and demand in the foreign exchange markets. Strictly speaking, this implies that intervention by the government should be absent.

Floating or variable rate interest   Interest on an issue of securities which is not fixed for the life of the issue, but is periodically set according to a predetermined formula. The rate is usually set at a margin or spread in relation to a specified money-market rate, such as LIBOR.

Floating rate note (FRN)   A short-term floating interest rate security. The interest rate is pegged to LIBOR, and is adjusted semi-annually. These securities are attractive to investors during periods of rising interest when fixed rate bonds are subject to depreciation.

Floating rate payer   A party that makes swap payments calculated on the basis of a floating rate.

Floor   A minimum interest rate.

Flowback   The sale of shares, originally placed with overseas investors, back into the domestic market by those investors.

Foreign bond   A long-term security issued by a borrower in the capital market of a country other than the borrower's. Usually underwritten by a syndicate from one country and sold on that country's capital market, the bond is denominated in the currency of the country in which it is sold.

Foreign Credit Insurance Corporation   A private association of leading US insurance companies, affiliated to Eximbank, that provides short- and medium-term credit insurance to exporters, enabling them to obtain or offer better financing terms.

Foreign currency bond   An issue where the coupon is paid in a different currency from that of denomination of principal.

Foreign direct investment   *See* direct investment.

Foreign exchange   Currency other than the one used internally in a given country.

Foreign exchange trader   One who stands ready to buy and sell currencies out of inventory and expects to earn a profit for the costs and risks incurred.

Foreign tax credit   Home country tax credit given against domestic tax in respect of foreign taxes already paid on foreign-source earnings.

FOREX   Foreign exchange.

Forfaiting   The discounting at a fixed rate of interest of term bills of exchange without recourse to the drawer.

Forward contract   An agreement to exchange specified amounts of currencies of different countries at a specified contractual rate (the forward rate) at a specified future date.

Forward exchange market   The market involved with forward contracts for exchange of currency at some future date. The usual forward maturities are for one, two, three, six and twelve months, although contracts for other maturities may be negotiated.

Forward/forward swap   A pair of forward exchange contracts involving a forward purchase and a forward sale of a currency, simultaneously entered into, but for different maturities. Sometimes called a forward swap.

Forward margin   The difference between the forward rate and the spot rate of currency.

Forward option contract   *See* optional date forward contract.

Forward premium (or discount when negative)   The difference between the forward and spot rates, expressed either as an annualized percentage of the spot exchange rate or as so many cents or pfennigs. When forward currencies are worth more than the corresponding spot amount, the stronger currency is at a premium; the weaker currency is at a discount.

Forward rate   The rate quoted today for delivery at a fixed future date of a specified amount of one currency against another.

Forward swap *See* forward/forward swap.

FRA Forward rate agreement or future rate agreement. Essentially an over-the-counter version of a short interest rate future.

Franked income Income that has already been subject to corporation tax.

Free cash flow The net figure obtained by deducting from cash generated by operations or by an investment that cash which has been absorbed by operations or by the investment. Free cash flow disregards all cash flows to do with financing.

FRN *See* floating rate note.

Front-end fee The commission payable at the start of a financial arrangement.

FT-SE100 A real-time weighted arithmetic average of the equity market capitalizations of the 100 largest UK companies on the International Stock Exchange, London.

Functional currency The currency of the main economic environment in which a multinational operates. It is normally the currency of the environment in which the firm primarily generates and expends cash.

Fundamental analysis A branch of security analysis based upon attempts to value securities in accordance with estimated future profits and cash outturns.

Futures contract A standardized foreign exchange or interest rate contract written against the exchange clearing house for a fixed number of foreign currency or interest rate units and for delivery on a fixed date. Because of their standardization, futures contracts have a deep secondary market.

FX Foreign exchange.

G7 *See* Group of Seven.

G10 *See* Group of Ten.

Gamma The rate of change of an option's delta with respect to the underlying price.

Gilt or gilt-edged Fixed interest, sterling-denominated securities issued by the UK government. They derive their name from the gold edge on the original certificates, subsequently replaced by green certificates.

Glass–Steagall Act The US legislation which prevents commercial banks from owning, underwriting or dealing in corporate shares and bonds. There have been recent moves to amend this legal restriction.

Globalization The trend of bringing major financial markets across the world closer together through technological innovations in communications.

Gold standard A monetary agreement under which national currencies are backed by gold and gold is utilized for international payments.

Group of Seven Seven major industrial nations whose ministers meet on a periodic basis to discuss and agree on economic and political issues. It comprises Germany, France, Italy, the United Kingdom, Canada, Japan and the United States.

Group of Ten Ten major industrial countries – Germany, France, Belgium, the Netherlands, Italy, the United Kingdom, Sweden, Canada, Japan and the United States – that agreed in 1962 to stand ready to lend their currencies to the IMF under the General Arrangements to Borrow. The Group of Ten has taken the lead in subsequent changes in the international monetary system.

Hard A market is said to be hard if prices are rising.

Hard currency A strong, freely convertible currency. A strong currency is one that is not expected to devalue within the foreseeable future.

Head and shoulders A chart pattern which approximates to the shape of a person's head and shoulders, implying a fall in share prices.

Hedging The generation of a position in a given currency in the forward market or in the money market with the purpose of matching it against the net exposure position as evidenced by the balance sheet. The purpose of hedging is to make the net position for a particular currency at a given date equal to zero. The accounts included in the exposed balance sheet items are determined in accordance with accounting rules. *See also* covering.

Historical exchange rate The foreign currency exchange rate in effect on the date when an asset or liability was acquired.

Holding company A legally constituted company that may not carry on any trade or industry, but has a controlling interest in one or more subsidiary companies.

Hot money Speculative bank deposits that are moved around the international money market to take advantage of interest rate and currency movements.

IBFs *See* international banking facilities.

ICCH *See* International Commodities Clearing House.

Illiquid A security or a market that is lacking activity.

IMF *See* International Monetary Fund.

IMM *See* International Monetary Market.

Income statement exposure Arises as a result of the process of translating income statement items denominated in foreign currency into group income statements denominated in the parent currency.

Inconvertible currency A currency that cannot be converted into other currencies because of exchange control restrictions.

Indexing In some countries the practice of adjusting debt by some measure of inflation to preserve the purchasing power of the debt in constant monetary units. In Brazil, indexing is applied to wages, business accounts and debt.

Indirect quote A rate of exchange quoted in terms of x units of foreign currency per 1 unit of home currency.

Initial margin The amount of margin needed to set up a position in a futures market.

Instrument A generic term for securities, ranging from debt to negotiable deposits and bonds.

Inter-bank rate The rate at which banks offer and bid for funds as between each other.

Inter-company trade Trade flows between fellow affiliates of the same group of companies.

Interest arbitrage The international transfer of funds to a foreign centre, or the maintenance of funds in a foreign centre with the intention of benefiting from the higher yield on short-term investment in that centre. *See* covered interest arbitrage *and* uncovered interest arbitrage.

Interest rate differential The difference between short-term interest rates prevailing in two money centres at a given moment. Sometimes called interest rate spread.

Interest rate exposure The risk of loss arising from possible interest rate movements.

Interest rate futures Futures contracts which relate wholly to levels of interest rates.

Interest rate guarantee (IRG) An indemnity sold by a bank or other financial institution protecting the purchaser against the effect of future movements in interest rates.

Interest rate parity The condition that the interest differential should equal the forward differential between two currencies.

Interest rate spread *See* interest rate differential.

Interest rate swap An agreement between two parties in which each agrees to pay to the other an amount calculated by reference to interest that would accrue over a given period on the same notional amount but using a different rate of interest.

Intermediary company A vehicle company used as a conduit for the transfer of funds between fellow affiliate companies.

Intermediation The activity of a bank or similar financial institution in taking a position between the two parties to a transaction in such a way as to accept a credit or other commercial risk.

Internal exposure management technique Tactics related to the business of the multinational which do not use third-party contracts, but are aimed at reducing exposed positions or preventing exposure from arising or exploiting possible future exchange rate movements.

International Banking Act 1978   US legislation designed to remove many of the competitive advantages that foreign banks had over their domestic US counterparts. Thus the Federal Reserve Bank is now authorized to impose reserve requirements on foreign banks and there are restrictions on their ability to take deposits nationwide.

International banking facilities (IBFs)   Free monetary zones in the United States that can be established by certain corporations and by US branches and agencies of foreign banks. The IBFs accepting foreign deposits are exempted from reserve requirements and interest rate restrictions and can make loans to foreign borrowers. The impact of their operations is that some dollars deposited in time deposits in the United States effectively become Eurodollars.

International Commodities Clearing House (ICCH)   The central guarantee organization which clears contracts on LIFFE.

International Fisher effect   The hypothesis that the interest differential between two countries should reflect the future change in the spot rate. Also called Fisher's open hypothesis.

International Monetary Fund (IMF)   An international organization created by the Bretton Woods Agreement in 1944 to promote exchange rate stability. The objectives of the fund include supervising exchange market intervention by member countries, providing the finance needed by members to overcome short-term payments imbalances, and encouraging monetary co-operation and international trade among nations.

International Monetary Market (IMM)   A centralized market in Chicago where currency and financial futures contracts, among others, are traded.

In the money   A call option when its strike price is less than the value of the underlying security price. It also applies to a put option when the strike price is higher than the current price of the underlying security.

Intrinsic value   The difference between the strike price of an option and the current market price of the underlying security where the option has value.

Investment bank   A US term for a merchant bank.

Investment grade   A bond rated BAA or above by Moody's or BBB or above by Standard and Poor's.

Issue price   The price at which securities are sold on issue.

Issuing bank   The bank that issues a letter of credit. It is usually the buyer's bank.

Issuing house   An institution or agency that organizes the arrangements associated with an issue of securities.

Junk bond   A high-yield bond that is deemed to be below investment grade which became popular as a means of financing corporate takeovers and management buyouts.

Lag   To defer payment of a debt. A firm with a subsidiary in a country with a hard currency may encourage the subsidiary to lag its payments in order to take advantage of a possible revaluation of the hard currency or devaluation of the subsidiary's currency.

Law of comparative advantage   According to this hypothesis, a country will specialize in producing, and will export, those goods that it can produce relatively cheaply compared with foreign countries. It will import those goods that it can produce only at relatively high cost.

Lead   To prepay a debt. A company with a subsidiary in a country with a soft currency may encourage the subsidiary to prepay money due to countries with harder currency to avoid the adverse impact on cash flow of devaluation by the country with soft currency.

Lead manager   The main organizer of a new issue, such as a bank or broker, responsible for the overall co-ordination and distribution of an issue and the documents associated with it. The lead manager is also likely to appoint co-managers, to determine the initial and final terms of the issue, and to select the underwriters and the selling group.

Lender of last resort   A concession given to a select number of financial institutions whereby their central bank agrees to provide them with funds if they should get into difficulties.

Letter of awareness   A formal letter written to a lender, normally by a parent company, acknowledging its relationship with another group company and its awareness of a loan being made to that company. It is the weakest form of comfort letter. Such letters do not constitute a guarantee, but may nevertheless involve a significant moral commitment on the part of the writer.

Letter of comfort   A document that indicates one party's intention to try to ensure that another party complies with the terms of a financial transaction without guaranteeing performance in the event of default.

Letter of credit   A letter issued by a bank, usually at the request of an importer, indicating that the opening bank or another will honour drafts if they are accompanied by specified documents under specified conditions.

LIBOR   *See* London inter-bank offered rate.

LIFFE   *See* London International Financial Futures Exchange.

Liquidity   The ability of a business to pay its debts as they fall due.

Liquidity preference   A wish to hold near-liquid assets at the cost of a lower return.

Liquidity premium   Normally, the degree by which prices are reduced and interest rates raised because a fixed income security is not easily traded.

Listed security   A security that is quoted and traded on a major stock exchange.

LOC backed   Letter of credit backed. An issue, usually of commercial paper, backed by a bank letter of credit – effectively a bank guarantee.

Lock box system   A method of centralized collection of remittances operated by banks in the United States on behalf of their corporate customers in order to reduce the float time on inter-state money transfers.

Lombard rate   A German term for the rate of interest charged for a loan against the security of a pledged promissory note. Particularly used by the Bundesbank, which normally maintains its Lombard rate at about 0.5 per cent above its discount rate.

London inter-bank bid rate (LIBID)   The rate at which the major banks will bid to take deposits from each other for a given maturity, normally between overnight and five years.

London inter-bank mean rate (LIMEAN)   The average of LIBID and LIBOR.

London inter-bank offered rate (LIBOR)   The interest rate at which prime banks offer deposits to other prime banks in London. This rate is often used as the basis for pricing Eurodollar and other Eurocurrency loans. The lender and the borrower agree to a mark-up over LIBOR: the total of LIBOR plus the mark-up is the effective interest rate for the loan.

London International Financial Futures Exchange (LIFFE)   A centralized market in London where standardized currency, currency options and financial futures are traded.

Long   In the UK government bond market, a security with a maturity of more than fifteen years. In the US treasury bond market, a security with a thirty-year maturity.

Long position   Having greater inflows than outflows of a given currency, or more assets than liabilities in a given currency.

Long term   In bond markets, bonds with initial maturities of more than seven years. In terms of company balance sheets, debts with a maturity of more than one year.

Maintenance margin   The amount by which an initial margin for a future position must be topped up.

Managed float   A floating exchange rate system in which some government intervention takes place. Also called a dirty float.

Marginal tax rate   The rate of tax due on additional amounts of taxable income.

Margin call   In futures contracts, a requirement to provide more maintenance margin.

Marker rate   A generic term for a base interest rate defined in a loan agreement to which the spread is added in order to establish the interest rate payable on a variable rate loan.

Mark to market   The procedure for revaluing a security, swap, commodity or futures contract according to current market prices.

Matching   A process whereby a firm balances its long positions in a given currency (assets, revenues or cash inflows) with its offsetting short positions (liabilities, expenses or cash outflows). The remaining (unmatched) position is the net exposure in that currency.

Material adverse change   The clause in a loan agreement or similar contract under which the loan will become repayable in the event that there should be a serious (or material) deterioration in the borrower's credit standing. The clause is used by banks as a substitute where they are not able to negotiate a stronger covenant such as a borrowings limitation clause or a ratio covenant. The difficulty with such clauses lies in the definition of materiality. The normal wording in the loan agreement gives no indication of how to interpret the clause. Attempts to define materiality are almost certain to have the effect of changing the clause into a ratio covenant.

Maturity or final maturity   The date when the principal or nominal value becomes payable to the holder of a loan or bond.

Maturity (or settlement) date   The date on which a contract is due to be settled.

Maturity structure   The expression used to describe the borrower's repayment obligation. The term may be used either in relation to a specific loan or to describe the composite repayment obligation arising from a company's total portfolio obligations.

Medium term   In bond markets, bonds with initial maturities of between three and seven years. In money markets, maturities of more than one year.

Merchant bank   A specialist bank that carries on a bank business and also acts as an adviser to companies, including assisting on flotations of new issues of shares and bonds.

Middle price   The average of a bid and an offer price.

Mismatch   A situation where assets and liabilities in a currency do not balance in either size or maturity.

Momentum analysis   *See* chartism.

Monetary/non-monetary method   A foreign currency translation method. Non-monetary assets and liabilities are translated at their historical exchange rates, while monetary items are translated at current exchange rates.

Monetary policy   Those instruments, such as interest rates and term controls, at the disposal of government for influencing the timing, availability and cost of money and credit in an economy.

Money market   Financial institutions and dealers in money and credit.

Money market basis   The method used to compute accrued interest on CDs and FRNs. The rate is multiplied by the number of days elapsed and divided by the number of days in the accounting year.

Moratorium   Authorization of suspension of payments by a debtor for a stated time.

Multilateral netting   A process where affiliates within multinationals offset their debtor and creditor positions with the rest of the group as a whole, so that a single net inter-company receipt or payment is made each period to settle indebtedness.

National Association of Securities Dealers Automated Quotations (NASDAQ)   A US automated securities price collection and dissemination service for over-the-counter securities traders.

Negatively sloping yield curve   A yield curve where interest rates in the shorter dates are above those in the longer. This occurs when interest rates are expected to fall.

Negative pledge   The covenant in a loan agreement by which a borrower undertakes that no secured borrowings will be made during the life of the loan, or ensures that the loan is secured equally and rateably with any new secured borrowings.

Negotiable instrument Any financial instrument such as bills of exchange, promissory notes, cheques, bank notes, CDs, share warrants, bearer shares or bearer bonds, the title of which passes by mere delivery, without notice to the party liable on the instrument, and in which the transferee in good faith and for a consideration of value acquires an indefeasible title against the whole world.

Net position The overall position given by the sum of long and short positions.

Netting A procedure by which affiliates within a multinational group net out inter-company trade or financial flows and only pass the net amount due.

Nominal exchange rate The actual exchange rate.

Non-callable An issue of securities where the holders cannot redeem the security before its stated maturity date.

Non-performing loan A bank loan that has stopped earning interest and where the borrower is likely to default on the principal.

Note *See* promissory note.

Notional amount The amount (in an interest rate swap, forward rate agreement, cap or floor) or each of the amounts (in a currency swap) to which interest rates are applied in order to calculate periodic payment obligations.

OECD *See* Organization for Economic Co-operation and Development.

Off-balance sheet finance Any form of finance that does not result in a corresponding liability appearing on the company's published balance sheet. Obviously, on double-entry principles the asset being financed cannot appear either. The impact of such financing methods is to show the company's gearing at a lower level than it usually is. Lenders are rarely deceived by such transparent devices.

Offer price *See* ask price.

Official reserves Holdings of gold and foreign currencies by the official monetary institutions of a country.

Offshore finance subsidiary A subsidiary company incorporated overseas, usually in a tax-haven country, whose function is to issue securities abroad for use in either the parent's domestic or foreign business.

Open contract A futures contract that has been bought or sold without the deal having been completed or offset by subsequent sale, purchase, actual delivery or receipt of the underlying financial instrument.

Open interest Contracts not yet offset by futures contracts or fulfilled by delivery.

Open outcry A kind of auction system used by futures markets under which all bids and offers are made openly by public, competitive outcry and hand signals.

Open position The difference between the amount of a foreign currency owned or receivable and the total of the same currency payable under definite contracts. If one exceeds the other, there is an open position. If the amount held and receivable exceeds the amount payable, there is said to be a long position; if the amount held or receivable is less than the amount payable, it constitutes a short position.

Opportunity cost The rate of return on the best alternative investment available, or the highest return that will not be earned if funds are invested in a particular project or security.

Option A contract providing the holder with the right but not the obligation either to buy from or sell to the issuer a given number of securities at a fixed price at or over a specified time.

Optional date forward contract A forward exchange contract in which the rate is fixed but the maturity is open, within a specified range of dates. Sometimes called a forward option contract or an option forward contract.

Option forward contract *See* optional date forward contract.

Option premium   The price paid to the seller of a foreign exchange option for the rights involved.

Option swap   A right to enter into a swap on or before a particular date. Also called a swaption.

Organization for Economic Co-operation and Development (OECD)   An organization that provides for inter-governmental discussion in the fields of economic and social policy. It collects and publishes data and makes short-term economic forecasts about its member countries.

Out-of-the-money   A call option when its strike price is greater than the current price of the underlying security. It also applies to a put option when its strike price is less than the current price of the underlying security. In other words the option has no intrinsic value.

Outright forward rate   The forward rate expressed in pounds or dollars per currency unit, or vice versa.

Overshooting   As overvalued but applied to the value of a particular currency.

Parent country   The country in which the parent company of a multinational group is located.

Parent currency   The currency of the parent company of a multinational group.

***Pari passu* clause**   The covenant in a loan agreement by which a borrower binds itself to ensure that the loan will rank equally with its other defined debts.

Parity   The official rate of exchange between two currencies.

Parity grid   The matrix of bilateral par values for the currencies of members of the European Monetary System. This grid establishes the intervention prices between which member governments are obliged to maintain the exchange value of their currency in terms of every other group currency.

Par value   Under the Bretton Woods fixed exchange rate system, the par value of a currency was that value measured in terms of gold or the US dollar that was maintained at a fixed rate relative to gold or the dollar.

Pip   The most junior digit in a currency quotation.

Plain vanilla   An issue of securities that lacks any special features.

Point and figure chart   A type of chart in the form of Xs and 0s which represent price changes independent of time.

Pooling   The transfer of excess affiliate cash into a central account – the pool – usually located in a low-tax country, where all corporate funds are managed by corporate staff.

Portfolio investment   The purchase of a foreign financial asset with the purpose of deriving returns from the security without intervening in the management of the foreign operation.

Positively sloping yield curve   A yield curve where interest rates in the shorter periods are below those in the longer. This is the normal form of yield curve.

PPP   *See* purchasing power parity.

Premium   The amount by which a currency is more expensive in the forward market relative to the spot price.

Prime rate   A US banking term to indicate the rate at which banks are prepared to lend to borrowers of the highest standing.

Private placement   A type of placement where new securities are sold by the lead manager to a limited number of investors, usually its own clients, rather than being offered to a wide public.

Project finance   A term financing arrangement, usually on a limited recourse basis, under which funds are provided for a specified project by banks against the security of the project cash flows.

Promissory note   An unconditional promise in writing signed by one party engaging to pay on demand or at a fixed or determinable time a sum certain in money to or to the order of a specified person or to the bearer, but not legally binding until delivered to the payee or bearer.

Prospectus   A document that details the nature, price and timing of an issue of securities to be made to a wide public. It is usually prepared by the issuer's adviser or sponsor and contains an historical record of earnings performance and, possibly, some form of future profit.

Purchasing power parity (PPP)   The hypothesis that, over time, the difference between the inflation rates in two countries tends to equal the rate of change of the exchange rate between the currencies of the countries concerned.

Put option   The right, but not the obligation, to sell an amount of foreign exchange at a specified price within a specified time.

Puttable   A security where there is a provision to redeem prior to maturity at the discretion of the lender.

Random walk   A term implying that there is no discernible pattern of travel. The last step, or even all the previous steps, cannot be used to predict either the size or the direction of the next step.

Ratio covenant   An undertaking given in a loan agreement by the borrower that it will operate its business within a financial constraint specified in the form of balance or other financial ratios.

Rational expectations   A concept implying that the market forms expectations in a way that is consistent with the actual economic structure of the market. The prices that result in the market place represent an average of all investors expectations.

Real effective exchange rate   A rate calculated by dividing the home country's nominal effective exchange rate by an index of the ratio of average foreign prices to home prices. If purchasing power parity is holding, the real effective exchange rate should remain constant.

Real exchange rate   The value of a currency in terms of real purchasing power. It is calculated by comparing the price of a hypothetical market basket of goods in two different countries, translated into the same currency at the prevailing exchange rate. It is useful in measuring the price competitiveness of domestic goods in international markets.

Real return   The rate of return of an asset after adjusting for inflation.

Recourse   A source of help should, for example, a bill be dishonoured at maturity. The holder would have the right of recourse against any of the other parties to the bill, unless expressly negated.

Redemption   The purchase and cancellation of outstanding securities through a cash payment to the holder.

Registered security   A security where ownership is recorded by a registrar in the name of the holder or a nominee. Title can be transferred only with the endorsement of the registered holder.

Regulation Q   A US regulation, now phased out, of the Federal Reserve system that established a ceiling on interest rates on time deposits. Banks were forbidden to pay interest on deposits with maturities of less than 30 days. Regulations played a significant role in the original growth of the Eurodollar market.

Reinvoicing vehicle   A vehicle company that performs group exposure or liquidity management functions. Goods exported from or imported to an associated company are shipped direct to the third party or to the associate as the case may be, but invoicing is performed via the reinvoicing vehicle. Title to the goods and payment are thus channelled through the vehicle.

Rescheduling   The renegotiation of the terms of an existing debt obligation, often in the area of sovereign debt.

Reserve requirements or reserve asset ratio   The percentage of different types of deposit or eligible asset which member banks must hold with their central bank.

Resistance level   A chartism term denoting a level of prices at which a movement has historically faltered or stabilized.

Revaluation   An increase in the spot value of a currency (UK parlance). A change – either an increase or a decrease – in the spot value of a currency (US parlance).

Revolver   *See* revolving credit facility.

Revolving credit facility   A loan that allows the borrower to draw down and repay at its discretion for a specified period. Sometimes called a revolver.

Roll over   When a forward exchange contract is about to mature a new forward contract is entered into to extend the original maturity date.

Round tripping   An opportunity to undertake arbitrage which arises when a bank's customer can draw from overdraft facilities and deposit the proceeds in the money markets at rates which exceed the cost of the overdraft.

Same-day funds   Funds with good value at the end of the business day on which the order to transfer the funds is made.

Samurai bond   A yen-denominated bond issue made in the Japanese market by a foreign (non-Japanese) issuer.

SDR   *See* special drawings right.

Second Amendment   This amendment to the Articles of Agreement of the International Monetary Fund, ratified in 1978, allows members more flexibility in the management of exchange rates than under the Bretton Woods system. It also increases the supervisory responsibilities of the IMF and makes the special drawing rights more attractive as reserve assets.

Secondary market   The market in which securities are traded after issue. Also called the 'after-market'.

Securitization   The process of packaging assets and liabilities such that they can be sold and traded in markets. This allows the financial institution that originates the deal – a mortgage, a car loan, etc. – to sell the asset to other investors, thus freeing its capital for alternative uses.

Self-financing loan or self-liquidating loan   A loan that is to be used to acquire assets that will produce sufficient return to meet the interest obligations and repay the principal.

Settlement date   The day upon which payment is effected and securities are delivered.

SFAS 52   A US accounting standard in force from December 1981, concerning translation of foreign currency financial statements. Results must be measured in the functional currency of the foreign entity, except in the case of high-inflation countries. Translation is done using the all-current method, with transaction losses showing up on the group's income statement and translation losses on the group's balance sheet.

Shallow discount bond   An expression used for UK tax purposes to refer to a bond issued in the primary market at a price exceeding 90 per cent of its face value.

Short   A UK government bond with a maturity of less than five years.

Short dates   A dealing term meaning periods up to one week, but sometimes used to refer to periods up to a month.

Short position   A situation in which the anticipated outflows of a currency exceed the anticipated inflows of that currency over a period of time. Also refers to a net liability, net expense or net cash outflow position in a currency.

Short term   In bond markets, bonds with initial maturities of less than two years. In company balance sheets, debt with a remaining maturity of less than a year.

Sight deposits   Current accounts, overnight deposits and money at call. Deposits with longer maturities are term deposits.

Sight draft   A bill of exchange that is due when presented.

Sinking fund   An amount in cash or securities periodically set aside by a borrower to redeem all or part of its long-term debt issues.

Smithsonian Agreement   This began the first stage of the multilateral exchange rate realignments that followed the collapse of the Bretton Woods system of international monetary relations.

Snake   The European system of exchange rate setting created in April 1972 and superseded in 1979 by the European Monetary System.

Society for Worldwide Inter-bank Financial Transfers (SWIFT)   A standardized electronic message transfer service designed to send and confirm instructions concerning funds transfers associated with international payments in the major industrial countries.

Soft   A market is said to be soft if prices are declining. A currency may also be described as soft if there is excess supply and an expectation that its value will fall in relation to other currencies.

Soft currency   A weak currency whose convertibility is, or is expected to become, restricted.

Sovereign debt   The loans outstanding of individual countries, usually negotiated by their respective governments.

Sovereign risk   (a) The risk of government default on a loan made or guaranteed by it. (b) The risk that the country of origin of the currency being bought or sold will impose foreign exchange regulations that will reduce the value of the contract.

Special drawing rights (SDRs)   A form of international reserve asset created and ratified by the IMF in 1969. SDRs have their value based on a weighted average of five widely used currencies.

Specific risk   Another name for unsystematic risk.

Spot/forward swaps   The simultaneous spot purchase or sale of a currency and a countering sale or purchase of the same currency in the forward market.

Spot market   The currency market for immediate delivery, although, in the spot market, delivery is usually two working days after the transaction date.

Spot rate   The price at which foreign exchange can be bought or sold for immediate delivery. In practice spot deals are settled two working days after the transaction date.

Spread   The difference between bid and ask prices in a price quote. Also the amount of interest, expressed in percentage terms or basis points, over the marker rate which the borrower must pay on a short-term or variable rate loan.

Standard deviation   The positive square root of the variance. This is the standard statistical measure of the spread of a sample.

Stop loss   An order to sell a financial instrument when its price falls to a specified level.

Straight bond   A bond issued in the primary market which carries no equity or other incentive to attract the investor, the only reward being an annual or semi-annual interest coupon.

Strike price   The price at which an option may be exercised.

Subordinated security   An issue that ranks below other debt in right of repayment on liquidation.

Sub-underwriter   A member of a new issue syndicate who agrees to buy a certain proportion of the issue from the managers should the issue be undersubscribed. They receive an underwriting fee and a selling concession on the principal amount of the securities for which they may subscribe.

Supplier credit   One of the two main techniques by which the ECGD supports UK companies in winning and financing projects overseas, where credit terms form an integral part of the commercial contract between supplier and customer. Under such an arrangement, that part of the contract price for which the supplier is at risk is secured by promissory notes issued by the customer and guaranteed unconditionally by the ECGD.

Support level   A term used in chartist analysis to describe when a security or commodity price has repeatedly fallen to a certain price, but has then recovered.

Swap   Where a given currency is simultaneously purchased and sold, but the maturity for each of the transactions is different. The term is also used, generically, to cover interest rate swaps and currency swaps.

Swap rate   The difference between spot and forward rates expressed in points – that is, in terms of 0.0001 of a currency unit.

Syndicated loan   A loan by a group of banks, normally on a floating rate basis, at a predetermined margin over short-term interest rates.

Synthetic position   An option or futures position that has the same risk–return characteristics as another position.

Systematic risk   The volatility of rates of return on stocks or portfolios in relation to changes in rates of return on the whole market. Also known as market risk, it stems from such non-diversifiable factors as war, inflation, recessions and high interest rates. These factors affect all firms simultaneously; hence this type of risk cannot be eliminated by diversification.

TARGET   Trans-European Automated Real-time Gross settlement Express Transfer system, a payment system linking together one real-time gross settlement system in each participating member state in EMU to enable same-day, cross-border transfers throughout the euro zone. TARGET is open 7am–6pm Central European Time, each TARGET operating day.

Tax break   A generic term for specific financial arrangements or instruments that attract an exemption from or reduced liability to different forms of taxation.

Tax haven   A country that imposes little or no tax on the profits from transactions carried on or routed through that country, especially income from dividends and interest.

Tax sparing   A Euromarket term (mainly) for a debt that is covered by a double exemption from withholding tax, enabling lenders to offer narrow margins over the reference rate.

Technical analysis   A branch of market analysis based upon the study of price movements and the forecasting of future movements from past movements.

Temporal method   A foreign currency translation method. The translation rate adopted preserves the accounting principles used to value assets and liabilities in the original financial statements. Thus items stated at historic cost are translated at historic exchange rates: current exchange rates are used for items stated at replacement cost, market value or expected future value.

Tender   A method of issuing securities where allotment takes place according to the higher bids received.

Term deposits   Deposits, including certificates of deposit, for terms longer than sight deposits. *See* sight deposits.

Term loan or credit   A bank advance that is for a specified period of time.

Term structure   An explanation of the framework for establishing money-market interest rates based upon cash flows and maturity or holding periods.

Thin   A market with low trading volumes and poor liquidity.

Time value   The value of an option taken as the difference between the premium and the intrinsic value. Time value decreases as the expiry date comes nearer.

Tombstone   An advertisement placed by banks shortly after a new Eurobond issue to record their part in its management and sale.

Traded option   An option that is itself tradable on a securities market.

Transaction date   In foreign exchange markets the date on which a foreign exchange contract is agreed.

Transaction exposure   The extent to which a given exchange rate change will affect the value of transactions denominated in foreign currency.

Transfer price The price at which one affiliate in a group of companies sells goods or services to another affiliated unit.

Translation exposure *See* accounting exposure.

Treasury bill or T-bill A UK or US government short-term debt instrument normally issued at a discount.

Treasury note A US government coupon security with a maturity of not less than one year and not more than ten years.

Triangulation When converting from one national currency unit within EMU to another, the conversion must be done via the euro. This method is known as triangulation.

Turn The difference between the bid and offer prices quoted by an individual market-maker.

Uncovered interest arbitrage A process of borrowing a currency and converting it to a second currency where it is invested. The arbitrageur aims to earn profit from the relative interest rates received and paid. Unlike covered interest arbitrage, the currency in which the arbitrageur invests is not sold forward; instead the arbitrageur waits until the maturity of the investment and then sells the second currency spot for the original currency. Also, unlike covered interest arbitrage, the uncovered version is risky.

Undated A security which has no definite maturity date, but may be redeemed at the discretion of the issuer.

Underlying asset The asset on which an option or warrant is based.

Underlying security The security on which an option or futures contract is written.

Undervalued A security, rather than a market, whose price is considered to be lower than that indicated by fundamentals.

Underwrite Undertake to buy unsubscribed securities on a given date at a particular price, thus guaranteeing the full proceeds to the borrower.

Underwriting agreement This states the obligations of each of the sub-underwriters to the managers of a security issue.

Underwriting group Bankers who receive a commission for underwriting a new issue.

Unsecured Bonds that entitle the holder to no recourse to specific assets in the case of default.

Unsystematic risk That part of a security's risk associated with random events which do not affect the economy as a whole. Also known as specific risk, this refers to such things as strikes, successful and unsuccessful marketing programmes, fire and other events that are unique to a particular firm. Such unsystematic events can be eliminated by portfolio diversification.

Value at risk (VAR) A single number estimate of how much a company can lose due to the price volatility of the instrument it holds, for example, a fixed rate bond or an unhedged currency payable/receivable. More precisely, it defines the likelihood of potential loss not exceeding a particular level, given certain assumptions.

Value date The date on which payment is made to settle a deal. A spot foreign exchange deal on Wednesday will be settled on Friday, so Friday is the value date.

VAR *See* value at risk.

Variance of the probability distribution The expected value of squared deviation from the expected return.

Variation margin Generally, the funds required to bring the equity in an account back up to the initial margin level. Used in the futures market where margin trading is permitted.

Vendor placing The sale of equity which has been issued in settlement of the cost of an acquisition of assets, with the objective of ensuring that the vendor of the assets so acquired receives cash instead of paper.

Volatility The variability of movements in a security's price.

Warehousing   Entering into a swap without having entered into a matching swap, but with the expectation of hedging either through a matched swap or a portfolio of swaps.

Warrant   A negotiable instrument granting the holder an option to subscribe for new equity in the issuing company at a predetermined price.

Window   A time during which certain deals can occur because of particular market conditions. For example, it may be possible to issue certain types of security because of ruling investor sentiment that is not expected to last.

Withholding tax   A tax collected by the source originating the income as opposed to one paid by the recipient of the income after the funds are received. Thus a withholding tax on interest payments to foreigners means that the tax proceeds are deducted from the interest payment made to the lender and are collected by the borrower on behalf of the tax authorities.

Yankee bond   A US dollar-denominated bond issue made in the US market by a foreign (non-US) borrower.

Yield   The amount of interest payments as a percentage of the amount lent or borrowed.

Yield curve   A diagrammatic representation of interest rates prevailing on a class of securities that are alike in every respect other than term to maturity. A yield curve may slope upwards or downwards or be flat.

Yield to maturity   That discount rate which equates the sum of the present value of the future stream of income payments and the present value of the principal repayment at maturity with the market value of a security.

Zero-coupon bond   A bond that bears no annual interest charge but is, instead, sold at such a discount as will result in the rolled-up interest cost being settled by its redemption at par.

Zero-coupon swap   A swap in which a fixed rate payer makes a single payment, on the maturity date, and the other party makes payments periodically.

References

Abdullah, F.A. (1987), *Financial Management for the Multinational Firm*, Prentice Hall, Englewood Cliffs, NJ.

Abuaf, N. (1988), 'The nature and management of foreign exchange risk', *Midland Corporate Finance Journal*, **4** (3) in J.M. Stern and D.H. Chew Jr (eds) (1988), *New Developments in International Finance*, Basil Blackwell, Oxford.

Abuaf, N. and Jorion, P. (1990), 'Purchasing power parity in the long run', *Journal of Finance*, **45** (1), 157–174.

Adler, M. (1982), 'Translation methods and operational foreign exchange risk management', in G. Bergendahl (ed.), *International Financial Management*, Norstedts, Stockholm.

Adler, M. and Dumas, B. (1977a), 'The microeconomics of the firm in an open economy', *American Economic Review*, **67** (1), 180–189.

Adler, M. and Dumas, B. (1977b), 'Default risk and the demand for forward exchange', in H. Levy and M. Sarnat (eds), *Financial Decision Making under Uncertainty*, Academic Press, London.

Adler, M. and Lehmann, B. (1983), 'Deviations from purchasing power parity in the long run', *Journal of Finance*, **38** (5), 1471–1487.

Aggarwal, R. (1977), 'Multinationality and stock market valuation', *Financial Review*, Summer, 45–46.

Agmon, T. and Lessard, D.R. (1977), 'Investor recognition of corporate international diversification', *Journal of Finance*, **32**, 1049–1056.

Alexander, D. and Nobes, C. (1994), *A European Introduction to Financial Accounting*, Prentice Hall, Hemel Hempstead.

Alexander, G.J., Eun, C.S. and Janakiramanan, S. (1988), 'International listings and stock returns: some empirical evidence', *Journal of Financial and Quantitative Analysis*, **23** (2), 135–151.

Aliber, R.Z. (1975a), *Monetary Interdependence under Fixed and Floating Exchange Rates*, Mimeo, University of Chicago, IL.

Aliber, R.Z. (1975b), *The Short Guide to International Corporate Finance*, Mimeo, University of Chicago, IL.

Aliber, R.Z. (1979), *Exchange Risk and Corporate International Finance*, Wiley, New York.

Aliber, R.Z. (1983), *The International Money Game*, 4th edition, Macmillan, London.

Aliber, R.Z. and Stickney, C.P. (1975), 'Accounting measures of foreign exchange exposure: the long and short of it', *The Accounting Review*, **50** (1), 44–57.

Allen, H.L. and Taylor, M.P. (1989), 'Charts and fundamentals in the foreign exchange market', *Bank of England Discussion Papers*, **40**.

Allyannis, G. and Ofek, E. (2001), 'Exchange rate exposure, hedging, and the use of foreign currency derivatives', *Journal of International Money and Finance*, **20**, 273–296.

Almeida, A., Goodhart, C. and Payne, R. (1998), 'The effects of macroeconomic news on high frequency exchange rate behaviour', *Journal of Financial and Quantitative Analysis*, **33** (3), 383–408.

Armington, P.J. (1977), *Floating Exchange Rates: The Balance of Payments and the Global Equilibrium of Asset Markets*, Forex Research Papers, No. 3, July, 3–12.

Artis, M. and Taylor, M.P. (1990), 'International financial stability and the regulation of capital flows', in G. Bird (ed.), *The International Financial Regime*, Surrey University, Guildford.

Bailey, W. and Stulz, R.M. (1990), 'Benefits of international diversification: the case of Pacific basis stock markets', *Journal of Portfolio Management*, **16** (4), 57–61.

Baillie, R.T., Lippens, R.E. and McMahon, P.C. (1983), 'Testing rational expectations and efficiency in the foreign exchange market', *Econometrica*, **53** (3), 553–563.

Baillie, R.T. and McMahon, P.C. (1989), *The Foreign Exchange Market: Theory and Econometric Research*, Cambridge University Press, Cambridge.

Bain, J.S. (1956), *Barriers to New Competition*, Harvard University Press, Boston, MA.

Baker, J.C. and Beardsley, L.J. (1973), 'Multinational companies: use of risk evaluation and profit measurement for capital budgeting decisions', *Journal of Business Finance*, **5** (1), 38–43.

Balassa, B. (1964), 'The purchasing power doctrine: a reappraisal', *Journal of Political Economy*, **72**, 584–596.

Barca, F. (1995), 'On corporate governance in Italy: issues, facts and agenda', paper presented at OECD Conference on the Influence of Corporate Governance and Financing Structures on Economic Performance.

Barnett, G. and Rosenberg, M. (1983), 'International diversification in bonds', *Prudential International Fixed Income Investment Strategy*, **2**.

Barone-Adesi, G. and Whaley, R. (1987), 'Efficient analytic approximation of American option values', *Journal of Finance*, June, 301–320.

Bavishi, V.B. (1981), 'Capital budgeting practices at multinationals', *Management Accounting*, August, 32–35.

Beckman, R.C. (1969), *Share Price Analysis*, Investors Bulletin, London.

Belk, P.A. and Glaum, M. (1990), 'The management of foreign exchange risk in the UK multinationals: an empirical investigation', *Accounting and Business Research*, **21** (81), 3–11.

Bell, S. and Kettell, B. (1983), *Foreign Exchange Handbook*, Graham & Trotman, London.

Berglöf, E. (1988), *Owners and Their Control over Corporations – A Comparison of Six Financial Systems*, Ministry of Industry, Stockholm.

Berkman, H. and Bradbury, M.E. (1996), 'Empirical evidence on the corporate use of derivatives', *Financial Management*, Summer, **25**, 5–13.

Bilik, E. (1982), *Forecasting Accuracy of Forward Exchange Rates and the Efficiency of the Market for Foreign Exchange: An Enquiry into the Performance of the Foreign Exchange Forecasting Industry*, unpublished PhD Dissertation, Ohio State University, OH.

Bilkey, W. and Tesar, G. (1977), 'The export behaviour of smaller Wisconsin manufacturing firms', *Journal of International Business Studies*, **8** (1), 93–98.

Bilson, J.F.O. (1975), 'Rational expectations and the exchange rate: theory and estimation', Paper presented on 30 December to the American Economic Association, Dallas, TX.

Bilson, J.F.O. (1979), 'Leading indicators of currency devaluation', *Columbia Journal of World Business*, **14** (4), 62–76.

Bilson, J.F.O. (1981), 'The speculative efficiency hypothesis', *Journal of Business*, **54** (3), 435–451.

Black, F. (1976), 'The pricing of commodity contracts', *Journal of Financial Economics*, **3**, 167–179.

Black, F. and Scholes, M. (1972), 'The valuation of option contracts and a test of market efficiency', *Journal of Finance*, **27**, 399–418.

Black, F. and Scholes, M. (1973), 'The pricing of options and corporate liabilities', *Journal of Political Economy*, **81** (3), 637–659.

Blake, D., Beenstock, M. and Brasse, V. (1986), 'The performance of UK exchange rate forecasters', *Economic Journal*, **96**, 986–999.

Blume, M.E. (1974), 'Unbiased estimators of long-run expected rates of return', *Journal of the American Statistical Association*, **69** (346), 634–638.

Bodurtha, J.N. and Courtadon, G.R. (1987), 'Tests of an American option pricing model on the foreign currency options market', *Journal of Financial and Quantitative Analysis*, **22**, June, 153–168.

Bonbright, J.C. (1937), *The Valuation of Property*, McGraw-Hill, New York.

Booth, J.R., Smith, R.L. and Stolz, R.W. (1984), 'The use of interest futures by financial institutions', *Journal of Bank Research*, Spring, 15–20.

Boothe, P. and Longworth, D. (1986), 'Foreign exchange market efficiency tests: implications of recent empirical findings', *Journal of International Money and Finance*, **5**, 135–152.

Bosner-Neal, C. Roley, V.V. and Sellon, G.H. Jr. (1998), 'Monetary policy actions, intervention and exchange rates: a re-examination of the empirical relationships using federal funds rate target data', *Journal of Business*, April, 147–177.

Branson, W.H. (1968), *Financial Capital Flows in the US Balance of Payments*, New-Holland, Amsterdam.

Brasse, U. (1983), 'The inaccuracy of exchange rate forecasting devices in the UK', *City University Business School Economic Review*, City University, London.

Brealey, R. and Myers, S. (1996), *Principles of Corporate Finance*, 5th edition, McGraw-Hill, New York.

Brigham, E.F. and Gapenski, L.C. (1997), *Financial Management: Theory and Practice*, 8th edition, Dryden Press, Forth Worth, TX.

Brouthers, L.E. and Werner, S. (1990), 'Are the Japanese good competitors?', *Columbia Journal of World Business*, **25** (3), 5–11.

Buckley, A. (1992), *Multinational Finance*, 2nd edition, Prentice Hall, London.

Buckley, A. (1996), *International Capital Budgeting*, Prentice Hall, London.

Buckley, A., Buckley, P., Langevin, P. and Tse, K. (1996), 'The financial analysis of foreign investment decisions by large UK-based companies', *European Journal of Finance*, **2** (2), 181–206.

Buckley, A., Tse, K., Rijken, H. and Eijgenhuijsen, H. (2002), 'Stock market valuation with real options: lessons from Netscape', *European Management Journal*, **20** (5), 512–526.

Buckley, P.J. (1983), 'New theories of international business: some unresolved issues', in M.C. Casson (ed.), *The Growth of International Business*, Allen & Unwin, London.

Buckley, P.J. and Casson, M. (1976), *The Future of the Multinational Enterprise*, Macmillan, London.

Buckley, P.J. and Casson, M. (1979), 'A theory of international operations', in M. Ghertman and J. Leontiades (eds), *European Research in International Business*, North-Holland, London.

Business International (1977), 'Evaluating foreign operations: the appropriate rates for comparing results with budgets', *Money Report*, 20 May, 154.

Business International (1979), 'Policies or MNCs on debt/equity mix', *Money Report*, 21 September, 319–320.

Cantor, R. and Packer, F. (1994), 'The credit rating industry', *Federal Reserve Bank of New York Quarterly Review*, **19** (2), 1–26.

Capaul, C., Rowley, I. and Sharpe, W.F. (1993), 'International value and growth stock returns', *Financial Analysts Journal*, **49** (1), 27–41.

Carsberg, B. (1983), 'FASB 52: Measuring the performance of foreign operations', *Midland Corporate Finance Journal*, **1** (2); in J.M. Stern and D.H. Chew Jr (eds) (1988), *New Developments in International Finance*, Basil Blackwell, New York and Oxford.

Cassal, G. (1921), *The World's Monetary Problems*, Constable, London.

Casson, M.C. (1982), 'Transaction costs and the theory of the multinational enterprise', in A.M. Rugman (ed.), *New Theories of the Multinational Enterprise*, St Martin's Press, New York.

Caves, D.W. and Feige, E.F. (1980), 'Efficient foreign exchange markets and the monetary approach to exchange rate determination', *American Economic Review*, 70, 120–134.

Caves, R.E. (1982), *Multinational Enterprise and Economic Analysis*, Cambridge University Press, New York.

Cavusgil, S.T. (1982), 'Some observations on the relevance of critical variables for internationalisation stages', in M.R. Czinkota and G. Tesar (eds), *Export Management: an International Context*, Praeger, New York.

Cavusgil, S.T. and Nevin, J.R. (1980), 'A conceptualization of the initial involvement in international marketing', in C.W. Lamb Jr and P.M. Dunne (eds), *Theoretical Development in Marketing*, American Marketing Association, New York.

Chance, D.M. (1986), 'Empirical tests of the pricing of index call options', *Advances in Futures and Options Research*, **1**, 141–166.

Chandler, L. (1948), *The Economics of Money and Banking*, Harper & Row, London.

Chang, T.C. (1986), 'Empirical analysis of the predictors of future spot rates', *Journal of Financial Research*, Summer, 153–162.

Chiras, D.P. and Manaster, S. (1978), 'The information content of stock prices and test of market efficiency', *Journal of Financial Economics*, 6, 213–234.

Choi, F. and Czechowicz, J. (1983), 'Assessing foreign subsidiary performance: a multinational comparison', *Management International Review*, 4, 14–25.

Cholerton, K., Pieraerts, P. and Solnik, B. (1986), 'Why invest in foreign currency bonds?', *Journal of Portfolio Management*, **12** (4), 4–8.

Chrystal, K.A. and Thornton, D. (1988), 'On the information content of spot and forward exchange rates', *Journal of International Money and Finance*, 7, 321–330.

Clark, E., Levasseur, M. and Rousseau, P. (1993), *International Finance*, Chapman & Hall, London.

Clifford, M.E. (1989), 'Foreign exchange hedging at Intel', *The Treasurer*, November, 26–29.

Coase, R.H. (1937), 'The nature of the firm', *Economica*, 4, 386–405.

Cochran, S.J. and Mansur, I. (1991), 'The interrelationships between US and foreign equity market yields: tests of Granger causality', *Journal of International Business Studies*, **4**, 723–736.

Collier, P.A. and Davis, E.W. (1985), 'Currency risk management in UK multinational companies', *Accounting and Business Research*, Autumn, 327–335.

Collier, P.A., Davis, E.W., Coates, J.B. and Longden, S.G. (1990a), *Multinational Companies and the Management of Currency Risk*, Prentice Hall, Englewood Cliffs, NJ.

Collier, P.A., Davis, E.W., Coates, J.B. and Longden, S.G. (1990b), 'The management of currency risk: case studies of US and UK multinationals', *Accounting and Business Research*, **20** (79), 206–210.

Collins, J.M. and Sekely, W.S. (1983), 'The relationship of headquarters country and industrial classification to financial structure', *Financial Management*, Autumn, 45–51.

Cooper, I. (1993), *Arithmetic versus Geometric Mean Risk Premium: Setting Discount Rates for Capital Budgeting*, London Business School Institute of Finance and Accounting Working Paper No. 174.

Cooper, I. and Franks, J. (1987), 'Treasury performance measurement', *Midland Corporate Finance Journal*, **4** (4); in J.M. Stern and D.H. Chew Jr (eds) (1988), *New Developments in International Finance*, Basil Blackwell, New York and Oxford.

Cooper, I. and Kaplanis, E. (1994), 'Home bias in equity portfolios, inflation hedging and international capital market equilibrium', *Review of Financial Studies*, 7, 45–60.

Copeland, T., Koller, J. and Murrin, J. (2000), *Valuation*, 3rd edition, Wiley, New York.

Cornell, B. (1977), 'Spot rates, and market efficiency', *Journal of Financial Economics*, 5, 55/65.

Cornell, B. and Dietrich, J.K. (1978), 'The efficiency of the market for foreign exchange market under floating exchange rates', *Review of Economics and Statistics*, **60** (1), 111–120.

Cox, J., Ross, S. and Rubinstein, M. (1979), 'Option pricing: a simplified approach', *Journal of Financial Economics*, 7, 229–264.

Cox, J.C. and Rubinstein, M. (1985), *Options Markets*, Prentice Hall, Englewood Cliffs, NJ.

Cumby, R.E. (1990), 'Consumption risk and international equity returns: some empirical evidence', *Journal of International Money and Finance*, **9** (2), 182–191.

Cumby, R.E. and Huizinga, J. (1988), *The Predictability of Real Exchange Rate Changes in the Short and Long Run*, Mimeo, University of Chicago, IL.

Cumby, R.E. and Mishkin, F. (1984), *The International Linkage of Real Interest Rates: The European Connection*, National Bureau of Economic Research, Working Paper No. 1423.

Cumby, R.E. and Obstfeld, M. (1984), 'International interest rate and price level linkages under flexible exchange rates: a review of the evidence', in J.F.O. Bilson and R.C. Marston (eds), *Exchange Rate Theory and Practices*, University of Chicago Press, Chicago, IL.

Cvar, M.R. (1986), 'Case studies in global competition: patterns of success and failure', in M.E. Porter (ed.), *Competition in Global Industries*, Harvard Business School, Boston, MA.

Dallas, G. (1990), 'A rating agency view', *The Treasurer*, July – August, 26–27.

Davis, E.P. (1995), *Pension Funds, Retirement-income Insurance and Capital Markets: An International Perspective*, Oxford University Press, Oxford.

Davis, E., Coates, J., Collier, P. and Longden, S. (1991), *Currency Risk Management in Multinational Companies*, Prentice Hall, London.

Davis, H. (1989), *Financial Products for Medium-sized Companies*, Globecon Group, New York.

de Bondt, W. and Thaler, R. (1985), 'Does the stock market overact?', *Journal of Finance*, **40**, 793–805.

de Grauwe, P. (1988), 'The long swings in real exchange rates: do they fit into our theories?', *Bank of Japan Monetary and Economic Studies*, 37–60.

Demirag, I. and Goddard, S. (1994), *Financial Management for International Business*, McGraw-Hill, New York.

Dichtl, L.E.M., Liebold, M., Koglmayr, H.G. and Muller, S. (1983), 'The foreign orientation of management as a central construct in export centred decision making processes', *Research for Marketing*, **10**, 7–14.

Dimson, E. Marsh, P., and Staunton, M. (2002), *Triumph of the Optimists*, Princeton University Press, Princeton, NJ.

Donaldson, J.A. (1987), *Corporate Currency Risk*, 2nd edition, *Financial Times* Business Information, London.

Dooley, M.P. and Shafer, J.R. (1976), *Analysis of Short Run Exchange Rate Behaviour: March 1973 to September 1975*, International Finance Discussion Papers No. 76, Federal Reserve System, Washington, DC.

Dornbusch, R. (1976), 'Expectations and exchange rate dynamics', *Journal of Political Economy*, **84**, 1161–1176.

Doukas, P. (1983), *The Exposure of US Multinational Corporations to Foreign Exchange Fluctuations Arising from the Translation of Financial Statements of their Foreign Subsidiaries*, PhD dissertation, Dept of Economics, New York University.

Doyle, P., Saunders, J. and Wong, V. (1992), 'Competition in global markets: a case study of American and Japanese competition in the British market', *Journal of International Business Studies*, **23** (3), 419–442.

Driskill, R.A. (1981), 'Exchange rate dynamics: an empirical investigation', *Journal of Political Economy*, **89** (2), 357–371.

Drummen, M. and Zimmermann, H. (1992), 'The structure of European stock returns', *Financial Analysts Journal*, **48** (4), 15–26.

Dufey, G. and Srinivasulu, S.L. (1983), 'The case for corporate management of foreign exchange risk', *Financial Management*, Winter, 54–62.

Duker, K. (1989), 'Derivative products', *The Treasurer*, November.

Dukes, R.E. (1978), *An Empirical Investigation of the Effect of Statement of Financial Accounting Standard No. 8 on Security Return Behaviour*, FASB.

Dunning, J.H. (1977), 'Trade location of economic activity and the multinational enterprise: a search for an eclectic approach', in B. Ohlin, P.O. Hesselborn and P.M. Wijkman (eds), *The International Allocation of Economic Activity*, Macmillan, London.

Dunning, J.H. (1985), *Multinational Enterprises, Economic Structure and International Competitiveness*, John Wiley, Chichester.

Dunning, J.H. (1988a), *Explaining International Production*, HarperCollins, London.

Dunning, J.H. (1988b), 'The eclectic paradigm of international production: a restatement and some possible extensions', *Journal of International Business Studies*, **19** (1), 1–31.

Dunning, J.H. and Archer, H. (1987), *The Eclectic Paradigm and the Growth of UK Multinational Enterprises 1870–1983*, University of Reading Discussion Papers in International Investment and Business Studies, No. 109.

Dunning, J.H. and Rugman, A.M. (1985), 'The influence of Hymer's dissertation on the theory of foreign direct investment', *AEA Papers and Proceedings May*, **75** (2), 228–232.

Edelshain, D.J. (1995), *British Corporate Currency Exposure and Foreign Exchange Risk Management*, unpublished PhD Thesis, London Business School, London.

Edison, H. (1985), 'The rise and fall of sterling: testing alternative models of exchange rate determination', *Applied Economics*, **17**, 1003–1021.

Edison, H.J. (1987), 'Purchasing power parity in the long run: a test of the dollar/pound exchange rate (1890–1978)', *Journal of Money Credit and Banking*, August, 376–387.

Edwards, S. (1983), 'Exchange rates and "news": a multicurrency approach', *Journal of International Money and Finance*, **1** (3), 211–224.

Eiteman, D.K., Stonehill, A.I. and Moffett, M.H. (2001), *Multinational Business Finance*, 9th edition, Addison-Wesley, Boston, MA.

Elliott, G. and Ito, T. (1995), *Heterogeneous Expectation and Tests of Efficiency in the Yen/Dollar Forward Foreign Exchange Rate Market*, NBER Working Paper, No. 5376, December.

Emmer, E. (1984), 'Debt rating', *The Treasurer*, April.

Engle, R.F. and Granger, C.W.J. (1987), 'Co-integration and error correction: representation, estimation and testing', *Econometrica*, **55**, 251–276.

Erb, C.B., Harvey, C.R. and Viskanta, T.E. (1995), 'Country risk and global equity selection', *Journal of Portfolio Management*, **21** (2), 74–83.

Evans, T.G., Folks, W.R. Jr and Jilling, M. (1978), *The Impact of Statement of Financial Accounting Standard No. 8 on the Foreign Exchange Management Practices of American Multinationals: An Economic Impact Study*, FASB, Stamford, CN.

Everett, R.M., George, A.M. and Blumberg, A. (1980), 'Appraising currency strengths and weaknesses: an operational model for calculating parity exchange rates', *Journal of International Business Studies*, **11** (2), 80–91.

Ezzell, J.R. and Miles, J.A. (1983), 'Capital project analysis and the debt transaction plan', *Journal of Financial Research*, Spring, 25–31.

Fama, E.F. (1975), 'Short-term interest rates as predictors of inflation', *American Economic Review*, **65** (3), 269–282.

Fama, E.F. and French, K.R. (1988), 'Permanent and temporary components of stock prices', *Journal of Political Economy*, **96**, 246–273.

Fama, E.F. and French, K.R. (1992), 'The cross-section of expected stock returns', *Journal of Finance*, **47**, 427–465.

Fama, E.F. and Schwert, G.W. (1977), 'Asset returns and inflation', *Journal of Financial Economics*, **5**, 115–146.

Feizer, G. and Jacquillat, B. (1981), *International Finance: Text and Cases*, Allyn and Bacon, Boston, MA.

Finnerty, J.E. and Nunn, K.P. Jr (1985), 'The determination of yield spreads on US and Euroland spreads', *Management International Review*, **2**, 22–33.

Fisher, L. and Lorie, J.H. (1968), 'Rates of return on investments in common stock: the year by year record, 1926–65', *Journal of Business*, **41** (35), 291–316.

Fleming, J.M. (1962), 'Domestic financial policies under fixed and flexible rates', *IMF Staff Papers*, November.

Fletcher, D.J. and Taylor, L.W. (1994), 'A non-parametric analysis of covered interest parity in long-date capital markets', *Journal of International Money and Finance*, **13** (4), 459–475.

Folks, W.R. Jr and Stansell, S.R. (1975), 'The use of discriminant analysis in forecasting exchange rate movements', *Journal of International Business Studies*, **6** (1), 33–50.

Franks, J.R., Broyles, J.E. and Carleton, W.T. (1985), *Corporate Finance: Concepts and Applications*, Wadsworth, Belmont, CA.

Franks, J., Mayer, C. and Rennebog, L. (1995), *The Role of Takeovers in Corporate Governance*, mimeo, London Business School, London.

Fraser, P., Helliar, C.V. and Power, D.M. (1994), 'An empirical investigation of convergence among European equity markets', *Applied Financial Economics*, **4**, 149–157.

French, K.R. and Poterba, J.M. (1991), 'Investor diversification and international equity markets', *American Economic Review*, **81**, 222–226.

Frenkel, J.A. (1977), 'The forward exchange rate, expectations and the demand for money: the German hyperinflation', *American Economic Review*, **67**, 653–670.

Frenkel, J.A. (1979), 'Tests of rational expectations in the forward exchange market', *Southern Journal of Economics*, 1083–1101.

Frenkel, J.A. (1980), *Exchange Rates, Prices and Money, Lessons from the 1920s*, American Economic Association Papers and Proceedings, pp. 235–242.

Frenkel, J.A. and Froot, K.A. (1990), 'Chartists, fundamentalists and trading in the foreign exchange market', *American Economic Review*, **80** (2), 181–185.

Frenkel, J.A. and Levich, R.M. (1975), 'Covered interest arbitrage: unexploited profits?', *Journal of Political Economy*, **83** (2), 325–338.

Frenkel, J.A. and Levich, R.M. (1977), 'Transaction costs and interest arbitrage: tranquil and turbulent periods', *Journal of Political Economy*, **85** (6), 1207–1224.

Friedman, M. and Schwartz, A.J. (1963), *A Monetary History of the United States, 1867–1960*, Princeton University Press, Princeton, NJ.

Friedman, M. and Schwartz, S. (1982), *Money, Interest Rates and Prices in the United States and United Kingdom: 1867–1975*, University of Chicago Press, Chicago, IL.

Fuller, R.J., Huberts, L.C. and Levinson, M.J. (1993), 'Returns to E/P strategies higgledy-piggledy growth, analysts' forecast errors and omitted risk factors', *Journal of Portfolio Management*, **19** (2), 13–24.

Gailliot, H.J. (1970), 'Purchasing power as an explanation of long-term changes in exchange rates', *Journal of Money, Credit and Banking*, **2**, 348–357.

Galai, D. (1977), 'Tests of market efficiency and the Chicago Board Options Exchange', *Journal of Business*, **50**, April, 167–197.

Galve Gortiz, C. and Salas Fumas, V. (1993), Propriedad y resultados de la gran empresa Espanola, *Investigaciones Economicas*, **17** (2), 207–238.

Garlicki, D.T., Fabozzi, F.J. and Fonfeder, R. (1987), 'The impact of earnings with FASB 52 on equity returns', *Financial Management*, Autumn, 36–44.

Garman, M.B. (1976), 'An algebra for evaluating hedge portfolios', *Journal of Financial Economics*, **3**, October, 403–427.

Garman, M.B. and Kohlhagen, S.W. (1983), 'Foreign currency option values', *Journal of International Money and Finance*, **2**, 231–237.

Garner, C.K. and Shapiro, A.C. (1984), 'A practical method of assessing foreign exchange risk', *Midland Corporate Finance Journal*, **2** (3); in J.M. Stern and D.H. Chew Jr (eds) (1988), *New Developments in International Finance*, Basil Blackwell, New York and Oxford.

Géczy, C., Minton, B.A. and Schrand, C. (1997), 'Why firms use currency derivatives', *Journal of Finance*, **52**, 1323–1354.

Geske, R. and Roll, R. (1983), 'The fiscal and monetary linkage between stock returns and inflation', *Journal of Finance*, **38**, 1–30.

Gibson, W.E. (1970), 'Price expectations effects on interest rates', *Journal of Finance*, **25**, 19–34.

Gibson, W.E. (1972), 'Interest rates and inflationary expectations', *American Economic Review*, **62** (5), 854–865.

Giddy, I.H. (1978a), 'What is FAS No. 8's effect on the market valuation of corporate stock prices?', *Business International Money Report*, 26 May, 1665.

Giddy, I.H. (1978b), 'The demise of the product cycle model in international business theory', *Colombia Journal of World Business*, **13** (1), 90–97.

Giddy, I.H. and Dufey, G. (1975), 'The random behaviour of flexible exchange rates', *Journal of International Business Studies*, **6** (1), 1–32.

Godfrey, S. and Espinosa, R. (1996), 'A practical approach to calculating costs of equity for investment in emerging markets', *Journal of Applied Corporate Finance*, **9** (3), 80–89.

Goetzman, W.N. and Jorion, P. (1999), 'Re-emerging markets' *Journal of Financial and Quantitative Analysis*, **34**, 1–32.

Goetzman, W.N., Li, L. and Rouwenhorst, K.G. (2001), 'Long-term global market correlations'. Working paper. Yale School of Management.

Goodman, S.H. (1978), 'No better than the toss of a coin', *Euromoney*, December, 75–85.

Goodman, S.H. (1979), 'Foreign exchange rate forecasting techniques: implications for business and policy', *Journal of Finance*, May, 415–427.

Goodman, S.H. (1980), 'Who's better than the toss of a coin?', *Euromoney*, August, 80–89.

Goodman, S.H. (1981), 'Technical analysis still beats econometrics', *Euromoney*, August, 48–59.

Goodman, S.H. (1982), 'Two technical analysts are even better than one', *Euromoney*, August, 85–96.

Goodman, S.H. and Jaycobs, R. (1983), 'Double up and prosper', *Euromoney*, August, 132–139.

Graham, E.M. (1990), 'Exchange of threat between multinational firms as an infinitely repeated non-cooperative game', *International Trade Journal*, **4** (3), 259–277.

Graham, J.R. and Smith, C.W. Jr. (1999a), 'Tax incentives to hedge' *Journal of Finance*, **54**, 2241–2262.

Graham, J.R. and Smith, C.W. Jr. (1999b), 'Tax progressivity and corporate incentives to hedge' *Journal of Applied Corporate Finance*, **12** (4), 102–111.

Granger, C.W.J. (1986), 'Developments in the study of cointegrated economic variables', *Oxford Bulletin of Economics and Statistics*, **48**, 213–228.

Griffin, P. (1979), *FASB Statement No. 8: a review of empirical research on its economic consequences*, Graduate School of Business, Stamford University Research Report, No. 482, January.

Grubel, H.G. (1965), 'Profits from forward exchange speculation', *Quantitative Journal of Economics*, May, 248–262.

Haache, G. and Townsend, J. (1981), 'A broad look at exchange rate movements for 8 currencies', *Bank of England Quarterly Bulletin*, **21** (4), 489–509.

Haegele, M.J. (1974), *Exchange Rate Expectations and Security Returns*, PhD Dissertation, University of Pennsylvania, PA.

Hakkarainen, A, Kasanen, E. and Puttonen, V. (1994), *Exchange Rate and Interest Rate Risk Management in Major Finnish Firms*, Helsinki School of Economics and Business Administration, Helsinki.

Hakkio, C.S. (1981), 'Expectations and the forward exchange rate', *International Economic Review*, **22**, 663–678.

Hakkio, C.S. (1986), 'Does the exchange rate follow a random walk? A Monte Carlo study of four tests for a random walk', *Journal of International Money and Finance*, **5** (2), 221–229.

Haner, F.T. (1979), 'Rating investment risks abroad', *Business Horizons*, **22** (2), 18–23.

Hansen, L.P. and Hodrick, R.J. (1980), 'Forward exchange rates as optimal predictors of future spot rates: an econometric analysis', *Journal of Political Economy*, **88** (5), 829–853.

Haugen, R.A. (1999), *The New Finance: The Case Against Efficient Markets*, 2nd edition, Prentice Hall, Upper Saddle River, NJ.

Haugen, R.A. (2002), *The Inefficient Stock Market: What Pays Off and Why*, 2nd edition Prentice Hall, Upper Saddle River, NJ.

Haugen, R.A. and Baker, N.L. (1996), 'Commonality in the determinants of expected stock returns', *Journal of Financial Economics*, **41**, 401–439.

Haushalter, G.D. (2000), 'Financing policy, basis risk and corporate hedging: evidence from oil and gas producers', *Journal of Finance*, **55**, 107–152.

Helpman, E. and Krugman, P. (1985), *Market Structure and Foreign Trade*, MIT Press, Cambridge, MA.

Hennart, J.F. (1988), 'Upstream vertical integration in the aluminium and tin industries', *Journal of Economic Behaviour and Organization*, **9**, 281–299.

Hennart, J.F. (1991), 'The transaction cost theory of the multinational enterprise', in C.N. Pitelis and R. Sugden (eds), *The Nature of the Transnational Firm*, Routledge, London.

Herring, R.J. and Marston, R.C. (1976), 'The forward market and interest rates in the Eurocurrency and national money markets', in C.H. Stern, J.H. Makin and D.E. Logue (eds), *Eurocurrencies and the International Monetary System*, American Enterprise Institute, Washington, DC.

Hicks, J.R. (1946), *Value and Capital: An Enquiry into some Fundamental Principles of Economic Theory*, 2nd edition, Oxford University Press, Oxford.

Hilley, J.L., Breidleman, C.R. and Greenleaf, J.A. (1981), 'Why there is no long forward market in foreign exchange', *Euromoney*, 95–103.

Hodder, J.E. (1986), 'Evaluation of manufacturing investments: a comparison of US and Japanese practices', *Financial Management*, Spring, 17–24.

Hodder, J.E. and Senbet, L.W. (1990), 'International capital structure equilibrium', *Journal of Finance*, **45** (5), 1495–1516.

Hodgson, J.A. and Phelps, P. (1975), 'The distributed impact of price level variation on floating exchange rates', *Review of Economics and Statistics*, **57**, February, 58–64.

Hodrick, R.J. (1987), *The Empirical Evidence of the Efficiency of Forward and Futures Foreign Exchange Markets*, Harwood, Chur, Switzerland.

Holland, J.B. (1993), *International Financial Management*, 2nd edition, Basil Blackwell, Oxford.

Hood, N. and Young, S. (1979), *The Economics of Multinational Enterprise*, Longman, London.

Hooke, J.C. (1998), *Security Analysis on Wall Street*, John Wiley, New York, NY.

Howe, J.S. and Kelm, K. (1987), 'The stock price impacts of overseas listings', *Financial Management*, Autumn, 51–56.

Howe, J.S. and Madura, J. (1990), 'The impact of international listings on risk: implications for capital market integration', *Journal of Banking and Finance*, **14** (6), 1133–1342.

Hsieh, D.A. (1982), *Tests of Rational Expectations and No Risk Premium in Forward Exchange Markets*, National Bureau of Economic Research Working Paper No. 843.

Huang, R. (1984), 'Exchange rate and relative monetary expansions: the case of simultaneous hyperinflation and rational expectations', *European Economic Review*, 24 (2), 189–195.

Hughes, J.S., Logue, D.E. and Sweeney, R.J. (1975), 'Corporate international diversification and market assigned measures of risk and diversification', *Journal of Finance and Quantitative Analysis*, **10** (4), 627–637.

Huizinga, J. (1987), *An Empirical Investigation of the Long-run Behaviour of Real Exchange Rates*, Carnegie-Rochester Conference on Public Policy.

Hunter, J.E. and Coggin, T.D. (1990), 'An analysis of the diversification benefit from international equity investment', *Journal of Portfolio Management*, **17** (1), 33–36.

Hymer, S.H. (1960), *The International Operations of National Firms: A Study of Direct Foreign Investment*, MIT Press, Cambridge, MA.

Ibbotson, R.G. and Sinquefield, R.A., *Stocks, Bonds, Bills and Inflation Yearbook*, Ibbotson Associates, Chicago, IL (published annually).

International Monetary Fund (1992), *International Financial Statistics*, June.

Isard, P. (1977), 'How far can we push the law of one price?', *American Economic Review*, 67, 942–948.

Jacque, L. and Hawawini, G. (1993), 'Myths and realities of the global capital market: lessons for financial managers', *Journal of Applied Corporate Finance*, **6** (3), 81–90.

Jacquillat, B. and Solnik, B. (1978), 'Multinationals are poor tools for international diversification', *Journal of Portfolio Management*, **4** (2), 8–12.

Jenkins, R.L. (1995), *Corporate Management of Exchange Rate Misalignment – the Experience of UK Firms 1972–82, 1987–92*, unpublished PhD Thesis, London School of Economics, London.

Johanson, J. and Vahlne, J. (1977), 'The internationalization process of the firm: a model of knowledge development on increasing foreign commitments', *Journal of International Business Studies*, **8** (1), 23–32.

Johanson, J. and Wiedersheim-Paul, F. (1975), 'The internationalization of the firm: four Swedish case studies', *Journal of Management Studies*, October, 305–322.

Johnson, D.R. (1990), 'Co-integration, error correction, and purchasing power parity between Canada and the United States', *Canadian Journal of Economics*, 23, 839–855.

Judge, A. (2001), *The Economic Determinants of Corporate Hedging: An Empirical Analysis of UK Non-Financial Firms*, Unpublished PhD thesis. London Guildhall University.

Kaserman, D.L. (1973), 'The forward exchange rate: its determination and behaviour as a predictor of the future spot rate', *Proceedings of the American Statistical Society*, 417–422.

Kay, N.M. (1983), 'Multinational enterprises: a review article', *Scottish Journal of Political Economy*, **30** (3), 304–312.

Keane, S.M. (1983) *Stock Market Efficiency: Theory, Evidence and Implications*, Philip Allan, Oxford.

Kendall, N. and Sheridan, T. (1991), *Finanzmeister: Financial Manager and Business Strategist*, Pitman, London.

Kettell, B. (1979), 'Is the forward rate an accurate predictor of future spot rates?', in T.W. McRae and D. Walker (eds), *Readings in Foreign Exchange Management*, MCB Publications, Bradford.

Khoury, S.J. and Chan, K.H. (1988), 'Hedging foreign exchange risk: selecting the optimal tool', *Midland Corporate Finance Journal*, **5** (4), 40–52.

Kidwell, D.S., Marr, M.W. and Thompson, G.R. (1985), 'Eurodollar bonds: alternative financing for US companies', *Financial Management*, Winter, 18–27.

Kim, M.J., Nelson, C.R. and Startz, R. (1991), 'Mean reversion in stock prices: a reappraisal of the empirical evidence', *Review of Economic Studies*, **58**, 515–528.

Kim, S.H., Farragher, E.J. and Crick, T. (1984), 'Foreign capital budgeting practices used by the US and non-US multinational companies', *Engineering Economist*, **29** (3), 207–215.

Kindleberger, C.P. (1969), *American Business Abroad: Six Lectures on Direct Investment*, Yale University Press, New Haven, CT.

Klemkosky, R.C. and Resnick, B.G. (1979), 'Pull–call parity and market efficiency', *Journal of Finance*, **34**, December, 1141–1155.

Knickerbocker, F.T. (1973), *Oligopolistic Reaction and Multinational Enterprise*, Harvard University Press, Boston, MA.

Kohlhagen, S.W. (1978), *The Behaviour of Foreign Exchange Markets – A Critical Survey of the Empirical Literature*, New York University Press, New York.

Kojima, K. (1978), *Direct Foreign Investment: A Japanese Model of Multinational Business Operations*, Croom Helm, London.

Kravis, I.B. and Lipsey, R.E. (1978), 'Price behaviour in the light of balance of payments theories', *Journal of International Economics*, May, 193–246.

Krugman, P. (1978), 'Purchasing power parity and exchange rates: another look at the evidence', *Journal of International Economics*, May, 397–407.

Kwok, C.C.Y. and van de Gucht (1991), 'An empirical examination of foreign exchange market efficiency: Applying the filter rule strategy to intra-daily DM/$ exchange rates', *Journal of International Financial Management and Accounting*, Autumn, **3** (3), 201–218.

Lakonishok, J., Shleifer, A. and Vishny, R.W. (1994), 'Contrarian investment, extrapolation, and risk', *Journal of Finance*, **49**, 1541–1578.

Lall, S. (1979), 'The international allocation of research activity by US multinationals', *Oxford Bulletin of Economics and Statistics*, **41**, 313–332.

Lannoo, K. (1994), *Corporate Governance in Europe*, mimeo, Centre for European Policy Studies.

le Baron, B. (1999), 'Technical trading rule profitability and foreign exchange intervention', *Journal of International Economics*, October, **49**, 125–143.

Leland, H.E. (1984), *Option Pricing and Replication with Transactions Costs*, Working Papers, No. 144, Institute of Business and Economic Research, University of California, Berkeley.

Lessard, D.R. (1976), 'World, country, and industry relationships in equity returns: implications for risk reduction through international diversification', *Financial Analysts Journal*, **32** (1), 32–38.

Lessard, D.R. (1996), 'Incorporating country risk in the valuation of offshore projects', *Journal of Applied Corporate Finance*, **9** (3), 52–63.

Lessard, D.R. and Lorange, P. (1977), 'Currency changes and management control: resolving the centralization/decentralization dilemma', *Accounting Review*, July, 628–637.

Lessard, D.R. and Shapiro, A.C. (1983), 'Guidelines for global financing choices', *Midland Corporate Finance Journal*, **1** (4); in J.M. Stern and D.H. Chew Jr (eds) (1988), *New Developments in International Finance*, Basil Blackwell, New York and Oxford.

Lessard, D.R. and Sharp, D. (1984), 'Measuring the performance of operations subject to fluctuating exchange rates', *Midland Corporate Finance Journal*, Fall, 18–30; in J.M. Stern and D.H. Chew Jr (eds) (1988), *New Developments in International Finance*, Basil Blackwell, New York and Oxford.

Levi, M.D. (1990), *International Finance: The Markets and Financial Management of Multinational Business*, 2nd edition, McGraw-Hill, New York.

Levi, M.D. (1996), *International Finance: The Markets and Financial Management of Multinational Business*, 3rd edition, McGraw-Hill, New York.

Levich, R.M. (1978), 'Further results of the efficiency of markets for foreign exchange', in J.A. Frenkel and H.G. Johnson (eds), *Managed Exchange Rate Flexibility: The Recent Experience*, Federal Reserve Bank of Boston, Conference Series No. 20, Boston, MA.

Levich, R.M. (1981), 'How to compare chance with forecasting expertise', *Euromoney*, August, 61–78.

Levich, R.M. (1982), 'How the rise of the dollar took forecasters by surprise', *Euromoney*, August, 98–111.

Levich, R.M. (1983), 'Currency forecasters show the way', *Euromoney*, August, 140–147.

Levich, R.M. and Thomas, L.R. (1993), 'The significance of technical trading-rule profits in the foreign exchange market: a bootstrap approach', *Journal of International Money and Finance*, **12** (5), 451–474.

Levin, J.H. (1986), 'Trade flow lags, monetary fiscal policy and exchange rate overshooting', *Journal of International Money and Finance*, **5** (4), 485–495.

Levitt, T. (1983), 'The globalization of markets', *Harvard Business Review*, **61** (3), 92–102.

Levy, E. and Nobay, A.R. (1986), 'The speculative efficiency hypothesis: a bivariate analysis', *Supplement to the Economic Journal*, **96**, 109–121.

Levy, H. and Sarnat, M. (1994), *Capital Investment and Financial Decisions*, 5th edition, Prentice Hall, New York.

Lewent, J.C. and Kearney, A.J. (1990), 'Identifying, measuring and hedging currency risk at Merck', *Journal of Applied Corporate Finance*, **2** (4), 19–28.

Lighterness, T. (1987), 'Managing economic exposure: the Rio-Tinto Zinc Corporation plc', *The Treasurer*, February, 13–15.

Lo, A.W. and MacKinlay, A.C. (1988), 'Stock market prices do not follow random walks: evidence from a simple specification test', *Review of Financial Studies*, **1**, 41–66.

Logue, D.E. and Oldfield, G.S. (1977), 'Managing foreign assets when foreign exchange markets are efficient', *Financial Management*, Summer, 16–22.

Logue, D.E. and Sweeney, R.J. (1977), 'White noise in imperfect markets: the case of the franc/dollar exchange rate', *Journal of Finance*, **32**, 761–778.

Luostarinen, R. (1977), *The Internationalization of the Firm*, Acta Academic Oeconomica Helsingiensis, Helsinki.

MacBeth, J.D. and Merville, L.J. (1979), 'An empirical examination of the Black–Scholes call option pricing model', *Journal of Finance*, **34**, December, 1173–1186.

MacDonald, R. (1983), 'Tests of efficiency and the impact of news in three foreign exchange markets: the experience of the 1920s', *Bulletin of Economic Research*, **35** (2), 123–144.

MacDonald, R. (1988), *Floating Exchange Rates: Theories and Evidence*, Unwin Hyman, London.

MacDonald, R. and Young, R. (1986), 'Decision rules, expectations and efficiency in two foreign exchange models', *The Economist*, **134** (1), 42–60.

Macrae, V. (2003), *Financial Risk Measurement and Management in Dutch Firms*, Unpublished PhD thesis. Nyenrode University, The Netherlands Business School.

Madura, J. (1989), *International Financial Management*, 2nd edition, West Publishing Co., St Paul, MN.

Madura, J.C. (2003), *International Financial Management*, 7th edition, Thomson South-Western, Mason, Ohio College Publishing.

Madura, J. and Nosari, E.J. (1984), 'Speculative trading in the Eurocurrency market', *Alron Business and Economic Review*, **15** (4), 48–52.

Magee, S.P. (1981), *The Appropriability Theory of Multinational Corporation Behaviour*, University of Reading Discussion Papers in International Investment and Business Studies, No. 51, Reading.

Makin, J.H. (1977), 'Flexible exchange rates, multinational corporations and accounting standards', *Federal Reserve Bank of San Francisco Economic Review*, Fall, 44–45.

Makin, J. (1981), 'Discussion', *Journal of Finance*, May, 440–442.

Maloney, P.J. (1990), 'Managing currency exposure: the case of Western Mining', *Journal of Applied Corporate Finance*, **2** (4), 29–34.

Manzur, M. (1990), 'An international comparison of prices and exchange rates: a new test of purchasing power parity', *Journal of International Money and Finance*, 9, 75–91.

Mark, N. (1990), 'Real exchange rates in the long-run: an empirical investigation', *Journal of International Economics*, **28**, 115–136.

Mark, N. (1995), 'Exchange rates and fundamentals: evidence on long-horizon predictability and overshooting', *American Economic Review*, **85** (1), 201–218.

Marston, R.C. (1976), 'Interest arbitrage in the euro-currency markets', *European Economic Review*, 7 (1), 1–13.

McClain, D. (1983), 'Foreign direct investment in the United States: old currents, new waves, and the theory of direct investment', in C.P. Kindleberger and D.B. Audretsch (eds), *The Multinational Corporation in the 1980s*, MIT Press, Cambridge, MA, pp. 278–333.

McGoun, G.E. (1987), *The Value of American Stock Listing on Foreign Stock Exchanges*, unpublished PhD thesis, Indiana University.

McKinnon, R.I. (1979), *Money in International Exchange*, Oxford University Press, Oxford.

McManus, J.P. (1972), 'The theory of the international firm', in G. Paquet (ed.), *The Multinational Firm & the Nation State*, Collier-Macmillan, Toronto.

McNown, R. and Wallace, M.S. (1990), 'Cointegration tests for purchasing power parity among four industrial countries: results for fixed and flexible rates', *Applied Economics*, **22**, 1729–1737.

McRae, T. and Walker, F. (1980), *Foreign Exchange Management*, Prentice Hall, London.

Meese, R. (1990), 'Currency fluctuations in the post-Bretton Woods era', *Journal of Economic Perspectives*, **4** (1), 117–134.

Meese, R. and Rogoff, K. (1983), 'Empirical exchange rate models of the seventies: do they fit out of sample', *Journal of International Economics*, February, 3–24.

Meese, R. and Rogoff, K. (1988), 'Was it real? The exchange rate differential relation over the modern floating exchange rate period', *Journal of Finance*, **43**, 933–948.

Mehra, R. and Prescott, E.C. (1985), 'The equity premium: a puzzle', *Journal of Monetary Economics*, **15**, 145–61.

Meister, I.W. (1970), *Managing the International Financial Function*, The Conference Board, New York.

Merrill Lynch (2000), *Size and Structure of the World Bond Market: 2000*, Global Fixed Income Research Team, Merrill Lynch.

Michalet, C.A. and Chevalier, T. (1985), 'France', in J.H. Dunning (ed.), *Multinational Enterprises, Economic Structure and International Competitiveness*, Wiley, Chichester.

Michie, R.C. (1992), 'Development of stock markets', in P. Newman, M. Milgate and J. Eatwell, (eds) *The New Palgrave Dictionary of Money and Finance*, (1) 662–8, Macmillan Press, London.

Miles, J.A. and Ezzell, J.R. (1980), 'The weighted average cost of capital, perfect capital markets and project life – a clarification', *Journal of Financial and Quantitative Analysis*, September, 719–730.

Millar, W. (1990), 'New directions in financial risk management', in W. Millar and B. Asher, *Strategic Risk Management, Business International*, January.

Mishkin, F. (1984), 'Are real interest rates equal across countries? An empirical investigation of international parity conditions', *Journal of Finance*, 39, 1345–1358.

Mittoo, U. (1992), 'Additional evidence of integration in the Canadian stock market', *Journal of Finance*, 47, 2035–2054.

Moazzami, B. (1990), 'Interest rates and inflationary expectations', *Journal of Banking and Finance*, 14 (6), 1163–1170.

Modigliani, F. and Miller, M.H. (1958), 'The cost of capital, corporation finance and the theory of investment', *American Economic Review*, 48, 261–297.

Modigliani, F. and Miller, M.H. (1963), 'Taxes and the cost of capital: a correction', *American Economic Review*, 53, 433–443.

Modigliani, F. and Sutch, R. (1966), 'Innovations in interest rate policy', *American Economic Review*, May, 178–197.

Montier, J. (2002), *Behavioural Finance*, John Wiley & Sons, Chichester, UK.

Moran, T. (1974), *The Politics of Dependence: Copper in Chile*, Princeton University Press, Princeton, NJ.

Morgan, J.E. (1986), 'A new look at debt rescheduling indicators and models', *Journal of International Business Studies*, Summer, 37–54.

Mundell, R.A. (1967), *International Economics*, Macmillan, London.

Murenbeeld, M. (1975), 'Economics for forecasting exchange rate changes', *Columbia Journal of World Business*, Summer.

Mussa, M. (1982), 'A model of exchange rate dynamics', *Journal of Political Economy*, 90 (1), 74–104.

Myers, S.C. (1974), 'Interactions of corporate financing and investment decisions – implications for capital budgeting', *Journal of Finance*, 29, 1–25.

Nair, R.D. and Frank, W.G. (1980), 'The impact of disclosure and measurement practices on international accounting classifications', *Accounting Review*, July.

Nagy, P. (1984), *Country Risk*, Euromoney Publications, London.

Neely, C.J. (1998), 'Technical analysis and the profitability of U.S. foreign exchange intervention', *Review*, Federal Reserve Bank of St. Louis, July/Aug, 3–17.

Nobes, C. (1992), *International Classification of Financial Reporting*, Routledge, London.

Nobes, C. and Parker, R. (1998), *Comparative International Accounting*, 5th edition, Prentice Hall, Hemel Hempstead.

Nobes, C. and Parker, R. (2002), *Comparative International Accounting*, 7th edition, Prentice Hall, Hemel Hempstead.

Oblak, D.J. and Helm, R.J., Jr (1980), 'Survey and analysis of capital budgeting methods used by multinationals', *Financial Management*, Winter, 37–41.

Obstfeld, M. (1995), 'International currency experience: new lessons and lessons relearned', *Brookings Papers on Economic Activity*, 1, 119–220.

OECD (1992), *Economic Outlook*, June, 51.

Ohmae, K. (1985), *Triad Power*, Free Press, New York.

Ong, L.L. (2003), *The Big Mac Index: Applications of Purchasing Power Parity*, Palgrave Macmillan, London.

Oster, S.M. (1990), *Modern Competitive Analysis*, Oxford University Press, Oxford.

Oxelheim, L. (1984), *Foreign Exchange Risk Management in the Modem Company: A Total Perspective*, Scandinavian Institute for Foreign Exchange Research, Stockholm.

Oxelheim, L. (1985), *International Financial Market Fluctuations*, Wiley, Chichester.

Oxelheim, L., Stonehill, A., Randøy, T., Vikkula, K., Dullum, K.B. and Modén, K.M. (1998), *Corporate Strategies to Internationalise the Cost of Capital*, Copenhagen Business School Press, Copenhagen.

Oxelheim, L. and Wihlborg, C. (1987), *Macroeconomic Uncertainty: International Risks and Opportunities for the Corporation*, Wiley, Chichester.

Oxelheim, L. and Wihlborg, C. (1989a), 'Competitive exposure: taking the global view', *Euromoney Corporate Finance*, February.

Oxelheim, L. and Wihlborg, C. (1989b), 'Taking the sting out of economic exposure', *Euromoney Corporate Finance*, March.

Papell, D.H. (1985), 'Activist monetary policy, imperfect capital mobility, and the overshooting hypothesis', *Journal of International Economics*, May.

Pedersson, G. and Tower, E. (1976), *On the Long and Short Run Relationship between the Forward Rate and the Interest Parity*, Mimeo, Duke University, Durham, NC.

Persen, W. and Lesig, V. (1980), *Evaluating the Performance of Overseas Operations*, Financial Executives Research Foundation, New York.

Phylaktis, K. (1992), 'Purchasing power parity and cointegration: the Greek evidence from the 1920s', *Journal of International Money and Finance*, **11**, 502–513.

Pigott, C. and Sweeney, R.J. (1985), 'Purchasing power parity and exchange rate dynamics: some empirical results', in S.W. Arndt, R.J. Sweeney and T.D. Willett (eds), *Exchange Rates, Trade and the US Economy*, Bellinger, Cambridge, MA.

Pippinger, J.E. (1973), 'The case for freely fluctuating exchange rates: some evidence', *Western Economic Journal*, September, 314–326.

Pippinger, J.E. (1986), 'Arbitrage and efficient markets interpretations of purchasing power parity: theory and evidence', *Economic Review*, Federal Reserve Bank of San Francisco, Winter, **1**, 31–48.

Poole, W. (1967), 'Speculative prices as random walks: an analysis of ten times series of flexible exchange rates', *Southern Economic Journal*, April, 468–478.

Popper, H. (1993), 'Long-term covered interest parity: evidence from currency swaps', *Journal of International Money and Finance*, **12** (4), 439–448.

Porter, M.E. (1980), *Competitive Strategy: Techniques for Analysing Industries and Competitors*, Free Press, New York.

Porter, M.E. (1985), *Competitive Advantage: Creating and Sustaining Superior Performance*, Free Press, New York.

Porter, M.E. (1986), 'Changing patterns of international competition', *California Management Review*, **28** (2), 9–39; in H. Vemon-Wortzel and L.H. Wortzel (eds) (1991), *Global Strategic Management: The Essentials*, 2nd edition, Wiley, New York.

Porter, M.E. (1990), *The Competitive Advantage of Nations*, Macmillan, London.

Poterba, J.M. and Summers, L.H. (1988), 'Mean reversion in stock prices: evidence and implications', *Journal of Financial Economics*, **22** (1), 27–59.

Rajan, R.G. and Zingales, L. (1995), 'What do we know about capital structure? Some evidence from international data', *Journal of Finance*, **1** (5), 1421–1460.

Rajan, R.G. and Zingales, L. (1998), 'Which capitalism? Lessons from the East Asian crisis', *Journal of Applied Corporate Finance*, **11** (3), 40–48.

Rawls III, S.W. and Smithson, C.W. (1990), 'Strategic risk management', *Journal of Applied Corporate Finance*, **2** (4), 6–18.

Richards, T. (1993), *A Review of Purchasing Power Parity between Australia, New Zealand and the UK using Cointegration Techniques*, MBA Dissertation, Stirling University, Stirling.

Ritter, L.S. and Urich, T. (1984), *The Role of Gold in Consumer Investment Portfolios*, Monograph Series in Finance and Economics, Salomon Brothers Center for the Study of Financial Institutions, Graduate School of Business, New York University, New York.

Robinson, B. and Warburton, P. (1980), 'Managing currency holdings: lessons from the floating period', *London Business School Economic Outlook*, **4** (5), 18–27.

Rodriguez, R.M. (1980), *Foreign Exchange Management in US Multinationals*, D.C. Heath, Lexington, MA.

Rodriguez, R.M. (1981), 'Corporate exchange risk management: theme and aberrations', *Journal of Finance*, **36** (2), 427–444.

Rodriguez, R. and Carter, E. (1984), *International Financial Management*, 3rd edition, Prentice Hall, Englewood Cliffs, NJ.

Rogalski, R.J. and Vinso, J.D. (1977), 'Price variations as predictors of exchange rates', *Journal of International Business Studies*, **8** (1), 71–83.

Rogoff, K. (1996), 'The purchasing power parity puzzle', *Journal of Economic Literature*, June, **34**, 647–668.

Roll, R. (1979), 'Violations of purchasing power parity and their implications for efficient international commodity markets', in M. Sarnat and G. Szego (eds), *International Finance and Trade*, Bellinger, Cambridge, MA.

Roll, R. (1993), *Work in Progress Paper*, Whittemore Conference on the International Capital Acquisition Process, May, Amos Tuck School, Dartmouth.

Roll, R.W. and Solnik, B.H. (1975), *A Pure Foreign Exchange Asset Pricing Model*, European Institute for Advanced Studies in Management, Working Paper.

Ronstadt, R. (1977), *Research and Development Abroad by US Multinationals*, Praeger, New York.

Root, F.R. (1978), *International Trade and Investment*, South-Western Publishing, Cincinnati, OH.

Ross, D. (1990), *International Treasury Management*, 2nd edition, Woodhead-Faulkner, Cambridge.

Ross, D., Clark, I. and Taiyeb, S. (1987), *International Treasury Management*, Woodhead-Faulkner, Cambridge.

Ross, S.A., Westerfield, R.W. and Jaffe, J. (1999), *Corporate Finance*, 5th edition, Irwin/McGraw-Hill, New York, NY.

Rubinstein, M. (1985), 'Non parametric tests of alternative options pricing models using all reported trades and quotes on the 30 most active CBOE options classes from August 23, 1976 through August 31, 1978', *Journal of Finance*, **40**, June, 455–480.

Rubinstein, M. (1994), 'Implied binomial trees', *Journal of Finance*, **49** (3), 771–818.

Rugman, A.M. (1980), 'Internationalization as a general theory of foreign direct investment', *Weltwirtschaftliches Archiv*, **116**, 365–379.

Rugman, A.M. (1981), *Inside the Multinationals: The Economics of Internal Markets*, Columbia University Press, New York.

Rugman, A.M. (1986), 'New theories of the multinational enterprise: an assessment of internalization theory', *Bulletin of Economic Research*, **39** (2), 101–118.

Rugman, A.M. and Hodgetts, R.M. (2003), *International Business*, 3rd edition, Pearson Education Ltd, Harlow, UK.

Rush, M. and Husted, S. (1985), 'Purchasing power parity in the long run', *Canadian Journal of Economics*, **1**, 137–145.

Samuelson, P.A. (1974), 'Analytical notes on international real-income measures', *Economic Journal*, 595–608.

Sandilands Committee (1975), *Inflation Accounting*, Cmnd 6225, HMSO, London.

Saudagaran, S.M. (1988), 'An empirical study of selected factors influencing the decision to list on foreign stock exchanges', *Journal of International Business Studies*, Spring, 101–127.

Schulmeister, S. (1987), *An Essay on Exchange Rate Dynamics*, Discussion paper IIM/LMP 87–8, Wissenschaftszentrum Berlin for Sozialforschung.

Schulmeister, S. (1988), 'Currency speculation and dollar fluctuations', *Quarterly Review*, Banca Nazionale del Lavoro, **167**, 343–365.

Severn, A.K. (1974), 'Investor evaluation of foreign and domestic risk', *Journal of Finance*, **29**, 545–550.

Shao, L.P. and Shao, A.T. (1993), 'Capital budgeting practices employed by European affiliates of US transnational companies', *Journal of Multinational Financial Management*, **3** (1/2), 95–109.

Shapiro, A.C. (1978), 'Capital budgeting for the multinational corporation', *Financial Management*, Spring, 7–16.

Shapiro, A.C. (2003), *Multinational Financial Management*, 7th edition, John Wiley, New York.

Shapiro, A.C. and Rutenberg, D.P. (1976), 'Managing exchange risks in a floating world', *Financial Management*, Summer, 48–58.

Shastri, K. and Tandon, K. (1986a), 'Valuation of foreign currency options: some empirical tests', *Journal of Financial and Quantitative Analysis*, **21**, June, 145–160.

Shastri, K. and Tandon, K. (1986b), 'An empirical test of a valuation model for American options on futures contracts', *Journal of Financial and Quantitative Analysis*, **21**, December, 377–392.

Shefrin, H. (2000), *Beyond Greed and Fear*, Harvard Business School Press, Boston, MA.

Shiller, R.J. (1989), *Market Volatility*, MIT Press, Cambridge, MA.

Shleifer, A. (2000), *Inefficient Markets*, Oxford University Press, New York.

Shleifer, A. and Vishny, R. (1995), *A Survey of Corporate Governance*, paper presented at the Nobel Symposium on 'Law and Finance' in Stockholm.

Silber, W.L. (1994), 'Technical trading: when it works and when it doesn't', *Journal of Derivatives*, Spring, **1** (3), 39–44.

Siegel, J.J. (1996), 'The equity premium: stock and bond returns since 1802', in P.L. Cooley (ed.), *Advances in Business Financial Management*, 2nd edition, Dryden, Forth Worth, TX.

Siegel, J.J. (2002), *Stocks for the Long Run*, 3rd edition, McGraw Hill, New York.

Smithson, C.W. (1987), 'A LEGO approach to financial engineering: an introduction to forwards, futures, swaps and options', *Midland Corporate Finance Journal*, **5** (4), 16–28.

Soenen, L.A. and Aggarwal, R. (1989), 'Cash and foreign exchange management: theory and corporate practice in three countries', *Journal of Business Finance and Accounting*, **16** (5).

Solnik, B. (1973), 'A note on the validity of the random walk for European stock prices', *Journal of Finance*, **28**, 1151–1159.

Solnik, B. (1974), 'Why not diversify internationally rather than domestically?', *Financial Analysts Journal*, **30** (4), 48–54.

Solnik, B. (1988), *International Investments*, Addison-Wesley, Reading, MA.

Solnik, B. and Noetzlin, B. (1982), 'Optimal international asset allocation', *Journal of Portfolio Management*, **9** (1), 11–21.

Solomon, E. (1963), *The Theory of Financial Management*, Columbian University Press, New York.

Srinivasula, S.L. (1983), 'Classifying foreign exchange exposure', *Financial Executive*, February, 36–44.

Stanley, M.T. and Block, S.B. (1983), 'An empirical study of management and financial variables influencing capital budgeting decisions for multinational companies in the 1980s', *Management International Review*, **23** (3), 61–72.

Stapleton, R.C. and Subrahmanyam, M.G. (1977), 'Market imperfections, capital market equilibrium and corporation finance', *Journal of Finance*, **32**, 307–321.

Stehle, R.H. (1977), 'An empirical test of the alternative hypothesis of national and international pricing of risky assets', *Journal of Finance*, **32** (2), 493–502.

Steil, B. (1993), 'Corporate foreign exchange risk management: a study in decision making under uncertainty', *Journal of Behavioural Decision Making*, 6, 1–31.

Steil, B. (1996), *The European Equity Markets*, Royal Institute of International Affairs, London.

Stein, J.L. (1965), 'The forward rate and interest parity', *Review of Economic Studies*, 32,113–126.

Stewart, G.B. (1983), 'A proposal for measuring international performance', *Midland Corporate Finance Journal*, Summer, 56–71; in J.M. Stern and D.H. Chew Jr (eds) (1988), *New Developments in International Finance*, Basil Blackwell, Oxford.

Stobaugh, R. (1970), 'Financing foreign subsidiaries', *Journal of International Business Studies*, Summer.

Stobaugh, R.B. (1979), 'Financing foreign subsidiaries of US-controlled multinational enterprises', *Journal of International Business Studies*, Summer, 43–64.

Stonehill, A.I. and Dullum, K.B. (1982), *Internationalising the Cost of Capital*, Wiley, Chichester.

Stonehill, A. and Nathanson, L. (1968), 'Capital budgeting and the multinational corporation', *California Management Review*, Summer, 39–54.

Stopford, J.M. and Turner, L. (1985), *Britain and the Multinationals*, Wiley, Chichester.

Sundaram, A.K. and Logue, D.E. (1996), 'Valuation effects of foreign company listing on US exchanges', *Journal of International Business*, **27** (1), 67–88.

Takagi, S. (1991), 'Exchange rate expectations: A survey of survey studies', *IMF Staff Papers*, **38** (1), 156–183.

Taylor, D. (1982), 'Official intervention in the foreign exchange market, or, bet against the central bank', *Journal of Political Economy*, **90** (2), 356–368.

Taylor, M. and Allen, H. (1992), 'The use of technical analysis in the foreign exchange market', *Journal of International Money and Finance*, June, 304–314.

Taylor, M.P. (1988), 'An empirical examination of long-run purchasing power parity using cointegration techniques', *Applied Economics*, **20**, 1369–1381.

Taylor, M.P. (1992), 'Dollar–sterling exchange rate in the 1920s: purchasing power parity and the Norman Conquest of $4.86', *Applied Economics*, **24** (8), 803–811.

Taylor, M.P. and McMahon, P.C. (1988), 'Long-run purchasing power parity in the 1920s', *European Economic Review*, **32**, 179–197.

Taylor, M.P. and Peel, D.A. (2000), 'Nonlinear adjustment, long-run equilibrium and exchange rate fundamentals', *Journal of International Money and Finance*, **19** (1), 33–53.

Teece, D.J. (1976), *The Multinational Corporation and the Resource Cost of International Technology Transfer*, Bellinger, Cambridge, MA.

Teece, D.J. (1986), 'Transaction cost economics and the multinational enterprise', *Journal of Economic and Business Organization*, **7**, 21–45.

Thaler, R. (1998), 'Giving markets a human dimension', in *Mastering Finance*, FT Pitman Publishing, London.

Thomas, L.R. (1985), 'A winning strategy for currency-futures speculation', *Journal of Portfolio Management*, **12** (1), 65–69.

Thomas, L.R. (1989), 'The performance of currency hedged foreign bonds', *Financial Analysts Journal*, **45** (3), 25–31.

Thygesen, N. (1977), 'Inflation and exchange rates', *Journal of International Economics*, **8**, 301–317.

Treuherz, R.M. (1969), 'Forecasting foreign exchange rates in inflationary economies', *Financial Executive*, February, 57–60.

Triffin, R. (1960), *Gold and the Dollar Crisis*, Yale University Press, New Haven, CN.

Tucker, A. (1990), 'Exchange rate jumps and currency options pricing', in S. Khoury and R. Haugen (eds), *Recent Developments in International Banking and Finance*, Lexington Books, Lexington, MA.

Tucker, A., Madura, J. and Chiang, T.C. (1991), *International Financial Markets*, West Publishing Co., St Paul, MN.

Tucker, A. and Pond, L. (1988), 'The probability distribution of foreign exchange price changes: tests of candidate processes', *Review of Economics and Statistics*, November, 638–664.

Tucker, J. (1994), 'Capital structure: an econometric perspective in Europe', in J. Pointon (ed.), *Issues in Business Taxation*, Avebury.

Tufano, P. (1996), 'Who manages risk? An empirical examination of risk management practices in the gold mining industry', *Journal of Finance*, **51**, 1097–1137.

United Nations (1993), *World Investment Report of the Transnational Corporations and Management Division of the United Nations*, United Nations, Geneva.

Upson, R.B. (1972), 'Random walk and forward exchange rates: a spectral analysis', *Journal of Finance and Quantitative Analysis*, 7 (4), 1897–1905.

Vernon, R. (1966), 'International investment and international trade in the product cycle', *Quarterly Journal of Economics*, **80**, 190–207.

Vernon, R. (1977), *Storm over the Multinationals*, Harvard University Press, Cambridge, MA.

Viren, M. (1989), 'The long run relationship between interest rates and inflation: some cross country evidence', *Journal of Banking and Finance*, **13** (4/5), 571–588.

von Furstenberg, G. (1983), 'Changes in US interest rates and their effects on European interest and exchange rates', in D. Bingham and T. Taya (eds), *Exchange Rate and Trade Instability: Causes, Consequences and Remedies*, Bellinger, Cambridge, MA.

von Neumann, J. and Morgenstern, O. (1944), *The Theory of Games and Economic Behaviour*, Princeton University Press, Princeton, NJ.

Welch, L.S. and Luostarinen, R. (1988), 'Internationalization: evolution of a concept', *Journal of General Management*, **14** (2), 34–35.

Wells, L.T., Jr (ed.) (1972), *The Product Life Cycle and International Trade*, Harvard University Press, Boston, MA.

Wicks Kelly, M.E. and Philippatos, G.C. (1982), 'Comparative analysis of the foreign investment evaluation practices by US-based manufacturing multinational companies', *Journal of International Business Studies*, **13** (3), 19–42.

Williamson, J. (1994) 'Estimates of FEERs', in J. Williamson (ed.), *Estimating Equilibrium Exchange Rates*, Institute for International Economics, Washington, DC.

Williamson, O.E. (1975), *Markets and Hierarchies: Analysis and Antitrust Implications*, Free Press, New York.

Williamson, O.E. (1979), 'Transaction cost economics: the governance of contractual relations', *Journal of Law and Economics*, **22** (2), 233–262.

Wilmott, P. (1998), *Derivatives*, John Wiley, Chichester.

Wilson, M. (1990), 'Empirical evidence of the use of a framework of risk and return in capital budgeting for foreign direct investment', *Managerial Finance*, **16** (2), 25–34.

Wong, S.K.O. (1978), *The Forward Rate as Predictor of the Future Spot Rate*, MBA Dissertation, University of Bradford.

Yeager, L.B. (1958), 'A rehabilitation of purchasing power parity', *Journal of Political Economy*, December, 516–530.

Index

Note: Emboldened page numbers indicate **chapters** and definitions in **glossaries**.